PRAISE FOR CLIMBING STRONGER, FAS

"A climbing education is best described by Bruce Lee: what is specifically your own.' Layton's book is a va which climbers of any discipline can choose what works best for them." –Tico Allulee: AMGA Rock and Alpine Guide Extraordinaire

"Vital information! I wish I had this information when I began climbing. There is such a gold mine of information here that it almost feels like cheating." **–Fred Beckey: Author of The Cascade Alpine Guide series, Range of Glaciers, Challenge of the North Cascades, Mount McKinley: Icy Crown of North America, The Bugaboos: An Alpine History (and one of the most accomplished climbers to ever have lived)**

"I like what I see...spoken in a voice of someone both determined to help others learn and someone with insight. The ground cover[ed] is enormous. This is not a chest-thumping attempt to show off what you know. It is an honest, provocative analysis of what a serious climber should be thinking about 365 days a year. Seasoned climbers may or may not agree with every sentence in this expansive coverage. But no one can argue that you have offered a series of topics that every climber should eventually delve into if they wish to reach the highest levels of the discipline." **–Carlos Buhler: Author for National Geographic, Motivational Speaker, Extreme High-Altitude Alpinist, Recipient of the Underhill Award, Mugs Stump Award, and the Spitzer Award**

"Layton has written the magnum opus on the subtleties of the art of climbing. While other books dance around the art and science of climbing, this book tackles subjects head on in an uncompromising and refreshing way." **–Cameron Burns: Author of "Selected Climbs of the Desert Southwest", "Climbing Colorado's Fourteeners", "Kilimanjaro& East Africa: Climbing and Trekking Guide", "Colorado Ice Climber's Guide", and pioneer of hundreds of desert climbs**

"Mike Layton's recent effort is grand in scale. I have never seen anyone put together this sort of climbing reference in such detail. There are few mountaineering books I think mandatory reads. M.F. Twight and S. House are two of the authors. Mike Layton's recent effort is in that small elite group of North American authors. Job well done!" - **Dane Burns: Accomplished Alpinist, Ice Climbing Equipment Manufacturer, and Editor at Coldthistle**

"Concise, comprehensive, and informative. Everything a modern, do-it-yourself alpine athlete needs to succeed. I wish all of my patients would use this book and wouldn't end up in the ER in the first place." -**Erik Denninghoff, M.D.: Emergency Room Physician and Climber**

"Dr. Mike Layton has been a friend and colleague for several years now and to this day it still amazes me the amount of knowledge and passion for climbing that this man has! Not only does his passion for climbing fuel his own athletic aspirations but also, it fuels his desire to help others achieve what he has through proper planning and preparation for an ascent. On the pages of this book you will find invaluable information on how to be more prepared for the task at hand and you will find that even though climbing, while seemingly rudimentary, can be as involved as you wish it to be!" -**Erik DeRoche MS, DC, CSCS: Chiropractic Sports Physician, Professional Triathlete, Co-Owner of Run Without Limits**

"WOW! This book is extensive. Climbing is so basic in its fun factor and origins in our human desire to get up ANY terrain put in front of us. Climbing is so basic, yet there are so many complexities to the movement, training, gear, logistics, lifestyle, and more. I give big kudos to Michael for taking it all on. There is a ton of information in this book. You want info, you've got it in a mega dosage". - **Hans Florine: Professional Speed Climber and Record Holder for the Nose on El Capitan**

"I am a big believer of training in a gym to improve my climbing. I focus on a climbing goal to help keep me motivated as well. I use my time in the weight room to work on power and endurance. I also use the time to meditate and visualize success with my climbing project. I encourage others to get educated with books like this to help build a training program that is right for you." **Dawn Glanc: AMGA Mountain Guide, Winner of the 2009, 2011 Ouray Ice Comp Women's Division, and 2012 Teva Winter Games**

"This second edition contains more information than most climbers could hope to learn in a lifetime. Benefiting from Layton's years of dedication to the craft of climbing and his professional experience, this book is clearly the most exhaustive text on all of the many nuances of climbing has ever been written. The book you hold in your hands may well be the best one-stop-shop for advanced topics in climbing available today." - **Kurt Hicks, AMGA Certified Rock & Alpine Guide, Founder of the Washington Anchor Replacement Project, and Author of the Upcoming Snoqualmie Rock Climbing Guidebook**

"This book is the go to guide and bible of everything rock climbing from a how to climb guide to injury prevention. I highly recommend for every climber, novice to advanced." -**Emily Kiberd, DC**

"Layton's years of mountain experience and passion absolutely shine through. It's a boiled down encyclopedia of absolute best climbing practices that can only have been gleaned from years on the sharp-end of all varieties of mountain environment. Layton has landed on a winning recipe of delivering the full package to the modern climber. This book is all about providing climbers of all types with the most efficient, logical and thoughtful methods of improving your vertical game, and the trick is to read these sections as you need to build that strength. There's an endless flow of nuggets that just can't be gained from any other way (up until now!) than by suffering through the trials and tribulations of the sharp end. Even the most experienced rope guns and hardened mountaineers will be able to glean some gems from this collection of wisdom." – **Lyle Knight: Author of "Central BC Rock," Accomplished First Ascensionist**

"When Mike sent me a copy to read over, he asked me to let him know if I had anything to add or if I thought something was missing. Instead, the amount of knowledge and information I gained from reading the book was overwhelming, the book covers all aspects of climbing technique, mental training, clothing, injury prevention and strategies for success in the mountains. Thanks Mike for providing the most comprehensive advanced climbing manual I've ever read' - **Marc Andre-Leclerc: Squamish Soloist, Speed Climber & First Ascensionist**

"This book is terribly comprehensive. It has everything that an advanced level climber could want, from training information to technical information. An awesome resource! I can assure you that it will be added to the reading list for American Alpine Institute clients. I imagine that other guide services will do the same throughout the United States in Canada." -**Jason Martin: American Alpine Institute Director, Author of "Rock Climbing: The AMGA Single Pitch Manual", "Fun Climbs Red Rocks", & "Washington Ice: A Climber's Guide"**

"Anyone doing any type of climbing at any level can benefit from the first half of this book. This information gives the climber a better understanding of how their own body works. The second half, practical and technical, gleaned from years of experience on peaks and crags is the icing on the cake." -**Ian McEleney: Professional Mountain Guide and First Ascensionist**

"Layton nailed it! This book is destined to become the bible on climbing stronger, faster, and healthier. No other book on these subjects offers such thorough and up to date information. Dr. Layton has written the 'New Testament' for climbers." -**Jim Nelson: Author of "Selected Climbs in the North Cascades" Volumes I & II, owner of Pro Mountain Sports, and Accomplished First Ascensionist**

"This is an amazingly comprehensive book for any climber who wants useful information on the pre, during and post climbs to enhance their performance, with an added bonus of knowing it comes from a reliable source. I'm still not sure how he did it, this is a [word deleted] ton of info." – **Linda Nordhus, DC**

"What makes hard alpine routes difficult isn't the climbing itself, but the logistics and knowhow to successfully deal with the situation at hand. Success begins before you get off the couch and decisions last well beyond the summit. Mike Layton's new book not only gives you the tools you need to succeed, but also shows you why and how to use them. This is a very useful book for all climbers!" -**Craig Pope, World-Class Alpinist**

"This book is a thoroughly comprehensive modern look at climbing healthy and smart for the long run. Having a medical perspective makes his training and injury prevention sections particularly strong." - **Clay Watson, PT & First Ascensionist**

"Back when we were learning to climb, we did so by beating our heads against the wall. Nowadays you can just use this book." -**Wayne Wallace: Pacific Northwest Legend**

"Climbers of all disciplines will find this a valuable resource for improving their fitness, skill and performance. It is packed with useful information that is a reflection of Mike's broad experiences as both an alpinist and a health care professional." -**Mark Westman: Accomplished Alaskan Extreme Alpinist**

CLIMBING STRONGER, FASTER, HEALTHIER:
BEYOND THE BASICS

Second Edition

MICHAEL A. LAYTON, DC

Climbing Stronger, Faster, Healthier: Beyond the Basics
Second Edition

Copyright 2009, 2014 by Michael Layton

ALL RIGHTS RESERVED. No part of this book may be reproduced or transmitted in any form or by any means, electronic or mechanical, including photocopying and recording, or by any other information storage and retrieval system, except as may be expressly permitted by the 1976 Copyright Act or in writing from the publisher. Requests for permission should be addressed to chiroclimber@gmail.com

First Edition: First Printing: October 2009, Second Printing: November, 2009
Second Edition: June 2014

Cover and Book Design by: Michael A. Layton
Front Cover Photograph copyright 2014 by Ben Herndon
Back Cover Photograph copyright 2014 by Wayne Wallace
All photographs and Illustrations Michael Layton Collection unless otherwise noted
Illustrations copyright 2014 Michael Layton unless otherwise noted

ISBN-13: 978-1499656671
ISBN-10: 149965667X

For additional copies and updated information
sites.google.com/site/climbingbeyondthebasics
facebook.com/Climbing.Stronger.Faster.Healthier
chiroclimber@gmail.com

!!!WARNING!!!

THIS BOOK DESCRIBES TRAINING TECHNIQUES FOR DANGEROUS ACTIVITIES. BOTH THE ACTIVITIES AND THE TRAINING TECHNIQUES DESCRIBED CAN CAUSE SERIOUS INJURY AND/OR DEATH. BY YOUR USE OF THIS BOOK, YOU AGREE TO THE FOLLOWING:

USE THE INFORMATION CONTAINED IN THIS BOOK AT YOUR OWN RISK. THE TECHNIQUES, IDEAS AND SUGGESTIONS PRESENTED IN THIS BOOK SHOULD NOT BE CONSIDERED MEDICAL ADVICE, AND THEY ARE NOT INTENDED TO REPLACE CONSULTATION WITH A QUALIFIED MEDICAL PROFESSIONAL. THE ADVICE AND INFORMATION GIVEN IN THIS BOOK ARE THE AUTHORS' OPINIONS. ANY APPLICATION OR USE OF THE TECHNIQUES, IDEAS, AND SUGGESTIONS CONTAINED HEREIN IS AT THE READER'S SOLE DISCRETION AND RISK. THE AUTHORS, PUBLISHER, DISTRIBUTOR, AND/OR ANYONE ELSE CONNECTED WITH THE CREATION, MARKETING, AND/OR SALE OF THIS BOOK (COLLECTIVELY REFERRED TO AS THE "AUTHORS") MAKE NO WARRANTIES, EXPRESS OR IMPLIED, OF ANY KIND IN CONNECTION WITH THIS BOOK, INCLUDING WARRANTIES OF SAFETY OR FITNESS FOR ANY PARTICULAR PURPOSE, AND EXPRESSLY DISCLAIM ANY WARRANTY REGARDING THE ACCURACY OR RELIABILITY OF THE INFORMATION CONTAINED HEREIN. THE AUTHORS ASSUME NO LIABILITY OR RESPONSIBILITY OF ANY TYPE TO ANY PERSON OR ENTITY FOR ERRORS CONTAINED HEREIN, OR FOR ANY SPECIAL, INCIDENTAL, OR CONSEQUENTIAL DAMAGE CAUSED OR ALLEGED TO BE CAUSED, DIRECTLY OR INDIRECTLY, BY THE INFORMATION PRESENTED HEREIN.

THE ACTIVITIES DESCRIBED IN THIS BOOK CARRY A SIGNIFICANT RISK OF PERSONAL INJURY OR DEATH. DO NOT PARTICIPATE IN THESE ACTIVITIES UNLESS YOU ARE AN EXPERT, HAVE SOUGHT AND OBTAINED QUALIFIED PROFESSIONAL INSTRUCTION OR GUIDANCE, ARE KNOWLEDGEABLE ABOUT THE RISKS INVOLVED, AND ARE WILLING TO ASSUME PERSONAL RESPONSIBILITY FOR ALL RISKS ASSOCIATED WITH THESE ACTIVITIES. THE LEARNING AND/OR PRACTICE OF SUITABLE TECHNIQUES AND SAFETY MEASURES IS YOUR SOLE RESPONSIBILITY, AND YOU ASSUME ANY AND ALL RISKS ASSOCIATED WITH THE PRACTICE OF TECHNIQUES DISCUSSED HEREIN. IF YOU ARE UNWILLING TO ASSUME THESE RISKS, DO NOT USE THIS BOOK, OR UNDERTAKE THE ACTIVITIES OR THE TRAINING TECHNIQUES DESCRIBED HEREIN.

CERTAIN HEALTH CONDITIONS CONTRAINDICATE EVEN SEEMINGLY SAFE ACTIVITIES IN THIS BOOK. IF YOU HAVE ANY HEALTH CONDITIONS, INCLUDING PREGNANCY, YOU MUST CONSULT WITH A DOCTOR BEFORE ATTEMPTING ANY ACTIVITIES CONTAINED WITHIN.

Regardless of what is contained inside the pages of this book, you must accept responsibility for your partner (even in the gym) and yourself. Accidents and Injuries are your fault. You are not the victim, you chose this path.

Acknowledgments

Huge thanks for helping above and beyond the call of duty for volunteering your time: Ben Herndon, Chris Simmons, Chris Chlebowski DC ND, Clay Watson PT, Craig Pope, Emily Kirberd DC, Ian McEleney, James Garrett R.N., Jay Hack, Kurt Hicks, Linda Nordhus DC, Marc-Andre Leclerc, Steve Elder, Tico Allulee, Tyler Adams, & Willie Benegas. And especially, my favorite partner and wife, Britne.

My Climbing Partners, Peers, and Mentors: Aaron Loffler, Adam Riser, Alan Rousseau, American Alpine Club, American Alpine Institute, Andrew Wexler, Angela Hawse, Beau Carrillo, Bill Amos, BJ Graham, Blake Herrington, Brian Eckerling, Brian Waters, Bryan Schmitz, Cameron Burns, Carlos Buhler, Carolyn Hansen, Carolyn Parker, Cascadeclimbers.com, Chris Gonzolez, Coley Gentzel, Colorado Mountain College, Cory Bennett, Craig Hook, Dane Burns, Darin Berdinka, Dave Leahy, Dawn Glanc, Derek Elliot, Dylan Taylor, Eric Denninghoff MD, Eric Johnson, Eric Linthewaite, Eric Wehrly Phd, Eric Wolfe, Erik DeRoche DC, Fern Webb, Fred Beckey, Front Climbing Gym, Garth Sundem, Gavin Ferguson, Gene Pires, Graham Williams and Cilogear, Hans Florine, Jason Martin, Jim Nelson and Pro Mountain Sports, John Frieh, John Kear, John Roper, John Scurlock, Jonathon and Rachel Spitzer, Jordan Peters, Josh Thompson, JP Rhode, Julia Niles, Justin Thibault, Karsten Duncan, Kathleen and Peter Hirst, Lane Brown Phd, Lee Lazarra, Luke Distelhorse, Lyle Haugsven, Lyle Knight, Matt Anderson, Matt Schonwald, Matt Wade, Mark Allen, Mark Westman, Marcus Donaldson, Mike Bahn, Mike Morris, Mikey Schaefer, Momentum Climbing Gym, Mountainproject.com, Nick Dolecek, Peggy Drinkwater (RIP), Pete Gualiardo, Peter Zabrok, Rachel Cox, Rachel Spitzer, Rebecca Roseberry, Robert Rogaz, Robert Yoho MD, Roger Strong, Rolf Larson, Ross Peritore, Ryan Lurie, Sara Stewart, Scott Decapio, Seth Hobby, Shane DeMars, Shingo Ohkawa, Sky Sjue Phd, Stacy Sims Phd, Sunny Jamshedji, Ted Coxsworth, Tim Sharks, Tina Moore DC ND, Todd Miller and Annaliese Eipert, Trisha Hirst, Tyson Bradley and Utah Mountain Adventures, University of Western States, Wayne Wallace, Western Washington University, & Zac Gearhart.

Thanks to the following people and companies and people for the use of their photos not already listed: Alpkit, Armaid, Arm Relief Massager, Atomik, Backcountry.com, Black Diamond, Blank Slate Climbing, Bodyblade, Brandon McPhail, Brooks Range, CAMP USA, Climbing Technologies Climb Tech, Clint Cummins, Concept2, Dave Elder/Cathy Pierce, David Tennant, DMM, Dustin Clelen, E-Climb, Edelrid, Edward Hartouni, Fat Grips, Feathered Friends, Flylow, Grip4orce, Grivel, Hive, Hyperlite Mountain Gear, Ian Roth, Iceholdz, IME Salt Lake, IronMind, James Arnold, JetBoil, Josh Kaplan, Katabatic, Klymit, Kurt Haire, La Sportiva, Liberty Mountain, Mammut, Metolius Climbing, Monty Lamb, Moon Climbing, Mountain Momma, Needlesports, New England Ropes/Maxim, Nunatak, Pettibon, Petzl, REI, Rock Exotica, Runoutcustoms, Russ Walling, Ryan Megenity, Salt Lake Running, Scarpa, Scott Carson, Sic Grips, TJ Brumme, Totem Cams, Trackers Skishoes, Ursack, Versaclimber, Washington Anchor Replacement Project, Wild Country, Yates, and Zac Robinson.

To all my climbing partners past, present and future!

and

<u>To all the readers who enjoy a love of climbing, knowledge, and the outdoors - I hope this book helps you on your journey!</u>

Foreword By Willie Benegas

Are you an aspiring climber who is always looking to learn the secrets of the trade? Well here they are. Michael has managed to compile an incredible amount of the best tips for climbing. From mountain safety, technical skills, and health, this book has it all. It is never too late to learn new climbing techniques. If you are planning to do a road trip across America chasing the classic climbs or mountaineering expeditions, use this book. Always practice, practice, practice, and of course have fun!!!

Willie (Guillermo) Benegas
June 4, 2014
Katmandu, Nepal

Wille is a legendary Guide and Patagonian native and co-owns Benegas Brothers Expeditions with his brother, Damien. Willie holds a record breaking 11 for 11 summits guiding Mt. Everest, has climbed El Cap over 80 times, and Aconcagua over 50 times. He is an accomplished first ascentionist, setting testpiece alpine rock and ice routes including "Book of Shadows" on the Nameless Tower in Pakistan (Grade VII A4, WI4, 5.10+) , winner of Climbing's Golden Piton Award for the "Crystal Snake" on the north face of Nuptse, 2010 AMGA Guide of the Year, is an athlete for the North Face and La Sportiva....and the list goes on and on. But more than anything, Willie Benegas is a great guy!

Introduction to the Second Edition

THIS IS NOT A "TRAINING FOR CLIMBING" OR "HOW TO" BOOK
THIS IS A TOOLBOX: A REFERENCE TO ADD TO YOUR KNOWLEDGE OR SPRINGBOARD FOR FURTHER INQUIRY

I decided to write a second edition from scratch. This and almost every sentence in this book are completely re-written based on feedback, a serious amount of introspection, and field research. While many subjects are repeated from the first edition, this could very well be a totally different book.

The book is divided into three parts. The first revolves around preparing physically and mentally from training to practicing skills. The second part tackles being healthy – from nutrition to rehabbing injuries, to first aid. The third and final part deals with climbing specific information applicable in the field.

The first thing you will notice is that the training section is radically different and does not employ a one size fits all program. This edition leaves much more responsibility to the reader to create their own program and set of exercises. I liked the philosophy of condensing it all down into one simple program, but it just didn't hold water unless you were some super-all-around-climber who had unlimited time to train and climb. I had to re-invent the paradigm of training into a goal-oriented focus and incorporate new methods of training like CrossFit-style workouts, functional training, and just pure climbing for training. The training section of this edition focuses on goal-oriented training and should provide drastically noticeable improvements in your climbing. I have also added a mental training chapter to address the most common reasons for failure and how to avoid and plan for them.

The health section greatly expands on the information provided in the first edition, providing much more detail and more topics relevant to climbing related health concerns. I tried to keep this chapter as climbing specific as possible. However, most of the information could be as relevant to climbers as it is to anyone.

The final section addresses advanced climbing techniques, planning, and is also a general catchall for tips, tricks, and suggestions. This section is intended for climbers who already know the basics and is not an instruction manual. There are some detailed instructions and basic information presented for continuity's sake and for experienced climbers who are mainly familiar with their specific type of climbing. It was difficult to choose what information to skip or gloss over, and I apologize if doing so comes off as arrogance. I also could not cover every single advanced climbing system in the book. I kept out the information I felt is redundant, overkill, extremely esoteric, very basic, or worthy of an entire book on its own. I also either just plain don't know the information, or no one in my research has bothered mentioning it to me. I have provided references to texts and resources to direct those interested in learning more. The point of the last section is to provide a handy reference for complicated systems and ideas so you don't have to buy an entire book on a subject when you only want a refresher course. The other point of the last section is similar to the training section: to provide options and ideas to help you customize your personal climbing style. I hope you question everything, and don't take anything as gospel. It's up to you to make your own decisions.

I have tried to incorporate all climbing disciplines from big wall expedition climbing to cragging to bouldering. It may appear that trad, ice, and alpine climbing have preferential treatment in this book. There is a lot of overlap between the disciplines, and some aspects of climbing are just more gear oriented and technically complicated than others. There would be too much repetition if I addressed every discipline with the same or similar information. I tried to keep the prose to a minimum once again, but compared to the first edition, I failed miserably. I also broke my rule of not having any forms or charts to fill out, but I still left out all the fluffy useless filler. I purposefully left out detailed explanations, terms, and the like to keep the focus on doing rather than explaining. If you want research studies, better explanations, and more definitions, you will have to do your own data mining.

Remember, this is a "beyond the basics" book. I explain physics or physiology only to emphasize the importance of something. Some subjects, especially basic ones, get little to no mention. Besides this verbose introduction and a few subjects I couldn't resist ranting on about, most of the book is an onslaught of information. I feel that too much non-essential information drowns out the useful information, and I would rather the reader do his or her own research if they don't understand, disagree, or want more information on a subject. There are too many books out there on a single subject (won't name names) that after 200+ pages of print, you're left feeling empty – just a bunch of verbal diarrhea. Everything in this book has purpose and immediate applicable use. If I state something totally obvious, I apologize, but occasionally things only seem obvious when you become aware that they exist. For example, if a self-help book said, "don't be so angry about stuff" or a training book just said "try harder" you'd probably think "no kidding". Of course in retrospect, you may agree that those seemingly obvious realizations are not only true, but have huge significance. The basic, "duh" information is included because it is extremely important and is sometimes forgotten.

You may also be wondering, "who the hell is Mike Layton and why should I accept his opinion and biased presentation of information"? If you wondered that then you get an A+ in critical thinking. You should not accept anything presented here as gospel, or even correct. Although I do interject my person opinions, I try to keep it to a minimum and make it obvious when I do. Any unreferenced information (except my opinionated editorializing) comes from the combined experience of hundreds of climbing partners, teachers, and professional classes. I have had this book reviewed by experts in each field, and if their opinion differs from mine I made sure to alert the reader.

My real goal in this new edition is actually a selfish one. I can't remember all of this stuff and need constant reminders from everything from fancy rope tricks to training so I can stop climbing as terribly as I sometimes do. My goals in this and the previous edition are not monetary (as proved by the 1st edition sales), or two prove how much I know or show off. This will be my go-to book. And why not share it? I hope you share your feedback, things I screwed up, and things I should add. I'll be honest. I put a lot more effort into the 2nd edition than I did the first! Hopefully a 3rd edition is a LONG way off.

Information taken from other publications is referenced, but information taught to me from climbing partners, peers, or teachers is not. Photos, diagrams, and illustrations that I did not take or create are credited and copyrighted by those credited. Thanks again to all who contributed. The entire book was written, edited, designed, and published by yours truly.

FEEDBACK AND UPDATES

I would greatly appreciate any feedback on the subject matter contained in this book. If there is a topic you would like to see in the next edition, you have a difference of opinion on the subject matter, have new ideas on gear, or have any other ideas, comments, or photos you would like to share for new editions, please contact me. This book can't get much better without your input. Hopefully you learn at least one trick or exercise that will improve your climbing from reading this book that made it worth the cover price. If you feel others could benefit from this book, please spread the word or give it a good review on Amazon or a similar site as marketing makes me want to curl up and die.

Sincerely,

Michael A. Layton, DC
June 5, 2014 Sandy, Utah

Contact, Links, and Updates
http://sites.google.com/site/climbingbeyondthebasics
www.facebook.com/Climbing.Faster.Stronger.Healthier
chiroclimber@gmail.com

Table of Contents

Part I: Climbing Stronger
Chapter One: Training Basics
Important Concepts p.23
Limits of this Book
Where's a Suggested Routine?
Training Theory
Evaluating Your Fitness
About the Exercises
Breathing and Posture
Beginning Training
Benefits of Training Beyond Climbing
 -Weight Gain
How Long to Train
Protocols
Reps and Sets
Weight and Intensity
 -Tricking the Central Governor
Types of Movements
 -Physics of Moving a Load
 -Isotonic Movements: Concentric and Eccentric
 -Isometric
 -Isokinetic Movement
 -Plyometric Exercises
 -Proprioceptive Exercises
 -Closed vs. Open Chain
 -Slow Twitch and Fast Twitch Muscles
Other Types of Exercise
 -Functional Exercises
 -Agonist, Antagonist, Stabilizers, & Core Muscles
CrossFit & Similar Programs

Weight Protocols p.34
Endurance
Strength
Strength-Endurance
Power
Cycling Between Protocols
Making an Interesting Workout of the Day (WOD)
Basic Order of Protocols
Basic Order of Exercises

Equipment p.37
The Gym
Building a Climbing Wall
 -Decorating the Wall
 -Wooden Cracks
 -Moonboard
Non-Climbing Specific Gym Equipment

Chapter Two: Preparation and Prevention
The Warm-Up and Cool Down p.45
Benefits of the Warm-Up
Warm-Up Basics
Post-Routine Cool Down
Climbing
Aerobic
Full Body
Neck
Hand, Wrist, and Elbow
Shoulder
Scapula
Lumbar
Core Stability
Hip
Knee
Foot & Ankle
Balance
Additional Balance Training
Yoga and Pilates

Intense Core p.70
Abs Isometric
Abs General
Lateral Benders
Lumbar

Antagonists and Stabilizers p.81
Shoulder Pushing
Shoulder Stabilizer
Functional Shoulder
Chest Pulling
Arms Pushing (Triceps)
Wrist and Hand Stabilizer and Antagonist
Lower Body Antagonist and Stabilizer

Stretching p.92
Benefits of Stretching
Basic Stretching
Active Stretching
 -Contract Relax, Antagonist Contract (CRAC) Method
 -Contract Relax Technique
 -Post-Isometric Relaxation
 -Active Range Resistance

-Post-Facilitation Technique
-Active Release or Flossing Technique
Whole Body
Neck
Chest
Nerve
Shoulder and Arm
Hand and Forearm
Hip and Thigh
Leg
Lumbar

Chapter Three: Non-Climbing Supplemental Exercises
Upper and Lower Body p.113
Upper Body Supplemental
Lower Body Supplemental
Upper and Lower Body Combination
Cardiovascular Training p.124
Benefits of Cardio Training
Aerobic and Anaerobic Training
Heart Rate and Intensity
Aerobic Protocols
Programming Cardio
Cardio Exercises
Running Technique
Training at or for Altitude

Chapter Four: Climbing Specific Exercises
Strength, Power, Technique, Endurance, and Combination Protocol Exercises p.131
Strength
-Grip
-Wrist & Forearm
-Biceps, Lats, & Shoulder
-Core
Strength-Endurance
Power
Power (and Strength) Endurance
Endurance
Skills p.147
Skill
Falling
Fast and Dynamic
Slow and Static
Balance
Route-Finding
Movement
Foot

Hand and Grip
Crack
Feedback
Combination
Specific Conditions
Specific Discipline
-Bouldering and Sport
-Trad
-Snow, Ice, and Mixed
-Big Wall
-Alpine and Mountaineering
-Other
Ability p.164
Developing Ability Exercises
Applying Ability Exercises

Chapter Five: Programming
Making and Planning for Your Goals p.167
Goals
Training for Your Goals
Break it Down
Set Basic Goals
-Setting Short to Long-Term Goals
Breaking Down the Goals
Pyramids
Monthly Schedule
Scheduling for Different Types of Climbing and Seasonal Overview
Assessing Other Weaknesses and Planning to Train for Them p.171
Physical Imbalances
Health Concerns
Lifestyle Habits, Logistical Issues, and Stressors
Technical Skills
Bad Climbing Habits
Periodization p.174
Separating Out Skills and Ability from Phases and Protocols
The Foundation Phase
Strength Phase
-Sub-dividing the Strength Phase
Endurance Phase
Rest Phase
Cramming Phase
Performance Phase
Combining or Altering Phases
Starting the Cycle Again
Fitting in Aerobic Training

Alternate Phases for Hard Endurance
  Rock, Ice, & Alpine Climbs
Putting the Plan Together p.178
Graph and Journal
Tweaking the Plan
Fitting it In
Rest
Sleep
Training for High-Level or Unique Climbs
Getting in More Pitches
-Bad Weather
-Dawn and Dusk Patrol
-No Partner
Training on a Climbing Trip
Missing Exercises and Days
Off-Season Phase
Plateau
-Try Harder!
Staying Motivated
-Taking a Break
-Burning Out, Training After an Injury, or
  After a Trip
Chapter Six: Mental Training
Ego p.187
Critical Thinking
Comparing Yourself to Others
Know Yourself
Expectations
Grades, Quality, and Why We Climb
Performance Anxiety
Clearing the Mind
Fear p.193
Being in Control
Disconnect Yourself from the Situation
Plan for the Worst at All Times
Manageable Bits
Basic Checklist
Will p.196
Trying Harder
Willingness to Suffer or Commit
Willingness to Change
Bailure
Motivation p.200
Have Fun, Stay Positive
Partners
Get Out of a Rut
Get Psyched
Visualization, Meditation, and Biofeedback

Using Measurements
Loss-Punishment and Gain-Reward
Top 10 Reasons For Unexpected Failure

Part II: Climbing Healthier
Chapter Seven: Nutrition
General Health and Performance p.206
Eating Well
Taking Vitamins and Supplements
Ergogenic Aids
Food Pyramid
Ratio of Carbohydrates, Fats, Protein
Carbohydrates
-Types of Carbs
Fats
-Fat Supplements
-Fat Loading
Proteins
Micronutrients, Vitamins, Minerals, &
  Supplements p.212
Multivitamins
Electrolytes and Minerals
Antioxidants
B-Vitamins
Fiber
Probiotics
Krebs Cycle Supplements
Amino Acid & Protein Supplements
Adaptogens
Energy and Alertness Supplements
Other Fat Metabolism, Protein, and
  Glycogen Sparing Supplements
Other Vasodilators
Hormones and Steroids
Weight Management p.222
Body Fat
Weight Loss
-Exercise
-Diet
-What to Eat
-What Not to Eat
-Timing
-Cheat Day!
-Cold
-Etc.
Fasting
Weight Disorders
Gaining Weight

Planning Food and Water p.229
Energy Requirements
Water Requirements
Food Weight
Refueling and Rehydrating
Carb Loading
-Glycogen Dumping
Water Loading (Hyperhydration)
Eating to Recover
Planning Water
-Sports & Electrolyte Drinks
Chapter Eight: Health Concerns
Field and Travel Medicine p.236
Life Threatening Conditions
-Other Need to Know Information
First Aid Kit
Diseases
-Diarrhea
-Colds and Flu
-Skin and Wound Infection
-Insect or Animal Borne
-Food Borne
-Worms
Minor Injuries
-Minor Cuts
-Boils and Abscesses
-Poison Ivy and Oak
-Sweating
-Chafing and Blisters
-Dry Skin and Calluses
-Foot Problems
-Eyes
-Teeth
Environmental Injuries
-Altitude and Cold
-Cold
-Heat
Who to See and How to Be Seen p.254
Second Opinions
Manual Therapy Practitioners
-Chiropractors
-Physical Therapists
-Massage Therapists
-Acupuncturists
-Athletic Trainers, Coaches, and Personal Trainers
-Other Manual Therapists
Non-Manual Therapy Practitioners

-Allopathic Doctors
-Nurses and Physician Assistants
-Naturopathic Doctors
When to Go to the Doctor or Hospital
History, Physical, Testing, Diagnosis, and Treatment
NMS Basics p.262
Reasons for Injury
-Technique
-Genes
-Nutritional and Other Chemical Reasons for Injury
-Biomechanical Imbalances via Movement
-Biomechanical Imbalances via Posture
-Biomechanical Imbalances via Shortening and Stretching
-Biomechanical Imbalances via Muscles
-Overtraining
-Common Inhibited or Weak Muscles
-Common Overpowered Stabilizer and Antagonists
-Common Tight Shortened Muscles
-Commonly Tight Overstretched Muscles
Pain Patterns
-Common Trigger Points
Stages of Injury Repair
-Acute and Sub-Acute Phase
-Inflammation
-Repair Phase
-Remodeling Phase
-Chronic Phase
-When to Push Through Pain
NMS Treatments p.273
Acute Treatment "PRICED"
Protective Devices and Immobilization
Compressive Devices
Supportive Devices
Physical Modalities
-Heat
-Cold
-Alternating Hot and Cold
-Electricity
-Sound
-Light
-Vibration
Manual Therapies
-Massage: Compression and Friction

-Stretching
-Joint Manipulation
-Continuous Passive Motion (CPM)
-Movement Therapies
-Muscle Activation Techniques
Drugs
-Foods to Avoid for Pain and Inflammation
-Pharmacologic Pain and Inflammation Drugs
-Pain and Inflammation Supplements
-Osteoarthritis (OA) and Degenerative Joint Disease (DJD) Supplements
-Tendon Repair Drugs and Supplements
-Tissue Repair Drugs and Supplements
Exercise and Stretches
Surgery
Weight Loss, Nutrition, Cardio, Heavy Lifting, and Healthy Living
Sketchy Treatments
Treatment Plans
Quick Treatment Reference p.295
Treatment Summary
Rehab Basics
Order of Exercise Progression
Exercises
NMS Injuries by Tissue Type p.296
What Exercises Should I Do?
Bones
-Fracture
-Avulsion or Rupture
-Dislocation
-Bone Bruise
-Spurs, Bunions, and Malformations
Joints
-Subluxation and Joint Dysfunction
-Arthritis
-Capsulitis and Contracture
-Articular Connective Tissue
-Bursitis
Tendons and Ligaments
-Sprain
-Tendinitis, Tendinosis, Tendinovaginitis, Tendinosynovitis
Muscles
-Strain
-Bruise
-Deactivation, Shortening, and Tightness

-Cramps
-Fascia
-Compartment Syndrome
-Rhabdomyolysis
Nerves
Blood Vessels
Average Healing Times
NMS Upper Body Conditions p.307
Head and Neck Pain
-Head and Neck Posture
-Neurologic Neck Pain
-Headaches
-Neck Key Movement Patterns
Mid Back/Chest Pain
Thoracic Outlet Syndrome (TOS), Shouldergenic Neuropathies, Referred Pain
Shoulder Pain
-Shoulder Instability
-Frozen Shoulder
-AC Sprain and Broken Clavicle
-Shoulder Key Movement Patterns
Arm and Forearm Pain
-Arm Posture
-Arm Sprain/Strain
-Epicondylitis (Golfers and Tennis Elbow)
-Nerve Pain of the Elbow/Forearm
Wrist and Hand Pain
-Nerve Pain in the Hands and Fingers
-Dupuytren's Contracture
-Ganglion Cysts
Finger Pain
-Finger Sprain
-Finger Fracture and Dislocation
-Other Common Finger Avulsions
NMS Lower Body Conditions p.321
Low Back Pain
-Low Back Posture
-Low Back Key Movement Patterns
Hip, Thigh, and Groin Pain
-ITB Syndrome
-Key Movement Patterns for the Hip
Knee Pain
Lower Leg Pain
Ankle Pain
Posterior Ankle and Heel Pain
Foot Pain
Foot Abnormalities

Footwear and Orthotics
Other Selected Conditions p.336
Check-Ups
Other Selected Conditions
-Allergies and Sensitivities
-Chronic Fatigue, Adrenal Insufficiency,
   Fibromyalgia, & Depression
-Gastrointestinal Problems
-Sleep and Stress
Unhealthy Vices
-Smoking
-Alcohol
-Marijuana
Age Related Conditions
-Kids
   -Congenital Malformations and End
   Plate Injuries
-Getting Older
   -Skin Cancer
   -Genetic Diseases
   -50's and Older
Pregnancy

Part III: Climbing Beyond the Basics
Chapter Nine: Equipment Planning and Use
Camping, Approach, and Basic Gear p.347
Ultralight vs. Durable Gear
Methods of Travel
Backpacks and Ditty Bags
-Fit
-Approach Pack
-Climbing and Approach Pack
-Day Pack
-Haul Bags
-Sleds
-Poop Tubes
-Pack Covers
-Stuff Sacks
Poles
Sleeping Systems
-Fill: Down or Synthetic
-Staying Warm and Asleep
-Where to Sleep
-No Sleeping Bag
-Sleeping Bags and Pads
-Vapor Barrier Liners (VBL) and Over Bags
-Single Wall Tents and Tarps
-Double Wall and Base Camp Tents
-Portaledges
-Caves and Igloos
-Misc. Tent Info
Cooking Systems
-Stove Purpose
-Car Camping Stoves
-High Efficiency Stoves
-Liquid Fuel Stoves
-Liquid Fuel
-Canister Stoves
-Canister Fuel
-Stove Accessories
-Minimalist Stove Options
-Pots
-Eating Container Logistics
Water
-Water on the Go
-Purifying Water
-Water Bladders
-Water Bottles
Planning Food
-Camping and Cragging
-Alpine Trips
-Breakfast
-Lunch
-Post Climb/Pre-Dinner
-Dinner
-Alcohol
-Caching Food
-At the Car
-Make Your Own
Navigation and Communication
-Binoculars and Scopes
-Cameras
-Compass and Altimeter
-GPS
-Maps and Topos
-Wands
-Wind and Temperature
-Lighting
-Communication Devices
-Recharging Batteries
Fire Starting
Leave No Trace and Hygiene
-Pooping
-Peeing
-Showers
-Sanitation

Luxury Items
Clothing p.400
Materials and Use
Heat Loss
-Body Regions
-Evaporation
-Conduction
-Radiation
-Convection
Clothing by Body Area
-Head
-Eyes
-Torso
  -Base Layers
  -Mid-layers
  -Outer-layer
  -Optional Uppers
-Legs
-Knees
-Hands
  -Tape Gloves
-Feet
  -Summer Footwear
  -Winter Footwear
  -Gaiters
  -Lacing Systems
  -Moldable Liners
  -Rock Shoes
Drying, Cleaning, and Repairing Clothes and Gear
-Fabric Repair
General Climbing Gear p.429
Marking Gear
Helmets
-Reasons to Wear a Helmet
-Reasons Not to Wear a Helmet
-Bad Reasons to Not Wear a Helmet
Harnesses
-On Your Harness
Chalk
Belay/Rappel Devices
Carabineers
-Lockers
-Non-Lockers
Ropes
-Single Ropes
-Double Ropes
-Impact Force
-Length
-Rope Treatments
-Sheath
-Rope Marking
-Haul and Tag Lines
-Pull Cords
-Rope Care
-Carrying the Rope
Slings and Draws
-Nylon and Dyneema
-Shoulder Slings and Quickdraws
-Double Length Runners
-Load Limiters (Screamers)
-Stick Clips
-Tat
Big Wall Gear
-Ascenders
-Hauling Devices
-Fifi Hooks and Daisies
-Ladders
-Hammers
-Belay Seat
Ice and Snow Gear
-Ice Axes
-Ice Tools
-Crampons
-Miscellaneous Ice Gear
Rock and Ice Protection p.473
How Much Pro?
Standard Rack
Racking
Fixed Gear
Natural Rock Pro
Nuts
Tricams
Hexes
Pins
Hooks
Heads
Cams
-Cam Angle and Range
-Cam Features
-Sizing
-Stuck Cams
-Cam Repair and Maintenance
Big Bros
Slider Nuts
Crash Pads and Shields

Natural Ice Gear
Pickets
Flukes
Ice Screws
The 3 to 25 Essentials p.500
Bolts and Anchors p.502
Types of Bolts
-Expansion Bolts
-Glue-Ins
-Sketchy Bolts
-Removable Bolts and Hangerless Studs
-Size and Length
Hardware
-Power Drills
-Bits
-Hangers
-Hammer
-Wrench
-Blow Tube and Brush
-Carrying Cases
-Glasses
-Glue
Placing Bolts
-The Basics
-Location
-Drilling
-Cleaning
-Installing the Bolt
-Drilling on Lead
-Overhanging Terrain
Hand Drilling and Emergency Bolt Kits
Bolted Anchors
Replacing Bolts and Anchors
Chapter Ten: Backcountry & Climbing Skills
Backcountry Travel p.515
Navigation
-Magnetic vs. True North
-Triangulation
-Orienteering
 Whiteouts
-Lost Without a Map and Compass
Approaches
River and Lake Crossings
Wilderness Survival
Bear, Moose, and Mountain Lion
Weather p.523
Before You Go
-Pressure and Temperature Gradients
 Impact on Weather
-Decoding Vague Forecast Descriptions
 In the Field
-Barometer or Altimeter Forecasting
-Cloud, Temperature, and Barometer
 Predictions
-Wind Predictions
-Cloud Predictions
-Sun and Moon Predictions
-Time of Day Predictions
-Snow Predictions
-Lightning and Storms
-Temperature and Altitude
Avalanche Safety p.532
Understanding Snowpack
Predicting Avalanche Conditions
-The Big Three Variable Factors
-Slope Angle
-Aspect
-Terrain
-Snowpack and Stability Tests
Equipment
Travel
If Caught
Deciding Avalanche Risk
Snow Travel p.539
Rope Team Systems
Moats, Bergschrunds, and Cornices
Camp
Maximizing Success p.544
Avoiding the Pump
-Finding Rests
-Using Holds More Effectively
-Moving Effectively
-Moving & Maintaining Your Base of
 Support
-Planning Your Pitches
Redpoint and Onsight
-Redpointing Strategies
-Onsight Strategies
-Moving Fast
Specific Discipline Strategies
-Crack Technique
-Placing Gear
-Offwidths and Chimneys
-Choss
-Big Walls
-Ice & Mixed

Before You Go
Chapter Eleven: Technical Systems
Anchors p.562
Anchor Forces
Sling and Rope Strength
Building Anchors
-Poor Anchors
-Good Anchors
-Using the Rope
-Standard Setups
-Equalettes and ACRs
-Fixing a Rope to the Anchor
Tying In
Belaying p.573
Belaying the Follower(s)
Belaying the Leader
-Fixed Point Belay
Leading p.578
Avoiding Anchor and Ledge Falls
Protecting Roofs & Trapping the Rope
Protecting the Follower
Ditching the Lead Pack
Aiding
-French-Free and Pre-Clipping
-Using the Gear You Have
-Using Aiders
-Great Setups For Quick Aiding
-Emergency Aid Kit
Inexperienced Partner
Following p.587
Ascending the Rope (Jugging)
-Texas Kick System
-Frog System
-Two Ascender and Aider System
-Cleaning Gear, Low Angled, and Sketchy Jugging
Following a Traverse
Following A Pendulum
-Following a Longer Pendulum
Descending p.599
Single Pitch Rappelling/Lowering
Anchoring the Rope
Rope Management
Rappelling Safety
Pulling the Rope/Rappel Sequence
Lowering
Speedy Rappelling
Other Ways Off

Problematic Rappel Situations
-Bailing on a Big Wall
-Passing the Knot on Rappel
-Rappelling Traverses and Overhangs
-Rappelling and Lowering Haul Bags (or Victims)
-Not Enough Rope
-Anchor Far to the Side
Stuck Ropes
-Rope Immediately Stuck
-Both Ends Down
-Only One End Down
Retrievable Anchors
-Sling Retrieval
-The Daisy Chain of Death
-The Death Macramé
-The Fiddle Stick of Death
-Retrievable Ice Axe, Picket, Ice Screw, Wood Block, & Sandbag of Death
-The Fifi of Death
Hauling p.625
Ratchets and Progress Capture Pulleys
Haul Systems
-1:1 Hauling
-2:1 Hauling
-3:1 Hauling
-5:1 Hauling
-6:1 Hauling and Crevasse Rescue
  -C to a Z
  -Z to a C
-9:1 Hauling
Special Hauling Situations
-Lowering Out the Bag
-Avoiding the Big Bag
-Docking Cords and Far End Hauling
-Solo Hauling
Rope-Soloing p.641
Toprope Soloing
Self-Belay Systems
-Types of Devices
-Basic Setup
-Solo Anchors
-Rope Management
Speed Climbing Systems p.648
Safe Methods
-Blocking Leads
-Teams of Three and Four
-Fix and Fire

Other (More Dangerous) Methods
-Simulclimbing
-Tiblocing
-Simul-Soloing and Short Roping
-Short-Fixing
-Short-Tagging
-Movable Anchor
-Yosemite Loop
-The Infinite Loop
-YoGo Method
Rescue and Self-Rescue p.656
To Bivy or Descend
Calling for Rescue
Have a Plan
Practicing Skills You Already Know
-Important Skills to Practice
Transfer the Victim's Weight Off of You
Lowering Past a Knot
Rescuing the Leader
Carrying a Victim
-On the Wall
-On the Ground
Chapter Twelve: Other Aspects
First Ascents, Ethics, and Stewardship p.663
First Ascents
-Grants
-Impact of Your New Route
-Being a Jerk About Your First Ascent
Bolting Impact and Ethics
Chopping Routes/Gear
Replacing Fixed Gear
Leave No Trace
Etiquette
-The Ethics Committee
-Good Beta
-Noise Pollution and Dogs
-Waiting in Line and Passing
-Helping/Rescuing Another Party
Giving Back
Traveling and Back Home p.671
Travel and Lodging
-Vehicle Setup
-Car Trouble
-Free Camping
-Huts, Hostels, and Couches
-Cheap Travel
-Flying Logistics
-Jet Lag and Travel Fatigue

Road Trips and Extended Stays
-Finding Partners
-The Opposite Sex
-Food
-Jobs and Money
-Down Time
International Travel and Expeditions
Insurance
Back to Civilization
-Back to the Car
-Back At Home

Appendixes
Exercise List p.684
Gear List p.686
References p.690

Part I: Climbing Stronger

Chapter One: Training Basics

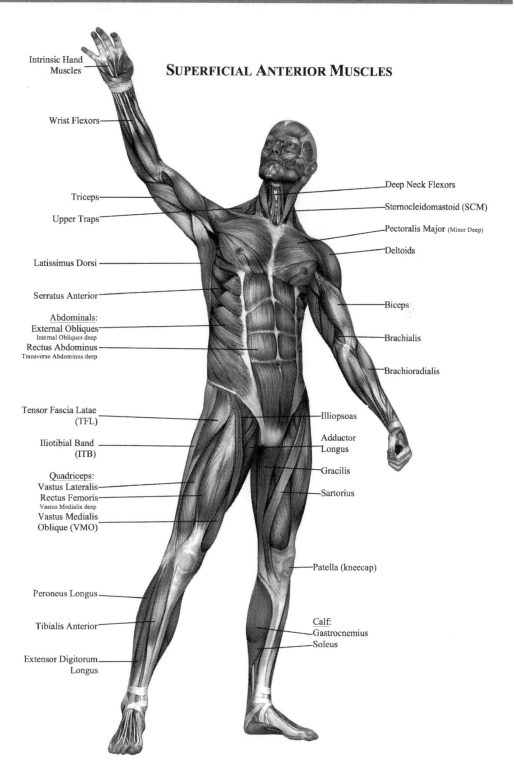

Superficial Posterior Muscles

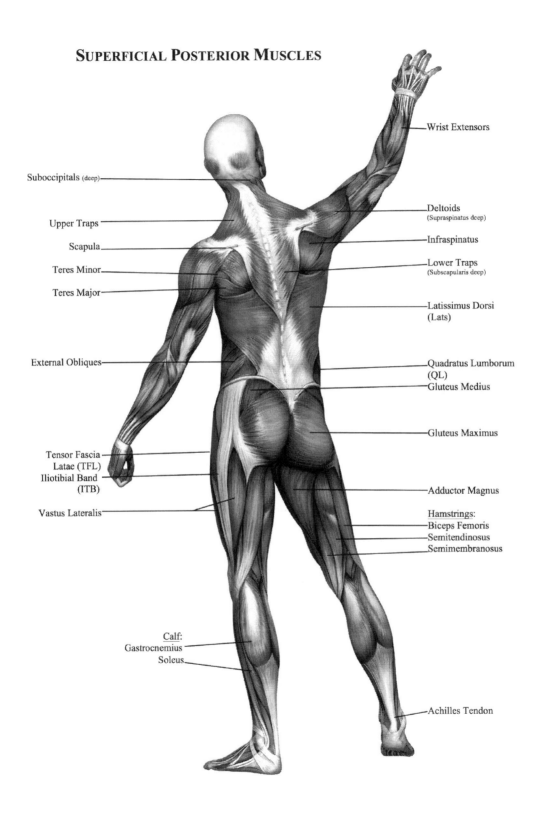

IMPORTANT CONCEPTS

LIMITS OF THIS BOOK

This book is by no means the best resource on training available. The cutting edge of training is taking place in garage gyms, or by high end climbers and coaches who spend their lives and livelihood dedicated to training. Science is a long way behind in the advancement of training for climbing, mainly because of the extreme specialization that takes place: every route and goal requires different training. This isn't baseball. No one training program is perfect or can be applied to every route or every climber. There are too many venues. Following a mountaineering plan by a high-end high altitude climber will be radically different to that of a sport climber or boulderer. You need to use your imagination, creativity, and your brain. There are also so many exercises out there for climbing, weight training, and general fitness and there is no way I can present them all. Use the book as a tool that can be adapted or discarded for a better tool for the job.

The purpose here is to take an extremely complex performance based skill, break it down, apply basic training and physiologic principles, and then provide a framework you can apply what you want out of it. Everything is just a suggestion. It may not apply to your body, type of climbing, or your mindset. Hopefully I've left it flexible enough to allow you to change what you need, or add what you want. If you see something in another book, video, website, or something your buddies do differently that you like better, then try it out. You don't have to do a single exercise I mentioned in this chapter, but you can still be able to use the programming or periodization chapters to guide your progress.

Where's a Suggested Routine?

One of the big changes of this edition is there are no suggested routines. The pressure to add this was huge, but I believe it would be a huge disservice to include one. The amount of exercises listed are overwhelming taken out of context of this whole section. I have listed the exercises in order as they appear in the appendix, *starred* some favorites, and included a huge section on programming and periodization to help you. But just like in the rehab section, even two similar goals (or injuries) can drastically vary in the approach with an infinite amount of ways to go about addressing them.

Here's what I suggest (explained in detail in the programming sections): Read all of Part I (and Part II if dealing with a health problem) first. I explain how to order your training in terms of a long term plan and weekly plan (periodization) and in what order to do your training for each section. I have ordered all the exercises by type (warm-up/rehab, supplemental, climbing specific, etc..), and body body area to help you.

After you have an idea of what you think you need to train, go back and cherry pick exercises and routines that can help fit your goal. The main point is to know what you want, know what you need, and then most important: be organized and thoughtful.

TRAINING THEORY

Since climbers tend to be cheap, and the sport still hasn't caught the status of sports like baseball or triathlons, there hasn't been much true scientific research done on training for climbing. Even so, exercise science in general has never really been top-notch in terms science. There are a ton of books on climbing training and technique, including this one, but most of the information is circumstantial evidence (it worked for you so it must be true), and is one of the worst kinds of evidence. It is evidence based upon trial and error, popularity, or because top climbers are doing it. Circumstantial evidence becomes more valid as it maintains its positive outcomes, which is basically group trial and error. Some top climbers could be top climbers if they drank beer all day and the only training they did were the routes they climbed. In other words, their hyped up form of training may not have had an actual effect, but because they are so good, you assume that it does.

The one thing that has held true for training for climbing is that the best way to train for climbing is by going climbing (unless you are attempting grade VI climbs, 5.13s, or high altitude alpine climbs). I will try and maintain this concept throughout this section. Another thing that can be done is to take principles that work well in other sports and apply them to climbing. The concepts that work best are specificity and transference. The more climbing specific you make an exercise, the more it will transfer into climbing, and visa-versa. A similar concept is the SAID principle, or that the human body Specifically Adapts to Imposed Demands. To add to this is the theory of overload and progression, or by training with continually increasing intensity and duration than in a real-life climbing situation, you should be able to meet the demands of the climb and more. A good rule of thumb, but not always applicable, is to increase your volume or intensity by 10% a week.

Unfortunately the principle of reversibility means that your gains can also be lost, so you need to continually overload and progress. Finally the principles and theories of variation, moderation, individual differences, and diminishing returns collectively state that to get better you need to mix it up and rest, what works for one person may not work for you, and there is only so much payout you can milk from a certain form of training. The next best idea is that to learn a complex skill, parts must be broken down into manageable learnable bits to learn them, and then reassembled back together to perform well.

The concepts of strength training can be applied by applying concepts such as periodization, programming, strength, endurance, power, recruitment, efficiency, cardiovascular training, adaptation, anatomy, physiology, psychology, neurology, and the rehabilitative medical fields. The best concepts to apply are common sense and critical thinking by challenging everything we do. It's cool to see the climbing community making it up as we go. It is such a complex sport that we should be proud of what has been discovered. All of these concepts are integrated into the principles behind this training section.

EVALUATING YOUR FITNESS

For pure climbing purposes, the best way to evaluate your fitness is to just slap a label on what level you climb. Obviously it's more subjective than that, but it's still the bottom line. Technique is an essential part of climbing fitness, but there are no gold standard tests to evaluate your technique. This book will guide you through picking apart different techniques and training the areas you need. There are many tests available to gauge more quantifiable aspects of physical fitness that evaluate muscle imbalance and flexibility. I designed this book to help you tease out these imbalances by going through the exercises, and give yourself a pass/fail. If you fail, then simply practice the exercise by making it easier to get started, and then progressively harder. I did not include specific tests to identify problems or imbalances simply because there are too many and no one test is better than another. I have included in the reference section at the end of the book several texts that do an excellent job at this.

For gauging cardiovascular fitness many people use indicators such as maximum heart rate, resting heart rate, VO2 max, and anaerobic endurance (RAST Test). The first three values are extremely subjective between individuals, and are really more useful for gauging over-training and exercise intensity. However, they can be improved upon. VO2 max is a favorite cardio indicator, but it is essentially meaningless information without actually getting an accurate test at an exercise physiology lab at a local hospital or university. Even then, what are you going to do with that information besides boast or bemoan about it? If you feel you are lacking in aerobic ability then you should train more regardless of your score.

For climbers, the main area where aerobic ability is needed is at altitude or speed climbing, and someone with a high VO2 max could perform terribly compared to someone with a lower score! Use your scores as a baseline to gauge improvement. Anaerobic endurance is measured via the RAST Test if you are interested in finding your score. For more information on testing you aerobic potential, see the suggested reference texts at the end of the book. All that matters is that you know your weaknesses for the type of climbing you want to do and train them. Getting better at an exercise, or better yet, climbing better, will tell you that your fitness or skills have improved.

ABOUT THE EXERCISES

There are a ton of exercises in this section. Remember to keep your focus on climbing the medium you want to train for as much as possible. Don't skip climbing because you need to spend time in the gym, unless you have to rehab an injury, have severe imbalances that need to be addressed first, or need to develop a baseline of fitness for non-technical aspects of a climb. Train with a goal in mind, and remind yourself of that goal every time you hit the crag or gym. I will begin by discussing all the exercises, how to do them correctly, and some specific comments about when to do them. This will be followed by a lengthy discussion of how to program the exercises into an effective training program. I have included most rehab exercises in the initial training section to make them prehab exercises. Any exercise than can be done one arm or leg at a time should be done that way if possible with some exceptions. Climbing is generally done one limb at a time, so it's best to train that way.

BREATHING AND POSTURE

I have tried to include postural tips for all the exercises, but also tried to avoid repeating myself over and over. Here are the basic postural principles to avoid injury and train correct automatic patterns for when the exercise gets put into use in real-life, which is in this case, climbing.

> Breathe out during exertion. This is important because it helps prevent your blood pressure from getting too high, and straining too hard which will prevent hernia. Breath out slowly through pursed lips, and engage your transverse abdominals by drawing your abs in (don't suck in your gut). Breathe in by expanding your stomach, as if inflating it like a balloon – not by filling up the upper part of your lungs and raising your shoulders up to your ears.

> If you are not moving one of the following body parts during exercise, keep them in this position: Chin pulled in (not back or down) as if making a double chin, set the shoulder blades down and in with an active squeeze, shoulders relaxed, chest high, pelvis neutral (not tipped forward or backward), transverse abs engaged (your abdominal corset), pelvic floor engaged (the stop-peeing muscles), knees slightly bent, feet shoulder width apart or in a fencer's stance, feet slightly turned out, and foot arches tense.

BEGINNING TRAINING

When you first begin your training, you will need to make a whole lot of changes along the way. It is a really good idea to schedule in a week of trial and error. During this week, try out the exercises to find out how long your exercise sessions really take.

Never take seemingly basic or easy exercises lightly. There's a good chance you are doing it wrong. Complex tasks are built upon basic skills. Remember the Karate Kid? So wax on/wax off the stupid breathing exercise, the annoying footwork drills, etc. If you have indeed mastered it, then of course move on, but re-check your form by re-visiting it, or better yet, teach it to someone.

You may find that you can do a lot on day one or week one of your training. Don't! Your connective tissue and nervous system needs time to adapt. Starting out running out of the gates is admirable, but will definitely lead to pain, possibly injury, and most likely pushing your training back even further. Most attempts at training stop after a few days to a month. Follow the 10% rule to give the rest of your body time to catch up – you're not just training muscles.

> Only add 10% more weight, time, or intensity each week.

BENEFITS OF TRAINING BEYOND CLIMBING

This list could go on for a while, but I'll keep it brief. Exercise improves your mood, love life, and energy levels. It helps you lose weight, and fight all sorts of systemic diseases like diabetes to name one. Your chances of living longer are increased. Weighted training strengthens bones, tendons, ligaments and other connective tissue that are important in avoiding injuries and growing old (general mobility to osteoporosis).

Weight Gain

Weighing less most certainly helps you climb. You should not gain significant weight by following the training program in this book. You really need to train hard and in a different way to bulk-up, and many body-types with certain genetics simply cannot bulk-up. If you are fairly de-trained you may develop more overall muscle tone, but the benefits of that should be glaringly obvious. The benefits far outweigh the gains in performance.

Weight gains from increased forearm strength are minimal considering the size of the forearm in proportion to the rest of your body. Cardio and leg exercises shouldn't give you bigger legs, just stronger. If you want to stay an anorexic sport climber then by all means, skip some exercise – just come back to them when you plateau or get injured. On the flip side, muscle does weigh a lot more than fat; so don't be discouraged because the scale may be reading new muscle replacing old fat.

HOW LONG TO TRAIN

Make the majority of your time spent actually climbing for technical proficiency. A day of outdoor climbing can last from dawn to dark. When you are in your normal workday/school schedule, time becomes an issue if you need to supplement your climbing with other exercises. A warm-up should take about 15 minutes, stretching about the same amount of time (or an hour yoga class), and the weight room could last an hour and a half if you are doing a long list of easier high rep, one arm/leg at a time conditioning exercises. If training for a long demanding alpine climb your endurance training could take hours.

Building your foundation is by far the longest time requirement because there are just so many exercises you could do. Many people drop out after a week or so. Either stick with it, or skip it and possibly get injured or have weaknesses holding you back. Luckily, the more you progress you make in your training, the less gym time will be needed. If you have a lot of imbalances and rehab issues, or are fairly de-trained, don't be in a time crunch to get through the initial foundation phases. If you are in tip-top all-around shape you can skip a large part of the initial phase to save time, adding in supplemental exercises when time allows.

Protocols

There are many different ways to do one exercise. I have listed a few specific protocols that group the above variables into formulas that isolate different performance results: strength (hypertrophy), power (maximum recruitment), endurance, technique, and a combination of these protocols.

Changing the variables will take doing an exercise from one protocol and place it into another protocol. I have divided the exercises into: warm-up, climbing, non-climbing, and cool down. Rehab exercises fit into either the warm-up or non-climbing category, or if extremely rehab specific, are done independent of training. Climbing exercises are divided into skills & ability (which do not fit into protocols), drills (sub divided into protocols) and non-climbing exercises are sub-divided into the protocols and by body area or technique. Aerobic protocols are almost identical, however I call them aerobic endurance, aerobic threshold, and anaerobic threshold.

> The basic elements you can change are the speed at which you perform the exercise, how many reps you do at one time or how long you hold a posture for, how many sets you perform, how much weight you used, or if you chose to do the exercise isometrically, concentrically, eccentrically, and/or with an element of instability.

Reps and Sets

Reps (repetitions) are how many times you repeat the movement without resting. Sets are how many times you perform the number of reps.

Example: 8 reps 3 sets. Lift the weight eight times and rest. Do this two more times. Failure means you cannot complete another rep. *If on your 20th pushup you collapse before you complete it, you failed and therefor completed 19 pushups. The 20th did not count. Or if you lift 95 pounds, but struggle and can't finish lifting 96 pounds, your max is 95 pounds.*

It is better to just do one full set and move onto another exercise if your time is limited. Changing the reps and weight will alter the desired benefit of the exercise from endurance training to power training. Changing the number of sets will determine the lasting benefit of the exercise. Each set performed has diminishing returns, and the first set is by far the most beneficial. In general, two sets is a great compromise between gains earned and time spent. Beyond two or three sets will wind up training your cardiovascular system's aerobic or anaerobic conditioning, or will be training your nervous system to learn the exercise as a skill.

If you cannot finish a set in the desired protocol you are using the wrong amount of weight and number of reps/time for the protocol you are training. If it's at bodyweight and you cannot finish, find a way to take weight off with tubing or props. If one side can do fewer reps than the other, you've got an imbalance. It's okay if the imbalance is only 2-3 reps off at medium to low weight. If there is a bigger discrepancy in the number of reps you can do on each side at low to medium weights, then do another set on the weaker side and also start with that side first. With heavy weight reps, the discrepancy becomes more pronounced. Even a one-rep discrepancy at max or near maximal exertion can be a moderate to severe imbalance. That side may need additional endurance and strength training. Tossing in another set could be okay, but it could also be too much.

A neat thing about our bodies and brains is neurologic crossover. That is, by training one side, the other side actually gets stronger too! Start with the weakest side first. Resting between reps also changes the intensity. If you want the additional benefit of endurance and anaerobic threshold training, then rest just enough to avoid puking or passing out. Rest between reps for power training is extremely important to be able to exert maximum effort and staying uninjured. Resting between sets should be just long enough to provide just enough recovery to do another set. This means 0-20 minutes depending on how intense the exercise is. A great way to cheat is to exercise other muscle groups during this rest. You'll need to eat or drink quickly digestible carbs to keep from crashing. You can also overtax your endocrine system with too much stress and high intensity cross training. Just how many days to rest between doing an exercise again will be discussed later.

WEIGHT AND INTENSITY

Your max (maximum) is the amount of weight where you can only do one rep. Another way to find your max without breaking or straining something is to find your 5 rep max and multiply it by 1.2. *Example: You can lift 50 pounds five times before failure. 50 x 1.2 = 60 lbs. max.*

It is very important to decide whether to scale back the weight to a more manageable weight to complete the number of reps. If you are doing an endurance building exercise that is bodyweight only, use a piece of furniture or a heavy rubber band to remove some weight. If you are doing hypertrophy or power exercises, drop the poundage until you can complete the reps to failure. Doing this the other way (keeping the same weight and dropping or increasing the reps) will put you in another protocol category and not accomplish what you are training for.

Every exercise needs to be done at an intensity hard enough to fail in the chosen amount of reps. The point of training is to make the exercise mimic a real-life activity (from maintaining posture, slogging uphill, to climbing moves) but making it much harder than the actual activity itself. Why cheat yourself? Exercising can be fun, but there are lot more fun things I'd rather be doing, and working for no reason is what most of do at our jobs. The only benefit for training below this intensity is to warm-up, or to prepare joints and ligaments for higher loads to come.

Gauge intensity by feel instead of math. In other words, if you're trying to lift 85% of your max (say 100 lbs.) and the math says this is 85 lbs., but you don't fail by the last rep, then increase the weight. Drops some weight if it's too heavy. Finally, add more weight when you start getting bored with an exercise – it probably means you got stronger. If you aren't sure if it is time to add more weight (remember you are training to get stronger, so you should be getting stronger and your weights won't stay fixed), then add more weight and see what happens. You could be failing at the last rep because you expect to (this is very important in climbing as well). For stability exercises and exercises using bodyweight or light weights, failing is achieved when a burning sensation or lots of shaking occur. Pushing beyond this will lead to injury.

After about 3 weeks of training (more or less) you'll notice that you may have jumped a level in the amount of weight or reps you can perform. This is because that most strength and endurance gains during this time are actually because of neurological adaptations that have taken place. Your brain has driven the route enough times now to find the best possible shortcut. This will continue to occur each time you make major changes to your training. You may have actually been much stronger than your brain let you, so find out by increasing weight or intensity. Not only increase volume by adding weight, but also increase volume by number of days a week. Start small 1-2 days a week and progress to more days a week (3-5).

The more proficient you become at an exercise, the more efficient you become, and your muscles and cardiovascular system will be less taxed. This is good because becoming efficient in a movement or skill will hopefully transfer into your climbing endeavors, but may not be so good while specifically training a muscle group, or heart and lungs. Train to be good at climbing, not to be good at the exercise. If you are really good at an exercise or aerobic sport, you may want to switch things up or realize that you may have to increase the intensity. Doing exercises at high intensity you are not proficient at will also increase the chance of injury.

Tricking the Central Governor
Our brains have a central governor that limits our physical potential in order to keep a reserve in store for emergency use; similar to the governor in newer cars that won't let you drive past a certain speed. Hardcore endurance athletes have come up with ways to trick the central governor. Don't push it for training, but being able to dig deep is needed for extreme performance or for actual emergency use on a long climb when things hit the fan and you can't afford to tire out. When the central governor says that's enough, we call it "hitting the wall".

Fear can trick the central governor to give you a bit more energy. Luckily fear comes naturally when you are in trouble (or perceived trouble), but it's pretty hard to trick yourself into pretending to be afraid. Utter, mortal fear helps to dig the deepest, but it also makes bad decisions and poor technique - just when you need it most. The more useful trick is the promise of good things to come for your body.

A brief rest may not actually help your body recover, but it can trick your brain into thinking more rest will be coming. Consuming some fat, the nutrient that says to your inner caveman that you just killed an animal and will have plenty of food and rest for a while, can trick your brain into letting you have the reserve of glycogen stored in your liver. Eating or drinking easily accessible carbs like glucose also calms the central governor, making it think you aren't quite at the wall. Even swishing sports drink around in your mouth and spitting it back into your bottle can be enough, and is a great strategy if your actual food and water supplies are low and you need to finish the climb.

Remember, the central governor is there for a reason, and by tricking it and actually using up your reserves will lead to a major crash. If you use it up and you aren't done with the climb, you could get into really big trouble, even die. Maybe you should seek retreat options or bivy. Check out the crazy stories from cyclists have had during a non-stop (yes, non-stop) bike race across the United States, how they trick the central governor, and some of the tragedies that have occurred because of this (source: RadioLab).

Types of Movements
The Physics of Moving a Load
Acceleration is a change in velocity over a change in time. Force = mass times acceleration. Work = force times distance. Power = work divided by time. The bottom line is to efficiently climb without tiring out, we want to do less work. Distance, mass, and gravity are constant. So what can you do to change things? You can climb quickly to shorten the time, or climb with acceleration to decrease the force. Acceleration is the

key, and in climbing that means dynamic movement. In weight training, acceleration is the key to moving loads that are way too heavy for a slow static lift. There are pros and cons to this. The pros are that the skills in training will translate towards skills in climbing. The cons are that one of the reasons to train is to make things harder than in real-life situations.

Isotonic Movements: Concentric and Eccentric

A concentric exercise is one where you shorten a muscle to move a load. This is your standard weight-lifting move. Use concentric contractions for most exercises. Eccentric contractions are the opposite of concentric. A muscle is lengthened to slow down or stabilize the movement of a load. This is a good rehab movement or a good stabilizer muscle movement to incorporate. Eccentric contractions are stronger than concentric and training one does not always train the other. Most of the exercises will be listed in their standard way, either eccentric on concentric. I urge you to experiment by taking a standard concentric exercise and making it eccentric. Usually this entails doing a concentric contraction, then prolonging the lowering phase.

Isometric

This means to hold load without moving a joint. Isometric training can be similar to endurance in that it usually trains postural muscles, but it also recreates climbing specific movements since you need to maintain body position statically for long periods of time in climbing. It is more boring and time consuming, but incorporating isometric holds is essential.

Isometric training trains your body in 20° increments, so it is best to pick 3-4 angles. *For example: fully flexed, 90°, 120°, and 150° (just below fully extended).*

Besides a static hold, another way to incorporate isometric training is to perform extremely slow concentric to eccentric reps to isolate all the angles at or near bodyweight.

Isokinetic Movement

Isokinetic is the secret brother to isometric and isotonic movement. An isokinetic movement can be concentric or eccentric, but the amount of force exerted is constant through the range of motion. In almost every exercise done in the gym or in the real world, the load lifted exerts a different amount of force through the range of motion. This is especially noticeable when using resistance tubing – it starts easy but gets harder. Training isometrically in various angles is one solution, but sometimes power must be applied from a weird angle as well. The only reason I'm mentioning this form of almost theoretical movement is because climbers need to exert maximum force with their joints in weird positions, and that climbers are very creative and maybe one of you will come up with some interesting training with amazing results. There are very expensive machines that create an isokinetic contraction, but it can also be accomplished by having a friend apply changing resistance against your limb to mimic an isokinetic movement.

Plyometric Exercises

These are quick, explosive movements, usually done in succession. Plyometric exercises are similar to power training, but the speed of contraction is more important than the weight used. Jumping is a classic example, or in climbing, the dyno. Other climbing movements are quickly grabbing a handhold, swinging your ice tool, or hopping talus and boulders. Tossing medicine balls with a partner or against a wall are standard plyometric exercises. Taking a standard exercise and making it plyometric can cause injury and may not be extraordinarily helpful. Try and train movements in climbing or climbing-related activities that could benefit from quick explosive movement. Training slowly or isometrically helps for holding static positions, but training plyometrically in fast repetitive powerful bursts help training to climb fast and efficiently.

Proprioceptive Exercises
Proprioception means your body's awareness of its location in space and time. These exercises are vital in rehabbing an injury, especially those due to poor technique or posture. A proprioceptive exercise challenges a muscle group by adding an element of instability such as taking away vision, making a surface unstable, or moving a joint through a range of motion extremely rapidly. The better proprioception you have in a particular joint or group of joints, the less likely it is that you will injure that area and vice versa. In fact, injuring a joint actually damages the proprioception and increases the likelihood for re-injury.

Many exercises, especially in the warm-up section, are proprioceptive exercises. However, you can make many traditional exercises more difficult by adding an element of instability by doing the exercise on a **suspension trainer, rings, furniture sliders, a Swiss ball, Bosu ball, foam roller, wobble board**, while simultaneously performing another exercise, or using spring-like weight such as a **Bodyblade** (or even a Shake Weight!). If there's an option to do an exercise by adding instability, do it.

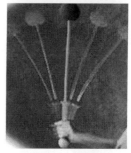

Courtesy Bodyblade®

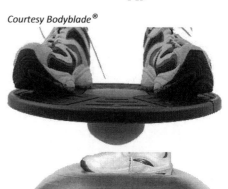

Furniture sliders, BOING, BodyBlade, wobble board, and Bosu Ball. Swiss balls, rings/suspension, and foam rollers are shown in exercises later.

Closed vs. Open Chain
You can move an object (open chain) or use the object to move you (closed chain). Climbing consists almost entirely of closed chain movements. You don't move the cliff -

you use the cliff to move your body. Swinging ice tools is an example of an open chain climbing movement. Pushups would be a closed chain exercise while bench presses would be an open chain. Squats are closed chain while leg press machines are open chain. Closed chain exercises are generally more applicable for climbing, and train more of your body instead of just one specific muscle. Open chain exercises are better for training precision movements. It takes creativity to turn an open-chain exercise into a closed chain exercise. For example a military press becomes closed chain as a handstand pushup.

Slow Twitch and Fast Twitch Muscles
Skeletal muscle can be broken down into two major groups: type I (slow twitch) and type IIa/IIb (fast twitch). Type IIa is an in-between with properties of both. Basically type I fibers are much more efficient at metabolizing glycogen and are more aerobic than type-II, which excel at anaerobic metabolism. This translates into type I fibers can contract longer for posture and endurance, and type II are more adapted to quick, powerful bursts. The ratio of fiber type in a particular muscle group is genetic, and can be a factor in performance. There is evidence that you can change fiber type through training. This is all just FYI to be complete, please don't waste your time trying to change muscle fiber type unless you really think it's the limiting factor in your climbing – and you'd better be a super-alpinist or a 5.15/V13 climber if you're considering.

OTHER TYPES OF EXERCISE
Functional Exercises
Functional exercises combine multi-joint movements that mimic basic patterns you do in life. The more functional you can make an exercise, the more it translates into activities. Single joint repetitive exercises only build strength for that specific movement. This is good for fine-tuning weak link muscles or for rehab, but an inefficient waste of time for general conditioning. You can also save a great deal of time by combining exercises into more functional exercises. For example a clean and jerk combines lifting, squats, and an overhead press and plyometric power. Start by isolating movements for strength gains, and progress to function exercises for gains in performance.

Agonist, Antagonist, Stabilizers, and Core Muscles
Agonists are the muscles that move the joint in the direction you want it to go, and antagonists slow the agonists down to make a controlled movement. For convention, I am labeling the prime movers in climbing as agonists, and the muscles that stabilize or work eccentrically as antagonists. The agonist muscles get their training focus during the strength phase and are mostly contained in the climbing drills section or in the legs section, and the antagonists get the most attention during the foundation phase except some key pushing exercises that need more extensive training. For convention I am calling some muscles of the spine and hip Core Muscles. The prime movers of the core (abs and lumbar) are trained slightly differently since they need to be much stronger than the other core muscles and stabilizers for climbing.

CrossFit (and similar programs)
"How do you know someone does CrossFit? -They tell you."

I am going to sound like a waffling politician here, and will probably get more than a few emails regarding this! My use of the term CrossFit can be swapped out with any of the other high intensity workout regimes that have become so popular. Programs that have individual, tailored training that appear to be "CrossFitty" may not apply to my reservations outlined below.

My biggest concern is how injury prone the workouts are. It's hard not to succumb to peer-pressure during the classes. The peer pressure is a benefit since you'll work harder than you ever would on your own. But having fifteen people screaming at you to "come on!" while trying to finish your 50th poorly executed pull-up can make you push past the limits of your joints and muscles. CrossFit has you do a lot of overhead weights and squat-based exercise at high reps or very high loads that are really dangerous if done improperly. The warm-up for CrossFit is generally inadequate, and the cool down and stretching at the end is almost nonexistent (may vary by gym). This is a recipe for shoulder, neck, and low back blowouts.

The CrossFit theory of muscle confusion will not help you be a better climber except for wallowing around in steep Alaskan snow and shoveling snow caves. The muscle confusion theory also makes it very difficult to get stronger in a certain area because you don't do that exercise enough times within a certain time-frame – there is no periodization or progression. If you don't have any lurking injuries and want to get fit as hell, CrossFit isn't a bad place to be.

The problem is that CrossFit does not allow you to get better at one thing – it's too random and brief. You may actually lose performance in a certain area. Many people complain that instead of getting stronger, they get good at being more efficient at doing the exercises, or that form is sacrificed over finishing a set. Since the skills in CrossFit have barely any sport-specific transference, getting better at CrossFit is fairly useless. The goal of weight training should be physiologic changes, not neurological adaptation. Adaptation should occur in sport-specific modalities.

If weight loss is a concern, CrossFit is not the best program. It doesn't last long enough. The weight loss stories from CrossFit are most likely occurring because of diet changes and doing other exercise on top of the workouts outside of class. Also, you can work so hard at CrossFit that you could succumb to rhabdomyolysis. Rhabdo is a condition when you break down so much muscle tissue that your suffer from kidney damage. This is probably not a concern for most, but if you find yourself working out that hard almost daily, you could be in jeopardy.

Finally, CrossFit embraces certain things with cult-like status without much critical thinking involved by the followers or "disciples". One of the cult-like embraces is following the Zone Diet. The Zone Diet is not the be-all-end-all of dieting. I'll discuss dieting later, but really with anything in life, give yourself a reality check to see if you're engaging in cult behavior. Besides nutrition, I seriously doubt if most CrossFit coaches have any formal training in what they teach besides training from other CrossFit members or classes, and I don't care who originally invented the theories. Many CrossFit coaches prescribe medical advice and even perform manual therapy on clients...not sure how legal that is.

That said, CrossFit and other programs are pretty good off-season workouts or for getting back in shape. Again, if you aren't suffering from any lingering injuries and need an extra push to get back in shape, I would recommend CrossFit (and the other programs mentioned) for a 1-3 month period. If you are really out of shape, then I would avoid them - they are just too intense and instead of "scaling back" with these programs, your time and money would be better spent on something else until you're ready

Weight Protocols

There is no distinct line drawn between endurance, strength, and power. The sets, reps, and times given for each protocol are just considered to be standard for that protocol. Changing the weight, reps, or time in a protocol will slide the desired effect from endurance to strength to power gains. Transference of protocols only slides one way: from power down to endurance. Endurance will not train strength, but strength can train for some endurance. Transference will diminish the farther you get away from one protocol to another. Feel free to tweak everything to fit your desired outcome.

Endurance

Endurance does not train for strength or power, only endurance. This is good training for postural muscles and stabilizers, or training a muscle or ligament for all day type movements. You can also train for skill. Endurance training is mostly a neurological adaptation – your brain does some re-wiring to make doing these movements as efficient as possible. You will actually lose some strength gains by training endurance. Endurance training is a good starting point to get weak muscles used to work and fully activated by your nervous system. But it's also a good place to end training for some areas because again, you can't train strength by training endurance. So it may be a good idea to get a muscle nice and strong, and then wire it for endurance. It also depends on the type of climbing you plan to do. You can steadily increase weight for endurance training, but progress is much slower. Only increase weight for exercises that would be too difficult to strength train for. Once you can do a high level of reps at bodyweight or low weight, switch to a strength protocol, and then come back and buff it out with endurance training at a higher weight or intensity. Some exercises are too dangerous to be in any other protocol but endurance.

> **Endurance**
>
> Basic endurance training consists of 1-6 sets of 20-50 reps generally at body weight to failure that is usually gauged by fatigue, burning, shaking, or loss of form. Perform statically (isometric) or at a slow speed. You can train 4-7 days per week for this protocol depending on the difficulty of the exercise.
>
> Below are some suggested endurance workouts:
> - Pick a few (3-10) exercises and cycle between each exercise and do sets of 50-40-30-20-10 reps
> - Perform 30 reps 3-10 exercises or 50 reps 3-10 exercises. Or just follow the general rule for a single exercise.
> - Hold a position for 1-2 minutes
> - Perform an exercise that is usually not held isometrically (a repetition exercise) extremely slowly.

Strength

Strength builds muscle (you may gain some weight) and makes you the sorest post-work out, also known as **delayed onset muscle soreness (DOMS)** which is frequently mistaken for pain due to injury – you can push through it and it should go away completely within a week or so of regular training. DOMS is caused by micro-tears in muscle from new demands and is safe. Strength training also taps into your endurance, so luckily you are killing two birds. Pick a goal for strength training and gradually increase weight, but not the number reps and sets.

> **Strength**
> - Weight should be 85% of your one rep max. Perform 5-10 reps at slower speed for 2-3 sets. Isometric exercises would be held for 10-30 seconds to failure.
> - You can train up to 3-4 days per week under the strength protocol and rest 1-2 days between training a muscle group.

> A sample strength workout could be
> - **3 sets of 3-7 exercises, or simply using the guidelines one exercise at a time**
> - **Short duration 3-8 second holds, using weight to failure**

STRENGTH-ENDURANCE

Strength-endurance trains you to be able to perform multiple bursts of sub-maximal strength over and over. This isn't really a new protocol, but a way to gap the spectrum between endurance and power since many climbing activities fall somewhere between the two. The starting and ending weights will vary with the exercise. Experiment with how much weight you will need. You should be able to do the first few sets without too much struggle, but should be a dripping pile of useless meat by the end.

> **Strength-Endurance**
>
> Use between bodyweight to 85% max weight in order to fail by the end of the final set.
>
> You can perform strength-endurance exercises 2-3 times a week max for each muscle group with 2-3 days of rest in between.
>
> Here are some ways to train for power endurance:
> - **Tabata Protocol**: 20 seconds of work / 10 seconds of rest. 8 minutes of this is a standard duration.
> - **Little Protocol**: 60 seconds of work / 75 seconds of rest. 8-12 minutes total time is standard.
> - **Fartlek Protocol**: 2 to 1 ratio of work to rest lasting 9-20 minutes.
> - **Compromised Rest**: 30 seconds of work with 30 seconds of isometric holds. A great may to mimic difficult climbing and to work stabilizers!
> - **High to Low Reps**: Sets of 21–15-9 reps (or other numbers of your choosing). Two to four exercises per set are standard.
> - **Time Pyramids**: 1 min, 2 min, 3 min...5 min...1 min. Decrease weight up the pyramid, and increase it down.
> - **Breathing Ladders**: These are excellent ways to combine strength and aerobic endurance at the same time, and great for climbing. For every rep you do, rest an equal number of breaths. Either start from the top 1 rep 1 breath or bottom *(example 10 reps 10 breaths)*. You can even do pyramids (1...10...1).
>
> Also, check out some of the WODs (workout of the day) over at popular training centers and blogs for ideas – but tailor them to your needs.

POWER

Power trains to use all of your strength (max recruitment) for one explosive movement. You don't normally recruit every muscle fiber for a given motion. Training to recruit as many fibers as possible allows you to use as much strength as possible in a short amount of time. This phase is not for core, antagonist, or stabilizer muscles. Don't make a workout like the other protocols that has you running around doing a bunch of different lifts for the power protocol. Take your time here to avoid injury. Do a few warm up sets of higher reps to build up to your final weight. Lift quickly.

> **Power**
> - 6 sets of 1-3 reps at 95-100% max.
> - Train one day per week, occasionally two, under the power protocol for each muscle group and give that group at least 2-3 days' rest in between.
>
> Some different ways to train are:
> - **3-6 sets of increasing weight with a rest, then 6 sets of 1-3 reps at max**
> - **Isometric holds for a moment to 4 seconds to failure**

CYCLING BETWEEN PROTOCOLS

Cycle between strength, power, and strength-endurance protocols, but try not to exercise the same muscles under more than one protocol in a day to reduce your chance of injury. It depends on what your emphasis is in order to decide what ratio of each protocol you choose to use for a given exercise, but be sure to follow the maximum days per week for each protocol with adequate rest. A basic schedule for a muscle group could be 2 days of strength, a day of power, and a day of strength-endurance and rest the rest of the week. This would accommodate the rest recommendations given for each protocol and give you a solid rest at the end of the week.

Exercises that are performed under the endurance protocol are generally not suitable to mix and match with the other protocols, or are meant as an introduction to the exercise. If endurance exercises get too easy or you run out of energy before you're muscles weaken, switch to a strength protocol until more weight can be tolerated, then switch back with that weight under the endurance protocol.

MAKING AN INTERESTING WORKOUT OF THE DAY (WOD)

Making cool-looking WOD's, like those seen in high profile training sites and groups, is not necessary. You can benefit by sticking with just doing one exercise at a time and then moving on to the next. This can get boring, and it may help to motivate you and provide higher intensity than you thought (central governor). Before making a WOD, plan out what exercises and protocols for that you think are appropriate. Look at the prescription for each protocol and some of the suggested ways to implement that protocol and put together either a timed WOD or a WOD that has a pre-prescribed number of reps and sets. To make it fun and doable, it has to flow well. To make it safe you need to follow the guidelines. You can mix and match all the climbing, non-climbing, and preventative exercises together or group them in teams.

BASIC ORDER OF PROTOCOLS

Not all exercises will go through the full cycle or hit every protocol

- **General Endurance**: Build a foundation to avoid injury
- **Strength**: Build new muscle
- **Strength Endurance**: Get new muscle ready for prolonged exertion and stress
- **Power**: Maximize the use of new muscle
- **Specific Endurance**: Regain endurance lost to simulate new demands

BASIC ORDER OF EXERCISES

When scheduling a workout, ordering the exercises is moderately important to prevent injury and receive maximum benefit from the each exercise. Re-order these if, say, climbing ability is really important for the day, but you still want to exercise, or don't have time before or after one or the other.

- Warm Up – Range of Motion, Muscle Activation, Dynamic Stretching
- Core, Stability, Agonist, and Rehab Exercises
- Climbing Specific Strength/Endurance
- Climbing Skills
- Climbing Ability
- Weight Training High Loads Low Reps
- Weight Training Low Loads High Reps
- Plyometric
- Aerobic
- Fatigued Skill Training
- Stretch

Equipment

By no means is this a complete list of exercise equipment out there, and likewise, by no means do you need to own a single item on this list. Besides some suggested aerobic equipment and a squat rack, I've left out a lot of expensive home gym equipment. Many items can be made yourself, with everyday items, or just your body. Remember, we're training for climbing here.

The Gym

You don't need to belong to a gym or a rock gym to get better – it just really helps. There are plenty of home exercises and outdoor training you can do with little to no equipment. If you don't live near accessible rock or ice, and have no climbing gym (or your climbing gym is limited) consider building a home wall and gym. Explore your neighborhood for buildings and objects that can provide you with training opportunities.

Building a Climbing Wall

Building a basic wall is actually pretty easy and cheap. I have little to no carpentry skills, and managed to make a passable wall with several panels for $300 worth of holds, wood, and screws. Metolius and Atomik have excellent free online instruction manuals on how to build a home wall, some Internet searching will provide you with additional ideas, and there is an excellent book called "Building Your Own Climbing Wall" by Steve Lange (2012). A home wall should be built mainly to do repetitive laps for finger strength training if you have limited space.

Do all of your design and measuring first since Home Depot will cut your wood for free! Unless you plan on just leaning your wall against your house or a tree, which is an excellent option, you'll need some basic trigonometry skills or an online triangle calculator. Check, check, and recheck. Then check again. Remember that the actual size of the wood you buy will be slightly smaller than its advertised dimensions. You'll need some tools, but I managed to build mine with only hammer and a $15 cordless drill.

The climbing surface of the wall is made by joining ¾" thick 4'x8' ACX plywood sheets framed by 2"x4" studs with another 2"x4" stud in the middle. Use 2"x6" studs if making a larger wall. Be sure to put at least a 10" kicker board at the base. If you can only have one panel, make it a 50° overhanging angle (relative to the ground, not the wall which would be a 40° angle). If you have room for two, make the other wall 10-20°. If you've got enough room, have the two panels face each other so you can put a roof between them. You could also make the panel pivot to adjust the angle.

Stack your panels together and drill ½" drill bit holes to install t-nuts in for your holds. Drill a lot so you have many options. Now hammer in t-nuts into the back of the wall in the holes you just drilled. If you want holes where the framing 2"x4"s are, you'll have to pre-drill into those 2"x4"s before adding the t-nuts. Drill and install the t-nuts first, before framing your panels! The panels can be supported by either drilling a piece of wood into your ceiling studs and leaning the wall into that (cleaner looking), or make it free standing by using support studs. Use 3" wood screws and pre-drill the holes so you don't strip the screws.

To reinforce your joints use various metal connectors. This will reduce the amount of other support architecture needed and make the whole thing look cleaner. You don't have to cut your joints at angles if your wall overhangs. Cutting at angles will certainly look better and cleaner, but getting it right is tricky business. If you don't cut at angles, you will need to screw in various connecting boards so your joints don't slip out of place. I drilled two kicker boards together and placed the wall panel in the groove between the two and reinforced it with scrap wood and screws.

You'll also want some mattresses to fall on – don't skimp on this.

Header Joists for anchoring into wall and ceiling studs

Joist hangers for frame

Kicker board added

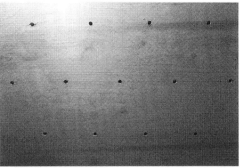
Grid drilled for t-nuts

T-nuts installed behind panels

Installing wall panels. Above 6 photos courtesy Adam Riser and backcountry.com

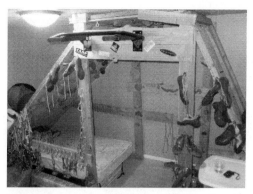

Self-supported wall. Hangboard opposite pull-up bar. Roof allows suspension trainer, pulleys, etc.

If you have limited space or can't even mount a fingerboard because you're renting, make a freestanding wall. For just a fingerboard you can make a short A-Frame base and extend the upper beams above the base to mount a fingerboard on. There are also some fingerboards that cam in a doorway similar to some pull-up bars. For system training you can make a narrow overhanging wall with just enough width to make it shoulder width. Leaning a wall outside against a tree or wall, or taking advantage of the underside of a flight of stairs are also other ideas for those with limited room. If you can afford one, treadwalls can be an excellent tool, but I'd start first by building your own wall.

Left Photo courtesy Dustin Clelen

Above photo courtesy The Blank Slate

Decorating the Wall

Now you can decorate the wall with **holds**, make storage shelves behind the panels, paint it, and slap stickers all over it. Adding extra 2"x10" panels for a **fingerboard(s), pull-up bar, pulleys** (to take weight off, homemade cable machine etc.) can make your wall more useful to train on. A good place to find climbing holds are in local classifieds, climbing forums, and at climbing gyms. You can even make your own plastic holds (search the web for how to), or by drilling through real rocks you've collected. Some companies manufacture limestone-like drytool holds. Get some **jibs** (tiny screw on holds) for your feet. Have some big jugs nearby your smaller holds. The goal should be to make it as hard as possible without being so hard that you injure yourself. If you can only have one set of holds on your wall, make them system holds. For **systems-type training or campus boards**, sanding down wood for different types of grips is cheap and very customizable. Rounded "logs" can make good slopers, as can a half a PVC pipe covered in decking tape. Atomik makes Pull-up Bombs for **open grip floating hold training**, as does G-Strings, Metolius (Rock-Rings), and Icetoolz. Several companies make system training holds, most notably Nicros for their HIT Strips, as well as Atomik, Revolution, Franklin and others.

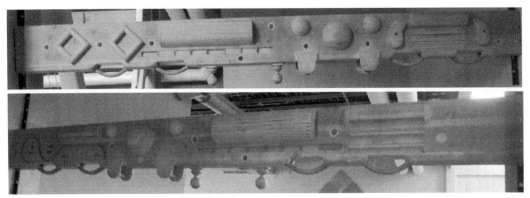

Poutre boards (Momentum Climbing Gym. Sandy, UT)

Adding **bolt hangers** is useful for drytool training, hanging **rock rings**, suspension trainers, or floating holds. **Specialty training holds are available for drytooling, or fully swinging your tool** (Iceholdz). Don't waste your time installing the dense foam some climbing gyms have available you can swing in – it is just too easy. You can also use scrap wood to hook, swing at, and create little divots on the wood face for hooking. Alpkit sells something called a **FigFour** that is similar to the shaft of a leashless icetool and has loops connected to the ends. The loops are swung onto the wall and loop around rock holds to simulate ice climbing movement.

Campus rungs can be bought commercially as well. A decent campus wall should be at least 4'x4' and begin 4' off the ground (head height is best) with rungs 6" apart with a 15° angle is space is limited. You can change it up by varying the angle between vertical to 30°, and the thickness and incut on the campus rung.

Wooden Cracks

To make wood cracks you'll need at least two high quality 2"x10"s (2"x8"s are ok) connected with threaded bolts. Check the wood for knots and splinters. Drill two holes at the top and bottom on each piece (clamp the boards together so the holes are equidistant), and drill holes 1" from the back of the boards every two feet. Slide the bolts through with washers and nuts on each side of every board and adjust the nuts on the threaded bolts to

Hit Strips and campus rungs

create a unique crack size between each board you are using. Adjusting the bolts differently, thereby bending/warping the wood can also vary the crack size. Too much and you will break it. It is a matter of choice whether to sand the wood, paint it, or create textured paint by throwing sand into the paint. You can go crazy and build all sorts of sizes and shapes and changing corners, but this requires a lot of space, money or resources, and carpentry knowledge. I recommend starting with slightly overhanging off fingers, tight hands, ring-locks, off fists just slightly too small for a knee jam, and a nasty off-width. Tips may be a bit too brutal for wooden cracks (but give it a try if you want).

Secure finger, hand, and fist jams don't require as much practice to master, so you may want to save time, money, and space on these sizes. If you have the money, Atomik sells pre-fab plastic adjustable cracks. Horizontal ceiling cracks of various sizes are also a valuable training tool for specific routes.

Above photo courtesy Atomik

Above photos courtesy Alan Rousseau

Above three photos courtesy Edward Hartouni

Moonboard

A Moonboard is a home built bouldering wall system available from moonclimbing.com. On the website you'll find detailed instructions on how to build one. The advantage to this system is that the board and holds are standardized. You can re-create boulder problems from the online resource, or create and share your own. Almost like a Facebook for boulder problems. This is a great idea. It streamlines wasted trial and error time to create your own problems, and takes away personal bias in creating problems.

Above photo courtesy David Tennant

Left photo courtesy Brandon McPhail, Right courtesy Moonboard

NON-CLIMBING SPECIFIC GYM EQUIPMENT

Here's a list of some home gym equipment that you may find useful. Most required equipment is listed in each exercise. Be extremely creative and don't waste too much money here. Many of the items are provided free by nature or can be crafted with some ingenuity. Google around to find homemade ways to make some of this stuff. One useful site is rosstraining.com. Instead of spending a ton of money at once, wait until you need something before you buy it.

- **Ab Mat** – Useful for floor crunches to keep your lumbar spine curved and it adds a bit more difficulty by increasing the angle a bit. A small firm throw pillow can do instead.
- **Ab Wheel** – Buy one or make your own.
- **Ankle, Wrist, and Weight Vest** – Ankle and wrist weights can add difficulty for core stability type exercises or for pull-ups and step-ups. A weight vest centers the weight best for added climbing weight, but a backpack filled with free-weights works. Also, training with a heavy pack is useful for training to climb with a pack on. Feel free to do an entire exercise routine with a weight vest on.
- **Balance Board** – Inflatable balance boards are great for training balance, or for making some exercises more unstable (therefor more difficult). A full complement of balance boards would be a 2-directional, 4 directional, omni-directional board, an Aeromat, followed by balance mats or shoes.
- **Box Jump** – Make your own with scraps from your climbing wall. 21" is a good height for a nice tall jump. If you're less than 5'8" scale it down. Easy to make your own.

- **Cable Machine** – The best ones out there have two adjustable arms you can raise and lower, and have several grips like a thick rope, single handle, double handle, and straps for your arms and legs. These are very expensive, and you can definitely get away without one. Most decent gyms have at least one of these. With a couple pulleys and a cable you can make your own cable machine. Or you can use rubber tubing and bands.
- **Countdown Timer, Interval (HIIT) Timer, or Smart Phone App**: Your own electronic motivator and reality check.
- **Dry Erase Board** – Useful for writing down goals, progression, and WODs.
- **Dumbbells** – Adjustable ones are cheaper and more space friendly. There are two basic kinds: one has the weights on it, the other you can add weights too. I like the latter so I can use the weights on their own for other exercises.
- **Electronic Training Assistants** to keep track of progress. There are too many to choose from. More useful for losing weight and aerobic activities, but technology is exploding on this one.
- **Foam Roller** – You can get a long one for core exercises, or a short one for massaging your ITB or gluts.
- **Free Weights** – A few 5 and 10 lb. weights and a couple 25 lb. weights lying around can be used for many different exercises.
- **Furniture Sliders** – Some genius used furniture sliders to do exercises normally done with a suspension trainer to save space and cost.
- **Grip Trainers** – There are many kinds from squeeze balls (some have finger bands to do extension exercises as well), to doughnuts, to individual finger trainers, to heavy-duty squeezers, to gyroscopic balls.
- **Gym Mat** – Puzzle piece mats are great cheap ways to pad your gym. Individual pieces are useful for road trips for knee padding and sitting on at camp.
- **Hypobaric Chamber or Breathing Trainer** – For the rich or super-fancy gym. Train at attitude for those big expeditions, or acclimatize in your bedroom while you sleep. Breathing trainers will be discussed later.
- **Journal** – Even more useful for writing down your daily exercises
- **Jump Rope** – The best jump rope is probably the cheapest looking – the Ultra Speed. One company that makes it is Rogue Fitness, but I've found similar ones online for cheaper.
- **Kettlebells** - Make your own adjustable ones with threaded pipes, hose clamps and free weights.
- **Lighting** – A desk lamp is useful for lighting up your climbing wall, and Christmas lights are always festive.
- **Medicine Balls** – Make your own by filling a basketball with sand and gluing it shut. 12 and 24 pound balls are a good start.
- **Pull-Up Bar** - A fingerboard or floating holds will do. There are several doorway models.
- **PVC Rod** – 1" thick and cut to a bit more than full arms width apart. Good for shoulder mobility.
- **Resistance Bands and Tubing**: Regular rubber bands work well for fingers, heavy weight lifting bands work well for taking body weight off, and thinner tubing with handles and door attachments are good for general exercises, rehab, and travel. Sheet-like resistance bands are good for rehab and stretching. However, resistance bands don't provide as sustained of a load for the range of the movement (hard to start, easier once you get going) as a cable machine.
- **Rower, Stationary Bike, Treadmill, Elliptical**, etc. – For those cold or rainy days. By far the best rower is made by Concept2, the best bike is the Schwinn Airdyne, and you're on your

own for the rest. If you have the space and funding, a treadmill desk for work/study is a godsend.
- **Squat Rack and Olympic Weights**. Rogue Fitness makes excellent weights because they bounce and you can drop them.
- **Step-up bench** – Just below knee height and wide enough for both legs. Easy to make your own.
- **Stereo System** – Goes without saying
- **Suspension Trainer or Gymnastic Rings** – There are great to make a standard exercise more unstable. There are commercial sets like the TRX, but it's really easy to make your own. Get creative. Aiders, daisy chains (especially adjustable ones), accessory cord, and rock rings work well.
- **Swiss Ball** – Aka stability ball, core ball, gym ball, exercise ball, etc. Great for intro stability training, or making some exercises more challenging. Also fun to sit in instead of a chair for short periods.
- **Weight Bench** – You could use a chair or the kitchen table.
- **Weight Machines** – You don't need to buy any weight machines, and most gyms have a good selection. The most useful machines help with rows, lat pulls, calf raises, leg press, hamstring curls, and bench press only because spotters aren't needed for very heavy weights. Free weights are more than acceptable substitutes.
- **Wrist Wraps** for squats or heavy lifting – protect your wrist from hyperextension with wrist wraps when doing very heavy lifting
- **Yoga Mat** – The extra friction helps you sliding on the linoleum or inhaling dog hair from the carpet. A closed-cell foam camping mat works just as well.

A really good gym would have a Moonboard wall, a wall with HIT strips and system holds, and a split wall with campus rungs (one side steep one side vertical) of various sizes - all with a decent kicker board. There would be several fingerboards and wood strips to move between and a couple pulleys to take weight off. The ceiling would have a few roof cracks in various sizes and some floating holds and gymnastic rings hanging down. If you have the height, put in some tall cracks of the hardest sizes as well. A stable weight bench and plates that can be used in adjustable kettle and dumbbells, a rower or Airdyne, PCV pipe, and a box jump rounds it out!

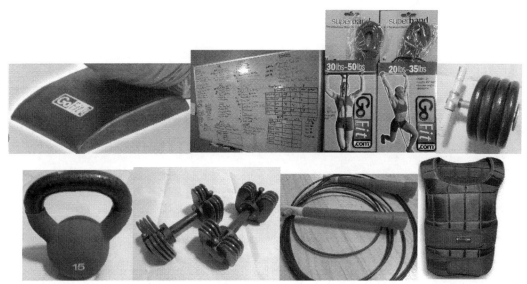

Ab mat, dry erase board, weight lifting bands, homemade kettlebell, adjustable dumbbells, speed jump rope, and weight vest

Chapter Two: Preparation and Prevention
The Warm-Up and Cool Down

Benefits of the Warm-Up
Before you launch into some serious training or climbing exercises, you'll want to first warm up, and also train antagonists and core musculature that shouldn't be trained when exhausted to prevent injury.

The purpose of the warm-up is to literally warm-up the body by increasing blood flow and expending energy to loosen muscles, connective tissue and joints, bring your joints through a full range of motion, and activate functional motor engrams (neurological pathways that regulate automatic proprioceptive feedback and control of specific complex movements). This will help reduce injury and improve training by increasing the active range of motion to prevent tears and increase movement, fire up circuitry so proprioceptive feedback and motor engrams are booted up, and get oxygen and nutrients to the cells and waste out more efficiently. You will read in the stretching section that slow steady stretching can reset your proprioceptors, but the dynamic stretches in the warm-up do not hold a position long enough to interfere with proprioception. There is just enough quick (but not forceful) stretching with dynamic stretching (not to be confused with active stretching) to sneak in some flexibility gains without increasing the chance of injury.

Warm-Up Basics
A basic warm up before any routine or climb should take about 15 minutes, although an entire session could be spent just on warm-up exercises. For hard redpoints or onsights you could easily spend an hour to a half day warming up. At the crag the hike in usually accomplishes this, but you still need to move your upper body around for at least 5 minutes. Stretches here should not be held for more than a second at the end range of motion.

Some of the warm-up exercises are also excellent rehab exercises. If a warm-up is difficult, put it on your list and make your goal full range of motion, perfect form, and the recommended amount without too much burning or pain. Some of the warm-ups are meant as learning tools or core exercises to help with imbalances and don't need to be continued once mastered. Some warm-ups are just good to do more than occasionally and I have *starred* my favorite go-to warm ups. Go through all the warm-ups and practice the ones that are difficult, because being unable to do a particular warm-up exercise well could mean an imbalance or weak-link. A warm-up that also includes exercises that address imbalances could last a while and be your entire non-climbing exercise routine for a few weeks. None of these warm-ups should interfere with climbing immediately afterword (they shouldn't tire out climbing muscles). If they do, you either need to eat more, or spend a lot of separate time to do the more difficult exercises you feel need to be mastered.

These exercises should be followed under endurance protocols (high reps or longer holds). Only use the strength protocol if you feel you are particularly weak and need to advance to a higher amount of weight to be balanced before returning to the endurance protocol. Some of these warm-ups could be considered part of the "non-climbing" exercises, but I chose to put them in here, as they are easier, and once mastered, not necessary to add in except for a quick warm-up.

Try and get a good mix of cardio and different body areas for your warm-up, but doing every exercise here would take half the day. If an exercise is too easy or you've finally mastered it, move on to something else or make it harder, but don't completely write them off. After a long period of climbing, training, driving, sitting, or hiking, there's a good chance a movement pattern got detrained or a muscle got tight.

Reps, sets, and times given are guidelines to aim for or exceed, not to force! Reps given are for one side or one direction of movement only, so do the same amount for every side and direction. Going slow (even very slowly) is more effective for most of these warm-ups than trying to fly through reps, especially for the exercises that require co-ordination and balance.

Post-Routine Cool Down

A cool down is highly recommended after an intense physical workout. Going straight to work or sitting in a car immediately afterwards is going to cause problems down the line. After exercise, it is recommended that you engage in light stretching or mild cardio afterwards so your muscles and connective tissue do not contract.

> Eat a meal immediately afterwards of 2 calories (0.5 gram) of carbs for every pound you weigh, 20-25 grams (80-100 cal) total of protein, and 16 oz. of liquid. Do this to keep from crashing and to use proteins for muscle building and recovery.

Ice sore muscles (balm feels good but does little) and try and stay away from the Ibuprofen or other NSAIDS unless you are fighting acute inflammation. Ice baths or alternating hot and cold showers (end on cold) help flush the system, reduce overall inflammation, and if done just before bed, and actually help you sleep. More information on the pros and cons of icing will be discussed later. Post exercise is also a great time to have manual therapy done by someone or by yourself since your muscles and ligaments are at their most pliable state.

Climbing Warm-Up
Climbing 2+ pitches
If you are just going to use climbing for your warm-up, really overly exaggerate reaching with your arms and legs, and try and achieve full range of motion. Just about

everyone should do at least a pitch or two of climbing as their standard warm-up regardless of whatever other exercises you do. This is a great time to practice your skills. You can gradually increase the difficulty until a few letter grades below your redpoint project or just below or at your onsight limit if you are trying for a hard send that day. It seems counterintuitive, but this will actually decrease the chances of getting flash-pumped. Take a long active break before climbing the hard stuff including stretching, massage, and active range of motion exercises.

Aerobic Warm-Ups
Abdominal Breathing
This exercise will train you to breathe more efficiently, keep your shoulders away from your ears, and give you a form of breathing to help you when you are freaked-out or over-working on a climb and need to chill out. Breathe in through your nose while expanding your belly, not your chest. Fill your lungs. Keeping your shoulders down and relaxed, breathe out slowly through pursed lips (this lowers blood pressure). While breathing out, contract the girdle of muscle that wraps longitudinally around your body like a corset, called the transverse abdomens. This draws your stomach in, but doesn't pull it in like you would when sucking in your gut.

There are two other muscles to contract to push out the air – one above and one below to create a "balloon" of muscles. The upper muscle is your diaphragm that you push down by and is activated by mildly bearing down, as if having a bowel movement. The lower muscle(s) is your pelvic floor and is activated by using the same muscle contraction you would as if stopping a flow of urine mid-stream (like a Kegel exercise). Pretty complicated for something you do 12 times a minute on average! This warm-up is worth practicing a few times on occasion to wire yourself to instinctively breathe like this when you are exercising or are gripped.

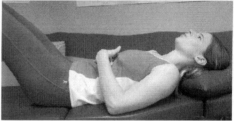

Notice how the back arches and flattens as the stomach pushes out and draws in

Cardio 5+ minutes
Row, jump rope, run, spin, etc. at a very brisk pace for 5 or more minutes. This is a key part of the warm-up and should not be skipped. Hiking in at a brisk pace counts.

Full Body Warm-ups
Overhead Air Squats x 20
Grab your trusty PVC rod, ski pole, or broom a bit longer than shoulder width apart. The tighter your pecs and shoulders, the farther apart your arms will be to the side and in front of your head. Hold the rod up, actively pushing your arms up. Now do an air squat.

Squat Form
Feet a bit more than shoulder width apart, feet slightly turned out. Keep your head neutral and your chest high to maintain lumbar curve throughout the motion. Begin the squat by pushing your butt straight back. Go to full depth and quickly come back up. As you go down, push your knees out to the side slightly. Try and keep your knees from going too far in front. The farther forward they go, the more strain you put on your knees. Keep your heels on the ground the entire time. Squats take time to

master and this quick, repetitive warm-up helps wire the correct form. This is an excellent low back, leg, hip and shoulder warm-up. Check your form! Is your chest still high? Arms still active? Weight still on your heels?

A less tight individual would have their chest higher and arms overhead!

Squat Jumps x 20
Explode up from the bottom of a jump, raising your arms above your head at the top.

Burpees x 10
See the non-climbing supplemental exercises for a detailed description, but essentially a pushup into a jumping jack. Good warm-up for bicep intensive climbs.

Inchworms x 10
Bend down to the ground as if you were trying to touch your toes (knees straight), but continue from the ground to walk your hands out in front of you as far as you possibly can. Reverse back up to standing. Another excellent full-body warm-up.

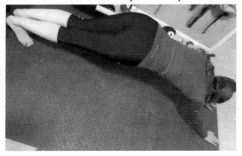

Foundation Exercises
The books, "Athletic Body in Balance" & "Movement" by Cook (2003, 2010), and "Foundation: Redefine Your Core" by Goodman & Park (2011) both have excellent proprietary exercises that focus on correcting and strengthening core full body movement patterns that I highly recommend. Cook describes five essential movements and steps to correct faults in those movements, while Goodman & Park have a series of 10 multi joint exercises. The exercises presented in this book will more than achieve the same results, but these are so good that I couldn't help but mentioning their existence.

Weighted Postural Training
Mentioned more in the rehab section, adding weights to areas with poor posture and either sitting on a wobbly surface or walking on a treadmill can strengthen a particular area.

Headweights to correct forward head posture, shoulder and hip weight to correct a low shoulder or hip. Courtesy The Pettibon System. (FYI - No concrete evidence that a reduced spinal curve contributes to arthritis, headaches, poor health, etc.)

NECK WARM-UPS

Constantly looking up really screws up climber necks. These warm-ups help loosen up the tight muscles behind your head, and strengthen the weaker deep neck flexors that keep things where they should be.

Neck Retractions x 25

Keep your shoulder blades pulled actively down and in. Now pull your chin straight back (no nodding) like you're going to make a double chin. Hold for a few moments and relax. You can do it against the wall with a squishy ball for extra resistance.

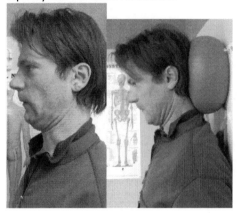

Isometric Neck Retractions 30 sec–1 min

Lie on your back and pull your chin in like the neck retraction. Now hover your head just slightly above the ground, keeping your head retracted. Hold for 30 seconds. Do it again. Next, flip over (face down and preferably off the end of something so you're not breathing into the floor) and do the same thing 30 sec twice.

Isometric Hold 1 minute

This is really only a useful exercise for neck rehab, or chronic neck pain. Lay off the end of a bed or surface with a drop off. Hold your head in a neutral position for one minute. To get the back of your neck, lay face down. To get the front of your neck go face up. To get the sides, lay sideways. Being able to hold your neck steady for 1 minute is a good time to shoot for.

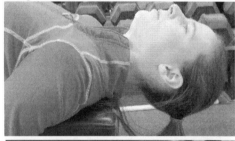

AROM Reps x 50
Another neck rehab or chronic neck pain warm-up. To exercise the side you want, follow the instructions above, but instead of just holding your head, flex it forward, backward, or to the side. You can do rotation also by turning your head to the left or right depending on which way you are lying. You can do this sitting or standing by actively pushing your head into an object with mild resistance (like a Nerf ball) or spring. 50 reps in each direction is a good goal.

Face Clenches
Squint your eyes and grimace, relax, and repeat. Good exercise to keep you relaxed on a pitch.

!!!No Neck Rolls!!!
Rolling your head around may help warm-up your neck, but the stress it places on the joints, discs, and nerves in your neck makes it not worth it. So don't do it.

<u>Hand, Wrist, Elbow, & Finger Warm-Ups</u>
Chinese Balls, Therapy Putty, and Squeeze Balls
This is mostly for rehab, but is actually a pretty good warm-up for anyone with over-developed forearms or stiff hands. Work the two balls, putty, or squeeze ball around your hand. Also works to develop intrinsic muscles of the hand.

Wrist Circles
Roll your wrists around in both directions.

These next four exercises can be done very quickly together for a great hand/finger warm-up between pitches.

Flipper
Lock your elbows and quickly flip your wrists up and down emphasizing extension.

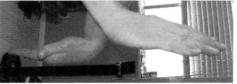

The Groper
Quickly curl your fingers at all the upper two joints quickly and repeatedly

Finger Spreads
Quickly spread your fingers apart as far as possible repeatedly.

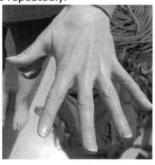

Pronate/Supinate
With your arms and wrist straight, turn your wrist up and down quickly.

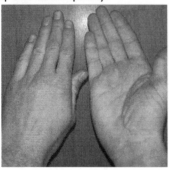

Alphabet
This exercise is mainly useful for rehabbing wrist injuries. Make a fist and write the alphabet in the air, pretending you are holding a paintbrush. This active range of motion exercise helps move your wrist in all directions multiple times. Write out about 100 letters worth of movement.

Screaming Barfies
Some good warm-ups before a pitch of ice are jumping jacks combined with squats, windmills, shoulder shrugs, and the speed skater. For shrugs, pause at the top and keep your arms straight with palms forward for maximum blood flow. The speed skater is just rapidly swinging your arms front to back. Thanks to Kelly Cordes in his blog postings for some of these suggestions.

Jumping Jacks and Squats

51

Windmills and Shoulder Shrugs

Speed Skater

SHOULDER WARM-UPS

The next four exercises help loosen up the shoulder muscles. Shoulders are generally fairly flexible joints – sometimes too flexible.

But even extra loose shoulders generally have tight muscles (but loose joints). It's a delicate balance with an unstable shoulder, but a side of tight muscles may be overpowering another side of loose capsule or muscle. Go to town if your shoulders are just tight. Adding a PVC rod can help you get more range of motion on some of these exercises.

Arm Circles/Scissor 10-20

Make small and large forward and reverse circles with your arms outstretched to the side (40 total circles). Next, scissor your arms horizontally across your chest and out. Going slowly trains supportive shoulder musculature, and quickly helps warm-up the joint. The best shoulder warm-up.

Circles

Sissors

Shoulder Sweeps x 10-20

With your PCV rod or what have you, hold the rod as far apart as needed to do the following: Keeping your arms straight, bring the rod over your head and behind your back, and come forward again. You can vary the direction and speed of the sweep to isolate various areas. One of the best shoulder warm-ups.

High Reaches x 10-20
Reach high alternating arms like you are mimicking climbing a ladder. Feel free to step high with your legs, but you may want to do this exercise in private to avoid mockery.

Around the World x 10 *The Clap* x 20
Keeping your arms straight, swing your arms from your side to over your head. Cross at the top and come back down. You could also do this quickly, clapping your hands at the top and coming back down without crossing over.

Empty Can Raise x 10
Start palms down, arms down and 30° out to the side. Raise your arms up while turning your arms in as if emptying a can. Stop when arms are parallel to the ground. A good rotator cuff warm-up or shoulder rehab exercise.

Field Goals x 10
With your arms and elbows at 90° each, rotate your arms frontwards and backwards. Do this with your arms pointed up, and also down. A good rotator cuff warm-up or shoulder rehab exercise. Use a PCV rod to get a little more reach.

Toy Soldier x 20
Lock your arms at your side, thumbs up. Quickly flex and extend your arm at the shoulder.

Pec and Lat Foam Roller x 25
Lay on a foam roller on your spine so your head is resting on it. Alternatively flex and extend straight arms up over your head slowly for the lats. For the pecs, bend your arms and elbows at 90° and alternate bringing your elbows to the floor and together.

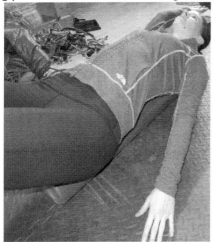

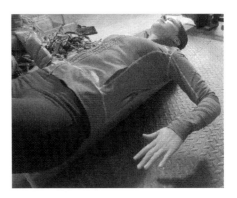

Weight Balance x 2 min
Grab a kettlebell or hold a dumbbell vertically so you are balancing the weight in your hand. Hold your arm up 90° to your body and your forearm 90° to your arm. Walk around balancing the weight for 1-2 minutes. If you can balance it for 2 minutes without too much shaking or lowering the weight, you're fine. 10-30 lbs. Good shoulder rehab warm-up.

Kipping Pull-Ups x 10
See the climbing specific exercises. A good shoulder and core warm-up if your form is good and it's not too taxing.

The next three exercises are really only useful in rehabbing a shoulder injury.

Circumduction

Lean over and dangle your arm. Use gravity and your body (but not your shoulder muscles) to move your arm in circles in both directions. Vary the size of the circle. You can progress by holding onto light weights: from a soup can to a gallon milk jug.

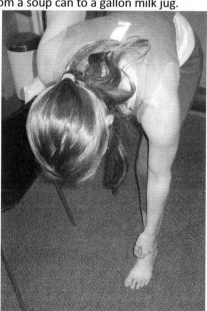

Wand ROM

Grab a PVC pipe or broomstick with both hands, shoulder width apart. Use your good arm to passively push or help your other arm in various directions: to the side, rotating, behind your back, and up to your head. Light active muscle stretching techniques may also help.

Wall Walks

Stand arm's length from a wall and walk your fingers up and down the wall. Next, do this to the side.

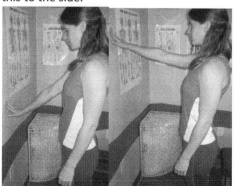

SCAPULA WARM-UPS

The following warm-ups help prevent shoulder, neck, and thoracic (upper back) issues.

Serratus Punch x 50

The serratus anterior muscle helps protract your scapula (shoulder blade) and keep your shoulder joint stabilized. There are a few ways to do this exercise.

Lying on a weight bench, scoot over until your shoulder blade is off the table. Use a dumbbell or tubing heavy enough to do. Stick your arm straight up and punch your arm up without moving anything but your shoulder blade. If you can fire off 50 with a pretty heavy weight (35-50 lbs.) you're doing well. Can also be done standing with a cable machine.

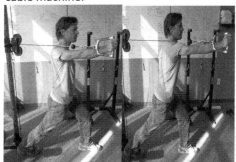

You can also do this as part of a push up, or a push up on a suspension trainer or Swiss ball. At the top of the pushup, push your arms out a little more (although pushups aren't great warm-ups).

Reverse Dips x 50

Grab a pair of rings, your suspension trainer, a dip-station, or sitting on a chair if your arms are long enough. With straight arms, lower yourself down and push yourself back up using your lower traps. The lower traps help pull your shoulders down and back for proper shoulder and thoracic alignment.

Wide Grip Lat Pulls x 25

Get a very wide grip on a lat pull down bar using cables or tubing, pull up bar using body weight, or spread out rock rings. Using only your lower traps, do a very small pull down. Another good lower trap exercise.

Shoulder/Scapula Rolls x 20

Lightly bring your shoulders up. Now squeeze your shoulder blades together and draw them down and in. Do this in one fluid motion and hold for a moment when your shoulder blades are pulling down and in. This trains your scapular stabilizers to hold correct scapula position.

Angels x 20

Almost an identical warm-up to the shoulder rolls above, except that arm movement is added. Lie on the ground or stand against the wall. The surface your shoulder blades press against helps provide some resistance. With your forearms and arms held out in a 90°/90° angle, make "snow angels". Try and keep your arms flat against the wall/ground with thumbs out and pinkie fingers against the surface. Try and create most of the motion from your shoulder blades and not your arms. Really squeeze down and in.

LUMBAR WARM-UPS
Cat / Camel x 10-20

If you've got a stiff low back, get on your hands and knees. Arch your back like an angry cat and then extend it like the dip between a camel's hump. Repeat until your loosen up. This and the next exercise are good for low back rehab.

Active Knee to Chest x 10-20
Lie on your back and hug your knees to your chest. Now pump your knees closer to your chest, rocking just a bit onto your upper back. This helps stretch you lumbar muscles and open up your discs.

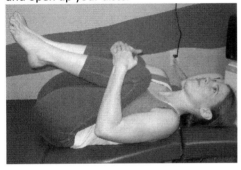

Pelvic Tilts, Circles, Fig 8 x 10-20
A good low back rehab warm-up, or for those with poor core coordination. Just because you are strong, doesn't mean you have good low back coordination. That can lead to many low back, lower limb, even neck problems in the future. Sit on a ball or balance pad and rock your pelvis forward and backward using your abs and gluts respectively. Your upper body should be still (arching and flexing your spine is cheating). The movement should only be in your pelvis. If this is still a puzzle, try going side-to-side. Progress into circles, then a fig-8 pattern. The most important movement is still rocking your hips forward and back (anterior and posterior pelvic tilt).

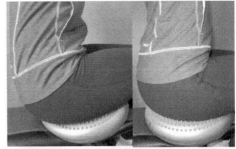

Pelvic Tilts with Abdominal Breathing (and Neck Retractions and Angels) x 20
This exercise combines pelvic tilts with abdominal breathing to strengthen your low back. When combined with neck retractions and angels, you have the ultimate basic core exercise. Get good at doing this, and you will be building on a properly trained base of support. Start by doing this on your back with knees bent. On the inhale, your belly expands and pelvis rock forward, arching your back slightly. On the exhale, contract all those abdominal and pelvic muscles, and tilt your pelvis back FIRMLY pressing your back into the floor. Pretend like you're squeezing an orange. Hold the final contraction for a few moments. Add neck retractions and angels on the exhale for the full exercise.

Now try it sitting on a Swiss ball. This is bit more difficult. Instead of pressing your low back into the table, roll your hips back and pretend you are trying to pop the ball by pressing down into the ball. Add angels and retractions.

The next two exercises strengthen the low back, but much more gently and can be used as a warm-up or low back strengthening exercise.

Superman x 1 min

Lay on the ground (easiest), a weight bench (harder) with your torso off the table and legs wrapped under it to keep you on, or on a Swiss ball (hardest) with your feet against the wall. Stick your arms out in front of you and hold it there until you can't. You will have to arch your back slightly if you are just doing this on the ground. 1 minute on a weight bench is pretty good isometric low back strength. Don't add weight!

Swimmer x 50

Lay on the ground face down with straight arms and legs extended. Alternate opposite arm and leg kicks up in the air. Add ankle and or wrist weights.

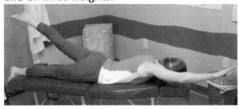

Core Stability Warm-Ups

There's low back and ab strength, and then there is the coordination involved in using your muscles together. The following exercises engage muscles of the abs, low back, and hip – making them work together. Core stability trains you to move as a unit, and these exercises are the foundation of a strong core. A strong core is a secret weapon to staying pain-free and climbing well. Failure means coming out of form or falling over. Good form means no shaking, dropping or raising your hips or having your body become unleveled. Focus more on the exercises that are hard or sides that are weaker.

Dead Bug on Foam Roller x 50

Lay on a full sized foam roller with your head resting on the top. Extend opposite arm and legs. Start by just lifting your heels alternately, then your feet alternately, and then your knees alternately. The real "dead bug" finally alternates lifting your whole leg along with your opposite arm. Add challenge by adding ankle and wrist weights. Make it easier by not using a foam roller.

Quadruped x 50

Place both knees on a foam roller lying horizontal to your body. Place your hands on the floor in front. Extended opposite arms and legs out straight. Add challenge by using wrist and ankle weights, or by placing your hands on a wobble board(s). You can also offset your hands placing your hands together on opposite sides. Pushing your knee into a Swiss ball adds a little hip flexion work.

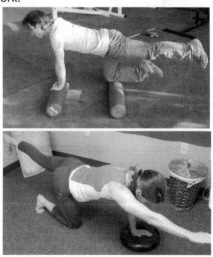

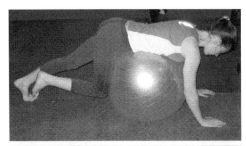

Last two – rotate pelvis up and down for an optional twist.

Bridge x 1-2 min or 50 reps

Lay on your back with your knees bent. Bridge your hips up until your body is level, hovering your arms above the ground. Hold it there for time (1-2 min), or repeat lifting your hips up and down (50 times). There are many ways to make this exercise more difficult. To add weight, you can place a weight on your lap. You can squeeze a ball between your legs to work the adductors, or place a resistance band across both knees to work the abductors. To work the gluts and hip flexors, at the top of the bridge, extend one leg and lift it up and down, keeping good form. Hover your arms just above the floor for extra challenge. You could add ankle weights to increase the difficulty. Also try it with a level of instability by lying on a Swiss ball or wobble board. Being able to keep the bridge for two minutes, 25 leg lifts each side, and 50 hip lifts is a good place to be.

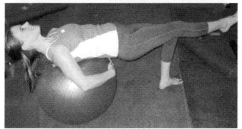

Reverse Bridge x 10

Lie on your back with both legs on a Swiss ball and bridge up, and hover your hands above the floor. Now try and lift one leg up at a time. You can do hip dips, add weight to your stomach, or add ankle weights to mix it up. You can do hamstring curls in the reverse bridge by rolling the ball towards you with either both feet, or just one foot. To increase the instability, place one leg in a suspension trainer or gymnastic ring, bridge up, and raise and lower the other leg.

Helicopter
This one is fun! Attach a weighted ball to a rope or strong cord and spin it around over your head. Keep your low back and pelvis stable. Be careful!

Floor Roll
On your hands and knees with your hips/knees at 90° each, try and rotate your body around 360° while keeping your low back completely stable and in a neutral pelvis. If this is too hard try it standing against the wall with your hands or elbows against the wall.

Hip Warm-Ups
Hips are one of the least mobile joints in our body due to tight muscles and joints, especially the hip flexors, hamstrings, and abductors (pulls your leg and limits "the splits"). All but the yoga master will probably need to focus more here than anywhere else for loosening up.

Leg Kicks x 20
Stand on one leg and hold onto something for support. Briskly swing your leg forward and back reaching as far as you can with your foot. You can also swing is left to right. You can do this laying on your side as well. A great hip warm-up.

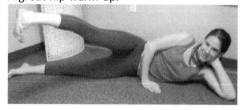

Rapid Toe Touches x 20
Stand with both feet together, and quickly bend and try to touch your toes rapidly. A good low back and hip warm-up.

Lunges x 20
Quickly lung forward, finishing with a deep quick stretch of your hip flexors. Bring both arms up straight overhead with each step. Try and keep your back knee from going over your toes. A good leg and hip warm-up.

Lunge Jumps x 20
Explode up from the bottom of a lunge. Bring your arms above your head at the bottom of the lunge.

Over Under x 5-10
This is an excellent warm up for hip mobility and your leg adductors (opposite of abductors). Pretend there is a fence you can barely high-step over that you are standing immediately to the left or right of you. Reach high with the closer leg and step over, then the other. Whoops, you forgot something, better slide back under it! Do a deep side lunge to slide under it, getting a good groin stretch, and follow through with the other leg. Now repeat facing the other way, starting with the other leg and sliding the opposite direct as before.

Dynamic Hip Stretch x 5
Do a low lunge and get a quick ½-1 second hip flexor stretch. On the forward leg, turn out of the lunge into a piriformis stretch (leg pointing into center, thigh straight ahead), hold for a brief moment, and quickly switch legs and do the same thing. Another excellent hip mobility warm-up.

Glut Squeeze and *Pumps* x 50
These exercises helps to strengthen your gluts and helps activate them as many people have chronically inhibited gluts which can lead to back and lower limb problems. The glut squeeze is the easier version. Lie on your stomach and just squeeze your butt cheeks together. Hold for a moment and relax.

Pumps are started on your hands and knees. Extend your thigh to parallel with the ground with your knee at 90° and your leg pointed at the sky and your foot parallel with the ground. Now pump your heel toward the sky as high as you can without torquing your pelvis, and come back to parallel. 50 times each leg without severe burning is what you are trying to achieve. Add ankle weights to increase difficulty, or somehow attach rubber tubing to your knee and the ground.

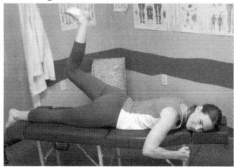

Standing Hip Dips x 50
This exercise trains your hip abductors and quadratus lumborum and is an excellent closed-chain exercise compared to other hip abduction exercises. Stop once you can do 50 on each side. Stand on one leg. Let your pelvis fall to the side you aren't standing on, but keep your torso and leg straight. Using the muscle you just let go slack, straighten your hip back out. You could hold a dumbbell on the leg you have up to make it more difficult.

The next few exercises focus on hip abductors and rotators and may or may not be that helpful. If you have low back, hip, S/I, knee, or foot problems you may want to see if there are any weak spots.

Leg Circles x 50
Lay on your side with feet slightly scissored apart. Pointing the toes and foot down on the upper leg, make tiny, then large circles in both directions. Ankle weights add difficulty. Going slowly helps strengthen supportive hip muscles and quickly helps warm up the joint.

Clamshell x 50
Lay on your side with your thighs together on the ground, but with your legs bent together at the knees and in the air. Now open up your legs, like a clamshell. When your legs are open, straighten out the upper leg, and then reverse the motion, but always keeping your legs in the air. An ankle weight and or a band around your thighs will add difficulty.

Side Leg Raise Lower x 50
Lay on your side with your legs together. Raise and lower your upper leg with your foot turned down, pointing towards the floor. Lift your leg up and down. An ankle weight or band around your thighs will make it harder.

Double Leg Raise Lower x 25

Same as above, but both legs travel up and down together. Harder, so 25 is a good number to reach. Ankle weights will make it harder.

Lower Leg Raise x 50

This isn't really that important of an exercise, as most of us will have strong inner thighs (adductors). I included this only for those with weak inner thighs. You won't target fat here (or anywhere) by exercising it, so if flabby thighs are your problem, this exercise will not help you. There are many other inner thigh exercises, this is just one of them.

Lay on your side and cross your upper leg over the top of your lower leg. Bring the lower leg up to the knee of the crossed over leg and back to the floor repeatedly. Ankle weights will add difficulty, or somehow attach a band to the lower leg. Thigh Masters work well, as does a hand grip strength trainer squeezed between your knees, or tubing attached on the outside of both legs and squeezing both knees together.

Knee Warm-Ups

The following exercises are mainly used for Knee Rehab

Knee Extension

Knee extension is key in rehabbing knee injuries, but don't use a knee extension machine through its full range of motion as it places too much stress on the knee. Start by exercising both end ranges of knee extension. The first form of knee extension focuses on the last few degrees of extension (terminal knee extension) and can be started early.

The easiest method has you sitting on the floor, leg extended with a towel bunched up under your knee. Press your knee into the towel and hold for six seconds. The towel should be firm and bulky enough that your foot elevates off the floor about six inches by pressing down. Add ankle weights as you gain strength.

You could also stand up and use a resistance band attached behind your knee and anchored in front as you pull your knee in, or attach the band ankle to ankle and extend the lower leg you are working on. Do not use your hip flexors to help you for this exercise.

The other form of knee extension focuses on the first few degrees of leg extension at the knee. You can sit on a chair with a band behind you and attached at the ankle while extending your leg about 45° with your foot turned out slightly. The can be done on a leg extension machine as well as long as you don't fully extend. A more advanced exercise is to place the band a little higher up behind you, start with your leg and knee fully flexed, and push out all the way.

Eccentric Quad Machine
This is best done on a quad machine. Extend both legs, remove the good leg, and lower back down with the bad leg. Start with low weight and build up so you don't overload by accident.

Straight Leg Raise
Lay on your back and practice raising your leg up and down with your knee straight and foot turned out a few degrees. Add weight or tubing to progress. Keeping your knee locked will help you emphasis the focus on your quads over your hip flexors.

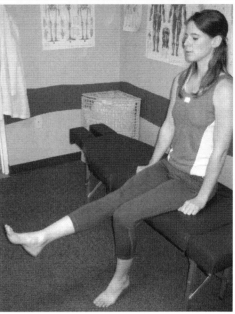

Reverse Lunge
Instead of lunging forward, lung backward.

Quarter and ½ Squats
Squatting is very important for knee rehab, but begin by only going down ¼ or halfway down.

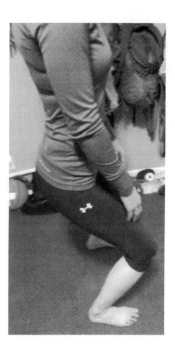

D1 Soccer Kick

The next two exercises are PNF exercises for the lower body, similar to the sword and seatbelt exercises for the shoulder. Stand with your body supported by a chair or rod, bring leg forward and slightly across body, foot turned outwards and toes pulled up similar to a soccer kick. Reverse the motion. Add ankle weights or use tubing.

D2 Snowplow

Standing supported, bring the leg forward and away from midline with hip turned in-wards like a snow play. Reverse the motion. Add ankle weights or use tubing.

Jumps / Hops

As you regain strength, practice small to progressively larger hops and jumps. Make a star pattern with some tape or just visualize it and practice jumping to all eight points while facing forward. You can advance by placing tubing around your waist to resistance or do it standing on one leg.

FOOT & ANKLE WARM-UPS
Alphabet Exercise x25

If you have stiff ankles or are rehabbing from an ankle injury do this warm-up. Using your big toe as the stylus, write the alphabet in the air. It doesn't actually matter what you write, as long as it's moved around in multiple random angles.

Toe and Heel Walk/Rock
Walk around on your toes and then your heels to warm-up your lower leg. Alternately, rock onto your heels then to your toes repeatedly. A good warm-up for calf straining climbs, hanging belays, or if you get shin splints running.

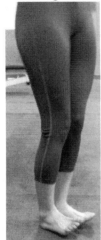

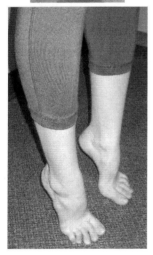

<u>BALANCE EXERCISES</u>
Balance exercises are good warm-up for those recovering from foot or knee injuries, or for those with poor balance. If you aren't rehabbing a neck, low back, knee, or foot injury, being able to stand on one foot for a full minute or 30 seconds with one foot on a wobble board/disc is good enough. If you find hopping around on talus fields is difficult, do more of these exercises. The following is an excellent progression to become a balance master. Switch to the next level if you don't lose balance within a few seconds.

Short Foot
This is an excellent exercise to strengthen weak feet, and can help with knee and back issues as well. The goal is to shorten the length of your foot (which increases the arch) without curling your toes. Try it with your hand to get the idea. You may need to start by using your hands to actively mold your foot and letting go, trying to hold the posture. Advance by doing it sitting and placing downward pressure on your knee. Next do it standing. Then try standing on one foot. Maintain good posture throughout.

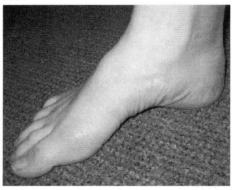

Maintain Short Foot posture for all the following exercises

Order of Unstable Surfaces:
- Floor Holding a Chair
- No Chair
- Pillow or Aeromat
- Unidirectional Rocker in Forwards Plane (front to back)
- Unidirectional Rocker in Sideways Plane (side to side)
- Bi-directional Rocker (forward and sideways)
- Omnidirectional Wobble Board or Inflatable Disc

> **Progression of Balance Exercises:**
> - One Leg Stand x 1 minute
> - One Leg Stand Eyes Closed x 30 seconds
> - Two Leg Unstable Surface Progression x 30 seconds
> - Progress to a more unstable surface starting at the top of the list then continue below:
> - 2 Leg Unstable Surface Progression: Eyes Closed x 30 seconds
> - 1 Leg Balance Board Progression x 30 seconds
> - *1 Leg Balance Board Progression: Eyes Closed* x 30 sec-1 min
>
> If you can stand on one leg with your eyes closed for a minute on an omnidirectional wobble board, you're doing great!

ADDITIONAL BALANCE TRAINING

You can also toss in some functional stability training to your balance training.

Sit to Stand

Put a rocker or wobble board under your feet while sitting on a chair. Try and stand up.

½ Foam Roller Walk

Take a few ½ foam rollers and lay them in a line. Try and walk on top of the foam rollers. Try it eyes closed.

Squats

During the progressions above try doing a ½ squat, then a full squat.

Ball Toss & Catch

Using the progressions above, catch and toss a weighted medicine ball from various directions.

Provocation

Using the progressions above, have someone (lightly) poke and shove you to get you to fall

Visual Tracking

Try and read a distant object using the above progressions, or have someone move an object randomly and track it with your eyes, but without moving your head

Slack Line

A climber's favorite camp activity and a great way to get an ankle injury. More fun than useful since by the time you can do this well, your balance is definitely good enough. This isn't surfing training. I don't even want to know what you are climbing if slack lining provided you with your key training.

Balance Lean

This is a great exercise for climbers because it is fairly practical. With good posture and moving only at the ankle joint, lean as far as you can forward, backward, or to the side keeping your feet flat on the ground. Try it one-legged.

YOGA AND PILATES

For those with the time, money, and inclination, Pilates studios use some pretty fancy equipment to provide some excellent core and stabilization training – check it out! A lot of gyms offer basic Pilates matt classes. There are many types of Yoga, but the type I would emphasize in a warm-up would be power-style yoga where isometric strength is incorporated to holding some fairly advanced poses.

INTENSE CORE

Many exercises under the warm-up are considered core, but the following are more intensive specific abdominal and lumbar exercises, and should be considered more weight-lifting type training than prehab/rehab or warm-up type exercises. The exercises can be done in any phase or protocol, but some are better served than others and I will offer suggestions for each type or specific exercise if necessary.

Most training plans have you doing core training that is more warm-up and imbalance training, like the exercises prescribed in the warm-up-up section. This is not enough. Of course you want a stable spine and balanced core, but for many the key to success vs. failure on many climbs comes from insufficient core strength. A strong torso initiates each move by initiating thrust, conserves limb energy and strength by maintaining balance and limiting excess movement. Training your core above and beyond will be your secret weapon. Keep the focus on abdominal flexion, but be sure to keep your lumbars and obliques up to speed. A good rule of thumb is do twice as much ab intense exercise as lumbar and twice as much lumbar as oblique (4:2:1), but be sure to do lumbar and obliques at least twice per week (and ab specific almost every session).

ABS ISOMETRIC
Side Plank x 2 min or 50 reps
Lay on your side with your feet stacked. Lift up on your elbow to a plank position. You can hold for time (2 minutes is great) or dip up and down at the hip for reps (50 each side). Weight around your hips will increase difficulty. You can splay your arm and leg out in a star pattern for the isometric hold to increase the instability. To get a hardcore oblique exercise, hold the upper arm straight up from a standard side-plank, and wrap it around under your hip in a long sweeping motion, twisting your spine but keeping your hips level. All of these variations focus more on your obliques, quadratus lumborum, erector spinae, and hip abductors than the other exercises.

Final photo: dipping hips up and down

Abdominal Plank x 2 min
Get into a downward facing plank position resting on your forearms. Hold good for 2 minutes. To make this harder, use a suspension trainer with either your arms in the rungs or your feet in the rungs, and mess with the height. You could also use a Swiss ball or wobble board for your arms or legs. Keep your heels touching to really add challenge. This exercise isolates ab stability more than the other exercises.

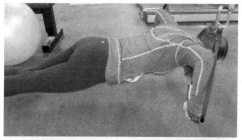

Supine Plank Twist

This exercise seems easy, but can be torture. Lie face up with your lower back to head hanging off the edge of a weight bench or table. You will need to have something to put over your feet to keep you from tipping off the table. Cross your arms over your chest and keep your torso in a rigid plank position. Without lifting up, turn your torso and upper body as one unit to the left and hold it there for three seconds. Return to neutral and without resting, turn to the right and hold for three seconds. Repeat five times for one set. Perform up to 5 sets.

Plank Twist

From a plank position, bring a knee towards the opposite hip and rotate. Or plank on two dumbbells and lift one up and towards the ceiling.

Front Levers & L-Sit 30 sec x 2 or 1 minute

Front levers are the champion isometric abdominal exercise, but they are extremely difficult to do. Levers can be done on a pull-up bar, hang-board, rock rings, or suspension system.

Work up to the full front-lever by starting with an L-sit or modified L-sit. Pull up to a 90° lock off. Hang with your legs sticking straight out and keep them there as long as possible. Repeat. If this is too hard, bend one knee so only one leg is sticking out and then switch legs.

A front lever keeps your entire body straight and parallel to the floor unlike the easier L-sit. You can modify it as well by bending one leg.

If you find it difficult to progress to the next level, try adding light ankle weights in an easier mode until you can progress further.

Try and work up to a 30 second hold x 2 or a full minute if you're going for master status.

ModifiedL-Sit (left)

Not quite a front lever (last pic)

100's

This is a Pilates exercise. Lie on your back and lift your torso until your shoulder blades are just off the floor and lift your legs (straight) off the floor. Hover your arms by your side and pump them up and down, counting to 100 (or more). Add difficulty by adding ankle weights, or by varying your leg angle (most difficult just off the floor).

ABS GENERAL

Follow the endurance, strength, or strength-endurance protocols for the rest of the abdominal and lumbar exercises unless noted otherwise. Some exercises lend themselves better to specific protocols than others.

The intense core exercises will have a much greater effect if you perform them slowly. Five seconds up and 4 seconds down is not an unreasonable amount of time for each rep. No one is counting but you, so there is no reason to whip through these. Try and do a few ridiculously slow!

Crunches

These are the missionary position of abdominal exercises. Posture is important to avoid neck or low back injuries. You can do these on the floor with an ab mat, or on a Swiss ball. *Warning: high-rep speed crunches can cause severe buttock irritation and bleeding – pad appropriately!*

The basic crunch is a sit-up, but only lift off the floor until your shoulder blades are off the floor. Do not jut your head forward or lead with your head! You can put your hands behind your head or across your chest. It doesn't really matter as long as you don't pull your head with your hands, or use the floor to push with. Lifting past shoulder blade height can stress the lower back, and the maximum benefit of muscle contraction is in the beginning stages of movement. Keep your feet from lifting off the ground. If your feet lift, lower the weight, or hook them under something until you are able to do so without support.

Performing a crunch through the full-range of motion from totally outstretched on the floor to touching your nose to your knees is more functional and more of a complete exercise. I recommend just off the floor for those with low to good ab strength, and full-extension with props (explained in a moment) for those with excellent abdominal strength (you can fire off 60 crunches no problem).

For the standard crunch (shoulder-blades off the ground), you can add weight by hugging a weight on your chest, or sitting on a Swiss ball with the weight in fully extended arms for a partially extended sit-up.

For all crunches you can vary what muscles you target by changing your leg position. Bent knees partially de-activate your hip flexors and target your abdominals, and legs in a butterfly position isolate the abs further. Generally your abs need a lot more work than your hip flexors.

You can also do a crunch on your hands and knees with an Ab Wheel.

Full Extension Crunches
To make a fully extended crunch more effective throughout the entire range of movement try placing a firm pillow under your back, or if you have a Bosu ball, lay over this. Extend your arms up over your head throughout the full crunch, but do not pull with your arms.

The champion exercise is a fully extended crunch with a person or prop actively pulling up on your feet! This exercise is most excellent and combined with a lever and oblique exercise, should make you an ab master. You have a few options. Have a friend pull up on your legs while doing a fully extended crunch just enough so you can resist and keep your feet on the floor. Use resistance bands or a cable machine and hook the bands/cables under your feet at a 45° angle.

With a wobble board

Wood Chop
One way to do a weighted fully extended sit-up without stressing your back too much is to use an overhead cable machine or resistance band. Grab the handle or rope attachment with both hands fully extended overhead, and crunch down, bringing the cable as far down as possible with your arms still overhead. Keep your back straight.

Oblique on right (but flex more ☺)

Hanging Sit-Ups
Another way to perform a sit-up is to vary the angle your body is in. Some weight rooms have slanted tables to perform slightly inverted crunches. You can take it to the extreme with gravity-boot sit-ups (great for offwidth climbers). Again, you can hug a weight in your chest to increase the difficulty as well.

Hanging from a bar and try to bring your knees to your elbows is similar in difficulty to a fully extended sit-up with leg resistance. You can add ankle weights for more difficulty. A less difficult version is to lock off at your arms (90° hang), bend your legs at the hip, and bring your knees to your chest. If you need to give your arms a break or save them for climbing, this can be performed at a captain's chair sit-up station. Offwidth climbers want to not only bring their knees to elbows, but also bring their feet up over their head.

Using a cable machine to lift on your legs while you try and keep them down.

Lying face down with your feet in a suspension trainer and doing crunches by bringing bended knees to your chest is a final excellent variation.

Incline bench with weight

Pike

To get some added instability for one of the most effective ab workouts out there, use a suspension trainer. Face the ground and place your feet in the suspension trainer. A pike means to make a V out of your body at the hip. So keep your arms and legs straight and pivot at the hip, attempting to bring your chest and knees together. You could make this really hard by having all four limbs in a set of suspension trainers. You can also do a Pike with an ab wheel or furniture sliders.

With homemade suspension trainer (etriers, adjustable daisy, handle grips from resistance bands)

Kettlebell Swing

This is yet another killer ab workout. But this exercise targets more than just abs – a full body functional workout. You can use a real kettlebell, make your own, or hold one end of a dumbbell. If you let go, make sure no one or anything expensive is in front of you. Form is very critical for this exercise – you can really hurt yourself.

Get in squat position and pick up the weight, letting it dangle with loose arms and shoulders. Movement is initiated by thrusting your hips forward! Dry hump that weight with a forceful hip thrust and send it up to almost just over your head. If it goes too far, you will hurt your shoulders and possibly get thrown backwards. Let the weight arc back down to starting position (much arm, core, and grip strength required here) and thrust that sucker back up. Keep perfect form and posture. Use enough weight to poop out after 30-75 swings and 2-3 sets. Although this is an endurance protocol (heavier weight would be severely unsafe), it will not feel like it. Prepare to be destroyed.

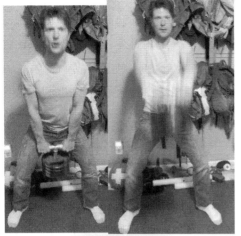

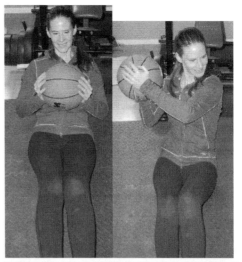

Medicine Ball Toss Sit-Up
You need a partner for this. Face each other in crunch position. Catch the ball at the top of the crunch, do a crunch, and toss is at the top. You can also do an oblique toss by starting in a twisted position or sit to the side of your partner. Like the kettlebell swing, this is another plyometric exercise for the abs. Ball shown below was filled with sand and patched.

Obliques
The standard way to transform a crunch into an oblique is to either bring your knees to your opposite elbow or your opposite elbow to your knee. Full-extension positions do not lend themselves to oblique crunches as easily to the amount of torque you would put on your back unless you use a cable machine. Try the wood-chop exercise but angle to the left and to the right instead. You can also lower the cable (or resistance band) to elbow height, stand sideways, and holding onto the cable with both hands, turn to the left or right. This last variation can stress the lumbar spine, and isn't as effective as other oblique exercises.

Bicycles
Besides adding an oblique twist to the standard ab crunches, you can reverse a basic crunch move by holding the top of the crunch isometrically and then bringing opposite elbows (with hands behind head) and knees together. This engages obliques slightly more than standard crunch done by just twisting to the left or right. This can also be done in a locked-off hanging sit-up, in a captain's chair, or suspension trainer.

Chop and Lift
This is an excellent functional isometric oblique exercise. It combines arm movement while holding a steady core. You need tubing or even better, an adjustable cable machine for this exercise. This is also a good shoulder exercise, however, the sword and seatbelt are more effective similar exercises. This is a good exercise to note and imbalance on your left or right side for both the chop and the lift.

To perform the chop, grab the cable (with a rope grip attachment if possible) like you would hold a baseball bat ready to swing (fists stacked and up near your head). You should be facing the machine (or door holding your tubing) with the cable/tubing at a 45° angle and your elbows at a 90° angle each. Again, the machine will not be to your side as the setup may suggest. Now, unlike a baseball swing, swipe a diagonal pattern from your head to your opposite hip using your shoulders and not your elbows (try and keep around a 90° elbow angle throughout). Keep your abs totally engaged. The weight should be heavy enough to just about make you lose balance and disengage your abs

Swiss ball, captain's chair, rings, cable twist

under the strength protocol. Switch hand position and go the other direction.

The lift is almost the same, except the motion is from your hips to your head. The cable or tubing will need to be placed at or near ground height for this to work. Also, the weight will need to be decreased.

The easiest way to perform this exercise is to kneel feet shoulder width apart then progress to standing. Next kneel in a lunge position with your feet directly in front of either other to minimize your base of support. Standing in this position will increase difficulty. You could further add instability, but it's best to end here and then add weight.

LATERAL BENDERS
You can also do the side plank and side-dips mentioned in the warm-up section for your lateral bend workout. These exercises work your obliques, quadratus lumborum, and erector spinae muscles.

Windmill
This is a good exercise to perform under the strength or strength-endurance protocols. A kettlebell works well with this exercise. Hold the weight above your head and keep it there. Look up at the weight throughout the exercise. Slide your opposite arm down your leg, bending your torso sideways at the waist. You can also hold two dumbbells in each hand and down by your side. Lean to the left and right.

LUMBAR
Lumbar exercises are tricky to prescribe weight and intensity for. Many people have an imbalance in their low back to ab strength and endurance. But excessively training your low back can cause injury to the muscles and discs. It is a fine line when to stop, and when to push through the pain of lumbar exercises. My advice is to start with lower reps and intensity, but increase the sets and frequency. After you have established trust in the integrity of your back, increase the reps per set and intensity of the exercises. See a doctor if even a few reps and sets at low weight cause severe

discomfort. If you experience pain into your legs or numbness, tingling, or weakness, see a doctor immediately.

Side note: Both hip, back, leg extension and hip flexion train your hamstrings as well.

Hip and Back Extension
These exercises are done prone off a weight bench, or using a Swiss ball. Lay off the bench or ball (using the underside of the bench or against a wall for foot support) and place your hands bending your head or folded across your chest. Both exercises train the back extensors. The hip extension trains the lower erectors more as a static unit for postural control, and the back extension trains your back extensors in a movement function. The difference is fairly slight, and I recommend hip extension as the "go-to" exercise. Hip extension is keeping the back straight and lowering towards the floor and back up to plank position. Do not hyperextend! Back extension has you curling your spine down, then back up. Use the endurance protocol and go slow to normal pace. Do not add weight unless you are an expert and really know what you are doing. It is not necessary to add weight, and I don't recommend it for anyone but bodybuilders. 50 reps is an excellent amount to shoot for.

Back extension

Hip extension

Lumbar Isometric Hold
Instead of lowering down, just hold it! Two minutes is an average hold time for those without back problems.

Leg Extension (Reverse Hypers) and Hip Flexion
Leg extension is pretty much the reverse of hip extensions, and can be done on a bench or a Swiss ball. Lower and raise straight legs. This exercise can be dangerous so do not hyperextend. Reverse hypers are leg extension, but with hyperextension at the end of the motion. Weight is also used. I still don't recommend hyperextending your lower back under stress, but it is a very common exercise. If anything, start by adding just ankle weights in the strength or strength-endurance protocol. Beyond that is your decision to make. Hip flexion is like the back extension, but you curl your legs in and out. If you added some tubing to your ankles or used the Swiss ball to push your knees deeply into, you would also be training your hip flexors.

Hip Flexion

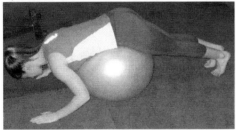

Leg Extension

Romanian Deadlift / Good Mornings

Both exercises have you standing and bending at the waist with a straight back (including a slight lumbar curve). Losing the curve and rounding your back will result in injury. To perform the Romanian deadlift, lift the weight in a squat position but keep your arms straight down. Now stand up straight, lifting with your low back and butt, not your arms. Repeat reps from the top of the squat position to standing before you put the weight back down. You can use an Olympic weight or dumbbell in each hand. This is best done under the strength or strength-endurance protocols as long as you are fussing around with weights. Good mornings are similar but you need a heavy-duty weight lifting band. Place the band under your feet and at the top of your shoulders/base of the neck. The exercise is the same as the Romanian deadlift. Perform this exercise under the endurance protocol. Another variation has you grabbing a cable pull machine behind your legs and extending your back to straighten upright.

Using an improvised weight lifting band

Hip Extension

Essentially a harder version of glut pumps, but done on a glut press machine.

Antagonists and Stabilizers

Like the core intensive exercises, there are plenty of examples of antagonist exercises presented in the warm-up section. The following exercises are more area specific and are meant for intensive isolated training – either for prehab or rehab intentions. Most of these should be done prior to an intensive training session.

Most of the exercises should be performed slowly to very slowly and under the endurance protocol except the pushing exercises that can be done under the strength protocol. The pushing exercises can be performed very slowly, but can also be done quickly as many pushing movements in climbing and in life are fast, explosive movements with a heavier load. True stabilizing muscles are best trained how they are used in real life. Slow concentric contractions do not stimulate a realistic environment. These stabilizers must be able to quickly contract to slow motion and then relax to allow motion so pure isometric exercises are less than ideal (although still useful).

Shoulder Pushing Exercises

Overhead pushing exercises using the shoulder can create a dangerous position for the shoulder. However, it is important to have strong overhead pushing muscles to prevent injury. The trick is to not overdo it, and stop when the first sign of pain occurs. Delayed onset muscle soreness is expected, but should not be sharp pain with movement, or an extremely deep dull ache. When your arms are above your head, the space inside your shoulder joint is decreased and muscles, tendons, and connective tissue can become inflamed or tear. The strict military press exercise is not listed since I believe this exercise is just too strenuous on the shoulder for climbers. Non-climbers can get away with a bit more shoulder risk. Shoulder presses are really just combined shoulder abduction with triceps extension. If you want a good stability exercise for this position, hold a weight above your head and walk around (already described).

Push-Press
Grab two dumbbells and hold them by your ears in a locked-off position. Push up quickly, and use some hip and knee extension for assistance to powerfully toss the weights up overhead. Use the strength or strength-endurance protocol, but start with light weights. Do not jut your head forward during the lift.

Handstand Pushup
This is the closed-chain version of the push-press, but is not done quickly. Start by facing the wall and somersaulting into position. Obviously be careful. To gain the strength for this skill you can be upside-down, but have your legs and knees over a table for balance support and to take half the weight off. Bodyweight using the reps for the strength protocol should be sufficient. This is a good exercise to develop pushing strength and balance. However, it is a bit far from reality where training for climbing is concerned.

See the non-climbing upper body exercises for more exercises that involve shoulder pushing, but combined with lower body movement.

Shoulder Stabilizer Exercises

The rest of the shoulder exercises should be done slowly and utilize endurance protocols. Isometric holds and eccentric contractions can be also thrown into the mix. Also, be sure to keep your shoulder blades actively squeezed down and in for the rest of the shoulder exercises.

External Rotation
Lay on your side and hold a weight in your hand so your elbow is resting on your hip and the weight is on the ground. It can help to put a pillow under the weighted arm to gain more range of motion. You can also do this exercise standing with a cable machine or using tubing. Externally rotate the arm at the shoulder, keeping the elbow at 90° until your arm is perpendicular to your body. Going farther can cause injury. The external rotator muscle stabilizes the powerful internal rotators, however, too much training can inflame the tendon and exacerbate or create shoulder pain. Follow the endurance protocol with occasional forays into the strength protocol.

Abduction
Lie on your side or stand with your arms straight and against your body. Lift the weight sideways. Do not continue past 90° and if pain is felt before then - stop there and repeat. Only follow the endurance protocol and do not overdo this exercise. This trains your supraspinatus muscle (especially in the first 30° of movement), which not only is an important shoulder stabilizer, but is the most commonly torn/injured shoulder muscle. Keep it in shape, but don't overtrain it. Start with very light weight or bodyweight. Can be done standing with tubing or a cable machine.

Field Goals
Field goals are basically bilateral external rotation exercises. Lay face down or stand and start the movement with elbows and shoulder at 90°. Rotate your arms at the shoulder until the weights are in plane with your body. Do not go behind your head. Use light weight and endurance protocols. The final "field goal" position can be done as an isometric hold lying face down holding weights, or with your feet on the floor and your hands in a suspension trainer. Hold for up to 30 seconds.

Y's (Shoulder Flexion)
Either stand holding some light weights, or lie face down on a weight bench doing the same. The exercise is raising outstretched arms to up overhead, but instead of your arms straight out ahead (like the letter H),

angle them 30° out to form the letter Y. This arm angle is known as "scaption plane" and provides perfect alignment between your arms and shoulder blades (scaption). Y's can be dangerous as well, so start with light to no weight, don't go too high, and use the endurance protocol. The final "Y" position can be done as an isometric hold lying face down holding weights, or with your feet on the floor and your hands in a suspension trainer. Hold for up to 30 seconds. Doing this exercise thumbs down isolates the supraspinatus more.

Horizontal Adduction
Lay face down on a bench with light weights in each hand. Hold both arms out straight to your sides (T-pattern). Either hold this position isometrically for up to a minute, or hyperextend your arms and squeezing your shoulder blades. The exercise can be done with palms up, down, or thumbs up. This can also be done on a suspension trainer with your hands on the trainer, your legs on the floor.

Shoulder Extension/Gorilla Pull
Lay on a weight bench holding med to light weights and your arms hanging down. With straight arms, extend your arms to parallel with your body, and repeat. This can also be held isometrically or done on a suspension trainer if you're strong enough. The Gorilla Pull is done standing, using heavier weight on a cable machine or tubing. Start with your arms by your side and feet in a split position/athletic stance. Without using any muscles to help you besides your shoulders, pull back both arms simultaneously.

Combining Field Goals through Extension
Lay face down on a table using weight in each hand, or with a suspension trainer. This can be done as one fluid movement, or hold each pose isometrically. Begin by making a field goal, then press arms into a Y. Lower your arms into a lower case-T and hyperextend slightly, then lower arms to your side and hyperextend slightly. Stop, rest, and repeat 2-4 more times.

Internal Rotation

Internal rotation is not recommended as most of us have already overdeveloped internal rotators. If you think they are weak or needed for a specific climb (bear hugs) then do it, but most likely other forms of training will prove more effective. Usually you only need to train this for recovering from shoulder surgery to get back to baseline, or for an unstable constantly dislocating shoulder. The motion is just the opposite of external rotation.

FUNCTIONAL SHOULDER EXERCISES
Sword and Seatbelt

The Sword and Seatbelt combine functional movement patterns useful in rehab, but can be used as a general shoulder prehab exercise or warm-up. Both exercises can use a cable machine or resistance tubing, or a Bodyblade, Gyroball, Flexbar, or even a Shake Weight to include proprioceptive training.

To perform the Sword, the cable or band must be below your waist. Grab the cable with your opposite hand and pretend you are pulling a sword out of a sheath. Use your shoulder to initiate the movement, and your external rotators, abductors, and deltoids to finish the movement overhead. Finish with pronating your hand. Repeat with the other arm.

To perform the Seatbelt, the tubing must be overhead. Grab the tubing with the opposite hand like you are putting on a seatbelt across your body. Use your lats to initiate the movement and your triceps to finish. Supinate your hand to finish.

Pay attention to what muscles perform what movement, and keep your shoulder blades down and in throughout the entire movement. If your shoulders rise, stop and start over. The use of rapid movement equipment like the Gyroball or Bodyblade causes you to "repeat" the exercise hundreds of times throughout the movement. Start with light weight and do 10 reps each arm/movement. Add weight as you gain proficiency.

Cross Body Lift and Press

I made this exercise up to create an extremely functional upper body exercise. Keep perfect posture, especially focusing on keeping your shoulder blades down and back (not up by your ears) and your pelvis neutral. Stop and correct when form is poor.

Place a dumbbell on the ground next to one foot. Bending only at the hip, grab the weight with the opposite arm and extend back up with a straight arm (your other foot may come off the ground). Next, using only your shoulder, pull the weight across your body until your elbow is cocked to 90°. Next, using only your shoulder and forearm, externally rotate and supinate (turn your palm up) your arm. Now do a biceps curl. Now pronate your forearm (opposite of supinate) so your palm faces in front. Do a push press and hold the weight overhead. Finish with a Windmill. Reverse the process. Since the weight will be easier for some of the movements, but difficult for others, perform the easier movement much more slowly. Each movement is already described separately as an individual exercise if one area needs more practice.

CHEST PULLING EXERCISES
The chest extensors are important stabilizers and postural muscles even though climbing is generally a pulling movement. The muscles of the upper back, especially the middle traps and rhomboids counteract the pull of the strong muscles of the chest, particularly the pecs (pectorals). They help also help maintain upright posture and can help avoid shoulder, neck, and mid back issues commonly felt by climbers.

Rows
Rows can be performed many ways. The one and two arm row isolates the rhomboids, but also trains the lats, which are generally strong.

Kneel on a weight bench or stand facing a cable machine or tubing. Pull back on the weight emphasizing a shoulder blade squeeze at the end. The two-arm row can be performed sitting or standing while using a cable machine or tubing. Pull back, aiming for mid sternum for mid traps and rhomboids, and navel for lower/mid traps and rhomboids. Follow the strength, strength-endurance, and even the power protocols.

To reduce the lat involvement, you can begin the rows from near the end range of movement, focusing on the shoulder squeeze more than the arm movement. Finally, you can use a suspension system. To isolate one arm at a time, lean back against the straps at about a 45° angle and pull your body in, trying not to twist too much. For both arms you can do the same using two handles, or you can try a supine position. Lean against the straps while holding your body up at just past horizontal to the ground, and your feet on the floor. Pull yourself up, focusing on the shoulder blade squeeze more than the arm movement. For the suspension trainer, use the endurance, strength, or strength-endurance protocols.

Reverse Fly

These are another good mid-back / rhomboid exercise. You can use a reverse fly machine at the gym, or lie on your stomach on a weight bench and hold dumbbells in each hand. In an arching movement with bent elbows, bring your arms out and up squeezing your shoulder blades together. Follow the endurance, strength, or strength-endurance protocols.

ARMS PUSHING (TRICEPS) EXERCISES

Triceps stabilize your arm flexors, and also concentrically help with mantles, swinging ice tools, belaying, and coiling ropes. They also help prevent biceps rupture or elbow pain. An eccentric version of the following exercise would be most easily done by slowly lowering yourself from a pull-up.

Dips

A suspension trainer is preferable for this exercise, however some form of parallel bars will suffice. You can also do dips off the side of a weight bench and with your feet on a Swiss ball for added instability. Start with arms fully extended, and lower yourself down, only bending at the elbows. Return to the starting position. Follow the strength or strength-endurance protocols.

Triceps Curl

Again, a suspension trainer is more useful here, but a dumbbell will do. To use a dumbbell, either stand or lay on a weight bench. Hold your arm straight up with the weight in it, and flex and extend at your elbow. To use a suspension trainer, lean against the straps facing the ground at a 45° angle (or more). Extend your arms at the elbow. Use the strength or strength-endurance protocols.

Hold for a killer ab workout too

One Arm Pull Down

This exercise better simulates overhead pull down movements in climbing. Use a cable machine or tubing overhead. You can either face towards or away for a slightly different angle. Stand almost directly underneath the cable. Pull down with your lats, and follow through with your triceps.

Hammer Throw

This is a good ice climbing exercise. Using a cable machine or tubing behind you at head height, grab the handle with your arm behind your head, and extend your arm forward, flicking your wrist at the end. You can also use a heavy hammer to simulate an ice tool. Follow the endurance protocol, and vary the speed from very slow to very fast.

WRIST AND HAND STABILIZER AND ANTAGONIST EXERCISES

The wrist and hand exercises should be done slowly and utilize endurance or strength protocols. Isometric holds and eccentric contractions can be also thrown into the mix.

If you've heard of only two antagonist climbing exercises, it's probably reverse wrist curls for the extensors and pronation exercises with a hammer. Why? Try to imagine what they do in climbing. When you are using your flexors to pull down on a hold, your extensors and pronators must work hard to keep your wrist in place. They already get plenty of practice holding on isometrically and eccentrically, so the goal is to scoop them up a bit by concentrically strengthening them. With an injury, you'd want to start from scratch and train them isometrically and eccentrically.

Reverse Wrist Curls

The better name should be wrist extension, but I'll stick with the lingo. Hold a dumbbell in your hand and support your wrist over your knee or the edge of a padded weight bench. Lower the weight slowly and raise it up. If you hear a lot of popping and cracking, try and support your wrist more, or try wrapping it. There are a lot of tiny bones and tendons in your wrist, and the sound is most likely tendons sliding over bones, and not bones grinding together. If the popping and grinding is painful, or intense, see a hand specialist. Use the endurance and strength protocols. Gyroscopic balls also effectively work your wrist extensors and can be found in various weights.

Weight on a String

Attach a weight to a string and a dowel rod. Roll the weight up with both hands to work your wrist flexors, and then unroll it to work your extensors eccentrically. This exercise is more useful for your extensors than it is for your flexors, but will train both. Use endurance or strength protocols.

Finger Extension, Finger Opposition, and Finger Abduction

To further work your hand extensors, you can wrap a moderately heavy rubber band around your fingers and thumb. Small bands can be placed between your thumb and each finger individually, or wrap twists in the rubber band for each finger and thumb so one finger doesn't overpower the others. The muscles worked are still in the forearm, however. There are no muscles in your fingers, and the muscles in your hand spread and squeeze your fingers and move your thumb. Metolius makes a squeeze ball with individual finger loops for extensor training, and Cando and TheraBand also make some unique training devices. They are worth the small cost. Also, try rigging a band to cause resistance by abducting the fingers to work intrinsic hand musculature. This is excellent prehab as well. Chinese Balls and Therapy Putty for the hand also provide good intrinsic hand exercise, as do gyroscopic balls.

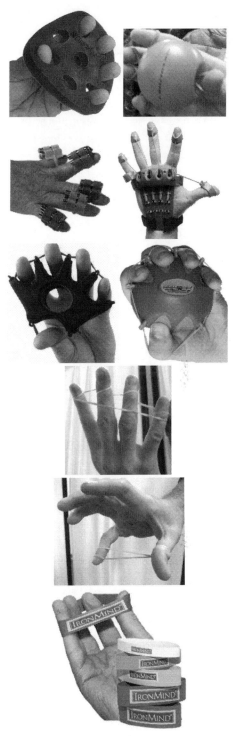

Final photo courtesy IronMind

Pronation

You can strengthen your pronators (and supinators) several ways. Arm flexion is generally coupled with supination, so it should follow to exercise the opposite for antagonist training. The easiest way to exercise is to use a sledgehammer, or tie resistance tubing to a hammer and hold the other end of the tubing with your other hand. In the same arm position as reverse wrist curls, turn your hand down. You can either let go and reset, or train the supinators by reversing back to starting position. Another easy way to practice is by grabbing a piece of tubing with both hands crossed over each other and palm up. Rotate your wrist down. You could also have the tubing anchored to something and just turn your palm down. For supination exercises just reverse the motion. Be creative. Finally, you can use a dumbbell, but having weight on both ends makes the exercise less effective. If you have adjustable dumbbells, you can remove the weight on one side – just like a sledgehammer. Use endurance and strength protocols. Isometric holds and eccentric contractions are useful as well.

Tyler and Reverse Tyler Twist FlexBar

TheraBand makes and excellent wrist training therapy device that looks like a giant Aussie licorice twist. It is designed for eccentric wrist extension and pronation. The Tyler Twist eccentrically works your extensors, and the Reverse Tyler Twist works the flexors eccentrically. You can progress using bars of different resistance. The basic exercise begins with the holding a twisted bar in both hands, and slowly letting the bar untwist with the involved arm. The exercise comes with the bar, and can be easily found on the Internet. This exercise is mainly useful for those dealing with wrist or elbow pain than solely for training your extensors.

Photo courtesy TheraBand

Radial and Ulnar Deviation

Don't forget that you can also move your wrist radially (like a hitchhiker) or towards the opposite, ulnar side. Radial deviation strengthens the outer lateral elbow (location of tennis elbow) and ulnar deviation strengthens the inner medial elbow (location of golfers elbow). Both can be exercised by grabbing tubing from above or below and laterally flexing the wrist. Radial deviators can also be easily trained by holding a hammer or half a dumbbell and flexing your wrist up towards your thumb (like hitchhiking). These exercises are mainly used for rehabbing wrist and elbow problems.

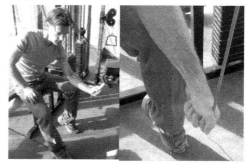

Lower Body Antagonist & Stabilizer Exercises

Many of the lower body antagonists and stabilizers are trained in the core, hip, functional routines, and especially the balance sections have already been described. More specific training is really only useful for rehab or for training for running and barefoot running. Use the endurance protocol. Most of these exercises can just use resistance against your own hand.

Tibialis Anterior

The tibialis anterior decelerates your foot as it pronates through the gait cycle, or raises your foot concentrically. This is the common location of shin splints. If it is very weak train it concentrically, but training it functionally is preferable. Walking around on your heels trains it to hold position, and walking as fast as possible without breaking into a run (prepare to be sore) will train it eccentrically. Lifting a dumbbell or tubing with your foot trains it concentrically.

Foot Eversion and Inversion

Turning your foot in (eversion) and out (inversion) are stabilizing movements in the gait cycle. Put your foot though a resistance band, hold it in your hand, and turn your foot. These are useful ankle sprain rehab exercises.

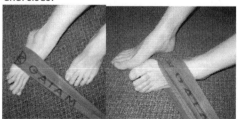

Leg Internal and External Rotation

Unless you are recovering from a hip operation, training internal or external hip rotation probably isn't very useful. First, check out the hip warm-up exercises. The best way to isolate this movement would be to attach resistance bands to your feet from either side, and turn you whole leg/thigh in and out. Keep your knees straight to avoid injuring your knee. However, using very light weight with a bent knee could help with late-stage rehab for knee problems. Internally and externally rotation your foot in this way with a bent knee won't target your hip.

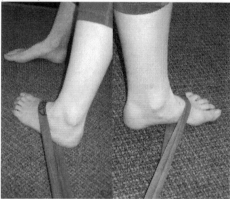

Toe Flexion and Extension

The short foot exercise in the balance exercises is a good internal foot strengthener. If you have really weak feet, you can try to strengthen your toe flexion by picking up a bowl of spilled marbles or objects of varying size, or placing a weight on the end of a towel and use your toes to scrunch up the towel. To practice extension, just curl and uncurl your toes a bunch or use hand resistance.

Toe Adduction and Abduction

Again, these exercises would be for someone having some sort of foot issue. To strengthen the toe adductors you would have to find something squishy with enough resistance to put between your toes to squeeze. To strengthen the abductors you could place a rubber band around your toes and try to spread them apart. For your big toe you could loop a rubber band around both big toes and squeeze them together, or cross the feet to spread them apart. Finally, for any of the above you can use light hand resistance for individual digits or movements.

STRETCHING

BENEFITS OF STRETCHING

Here's a bold statement: Most people do not stretch correctly and may be doing more harm than good. Muscles are tight for two reasons. The first reason is that muscles have physically shortened. The second and main reason is that they are tight is because the muscles are in a constant state of over-contraction because your nervous system is telling them to. Think of a leather belt. Stretching a piece of leather over time will indeed lengthen it. But if your belt is buckled (contracted by your nervous system), the best way to lengthen it is to first undo the clasp (reset the nervous system).

Your muscles and joints have built in sensors that tell your brain when and where your various body parts are in space and time. These sensor cells are called proprioceptors. Slow steady stretching can push the "reset button" on these proprioceptors. Studies have shown that changing your body's proprioception via stretching can actually decrease athletic performance and increase the risk of injury! An extreme example would be calibrating an electronic compass on a rollercoaster and then trying to navigate. Performing vigorous physical activity after recalibrating your joint sensors (by stretching) will make your sense of where things are slightly off.

Next, stretching before a solid warm up of at least fifteen to thirty minutes can also damage muscles by creating micro-tears and strains. Warm muscles are more pliable due to increased blood and warmth and you should notice that you will be much more flexible after you have completely warmed up. Muscles that are overly tight should be stretched after a warm-up for approximately thirty seconds, followed by some sort of proprioceptive drill or slow, easy climbing or training. However, stretching after activity will result in the greatest gains in long-term flexibility partly because you will have put your body through multiple cycles of your complete range of motion already.

Chronically over-tight muscles may be a sign of a muscle imbalance (the antagonist is weak), compensation (an injury elsewhere, or a postural or technique problem), or a joint may be hypermobile and injured and the muscle is protecting the area. On the other hand, overly flexible muscles are not as strong, and being tight can be genetic – it is okay to be tight as long as there is no pain and function is not limited. Remember, muscles are not the only thing limiting your range of motion or the only thing being stretched. From superficial to deep you have skin, fascia, muscles, ligaments, tendons, joint capsules, and bone holding you in place.

BASIC STRETCHING

Bring the desired joint to its first noticed resistance barrier – begin the stretch here. Slowly move into a deeper stretch, holding at least twenty seconds. Relax slightly out of the stretch and repeat for another twenty seconds or more.

If a muscle is insanely tight you will need to increase the duration and frequency of the stretch. You may have to make a muscle your "project" for a month by stretching it 3-5 times per day and for up to 5 minutes or repeated 30 second to one minute holds. Passive postural stretches where you aren't actively pushing should be held for 2 minutes and done three times a day. A multifunction alarm on a smartphone can help remind you. Stop if anything starts to hurt and back off the intensity of the stretch. For general maintenance, stretch the muscle group used for two 20 second reps after every climbing or training session.

ACTIVE STRETCHING

Active stretching tricks your nervous system (mainly via local reflex arcs, golgi tendon organs, and muscle spindles) into unclasping the last few notches on the belt, allowing you to get the deepest stretch possible. This form of stretching is an excellent way to get major gains by taking all of the physiological slack out of tight muscles. This type of stretching is also known as proprioceptive neuromuscular facilitation, or PNF, but the term should refer to repetitive functional training exercises instead.

Contract Relax, Antagonist Contract (CRAC) Method

Having a partner help you will provide the best results, but it is not necessary. You will need something to push against if doing the stretch alone, like a doorway, chair, or wall depending of the area to be stretched.

- Actively move the joint you want to stretch to almost the limit of how far you can stretch it. Do not stretch too deep to avoid injuring the muscle or joints.
- Push against your partner or solid object as hard as you can for five seconds to contact the muscle you are stretching. You partner should not push back, but just brace.
- Relax completely. Immediately repeat the above steps so that you wind up actively contacting the muscle for a total of three to four times.
- You need a partner for this step. From the fully stretched position, your partner will push and moderately shake the muscle back to its normal resting position while you try and resist – in other words – your partner will push (and shake) in the opposite direction as before.
- Finish with two rounds of slow steady stretching.

This procedure works best on large muscles groups over less mobile joints – primarily the hip.

Contract Relax Technique

Smaller muscles should be stretched via this technique using a slightly modified technique:

- Actively move into a stretch
- Use your hand, or if not possible, use an object like the wall to push back into.
- Lightly push for 5 seconds and relax
- Actively move farther into the stretch if possible, or just keep the same position. Do not force.
- Repeat 2-4 more times.
- Follow with 1-2 cycles of slow, steady stretching.

Above: hip flexor, TFL, piriformis, abductors, adductors, low back, QL

Post-Isometric Relaxation
In PIR a muscle is brought into tension very lightly, mainly to isolate the specific muscle. The muscle is then isometrically contracted very lightly as well for about 20-30 seconds and then relax. After this, the muscle is lengthened slightly more but not stretched and the process repeats. This helps isolate trigger points and focused areas of tightness within a muscle.

Active Range Resistance
You probably need a partner for this. Move your body part through its full range of motion in both directions while your partner applies resistance throughout. This will ensure that all reflex and stretch receptors are engaged for the full range of motion.

Post-Facilitation Technique
This is sometimes labeled Active Isolated Stretching. Activate the tight muscle in a mid-range position by pushing as hard as you can for 8-10 seconds and relaxing for two seconds. Now actively (on your own) move the joint to end range fairly quickly (but not so fast you tear something). A friend can help you guide the body part to end range and apply a little bit of overpressure for a deeper stretch. Hold for twenty seconds and relax. Repeat up to five times.

Active Release or Flossing Technique
One final type of active stretch, sometimes called flossing by CrossFitters, adds antagonist resistance while dynamically stretching a joint. For example, to "floss" the hip extensors, put an elastic band around your thigh attached in front of you while kneeling to activate the antagonist gluts. The band may need to be a weight-lifting band to provide enough resistance. While the band is pulling, contract your gluts, for example (the antagonist), and push your hip forward slowly and repeatedly through its full range of motion. Adding pinpoint compression via wraps, golf balls, or lacrosse balls can further help reduce scar tissue and adhesions. This is a combination of flossing and pin and stretch techniques.

Many active stretches are presented in the previous warm-up section. You can use some props like straps and PVC rods to assist pulling areas you can't reach. Also, rolling over a tight muscle with a foam roller is helpful. Some common uses of these devices are mentioned in some, but not all of these stretches. Be creative.

More information provided in Chapter 8 Treatments.

Two lacrosse balls taped together

Golf ball

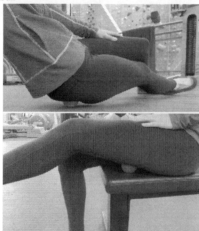
Lacrosse ball

Elbow with bike tube wrap and manual compression

Resistance and flossing band (bike tube)

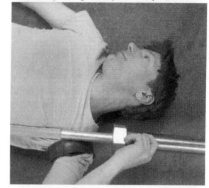
Flossing band and Olympic bar for extra compression

Foam roller with trigger point nubs

Whole Body Stretches
Relief Posture

This is an excellent whole body postural stretch, otherwise known as Brugger's Posture. Practice this often, especially during long periods of sitting and reading. Pull your chin straight back without nodding or looking up (make a double chin), pull your shoulder blades down and in, find neutral position in your pelvis, tighten your transverse abdominals and pelvic floor (draw your stomach in without sucking it in and use the muscles that stop urine flow), and if standing, do the short foot exercise (increase your foot arch without curling your toes). This is a good time to also practice abdominal breathing. Hold for 20 seconds. To increase the shoulder blade activity, you can place a band or tubing between your hands.

Yoga
Yoga classes are great ways to force you to stretch. Hatha Yoga is all the rage these days (hot yoga), but I don't think there is any benefit. An intense 30-minute warm-up should be enough to get ready. One more thing – you do not sweat out toxins (and your ischial tuberosity is NOT your "sits bones") in case your yoga teacher says so.

<u>Neck Stretches</u>
Neck retractions are described in the warm-up and can be done here. Only focus on the tight areas

Upper Traps
Pull your head to the side, keeping your shoulder down.

Posterior Cervicals and Levator Scapula
Pull your head straight down. Rounding your upper back can increase the stretch.

Neck, Sub-Occipitals, and Levator Scap
Pull your head diagonally towards the mid-point between your sternum and shoulder while looking at the opposite shoulder. Keep your shoulder down to increase the levator scapula stretch, and relax the shoulder and tuck your chin in to increase the sub-occipital stretch. To further increase the levator stretch, you can grasp your wrist on the involved side behind your back and pull it down during the stretch.

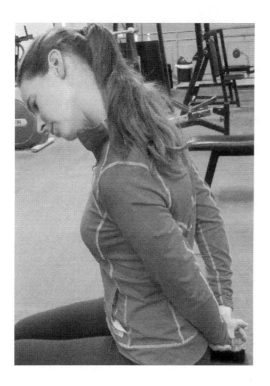

Sub-Occipitals
Pull your head diagonally towards the midpoint between your sternum and shoulder while looking at the same shoulder. Tuck your chin in.

Rotation
Turn your head as far as you can to the left or right and hold. You can use the modified active stretching described above. Do not stretch forcefully in this direction.

Extension
Tilt your head straight back and hold. You can do this laying on your back with your head off the end of a table or bed, or use the modified active stretching described above. Do not stretch forcefully in this direction.

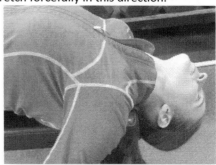

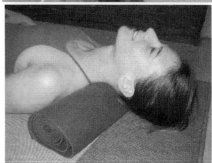

Scalenes
Tilt your head diagonally back and hold. You can do this laying on your back with your head off the end of a table or bed, or use the modified active stretching described above. Do not stretch forcefully in this direction.

SCM
Tilt your head diagonally back with your head turned to the opposite direction. You can do this laying on your back with your head off the end of a table or bed, or use the modified active stretching described above. Do not stretch forcefully in this direction. SCM is short for the sternocleidomastoid muscle.

Passive Neck Traction
These are good for post whiplash type injuries, chronic forward head posture, and reduced cervical curve. Pure vertical traction takes weight off the joints and discs, and extension traction helps restore cervical curve. There are several types of home neck traction. Saunders Company makes the best, but over the door counterbalance or spring loaded devices work well too. Cervical traction can misfire and create more pain and discomfort, so I cannot go into a how to –

follow the directions or ask your doctor. I will note, however, that to separate intervertebral space, 20-40 pounds of force may be necessary – more than was commonly recommended. Some people react very negatively towards cervical traction when compared to others with similar symptoms or conditions.

Bodyweight traction is a safe and effective way to passively stretch your neck into correct position. The best way to do this is by using a semi-soft cervical curve orthotic, often called a neck wedge. You can also hang your head off the edge of the bed, use a cylindrical cervical pillow, or a partially used paper towel roll. The correct procedure is as follows (so you don't curve the wrong part of your neck): Place the orthotic under your head and tightly against your shoulders – it should be at the very base of the neck. Let your head relax and hang for up to 15 minutes, but start with only a couple minutes.

Chest Stretches

Pectorals

Stand near a doorway and bend your arm and shoulders to 90°. Brace your arm against the doorway, and step forward slightly, pressing with your chest. Lowering your shoulder below 90° will stretch the upper pecs, and above 90° will get the upper pecs. Double up with both arms is possible.

Nerve Stretches

These stretches are a great way to help free up nerves when they act up (tingling, weakness, numbness).

Never Glide (Flossing)

To stretch the following nerves, hold for a moment, relax, and repeat to "floss" the nerve through the sheath. The goal is not to actually lengthen the nerve, but to free it up along the way from entrapments. Hold the stretch just before any tingling or numbness is felt

- **Ulnar Nerve**

To stretch the ulnar nerve, make thumb/forefinger glasses over your eyes. Seriously. To get the ulnar nerve at the elbow do the triceps stretch.

- **Median Nerve**

Abduct your arm to about 110° with the same shoulder depressed, turn your head away, and extend your wrist and fingers.

- **Radial Nerve**

Depress your shoulder and turn your head away. Internally rotate your arm and abduct it slightly (10°). Supinate your hand, flex your wrist and fingers, and ulnar deviate your wrist.

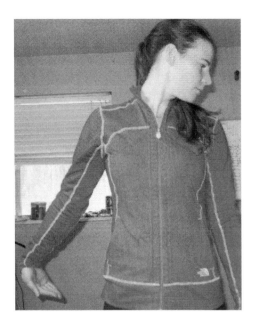

- **Musculocutaneous, Axillary, and Median Nerve**

Abduct your arm about 10° and turn your head away with the shoulder depressed. Externally rotate your arm, and extend your elbow, wrist, and fingers with your hand pronated.

SHOULDER AND ARM STRETCHES
Whole Arm

This is just like the pec stretch, but don't bend your elbows. To emphasize the hand and fingers, spread your fingers out so they just contact the door or wall.

Shoulder Traction / Bar Hang

Hang from a pull-up bar with your hands close together and palms facing forward. Hooks on wrist wraps help reduce muscle tension in the shoulder, and for fatigue if you can't hang on long enough. For frozen shoulder and impingement hang for three 2 minute sessions. Otherwise hang for 30 seconds to a minute. According to Dr. Kirsch in his book, "Shoulder Pain? The Solution & Prevention" (2013), a dead hang for a few minutes a day will stretch the coracoacromial arch and will help alleviate shoulder pain and rotator cuff injury. The danger zone for overhead activity is between 70 to 120° so this should not pinch the rotator cuff, and according to the study, it could actually reduce impingement. See the rehab section for more info.

Rhomboid Stretch
Interlace your fingers together, turn your palms forward, round your upper back, and push out with your arms. Stick a knee in between your hands to help push.

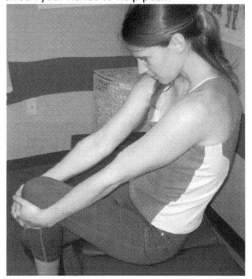

Latissimus Dorsi
To stretch your Lats (atissimus dorsi), kneel on the floor, place outstretched arms on a chair, table, or on the floor and press your chest towards the floor.

General Rotator Cuff
Place on arm behind your neck and the other behind your back and clasp hands. If you can't clasp hands use a small towel to bridge the gap. Pulling up gets the supraspinatus more, and pulling down gets the subscapularis more.

Subscapularis

Just like the Lat stretch, but bend your elbow to 90°. You can also use a PVC pipe or broom to perform it this way: grasp the end of a pole to the side of your head with other end of pole behind your arm. Bring your elbow forward slightly and bend the wrist back. Reach in front of your body with the opposite arm and grasp the lower end of pole. Pull the lower end of pole forward so the shoulder is externally rotated. You can also lay on your side with or without a firm pillow under your elbow and press down on your arm.

Supraspinatus

Place your hands on your hips and press your elbows forward. Or, place your hand banding your back and with your other hand, pull the elbow down and forwards.

External Rotators

To stretch the external rotators, or the infraspinatus and teres minor muscles, place one elbow inside the other elbow. Rotate the inner arm out. If you are very flexible you can lace your hands to help pull. You can use a pole in a stretch similar to the subscap stretch. Grasp pole at one end and position it overhead with other end of pole behind your opposite arm. Grasp other end of the pole with your hand positioned below the elbow. Position your elbow at the height of your shoulder. Pull the upper end of the pole forward so the shoulder is internally rotated. You can also lie on your back and hold onto a PVC rod with your arms and elbows up 90° each (field goal). Use the rod to rotate your arms back.

Posterior Capsule
Cross your arm across your chest, and hook your other elbow over that arm, pulling it in. You can also lay on the affected side with arm outstretched and rollover onto the arm.

Triceps
Bend your arm at the elbow, grab your elbow, and pull it towards your head. This also stretches the subscap if your traps are loose or you ulnar nerve at the elbow.

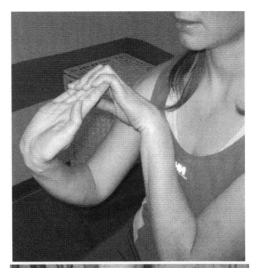

HAND AND FOREARM STRETCHES
Forearm / Wrist
There are several positions to stretch your forearms, but they all basically extend your hand at the wrist. Put both hands together behind your back in a prayer position. Grab your hand and pull it back. My favorite is to kneel on the floor and place your palms on the ground with your fingers pointed towards your knees.

Fingers
You can stretch your fingers one at a time by pulling them back. To get them all, place your fingertips together and push your palms in, or get on your knees like the above forearm stretch, put only keep your fingertips on the floor.

Gluteals
Lie on your back and pull your knee into your chest. To get the lateral gluts, pull your knee in diagonally. You can roll your butt across a foam roller to help.

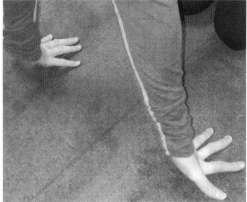

Wrist Traction
Put your wrist in a neutral position (not flexor or extended) and pull on it. You can sometimes find wrist traction devices (shown below).

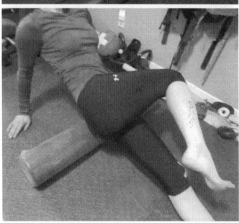

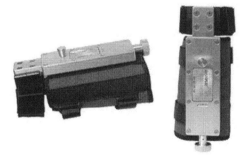

Low Squats
Get into a low squat position and hang out. This is a great compliment to the Egoscue stretch. Sit in a low squat position with feet flat on the floor and hold it for up to 30 minutes a day. This stretches the butt, low back, and quads but compresses the hip flexors so be sure to stretch those afterwards.

<u>**Hip and Thigh Stretches**</u>
As mentioned earlier, the hip is one of the main areas that need extra stretching, as it is often the tightest and good hip mobility is key in technical climbing moves.

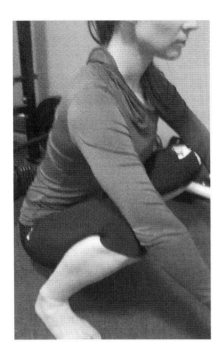

Piriformis
The key to stretching the piriformis is to externally rotate the thigh, using your lower bent leg as a lever. You can do it standing on one leg, standing with a chair or just below the hip surface, on your back, or laying forward.

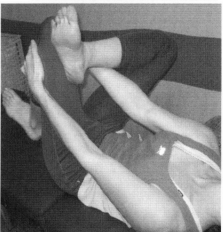
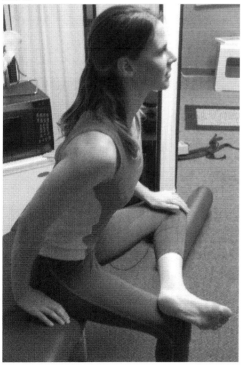

Hamstring

Your hamstring is composed in three muscles, the lateral semitendinosus, the medial semimembranosus, and the central biceps femoris. Turning your leg in and out will stretch those muscles more specifically. Also, the hamstring crosses two joints, making it more complex to stretch. Bending the knee will give a more proximal stretch while a straight leg will give a more distal stretch. Pointing the ankle will also disengage the calf (gastrocnemius and soleus).

The best way to stretch is to stand up straight, place the leg on a shorter surface like a chair or footstool, and lean forward keeping your body straight and leading with the chest. Active stretching is best done solo through a doorway. Hurdler's stretches (seated version) aren't as effective.

Psoas

The psoas (or iliopsoas group) is a commonly tight hip flexor (along with the rectus femoris in your quads). Stand or kneel in a fencer's stance with the involved side back. Keep your upper body and back straight and push forward at the hip. To actively stretch it with a partner, grab the unaffected knee to your chest, and dangle the affected limb off a low table or bench. To target your psoas more than your general hip flexors, slightly twist and rotate away for the side you are stretching.

Egoscue Stretch
This stretch is taken from Pete Egoscue and his Egoscue Method. It is a wonderful passive stretch that works on the hips and low back and can offer some real relief. Lie on your back and put the leg of the side you aren't stretching up on a support so the hip and knee are both bent at 90°. The other leg is straight and propped up at a level high enough that <u>your back isn't arched and is as flat as possible</u> on the floor. Relax until you feel your back relax and flatten, then lower your leg further. The goal is to get your leg flat on the floor with your back flattened on the floor as well. Feel free to take a nap; this stretch can take up to 45 minutes. If your leg rolls to the side use some books stacked to the side of your foot to keep it pointed at the ceiling.

Quads
The standard quad stretch is done standing or kneeling by pulling your leg behind your hip and touching your heel to your butt. A deeper stretch can be performed by placing the affected side knee on the floor directly against a wall so your leg and foot are vertically up on the wall. Take the unaffected leg and place it in front of you (like you are proposing). Lean back. The muscles of the quads from inner to outer are the vastus medialis, vastus intermedius, and vastus lateralis with the rectus femoris on top of the vastus intermedialis. The vastus medialis oblique (VMO) is the part of the vastus medialis that bulges near your medial knee when you extend your leg.

Groin
To stretch the adductors and some of the flexors of the groin/hip, sit in butterfly position with the soles of your feet touching. Lower your knees to the ground, and if you can press down with your elbows, try that. Lowering your head and/or rounding your upper back will give a good upper back stretch as well. You can also do this face down. To achieve more of a "splits" style stretch, stand with your feet a bit more than

shoulder width apart, turn the affected side in, and rock to the opposite side.

TFL and ITB

This stretches your tensor fascia lattea (TFL) and lateral gluts. You may feel it on your ITB (iliotibial band), but that is not a muscle. In fact your ITB is so fibrous and tough that stretching it is next to impossible and it usually feels tight due to the imbalance in your hams vs. quad strength/flexibility. Lengthening your TFL, hamstrings, or quads usually does the trick. You can first roll the outside of your thigh on a foam roller. To stretch, stand in a doorway and cross the affected leg behind the other. Use the doorway for support and push your affected side hip out to the side. This is a hard movement to discover. Experiment with the position of your hips and legs to find just the right spot. Another variation has you touching your toes with crossed legs.

Hip Traction

I wish there were more devices for hip traction besides having someone pull on your leg or hanging upside-down. Relieving pressure on the hip joint and stretching the capsule feels amazing. If you are feeling savvy, you could rig a 3:1 system using a harness, cord, pole, and a coffee cup. Good luck. Inversion, gravity boots, and manual therapy are probably the best bet.

Leg Stretches
Calf
To get a great calf stretch, stand with your heel off a platform or stair and drop your heel. You can also put your foot up against the wall and step forward.

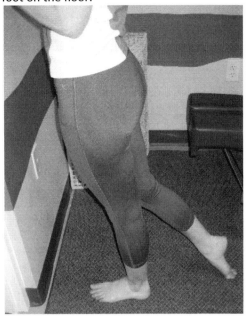

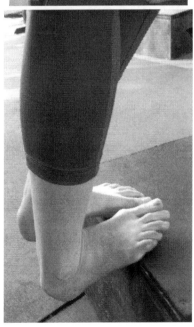

Tibialis Anterior
This is a difficult muscle to stretch, and is generally not necessary. Start sitting and put your foot behind you with the top of your foot on the floor.

Plantar Fascia Stretch
For tight feet or plantar fasciitis you can grab your toes and pull them back, roll them over a glass bottle, golf ball, or TheraBand roller.

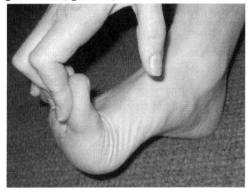

Lumbar Stretches
Pelvic Blocks
Pelvic blocks passively stretch your SI Joint (sacroiliac) and also open up your lower lumbar disc space. Shoes can substitute for the blocks. Placing both right over your hip crest and laying supine will open up the low back. Alternating a block under one hip crest and the other under the opposite hip flexor will open up the upper SI joint on the high block

side and the lower SI joint and the low block side.

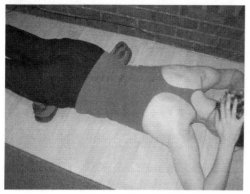

Extension, Lateral Flexion, Flexion
These can be done standing or over a Swiss ball. Bend backward, forward, and to the side bending at the hip. Raise your arms overhead for added leverage.

Cobra
Really an abdominal stretch, the cobra extends your low back that can be therapeutic for disc issues or arthritis. Lie on your stomach and press up with your hands.

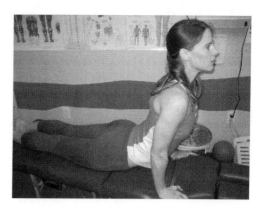

Rotation
Sitting, cross your leg and use your arms to rotate your body towards the crossing leg. On your back, lay just on the side of a firm couch or mattress (on the ground is acceptable). Grab the knee away from the edge and pull it over the edge, rotating your lower back. Use your arm to keep you from falling or tipping over. Don't force your back to pop.

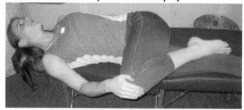

McKenzie and Williams Stretches

These exercises are mainly for those with low back pain with or without nerve involvement into their legs. To help centralize nerve or muscle pain you may find that you have a flexion or extension bias.

The McKenzie exercises help those with an extension bias. Start by lying face down with your hands near your ears. Prop yourself up as far as you can comfortable go, it may only be resting on your forearms to begin. At the top of your range, take six deep breaths, lower down, relax, and try again. Williams's exercises are for those with a flexion bias. Lie on your back and do the abdominal breathing and pelvic tilt exercise from the warm-up section. Next bring on knee to your chest and hold for a few breaths. Progress to both knees, active knee to chest, and then abdominal exercises. Knee raises on a captain's chair are good low-stress ab exercises for the back.

Lumbar Traction and Inversion

The most common form of lumbar traction is the inversion table. Luckily these aren't that expensive or dangerous. Saunders makes a home lumbar traction unit for about $500, but clinical grade intersegmental traction tables cost into the tens of thousands. Lumbar traction opens up your low back helping to hydrate discs, relieve pressure off nerves and discs, and stretches tight muscles and joints. Inversion therapy is also claimed to help with systemic conditions because of the redistribution of body fluids that gravitate down throughout the day. I can't really comment on validity of that claim. Doing lumbar and abdominal exercises during inversion can be made safer because there is much less load on the spine during exercise. Most people vary between 45° and fully inverted. Gravity boots used to be all the rage back in the disco days. They are actually pretty useful and cheap compared to an inversion table – just a bit more dangerous. You could you make your own with some ski boots, but do you want to trust your life or use of your legs to your handiwork? You'll need something to hang from. A pull-up bar works well, and bars that have grips sticking out perpendicular from the main bar help for dismounting. A good pair of boots have hook in the front, along with grasping stirrups to help you dismount. If you try inversion, start slow and have someone in the room to help you dismount. Some people react very negatively towards lumbar traction compared to others with similar symptoms or conditions.

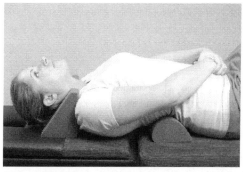

Neck and low back stretching with orthotics. The final photos shows a neck wedge. Courtesy The Pettibon System

Inversion, decompression unit, low back home traction, sacroiliac traction pillow

CHAPTER THREE: NON-CLIMBING SUPPLEMENTAL EXERCISES
UPPER AND LOWER BODY

The rest of these exercises are good for general weight training conditioning, especially in the off-season. Backpackers, skiers, mountaineers, alpinists, and ice climbers may find the lower body exercises helpful. But these exercises really didn't fit into any warm-up, prevention/preparation, or climbing specific exercise. For general weight training conditioning I'd also recommend CrossFit or similar programs.

UPPER BODY SUPPLEMENTAL EXERCISES
Pushups
An exercise staple for general fitness! There are some variations to try. Putting your feet on a Swiss ball (try one at a time) adds some instability, as does putting your hands in a suspension trainer. You can add weights in a backpack or vest, or try it one-armed. To add some serratus anterior work, protract your scapular at the top of the push up. Raising your chest off the floor with dumbbells, or something solid adds difficulty. A true push up has your chest touching the floor with every rep. Slow is better than fast. Use the strength or strength-endurance protocols.

Bench Press

Basically the same exercise as a pushup, but you can add more weight. I'd go with the pushup unless you are using the power protocol here.

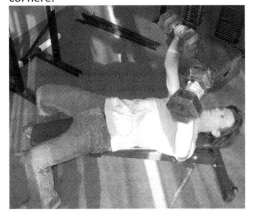

Medicine Ball Toss

Tossing and catching a heavy medicine ball works the chest muscles concentrically, eccentrically, and plyometrically. Use endurance, strength, or strength-endurance protocols. Squats shown below.

Pushup and Row Combo

This is a great example of combining exercises to maximize your time! Grab two dumbbells that meet the weight requirements for you one arm row. Use them to elevate your chest for a push up. Do a pushup, and a row with the dumbbell at the top.

Biceps Curl

This exercise specifically targets the arm flexors. You can do one at a time via dumbbells, or use a preacher bar or Olympic weights for both arms. You can also use a suspension trainer one arm at a time. Go slow, even very slowly. Use the strength, or strength-endurance protocols. Rupturing the biceps or causing shoulder problems at the shoulder attachment are very common climbing injuries.

Lower Body Supplemental exercises

The best way to train the lower body (hips, thighs, legs, and feet) is in the way you will use them almost all of the time – by moments that simulate balance, walking, or helping to pick an object up. That's what legs do! If this were a book for monkeys, the leg section would be as detailed as the arms.

Sport climbers and boulders can luckily skip leg training for the most part. One leg stands with weight can be useful in training to stand up onto a high foot, however. Backcountry skiers, alpinists, mountaineers, and ice climbers are the main group that might need to train their legs. Schedule leg training during the same period as you schedule your aerobic since both are used at the same time (slogging, carving turns, sprinting up the trail). Ice climbers don't necessarily need to schedule both together since cardio is as important for strict ice climbing as it is for other types of purely technical climbing. However, ice climbs sometimes have thigh deep post-holing for several hours involved in the approach compared to standard trad approaches. The functional exercises crossover into the cardio exercises and the best one would be the most similar to your goal (uphill hikes with a pack almost always works best). The other exercises are meant to help correct weak links. Skip them if they are strong enough for your goal.

Heavy squats are dangerous and form is of extreme importance. Beware of rounding your back and sacral nutation (your sacrum tips in or you lose neutral pelvis) at the very bottom.

The focus on the following exercises should be strength and endurance, not cardio.

Outdoor
Uphill hikes with a heavy pack, backcountry skiing, uphill runs, uphill mountain biking, and resort skiing (good for isometric strength) are the best in that order. Your legs should be

Lat Pulls
Behind the head lat pulls are a bad idea because of the high risk of shoulder and neck injury, and all of our pulling occurs in front of the head. Lat pulls are good supplemental pulling exercises, but climbing or at least pull-ups are much better. The only benefit to doing lat pulls on a cable machine is that it's easy to change weights out for the power protocol.

fully worked at the end. One of the better exercises to do is to fill your pack with collapsible water jugs (1-5 gallons) and slog uphill. Dump the water out on top.

Indoor
Weighted uphill treadmills, Stairmasters, or VersaClimbers can simulate the outdoor versions, but are so unbelievably boring. Again, go for leg strength and endurance instead of cardio by using the endurance or strength-endurance protocol.

Step-Ups
Using a solid platform at knee height step up and down alternating the leading leg. Increase the reps to 1,000 (500 per leg) and the weight to 40 pounds to simulate an uphill slog.

Box Jumps
This intense exercise adds plyometric strength. Jump onto a stable box or surface, landing on both legs. At the top make sure your legs and hips are fully extended. Jump back down and repeat in a fluid, dynamic motion. A standard box jump height is about 20", but can vary depending on size and skill. The higher the jump the better. Wear shin guards if you are in doubt of your ability to make the jump! I witnessed the world record by a guy in Salt Lake who was just normal height. I was scared for his shins. Use the endurance or strength-endurance protocol.

Side Step-Ups, Step-Downs
In addition to the step-up presented above, you can step to the side or face away from the platform and step down (and back up). Use the endurance or strength-endurance protocol.

Lunges

This is a pretty good exercise for skiers. A proper lunge is executed by keeping your upper body still and straight, and the final position of your front and back knee and hip at 90° each. Knee problems can develop if your front knee goes beyond your ankle or foot. Stop 2" from the ground. You can lunge forward or to the side, and also carry weights in your hand for added difficulty. To train plyometrically, skip forward, backward, and to the sides. Use the endurance or strength-endurance protocol.

Front Squat

The front squat is the king of lower body weight lifting exercises. Perfect form is absolutely critical (described in the warm-up). To re-cap: feet turned slightly out and shoulder width apart, knees slightly push out, lead with the butt, keep back rounded, avoid sacral nutation at the bottom (tail bone tips down), go to full depth, keep chest high. You can do high reps at bodyweight for the endurance protocol, including using a suspension trainer. For weighted front squats (strength, strength-endurance, or power), use an Olympic bar and keep the bar close to your chest with elbows fully bent and sticking out (upper arm parallel to floor). Wrists are bent and a wrist wrap can help. Use a spotter for high weights, especially the power protocol. Hold for one second at the bottom of the squat.

Goblet Squat
This is a great squat to work up to a full front squat. Grab a kettlebell or dumbbell up to your chin with both hands and squat down.

Wrist wrap for heavy squats

Back Squat
Same as the front squat, but the Olympic bar is positioned behind your head. This can place excessive strain on your shoulders, and do not rest the weight on your shoulders – you can bruise your lower cervical vertebra or shear it off the spine of the lowest cervical vertebrae if you drop the weight.

Reverse Squat
This is an interesting open chain version of the squat done with gravity boots. You can hold a weight to increase the load. You will most likely be using the strength protocol.

Wall Squat
Lean against the wall with your hips and legs at 90° and hold it there for as long as possible. Avoid using your arms for support. You can place a Swiss ball behind your back for some instability, or squeeze a ball between your legs or hold a resistance band open that is wrapped around your knees to additionally train adductors or adductors. Use the endurance protocol.

One-Leg Squat

Use a suspension trainer to aid in balance or stand on a platform to get more depth. Do a one-leg squat, flagging your other leg out. You can hold a heavy dumbbell in either hand, or use a cable from below. To add instability, attach a cable or band to either leg or stand on an unstable platform. This and Pistols are great exercises to determine if there is a general imbalance in your leg strength as well as training to stand up from a high step or rock-over move. Use endurance, strength, or strength-endurance protocols.

Leg Press Machine
The leg press machine is a substitute for the squat, although it is not nearly as effective. However, if you don't have access to Olympic weights or a spotter for heavy loads, it is an acceptable substitute.

Leg Extension Machine
Leg extension machines work your quads, but are exceptionally dangerous for your knee under moderate to heavy loads. Skip this one, or use light weights for rehab purposes only.

Pistols
This is like a one-leg squat, but instead of flagging your leg, stick it straight forward. Add weights as you progress. You can also use a suspension trainer for support. Use the strength or strength-endurance protocol.

Mountain Climbers

Using a suspension trainer, put your feet into the grips/rings and lay on your elbows or extended arms on some type of platform. Pump your knees up and then extend your legs for endurance.

Hamstring Curl

You may want to do some specific hamstring exercise if your hamstrings are less than 60-75% as strong as your quadriceps. The easiest way is on a hamstring curl machine, but you can attach resistance bands to your ankle while lying on your stomach or sitting on a chair. You can also use a Swiss ball by starting in the supine bridge position and rolling the ball towards you with your foot and bending at the knee, or by doing the same thing with your feet in suspension trainers (easy endurance exercises). Try and use the strength protocol to match your quads.

Calf Raises

Some of are blessed with giant calfs (gastrocnemius and soleus muscles), and some aren't. Train these if you require a lot of stemming or ice climbing. To train strength or strength-endurance use a calf-raise machine, hold some dumbbells or a weighted Olympic bar on your shoulders and lift yourself up by your ankles. To train endurance you can walk around on your toes for a while, or attach resistance bands to your feet and press forward.

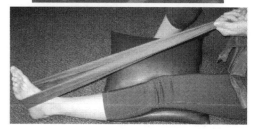

Pulling a Tire
Dragging around a tire or something heavy can help train you for slogging through deep snow or more specifically, pulling a sled.

<u>UPPER AND LOWER BODY COMBINATION EXERCISES</u>
The rest of these exercises are amazing function full body conditioning.

Turkish Get Up
The TGU is considered to be one of the best full-body functional exercises of all time. It's kind of complicated to describe. Google it if my instructions don't do it for you. There are a lot of subtleties involved that I can't get into in book format. A kettlebell works best. Start with light weight to figure it out, and then progress to the strength, or strength-endurance protocol.

- Keep your shoulder blades down and in, and look at the weight throughout the exercise. Lie on the ground, roll over, and grab the weight with both hands, and roll back onto your back. The weight is in both hands.
- Now, with the weight in just your right hand, press the weight straight up. Your right knee should be flexed up by your butt, and your left leg is straight and slightly abducted.
- Bend your right knee and plant your foot firmly onto the ground
- Lift the right shoulder off the floor, and then twist until you have to support your weight onto your left elbow. Pop off from your left elbow onto your hand, the hand should be slightly behind but out wide.
- Raise your butt and extended left leg off the floor. With your weight balanced on your left hand and right leg, begin to pass your left leg underneath you, knee and toes on the ground, ending up on a lunge type position. This "leg sweep" is fairly complicated, but essential. The reverse is even harder.
- Come out of the lung to stand up, hold the position, and then reverse the process to sit back down. Remember, the weight is above you on an outstretched arm at all times.

Thruster

Thrusters combine a squat with a push press. You can use dumbbells or an Olympic weight. The starting position is important. Your elbows should be as parallel to the ground as possible and your arms fully flexed at the elbow. Wrists are back or in neutral position. Wrist wraps can help with wrist pain. Dive down into a squat and thrust back up. At the top use your hips and knees to drive the weight over your head. Return to the starting position and repeat. Maintain perfect squat form during the squat. Adding a snatch, hang, clean, and or jerk will make it more functional, but take you farther from the intention of shoulder pressing here. Save those for off-season weightlifting training. Use the strength or strength-endurance protocol.

Wall Ball

Wall balls are similar to thrusters, but more plyometric and eccentric contraction are utilized. You will need a medicine ball (12-24 pounds are common weights) and a high wall to throw the ball into. Begin in a squat position only a few feet away from the wall, and hold the ball like the weights described in the thruster exercise. Powerfully come out of the squat and throw the ball up overhead (like the thrust) using momentum and your hips, aiming as high as you possibly can. Catch the ball overhead and decelerate it using your hips, and legs, but as little of your body/chest (or face) as possible, coming back into a squat. Repeat using the strength or power-endurance protocols.

Burpee

Jump down into a pushup (chest to the floor), and blast back up to a jumping jack. Clap at the top to be sure you are doing the complete range of motion. A high-speed plyometric combo exercise. You could also use dumbbells to do the pushups on, and then bust out a thruster. Use the endurance or strength-endurance protocol.

Sumo Deadlift High-Pull
You can use a kettlebell, Olympic bar, or dumbbell. Start in a wide squat position and grab the weight with both hands. In an explosive movement, come out of the squat, thrusting with your hips, drive the weight up to your chin. To do this as a pure arm exercise a cable machine with the pulley below you works best, aka a standing upright row. Use the endurance, power, or power-endurance protocol. This exercise can actually be a very good foundational training for dynamic climbing movements and dynos.

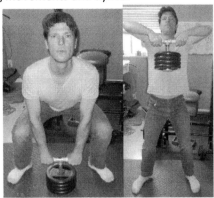

Olympic Lifts
Olympic lifts combine a basic functional movement (from picking something up to bringing it up over your head) with moderate to very heavy weights. These exercises are the staple of serious weight lifters. I recommend them only for general off-season conditioning. I have already explained some of the movements so far. Describing the rest would fill pages to include proper technique and form, and would seriously go beyond the scope and purpose of this book. A good CrossFit gym will teach you most of the basics. Warning: poor form will get you injured. Do not sacrifice form for weights or reps. Various Olympic lifts not described in the book: Snatch, Hang, Clean, Jerk, Power, Push, Press, Split, Catch, Drops, and combinations of these.

CARDIOVASCULAR TRAINING

BENEFITS OF CARDIO TRAINING

Even though cardiovascular (heart, lungs, blood vessels, and metabolism) exercise is not necessary for most climbing specific training or prehab for climbing, it is still useful to prehab against heart disease and is obviously helpful for alpinists and mountaineers. Training cardio is also useful for hard climbing to keep from getting winded. I will be using the term cardio(vascular) and aerobic interchangeable solely due to convention, even though anaerobic training is a major player.

Aerobic conditioning can double up with other types of training that keeps your heart rate high, or by performing exercises at a high intensity without rest. Aerobic exercise is necessary for "out of shape" individuals who are out of breath during roped climbing, approaching, descending, and also for alpinists and mountaineers. Training your cardiovascular system can help improve efficiency in all types of climbing, and efficient climbers climb better. Also, aerobic conditioning is good for your health, heart, mood, and your overall cardiovascular system. It also improves blood distribution to the capillaries of your muscles so you don't get pumped as quickly. It also helps flush out metabolic waste more efficiently, decreasing your pump. You can last longer and feel stronger by training aerobically. If your goal isn't aerobic intensive and you enjoy road biking, running, or mountain biking, do your aerobic training during those activities so it can be enjoyable for you.

One of the main reasons people hate cardio training is because it hurts and causes injury. Becoming proficient and efficient will make the pains go away – ribs and lungs need to get strong and become more elastic, and tendons and ligaments will strengthen. Follow the ten per cent rule: increase the intensity, time, or distance by 10% each week so you don't force connective tissue to go beyond its holding power. Do not push past bad pains in your joints: either stop, or slow down. Back off and try again. Knowledge of proper technique and equipment is also key to avoiding injury. Become knowledgeable. If you have an injury, you can easily change exercises. You can get a good cardio workout in with just your arms if need be!

Another excuse is that an exercise like running is too high impact. Study after study has shown that running is not only safe for your knees, it actually makes the joint stronger and healthier. This is not the case for extremely high impact activities like jumping off boulders. The problem is usually not with the exercise, but your technique or physical imbalance. Again, take to time to understand how to do these exercises correctly. Cardio training outside on very poor air quality days (smog or ozone), or running on a busy road (ever ran behind a school bus?) are worse for you than staying home and doing nothing but smoking a pack of cigarettes.

Aerobic and Anaerobic Training

These terms actually deal with how your cells utilize energy (ATP). By using oxygen, your cells can produce about 16 times as much energy (at peak efficiency). Lactic acid is a byproduct of anaerobic metabolism, and is a cause of soreness and pain during anaerobic exercise. However, you flush it out fairly quickly – it does not cause DOMS or become crystalized contrary to some poorly educated manual therapy practitioners). Exercise becomes anaerobic when your body cannot supply the working muscles and tissues with enough oxygen to meet its demands. Once an activity has become anaerobic, the clock begins to tick before your brain forces you to stop by signaling pain (otherwise cell death will occur).

Heart Rate and Intensity

To follow the protocols given below, you will need to be able to figure out your maximum heart rate – just like finding your maximum weight in the previous chapters. The best and most accurate way to find this out is to use a **heart rate monitor** and go all-out on a treadmill. There can be significant fluctuation in using a formula like:

$$\text{Max Heart Rate (HR)} = 208 - (0.7 * \text{Age in Years})$$

A heart rate monitor will be extremely helpful in objectively determining what intensity you should be exerting to stay in a protocol. Smartphones are getting better at finding your heart rate by using the phone's camera. Heart rate monitors that utilize a chest strap are still the best, but wrist only versions are quickly catching up.

AEROBIC PROTOCOLS

The following are similar to the weight training protocols, but tailored towards your cardiovascular system. Mountaineers and alpinists may need to spend more time in other heart rate zones. See "Training for the New Alpinism" (2014) by Steve House and Scott Johnston for more detailed info.

Aerobic Endurance
- 70-80% Max HR, 60-120 minutes

One to two hours moderate "jogging" pace. This protocol also helps build lung capacity, trains the heart, promotes vascularization into muscle tissues, and builds efficiency in your metabolism (including more mitochondria are built in your cells). It also strengthens lower body ligaments and tendons. High altitude and endurance climbers will actually need to spend more time below this level - discussed in the programming section. Also, if you are seriously out of shape, begin with an easier cardio program. This will help you from bonking during long days, climbs, and approaches.

Aerobic Threshold
- 80-90% Max HR. 12-15 minutes x 2

This protocol is similar to the strength protocol. It's called aerobic threshold because you are trying to push the boundary at which high intensity exercise becomes anaerobic. One way this is trained is by tricking your brain into letting you push further (see Tricking the Central Governor). Your body will also learn tricks into becoming more efficient so there is less demand for oxygen. The benefits of aerobic endurance are also included. Take a break and recover by moving at low intensity to flush the system for a few minutes before beginning the second set. This is great training to keep the pump away or to perform at high intensity for longer.

Anaerobic Threshold
- 100% all-out effort. 30-60 seconds x 5

This is very similar to the power protocol, and will most likely destroy you. If you have injuries or are in good to worse shape, wait until you are more conditioned. This trains you to be able to work harder under an oxygen starved environment for longer. It also helps speed up flushing of metabolic waste. Don't plan on being able to do much after this. This will help you to recover from a pump faster, and perform high exertion activities without as much need for recovery. When you are done with a rep, try and minimize the time it takes to get back on the horse and do it again, but you'll probably need at least a couple minutes if not more. You actually want to maximize the amount of metabolic waste to make this exercise effective. Standing motionless between reps is one way to stay lactic acid saturated! It's harder to do this outside with the exception of running up a hill. Treadmills at an incline and rowing machines work well.

PROGRAMMING CARDIO

Aerobic training doesn't need to be programmed in at any specific time, but it helps to cluster your aerobic training instead of spreading it out. If your goal is aerobic intensive, plan on 1-3 months of 3-4 times per week of gradually increasing intensity. It can help to schedule your lower body leg training during your cardio phase. If you just want to experience some cardio gains for general fitness do one of each aerobic protocol a week until it doesn't hurt and you're not completely out of breath (1-2 months). Actual activity for your sport will drastically reduce the amount of cardio and leg training. A few long approaches with a heavy pack, or a few days backcountry skiing are far superior to all other types of cardio training and will help train your legs as well.

Cardio Exercises

Modify any of the following examples to fit into your selected aerobic protocol.

High Intensity Circuit Training
Any form of exercise will train the cardiovascular system depending on the intensity. Cycling through multiple exercises at a high intensity without much resting can provide as much cardio training as a run.

Speed Climbing
To keep your training as climbing related as possible, you could double up cardio with climbing. You won't necessarily have to climb really fast, but climb at high intensity with small breaks. I would actually recommend against this as your main form of cardio. Give your climbing muscles a break.

Trail Running
Trail running is not only more scenic, but it provides you will more uphill opportunities. Unless you have a several miles of uphill road, regular jogging won't provide you with the type of aerobic training useful for climbing except to get back in shape and train the ligaments of your foot and ankles.

Hiking or Skinning Uphill
You may need to toss some rocks or collapsable water jugs in a pack to up the intensity without breaking into a jog. This is probably the best form of cardio you can do.

Mountain Biking and Road Biking
Only the uphill sections will help unless you can really haul on the flats. Be sure to have good form and a well-fitted bike.

Spin Cycle
You have to be motivated to keep up the intensity. The Schwinn Airdyne is the best choice to maintain a high intensity, and can really blast you good. Keep good form and fit your bike accordingly. Spin classes are fun diversions if you belong to a gym.

Schwinn Airdyne

Treadmill
You will need one with variable incline. Adding weight can help simulate and train the pains of backpacking. This, and the elliptical, is where you will find most of the gym drones wasting their time and gym membership.

Elliptical
It is difficult to get it go fast enough for climbing related aerobic intensity. The elliptical is nice because it is very low impact, but it can actually be hard on the knees and ankles since you don't pick up your feet. Ones with arm bars are nice to warm-up your arms and legs.

Stairmaster
This is a great machine for climbing related cardio training. Adding a pack with some weight helps to increase the intensity to high gear. There are small portable step-only Stairmaster-like devices available for cheap. I have not tried them, but can only assume that you get what you pay for.

Very cool stair climber

VersaClimber
This is like a Stairmaster with an arm component. If you can afford it, or are lucky enough to have one at your gym, I suggest hopping on one.

Photo courtesy VersaClimber

Rowing Machine
Rowing machines (or actual outdoor rowing) provide some of the best full body cardio training there is, although proper form is key. It's like performing hundreds of squats and rows at the same time. Great for your arms, chest, legs, butt, and back. The Concept2 rower is by far the best machine to buy. I'd almost say don't get anything else. This exercise, the Airdyne, and the VersaClimber are the best of the indoor cardio workouts.

Photo courtesy Concept2

Cross-Country Skiing
You're outside, fresh winter air, it's fun, and you're doing a fairly transferrable skill: what could be better? If you grew up in the 1970's, maybe you can get your parents' Nordic Track out of their basement?

Jump Rope
Jumping rope, especially with a Speed Rope, can get your heart rate going in no time. It's also one of the cheapest pieces of cardio equipment you can buy considering you can do it barefoot. Good form is necessary or you'll be stopping and starting with bruised shins. One way to get the heart rate way up is to practice double-unders: getting the rope to pass under you twice in one jump. You can even try your luck for the elusive triple-under.

There are many other forms of aerobic activity you can perform, such as: swimming (logistically difficult), roller blading, skateboarding, dancing, etc. It really doesn't matter what as long as you can maintain intensity and not get hurt. The more transference of skill the better.

RUNNING TECHNIQUE

There are three mainstream running techniques out there: Evolution Running, Chi Running, and Pose Technique. CrossFitters have latched onto the Pose technique, Chi Running is the most widely recognized, and Evolution Running, although excellent, isn't as popular. The best one is the one that fits your body and style, so you may have to shop around. To sum up the techniques, I'd offer that Chi may not be the fastest technique, but uses a more relaxed form. Pose method relies on coming in and out of specific postures. Evolution Running focuses on minimizing wasted energy through excess movement and using larger muscle groups to do most of the work. You can find a lot of information and videos on the Internet, and both Chi and Evolution have excellent instructional videos that are way better than reading a book about it.

All the techniques encourage either a midfoot strike (Chi) or forefoot strike (Chi and Evo). No matter what your speed, all encourage a cadence of 180 beats per minute (bpm) and a metronome is useful. Also, propulsion is gained by leaning your body forward. The more your lean (fall forward) the faster you go. Keep a neutral pelvis, erect posture, tight core, and relaxed limbs. Don't lead with your head, and keep your shoulders relaxed. Your feet should point straight ahead with mild foot pronation. Land with your foot directly beneath your hips (not in front). Use your body's elastic recoil upon foot-strike.

Techniques differ on what exactly to do with your legs in propulsion and return. Here's my take: Use your gluts to pull back. Don't use your quads to straighten your knee to push off, or your hams to pull your legs back. Keep your knees slightly bent for the full cycle and flick your heel towards your butt on the follow through. Your arms should also pump at 180 bpm, be at a 90° bend, and your arm swing should not pass centerline.

When climbing hills use hip and knee extension, driving your knee vertically, and pulling your feet toward the ground (kick the ground). Downhill technique uses forward lean and your foot strike is slightly behind. Followers of these programs will probably gag and scoff at my bastardizatoin of the three techniques.

TRAINING AT OR FOR ALTITUDE

Being fit for some reason does not affect how you will be affected by altitude. Obviously you'll be relatively fitter compared to someone less fit, but may only get a slight advantage when protecting yourself from altitude-related sicknesses. That said, I would want to be in the best aerobic shape of my life if I were planning on climbing at altitude.

There are some training tricks you can employ to train for becoming more acclimatized. First, the more time spent at altitude the better, and I'll get into this and more in the altitude section later in the book. Exercising at high altitude isn't like having extra training weight of less air. It's more like training without eating. The best training at altitude can offer is to help with getting used to what it feels like to work hard with less oxygen, so a few of your sessions should be done higher-up. Some gyms have hyperbaric chamber that allow you to simulate training at altitude.

If you can sleep and live at a high altitude but train at a low altitude, you get the best of both worlds. If you have enough money, you could invest in a **high-altitude chamber** for your bedroom to acclimatize. There are even some **masks** you can sleep with. Before any high altitude summit, plan on some less technical training hikes that reach a comparable altitude. For instance, if you're going up Mount Rainier, climb some lower nearby volcanoes or hills first. Spend the night on top if you can. Spend a few days in Leadville, Colorado and climb an easier fourteener if planning on hitting up the Diamond on Longs Peak. Claims that there is less oxygen near the poles (like Denali) aren't necessarily true; the difference in pressure is negligible (~100 feet difference).

Powerbreathe, Elevation Training Mask, and Breathing Training Programs
You can train your inspiratory muscles to increase your respiratory volume - possibly a great exercise for everything from high-output approaching, slogging, climbing, and for high altitudes. Both products, Powerbreathe and Elevation Training Mask claim that breathing in with resistance and breathing out slowly and passively trains the muscles of your ribcage and diaphragm, and stretches your alveoli. The Training Mask also claims that the decreased O2 simulates high altitude, and it also makes more CO2 available that in theory (Bohr Effect) makes oxygen more available for use. Claims are increased aerobic capacity, V02 max, aerobic and anaerobic thresholds, oxygen efficiency, and energy production. The Powerbreathe's program takes about 5 minutes per day of exercise for about six weeks, and the Training Mask 2.0 is a bit more intense. Check out the book "Breathe Strong Perform Better" by Alison McConnell (2011) for a manifesto on breathing and training. She did invent the Powerbreathe device, so there is a strong plug for her device.

So is this for real? Some studies have shown positive results, while others have shown control groups actually getting better results! Here's my take… Training at altitude has time and again been shown to be less effective, if not detrimental on the training effect. Training low in an O^2 rich environment and living high to achieve physiologic changes is the standard paradigm. But I still think it is excellent training! Why? Because I do think these devices strengthen lung musculature, help you practice slow exhalation, and train your lungs to expand to their fullest during really hard exertion.

Which brings us to breathing training programs. There are a lot of them, and most sport images of new-age wanna be's floating around and looking super-peaceful – and websites scroll on forever (my #1 sign of a bad source of Internet information) with links, gif files, and references everywhere. That said, breathing is pretty damn important, and we do it wrong all the time. Unless I find a credible program, practice the abdominal breathing exercise I gave you. It is true that slow exhalation is tied directly into your heart rate, blood pressure, and oxygen/carbon-dioxide regulation. Pursing your lips, or plugging a nostril with your finger (on the outside!), and breathing slowly out will lower your heart rate and blood-pressure...but only while you're doing it. Practice may help remind you to correctly breathe on a climb.

Chapter Four: Climbing Specific Exercises
Strength, Power, Technique, Endurance, and Combination Protocol Exercises

Did you skip to this section? If you don't want to bother with anything in the chapters before this point, but still want to have some sort of well-rounded fitness, I'd suggest CrossFit, Mountain Athlete, Gym Jones, or any bootcamp style exercise routing (Sealfit, P90X, etc.). You can take group exercise classes, use exercise videos, or find exercise routines online.

Drytool-snowshoe-bouldering. Photo courtesy Peter Hirst

Every other sport incorporates major time into practicing drills and skills. Well, you should too. The following protocols and exercises, or drills, train climbing specific muscles. The exercises are divided into similar protocols as the non-climbing specific exercises with the addition of technique. Technique in this section is more of a byproduct than an actual protocol. The skills section, which does not follow the strength and similar protocols, is where the core of skill training takes place. Repeated overload practice of climbing related movements are different from skills in that they promote strength over learning. The exercises are divided up into protocols, and should be scheduled during what "phase" you are training in (see programming). It is best to omit these exercises from your foundation phase (you should be practicing skills and ability there). The protocols follow the strength, power, and endurance guidelines already presented. More rigid guidelines for sets, reps, time, and rest will be presented for the exercises, but feel free to create your own. Performing exercises under different protocols in the same day greatly increases your risk of injury.

Just as the non-climbing exercises already presented are not absolutely necessary to train for climbing, the following exercises are also supplemental. They are meant to work weak links in strength in addition to the bulk of your training. There may come a time when only working on skill and ability through climbing starts to provide diminishing returns and you may want to focus your time here to develop a stronger base.

Think of the non-climbing specific exercises as your absolute base. Not having a solid base can have far reaching effects in your climbing performance, especially with an injury or major imbalance. But your base can only take you so far and returns are greatly diminished after a foundation is set. A little goes a long way, and visa-versa. The same is true for these exercises – you only need to be so strong in your climbing specific muscles to climb at a particular grade. These are your 2nd tier in climbing fitness. Skills (technique) have far reaching effects and require constant practice and training. You could sneak up a climb that should be above your ability by skill alone.

A note on interval training: interval training in climbing training means climbing, resting, and climbing again. Several common methods are described here (4x4's, timed climbing, pyramids, etc.). You can develop hundreds of unique interval training exercises by varying the grade and type of climbing, length of the climb (number of moves), the amount of rest in between climbs, and the number of sets and reps to train strength, power, endurance and combinations of the three.

STRENGTH EXERCISES

- **2-4 per week maximum; rarely in a row.**
- If specific weights and times are not given for an exercise, follow the strength protocol suggestions in Chapter One.

Grip Training

Most grip strength comes from your forearm, but your hand (not fingers) does have muscles in it that can get tired first in certain types of climbing, like ice climbing, hand jamming, and pinches.

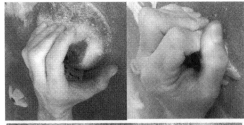

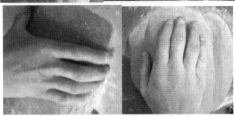
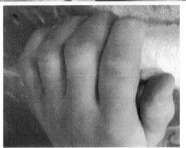

½ crimp, full crimp, 3-fingers, wide pinch, sloper, open hand

Fingerboards (Grip Specific)

Fingerboards and rock rings are the most climbing specific exercises to training grip and finger strength. Varying from the routine provided trains other protocols, not strength, and there are better exercises to accomplish those goals. Tendon injuries are common with over training or improper use, so tape your finger if it is prone to injury. Taping won't allow that tendon to react to stresses applied to it and strengthen if you continually use tape.

Holds
- Fingerboard Grips: ½ crimp, open hand, 3 finger index to ring finger, 3 finger middle to pinky finger, and wide pinch (optional: 2 finger combinations, full-crimp, sloper). Vary the edge depth and sloping angle of the holds.
- Ice tools: (Tools, Dowels, Padding) lock off, 90°, 120°, 150°, straight arm, and staggered.
- Pinch Grips: Blocks, Balls. (Atomik, Rogue, IronMind, Wood, other DIY)

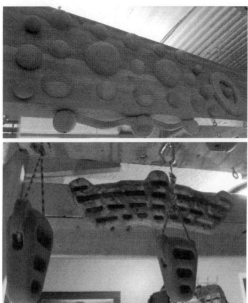

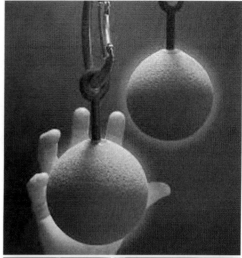

Above three photos courtesy Atomik

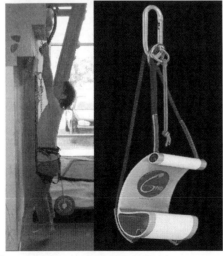

Above right photo courtesy SicGrips/Gstring

To train, start with the most difficult grip (most likely the three finger middle through pinky grip) and end with the easiest (most likely the open hand). There is little need to train one or two finger pockets unless the route you're training for demands it. Training the two sets of 3 fingers is close enough and the injury prevention gains offset any minor advantages to training 2 finger pockets. However, training 2 finger pockets carefully will stress those tendons enough to build up more strength in those tendons. Chalk up and slowly pull yourself up so you don't pop off which could blow a finger pulley. Hang with your elbows slightly bent to reduce the chance of an elbow or shoulder injury. Try and get both holds a bit wider than shoulder width apart to reduce the stress on your shoulders. Cut your board in half and spread it out if needed. Rock rings allow your elbows to rotate and can be set at the perfect width, but don't offer as many hold combinations. Now hang there for 5-8 seconds. You need to add weight or take weight off so you stay on for the 5-8 seconds. Weight lifting bands, a foot on a chair or wall, or a harness and a weighted pulley can take weight off. Use two pulleys so the weights aren't interfering with your hang. Hang on a single grip for the 5-8 seconds, rest for five seconds, and hop back on the same grip for 5-10 reps. You may want to start with the shallowest grip and progress to deeper holds as the reps progress. After you finish a set of the most difficult grip, rest for a minute and move on to the next easier grip. After you have gone through all the grips you intended to train, you can do a 2nd (or 3rd) set.

When you progress and can hang for more than 5-8 seconds, add 5 more pounds. As you advance, vary the depth and angle of the different grips (sloping crimper, shallow pockets, etc.), but focus on weight and larger holds first. If time allows, try and train each hand separately, only using the other hand for additional support until both hands catch-up. Increasing hang time and decreasing rest will train anaerobic endurance more than strength.

A more advanced routine starts on the hardest grip, and fails at 7 seconds. Add more weight so you fail at 6 seconds. Repeat until you make it to a 2 second failure. Rest one minute and move on to a less difficult grip. This is very stressful on the joints and also takes time to know exactly how much weight to add. Two sets are probably more than enough.

If you are training on ice tools or dowel rods, use the TABATA or Little protocols instead (but still add weight until failure). You can thicken the grip on your tools with some pipe insulation or a towel wrapped in tape to increase the difficulty. Dowel rods will lessen the stress to your elbows, allowing them to rotate in more.

> **Fingerboard Exercises**
> - Two or three sets: Five to ten hangs on each selected grip (each hand individually or both) for 5-8 seconds. Five second rests between hangs, with a 1-minute rest between new grip positions.
> - Advanced Routine: Two sets: 6 reps of 7 second down to 2 second hangs per grip (each hand or both). 5 second rests with 1-minute rests between new grip positions.
> - Ice Tool Routine: Tabata or Little Protocol.

Hanging in various locked off positions on the fingerboard, rock-rings or ice tools has nothing to do with gaining grip strength – it just doubles up on exercises. Another way to save time is to incorporate various pull-up exercises (except the archer) into a fingerboard workout. This will be harder because you're only hanging for a few seconds and with weight.

There is an excellent app called Boulder Trainer (iPhone only for now) that shows photos of several popular fingerboards with a countdown timer.

Last three photos courtesy: IronMind, Grip4orce, Fatgripz

Grip Trainers: Grip Master, Hand Grips, Doughnuts, Squeeze Balls, and Gyroscopic Balls

There are several types of hand and finger trainers out there. Some are softer and more appropriate for rehabbing an injury or for a warm-up, and some (like the up to 365 lb. "Captain of Crush" from Ironmind) offer extremely heavy resistance. You can grip these (depending on your model) in several different ways. Check out the Ironmind website, they have a ton of useful training equipment. The following exercises are shown with a common finger trainer, but other products can use the same exercises.

Captain of Crush and V-Power gyroscopic ball

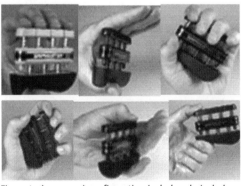

Finger trainer exercises: fingertip pinch, hand pinch, hand squeeze, hook grasp, thumb pinch, thumb squeeze

Gyroscopic balls spin at high rpm's and the centrifugal force creates resistance against your hand. These balls train isometric grip strength in your hands and forearms giving you the benefit of training grip and training antagonistic muscles at the same time. But just because it also trains antagonists, it still can lead to overtraining. The two best ways to grip the ball are like a baseball for more forearm involvement, and then with your fingertips for more hand specific involvement. Hold on as long as possible. You should be super-pumped! The best gyroscopic ball I have found is the red V-Power Ball and is made of solid metal. It can produce up to 60 lbs. of force. Besides training your hands and forearms, you can use it to train biceps, triceps, and shoulders. Doing the sword/seatbelt patterns (described earlier) with this is an excellent shoulder rehab exercise.

Farmer's Carry

This trains pinch strength. Pinch a weight or thick heavy object in your hand and hold it until you drop it. You can use some of the grip devices to attach to weights listed under the fingerboard exercises. Start with a 60 lb. or so weight, hold for a minute. Progress to a heavier weight and repeat.

Above right courtesy IronMind

Wrist and Forearm
Wrist and Finger Curls

Wrist and finger curls can be done in any protocol, but are most effectively done under the power protocol using an Olympic bar or finger combinations with a heavy dumbbell. To do wrist curls hold the weight in your palm and flex at the wrist. You may need to support your forearms on a bench, your legs, or a preacher bar. To do finger curls place the weight over your finger joints as close to the tips as possible and curl your fingers. You could finish with a wrist curl from the end of a finger curl. Depending on the weight, specificity, and time you want to commit, you can train combinations of one finger, two fingers, or three fingers. You may need to loop webbing over a dumbbell to put your combinations fingers through.

Ironmind Eagle Loops

Biceps, Lats, and Shoulder

The brachialis is actually the main flexor of the arm. The biceps brachii lays over it and looks bulkier, so it usually gets all the credit.

Pull-ups

Depending on the routes you want to climb, pull-ups may or may not help you. If your climbing is limited by upper arm and shoulder strength (biceps cramps or fatigue on long routes, big moves, overhangs, ice climbing, or aid climbing) then incorporate them into your training. If you can't do many, use a resistance band to take weight off so you can do more, and if you can do 5-10, then add weight. Rock-rings and dowel rods are better for your elbows since they allow them rotate, placing less medial and lateral stress on them. But unless you have elbow problems, don't let this be a limiting factor. Atomik Pull-Up Bombs and G-Strings are also an excellent choice for both shoulder, elbow and finger injuries because they rotate and you don't crimp as much as with other devices. Hands face palms out. Follow the strength, strength-endurance, or power protocols. Go slow to maximize the results. You may want to turn your palms in for a chin-up to mimic undercling moves occasionally. To add instability and reduce imbalance, attach a bar or dowel with cord so it will tip if one arm is pulling harder. Discontinue pull-up training once you find that it isn't becoming much of a limiting factor anymore.

Staggered / Archers

Staggered pull-ups (one hand is lower than the other) are excellent to build strength if one arm is weaker, but if that's not a problem, adding more weight has the exact same effect. "Archer" pull-ups are similar to staggered pull-ups, but are done on gymnastic rings (or any suspension training setup you've rigged). They differ from staggered pull-ups in that they add a slight amount of instability into the pull-up, and more isometric strength on the non-pulling side - making it harder. Have whatever you are gripping shoulder width apart or slightly more for the archer. One arm remains rigid, while the other does a pull-up. Vary the width of the grips and the angle of the rigid arm to change difficulty.

Kipping Pull-ups

Kipping pull-ups are popular in CrossFit, but are of little use for building strength. The only benefit in performing them is to learn how to do it well, in case you need to bust one out on a climb. You basically "cheat" by using momentum (swinging) and core thrusts to vault yourself up. If someone says they did a huge number of pull-ups, chances are they cheated with these. These are best trained in the endurance protocol as a warm-up. Be careful, you can hurt your back with these.

Concentric-Isometric-Eccentric (Frenchies)

One other type of pull-up, commonly referred to as a "Frenchie" incorporates isometric hangs into a pull-up. It is important to train your upper arm and shoulder isometrically since this is a very sport specific type of training. This is the best pulling exercise you can possibly do. It helps train lock-off strength and isometric strength with the addition of following through with a pull-up. If you find that you are too tired to pull through overhangs but still have pretty good grip strength, these are for you.

Hang straight arm for 5 second, raise to 120-150° and hold 5 seconds, raise to a 90° lock off and hold 5 seconds, and hold at a full lock-off at the top for 5 seconds. Lower and repeat. For extra effort, lower down and hold as well. Follow the strength protocol, and add weight if you need. You could totally skip all the pull-up parts, and just hold the lock-off at various angles for time. Or do really slow pull-ups. Switching to palms facing forwards helps to simulate underclings.

Negative Pull-Ups
This could actually have gone in the antagonist section. Once you do a pull-up, slowly lower yourself down. The slower the better. Add weight as needed.

Muscle ups
Muscle ups are best done on gymnastic rings for full-effect (rock rings should work well). Start with the rings about head height to arms reach, do a pull-up and switch into a press-up. Very difficult to figure out, but a good way to combine two exercises (pull ups and dips) and a pretty good way to practice mantling. Toss these in every once in a while if you are able to do them.

Lockoffs
Lockoffs train isometric strength and can be done in the strength protocol with added weight or combined with fingerboard exercises, or better still, in the strength endurance or endurance protocols. Hold at various angles (slightly flexed, 120°, 90°, 45°, and fully locked off). By doing lock-offs on an overhanging wall (feet on) you can flex your wrist at various angles as well to help isolate forearm lock-off strength. Find underclings to train on as well.

Core
Body Tension
To train body tension without just doing planks, L-sits, etc. you can do some exercises on the wall that also train footwork and balance. You can either keep your feet in one position or hands in one position. The steeper the wall as well as just one foot on, the harder. You can hold each position for a while, or do the exercise dynamically. You can also climb higher with each movement.

Find a scrappy foothold and stay on while traversing around with your hands until you pop off. Next, find a couple handholds and swing your foot over to each side on a distant foothold. Lower your legs down and do the opposite side or continue up and get the other side on the next move. You can also combine the two exercises into one by traversing your arms over, holding the position, swinging your legs out, and continuing on.

Strength-Endurance Exercises

- **2-4 x per week max, occasionally in a row**
- If specific weights and times are not given for an exercise, follow the strength protocol suggestions in Chapter One.

Figure Four and Nine

Mainly for the mixed climbers, but sport climbers and boulders may want to practice a few times (under skills) to have in their bag of tricks. Instead of a dyno, use these to get you past a baffling sequence. They help you get through overhanging sections or roofs statically instead of dynamically, and a figure-9 is often used to transition into or out of a figure-4. If you are not climbing at a difficult level, don't even bother with these. If you're at that point where you think you'll need to pull one of these bad boys out, add them into your training. Start by doing three sets of however many reps you can do until failure. Try them one armed once you've got the hang of it. Icetoolz produces hanging blocks of wood with holes sold as figure 4 trainers. You could easily make your own. This also trains lock-off strength.

Isometric strength comes into play quite a bit when training strength endurance. Try and incorporate isometric training when focusing on this aspect of your climbing. Frenchies, underclings, and lock off training are excellent supplemental exercises to do here. The more powerful, difficult, and dynamic the climbs you pick (you can't stay on very long at all) the more you train power-endurance.

System Holds

System hold training uses static holds for 5 seconds, then moving to another set of holds for another 5 seconds – usually doing this twice per side. One hand is doing the holding, feet off or on small jibs, while the other hand is off or stabilizes on a similar hold (can be a different hold if training for a sequence) 16" to the side. Transfer the weight to the other hand after the five seconds are up. Take a 3-5 minute rest, and repeat either on the same holds or new holds. 5 to 8 sets containing four five second holds total is a good amount. Add weight or vary the steepness if necessary. Use poor footholds to keep the focus on the arms and hands.

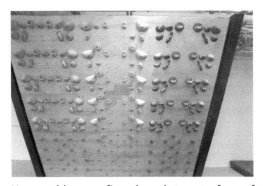

You could use a fingerboard, two to four of one kind of hold, wood slats and blocks, slopers, hard cracks – any type of hold you want to train. You can even train body tension training by holding positions like underclings, sidepulls, gastons, etc. If you are training for a specific climb, you can train for a particular sequence instead of using the same hold. Go bananas. Increasing your hang time or the amount of holds per set makes this more of a moving hang scenario. Check out this video for more info on system walls: http://vimeo.com/95868985

Timed Climbing, Laps or Moving Hangs
- 30 minutes or more (hour max) of continuous and difficult climbing (approx. 5-8 laps/pitches)
- 2-3 sets of 5-20 minute continuous climbing
- 1-3 sets of 20 minutes as many laps as possible
- 2-3 sets time Intervals: 1 min…2 min…3 min…5 min…3 min…1 min
- Time Limit Pitches/Problems: climb a pitch or problem until time runs out
- 3-4 sets of 2 laps on a 30+ move pitch or boulder problem, usually a grade below your onsight level. No rest between laps and 15-minute rest between sets.
- 3 sets of 3 laps on a 15-30 move pitch or boulder problem, usually at or near your onsight level. 2 min rest between pitches, and 15 min rest between sets.

Because you are not holding on for the entire time (you get a break when you switch hands or holds), this is strength endurance – not a pure endurance exercise. This is a lot easier done top-roping, bouldering, or well-protected sport climbing (especially traversing). Get as many laps in or traversing as you can. You want to be pumped out of your mind by the end of the session and fail at the end of the allotted time (for time intervals fail at end of every 1 – 5 minute round). Rest no more than 3 minutes while the clock is running. The longer your session, the easier the climbing needs to be and the less this becomes a strength activity and the more it becomes an endurance (which is fine, just plan your time/difficulty according to what you want out of it). The goal here is to stay on the wall for the allotted time (you can use your feet), but with enough weight, steepness, or crappy holds that you fail at the end of the time.

If going for a long time you'll need to lower the grade, if for a short time you'll want it hard. This is a great way to train for prolonging a pump. The shorter the time the harder the problem, and the heavier the weight the less you work endurance and the more you work strength. You can also set a time limit to finish a lap – the quicker your climb the more power you train. Rest until the time is up, and do it again. One way to stay on the wall indoors is to do a boulder problem, down-climb to another, and climb that, etc. You can do this on a fingerboard or system holds sans feet, or Moving Hangs, with a weight lifting rubber band to keep your weight low enough to stay on if needed. Rest as long as you climbed between sets.

You can also forget about the time and go for laps. One option is to lead a climb and to immediately lead it again. To develop strength endurance find a route about a number grade below your onsight level and climb it twice in a row without a rest. The route should be 30 moves or longer, so if you are bouldering you'll need to get more laps in. After a good rest, do a few more sets. To develop more power endurance you would pick a climb that on your second lap you will fall or barely be able to complete without a short hang, usually near your onsight limit. The route should be around 15-30 moves long. If you are bouldering you may need to do more laps. Do 3 laps with 2 minutes of rest between laps, get a solid rest, and do 2 more sets. For more endurance based laps, a timed set of laps will be more useful but you can set an arbitrary number of laps on easier climbs if you want.

An excellent training board

Pyramids

Pyramids and 4x4's are just another fun way to accomplish the same thing that laps or timed climbing do. For pyramids, pick your hardest onsight grade, and start 3 grades below that. Do four of the easiest, then 3 one grade harder, 2 a grade harder than that, and then your hardest. Reverse back down. If you find that you are so burnt by the top of the pyramid you can't even attempt to climb it, then back down the grades however many notches to be able to barely complete the hardest problem. It's great to pick a different problem for each, but you may have to climb routes more than once to get a full session in. That's totally fine for this exercise. It also helps to have done some of the harder problems before so you avoid wasting a lot of time to find out that a particular problem is either is too hard for you, or it requires a lot of beta/practice.
- 4xV-hardest minus (-) 3, 3xV-hardest-2, 2xV-hardest-1, 1xV-hardest, 2xV-hardest-1, 3xV-hardest-2, 4xV-hardest-3

4x4's (6x3's, 4x5's, 6x8's, etc.)

Do 4 sets of 4 boulder problems back to back with 3 min rest after each set, but no rest between reps. Start 2-4 V grades below your limit. If you're not bouldering, then just do 4-6 hard climbs on toprope. You can increase the workload by altering the number of sets, or number of boulder problems per set. If you are doing a monster like the 6x8, then start very easy.

Very Difficult Climbing

The goal here is to work on climbs that aren't impossible, but require many attempts of piecing together difficult moves. This helps you find new weaknesses, and can help hurdle out of a plateau. This is where top-roping, safe bouldering, homemade cracks, and Moonboards shine. Leading isn't important here.

Weighted Climbing or Bouldering

The only difference between this and timed climbing is that time is not a variable. You can just add a little weight on a hard climb so it seems easier when you try to redpoint it, or a lot of weight on an easier climb to get a strength exercise for the entire body. As a pure strength training exercise, this is more effective with more weight on easier climbs. As a tool for ability to achieve a redpoint, it is better done with less weight on difficult climbs. Use between 10 to 50 pounds added weight.

The following exercises have already been discussed under Strength:

Grip Trainers

Farmer's Carry

Lockoffs – These are very effectively trained here.

Pull-Ups

Staggered Pull-Ups/Archer

Frenchie- Frenchies are generally limited in their protocol by how many you can actually do with bodyweight. They usually fit in under strength or strength/endurance.

Negative Pull-Ups

Muscle-Ups

Figure Four and Nine

POWER EXERCISES

- 2 x week maximum, never in a row
- If specific weights and times are not given for an exercise, follow the strength protocol suggestions in Chapter One.

Power Dyno
This should be rarely done unless you are training for a single specific move. Practice dynoing to a horrible hold or a faraway hold. To make it safer, don't grab the hold to train launch power instead of contact strength.

Wrist and Finger Curls – presented under strength, but best done here.

Grip Trainers – presented under strength. You'll need the heavy duty ones.

Pull-Up – You will most likely need to use a lat-pull down machine to safely do this.

Muscle-Up – presented under strength. A power exercise if you can only do one or two, or by adding weight.

POWER/STRENGTH ENDURANCE EXERCISES

- **2-4 per week maximum occasionally in a row**
- If specific weights and times are not given for an exercise, follow the strength protocol suggestions in Chapter One.

The following exercises combine some aspects of strength and power with being able to hold on for a longer duration. They combine grip strength from fingerboard training or moving to difficult holds, power from campusing or moving from hold to hold, and endurance by increasing the reps or time spent.

Campusing
2-8 sets of 6-12 moves. Progress to rung 1,2,4; 1,3,5; 1,4,7; etc.
- Deadpoint (Touches when combined with Drop Downs)
- *Single Dyno, aka Laddering*
- Double Dyno
- Drop-Downs

Holds: 3 finger pads, 2 finger pads, 1 finger pad, ½ pad, and/or sloper. Usually the middle 3 fingers are used. Using fewer fingers is really dangerous. Rungs are spaced about 8-12 inches apart.

Campusing trains for explosive power and contact strength with some endurance by keeping the weight down enough to do more than just one or two moves (which would train power but would be extremely dangerous). Campusing is also a great way to get injured. Beginning climbers should skip this exercise altogether, and intermediate climbers should stick with deadpoints.

You can vary the intensity by steepening the angle, (20° is the generally accepted angle) or varying the depth (jugs to crimps) and surface (coarse to smooth). For the vast majority, a 20° wall with wooden rungs two knuckles deep should be more than enough. Smaller holds will train contact strength and longer reaches will train upper body power more. You can also create a set of slopers by sawing PVC pipes of varying diameter (bigger=harder) in half and covering them with deck (not duct) tape.

Deadpoints are the easiest and begin from a hang. Throw one hand to a higher hold still holding onto the start hold with the other hand, and then match with the other hand. Repeat, starting with a new leading hand. Single dynos begin the same way, throw to a hold and stay on. Now throw your other arm to a higher hold. Double dynos are when you use both hands to throw for a higher hold. Drop downs train eccentric power and should be used more rarely since the injury rate is super high and there isn't much transition into useful climbing moves (although some routes and boulder problems do demand it). Drop downs can be added to deadpoints, single, or double dynos either on the way down, or just going from a starting hold to a higher hold and back to the starting hold.

From deadpoints to double dynos, progress by starting out going from rung 1 to 2 (2 to 3, 3 to 4 etc.), then rung 1 to 3 (3 to 5 etc.), 1 to 4, etc. Weighted campusing is just asking for trouble, but you can do it.

If you don't have a campus board try **No Feet Bouldering**, **Stacking Fingerboards** on top of each other, a **Bachar Ladder**, **Rope Climb**, or a

Pegboard to substitute (no finger contact strength gains for the last three). One arm traversing/climbing also help train for powerful contact strength.

Above photo courtesy James Arnold

Repetitive Hold Climbing or HIT Strips
- Holds: pinch, 3 finger sets, open hand, crimp, and full crimp - or icetools in bolts
- 1-2 sets of 20 moves (10 holds per hand) per grip. 2-3 min rest between each grip. Body weight to 10-40 lbs.

Repetitive hold climbing trains finger strength endurance with some power benefits by quickly moving from hold to hold. Repetitively climbing on the same hold is like a cross between fingerboard training and campusing. It is extremely effective. The following protocol is derived from Nicros's HIT Strips. You'll need a 50° wall and either a set of system holds (various companies, Nicros HIT strips being the most popular), or 4-5 of the same holds for both hands. The first set of holds needs to be high enough off the ground to be at head height when sitting, although higher is better. The rest should be spaced a foot and a half apart. Just like on the fingerboard, training two fingers is only slightly more effective than training 3 fingers but much more injury prone. The goal is to add enough weight per grip type so that you fail after about 20 moves (or 10 holds per hand).

Start with both hands on the bottom holds (and with the most difficult grip – probably pinch). You use your feet on the wall (unlike the campus board) to start and on the holds as you progress. Grab the next higher hold with each hand until you match at the top, and reverse the moves back down. Make sure you start with a new leading hand. Take 2-3 minutes rest, and repeat with the same hold. Then move on to a new grip cycle. If you can do 20 moves, add more weight. Ice climbers can use their tools on different types of holds, or by hooking bolt hangers, eye bolts, steps of an inverted ladder or staircase, or a jungle gym. If you don't have system holds or a wall, you could stack two fingerboards on a tilted frame or bump up and down between two holds with your feet on a chair for a simulated, but not quite as effective workout. Varying the angle, weight, and reps will alter the workout into different protocols, but there are better exercises for that.

Power Bouldering/Top Roping
This combines elements of strength and power with the endurance to stay on, but technique is also incorporated. Pick a few boulder problems or cruxes (you will have to lower to the crux each time on toprope) that are quite difficult for you. Rest 3 minutes, and then repeat 3-6 times. You should be pretty spent.

- Several very hard moves at or just above your limit that take about 10-20 seconds to move through. 3 minutes rest. Repeat 3-6 times.
- If the problem or crux section takes longer, rest 3 minutes after you "take" or fall and try again 3-6 more times.

Weighted Climbing – already discussed under strength endurance but adding a lot of weight puts this into more of a power-endurance category.

ENDURANCE

- **Can be done multiple days in a row 3-5 days/week**
- **If specific weights and times are not given for an exercise follow the strength protocol suggestions in Chapter One.**

As mentioned, endurance is already getting trained in the other protocols, although it gets less attention the more the weight is increased and time/reps decrease. Training just endurance also reduces your strength and power. Actual climbing exercises are best done under the endurance phase towards the end of your cycle when you are nearing the end of a training phase and ready to enter a performance phase. Suggestions for actual climbing endurance training will be detailed under the periodization chapter.

Training some climbing related exercises under the endurance protocol is either best done in a warm-up or to establish baseline fitness during your foundation phase, while some are good "finishing touches" exercises to train during your endurance phase. Those exercises are listed below.

Lockoffs – These are very effectively training here. Done at bodyweight until failure at least a minute (take weight off or add more weight if needed).
Kipping Pull-Ups
Grip Trainers
Farmers Carry
Frenchie – if you are strong enough to actually make this an endurance exercise.

The next three exercises are exercises for Aid Climbing. Ascending the rope with jugs can be pumpy as hell and give you horrible cramps. It helps to train for them. This will also help with hauling (as will squatting and leg press exercises)

Jugging with Weight
The best way to train is to just jug ropes repeatedly with a pack filled with rocks - you'll get way more pumped and become more efficient in the process.

Jumar Hang
- 1-2 Sets of 3 one-minute hangs.

On a 45° wall with your feet on some jibs, hold a vertically oriented bucket-handle grip or clip the top of your jumar into a bolt. You could also clip the jumar into a quickdraw to allow for more elbow rotation and to add some instability. Add enough weight so that you fail after one minute of hanging on one-handed. If this setup is too complicated for your wall, you can just do more isometric hangs on a pull-up bar. Hold the grip on the jumar so your wrist is radially deviated (hitchhiker position) and elbow flexed at 120-150°.

Jumar Hang and Squat
The setup is the same as above but squat up and down from a full hang to a lock-off. Do three sets at high reps (25-50 per side twice). Add weight if 25-50 reps is too easy.

Finally, here is an ice climbing version of the above exercise:

Ice Tool Squat and Reach
With tools in hand, begin in a deep squat and lunge up to a hold (or imagined point) at maximum extension, tap it, and come back down. Do two to three sets at high reps (25-50 per side twice). Add weight if 25-50 reps is too easy.

SKILLS

Whatever you do, don't skip this section! Practicing skills, even basic ones, at any level, is how you learn – and any good climber can tell you that technique, knowledge, and experience is just as important as being strong. Check out the Maximizing Success section for more information on applying skills.

These skill exercises are great to practice on warm-up climbs. However, they should be practiced every time you climb. In fact, you should schedule a few complete climbing sessions only focusing on skills. Vary the terrain for each skill if possible from:

- **Rock type** (granite, sandstone, limestone, basalt, quartzite, etc.)
- **Friction** (low, medium, and high)
- **Steepness** (slab, vertical, and overhanging).

Move to a new skill as soon as you have figured it out, and come back to it later when it becomes important again. Skill training should be part of your entire training program and is not affected by protocols or periodization, although intelligent timing of when to practice different skills is important. Some of the skills listed below are exercises, while some are just to keep you aware of a particular skill, and some are listed solely to remind you they exist. This is not a how to climb book, so my explanation of some skills will be very brief. See the appendix for references to help with any "how to" type questions.

The fastest way to get better technique is to climb more (especially bouldering outdoors). Work on technique on easier climbs. This is why certain areas with easy access to high quality fun and easier climbing produce better climbers: pure mileage. After you get a skill figured out, apply it to an actual climb as soon as possible. Some of these skills also incorporate some suggestions for actual climbing and how-to. See the "Maximizing Success" section for more info.

<u>FALLING SKILLS</u>
Practicing falling is one of the best exercises roped climbers can do – even boulderers. Incorporate falling as much as possible into your climbing. Just doing some practice falls occasionally is not enough; you need to make it a daily habit. Obviously falling can be dangerous, so some precautions must be taken. Assess the consequences of the fall and the quality of your gear before casting off. Your belayer or spotter needs to know your plan so they can adequately position themselves and pay in rope or provide a dynamic belay. Boulderers must have ade-

quate padding and trained spotters. Check out the second edition of "Better Bouldering" for detailed instructions on proper spotting and falling technique.

To really get falling dialed, you should do two falls per route (around 5-20 falls per climbing day) for a year, obviously making sure the route will lend a safe fall on it. That's a lot! Fall until it becomes as exciting as calling take. Try and stop using the words, "TAKE!" and "WATCH ME!" until they are actually useful to you. Saying "watch-me" constantly not only starts to permanently psych you out every time a situation even comes near being unsafe, but also we all know what happens when you cry wolf too many times. Yelling, "take!" or grabbing draws robs you of falling practice. If you need to take because right now you are more concerned with figuring out a sequence without distractions, then please do everyone a favor and clip "in direct", that is, clip a draw from your belay loop into the piece or draw. The other good reason for yelling take is because you don't want to fall on a piece of gear that you don't think will hold a fall, or a hard stretch of difficult runout, and need to rest before gunning to the next placement. If you yelled it and realized you were just being a wimp, you owe it to yourself to climb up a few feet and whip.

Falling Progression
WEAR A HELMET WHEN PRACTICING FALLING!
Roped climbers should start on a bolted route, or on gear with a backup toprope. Begin by falling right at the bolt. Next, fall at the bolt with a small bit of slack out. Then fall with the bolt at your feet. It is a good idea to take these short practice falls well up a route to provide some cushioning from rope stretch (at least past the 2nd bolt). After your comfort level increases, take some longer falls, making sure your landing is safe. Try some falls on a vertical wall, overhang, and slab. Try falling out of line with the bolt. Start by falling just left or right of the bolt, then a bit higher and further to the side. These can be dangerous if there is something to your side you can smack into. Don't do this if that is the case, wait for a better scenario. Practice falling above a roof and on an arête. One good way to incorporate falls is to fall just before clipping the anchor, that way you can still onsight or redpoint the route and get a fall in. If you have a climbing gym that has lead wall, this is a good place to start.

Falling on Gear
After you have learned to fall safely (probably around 100 practice falls) onto bolts, it's time to move on to falling on gear. Trusting your gear is extremely important to begin climbing harder trad lines. ALWAYS BACKUP YOUR GEAR FOR PRACTICE FALLS. This could mean being belayed on a slack toprope in addition to the lead line, falling on gear just above a bolt, or placing two or more bomber pieces just below the gear you plan on falling on. Don't look at the gear when you fall to avoid it popping out in your face. Fall on different types and sizes of gear from micro cams to nuts. Make sure you will be able to remove your gear after you fall on it. Shorter fall are best here to minimize your fall in case the gear blows. The goal for falling on gear is not to test the limits of your gear (and trashing your gear), but to become confident that your placements will hold a fall. Practice on different rock types, but pick zero star obscure routes if they are on soft or friable stone such as sandstone if you wind up breaking the rock when you fall.

Testing Sketchy Gear and Run Outs
Don't overlook learning experiences from falling when climbing. For example, let's say you just led a route and a section scared the crap out of you. Maybe you didn't trust the gear, or you felt that you ran it dangerously out (could be a sport climb too). Take the time to find out – the payoff will be a thou-

sand fold the time it takes to do so. There are a few ways to do this. If you didn't have the gear you needed below your questionable piece, re-climb the route with the correct gear but leave that original piece in and fall onto it.

To test the fall potential of a supposed runout, haul a pack up and toss it off with a second anchored rope onto the last piece from the end of the run out to see where and how it lands (add several extra feet for rope stretch). If it turns out totally benign, conquer your fear and take the whip yourself! If a questionable piece does not have the opportunity to have a backup (remember the option of a toprope backup) you could try a couple of things. After you get in a few bomber higher pieces or to the anchor, lower back down, clip a few slings to the piece, and jump up and down on the sling to test the piece. If you can, haul a bag full of rocks to simulate the weight of you falling (better have a burly bag and a clear landing zone). Many top climbers who climb routes with run-outs and thin gear will use some of these tricks to get a full evaluation of the risk and ways to mitigate that risk before attempting a lead.

Falling on Ice
It's not as easy to practice falling for ice climbers, and even a controlled fall could result in a crampon point catching or a puncture from a tool. Falling on ice climbs is totally unacceptable. However, you do need to trust your gear. Here's a solution: find an ice climb you can drop a haul bag filled with rocks off the top. Get a few beater ice screws (you will ruin them) and place them in good ice, questionable ice, and in just a few centimeters each. Huck the bag off the top until the screw fails. Hopefully you will discover that a screw can hold a fall on ice. The point is to help you become comfortable with your ice screws, not to make you climb over your head thinking that falling while ice climbing is safe in any way. If you fell while leading ice you royally screwed up and need to re-evaluate your actual ability.

Falling on Etriers
One of the scariest falls you can take is while standing in your etriers while aid climbing. It is an unnatural and awful fall, but if you're climbing anything over C2, it will probably happen. I don't recommend taking a practice fall on your aiders on anything less than mildly overhanging terrain—you will lose skin. But what you can do is practice dicey aid moves above an overhanging wall just above a bolt, nest of gear, or on slightly loose toprope. This is a great way to learn hooking. Hanging and bouncing on gear generates a lot of force, so you can rip off holds or widen cracks if you're on soft stone or on a flakey sport climb. Don't ruin a climb: go find a piece of crap to practice on.

Falling While Rope-Soloing
The last type of fall you could practice is on your rope-solo setup with a toprope backup. The Silent Partner is particularly important to take a few practice falls on since it doesn't lock up just by sitting down onto it. You need to know if it will actually do its job, especially on slabby terrain. Other devices should be tested as well. You need to know if you are setting it up correctly, how you will land, what orientations will cause the device not to work, if grabbing it causes the device not to lock, and if slow low-angle falls will be caught. Be backed-up via toprope when testing you solo device!

> **Fall Checklist**
> - Is any of my gear damaged (nylon/Dyneema slings and loops, cracks in cams and biners, wires on chocks, flat spots on rope, rough spots on biners – especially fixed ones)?
> - Is my knot and harness ok?
> - Are the bolts and gear safe?
> - If the gear blows, will the next piece hold a fall or result in hitting something?
> - Is the rock safe and stable?
> - Am I clipped properly (back-clip, extension, biners over an edge)?
> - Will the rope run over an edge?
> - Will the fall result in a pendulum (into the rock or sideways)? Can another rope be used to mitigate the pendulum?
> - Do I need to employ safer backups or simulate the fall with an object?
> - Are my legs behind the rope/will I fall upside-down?
> - What will I fall onto/into and with what body part?
> - Is my belayer going to do his/her job properly?
> - Do they expect me to fall?
> - Do they know to give me a dynamic belay?
> - Does the belay need to run or jump back and are they aware of this option?
> - Do I need to reduce the force on my gear (Revolver biner, screamers, loosen tie-in knot, tube-style belay device)?
> - Can I climb higher to a rest, or shake out to avoid a fall?

Whatever type of climbing you will be doing, the bottom line is to practice falling to remove doubt and uncertainty and to understand the consequences of a fall.

FAST AND DYNAMIC SKILLS

Climbing quickly and dynamically reduces overall energy expenditure by reducing time on the route and using elastic recoil to propagate up the route. Spring from one hold to the next. This is how you should be climbing when redpointing a route.

Climb Dynamically: Use your legs, hips, and arms like springs

Climb Fast: See how fast you can complete a climb on toprope

Practice Deadpoints and Dynos

Skip Holds: See if you can skip holds on a climb to minimize effort

Follow Through: How many sports require a follow-through as an essential skill? To keep momentum, practice following through difficult or scary moves. Sometimes looking ahead instead of in front of you can get you through a tough section. Unless the moves are incredibly sequential or the holds are hidden, try using your instincts instead of second guessing your movements.

SLOW AND STATIC SKILLS

Practice climbing as slowly and deliberately as possible. Feel each hold for the best possible grip and foot placement. Combining speed and efficiency of movement, while at the same time milking holds, finding rests and shaking out even though your excitement level wants you to keep moving are the skills needed to keep from being pumped and staying fresh throughout the climb.

Climb Slow: Every movement should have intention.

Find Rests: Try and find rests in as many places as possible, including just before, at, and after the crux.

Shake Out: Practice shaking out as much as possible to stay fresh through the entire climb. Raise your arms above your head during your shake out to drain venous blood back to the heart, and lower them to get a return of fresh oxygenated blood. If you don't have a good resting hold you can quickly flick your hands/arms between moves to avoid slowing down.

BALANCE SKILLS

Pay extreme attention to finding your center of gravity during each move, and after you complete each move. Keep weight over your feet, and maintain body tension after every move. Body tension means keeping your abs engaged and keeping your hips from dropping or sagging. Since you must pull perpendicular to a hold, you must sometimes move your body and flag to face the other direction so the center of gravity keeps you balanced on the wall. Proper hip position relative to foot position is just as important to maintain balance. Initiating movement from your center of gravity with good hip/foot position is key to saving arm strength and staying on the wall.

Men's center of gravity is slightly higher than women's. This means that men can generally make longer more dynamic moves by having their chest and feet higher up on the respective holds. Women can find better rests and perform more delicate and balancing moves, especially on slabby or techy terrain by being slightly lower on the hand and foot holds, but may have to make more intermediate moves. If your center of gravity is too high or too low you will get pumped more quickly, and also blow a foot or handhold. These are the skills necessary to climb difficult routes and to take the stress off of your arms and fingers.

Some drills you can perform to help you are:

Keep weight over your feet and maintaining body tension

Climbing with straight arms

Traversing or climbing with one arm behind your back. Also good for training contact strength.

Climbing with your body fully extended

Climbing with your body scrunched up

Rocking onto your feet after a high step

Climbing with the same hip in towards the wall as the hand you are gripping with while keeping a straight arm (if left hand grabs hold with a straight arm, turn left hip into the wall).

The core exercises in the climbing specific strength section that involves moving arms and or feet to develop body tension

Try and keep your hips under your handhold by changing foot position

Switch from a twistlock to a tripod, X, or frog position when resting or clipping.

Switch between an X, frog, backstep, drop knee, flag, and twistlock to find out what will establish the best base of support or will allow the best balance and reach to the next move.

Find no hands rests, or at least only use hands for balance. Practice finding these on various terrains such as slabs, arêtes, corners, etc. If working a route, try to make one lap up a rest finding mission.

Practicing balance skills on slopers will force you to find positions and movements of optimum balance. Other holds that will help improve balance are any hold that is not oriented in a straight down manner.

Moving your center of gravity over your feet by maintaining body tension and body position are key elements in steep climbing, weird moves, and keeping your arms from exerting all of the force. The next two skill sets (movement and feet) are really an extension of climbing balanced.

Movement Skills

Climbing with blocky, ladder-like or x-pattern movements won't get you up much more than easy face climbs. Practice doing laps on climbs by using the following moves as much as possible to find out where they are best suited.

Note: This is not an instruction manual on how to climb; I assume the reader already knows the majority of these moves.

The point is to have them listed here for reminder to practice them, and to remind you to use them more. Drop-knees, back-steps, twist-locks, flagging, and stemming should be second nature and used as much as possible.

Twist-Lock: Turn the same hip into the wall that your arm is reaching with to maintain balance and gain height. The outside edge of your shoe will gain more height.

Flagging: With only one foot on the wall, use the free leg to counter-balance your center of gravity. Practice flagging the inside and outside leg. Generally the flagging leg mirrors the activity of the opposite reaching arm. The outside edge of the shoe will get you more height.

Drop Knee: Pivot your leg so your knee points in or down the wall to balance your center of gravity. Don't forget to push with both feet. Reach with the arm on the side of the knee that is dropped.

Stem: Try stemming on various angles off corners and sloping holds to maintain balance and take weight off the arms. Stemming is your secret weapon, even on faces without corners.

Back-step: Almost like a drop-knee / stemming combo, but your drop-knee foot is stemming off of a lateral hold to stay balanced. Don't forget to push with both feet. A good way to "stem without stemming".

Frog-Step: Turn both knees out to assume a frog-style position to maintain balance and rest. Keep your arms straight.

X-Position: Arms and legs are splayed out in an "X" or "H" position. This is the most stable and restful position, but affords the least amount of reach and dynamic movement. Most climbers need to practice not using this position except when resting.

High-Steps and Rock-Overs: See what is possible by practicing long high-steps and rock-overs.

Heel Hook: Take advantage of the rubber on the back of your shoes. Underused, and an amazing way to find hidden rests.

Toe Hook: Hook your toes under holds and around corners to pull yourself in the wall for balance and resting. Great on steep routes and overhangs.

Kneebar: Try and find kneebars under roofs, and hidden features to get an excellent rest. Sticky-rubber kneepads help. This takes a lot of creativity, and I've been amazed where some climbers have found these!

Bicycling: This move uses opposing foot pressure with one foot pulling under a hold and the other foot pressing down on top to keep you into the wall on very steep climbs. Can be used on the same hold if it's big enough.

Lock-off and Straight Arm: Practice between keeping your arms straight to keep the weight on your skeleton and locked-off to keep the level-arm as short as possible. A good place to shake out. If you can't clip or rest without keeping your arm bent, it is ok to lose height by moving your feet down.

Cross-Through: On a lateral move, cross your arm through the other and avoid the barn door.

Step-Through: Like the cross-through but with your feet.

Rose Move: This is an extreme cross through when your whole body turns away from the wall.

Matching and Swapping Hands and Feet: Experiment what you can get away with by matching hands and swapping feet.

Roofs: Practice climbing through roofs.

Photo courtesy Ian Roth

Mantling and Down-Palming: There are many opportunities to seek out mantles at home, and around town. Many climbers blow it here! Down-palming is a great technique to save forearm strength, to gain height from a low hold, or to perform sideways moves.

Deadpoints, Single, and Double Dynos: It's a good idea to know what you are capable of by practice these. Pumping up and down doesn't help. Crouch down and spring up quickly. And believe!

Figure Four's and Nine's (see climbing specific exercises): These are very occasionally useful on long reaches below overhangs and bulges. Figure 4's are across the opposite leg, and 9's are on the same leg (usually used to move into a 2nd fig-4).

Steep to Slab: Sometimes getting onto low angle terrain from steeper climbing can be harder than the steep section below, especially if topping out onto slopers or onto thin (or no) ice. Resist the temptation to bend forward and do the "beached whale". This will cause your feet to blow. Keep your weight over your feet at all times and use your arms for balance. Work your feet as high as possible. If you need to, take small steps, smear, or high-step and rock over when high enough.

FOOT SKILLS
Velcro Feet: Once your foot touches a hold, it's stuck there until the next move. This will help with precise footwork.

Climbing with Fists: Make fists and try and climb some slabs and steeper stuff. Use your fists only for balance and try and climb with mostly good footwork. This is the same thing as climbing with tennis balls in your hand, but without the hassle of carrying tennis balls! If you can't resist opening your hand, put a sock over it.

Slab Climbing: Nothing makes you use your feet like some good old slab climbing. The steeper, slicker the crystals, and thinner the holds are, the better. Keep those heels down and smear while pressing into the wall rather than down on greasy holds. Soft shoes will help.

Approach Shoes: Do you really need your climbing shoes? Find out what you can and cannot climb with your approach shoes. You may find that you start to leave the rock shoes at home.

Timing pushing with your legs: Practice going for reachy moves from a stable tripod or frog position, from a high drop knee, or a balancey twist lock by pushing with your legs before or during arm movement. Going for crappy holds will emphasize the exercise.

HAND AND GRIP SKILLS

Practice the holds you are weaker on, and find ways to make a grip work more in your favor. *Starred* items are basic hand positions that you can train for on the fingerboard, systems holds, etc.

Soft Grip (and climbing relaxed): Try climbing with as soft a grip as possible. Exert as much force as you need to just barely keep you on the wall. As long as you are practicing this, you should also try and keep your body as relaxed as possible and pay attention to your breathing.

Velcro Hands: This is the same as Velcro feet, only with your hands. Once you touch a hold, you can't let go until the next.

Undercling: See how much pressure you need to exert, and where your feet need to be for maximum and minimum stability

Thumbercling: Use your thumb below a tenuous hold to provide counter-pressure

Gaston: Try and find Gastons in irregular places. A Gaston is best described as trying to pry open elevator doors.

Side-Pull: Experiment with how much force you need to apply and where your body needs to be for maximum and minimum stability. Find side-pulls off unobvious holds like slopers, cracks, and arêtes.

Reverse Side-Pull: This requires you to press rather than pull and requires balance and shoulder strength. It can be a dangerous position for your shoulder if you are experiencing problems.

Open-Handed Crimp: Try climbing with an open handed crimp (middle finger joints almost straight instead of bent at 90° and first finger joint slightly flexed instead of hyperextended) instead of a full crimp to save energy and prevent injury.

Crimp: Good practice for general grip strength. Practice a thumb wrap for added support. A real full crimp is the strongest finger intensive face hold position and requires slight hyperextension of the first finger joint. A half crimp does not hyperextend the first finger joint.

Fingernail (Vertical) Crimp: Usually found on tough slab climbs. See what you can move off of, and what fingernail length works best for you.

Sloper: Who doesn't need practice! Practice not only trying to grab and hold on to them, but also practice deadpointing to, and moving off of slopers – especially sloper mantles, traverses, and roofs.

Pinch: Try pinching holds you normally wouldn't to find new solutions to hard problems.

Pockets: Practicing on pockets builds individual finger strength (or causes injury). Experiment with pockets of various depths, angles of pull, and using one or two fingers.

Layback: Not really a type of hold, but more a type of movement. Practice finding out how much force you really need to apply with your arms vs. your feet. Practice how high up or down your legs need to be to find the maximum and minimum secure placements for resting and moving off of. Finally, practice placing gear on these.

Non-Traditional Holds: Try using down-pressure and palming, or using other parts of your upper body to apply force such as a wrist wrap over a hold when extra-pumped.

Compression: Pushing in using two opposing holds, especially on overhanging terrain with slopers or slabby holds (like a blunt arête) can save precious finger strength. You can also incorporate pressing in with both thighs, legs, and feet to stay on.

Cracks: Climb cracks of all sizes and practice the ones you have a lot of trouble with. A homemade simulator or visits to Indian Creek are worth the investment. There are tons of places to practice these, but Indian Creek (for every size and off-width), Vedauwoo (for off-width), and Yosemite (for the honest versions of Indian Creek) stand out as the primo places to practice. Wild Country has produced some excellent videos entitled "Crack School" on Vimeo.com to watch. Crack technique will be discussed later in the technical section, Maximizing Success.

ROUTE-FINDING SKILLS

Once you start climbing routes at your limit, finding the correct sequence of movements, rests, and hold positions will be your number one skill to make or break your ascent. All the technique and strength in the world can be lost if you don't climb the route correctly. Picking the correct time of day to adequately see all the holds can help a ton.

Visualization: More detail on visualization will be discussed later. However, I will assume you understand the concept. Pick a difficult route and study it well. Mimic the hand and foot motions on the ground repeatedly. Get on the route (leading is best) and do your best to onsight it. If you get mixed up, lower down from the difficult spot to the ground or your last good rest, and re-visualize. Once you figure it out, redpoint it. On your next visit to the wall, re-redpoint it after you've warmed up.

Trusting your Gut: Hop on a new route at or slightly harder than your onsight limit and give a 100% effort to try and onsight the route. Only try this exercise when you are feeling it as it could have the opposite effect if you aren't performing well physically and mentally. Briefly read the moves on the ground to the first two clips, and keep a wide field of vision, following through on moves and looking at least two moves ahead. If you screw up, hang, rest, and keep going.

New Area: If climbing at a new area or type of rock, hop a few routes a letter grade or two below your onsight level and pay attention to how the routes flow and the general feel and placement of the holds. Different walls at the same area may climb very differently.

FEEDBACK SKILLS

There are some specific things you can do to hone in on your general skill levels. The feedback exercises will make you a better climber and can help you get out of a climbing rut or plateau. Expect smartphones and watches to offer biometric feedback to "coach" or guide your workouts or performance. One smartwatch is already available that uses precise accelerometers and tools to track your movements. I have no idea how useful it is or may be. Check it out: www.climbax.co.uk/demo.html

Video Feedback: Most cameras and phones these days have a video camera on them, making this much more accessible than before. What better use than to have your partner film you climbing! If it's just you and your belayer, then you should either make sure they have a GriGri and can multitask, or wait until it's a threesome. Have them film you following as well. Pay them back the favor by doing the same for them.

Partner Feedback: Another way to get a good handle on your skills and weakness is just to flat out ask your partner, "What do I need to work on?" Start climbing with people better than you. Watch them and try and learn as much as you can. Climb with someone way better than you and specifically ask them for feedback. Try and break into a clique of climbers who are pushing themselves. Hanging with a group will expose you to more than just you and your partner.

Coach Feedback :A climbing team or individual coach can help, but it may be hard to find a team in your age group or a real climbing coach who knows what he or she is doing and not just a helpful parent or moronic gym employee.

Movies and YouTube: If you can stand getting your ego bruised by watching other people make things that would crush you look easy, then get some climbing movies or hop on the Internet (YouTube, Vimeo, Google search, blogs). Here you will be able to see how it's done. Watch first with enjoyment, but watch it again trying to visualize yourself performing the same moves. Hopefully you'll spot some of your errors by seeing how it should be done (and correct them of course). The American Alpine Club has an extensive library, and dirt bags can use the public library.

COMBINATION SKILLS

These next few exercises are great at taking skills and applying them by combining several skills into complex patterns.

Add-On: This is a fun exercise at the bouldering gym. A cleaning stick or laser pointer help. Have your partner point to hand and foot holds on a bouldering wall to make up a problem for you. You can alternate, or make a complete problem.

Weight Off: Your partner pushes up on your butt, or applies a heavy-handed toprope to take weight off so you can learn the moves.

Open Feet/Hands: Unless you're climbing at the most contrived outdoor crag ever, this has to be done at the gym. Allow yourself to figure out harder problems by allowing yourself extra holds for just the feet, or just the hands.

Down-Climb: Down climbing accomplishes three things. It helps you know what moves are reversible for use in future epic situations, gives you double-time on the route for strength and skills, it works eccentric muscles, and reversing moves may require different technique than just going up.

The next three suggestions are also in the Ability section but are great ways to engrain skills.
Top-roping: Don't dismiss the toprope! Top-roping provides you with access to applying skills on difficult climbs. Top-roping climbs at the very end of the day helps wire skills solid and gives you practice at climbing difficult moves when tired.

Re-Climbing Redpoints and Onsights: Just because you got to the top doesn't mean you did it well. Struggling to finish a climb without falling can engrain bad techniques by rewarding yourself with a pat on the back for redpointing or onsighting it. Get back on it and do it perfectly.

Vary the terrain: Apply skills you are developing by changing the rock-type, friction, steepness, and difficulty of the grade.

Climbs You Hate or Flail on: If you don't like a climb or flail on a climb that's within your grade, chances are these climbs are perfect at isolating your weak links. Make these climbs your new project.

SPECIFIC CONDITIONS SKILLS

Don't just climb on perfect days! To maximize your time climbing and to minimize bailing, it's a good idea to know what conditions you can really climb in. Also, you can get some good climbing in at the crag while everyone else is at home. Please, please, please, exercise some judgment and common sense before trying these, or at least hide the copy of this book from friends and family before you do something stupid.

The following exercises increase the chance of screwing up, so take extra precautions:
Night Climbing: Absence of light is no excuse. In fact night climbing can be a ton of fun, and not too bad with modern spot beam headlamps. Climb at night to see what you are comfortable with. Maybe you won't have a forced bivy and you will just keep climbing, or maybe you'll still do that long route even though there aren't as many hours of daylight left. Of course if route finding is complex, then you probably chose your route poorly. Also, finding the start of the climb and complicated descents can and should be avoided in the dark. *Here's a hidden bonus tip: wear two headlamps - one pointed forward and the other pointed down to see your feet.*

Cold Weather: How cold can you realistically climb in? It's probably a lot colder than you think. Once you warm up (or endure a route of hot aches), climbing rock at or around freezing isn't that bad. Try climbing in gloves and boots. Knowing how to climb, dress, and pack for cold weather is a lifesaving skill to have.

Cold Tolerance: Ok, this isn't a skill. But, repeated training in cold water can increase your body's tolerance to cold, mentally and physically. Cold water won't let your body get warm like it would doing an activity in the cold air, making it the perfect training medium.

Rain: Will a light rain really make it that much harder to climb? It's a good idea to know what your limit is in wet conditions to be able to decide whether to bail or not in a real situation.

Snow: If it's dry enough, you may find that a little snow isn't so bad!

Wind: This one really gets me. Not only is communication, rope management and rappelling difficult, but the mental strain can be worse. Know how to deal with wind.

The following exercises are counter-intuitive because strength and performance gains are greatest when your body's needs are taken care of. However, training in depleted states can offer some compensatory adaptations if used carefully and sparingly. The following exercises can be very dangerous:

Dehydration: Training dehydrated is really dangerous, but I will say that it can really help on long climbs, in hot dry areas, or at high altitude. Being fully hydrated is obviously the best way to train for performance gains, but if you are used to having water available all the time or are unaccustomed to climbing in harsh conditions then you may need to train in a dehydrated state. Have emergency water available and don't try this far from home. Knowing what your limits are when dehydrated, and overcoming/tuning-down your feeling of thirst can help you overcome a major obstacle in climbing which is not being able to carry enough water. No studies have shown that your body physiologically adapts to dehydration by this method, but experience has shown that your body can tolerate thirst and will conserve fluids after spending time in dehydrating environments.

Hunger: Just like thirst, if you are going to be doing something HUGE, then you need to have experience pushing on with depleted glycogen stores. It's also a good lesson in eating and drinking even if you don't feel like it, by finding out just how shitty your climbing and judgment can become. Again, have food handy just in case. Training in a depleted state, like in the morning before breakfast, has been shown to increase fat utilization and promote increased levels of HGH.

Exhaustion: You need to know what it's like to climb exhausted and how far you can push until exhaustion. The first is easy – go cragging without getting much sleep – either ridiculously early, or after a long awful day. The thought of climbing, even top-roping should conjure up an extreme sense of dread. The other end of the spectrum is to have a few total depletion days that involve climbing towards the end for at least a few hours. You can train, climb, and run - whatever. How far can you push yourself before your climbing takes a nosedive? This will train you to know when to stop pushing on a real climb, and hunker down.

Heat: How about climbing when it's blazing hot or muggy. For both, go to Arkansas in August (I didn't make it past opening the car door). Knowing how to climb, dress, and pack in the heat and humidity is pretty important for survival when it catches you off guard, or you climb in the Black Canyon.

Altitude: The best adage for using altitude to train is sleep high, train low. Your body will acclimatize and produce more red blood cells while at rest and then use the increased oxygen availability down low while training to increase fitness. If using a hyperbaric chamber, start at around 2500 meters and increase 500 meters every three-four days until you reach a simulated altitude of about 6,600 meters. However, just like the above exercises, training in a hypoxic state (at altitude) can help your body adapt the real demands you will place on it while at altitude. In fact, training at altitude can help increase the body's ability to utilize fat, buffer lactic acid, and increase the amount of red blood cells. One way to accomplish this is to train at a facility that has a hypoxic chamber and to train intermittently at altitude. Sessions should last between 60-90 minutes with the altitude fluctuating from your current altitude to the desired altitude every 5 minutes or so. Start at around 4000 meters, and increase the simulated altitude by 500 meters every three days until at about 6000 meters. After you have trained in this manner, you can also try more prolonged exposure at about 3,000 meters by starting slow and gradually increasing the intensity of training. One final method is to train under normal conditions using interval training. During the rest period, increase the altitude to about 4,500 meters. If training at altitude you may want to have your iron levels checked, and be sure to consume the RDA of iron in your diet. Do not supplement with iron above the RDA for your gender unless directed to by your doctor after a blood test.

The bottom line is that without knowing where your comfort levels are, it's easy to call it quits, or not even consider going climbing. On the flip side, knowing your limits can save your life. But if you know your limits, then a whole new world just opened up (see below). If only you can convince your partner. Wait! Do you really need a partner (see Maximizing Success and Rope-soloing)?

Specific Discipline Skills

There are a million other technique skills to practice as well as technical skills. The second part of this book deals with many advanced skills that should be practiced or learned. However, I want to include some style specific skills that I think should be emphasized.

Bouldering and Sport

The bulk of the skills in bouldering and sport climbing should be everything already presented from falling to feedback with the exception of some of the more advanced crack techniques. Here are some more:

New Shoes: Try out a whole bunch of new brands and types (board last, slip last, slipper, lace, Velcro, aggressively turned-down, aggressively asymmetrical) to see what works well for different types of climbing and rock type. You may be held back by simply wearing the wrong shoe. Experiment with tighter or looser shoes. Try out different types and thicknesses of rubber for future resoles.

Clipping – Sport climbers should practice smoothly clipping draws, correctly orienting them, and clipping to the side of, at, or slightly above a bolt if a better hold can be found. Try and keep your arms straight. Next practice clipping while moving past the bolt to keep momentum. Follow through the clip to grabbing the next hold.

Jamming – Learn to jam with your hands and feet by getting on some trad climbs. It's amazing how difficult some climbers can make a problem when they face climb around a perfectly good crack!

Figure 4 and 9 – You might want to practice these so they are in your bag of tricks. See the climbing specific exercises.

Trad

Trad climbers may want to practice a few more skills besides the many already mentioned.

Limiting Your Gear: Try climbing with just a single set, or smaller number of cams, or only using passive pro like nuts or tri-cams.

Use New Brands: If you only use Black Diamond, try borrowing a rack of Metolius for example. If you've never placed huge cams, big bros, ball nuts, RP's, offset nuts, or offset cams – try em out!

Different Shoes: Your Mythos or TC Pros may be holding you back – or be the ticket.

Find Unlikely and Difficult Placements: Even if there's a splitter crack right in front of you, try and find things to sling, thin cracks off to the side, under lips, and in pockets. Some difficult placements are protecting pin scars, flaring cracks, and wider cracks behind narrower lips.

Chockcraft: Try using your nuts sideways, equalize some opposing nuts, and try stacking nut placements.

Pitoncraft: Placing pitons AND trusting or backing up fixed pitons by having placed some yourself is a must-learn skill in the alpine. Start with knifeblades and angles, and then move on to fancier pins and stacking techniques.

Natural Pro: Use those slings! Try and see what you can sling or wrap with your slings. Don't forget about using knotted slings in constrictions.

Hand Drilling: Practice hand drilling on a small, out of the way rock or small bounder on granite and sandstone.

Linking Pitches: If anchors become your goal, or you always feel spent or have an empty rack by the anchor, try and use the full amount of your rope and either make an anchor or link pitches.

Back Cleaning: Get fast at placing intermediate placements to protect moves and short sections, then reaching down and yanking them out.

Harness vs. Sling: Experiment racking the cams you need on your harness if you are a shoulder sling type person.

Doubling Gear vs. Biners All-Around: If you are used to having a biner on every cam, and two biners on each sling, try and toss some like sized pieces on one biner, and throw some binerless or one-biner slings over your shoulder. I am not saying this is a better way since it is WAY slower on hard leads, but on easier technical climbs it saves weight. (I feel that such a mess is made by the end of the lead that the extra weight of the biners is worth it!)

Sport Climbing and Bouldering: Difficult trad climbs are often very similar to face cruxes or slab moves found in sport climbs or boulder problems. By practicing on bolt-protected faces or by bouldering, you can feel more comfortable executing difficult moves above trad gear. Focus your sport climbing and bouldering on the same type of rock that you want to lead on trad.

Snow, Ice, and Mixed

Ice climbers require mileage more than anything – even though leading and climbing routes you've never done is more fun, get lots and lots of toprope laps and mileage on easier routes every season.

Sinker Swings and Kicks: Practice getting sinker one-swing precise placements of both the tools and the crampons. Minimize second-guessing your swings and stomping around. Expend as little energy as possible for the best placement possible. Alpkit and

Schmools both make indoor ice-tool simulators to help with your swing (and to get some strength gains).

Photo courtesy Alpkit

Thin Ice: Practice thin ice by hooking and using small taps with both the tools and crampons.

Holding the Tools: Practice using the different grips on leashless tools (low, high, and working up the tool), matching hands, swapping hands, and stacking tools (hooking your own tool). Climbers trying to climb quickly over steep snow or low angled ice should practice or at least remind themselves to climb with their tools in the dagger position

Rock Moves: Try and start incorporating more rock climbing moves on the ice, especially stemming with your feet, but also many others for both the feet and the tools. Feet and tools don't have to always pull straight down.

X vs. T: Experiment with the "X"-position vs. the "T", but try and climb only in T position.

Climbing Fast: Practice cruising and getting into a rhythm. Use the skills you practice above to climb a pitch as quickly and as perfectly as possible. Top-roping mileage is the key to leading ice well.

Crampon Type: Climb with mono-points, dual points, and horizontal point crampons. Also give heel-spurs a try in varied ice and rock conditions.

Boots: Try climbing in clunky plastics to lightweight fruit boots.

Ice Conditions: Practice climbing and placing pro in wet ice, bullet hard ice, kicked out ice, chandelier, mushroom, hollow ice, and pillars.

Screw Placements: Practice placing screws with both hands at your waist, off to each side, and above your head. Practice placing screws on toprope in sketchy ice, in pillars, and thin ice. Practice placing them pumped as quickly as possible. Also practice keeping your screws on your harness vs. a gear sling.

Ice Features for Pro: Get some experience slinging icicles (and bounce testing them on TR if it's safe), slotting screws behind constrictions, making V-threads, and placing screws in weird places such as chopping a small pillar out and placing the screw straight up or down.

Angle Transition: Practice transitioning from steep to low angle ice

Resting: Practice shaking out on ice and rock, and keeping a loose grip, relaxed body, and your heels down.

Rock Type and Holds: Boulder traverse or toprope to experiment with tools on different type of rock: mainly limestone and granite. Try and find different holds from hooking micro edges and nearly invisible divots, to finding constrictions, finding small and wide pick cams, adz or hammer placement, stein pulls, and reverse stein pulls, and swings into turf or ice blob. Icetoolz sells indoor fake ice blobs to practice swings and hook, and distributes drytool simulator holds by Nicros. Icetoolz also makes stein-pull trainers (but you can make your own easily).

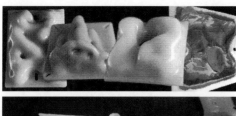

Ice holds, Steinpull trainer, hanging figure four block, courtesy IceHoldz

No Tools/Crampons: Toprope on rock and ice with only crampons (using your hands on the rock or ice) or only tools (using your boots on the rock or ice).

Pick and Tool: Try climbing hard ice or rock with an Alaska pick, a straight shafted tool, glacier ax, or a short 3rd tool. Also try out ergo tools with radical clearance, or just another company's version of your current tool.

Leashless, Umbilical, or Leashed: You need to get used to climbing with all three before committing yourself to leading, or climbing a long route.

Stashing Your Tool: When placing gear practice clipping your tool to your harness, placing it in a holster, between your pack strap and pack, over your shoulder, pinching it with the thumb and index finger of the tool still on the wall, in the ice, in your mouth, or a solid constriction.

Practice Clipping on Rock: Practice on bolts to get a rhythm established.

Rock Gear: Practice placing pitons in general, but also with a reverse curve hammer. Get used to placing tricams, ice beaks, warthogs, and offset nuts, as well as looking for unusual places like moss, dirt, and bushes or trees.

Big Wall

Without this just becoming a list of things you need to know how to perform to aid climb or wall climb, here are some specific skills that always need practice with some unique skills tossed in. A lot of the exercises in the rock paragraphs above are useful too. A good way to practice systems is to put an anchor bolt or two (like an eyebolt) in your ceiling stud, or sling a rafter that can hold bodyweight.

Aider Systems: Practice between using minimal gear (slings and cordalette), to a 2-aider, 3-aider, and 4-aider setup on, to different daisy chain (adjustable, standard, no daisy) and fifi hook combinations on a wall of varying steepness. A chain link fence, like the backstop on a baseball diamond, or closely bolted sport climb works well to focus on systems quickly instead of gear placements.

Jugging: Practice jugging with minimal gear (prusik) to using a two-ascender two-aider system to a one ascender / GriGri frog-style setup.

Hauling: Figure out how to setup a haul system with up to a 3:1 mechanical advantage, how to lower out the haul bag, rappel with the haul bag, and to solo with the haul bag.

Pendulums and Traverses: Practice tension-traverses, following traverses on jugs, doing quick pendulums and lower-outs off a fixed piece, and big pendulums. These definitely require practice if you're going solo.

Aiding Quickly: Spend time getting dialed, it takes time. Start with French-freeing in the most energy-saving manner possible, and progress to quickly placing, testing, and placing the next piece of gear to move up fast. Practice on a tall chain link fence or closely bolted sport climb.

Short-fixing and Rope-soloing: Get your rope-soloing dialed for faster climbing with a partner.

Placing Special Gear: Learn to place and deal with hooks, beaks, modified pins, copperheads, cam hooks, rivet hangers, offset cams, expanding cracks, and pin scars.

Alpine and Mountaineering
Self-Arrest: Practice on both sides, sliding on your stomach, back, head first, and feet first. Practice raising your feet if sliding with crampons on.

Minimal Gear: Practice self-arresting with a rock or piece of gear for rock routes starting on snow slopes. Practice climbing hard ice snow slopes with aluminum crampons over tennis shoes and a lightweight aluminum ax.

Ax and Foot Positions: Practice placing your feet in the (English terms) splayed, duck walk, front-point, and front-point/splayed position, as well as kicking steps, and locking your back knee on the uphill rest-step. Ax positions include: dagger (grabbing just shaft just below the pick), high dagger (hand around the shaft, pick, and adz/hammer), and cane (walking with the pick forwards).

Steep Snow Traverse: Practice maintaining stability by planting your shaft or pick before committing weight to the leg that needs to cross through. Practice coming about on switchbacks by maintaining stability, and stepping over the rope.

Glissading, Plunge-Stepping, and Scree Surfing: Practice staying in control sliding down safe slopes on your feet (no crampons!!), on your butt, and plunging down the slope by firmly planting your heels. Practice ruddering with your trekking pole. Also practice plunge stepping and glissading in loose scree.

Other
There are many other things you can practice like navigation, rappel ticks, speed tricks, self-rescue, and wilderness first aid. Go through the rest of the book and mark areas that need work or practice. Strength, technique, and technical skills are all equally important.

These suggestions for practicing skills will speed up your abilities by years of trial and error! Plan on being humbled, don't make excuses, but be honest about your abilities and worries. Try and use your brain to logically solve the problem, also using resources like books and the Internet, and always ask for help and feedback.

ABILITY

Ability means combining all of your fitness and skills into actually performing. Just training fitness, strength, and skills without applying them together will not provide results. A person could have every tool imaginable at their discretion, and have taken every academic class imaginable and still be totally useless. You have the skills and the fitness, but are you able to use them?

To get better at transferring new skills and fitness into ability, try the following progression in order of importance: bouldering, top roping, redpointing sport, redpointing, trad/ice/mixed, headpointing if applicable, and other skills practice. This should also be the bulk of your climbing training. You could theoretically climb every day, but most normal humans can only climb hard a few days in a row.

> **Ability training is done throughout the entire training program and is not subject to periodization or protocols.**

DEVELOPING ABILITY EXERCISES
Climbing in Your Comfort Zone and Ticking Routes
This is where most climbers spend the vast majority of their time, leading and toproping routes (cragging to multipitch) that are challenging, but still within their onsight range. There is absolutely nothing wrong with this, and it's where most of the fun is had – it's why most of us climb. But you won't get better very fast unless you are a beginner. Many people push themselves in their non-climbing specific training, but most don't push themselves outside of their comfort zone. If you're training, there's nothing wrong with climbing routes in this area, but save these for fun days, endurance days, and trips with a less-skilled partner, warm-ups, or testing out the water in a new area.

The rest of the exercises are where the real skills are applied and where you get better…

Redpointing
Redpointing means climbing a route with no falls and hangs. The difference between this and an onsight is that a redpoint will be something too difficult to climb on your first try. You have to work the route, and much learning takes place. A redpoint project could be a few routes just above your onsight limit, to something way over your head that could take years to complete. If you want to get better at lead climbing, this is where the main bulk of your climbing and training should occur. Redpointing is a hard mindset for many climbers to get into, especially those who like to rack up as many new pitches as possible. It really helps to have a partner with similar goals. Redpointing a route is extremely rewarding and the payback is huge. Start making redpoints a regular habit. For those of you who only do multipitch or alpine, it would be in your best interest to devote some time to cragging and working routes. One good redpoint exercise is to not be picky – if the route sucks, redpoint it anyway. If you don't like it, it probably means you'll be working your weaknesses.

Wire a Difficult Climb Solid
By getting a few distinct types of climbs totally wired (that is more than just redpointing something and calling it good) you'll be able to draw on this experience during other climbs. Choose a route that was uniquely challenging to you in some way and redpoint it. Come back to it a week or month later and redpoint it again. Keep repeating it until you climb it extremely well - that is, you have it "totally dialed". Doing this will create a mental library you can draw on, and use as benchmarks. Don't apply your feeling of mastery for this climb as a blanket for all climbs of its grade or nature. It can lead to complacency and inflated sense of your ability. If you can onsight something, then it wasn't hard enough. You will wind up onsighting plenty of climbs during your training – during your warm-up or filler climbs, or by accident when a redpoint attempt became an onsight! If the latter is the case either that route was graded too soft, or maybe it's a sign to start redpointing a little harder grades.

Head-Pointing
Headpointing routes (leading them with a toprope backup) is the best way to get better at difficult trad climbs, or even run-out sport climbs. Headpointing allows you to get the gear wired (and build gear placement skills). Check out the falling section on how

to gauge and mitigate risk on falls you don't want to take.

Very Difficult Climbing
Warm-up on a few routes first. The goal here is to work on climbs that aren't impossible, but require many attempts of piecing together difficult moves. This helps you find new weaknesses, and can help you hurdle out of a plateau. This is where top-roping or safe bouldering, homemade cracks, and Moonboards shine. You won't learn anything by trying to lead routes this hard. Cool down on something fun to ease your frustrations. This is also a strength-endurance building exercise depending on the type of climb.

Solo Top-Roping, Rope-Soloing, and Bouldering
Just because you don't have a partner, doesn't mean you can't go climbing or stop training. You won't be able to climb to the full limits of your ability, but at least you're trying.

APPLYING ABILITY EXERCISES
The whole point of training is to have something to show for it, otherwise you're only engaging in a Sisyphusian odyssey. Later in the Periodization section, I will discuss that after a cycle of training and a rest phase, you should apply your training in the performance phase. However, the ability exercises below can be applied in ANY phase. They are a great way to break up the monotony, gauge how you are doing, and rack-up much needed mileage and experience.

Onsighting or Revisiting an Old Climb
After you've trained a bit, are feeling particularly strong, and need a litmus test of your ability, go try and climb something that you didn't think you could before – or had tried before and couldn't. Onsighting is an excellent way to apply your skill to new terrain, but it is a goal and should be enjoyed mainly during the performance phase.

Strength-Endurance Climb
Pick a big long climb at or near your limit and come back destroyed, or rack up a ton of pitches in one day! This is a good exercise to do during the endurance phase.

Technique-Endurance Climb
Part of me even considered to just say "climb true 5.7 routes all day every day and you'll learn the skills necessary to climb 5.12". Racking up mileage and applying ability is much easier on easy to moderate terrain, and the rewards are outstanding. Some good ideas are a long easier alpine climb, multi-climb link-up, an El-Cap or Half-Dome day at the crag (i.e. do 20+ pitches of cragging in one day), a solo circuit at a local crag, or multi-discipline day (go skiing, rock climbing, ice climbing, etc. in the same day). Keep the grade at a level that you could literally climb from dawn till dusk (or longer!). Another good one for the endurance phase.

A Good Day Cragging
A great way to make the most out of a day of cragging and bouldering would be to warm-up on some fun looking easier routes, and then do a few favorites that are a little harder (since you already know the moves you won't use as much energy and you'll fire up the neurons). Now go work on your redpoint project, and climb a couple routes near the same grade to keep things fun and find new projects. Climb another easy pitch or two, or finish up by top-roping a pitch that is really hard and technique intensive.

Chapter Five: Programming

Programming: Making and Planning for Your Goals

Goals

You can't get better at everything by training for everything. Time and physical limitations will not allow this. You can be a jack-of-all-trades, but (you guessed it) a master of none. This section takes all the skills and exercises and makes a manageable plan out of them. One of the worst parts about training to get better is that you need to sacrifice a lot of personal "fun" climbing or focusing on ticking off all the classic routes in a bunch of different areas. The good news is that training with more focus starts getting fun once you start noticing improvement, and the satisfaction of finally climbing something with so much effort spent can become just as addicting as ticking off routes. This isn't a problem if your goal isn't to improve much in the grades, but that you want to be more physically fit doing the moderate climbs on your tick list. What you shouldn't feel is like that kid who was forced to stay at home practicing the piano while the other kids played outside. Unless of course you want to be an elite climber, especially in gym comps, then I'm sorry - you may have to become that kid. You have to make sacrifices.

The more closely you can recreate what you are training for in your training will help you reach that goal. To do this, your goal must be broken down into component parts and steps, then gradually put back together. Train at a high intensity for all of the component parts of your goal, practice each step, gradually combine steps, and increase the intensity until it matches and achieves your goal. Many of the components and steps are shared in many modalities of climbing, so if you train for enough goals, you may indeed become a master all around climber...but you may need to quit your day job since if you don't use it, you lose it. You don't have to do a single exercise in this book to succeed, they are only provided for you as tools. However, even if you have a serious aversion to exercise, you can still "train" by climbing intelligently. That's what this chapter is about.

Training for your Goals
Break It Down

Luckily, most of the different aspects of climbing are transferrable. That is, by getting better at one thing, you can transfer that new skill set towards something else. But, the other thing about climbing is that every climb requires a unique set of skills. The best way to get a handle on this is to break it down into the component parts.

- **Discipline**: Bouldering, Sport, Trad, Mixed, Ice, Aid, Alpine, and Mountaineering, and Peak Bagging. The order I presented the types of climbing has some significance. In general, technique transfers up that chain, but not down. Mountain and outdoor skills and wisdom generally flow in the reverse direction. In other words, a boulderer won't learn better technique by going mountaineering, but an alpine climber could by going bouldering. A mountaineer won't learn much about mountain skills (which are equally as important as technique in my opinion) by going bouldering, but a boulder will by going mountaineering.

You can break type of climbing down further:
- **Rock Type:** granite, basalt, limestone, sandstone, quartzite, gneiss, gritstone, tuft, and plastic (to name a few).
- **Steepness:** slab, vertical, and overhanging
- **Friction:** low, medium, and high

These can be even further broken down into type of holds, moves, etc. (which is what the skill section tries to break down). For example, training for vertical sport climbing on granite will help a vertical granite trad climber improve. The more similar the better. The best scenario would be if you are training for a 5.12 at your crag and you were able to specifically train at this crag progressing in the grades right there. The three basic types of rock climbing are **cracks, face holds, and slabs**. To be an all-rounder, train all three. The above works for mixed climbers, but ice climbing is more difficult to break down, especially since the same climb can change drastically over time. Steepness shouldn't change much, but the type of consistency and shape (dagger, curtain, gully, smear) can.

Set Basic Goals

Here's a basic question: what type of climbing do you want to do be great at and what type do you want to be good at? The best way to improve your climbing is to train and climb with a highly specific goal in mind. Climbing is just too complex (if not the most complex sport there is) with too many variables to train without a specific goal. It's a good idea to begin training for an easily attainable goal with your sights set higher. Once that goal is attained, train for another slightly harder goal. To get past the activation energy of actually beginning training, set an easy training goal. Start with something easy to avoid becoming overwhelmed too soon. If you have trouble getting into the habit of exercising, or training hard for a few days or week and wind up quitting, try something like 10 sit ups 10 pull ups and 10 pushups every day. This takes no time at all and you don't need to travel to the gym. Make a goto "too lazy to train" workout that so at the very least, you can do that every day. Remember the more climbing specific, the better, but at the same time, the easier it is for you to actually do it, the better. You need a goal. If you don't have one, just tear out each exercise from the book, stick it in a jar, and pull out a few to do today.

Setting Short to Long-Term Goals

Get out a piece of paper or boot up your computer and write down (the more specific the better): one goal for the new few months, each season, for the next year or two years if it's a big goal, your long term goals, and dream routes. They can be anything climbing related: getting good at particular skill, speed climbing, climbing at a particular grade, a specific route, whatever. Now look at your goals. Do they complement, or build upon each other? If they don't, re-evaluate your goals. This is not the place for wishful thinking. Next, write down a date when you expect to complete the goal. Obviously this is not set in stone, but it will help light a fire and also help for planning your training.

<u>BREAKING DOWN THE GOALS</u>

Next, answer the following questions. You can answer them for any of your goals. If, for example, your 1-2 year goal is the most important, and you're happy to climb whatever as long as you're improving, then just answer for your 1-2 year goal. There is plenty of food for thought throughout this book that I suggest leaving room to add more information.

✓ **What grade, type of climbing, and rock type (including steepness & friction) are you training for?** This just helps you start thinking about ways to break down your training.

✓ **What climbs help simulate this goal?**

Make a tick list of all the "important" climbs you've always wanted to do. Weed out the trivial climbs you can live without doing. You can't do them all. Now highlight the climbs that fit within your goal. They don't all have to be, say, granite crack climbs. There can be sport climbs in there too.

Mount Everest probably falls way outside your goal parameters if you want to do the Nose of El Cap in a day. The point here is to make sure you have mini goals to keep you happy, and to track your progress along the way. Some of the climbs could be technically harder than your main goal, some way easier (but should have some benefit like being really long or something).

✓ **Take your tick list and organize it by time of year, difficulty, type of climbing, and rock-type.**

At the top of your route tick list, list all the climbing areas by season that you want to climb that would be helpful in achieving your goal. Be sure and add some local areas that are very easy to access even if they don't quite fit the bill. Even if you don't do a lot of it, list out some cragging, bouldering, and top roping spots as well in order to keep you active if a trip doesn't go your way or during downtime.

Look at your tick list that you just created and you will see a natural progression dictated by the grade and by season. Easier sport climbs in winter could lead into easier trad climbs in the fall, etc. This isn't enough to make a real training plan, but it roughly outlines a plan for a long-term goal. Basically the closer you get to your goal's deadline, the closer all the attributes of your tick lists climbs should be to your goal.

✓ **What special techniques, skills, and physical requirements are needed?**

Next make a list of the from the abilities and skills sections needed to complete your goal and the grade you should be proficient in if necessary.

For example: generic crack climbing 11c, granite crack climbing 11b, slab 11a, off-width 10c, aid climbing A2, strength-endurance, technique endurance, finger strength, falling, hard topropes, redpoints and headpoints, climbing at night, jugging, falling.

Transfer this list of skills into your tick list. Do some of the skills you need to practice fit nicely into a climb or area? If so, put them there. Some skills may need constant work throughout the year. If a season doesn't have a climb or area on that list, write the skill in that season to remind you to practice it. Some skills only need to be practiced just before your goal. Add those to your list, giving yourself enough time to practice.

Pyramids

A good way to keep track of your progress is to make grade pyramids. Pyramids are only meant to keep track of progress and give you an idea what grades to climb at. Just because you completed a pyramid doesn't mean you magically can make a leap forward. It is just a useful tool. To create a pyramid, try and decide what your standard onsight level is for a particular area or type of climbing. The base of your pyramid will be one letter grade above that. It really doesn't matter how you construct the pyramid since it is just a reference tool, but the most common way to make a pyramid is the start with 8 routes one notch above your onside limit. The next level will have 4 routes one letter grade harder. The third tier contains two routes another letter grade harder, and the top will have one route one letter grade harder. You can only cross off a route in the pyramid if you redpointed or onsighted it fairly (no takes, hangs, or miracles).

Once you start ticking off routes and going beyond the numbers listed in your pyramid, add another grade to the right of the level of the same grade. Confused? Below is a sample pyramid that starts out at 10c (the climber can onsight 10b regularly) and tops out at 11b, shown in bold. But this climber's goal is to be able to regularly onsight 11a, so he or she would need to construct a pyramid that maxes out at 12b (shown in underline). This is only to create a visual tool to create some sort of order to the madness. It really shows that to feel comfortable onsighting 11b's with some consistency, this climber needs a solid foundation of easier routes, and some successes at much more difficult routes.

> **Sample Pyramid.** Goal is 11a onsight, current level is regularly able to onsight 10b. Two combined pyramids to show what needs to get redpointed to theoretically onsight at an 11a level.
>
> <u>12b</u>
> 12a 12a
> 11d 11d 11d 11d
> 11c 11c 11c 11c 11c 11c 11c 11c
> 11b 11b 11b 11b 11b 11b 11b 11b
> Desired Onsight 11a 11a 11a 11a 11a 11a 11a 11a
> 10d 10d 10d 10d 10d 10d 10d 10d
> Current Onsight: 10c 10c 10c 10c 10c 10c 10c 10c

Pyramids are a great way to keep track of your ability and provide motivation to improve. But remember, they don't really mean anything. This sample climber could theoretically jump a level or two and never climb a single 11a or 11b to finally reach being able to redpoint a 12b if that was his/her goal. If this climber found that he/she has about the same difficulty on 10d's as 11a's, then maybe skip the 10d's, up the ante, and raise the pyramid another notch. The only reason not to do this would be if a particular area's 10d have a totally different style and character than the 11a's. The climber would be missing valuable skill building. It's important to realize that to get better you need to be constantly pushing your ability level on harder stuff. You also need to keep in mind that gaining experience and wisdom take a different speed.

Make pyramids for each major type of climbing skill/technique that is involved in your goal. For instance, if 11b granite cracks is the grade you need to be proficient in, make that 11c base of your pyramid. If your goal has some other distinct types of climbing involved as well, make separate pyramids for those too. So if your goal is an 11b multipitch granite climb that has some 10c offwidth and 11a slab that you need to be extremely proficient in, make a pyramid for offwidth based at 10d, slab climbing with a base of 11b, and a general pyramid with a base of 11c. If your goal is to attain a successful redpoint of a certain grade, than that grade can be the top of your pyramid. This is just a fancy way of showing that if you want to be solid at something you have to have a solid base and try harder routes than it.

Keep track of the different variables mentioned before (type of climbing, steepness, type of rock, friction) and make sure you are training in a step-by-step way that slowly increases difficulty matching the conditions of your goal as closely as possible. If you have multiple types of climbing as your goal, then mix it up and expect slower progress. If your goal is ultra-specific, train that way.

By now you should have a basic plan of the type of climbing that needs to be trained for, and when and where you'll be training. At the bare minimum you can use the exercises under Skills and Ability to train for what you have written down.

Monthly Schedule

Now that you have the big picture, it's time to break things down into even more manageable pieces. Write down the months involved in your training period, and under each month take a few climbs from your earlier tick list and make those climbs that month's goal. You will need to follow a basic periodization of the different protocols of training that is detailed in the next chapter. After reading the next chapter, re-schedule periodization based phases into your monthly plan. It takes about 30 full training days or practice to reach a step forward in progress. To maintain that level, you must train and practice much longer, about six weeks of committed effort.

You should also answer these next few questions. Tweak your goal if the answers don't coexist with realistic expectations of reaching your goal, or find solutions to the answers. Tweak your goal if necessary.

- ✓ When, where, & how much can I climb outside?

- ✓ Is there time, money, partner, access to crags, and equipment limitations?

- ✓ How much time do I have? Is it enough, too much (set a bigger goal), or not enough (set a smaller goal)?

SCHEDULING FOR DIFFERENT TYPES OF CLIMBING AND SEASONAL OVERVIEW

If you sport climb, ice climb, trad climb, alpine climb, or whatever it becomes very important to set a time to start training for each type of climbing. You may even need to schedule different forms of the same style of climbing. For instance, sport climbers may climb overhanging shaded routes in the summer and slabbier routes in the spring, fall, or winter. Also, a particular area you frequent may be only climbable in certain times of the year and offer a totally different style of climbing. Summers could be slabby cracks in the PNW, fall and spring could be steep sustained cracks in the desert, and winters spent ice climbing, skiing, or sport climbing down South. Luckily, a lot of training overlaps but prepare for a minimum two months of training before your season starts unless it's a long season and you don't mind training during that season and reaching goals mid to late season. If you have many types of climbing you want to do, you may have to start training for your one type of climbing while doing another!

The best way I have figured out to reconcile this, or at least make things manageable, is to have extremely specific goals in each arena of climbing you want to excel at. So if your plan is to onsight a 5.12 granite trad climb and nothing else, but you still want to climb some ice in the winter because you simply can't granite crack climb during those months, don't train for ice climbing. Just go out, have fun, and focus your mental energy and what training you can on granite cracks. This may mean aiding some granite in the winter to keep the protection skill set up, or practicing whippers at the gym. If you have many different goals, draw a timeline. Highlight the seasons during which your various climbing activities occur. Now above your timeline, write in when you should begin training for the goals of those activities.

SEASONAL TIMELINE (EXAMPLE):
Month: Dec, Jan,   Feb, March, April, May, June, July, Aug,   Sept   Oct Nov
Activity: Skiing & Ice   Desert Crack   Cragging Alpine   Cragging Desert Sport/Trad
Train: *Gen Weights Crack   Grip   Redpoint Aerobic Grip   Crack   Ice Gen Weight*

ASSESSING OTHER WEAKNESSES AND PLANNING TO TRAIN FOR THEM

There probably are other things you need to train for besides just climbing ability. The most successful climbers know themselves (in a climbing sense) better. They admit to weaknesses and shortcomings and are constantly aware of finding and fixing these problems. Check out www.habitforge.com – it's a website that will email your reminders to help you change bad habits. ReMind Alarm is a great app that allow you to set specific reminder alarms throughout the day.

Physical Imbalances

Rehabbing will be discussed later in great detail, and with many tidbits thrown in throughout the book. If you have, are recovering from, or are chronically suffering from an injury, the time is now to fix it as much as you can. Schedule appointments with appropriate therapists or doctors. Take whatever medication or supplements you need to. Figure out whatever stretches and exercises you need to do. If the injury prevents you from training, or you have so much physical rehab that it consumes most of your free time – don't train for climbing yet. Recover and come back to this. Or change your goal to something realistic. Hopefully you just need to deal with a few exercises and stretches, and you can toss them into your daily training.

Start going through all the non-climbing exercises, warm-ups, and stretches, and mark down which ones are difficult and if a particular side or muscle group is especially weak or tight. You may develop an extensive list. At the top of the list should be difficult warm-ups and exercises in the core stability and antagonist groups. I've tried to mention better exercises to focus on as some really are meant solely for rehab purposes. Put the exercises into their appropriate categories (warm-up, core, antagonist, etc.). Do these exercises 2-4 days per week until they are no longer imbalanced or weak – then stop doing them. The more times you do them a week, the sooner you can stop doing them. Go back to these exercises a month or two later to be confident they are strong and stable. Some exercises in this list may be ongoing as part of a warm-up and prehab or done 1-2 times a week to maintain fitness.

You may want to get a head start on pulling and finger strength exercises if your hands, arms, and shoulders are imbalanced. But if you're doing pretty good, leave them for the strength phase (described later) as you'll gain upper body and finger strength by climbing routes.

Schedule the rehab exercises you need to do in your plan, putting them at the top of the list and plan on doing them 3-6 days per week. These exercises will be your non-climbing exercises for the foundation phase. Remember, for all exercises to try and gradually increase weight, time, and/or reps.

Health Concerns

This is a great time to take care of any health concerns, so schedule your doctor's appointment now and start eating healthy. Check out the health section for ideas. Keep track of positive or poor results from any of these concerns so you can chart your progress if applicable. The biggest concern for climbers is generally their body fat percentages. I will discuss some weight loss techniques later, but keep track of your weight and body fat in a place (like your monthly schedule) you can constantly look at and check your progress. For accurate weight and body fat measurement use the same scale, and use the same method of body fat testing to recheck. Smoking, alcoholism, and drug abuse are lifestyle concerns, but they are also health concerns. Now is the time to schedule a plan to quit. Schedule dealing with health concerns into your monthly plan.

Lifestyle Habits, Logistical Issues, and Stressors

The best offense is a good defense, and the best way to deal with obstacles is to know them and plan for them. Take some time and write down things in your life that could interfere with your goals and train or plan for them. Check out the mental training chapter for some ideas. What are your bad habits? They could be chemical dependence on drugs, tobacco, or alcohol. These will certainly limit your potential. They could be emotional, social, personal, climbing related, or indirectly related to climbing. Do some soul searching, challenge yourself. Start paying attention to this and you may find that you have habits that could affect your climbing you never even realized. See a counselor, and by talking with the help of a trained professional, you may discover things you never would on your own no matter how introverted you think you may be.

Are there logistical issues interfering with climbing that you can fix: a bad job schedule, no car, no partners, no nearby climbing or gym to train in? Almost everything has a solution or reasonable work around. Write them down and a plan of attack. Finally, what are the stressors in your life? Stress is a major health concern and nothing can limit your performance like it. Maybe one of the stressors is climbing itself. You may not be able to eliminate your stress save quitting your job and getting a divorce, but you can plan on how to deal with it. Remember, physical stress and pain are the only things that force you to react, and you can choose how to react to even those by training yourself.

Make a plan and schedule what needs to be done in your monthly schedule. Make firm dates and start searching for solutions and begin to fix the problems now. That nagging problem you may or may not be consciously dealing with could be the one thing holding you back.

Technical Skills
One of the last imbalances is a lack of climbing or outdoor knowledge. I will talk later in the book about some of these technical skills, but if you are just beginning learning about a new area of climbing and outdoor knowledge, read more specialized books, take a course, go with an experienced friend, or hire a guide. Even a goal that sounds simple, like bouldering, can have little hidden technical skill or bits of knowledge that can help you succeed. It's hard to know what you need to know without knowing, so read the rest of this book and check out the other resources. If your goal requires you to have a skill you don't know how to do, or are poor at that fits into your goal, then plan on learning it. Don't forget to practice once you have learned it. Schedule into your monthly schedule when and where you will learn and practice these skills. All climbers should practice self-rescue technique and brush up on first aid, wilderness medicine, and low/no-impact camping. If you can find someone willing to practice with you on these skills, make them a regular climbing partner. Even if their ability is less than yours, you will want this type of person tied into you.

Bad Climbing Habits
Besides climbing ability, technical skills, and strength issues, what else limits you during a climb? Maybe your belay change overs are too slow, you never drink or eat enough on or before a climb, you always bring too much or not enough of something, you bail constantly by overrating your skill or get scared, you sleep too later or stay up too late, you don't rest enough, or a whole host of other things. A lot will be addressed in other parts of the book, but you should be able to think of plenty right now. Stay aware of this question during future climbs, and while reading the rest of this book. Write these issues down and a plan of how to deal with them in your monthly schedule.

PERIODIZATION

By now you should have a goal or goals set with climbs picked out in a logical progression, along with specific skills and foundation exercises. But, if you were wondering when to do an exercise under a specific protocol, this is the place.

The time spent on each of the phases below are just estimates. When you are ready to move on, move on. If you need to come back, come back. There are pro and cons to how long you should spend on any given exercise, protocol, or phase. By staying in one place too long, you become stagnant and plateau. But, by mixing it up too much, it is hard to get good at something and improve. If you are really on top of your performance, you can mix and match phases at any point. If something is of extreme importance, it is probably best to train it until fully mastered. If something needs work but won't limit you too much, move on after you have accomplished what needed accomplishing. Make a mental and written note, and come back to it when time allows in order of importance.

In order to maximize your potential, you may need to progress through each phase before meeting your goal, depending on how hard it is. It is not important to plan out specifically what exercises or climbs you plan on doing in advance of a new phase (unless you need to make travel plans). The phases don't specifically change what exercise or climbs you wind up doing, but how you do them. The phases are more appropriate for adapting your climbing and non-climbing exercises.

SEPARATING OUT SKILLS AND ABILITY FROM PHASES AND PROTOCOLS

It is important that you differentiate skills and ability from the other exercise in this book. Skills and ability take priority far and above everything else and are not separated into the different periodization phases – you will perform and practice them all of the time. Almost every sport out there places the most time and concentration in training on skills and practice. In fact, most of your time spent training should be focusing on skills and applying them into ability. You can double up your skills during your ability training. There are no phases or protocols for actually going climbing. Skills and ability are meant to occur at the same time as the other training. Everything else is just extra training. Plan on selecting all the basic skills you need to work on. Practicing more basic skills will probably occur during the foundation phase, but they can drift well into the other phases. Try and make some kind of progression of increasing more and more difficult skills, but always be aware of the possible need to go back and work on basic skills occasionally.

THE FOUNDATION PHASE: SKILL BUILDING, REHAB, IMBALANCE CORRECTING, AND CONDITIONING. 1-2 MONTHS.

It is always best to build on a solid foundation. This phase is the get in shape, fix imbalances, and train basic skills and technique. This is the pain in the ass phase no one wants to do and has the highest level of dropout. Plan for it. If your goal is large, your foundation must be too. If your goal is simple, you could get away with skipping much of this phase – it all depends on what you want to get out of your effort. Joining a rock gym (if possible) is a very good idea here if your local crag doesn't help you or is too seasonal. If your climbing style requires aerobic training and leg work, schedule them into your monthly training most likely now, but if the timing isn't right, schedule them in a few months in advance of your goal. Start with aerobic endurance.

Now is the time to focus on weak muscles, tight muscles and joints, core exercises, abdominal and lumbar exercises, antagonist muscle exercises, early climbing ability progressions, basic skills and techniques, lifestyle modification, and lingering rehab issues. Endurance and strength protocols described in Chapter One are very useful here. Don't forget to start by scheduling your ability sessions (actual climbing) and revolve the rest of your training around those. You should be climbing 3-4 days per week.

Once you have completed the foundation phase, you will not need to spend as long on it during the next round of training – unless you have a new injury or have taken significant time off. When you land here again you should explore the exercises once again to see if you have new weakness or have eliminated old ones. Round two and above should hopefully only last a few weeks, or just stuck in occasionally during the strength phase.

> **The following would be a good progression example for the Ability portion of your foundation:** *Build a reasonable redpoint pyramid for leading in the gym or outside, topping out at a grade you feel is achievable in a month or so. Take lots and lots of falls. After a head start of a week or two on leading, add indoor or outdoor bouldering to your training, creating another pyramid for bouldering (the base would be something you fall off of half the time). When you begin working on your last few climbs start top-roping climbs at the top of your pyramid, and one to two letter grades harder. After finishing up sport climbing and bouldering take it another step further and begin new pyramids for crack and slab climbing. Finish each session with a hard toprope or two.*

STRENGTH PHASE – 1-2 MONTHS

During this phase you begin the climbing specific exercises listed in the exercise sections. Increase weight and intensity of non-climbing exercises by delving into the power, power-endurance, and strength-endurance protocols, and by doing some of the more difficult or functional exercises. Continue on with skills and any lingering exercises you still need to fix from the foundation phase as well as tossing in a few antagonist and stability exercises to stay healthy and balanced.

After a warm-up, climbing specific exercises should be scheduled before skills and ability to get the maximum strength training benefit from them. Actual climbing still takes priority if time or resources won't allow for the other exercises, but be creative when you hit the crag to try and re-create some of the drills by choosing routes that simulate the goals of the different exercises and skills.

Sub-Dividing the Strength Phase: Strength, Power, Power-Endurance, and Strength-Endurance

You have the choice during the strength phase whether to sub-periodize climbing and non-climbing exercises. You could prolong the strength phase by spending a few weeks each on strength, power, and endurance combinations. You can rotate through each protocol on a biweekly, weekly, daily basis, or mix and match for each training session by doing a little of each. One advantage of shorter cycles is that people tend to burn out and quit by having too much repetition. The disadvantage of shorter cycles is that you need time and repetition to get maximum benefit. If you start to get burnt or aren't noticing gains, switch it up.

The length may vary, but the order you do each strength protocol should remain the same. Start with strength, then power, power endurance, and finally strength endurance. Each protocol builds on the last. Train endurance during the foundation phase and during its own separate phase after you're done with the strength phase. Follow the guidelines of how many days per week each drill should or can be one. Plan on training climbing specific exercises about 4 days per week, and schedule in more specific skills. Continue with your ability practice (actual climbing) 3-4 days per week.

Climbers training for cardio should be focusing on aerobic and anaerobic threshold training, although your cardio program doesn't have to parallel your climbing training program.

ENDURANCE PHASE – A FEW DAYS TO 2 WEEKS

This phase is about getting in some serious climbing time. Stay out of the weight room. If your goal requires some specific techniques that are best practiced just before your climb, you may need to extend the endurance phase to hone these techniques in for practice, or if they aren't strenuous do them in the rest phase. Continue to warm-up and stretch. Keep your skills in the back of your mind, and your ability should be part of the route or climbs you are doing.

You should be doing long all-day climbing marathons, or if your goals are more mountaineering-based, long hard hikes preferably at altitude. If you are doing long multi-pitch routes, try and get in 2-3 big ones. If you are cragging or bouldering, then try and focus on climbing as many pitches / problems as possible for 5-8 sessions. Indoor climbers should be spending every possible moment in the gym doing routes. Toss in a few climbs/pitches near or at your limit, but make sure you can set an all-day pace. Climbers with leg and cardio intensive goals should be outside on terrain that simulates their goals as much as possible.

Endurance gains are lost quickly, which is a major reason why endurance is trained last. Strength does help train endurance, but not completely. At worst, strength training slows the decay of endurance gains. One thing to stress here is that this is not the performance phase. Don't schedule really difficult climbs. They will burn you out and make you climb like crap for the performance phase, or your goal. You may actually lose strength and ability if you push it too hard.

REST PHASE – 1-2 WEEKS

Before you are ready to actualize your goal, or mini goal, take a break. You should be drastically increasing your calorie consumption, sleeping at least 9 hours a night, and only doing light climbing/training (it can be technically hard, just not tiring) to keep yourself on your toes. Continue stretching and doing light cardio.

One round of these three phases may not be enough to get to your goal, and will certainly not make you as strong as possible. You need to cycle through over and over again. When you first begin, each phase will last much longer. Each time you cycle, you can cut back the length of the phases until you find a perfect mix.

CRAMMING PHASE 2-4 DAYS (OPTIONAL)

Sometimes big gains in performance are achieved by revisiting key core, large muscle group, and functional exercises along with additional climbing specific training using strength and power protocols just after the rest phase. This primes the muscles and movement patterns that were being processed during the rest phase. Hit it hard, but for no more than two hours a day, and give yourself an additional rest day or two.

PERFORMANCE PHASE – ONE CLIMB TO A FULL SEASON

This is what you spent the time training for. This phase can last for just one problem, pitch, route, or it can last a season. If it's more than just a one-time climb, keep playing with your skills, ability, warm-ups and stretching. Keep up your fitness by occasionally visiting some drills, aerobics, antagonist, core, climbing specific conditioning, and functional exercises. If you still have weaknesses, continue training those specifically. Factor in rest days or weeks during this phase. Your performance phase can cycle between periods of foundation, strength, power, and or skill development, endurance and rest as you move to different projects.

COMBINING OR ALTERING PHASES
You don't have to be totally stuck in a phase. Feel free to jump back and forth occasionally. The phases are meant to build on each other in a progression for a reason, but mixing things up occasionally can create "jumps" in performance. If the weather looks good and you have a partner that wants to do a long endurance route before you are in that phase – do it. You can also see what happens when you jump a level or two in your pyramid. Maybe you can totally skip the 10b's and make a leap in performance. Or stack on another 25 pounds. Sometimes a skill or exercise feels hard because you are used to it being hard. If you can successfully make a jump, then what was once hard now feels easy. You just got better.

One good approach is to cycle every two weeks between different protocols or phases. This allow you to stick with a group of exercises long enough to make gains in a particular area. Every two weeks, pick a focus that you want to get stronger in or better at.

STARTING THE CYCLE AGAIN
When you start training again your foundation phase can be a lot shorter (or skipped) depending on how much time you took off or what you lost during your performance phase.

FITTING IN AEROBIC TRAINING
Aerobic training does not have to coincide with the different phases. It totally depends on how cardio fits into your climbing goals.

It is better to cycle through the three types of cardio training (endurance, aerobic threshold, and anaerobic threshold) than to only train one at a time. If you are deconditioned in cardio, focus more heavily on aerobic endurance until you are able to withstand the more intense aerobic and anaerobic threshold training. If you are a fit runner, cycler, mountaineer, or alpinist you may only do cardio endurance training a few times a month or solely under the endurance phase, focusing your main efforts on threshold training. If you are focusing on short, high-intensity difficult pitches you may want to focus solely on anaerobic threshold and toss in aerobic threshold training occasionally. If cardio is a major limiting factor, start training as soon as possible. If you just want an edge and some benefit from cardio training, start a couple of months before your performance phase. To get any benefit from cardio training, however, you will need to get at least three cardio sessions in a week so it's best to concentrate your efforts.

ALTERNATE PHASES FOR HARD ENDURANCE ROCK, ICE, ALPINE, AND ALTITUDE CLIMBS
For those climbers attempting long hard endurance climbs like link-ups, multi-day traverses, massive alpine climbs, and big mountain climbs at altitude you will want to take a different approach to periodizing your training. The **general foundation phase** should be about 1-2 months getting back in shape and addressing imbalances. The **strength foundation phase** will also last 1-2 months, but the focus should be strengthening large muscle groups and lots of light to moderate cardio at 55-75% max HR.

The next phase is the **strength phase** and will last 3-5 months of sub-divided strength protocols: **power, power-endurance, and strength-endurance**. During this phase you will be spending a lot of time racking up milage on climbs. The climbs should be below your redpoint limit, however you will still want to occasionally get on some hard projects to stay sharp. The goal is to get fast and confident to move quickly over "moderate" terrain - be it a snow slog, or moderate rock/ice climb.

You will need to train cardio. If doing climbs at altitude or climbs that a ton of moderate terrain must be covered quickly you will need to do a lot of cardio. Begin training anaerobic endurance supplemented with moderate cardio still at 55-75% max HR. Move into slightly easier but still anaerobic efforts at 90-95% max HR. Spend several weeks training aerobic threshold by doing hour long hard efforts at 80-90%. Muscular strength begins by training maximum power, followed by power-endurance and strength-endurance protocols already outlined in detail. The next phase is a bit like the **performance phase**. This phase should last a few weeks to two months training for the technical aspects of your goal. This is when you get on progressively harder climbs that work up to and simulate your goal. Finally, visit the **rest phase** for 2-3 weeks.

PUTTING THE PLAN TOGETHER

You now have every tool to make a fully formed training plan. I am going to assume that you are starting with the foundation phase. Start by getting your monthly schedule and make sure it has everything on it and it makes sense. Your list of climbing skills, ability exercises, climbing specific exercises, warm-ups, and non-climbing exercises should already be organized by phases (foundation, strength, endurance, rest), season (where and what you'll be climbing), and by progressive difficulty (climbs and exercises). You should also have your list of climbing and non-climbing weaknesses, and self-improvements scheduled as well. The only thing left to do is to make a daily or weekly exercise plan.

GRAPH AND JOURNAL

This is just an idea on how to organize your training into a daily or weekly plan. Yours way may be better. Make a spreadsheet with a computer or graph paper. Label the top Foundation Phase and enter in the start date and projected ending date. Make the top columns days of the week. Make copies for additional weeks (but it will probably change as you tweak it). Now write in the first row "Warm-Up". You can refer to your list of exercises what your warm-ups are to save space. In the next row, write "Skills" to refer to the list of skills you will be training for during this phase. Next to the skills (and the other rows), write how many days per week you would like to practice them. The next row should be "Ability" exercises. You can just keep it at that and place an X to show what days you went climbing, or make groups like "redpointing", "offwidth", etc. It just depends on how many ability focuses you have going on at once. You can even write in the empty boxes how many pitches you climbed, the grades, or how many hours. Again, write how many days a week you want to practice Ability exercises. For the climbing specific exercises you may want to make a row for each individual or group of exercises labeled "Fingerboard", "Campusing", "Pull-Ups", "System Board", "Strength-Endurance", "Power-Endurance", etc. with how many days you plan on training each. For the non-climbing exercises make rows for "Core", "Antagonist", "Cardio", "Shoulder Rehab", "Other", etc. Your final row should be "Stretching".

If you have a lot of non-climbing exercises you can further separate them into body area (Legs, Chest, etc.), put them into alternating groups to avoid overdoing a body area or protocol (Group A exercises, Group B exercises, etc.), or just try and keep track of what you've done. If doing a lot of non-climbing exercises that requires a bit more organization like Cardio, you could break them down into protocols (Endurance, Aerobic Threshold, Anaerobic Threshold).

However you organize things, it is best that the end result is a simple page you can look at to see what needs to get done that week. Worry about making a spreadsheet for the other phases when you get close, as you will probably make significant changes by that time based on what happens during your foundation phase.

On the back of the page or on a white board you can list all the exercises in an organized fashion to refer just what those strength-endurance exercises are, for example. On the list of exercises you can write your current weight and reps and your desired goal. It can help to organize exercises by body area, type (core, antag, rehab, warm-up, functional, pulling, pushing, etc.), and how to do the exercise (eccentric, isometric, plyometric, concentric), and what protocol (endurance, strength, power, strength-endurance). Keeping your exercises super organized will not only help you pick and choose exactly how and when to do them now, but will give you a head start for future phases. You may even want to write in the exercises for future phases on your list so you'll have a master list you can always go back to.

You can add more rows if you need to keep track of other things like your weight, other weaknesses or lifestyle modifications, additional activities, or reminders. At the end of the week you could pencil in what you want to work on the next week. A good idea is to also keep a journal to write out exactly what you did every day to have a detailed training log. You may think you remember what you did, but after an unexpected break or after enough time passes, you'll want to see where you left off, or what needs to get done. Finally, writing in how long it takes to do an exercise or group of exercises will help you better manage your time.

After everything is down on paper you can start to plan on what days you'll do each row. Make sure to plan in rest days, avoid overdoing the suggested amount per week, and stacking too many hard protocols on top of each other or in a row. You may have to split each column (day of the week) into A.M. and P.M. to pack it all in.

TWEAKING THE PLAN
You'll probably tweak this list several times the first few weeks, so having it on your computer is a good idea. Don't get stuck on an exercise – if you've attained your goal for that exercise, cross it off. If you're hesitant to do so, come back to it in a couple weeks and re-check your progress on it. Remember to keep track of everything you did in a daily journal, and record the reps, weight, time, side that was difficult, etc. If you notice that say, only your left glut is weak during a core stability exercise, save time and only do that side. Or if only one side is tight, just stretch that side.

Keep track of your skills and climbing ability. Move onto new skills once old skills are mastered. Tick off your pyramids. Keep an eye on your monthly schedule to make sure you are on track. If you are pretty close, then just keep an eye on what you didn't finish; it may resolve itself in the other phases. If you are way behind, re-evaluate your goal or figure out what's keeping you behind. Decide if you need to spend more time on a phase, or if you can get away with jumping ahead. Finally, keep your eye on the goal and what's really important: climbing. If you find yourself obsessing over a tight hamstring, a weak external rotator, and a shaky core – get over it and move on.

Remember that you can double-up on some exercises by doing two things at the same time or one exercise that gets several muscle groups. Just don't cheap yourself. This is not set in stone. After a week of doing an exercise 3 times per week and you've brushed the cobwebs off, scale back to 1 time per week, or take it off the list for a while. Don't get caught up in doing exercises you think you should be doing because they are what you are used to doing or see others doing. Maybe your list of non-climbing exercises are all body weight and you notice that you are not doing any heavy lifting. Don't force an exercise in that you are already proficient in. The only exercises that you need to be doing are climbing specific exercises, even if that only includes outdoor climbing. Likewise, if your goal is general mountaineering, there is little reason to be doing things like campusing and fingerboard training.

Keep your climbing specific training fixed if possible. In other words, if you planned on climbing 4 days a week, schedule your other exercises around it, unless you are so weak and imbalanced that those need priority for a while. Try and pre-plan each week when you'll be able to go climbing. If this week you can only go Saturday and Sunday, schedule those in and now you have 5 days to do other training.

You can periodize your plan however you want. You may find that making a plan for the day at hand and just training what you feel needs work is perfect for you and your schedule, or you can only create or stick to a weekly plan. Mini cycles work well for most climbers who can never seem to stick to a long-term plan. Train one or more areas at a time, progressively increasing intensity/volume. Alternate your focus every couple weeks so that one area does not get too de-trained. Just sticking to a list of exercises and doing the same thing every week won't produce results, but it will probably keep you at your current level. This isn't a bad plan for staying fit during an extended performance phase, or when you simply don't want to spend a lot of time dealing with programming. Whatever your plan, the more you intelligently plan your day, week, month, or year instead of just randomly doing "whatever", the more you will improve. However, doing anything is better than nothing. You cannot regain lost time.

Fitting it In

It can become overwhelming if you have a ton of exercise and climbing plans. How to fit it all in takes organization, time management, determination, and sacrifice. Climbing comes first unless you have an injury to rehab or are totally plateaued. One way to fit it all in is to make a weekly calendar with your work or school schedule written in.

Try and make "groups" of exercises like: Aerobic, Performance Climbing, Antagonist and Core, etc., and have a good idea how long these take. Take your grouped training blocks and write down how many times a week you want to train them. Look at your work/school schedule and add up (realistic) free time to train. If you can plug your blocks of training in, great! If not, you need to prioritize and dump some exercises, rotate through exercise instead of repeating them, or save them for another phase or round of training. Look at recovery times for types of exercise and be sure to plan this in. Prepare to compromise and to not have this set in stone.

The first week or so, your workouts will take longer. As you get more efficient and maybe cross some stuff off, your times should decrease. It's a good idea to write down in your journal how long each group of exercises took. This way if you are looking at the clock and you have a half hour until you must leave, you will know what you can fit in and what needs to be sacrificed.

There are a few ways to fit training in throughout the day to cut down on your gym time. Can you split up your training in the morning, at lunch, your 15-minute break, and or after work? Is there anything you can do that won't interfere physically during your climbing days? Go through all of your selected exercises and note when you could be doing it, and stick it on a notecard in your pocket. Can you do any of the exercises on the phone, while cooking, watching TV? Can you combine some exercises or do two at the same time? You might need to plan your food and changes of clothes/equipment if you're running between school, work, and the gym. Also, bring some gear to work like a fingerboard if you can. Studies have shown that performance is best in the evening, but the best time to exercise is different for most people, so if you find that your energy levels are highest at a particular time of day, try and plan your training then. The same goes with planning times for your onsights and redpoints. Always have water and snacks handy.

> Your performance days while training should be 1.5 to 3 days post training. To be able to perform your best and recover from hard training you have a couple options.
> - By week: Follow every hard day by an easy day or two maxing out at 3 hard days a week and take 1 day off a week. If you are adapted you can do 2 hard days in a row, but still no more than 3 hard days per week.
> - By Month: 3 weeks on followed by 1 week off if training hard, 2:1 if training very hard.

REST

Training breaks your body down and rewires your brain and nervous system. Gains in strength and skill are built during your rest periods, known as the reminiscence effect. New tissue gets built and your brain sorts out new programs (kind of like when updates get installed on your computer and have to restart it for them to take effect). During periods of intense training you will need more rest. You may need to increase your sleep time to 9-10 hours a night after some hard days. Don't slip below 7 hours during your training. The amount of time to rest between exercises depends on how tired you are (if you are too tired to do the next set or exercise then wait!) and the type of training you are doing. For most exercises you just need a couple of minutes to recuperate. You can switch to an easy exercise while recovering to be efficient. Between hard climbs, plan on at least 20 minutes. Some exercises require 1-3 days before doing them again.

The most important thing do is listening to your body. It takes time to decide if you really need a break, or if you need to dig deep and push on. If you wake up with your heart rate racing, get a bad night's sleep, simple exercises sound exhausting, you start to get irritable, your sex drive plummets, or your climbing ability starts to take a nose dive, take a day or more off - even a week or two. It's ok if it throws off your schedule. Your schedule is not set in stone and if you're that tired, you've probably done a pretty good job and need a break. This may also be a sign that you programmed your training poorly and need to change up when you do your different exercises (maybe your body doesn't respond to doing pushups, dips, and pull-ups in the same day).

There are several things you can do during your rest period. The first is to eat eat eat, and eat. Dieters, this is a choice day to have your cheat day. This is a great time to go out to dinner, have a potluck or BBQ with friends, or to make your fancy breakfast. Stack on those calories, but also stuff your face with nutrient rich fruits and veggies.

Replenish your liver's depleted glycogen stores, healthy fats that are essential for your connective tissues and nerves, and vitamins, minerals and electrolytes.

Take your mind off climbing. Go to the library or bookstore, see a movie, or do a light activity that will delight your significant other like dancing, ice-skating, roller blading, fishing, or easy bike riding. Go on a fun easy climb you never would have bothered, or a hike. Get a massage. You may have noticed that I'm all about lists. I keep a list of all the fun city and mountain activities I never get to do because of work, school, or climbing.

Sleep
As mentioned, get more sleep. It is a much better idea to go to bed earlier to get more sleep than it is to sleep in longer. If you just can't fall asleep, don't force it. Get up at the same time every day, however. The idea is to get your body used to a normal cycle, and waking up at various hours won't help. When the alarm goes off or you become conscious regardless of an alarm, wake up. Staggering alarms, or hitting the snooze puts you into non-REM sleep and will make you more tired. Some smartphone apps measure body movements, and will wake you up when they predict your sleep cycle is in the lightest phase. Blue lights, like the **Phillips GoLight**, used right when you wake up will help get your body on a normal cycle. **Melatonin**, mentioned in the nutrition chapter, can also be taken for a short time before bed to also help get your body clock reset. Most people get the best sleep if they go to bed before 11 pm (in bed by 10:30) and feel the groggiest if they wake up between the hours of 7-9 am.

Cooler temps in the bedroom will help you fall asleep and stay asleep. A good mattress can do wonders for your sleep and body. Ice baths shortly before bed have been shown to knock you out as well. Don't drink alcohol, caffeine, or watch TV just before bedtime. Try and keep your exercise three hours before bedtime, although recent studies has started to debunk that you shouldn't exercise before bed so it's your call. Careful with midday naps, they can really screw up your schedule. When the clock hits a certain time, start your winding down process, and turn down the lights. Eat something before bedtime with some sugar, fat and protein, like a nut-based spread, so you don't wake up with low blood sugar that can make you really groggy. Sleep apnea, especially in overweight individuals, is another common cause of poor sleep.

Taking quality 20-minute naps can totally invigorate you. They also cut down on the amount of sleep you need, or they can totally screw up your sleep schedule. I know that if I nap, I do not have enough will power to do it for 20 minutes and I wind up totally screwing up my schedule. For those who can, some people have been known to live on only 20 minute naps scheduled every 4 hours! This could be helpful for those doing a multiday no sleep alpine climbs, or those with extremely hectic schedules. I'm not advocating not sleeping, but if you can't fit 8 hours of sleep in but you do have 20 minutes to spare, you may be able to endure a little better. It takes training to fall asleep fast enough during a 20-minute nap. Don't add extra time if you don't fall asleep – get up after 20 minutes regardless. For more information on using napping to cut down on the bulk of your sleep time, research "phasic sleep".

TRAINING FOR HIGH-LEVEL OR UNIQUE CLIMBS
Alpinists may need to focus on their legs, cardio, climbing endurance, and foundational exercises a lot more than other climbers. Your general weight training and cardio foundation phase could take 6-8 months if training for something huge, and include routine 10-16 hour days in the mountains several times a week. If it's just

long hard routes then plan on getting in 20 pitch days regularly. Likewise, hard general mountaineering objectives may need to spend most of the time training cardio and legs, doing an average of 2 hours cardio (700+ hours a year) per day.

There will be a point for some climbers that the training in this book won't work anymore. At this point their weaknesses become highly specific and difficult to train. Very few, if any, climbers can become a 5.12 generalist. Each difficult climb requires different training. The standard advice becomes a waste of words here because this type of climber already knows it (like take time off, climb somewhere else, go bouldering). There may be a few things you have not tried, however.

The first is video feedback of your attempts by you, and highly skilled others. One of you may find the key. Also, if you have the opportunity to watch someone else successfully climb the route, ask them detailed questions, videotape them, and have them watch you. The final piece of advice, and this applies to training for unique climbs (off-width, inverted cracks, etc.): create a simulation of the climb. Can you build a wall at home, or piece together several different climbs with similar moves, similar rock, steepness, gear, etc.? Try and climb these "simulations" at high reps and maybe even with some weight in the pack.

Get In More Pitches
Bad Weather
Build skills if conditions are good enough to at least toprope, practice aid climbing, ropework, rescue skill etc. Is there a cave or overhang to keep you dry? Can you bring a heater, puffy jacket, or build a leave no trace fire to at least belay near? If the sun is out and it's cold, can you find a South facing cliff or West facing cliff in the afternoon? If it's too hot can you climb in the a.m. and p.m. and chase the shade? If it's windy, sometimes changing crags or aspects can make a huge difference. The weather is always nice in the climbing gym.

Dawn and Dusk Patrol
Go climbing after a long day when you'd normally sit in front of the tube drinking beer, or super early hours before you'd normally get up and go to work. What about RIGHT NOW? Short sessions scheduled into a normal day a few days a week can be some of the best climbing sessions you can have, and the most productive. It's never crowed at 6 am.

Weekend or longer trips can be shortened by rain, driving, camping logistics, rest days, fatigue or mental exhaustion. They also can be more expensive. Pre/post work climbs can also be that extra something to make you a better climber. I know many 9 to 5'ers with families that get way more done with no weekend trips than some full-time climbers! More can be accomplished by training at your local area than you think, no matter how crappy it may be. Finally there's just something the low-light quiet of the crag at pre-dawn, and the paradigm shift between work and play in the same day.

No Partner
Rope-soloing doesn't have to be sketchy, especially if you can setup a toprope. Part Three has detailed instructions on how-to. If you actually get good at it (efficient that is), another world just opened up for getting out more. Go through your guidebook and check out those easier climbs you initially wrote off and solo them. If you don't want to solo with or without a rope, go check out areas for first ascents, or scout the approach, start, or descent off a climb you really want to do to maximize success.

Training On a Climbing Trip
If you will be away from home during one of your training phases, it would be a good

idea to have a list of exercises and gear to bring with you so you don't fall behind or lose ground. Bring your journal and write down a list of skills to work on while climbing to keep up your technique improvement such as: body tension, center of gravity, high stepping, climbing with a single rack, night climbing, etc. Next have a list of supplemental gear to bring along so you can train more effectively. Creativity helps, so plan ahead. For example: rock rings, suspension training system, running shoes, closed cell foam sleeping pad, a hand training device, and a TheraCane are highly portable.

Finally, list all of the exercises in your training program that you think you can do while on your trip. You may want to add some extra exercises not in your program for rest days. You may be able to find a tree to use your suspension system on. A picnic table, a pack with some rocks in it, and maybe some larger rocks for weights can mimic your exercise program. But, most importantly, tailor what you are going to actually climb towards your plan and goals.

Missing Exercises and Days
Although you really should stick to the plan, things come up you didn't plan for. If you can get in at least one day a week of climbing and or exercises that are highly important to your goal, do so. This will keep you at the same level for a while. I can't tell you for how long, but generally enough to ride it out. If you are really sick for a whole week, just start from where you left off, and at the end of the phase, decide if you need to tack on another week or few days. If you ran out of time and the exercise is important, make it the priority for the next day. But if your training plan is ambitious and time is limited, just let it go. If it's a climbing trip that interrupts your plan, then you may be focusing too heavily on non-climbing exercises because a climbing trip is the perfect training.

Let's say you can't get out climbing for quite some time, or you have an injury. Yes, you will have to make that time up, but during the meantime, continue with what exercises you can do. When you return to climbing, you may have to have two separate out of sync training plans. Guides and seasonal employees who work non-stop for chunks of time need to plan differently. Make a training plan for when you are working and one for when you are not. If for some reason you find yourself with free time and want to do more, go to the gym or outside and do some bouldering, or work on weak antagonists. Remember that endurance gains are quickly lost. You may be able to quickly regain your strength, but totally poop out on longer climbs. Training easier endurance routes may get you back up to speed much more quickly than doing shorter, harder routes. Another reason why a doing few long easy climbs makes you feel much stronger. After two months of ceasing training only 10% of muscular strength is lost, but 30-40% of muscular endurance is lost.

Off-Season Phase
For those of you with an off-season, those that need to give their fingers and toes a break, or folks that focus on a different sports during a particular time of the year, like skiers, you may want to change up your training to a more conditioning-based training program. I suggest that everyone take at least a month or two out of the year to recover from climbing and build a stronger foundation. This is where classes like Cross-Fit, Seal-Fit, Gym Jones, Mountain Athlete, Insanity, TRX, or P90X fit in nicely. There are a million DVDs, personal trainers, books, group classes, and online videos out there for general fitness. I would recommend a group class or posted workout of the day via Gym Jones, CrossFit, or Mountain Athlete over anything else. One of the best online general conditioning videos I've seen is Bodyrock.tv. I first scoffed at the scantily

clad, large breasted, wafer thin vixens on these videos, but when I was finally able to pay attention to the exercises, I was actually very impressed. One of the original trainers broke off and started her own series on YouTube called Zuzkalight, which is also excellent. Also, visit the exercises in the Upper and Lower Body Supplemental Exercises. You can add a lot of the next season's foundation phase into the off-season, but when beginning again, be sure to do foundation climbing exercises. Revisiting the foundation climbing exercises keeps you with a beginners mind so you force yourself to learn new things and find new weaknesses instead of plateauing.

PLATEAU

When you are a beginner you will improve dramatically by doing just about anything. In the vague mid-ground when you have lots of experience, but haven't continued to push yourself and try new things, or continue to improve on even basic stuff, you plateau. Once you get better and break out of that plateau, you will have more specific goals in sight. But to get off that plateau, you need to make sacrifices – do you want to? Why would you? Climbing harder opens up a whole new world of richness. Being able to do the North Ridge of Stuart in a day or Epinephrine off the couch with no directed climbing training is great. But don't you want to climb Astroman? The Nose in a day? Redpoint Coyne Crack? Go to Baffin and do a first ascent knowing you have the tools for a big hard wall? Unless you have some severe physical limitations, you can. One problem: it will be hard. As a guide friend of mine once told a client, "You're climbing a mountain. It's not supposed to be easy". You can still climb those long fun classics when you're 70, your significant other begs you, or you have a partner who can't climb at your level.

Try Harder!

Most people do not put the time in to train to climb hard. Good climbers either are always climbing and rack up literally thousands of pitches a year, or treat their training like a full time job. Try hard on the climbs you are on, and make the most out of your climbing day. You can probably do more. Depending on your goal some of your training days should be long and grueling. Don't expect much gain from casually doing exercises and training.

Don't forget that you will constantly need to increase both volume and intensity. Volume and intensity are similar to endurance and strength. In general start with increasing the intensity, then upping the volume. After the volume becomes tolerable, increase the intensity again!

Total plateau? Don't know what to train? That's like a kid saying I'm bored. Change up your type of climbing. Sure you tear it up at Indian Creek – how are you at crimpy run out slabs? Go do the North Face of the Grand Teton in awful conditions. Getting out of a plateau requires you to take a step back from your ego and desires to figure out what's really going on. Your concept of your actual ability is probably skewed if you continually fail or plateau. Back off and try slightly easier climbs, and revisit old neglected skills. High-level climbers have a different reason for plateauing. The better you get, the more specific your goals and your training needs to be. It could mean training one specific skill in very creative ways, and pairing your goals down to one single route – or changing the goal temporarily to something very similar, but slightly different. Then come back to it.

The Importance of Cragging and Moderate Climbs

If you're like me and only want to do long routes or difficult cragging, you may notice that you've hit a plateau or actually have gotten worse over the season. The detraining effect of just doing long routes is part physical and part mental. As mentioned, training endurance detrains strength and power over time. However, it is really mentally challenging to push yourself to make difficult, sustained, or desperate moves with pitches looming ahead, or the ground spinning below. I can't stress how important cragging (or bouldering) is to keeping yourself strong and sharp. Cragging will build back up the strength and power lost from a long day in the mountains, and the relaxed atmosphere will allow you to push it on the relatively short terrain. You can use the memories and experience from these cragging session when faced with a similar pitch high up on a long route.

The next topic, moderate climbing, has also been discussed numerous times, but scattered through this book. I want to reemphasis the extreme importance of this concept once more. Moderate climbing means climbing that you can do no problem - all fear and anxiety gone - but is difficult enough not to be boring. Remember how I mentioned that almost every sport besides climbing will find the bulk of training practicing skills and drills? You don't see videos of olympic athletes at training camp just going all out performing their full activity. I listed a ton of skills to practice, but honestly, the best venue to practice the bulk of your skills is on moderate terrain - and lots of it!

Throwing yourself on difficult climbs won't gain you much except an occasional success and some strength gains, but milage on easier routes will train your technique, hone your mind, and improve your skills. As mentioned, even moderate climbs contain the moves, holds, and gear as harder climbs do. A 5.12 climber climbs a 5.10 like a 5.10 climber climbs a 5.8. So if you're a 5.10 climber, doing a ton of 5.8's well will start to make that 5.10 seem easier. This applies to all types of climbers - from boulderers to alpinists. Just change the setting and type of training to mimic your desired venue. So next time you start to plateau, or you struggle on longer climbs, just try a day of moderate climbing and a day of cragging and you will be surprised at the results. If this convinces you, start to incorporate lots and lots of moderates and cragging into your routine.

STAYING MOTIVATED

Doing something is better than doing nothing. This is an essential concept. Time wasted is time lost, and the less you do, the easier it becomes to do nothing. Training and willpower require momentum. So no matter how you "train", make the best of your time. If exercise is part of your training and you're super busy, just doing 10 minutes a day will create momentum to get you to either do the same, or more the next day. Skipping out and saying, "I'll do it tomorrow" will most likely happen again, tomorrow. The same goes with all aspects of putting forth the willpower to make you a better climber: take the fall today, toprope that training lap, go out and learn that aid trick...whatever.

Entropy and age suck. Before you know it you'll be old, past your prime, and have lost the skills. If those things have already happened to you, you can always start today. It's never too late to start. It is very difficult to get over the mentality of, "I'll just wait until I start my new job," or "after I move into my new house". Life will always get in the way, sapping will power and motivation. Plan ahead, adapt, and stick with it. An all-or-nothing mentality will most likely degrade into the nothing end of the spectrum. It is also much more difficult to start from scratch.

Taking a Break
You have to have some "me" time. For some, this can just be an extended per-

formance phase, or going back to that tick list and doing some hard climbs or easier classics you're still dreaming about. The more active you are in climbing, the less training you'll need to redo later on.

Let's say you just broke into 5.11s and this opens up a vast potential of new routes you want to climb or put up. You may want to spend a couple years plateaued in this level on purpose. 5.10 is just as fun to a 5.10 climber as 5.12 is to a 5.12 climber. You may need to train periodically to maintain 5.11 or 5.12 status, however. Anyway, the mileage you put in is important to make you a solid 5.10, 5.11, or whatever level climber.

Sometime in your life, you'll probably need a total break from climbing. Maybe you're just sick of the stress of planning trips, finding partners, bailing because of weather, or maybe you want to focus on a career or a family. Don't freak out! So many people do this and get right back into things after a few years. You'll probably wind up enjoying climbing more than ever, and have the wisdom of having taken a step back in your favor. No matter how it is you take a break, whenever you get the itch to start again or break into new grades, let the training begin!

Burning Out, Training After an Injury, or After a Trip

When you get back from a trip, especially an exhausting one, it is hard to start training again. Besides all the post-trip crap you have to deal with (unpacking, emails, chores, grocery shopping, job duties, family, etc.), you may be too burned out to train for a bit. That's ok. Remember to refuel and recharge your battery by getting in some sleep, rest, and food – "the vacation from your vacation". Take as much time as you need, but set a start date in your calendar ASAP. Be sure to get back on the horse, since as mentioned, it will become harder and harder to get back into a routine the longer you put it off.

If you are injured, stay in shape by training whatever body part is not affected by your injury if possible. During your injury, take the time to re-tailor your plan to accommodate this minor to major setback. Take this time to learn new skills and practice old ones. Many times after an injury, you may actually climb better than ever because you will be forced to climb more thoughtfully.

Sometimes, especially after a very hard climb or an epic, your performance will take a nosedive. Climbing will feel like beating your head against a wall, and you will get burned out. If this happens, or you just get burned out for whatever reason, STOP and re-evaluate everything that you are doing to find your mental and physical block. One sure fix is to climb something you know will be fun and not overly challenging. Too many bad days, hard climbs, and epics will crush your spirit.

Chapter Six: Mental Training

EGO

It can certainly be argued that your mind is the most important aspect of climbing performance. Strength, skill and technique are only physical limitations. They are usually not the main reason for success or failure. This chapter will explore ways to manage your ego, fear, willpower, and motivation to keep you from failing or bailing. Planning, decision-making, and technical knowledge are also forms of mental training and are discussed many places throughout the book.

Without getting into strict psychological definitions, I'm going to use the term "ego" as how you view or want to view yourself and how you want or believe others to view you as. It is extremely important to ground yourself in reality if you are out of synch with "true reality" which is basically the mountain's point of view.

CRITICAL THINKING

Don't fall victim to Hype, it is one of the worst things in our climbing culture. Succumbing to hype means doing something, buying something, climbing something, or taking an attitude because it's cool. Challenge yourself and challenge the opinions of others. Ignore what idiots say on Internet forums, arguments online are bottomless pits of spray. Critical thinking is the most important skill you can have in climbing. Always ask yourself why, is there a better way, or is what I'm going a good idea. Always be self-critiquing of your negative ways of thinking and poor planning decisions. Be open to new ideas, and challenge your partner's decisions even if you just met. If you think something is a bad idea, be vocal and firm. Being polite can get you killed. Going along with the herd can lead from mild to grave things such as discomfort, wasted time or money, loss of self-confidence/respect, poor ethical decisions, epics involving you or others you pass your hype onto, and injury or death. However, when executing actual climbing moves, too much critical thinking can hinder your performance.

COMPARING YOURSELF TO OTHERS

Climb for yourself. Someone will always be better than you, the mountain will still be there, and many people in their 60's and 70's can climb hard too. Your goals are you own and you can't compare yourself to others. No one has the same experiences and background as you do. Does anyone really care what route you climbed, or how well you climbed it? Unless you're doing a major first ascent or repeating a serious test piece, you're not going to make into the magazines.

Yes, public high-end climbers do get a lot of respect, hype, groupies, and are put on a pedestal. But for every one of those, there are hundreds of low key hardcore climbers whose names are never dropped. It takes a lot of self-promotion to become one of those climbing "stars", and their time in the sun is short lived. In climbing films and magazines you are shown an edited version of those climbers – only their successes and high points of achievement. You don't see their failures (in life and climbing). Better climbers are not better people, even if some do act like it. Wanting to become a sponsored climber or competition winner isn't a bad goal. I'm just letting you know that it's not an easy life, and luck plays a huge role in success.

You also can't compare yourself to your climbing partners or others at the crag and the gym. Again, they don't have the same experiences you have had. If you see a great 5.14 climber at a new crag for him/her, you'll probably see him/her climbing 11's or easy 12's. Do the same – learn the rock by hopping on some 5.7's or 5.8's – don't expect to be sending 10d's. It is all relative.

That kid next to you who's climbing that sport route way better than you and has only been climbing for a year may a.)be lying b.)have been working that route constantly c.)only climb at that crag d.)only ever climbs sport routes e.)may be genetically gifted. In any event, none of that matters. Would you want to swap your broader experiences in climbing for that? If you're less genetically gifted, then your "handicap" may make you a better climber! If this experience made you realize that you've been lazy, or overly scared, or wasting time – then use this opportunity to make it a learning experience and apply that new self-discovery. If you don't apply it, then just be happy and have fun. What will demotivate you and cause self-hate would be to not apply this new information and not be content with your current performance compared to others.

Social media, Internet forums, and climbing media have made it very difficult to not care about what other people are doing. When you see 50 friends posting that they all just got back from a bunch of awesome climbs you want to do, you can feel that you should have been on every one of those trips – even if you just were on one yourself! Magazines, videos, Internet sites, advertisements, blogs, and journal publications are chock full of images and stories of thousands of people doing amazing things in amazing places. Our brains usually don't have to capacity to separate these out into rationale scenarios: every person is an individual, they didn't do all of these things, and you only see people at their best in a single moment of time. Odds are they individually had just as many rained out and sucky days as you did and hadn't been on a trip for 6 months prior. Most of the ads and a good majority of the photos and stories you see about others are also consciously or subconsciously trying to make you feel this way to boost their own egos, or to sell gear and magazines.

One of the worst ego traps you can find yourself in is worrying about telling your friends who you already told what route you were going to do, people camping next to you who asked what you did today, or even random hikers on the way down asking "did you make it?" that you bailed. I hear you, that just sucks. First, they don't really care. Maybe they will downgrade your status in their mind for a second or two (ouch!), but you and your failure will be quickly forgotten. They will fail at some point in the near future, and at many things in life as well. You will too. Get over it. It's just climbing. Another thing you can do is not being so judgmental about other climbers as well. Don't mock the newbie, the bad climber, or your friend that bailed on a route you cruised. If you stop judging, you will stop caring what they think. Suck it up, say you failed, and tell them why. You may be surprised at the stories of failure hardmen will tell you if you put your defenses down.

Besides the fact that some climbers are just plain able to grow stronger than you, are more genetically gifted than you, taller than you, have better centers of gravity than you, longer ape indexes than you, lighter than you, smaller/bigger hands than you, longer fingers than you, tendons are attached at more mechanically advantageous locations than you, better muscle fiber type than you….some climbers just more have natural "God-given" talent. Someone with similar proportions that has been climbing way less than you can just totally school you. This is natural talent, and the answer why they can climb so well when you can't. There's nothing you can do about this except put more fight and gumption into your climbing, and use it as another excuse to try harder! Making the best of the ability you have, be it climbing new remote routes, racking up serious mileage, or completing multiple linkups in your grade level (just to name a few), in my opinion, makes you a better climber than say, someone who can climb 5.13 but only climbs similar rock at local or destination crags.

KNOW THYSELF
You must truly know yourself and have the self-discipline to do so. It's ok not to, most of us don't. But to avoid wasted time and bailing/failing all over the place, you need to admit to yourself what you can and cannot do. Most climbers have an exaggerated picture of how well they climbed in the past. A lot of this has to do with how quickly

climbers improve in their first few years of climbing. Imagine that you've been climbing for several years and you are falling all over 5.11 routes, but five years ago you on-sighted or redpointed a few 5.11 routes. That experience gets stuck in your head because it was such an accomplishment for you at the time.

Memories of memories are just like copies of copies – they get distorted over time. So now you think "I used to be able to climb 5.11"! That's not true, you only climbed a few 5.11's and they were probably easy for the grade and matched your unique style. You may now have a much more solid base. The thing to do here is to find that grade (it will be different for all type of areas and rocks) where you need to broaden your base – not hammer at the top of your pyramid. For this climber, it may need to be climbing a lot more 5.10c's – way lower than that 5.11.

You need to know your physical and technical limitations. How long can you climb though a pump before falling? Practice this and actually fall due to physical inability. Good climbers know this, trust their gear, partner, and ability – and then go for it. Pushing through is safe if you know your limitations, gear, and options. It is not safe if you don't.

Getting a psych on for a hard climb is very helpful, but you must know that you can do it. Picking a hard climb in a grade that you've done only a few times and just hoping it works out will end up in failure or injury. Badly wanting to do routes you're not prepared for means you're succumbing to ego, or unwillingness to put the time in. Only occasionally can you treat a long hard route like a crag – working a pitch, pulling the rope, and trying the redpoint.

Doubt eats at the mind and affects performance. It's ok to push it at the crag if the gear is safe, but not on long routes or sketchy leads. Some other examples are: not being aware of your energy levels, planning poorly so you exhaust your energy levels, not knowing you've plateaued or doing nothing about it, too many failures, not trusting pro, equipment or partners, thinking failure is a bad thing, thinking a particular grade is easy, not being aware of fatigue or other issues that may make you climb poorer today and changing plans. Magical thinking will not change a climb, but it will offer a harsh wake-up call when reality sets in. Reading guidebooks and making plans with friends (especially if drinking) is a great way to create some extreme forms of magical thinking. It's amazing how weightless and effortless movement is when daydreaming about a climb.

One final thought is to try climbing without a guidebook. Make sure that there is enough gear and the bolts are spaced close enough to bail if necessary. You may be better than you think without the psyche of the grade causing you to fail by expecting to.

Expectations

Let go of expectations. Not all climbs and areas are equal, and everyone has bad days. Your only expectation should be to try your best at your current state of being, and that the climb is what it is. If a climb is long and hard, expect it to be long and hard. If the climb is full on, then expect to suffer. If you are frustrated that a climb totally stops you, then you have seriously misjudged yourself and the climb. Learn from it, and don't give a crap what grade it was or who climbed it. High expectations lead to disappointment, and low expectations lead to poor performance. If you start acting like an ass to your partner or find yourself having a temper-tantrum, your expectations are outta whack.

GRADES, QUALITY, AND WHY WE CLIMB

Climbing allows us to achieve our "moment of Zen". It allows us to have a sense of accomplishment in a world already mapped out and full of rules and responsibility. It is so very difficult to achieve financial and career goals – most of us never do. Once the school-job-marriage-house-kids thing plays out, our main societal goals are fulfilled. Those of us privileged enough to bother reading such a specialized book like this probably don't toil endlessly, live in war and chaos, or have many real hardships. You don't see people with real hardships out climbing…unless it is (or has been made) their job. So climbing may be the only time in our structured, corporate, sanitized life where one can actually make hard decisions, be creative, and be part of, not observer to, nature. It's almost like going to war, or watching "Fight Club" one too many times. But, if you are out to prove something to yourself or others (which is really to yourself because they don't care), you are doing it for the wrong reasons. You actually may not fail because of this – many great things have been done for this reason – but it's not worth it in the long run.

That said: a climb is what it is. It's a piece of rock that's basically just been sitting there for a few billion years. It doesn't give a crap if you climb it or not, a million years later it will probably still be there, and what you did on it will be long forgotten. Climbers personify the climb by interpreting it aesthetically and categorizing it. It's only rock climbing – you don't make the world or anyone better by doing it. Ants and lizards send your project upside-down all day long. There are climbs better than your project, and there will always be climbers better than you.

You can over glorify a climb – obsess over a route for whatever reason, wanting to do a route with an Ahab-like mentality. Maybe it's 5-stars, the longest, unrepeated, or the last on your list for that area. The problem with this mentality is that it closes you off from other opportunities. Let's say it takes two days of driving or hiking – maybe there's something closer: two days wasted. Maybe the 5-star climb has a line a mile long and there are tons of possibly fun 2-star climbs all over. Now let's say you fail. Fine, it could happen anywhere. Instead of waiting for all of the planets to align in your favor, you try again – and fail. Keeping an open mind and deciding when and where you're going to climb will give you a lot more experience and memories. And after you ticked your white whale?

Memories and feelings don't last too long, and you can't box up your experience and take it with you. Many climbers get post-climb depression after big climbs. A lot has to do with physical and mental exhaustion, but it can last. I'm not saying to not go climb a big long remote route or do an amazing 5-star route by the way. Just take the blinders off and realize you may be expecting more than you will receive. (On a side note: as a rule, the more stars a climb gets, the more sustained or old it is, so it can feel sandbagged. My wife won't climb anything 5.9+ put up by anyone named Lowe or pre-1980!)

It's been said before somewhere, but I'll say it again: "Grades Don't Mean Shit!" Grades can be all over the place, even at the same area. The scale isn't exactly linear in difficulty, and grades don't translate at all between different types of climbing or areas. Is a 5.12 sport climb as hard as a 5.12 off-width or slab climb? If that 5.11 is so impossibly hard only a few people can climb it, could 5.15 even theoretically exist? Why is that 5.9+ harder than the 10c? Grades also don't take into account physical differences between different people. Is a reachy crux the same grade if a short person sends it? Grades also don't take into account that you've never climbed at that particular crag or rock type. Many climbs were established before 5.10 "existed", and the followers of the old hardmen don't want to look like "total pussies" when they grade their modern routes at the crag. Many climbs have been established from climbers learning the ropes doing feel-good ratings at climbing gyms and establishing soft ratings at new areas. I have a feeling if the playing field were leveled, they would be very few 5.11 climbers out there.

So why care about grades? It's obvious that we need some sort of scale so we don't get in over our heads. But, just knowing a grade can make you fail your onsight due to expectations. Grades are good because they can direct you to climbs that push your ability without wasting too much time. Also, grades tell us that we are getting better or worse. They obviously give climbers something to talk about!

A great way to think about grades is that it's all 5.9! This pitch was a really hard 5.9, and the one before it was a pretty easy 5.9. I think the best way to grade something is by how much effort and calories you burned on the whole pitch, and at any one move. That whole pitch burned 1500 calories, and there was a three move section that burned a thousand of the combined total. In a way, 5.10 to a 5.12 climber feels like 5.8 to a 5.10 climber. Not just because the 5.12 climber is stronger – they may not be. They are climbing that 5.10 exactly like the 5.10 climber is climbing the 5.8 (because they are grabbing all the right holds in the best, most efficient way, etc.).

PERFORMANCE ANXIETY

Steve Blass Disease is named after a baseball pitcher who, at the top his career, became physically unable to throw a straight pitch for no apparent medical reason. It's basically an extreme form of performance anxiety. Competitions aside, most performance anxiety in climbing is between you and your ego.

Your ego can create a viscous circle. You expect to be able to climb a route so you lower your concentration, therefore lowering commitment, and you fail. The other scenario is that your perceived ability is lower than your actual ability and you fail because it's either too hard, or you realize what's happened and can't commit. Failing when fully committing is success in my opinion.

Anyway, you failed or realized you suck more than you thought you did. This lowers your self-confidence. So, subconsciously you don't expect to succeed next time. Now your concentration and commitment won't be really 100% even if you think they are. It's now a crapshoot if you succeed or fail. Success will be help break the cycle, but if you choke then seriously re-evaluate your perceived ability. Continuing climbing regardless will continue the spiral. Sounds like a crazy plan to keep that up? All of us wind up doing this at some point, or at many points in our climbing career. If you think you're doing this, swallow your pride, remember your past experiences, and go back to your training and spend some time building a more solid foundation.

Following too many pitches can add to your perceived ability and anxiety to lead. It's getting stuck in "client mode". Take a hard lead even if you don't want to. Don't let your partner do too long of a block or crux pitches before you become a permaclient. If you have chronic anxiety or generalized anxiety, then some anti-depressant medications can be very effective at treating this form of anxiety.

CLEARING THE MIND

It may sound like a contradiction: always be assessing the situation (see fear) but clearing your mind. During your visualization process (see maximizing success), think of any distractions to take your mind off the climb – negative thoughts, partner problems, expectations, fear, pro, run-outs, length, work, friends, money, love. Acknowledge them but then put them out of your mind. Relax your hands, feet, face, good posture, ab breathe. On the way up, continually and instantly assess risk, energy, strength, etc., but be decisive and commit. But most importantly – enjoy (or at least pretend to start a habit) the climbing. That's why you're here...right? One great way to clear the mind is to sing, either to yourself or loudly with your belayer.

Fear

Humans are just terrible at assessing risk and are idiots at rationalizing their fears. The media, and those in positions of power have known this for years. So get informed and be the one in control.

Being in Control

Being afraid is essentially feeling out of control. Thinking you're in control and actually being in control are two separate realities. A fear of success can stem from the feeling of not wanting to lose control. Routes get harder and they can get scarier. Sometimes hopping on more difficult terrain makes the gear gets thinner and run-outs increase. Ice climbing is a prime example, as ice conditions can get sketchier as they get more difficult. The same goes for long routes – the higher you climb, the further and further out of control you can feel. The more experience you get in the hills, the more the realms between feeling and being in control overlap. But feeling out of control leads to a fear of failure or success and not committing yourself 100%. Obviously more experience climbing helps, but so does experiencing mini epics. Getting caught in a non-life threatening rain shower, topping out in the dark, or bailing 12 pitches up with one rope successfully can desensitize you to scary things that don't wind up being so bad. Practicing falls is the ultimate confidence builder.

Water, darkness, cold, and falling are all things that can all be experienced safely and in control if you planned ahead for these things and don't climb past the point of no return. To exert control over seemingly uncontrollable situations you need to be aware of the dangers and have backup systems in place to cope. Backup systems mean bringing appropriate "just in case" gear: a minimal bivy kit, just a little extra food and water, and also being able to judge when and where on the route is "the point of no return".

This could mean being at a certain pitch by a certain time, a traverse or major overhang that would make it impossible or extremely difficult/dangerous to rappel from, or a last piece of gear before a difficult run-out. That's being in control – anticipating and evaluating the risk, planning for it accordingly, and then dealing with the risk until you decide the risk is unacceptable. Having holds break (or falling unexpectedly) is also something you can control by either testing holds and having other solid points of contact, or making sure you place enough gear to avoid ground or ledge falls - even on easy terrain. As great climber once told me, "Never pass up good gear!"

Avalanche, rock, and icefall, lightning, and bivying instead of bailing in a storm are the big bad boys that you should definitely plan for and not take lightly. These usually aren't much of a concern on most of the routes people climb. However, they are an objective that you can minimize the risk, but can never fully control. Bivying instead of bailing may seem like a good idea at the time, but the storm may wait you out and now you've just sat around wasting valuable time and resources. If you or your partner feels like any of those hazards are beginning to become an uncontrollable issue, then bail! You can climb with these risks, but your desire to climb must outweigh that danger. It's usually not the "hardmen" that do this, but average climbers with big agendas and egos. Yes, some big famous climbs have pushed through these deadly conditions, but those instances are rare. If you hear rock fall, dive under any available protection. If that's not available, and you're wearing a pack, turn your back to the wall. If not, turn to the side to minimize your width. In either case, cower and cover your neck with elbows tucked in front. Avalanches and lightning risk mitigation are described in detail later.

Another option is to go up instead of bailing, while remaining in control. One form of control is knowledge of your climbing ability and mountain sense. If you have great awareness of your ability and familiarity on the type of terrain you are climbing, then climbing within your limits is being in control. This is how climbers can remain fairly calm, or at least not hyperventilate and soil themselves during run-outs. You may be completely capable of cruising through a run-out but not have the knowledge of your ability to climb that run-out in control. And of course, committing to a run-out that you know you are not cable of doing is not being in control.

Free-soloers can be in almost total control because of their carefully honed self-awareness in their ability and knowledge of the rock they are climbing on. However, a loose rock, bee-sting, or slip will put them fully out of control. On hard leads or run-outs you need a reserve of previous climbs and experiences to draw on. How far can you climb or fish for pro before you actually get so pumped you fall? Can you deal with pulling a crux and then running it out on slightly easier terrain, or do you need to have that piece of gear in to comfort you after the crux? Do you understand the rock, what unknown holds should feel like, where cracks and pro opportunities usually arise? Could you down climb this? Will that piece hold a fall?

DISCONNECT YOURSELF FROM THE SITUATION

When you start to get gripped on a climb for whatever reason it can help to pretend you are somewhere else emotionally or physically. This is terrible advice in the real world for dealing with your problems, but in climbing all bets are off. Even if a climb feels desperate or you're starting to feel the grip of commitment, then laughing, smiling, singing, and joking around can help create a disconnect from the environment or situation. Being silly, goofy, and giving your partner shit (or taking it) can sometimes be the only way to make a gripping climb fun. Another tactic to disconnect yourself from the situation is to get a case of the "fuck its". We've all done this at some point – just grab the rack and go! Another "fuck it" mentality is to flip a switch and want to take the fall. This may psych you out of being too scared to continue leading and cause you to take on gear or down-climb.

If you're on lead and start to feel run-out, a stretch ahead looks dicey, or you find yourself sewing it up, pretend you are the belayer looking up at you leading. Even a piece of gear at your waist can start to feel a mile away, or a ten-foot run-out seems like death terrain. But you remember the times belaying when the leader was feeling the same way and you thought, "Come on man! You've got tons of gear, it's not that far, etc."

On long multipitch climbs the commitment can start to make each pitch ahead feel like you're spiraling out of control by going higher. Pretend like each pitch is on the ground and you are just getting in a big day of cragging. Cruxes that occur high up on a pitch always feel scarier even though your fall would probably be safer higher up. When cruxes are before the first bolt or piece, you usually crush it, even though a fall would be worse. Pretend like you are just starting out on the pitch when you get to a crux or an endurance pitch starts to take a mentally draining toll.

Give your ego some candy and pretend that you are being judged in a completion or featured in a badass climbing video - sound track and all. This can make you climb more efficiently with every move, and every move will have intent and follow-through with no wasted movements or moments.

Plan for the Worst at All Times
Climb with confidence in your ability, but with a general sense of distrust about everything else. At every point before (including packing for your trip) and during the climb, belay, rappel, whenever, think, "What would happen if..."

- I fell right now?
- My partner fell?
- That (fill in the blank) failed?
- I go any further? Could I still bail?
- A storm came in?
- It got dark?
- The climb gets too hard or takes too long to continue?
- My partner or I got hurt or knocked out and was unable to climb?

You have to plan ahead by bringing appropriate gear, knowing first aid, and knowing self-rescue. And you have to continually plan and assess during every stage and moment of the climb. See also the falling checklist. It's one thing to not bring a headlamp, raincoat, etc. on a climb that you can easily escape or at least endure with some modest amount of safety, but it is another to be unprepared on committing climbs.

Some climbs require speed for safety and too much extra crap could slow you down to the point of actually being unsafe. I'm going to go out on a big limb here by saying the "fast and light revolution" principles are being applied by climbers too often and on routes that do not demand this technique. The culprit? Hype! Is carrying 1-2 extra pounds (water, jacket, headlamp, emergency kit) really going to weight or slow you down so much that you can't finish the route or pull the crux? If the answer is yes, then you are a.) climbing a very difficult route and have total confidence in your ability and are accepting the consequences to achieve a lifetime dream climb, b.) climbing dangerously over your ability, putting yourself, partner, future rescuers at risk, and being irresponsible to your family, or c.) letting your ego run out of control because you heard one of your friends did the route in X amount of hours and you want to also.

Manageable Bits
Staring up at a huge intimidating objective first thing in the morning can overwhelm you so much your brain can make up amazing reasons to bail without ever leaving the ground. One way to control your fear is to chop things down into manageable, rational, bite-sized bits.

Remember that you can usually bail – even without established rap anchors or two ropes. It won't cost nearly as much as it cost you to buy and then not use all that gear, food, gasoline and time off it did to get you here. And think about how hard it's going to be to come back. And when you do come back, it'll be just like right now! Look at the topo for run-outs and big traverses that would be hard to bail from. Anything below that point is non-committing. Deal with decisions above that when you get that point. Just make it to there. Instead of freaking out on the climb and obsessing the whole time,

"I gotta make it to pitch 12, that's the point of no return", have fun and enjoy this part because you can. Divide out how many pitches you have to lead. On a 12-pitch climb you only have to lead 6. That's not so bad! Let your partner freak out about their pitches.

On your hard leads if you can get gear then you can at least climb a bit farther. When you get to the point where it's difficult but you still don't have gear, assess the consequences of a fall (see fall checklist). If the fall will be clean, climb until (just before) it won't be. If you get gear, then the process repeats itself. If not, then you should have been aware of the grade and seriousness of the pitch and just sucked it up because you know you won't fall. If you can't, then you succumbed to magical thinking when choosing this route. If it's a first ascent, negotiate with you and your partner if it's worth the risk. If not, down-climb to gear and bail. If you are scared to fall, but the grade is in your ability, a good mental trick is to think, "If this move was right off the ground I would have no problem."

If you are worried about the dwindling rack, realize that you can build an anchor before the established anchor, lower and back clean, or down climb to better gear and build an anchor there. After you are at an anchor, your pitch count is now lowered! You can rest while belaying, and hey, you can at least lead "just one more pitch". As the climb progresses, keep in mind that you can still bail. If you've climbed past the point of no return, realize that you based your decision to continue off the fact that the weather looks good, the rest is in your ability, you've climbed the majority of the route, the summit is almost in the bag, or the crux is over!

On very long routes, check your food and water rations and know that you have plenty to get you safely to the top, even if a night out is possible. Know that you brought at least the minimum amount of kit to keep you relatively dry and warm if it rains, snows, or you have to bivy. The storm may pass quickly, and another pitch or waiting for a couple hours couldn't hurt. The last few pitches or descent could be pretty straightforward, even in the dark. Finally: suck it up! This is why you are here. Would a bivy really be worse than bailing?

The suck it up mentality of psyching yourself up doesn't really work if the answers or endpoints of any of the above scenarios are negative ones (i.e., you could actually get into a pretty bad epic if you continue). You could also be such a hardman/woman that you just don't care, you're not bailing. If it's the latter, then why are you reading this chapter? If the case is the former, then continuing is an equation of risk vs. desire.

BASIC CHECKLIST
- Ability to climb to next gear
- Fall Checklist
- Enough gear to continue or build anchor
- Ability to retreat or down climb
- Weather
- Time
- Enough energy to continue
- Enough food, water, clothes, headlamp to continue/endure

WILL

Fancy equipment and elaborate training are no substitute for experience and willpower. Much harder routes have been done than you are I will ever know with cotton snowsuits, iron pitons, and an iron will. Courage and willpower are what make hardmen and women continue on.

Trying Harder

Take a look at yourself. Are you trying hard? I mean REALLY trying. Getting better requires a lot of commitment, but what most people don't get is that this means not just trying hard when you're training, but also when you are out climbing. Most climbers trying to get better can push themselves to the point of overtraining, but do not give it their all when climbing. This means giving it your all when you are actually climbing, and getting in the best possible day of climbing you can. You'd be amazed at how many pitches some great climbers get in during a cragging session, and during a season. Yes, you need rest, but you can push yourself a lot further than you think while scheduling your rests intelligently. This means less wasted time and more effort involved.

Could you have gotten up earlier, done more warm-up pitches, and gone running after a day of climbing? By setting a predetermined end point, you feel you have tapped out your reserves no matter how much you have done. Push your limits; what do you have to lose? What's so damned important about getting back to the car, back home, or off the climb? Those things usually wind up being more stressful anyway. The most important time to try hard is during an actual lead. Gains from giving your all on a single pitch are worth an entire season of overtraining.

Giving your all and trying hard is a great reason why CrossFit is so successful. You are peer pressured into trying as hard as possible in a workout you'd never subject yourself to. The goal is to get better. If you half-ass train, you get half-ass results. Same with climbing. If you want to get better, or maintain a high level, you need to put forth maximum effort like they do in a CrossFit class, only longer. Put forth maximum effort on the climb, during your whole day of climbing, and during your training season.

Even a little more effort equals a lot more results. One more try could mean the send instead of moving on to another climb. Ten seconds of pain, fear, and uncertainty could have gotten you through the crux before you yelled take or let go without fully committing. On more tenuous move could have made the send! Did your physical and technical limitations make you fall, or did fear or self-doubt? Sustained climbs start to beat you down psychologically, not just physically. Many climbers mentally quit if a move seems too hard, after they pulled the hard move and another one is coming up, or it's still a long way to the anchor. Practicing falling can help, but a lot of the time it's a fear of continuing on. The only way to beat this is to know your ability, acknowledge you're being a quitter, and start to make a habit of forcing yourself to continue on.

You can also try too hard by being too hard on yourself. Most of this stems from comparing yourself to others. If you are too hard on yourself, you will likely always fail and send you into a downward spiral of poor performance. A good example is if you're a 5.10 climber and always hopping on 5.10d's or sandbagged 5.9+ routes. 10d's (or highest end of any grade) and 5.9+ are usually sandbagged. You don't give yourself any credit for climbing a 10c because you think it's too easy and the 5.11a you just onsighted was way "too soft".

Willingness to Suffer or Commit

You can't give it your all, or control your fear if you aren't willing to suffer or commit. This makes climbing fairly unique. Many "normal" people have to be coaxed to let go at the top of an indoor climbing wall their first time. They have to suffer through the ordeal and they have to commit to let go and trust the rope. It's a big deal for them. Now take a look at what you do. It would probably turn that newbie into a catatonic bowl of jelly. But there are things we still clutch to as psychological safety blankets. The problem is that clutching that safety blanket is also holding you back. There is hopefully a gap between a rational fear of death and pain and what our tolerance is to accept danger and experience pain. We generally set our limit for risk and pain by our desire to climb something. The more you want to climb something outweighs other things in your life, the more you are willing to set the risk and suffering bar high. The problem, as stated in the fear section, is that the actual risk and your perceived risk could be way off. So the first step in willpower is to know the actual risk and to have experiences in similar situations.

The second step is to understand that future pain and fear are generally much worse than reality. Everyone knows the worst part in falling is before you fall. Thinking about getting wet and cold can get your heart racing (like just before you jump in that mountain lake). Your safety blanket keeps you on the dock, and you have to let go to jump in and commit. Experience helps you let go. Desire makes you jump.

Before you even start a climb, you need to decide what you are willing to suffer and endure, and to make sure the climb or situation fits within your parameters. When it comes time to actually climb you must be decisive and totally commit. After you have evaluated the pitch or section ahead and decided that the risk is acceptable there can be no negative thoughts or hesitation.

Climbing should be an experience-oriented sport. In other words, you must want to be there. If you don't want to be there, you have sabotaged your ability to commit. Sometimes an internal pep talk helps (you could just be being lazy or not trying hard enough), and sometimes you need to swallow your pride and tell your partner that you don't want to be here. Don't make up lies or fake an injury. If you do that, you need to seriously re-evaluate your relationship with your climbing partner. You may find out that he or she is actually an understanding human being and plans can be changed. If that's not the case, suck it up and just say no! You don't want to climb with that person anyways, and they probably don't want to climb with you. It's worth a bruised ego. Otherwise you are wasting their time and your own.

Pick an easier or more enjoyable climb, take a rest day, or figure out what it is (possibly in your life) causing you to not commit and fix it. Otherwise you'll be constantly bailing or not committing and your climbing ability will nose-dive. One of the biggest commitment killers is having to be at work, school, or the airport the next day. Be smart and realize this could affect your commitment by scheduling differently. If you only have weekends, go cragging. Save your days off or long weekends for the big send. It's not worth wasting time, money, and energy to go anyway and bail. The only other option is to be okay with being exhausted at work the next day, or dealing with being late. Faking sickness on the phone works great – just don't show up with a sunburn and bleeding hands.

The best climbers always have way less junk on them on long routes. Not because they're all jazzed up on "fast and light," but because they are more confident in their skills, and more willing to suffer and commit. However, some climbers, no matter what their ability or experience, have less fear, greater ability to suffer, and the ability to climb to the top no matter what. Know your limits. The biggest difference between a great climber and a mediocre climber is the overall effort, commitment, and desire put forth. This doesn't mean quitting your job and living out of your car to climb. It means when it comes down to the challenge, more effort and commitment are put forth and there is a strong desire to be climbing. Giving your best may not match your partner's, or even your own for that day. Plan intelligently.

It's kind of ironic, but sometimes climbers that just go cragging and decide to do a long hard route often succeed more than experienced alpinists. Why? Besides the fact that they are probably technically superior from cragging so much and practicing falling, not having a lot of experience with suffering and having things going wrong can be very beneficial (until things go wrong). If you know how much suffering sucks, you may climb more cautiously, bring more stuff, and not commit to scary moves.

WILLINGNESS TO CHANGE
Willpower also means the ability to recognize the need for a change in habits, and actually following through even though you desire something else. It means doing something that you know is good for you even though you would rather be doing something else. Giving in makes giving in easier the next time until you forget what you were trying to change, or irrationally rationalize yourself out of it. Not getting enough sleep is a sure way to trash your willpower, as is not eating or drinking enough.

It takes willpower to become self-aware, admit your weaknesses, and know your strengths. But it also takes willpower to do something about them. Change your mental focus when climbing from a passenger along for the ride, to an active learning participant. Learn from everything: mistakes and successes. The first step in learning from your mistakes is to admit you've made them. Next comes developing a logical plan to fix them. The hard part is to follow through and actually fix the mistakes. Learning from your success means actively thinking about how you are climbing. If you grab a desperate hold and crank through, log that experience by thinking about it. The next time that situation occurs you can draw on your previous experiences. If you don't actively think about it, you won't remember it. The best way to be successful again is to recreate previous successes. Find similar climbs when you want to be successful. When you are training you can throw yourself curveballs. But don't trick yourself into thinking that if you can do this, you should also be able to do something equally hard but much less similar.

Self-discipline is the key to being successful. This means taking the time to eat and drink, put on your belay jacket, look at the topo, or fix your shoes - even if you're freaked and just want to keep climbing to get it over with.

BAILURE
Bail mentality is self-fulfilling. If you start thinking about going down, you're probably going to bail. Once that thought or desire slips into your mind it eats away at your thoughts like a cancer. If this starts to creep into your brain, take a ten-minute time out. Chill. Smoke a butt (not that you have any, right?). Drink some water and eat some food, you may just be tired. Don't make hasty decisions, or let thoughts creep in that take on a life of their own and overpower you. You may change your mind after that harrowing lead while you belay your partner up, and he or she leads the next pitch. If it's bad, tell your partner. Give them the reins for a couple pitches. If they put up a fuss, odds are they want to bail too and aren't being mature enough to say so.

You will fail or bail when you feel like you should or are used to doing so. To counteract this purposefully (it won't just happen) keep going and try harder. Get a case of the "fuck it's". This is the feeling that Generals are trying to instill their doomed soldiers in their pep talks during epic war movies. Just "standing" there does nothing. Either go up or go down. You can tell an inexperienced climber by how slow it takes them between moves. Every movement is a counter reaction to overcoming fear by using the "fuck it method" of willpower. It may take a few tries to break out of this on each route. Sometimes knowing the grade or hearing about the route will spook you. Have your partner pick your routes for you, or just don't look at the guidebook. You are not beaten until you are beaten. Don't give in. Go until you have to start leaving gear.

Stop worrying about the "what-if's" on non-life threatening climbs. It's been done by less skilled climbers than you, with way worse gear, and in way worse conditions. It is so hard to bail and then come back again. Change plans way earlier in the game. Avoid "anchor syndrome." Try not to focus too much on the anchors ahead or next gear placement, but focus on the climb and experience itself. If you have to, fake it. Lie to yourself until your attitude actually changes. Bring too much protection to keep lack of gear out of the excuse list. Compare what you are leading or about to climb to other routes you've done successfully. 5.8 in the hills is 5.8 at the crags, and a crack or bolt is a crack or bolt. Don't let the arena hold you back from giving it your all. Some of the best sends come from a just go for it attitude. If you don't have that attitude and aren't confident, you will fail and not learn.

No matter what, try and redpoint the climb. Pretend you're a hardman that never quits. If you always bail - try to keep climbing and deal. Eliminate "take" from your vocabulary and stop saying, "watch me" all the time. Break that habit. Keep climbing – or actually have your partner give you slack! If you fall, be calm about it - don't scream and freak out. Use that energy to climb a little higher.

Motivation

As discussed, desire is key to successful climbing. To affect you desire, you need to do things to increase your motivation.

Have Fun, Stay Positive

If you feel like you're beating your head against the wall and are failing at hard climbs, or are starting to dread going climbing, dumb it down occasionally – do a fun easy route, or a bunch of easy link-ups. This is a guaranteed motivator. Fun should be your number one priority when motivation starts to drain.

The power of a positive mental attitude is incredible. Occasionally check to see if you're being negative, or thinking negatively. If you're thinking, "This sucks, I'm sacred, I want to go home, etc.," change it around. Try and focus on the positive: how beautiful it is outside, how interesting the climbing is, how most people don't get this kind of opportunity, how bored you'd be doing something else. Turn bad or uncomfortable situations into lighthearted jokes. Make difficult situations challenges to overcome, not ordeals to endure.

One way to stay positive and have fun is to force yourself to. You have to know you are lying to yourself. If you think you are having fun but really aren't – that's a much bigger problem. Anyway, a forced self-inflicted positive mental attitude can actually help change your perception. You're not brainwashing yourself because all points of view are basically brainwashing that you were unaware of and are used to. What happens is that you see things from a new (albeit forced) point of view. Once the new point of view gets enough exposure, you can begin to understand, empathize, and then possibly accept it. Faking it also creates a better partner dynamic, and time could actually become more enjoyable if your partner is happy.

Partners

A good climbing partner is most important piece of gear you can have. Find a good one and ditch the bad one. Listen to your gut if you feel sketched out by your partner and don't trust your life to a possible idiot. Peer pressure and friendly competition helps immensely. You and your partner's goals must match. Is getting to the top more important than the experience or the other way around?

Don't do a long or hard route with a bailer or newbie - even if you state you'll lead the rest of the pitches, they'll think of another reason to bail. However, sometime climbing with a newbie or someone less experienced can help boost confidence by teaching and giving feedback. That feedback and teaching helps you too. Sometimes climbing with a new partner can get you up a route you may have bailed on with a partner you are very familiar with. The awkwardness of not knowing a new partner can make both of you push a little harder and not speak up as much (mostly due to ego) about bailing or not wanting to lead a pitch.

Besides having similar goals on a route, a good partner has similar goals in the types of climbs that you like to do. Nothing helps your training more than having a friend who wants to train with you. You can share ideas, and push each other harder than you would alone.

There are pros and cons to having partners either way worse than you, on your level, or much better than you. If just starting out, you can learn a lot from a more experienced climber, but you lose out on ton of experience, wisdom, and basic knowledge by not making mistakes and by being quasi-guided. When you get more advanced, a better partner than you can fill in gaps of knowledge and technique that you may not get on your own, but you can also get frustrated by having everything always be hard. Climbing with someone worse than you is a great way to emphasize your own skill by teaching and also by watching a skill performed poorly. You get to do more leading as well. If you can't seem to find a great partner, start looking for people you discounted because of their inexperience. Someone truly psyched will catch up quickly. Creating a new climbing partner can involve a whole lot less wasted time than trying to change an old partner, or trying to find that perfect one.

Make sure your partner also has a positive attitude. They should cheer you on, encourage you to try harder, and talk you down when you are freaked out. Give more to your partner than you expect them to give to you. Share your food and water, be the team cheerleader. It will rub off and create an amazing dynamic. Bad partners are a huge reason for failure. They squash your psych and bail on trips or while on the climb at the last minute. If you feel that your partner is a major reason for failure or lack of climbing motivation, ditch them!

Other ways to find partners are to go on the Internet, put a flier up at work, school, or at the gym. Rope-soloing is a great way to have potential partners realize you've got your stuff dialed, and to feel sorry for you and offer a belay. Hanging out at a crag without a partner is scary. You must have a backup plan to keep yourself occupied. But it works for thousands of people – even in alpine areas. In fact, showing up partnerless in an alpine area really shows determination and makes a team of two feel sorry enough for you to tag along or a team of three to split up. Get people's emails who you have a nice conversation with and Facebook friend them. They may be the only person who has the same week or month of you do down the line.

Make sure you and your partner are on the same page as far as goals, knowledge (first aid, self-rescue, mountain travel, etc.), style of climbing (fast and light, normal and safe, etc.), and ability levels. Just because you're totally dialed in doesn't mean your partner is, and besides just holding a belay device, you must rely on your partner. If you're unsure of your partner, do a pre-climb shakedown somewhere easier and teach them your tricks, or assume the role of guide.

Assuming the role of guide with an unknown or weak partner means that you must rely on only yourself in sticky situations. The cardinal rule in this case is do not get hurt or put yourself in a situation that requires them to get you out of. Either climb something easier and safer and be on high alert, or be on uber-high alert, put in extra gear, and always err on the side of caution. Remember that if a climb requires a strong effort and skill set from both partners and yous hasn't prepared like you have, everything will ride on the lowest common denominator. It's up to you to motivate and communicate with your partner about being on the same page.

GET OUT OF A RUT
If your motivation has just tanked or you have totally plateaued, sometimes you need a change. Try and figure out what it is in your life that may be dragging you down. No one is more psyched than the climber that just quit his or her job, or dumped their significant other and headed out for that great road trip. Go to a new climbing areas and try different mediums. Nothing cures trad blues like low commitment sunny sport climbing days. Go climb a peak or easy ridge traverse to just enjoy being outside and moving quickly.

Road trip blues are easily cured by getting a motel room for one or two nights. Two nights allows you to not worry about checking out before 10 am and have a complete relaxation day while watching daytime TV. Multiday alpine climbs can feel like they just started if you bathe and wash your clothes.

Finally, you can always put your goal on the backburner for a while, or even change your goal if progress is awful or motivation is so low you forgot why it's your goal. The situation could be the reverse: you have no goals so you just plateau all over the place. Picking a goal, even just a single redpoint project, can really rejuvenate the psyche. Tick lists can be a constant reminder off all the goals you have to look forward to in climbing. Tick lists can also imprison you into climbing a route for the wrong reasons and you could miss out on getting a bunch of pitches cragging while you vainly try and tick off routes regardless if there are better things you could be climbing right now.

GET PSYCHED
A great way to get totally amped is to have **music mixes** for special occasions. Go through your music library and build a playlist with all of the songs that hit you hard emotionally (in a good way of course). Just one motivational song can change your entire perspective. Watching climbing movies is a really fun way to build psych and absorb technique just by watching. Buy a new guidebook. A new area with a host of superlatives about how awesome each climb is can get you planning that next adventure in no time. Keep a **motivational notecard** in your pocket like an alcoholic or someone quitting smoking would. This is especially useful on long climbs or before demanding routes. If your mind is racing with thoughts of fear or too much psyche, it's hard to remember ways to deal with stress, increase desire, and to manage fear, commitment, and will. If you are exhausted or hit a wall it's most likely because you need to eat and drink. Other reasons could

be the quality of the food you're eating, too much alcohol in your diet, stress and worries in life, bad quality or not enough sleep, or just not trying hard enough.

Visualization, Meditation, and Biofeedback
There have been several studies done where one group lifted heavy weights, while another really thought about lifting heavy weights. Yes, the visualization group actually got significantly stronger: 40-85% stronger. The studies didn't follow the two groups over time, and I bet that after a certain period the visualization group would reach a plateau. But, when visualization is combined with actual activity, the gains are greater than the sum of the parts. Visualization is not just limited to strength gains. It can be applied to learning a skill, losing weight, lifestyle and personality modification, etc. So when you are training, don't be absent-minded while performing an exercise or skill. Really think about it. Before you execute, think about how it will be (in a good way!). While you train, think about what you are doing, how it should go, and how it feels. After execution, go over in your mind what it was like, and how it could change. The more you repeat this, the quicker you will learn and the more you will be willing to commit with confidence.

At the base of your climb, take 10 minutes to run through a total visualization. Try and imagine with as many senses engaged as possible, how you will climb the route. The moment you start having negative thoughts, stop, think of something else (have a go-to thought), and try it again – until you've climbed the route successfully many times in your mind. Be sure to tell your partner what you are doing so he or she will not bother you.

When you begin to become overly excited on a climb, you need to have a system to chill out. Try abdominal breathing, breathing out slowly, relaxing your face, and relaxing of the muscles not directly keeping you attached to the wall. Having a mantra can help calm you down, and this usually is achieved by saying some calming phrase (serenity now!) and visualizing something relaxing. If you are afraid, go through the fall checklist, assess the situation after you've calmed down a bit, and try and remember other similar experiences and how you dealt with them before. Mantras don't have to be sayings, they can be actions or sounds. A good finger lock, incut hold, the clip of a carabineer, or thunk of an ice tool can train your to relax and maintain focus on the rhythm of climbing.

Hypnosis is a viable option to help you get your subconscious mind to do what you want it to do. There are plenty of scammy auido tapes and practitioners out there so watch your wallet. Brainwave synchronization is very similar to hypnosis, and is another tool you can try. Light, sound, and meditation are used to alter, change, harmonize, or sync brainwaves into appropriate states for relaxation, performance, and other uses. Again, this can be a very useful tool, or an exercise in draining your wallet. Biofeedback machines that measure heart rhythms, pulse, blood pressure, muscle contraction, temperature, brainwaves, and other physiologic signs of stress can also be very useful to mastering mind over body. There are several books, websites, software, apps, and devices out there. HeartMath and the Emwave machine, shaky evidence aside, can be very useful tools if taken with a small grain of salt.

Using Measurements
You can use measurements to motivate yourself. The measurements don't have to be just numbers. Take a photo of yourself before beginning training or weight loss, and then a new photo every month afterwards. Tick off grades on your pyramid. See how much longer you can climb before falling or taking. Be creative!

LOSS-PUNISHMENT AND GAIN-REWARD

If you find yourself succumbing to bad habits on a climb of any kind, you can set rewards and punishments deals for yourself. It turns out that behaviors are more motivated by fear of loss than they are modified by reward. But you won't enjoy climbing much if you wind up punishing yourself constantly. It is best to have both - not just a reward or punishment. The severity of the punishment or extent of the reward should be based on how serious the issue is. The consequences cannot be emotional: hating yourself, or thinking you are the best. This leads to creating negative self-fulfilling prophecies, and unrealistic expectations. The important thing is to make a deal with yourself and stick to the plan. Both reward and punishment could be strategic in that they both do things that make you a better climbing. They can also have nothing to do with climbing – the reward could be self-indulgent and the punishment could be withholding some sort of pleasure. The rewards and punishments need to matter to you. Also, the more tangible the prize or punishment, the better.

Part of the punishment must include introspective analysis of why you didn't succeed and what can be done differently next time. Increase the punishment if you didn't learn from your mistake during that next time. I heard a great story on the radio about a lady who wanted to quit smoking so badly that she decided that if she had another cigarette as long as she lived, she would have to donate money to the Klu Klux Klan! She thankfully hasn't had a smoke in 30 years. I doubt she would have quit if her motivation were to buy herself something nice if she went x-amount of weeks without a smoke. Another man had to write Oprah a check for $700 if he cheated on his diet. He did cheat, and sent her the money. However, he did not cheat again! Again, it's harder to lose what you have than to gain what you don't have. Finally, instead of trying to correct bad habits, you can also use rewards and punishments as motivators. You can make lighthearted games with yourself or climbing partner that have rewards and consequences. Friendly completion is a strong motivator.

TOP 10 REASONS FOR UNEXPECTED FAILURE (IN ORDER OF MOST TO LEAST COMMON)
1. Desire or perceived ability out of sync with actual difficulty or commitment required
2. Scooped by another party
3. Fear of falling or suffering
4. Climb requires a specific skill that needs more practice
5. Inadequate preparation: gear, weather check, route/approach/descent recon
6. Inadequate nutrition, hydration, rest
7. Not enough endurance for the entire route
8. Not enough strength endurance for a pitch
9. Not enough power for a move
10. Not enough strength for a move

Note how the first reason (and a few others) is a balance between ego, willpower, fear, and reality. If you can at least asses what indeed the reality of the situation is and accommodate for it, then you are much more likely to succeed. Expected failure is not failure. You would not grow or get better as a climber only getting on routes at or below your onsight grade. Finally, failure is a big reason why we climb. If everything were a given, would it be much fun? Even easy climbs aren't in the bag. Nothing should be a given and that's why you should give it your all.

PART II: CLIMBING HEALTHIER

Warning: *There are a myriad of health conditions and adverse reactions to everything in this book, but especially any drug, supplement, or nutrient that may have minor to serious contraindications. I can't go over them all – if you're putting something new inside of you, have a medical or genetic condition, and/or are on any prescription meds, it is up to you to check with your doctor and do your own research. This section is NOT a substitute for the advice and care of a qualified medical practitioner and should only be used as a supplemental reference or springboard for ideas.*

Chapter Seven: Nutrition

General Health and Performance

Eating Well
Climbers tend to push themselves to the point of depletion so proper nutrition is critical to success. Not eating and drinking well in terms of quality or quantity is a major reason for failure or low performance. The basic point of nutrition, aka "eating food", is to provide calories for energy, and to provide protein, vitamins, and minerals for building tissue and cellular function. Water is the body's medium for transport of nutrients within and between cells, maintaining blood pressure and osmolality, and thermoregulation.

Thermoregulation doesn't get enough emphasis when it comes to rehydrating. When we lose water blood becomes thicker so our heart pumps faster and this increases temperature. Blood also gets rerouted to the skin when the outside temperatures or your own body is too hot. This reduces the water and blood our muscles get, which is obviously bad for performance. To make matters worse, as muscles don't work well when too hot, the proteins that contract muscles, actin and myosin, don't engage due to denaturing. Finally and very importantly, water acts as an insulator to buffer temperature changes.

Despite gloom and doom prophecies of many food dictators, your body does a pretty darn good job of telling you when you need more food and water, and has evolved over many millions of years to get what it needs out of an omnivorous diet. One of the biggest moneymakers out there and biggest sources of misinformation, propaganda, and fear mongering are nutritional claims that sell radical life-changing diets and supplements for all sorts of real and imagined diseases and health conditions. A well-rounded meal of carbs, fats, and protein, with some fruits and veggies tossed in is about as much nutrition as most climbers need.

Unless you live in a 3rd world country, are in poverty, or have a genetic condition that I'm not going to cover here, a healthy bag of groceries will keep you covered. Even eating crap every so often is not going to hurt you. Yes, there is a lot of circumstantial evidence out there regarding what we eat contributes to cancer, diabetes, heart disease, obesity, Alzheimer's, autism, and the like. But so far we don't know what the specific culprits or amounts are. I would argue that there's just as much evidence out there that disproves those claims. My sneaking suspicion is that it has less to do with diet, and more due to stress, laziness, and genetics. But since we don't know, it is prudent to eat fewer artery clogging and processed chemical ridden foods – especially less refined sugar and additives. I'd be writing something completely different is this was a book for the fat and lazy general public. But climbers' biggest concerns are getting enough calories for the climb, recovery, and for losing body fat. This is the bottom line: eat well rounded meals, don't eat crap all the time, eat and drink enough to supply your energy demands, and get enough protein to compensate for your increased workload.

Taking Vitamins and Supplements
Most vitamins, nutrients, and herbal supplements are all over the place in terms of quality and bioavailability and you may not be getting what you think you're buying. The actual chemical in plant's purported health benefits may be totally unknown, you wind up eating the wrong parts, the concentrations may be wrong, the refining process may have damaged the ingredients,

the supplement may not be standardized, the wrong species may be used, the active ingredient may just get metabolized before it even reaches your cells, pills may just get passed through your bowels undigested, liquids may be better than powders or solids, and the amount and timing may be off - among other things. Unlike FDA regulated drugs (which have their own host of problems and issues), it's really anybody's guess. A big reason for all of this is that there's no money or major quality studies being done on supplements.

Before spending a single penny, do your own research. Try to find the abstracts from the actual studies. If you can find the whole study, you may find that the entire study is flawed. It's amazing what a crappy job some "scientists" do on nutritional studies. Most studies are side-projects, done by students, or are extremely biased studies done by the companies selling the supplement. Finally, taking ten different supplements with the same reported benefit may have an additive effect, have the same effect as just taking a full dose of just one of them, or may have no effect because the dose of each isn't high enough! The effects of most supplements are only noticeable after taking them for a few days to weeks. The benefit of many supplements may also be so slim (5% increase, etc.) that your efforts would be better spent finding other ways to achieve the same benefit. So unless you've reached a roadblock or are close to your genetic potential, you will probably get more gains from climbing more and training more, and spending your extra money on more trips.

I purposefully left off many recommended amounts on some vitamins and supplements because not only does gender and bodyweight matter, but also recommended doses change drastically as more research is done. It is easy to use Google to find a current study to find recommended doses if you decide to supplement outside of a healthy diet.

Ergogenic Aids

Ergogenic aids means performance enhancers. Sound like cheating? It depends on how you look at it. Anything you do in a positive way to improve your performance is a performance enhancer. Kind of like calling something a "drug." Anything you put in your body is a drug. It's up to you to decide, or the climbing community if you climb for non-altruistic rewards. I've included a list of commonly used supplements that or may not may improve your climbing, make you a cheater, or make you sick (vomit, GI distress, diarrhea).

Food Pyramid

The old food pyramid we all learned in school is wrong. Starches like potatoes, white rice, white bread, sugar, and white pasta are what make you fat and crash, healthy oils are good for you and don't make you fat or raise your bad cholesterol, and dairy is totally unnecessary if you get calcium elsewhere. Instead, **whole grains should compose your carbs, and nuts (and legumes), fruit, and vegies should be eaten in abundance. You can also eat plenty of eggs, fish, poultry, and pork**, but limit red meat and meats high in nitrates (processed meats) for their carcinogenic and artery clogging effects.

Ratio of Carbohydrates, Fats, Protein

Climbers who maintain a very active lifestyle should eat a ratio of approximately 50-60% carbohydrates, 30% healthy oils, and 10-20% proteins. During long high exertion climbs and extended bouts of training the ratio changes to a 4:1 carb to protein ratio (80% carbs and 20% protein), and a small amount of fat to avoid crashing.

Regular days of climbing (cragging, short multipitch, or inconsequential longer climbs) means just eating enough regular food and having a regular diet with a bit more emphasis on the carbs during the day and more protein and fat at dinner. Most climbs aren't constant high output activities similar to long distance running or cycling and you'll feel a lot better by simply eating real food.

CARBOHYDRATES

Carbohydrates (carbs) are sugars and starches used for short-term energy, and unused carbs are converted into fat or stored as glycogen in the liver and muscles. Glycogen is our carb reserve, mainly from muscle and some from the liver, and blood sugar is our immediate carb source. Glycogen is converted into glucose and enters the blood. Insulin from our pancreas allows the blood sugar to enter the cells for energy, and lowers blood sugar by doing this. Once in the cells, glucose is converted into ATP and mitochondria converts ATP into energy. Oxygen increases the amount of ATP produced by a substantial amount, known as aerobic metabolism. Lack of oxygen creates the byproduct lactic acid, which limits your ability to continue muscular contraction and causes pain, known as anaerobic metabolism. Lactic acid is quickly metabolized into energy when you get more oxygen or rest.

Foods are rated on their glycemic index and load: the higher the number the higher blood sugar and insulin response: your blood sugar spikes, then crashes. Type I diabetics don't produce enough insulin, and hypoglycemics produce too much. Producing too much insulin can result in Type II diabetes because you tucker the pancreas out. A sugar crash is a result of too much insulin being excreted because the glycemic index of the foods were so high your pancreas overshot the correct amount and blood sugar levels drop too low. High blood sugar and high insulin levels are literally toxic with serious long-term health consequences like an early death, blindness, or amputation. The simpler the sugar (higher glycemic index), the more quickly insulin is excreted. Insulin response during high levels of exertion is not an issue during glucose depletion since your body NEEDS this sugar. In other words, you are not going to crash eating pure sugar while exercising.

Types of Carbs
We only have so many calories of carbohydrates available in our bodies, so we want to be using fat as a fuel as much as possible. This is why we want to keep blood sugar low (to prevent insulin spike), but balanced by eating carbs that take time to enter the blood in our normal routine and in our pre-climb meals. Whole grains and carbs locked-up in foods like vegetables are the best source of complex carbohydrates. "White" carbs like bread, potatoes and rice are fairly simple carbohydrates and are a poor choice for maintaining normal blood sugar and glycogen levels. Stay far away from synthetic carbs "sweeteners". Most forms of climbing allow for digestion of all forms of dietary carbohydrates from whole grains to pure glucose, while high-exertion climbing mainly uses simple sugars like glucose, fructose or sucrose (combined glucose/fructose). If you need a quick boost or are hitting it hard non-stop all day, eat simple carbs. If you're eating to not get hungry and to provide you with your caloric needs (most forms of climbing), eat complex carbs. Tailor your carb diet accordingly.

The simplest carbs, like glucose, are absorbed the fastest, while more complex carbs need more digestion to be broken down. Glucose will get to your cells quicker, last shorter, and spike insulin higher. Simple carbs include glucose (aka dextrose), sucrose (table sugar), fructose (fruit sugar), and galactose (milk sugar). Due to complex metabolic pathways, not all sugars have the same effect on your pancreas, blood sugar, and health. More and more studies are showing just how bad sucrose and especially fructose are for you besides just the extra calories and the fat gain.

Sugar has become the "new fat" in terms of evil food products. **Glucose** is by far the best simple sugar for immediate energy and quick replenishment with the fewest side effects, followed by short-term use of **Sucrose**. Waxy Maize Starch (aka Vitago) had a short-lived fad because it apparently had a high molecular weight and low glycemic index. Theoretically it got absorbed quicker (because it was heavier), and had better effects on blood glucose – the perfect recovery sugar. There is absolutely no evidence to support this, and should be considered a total waste of money. **Maltodextrin** is a popular carb in energy products since it is a slightly more complex carbohydrate than glucose so it lasts slightly longer during the long haul. However, maltodextrin is digested slower and can cause GI upset during exertion. Although a simple carb, fructose gets digested slightly slower than maltodextrin. The more intense the exercise, the more you want to favor glucose followed by sucrose as your main source of carbohydrates since digestion slows and other sugars leave you bloated.

Fats

Besides being useful for fuel and storage of fuel, fat is used in many vital physiologic processes and for protection. There are many types of fat, but the main types we consume are in the form of saturated fat, unsaturated fat, and cholesterol. The bulkier or less dense the fat (LDL cholesterol and saturated fat) the worse it is for us: they clog our arteries and organs. Unsaturated fats are liquid at room temperature so they stay liquid at higher temperatures inside our bodies. If the fat gets digested and used as fuel or for cellular reasons, it doesn't matter the type (although just because you may be skinny and have a high metabolism does not mean you're arteries aren't clogged). Trans fats are made in the lab and wreak havoc on our system. Luckily it became a law to state levels of trans-fats on labels, so we are seeing a lot less of them in foods. They may soon be altogether banned. "Crisco" is a good example of a trans-fat (but is necessary in making delicious Southern-style cooking). Synthetic indigestible fats, like fake sugars also created in the lab, can't be good for you. They generally get pooped out.

Healthy oils are either **unsaturated**, aka **monounsaturated**, or at least partially unsaturated, aka **polyunsaturated**. Healthy oils can also reduce levels of bad (LDL) cholesterol and increase levels of good (HDL) cholesterol. Some goods oils to use are **olive and macadamia oils**. New research is showing that polyunsaturated fats may actually be worse for you compared to unprocessed forms of saturated fats. The jury is out on this, but erring the side of eating the most unprocessed and natural. Natural doesn't just mean unprocessed. It also means what the human animal would naturally eat. **Coconut oil** is high in saturated fat, so it should be used in moderation until more is known, but it has been shown to help regulate blood sugar, help with weight loss, and improve bone and dental health. It is a newcomer to the supplement world, so its benefits should be taken with a grain of salt. Apparently, coconut oil is not fully digested, but more goes directly to your muscles for energy than other fats.

Eating fat doesn't make you fat, calories do. Excess carbs are way more likely to become fat than the butter on your toast. Dieting or not, you should not feel guilty eating as many healthy fats as you want as long as your total calorie limit isn't overloaded. Excess fat is more easily excreted in your stool than excess carbohydrates. Too much fat intake can overwhelm your liver and gallbladder, and many overweight individuals have to have their gallbladder removed – kind of like diabetes of the liver.

Fats are used as energy in proportion to your energy output just like carbs. You burn the highest percentage of fats at rest (60%), and almost none at high levels of output. The "fat burning range" is really at rest! The goal in optimal climbing nutrition and dieters is the same – burn more fat than carbs. To do this we need to keep blood glucose levels low with a high insulin response during consumption of carbs. Fats have the most energy per weight and we have a vast amount stored compared to carbs, so it makes sense why climbers would want to burn fat over carbs. Fats are not converted into energy the same way carbs are, and the process takes longer to turn body fat into fuel.

Fat Supplements

One type of fat that is healthy, but our bodies don't produce on their own are **omega-3 fatty acids**. They are considered **essential fatty acids (EFAs)**, so we need to eat outside sources. Consuming EPA omega-3 fatty acids, like **fish oil**, over time gradually replaces the lipid (fat) containing cell membranes with this type of lipid. When cells have a high enough concentration of omega 3's, they inhibit the formation of prostaglandins, which create inflammation. Short-term inflammation is essential for repair, but long-term inflammation takes its toll on your bodies. Benefits of this supplement supposedly include almost everything under the sun, but the inflammation reducing properties, and to a lesser extent blood sugar lowering properties, are of the main interest to athletes. It is usually sold as fish oil, and you can get fish-burp free pills (highly recommended). Mercury contamination is a concern, so make sure you buy from a reputable company and the bottle says something about this. **ALA omega-3 fatty acids,** like **flaxseed oil**, are precursors to EPA fatty acids, and have less effect (but still some) because they are converted into other things.

A recent study has replicated results that consuming omega-3's, fish oil or fatty fish could increase the risk of prostate cancer in men by 70%! This is a classic example of misunderstanding data or misrepresenting statistics, as the study was observational (no one was given fish oil), the fatty acids were represented as a ratio, and no biologic mechanism was discussed. In other words, the subjects had a higher percentage but this could mean low levels of other types of fat. They could have been taking supplements because of pre-existing conditions! Correlation does not equal cause. So I still recommend taking these supplements unless more information comes out.

Medium-chain triglycerides (MCTs) are a form of lipid that are digested more quickly than other fats - almost as fast as carbs. Supplementing with these may help with endurance sports during activity by promoting fat oxidation. Too much will make you poop. You can add MCTs to your sports drink in a 1:5 MCT to Carb ratio. You can also take MCT pills before a climb – about 24-30 grams or 2-3 tablespoons two hours prior. The evidence is still out and these aren't cheap. MCTs are also recommended for those who have trouble keeping weight on, something not too concerning for climbers.

Fat Loading

Later on in this chapter carb loading will be discussed. However it has been shown that consuming a high fat diet (65% total intake) for 5-7 days prior to an event can help with fat utilization during aerobic activity (not anaerobic). In other words, you may burn a higher percentage of fat during submaximal exercise. You will need to replenish your glycogen stores the day or at least the night before from the high fat diet. You'll probably want to experiment with this well before any big day just in case it messes up your system.

PROTEINS

Proteins, like fats, have too many physiologic properties to list, but are the building blocks of our muscles. Amino acids are the building blocks of proteins. Our bodies break down proteins and use the amino acids to build new things. However, there are essential amino acids that need to be ingested because our body cannot produce them, but needs them.

Meat is an excellent source of protein if the fat is trimmed and isn't processed. The best pure protein supplements are **whey protein**, **casein**, and **soy protein**. Soy protein can negatively affect the thyroid and increase the risks of breast cancer in some cases, but has many other positive cancer fighting and health benefits. Vegetable proteins are often incomplete proteins because they don't have all of the essential amino acids in them. Bovine (or human) **colostrum** is another source used as a protein supplement. It is higher in protein and in antibodies than regular milk, but the verdict is out if it offers any benefit over other forms of complete proteins or for any immune protection, muscle growth, or recovery support. **Branched chain amino acids (BCAAs)** are a special class of essential amino acids based on their structure, and include **leucine, isoleucine, and valine** and have been shown beneficial in certain cases to supplement with (described later).

Protein is the second quickest form of energy available after carbs. Fat needs carbs to burn fat (they stoke the fire), so if carbs aren't available, your body turns to protein as its fuel. This is bad because the protein usually comes from muscle, and the by-products of protein metabolism create toxins (ammonia, urea, and uric acid) that are further metabolized and increase your blood pH, which throws off cellular function. After muscle, your body begins metabolizing other obviously important tissues composed of proteins.

One thing to keep in mind is that if no matter what percent fat you are burning, the harder you exercise the more calories are burned. So if you're losing weight and exercising, you still need to have more carbs so proteins don't get used. If carbs are available (and they should be), you only burn a small amount of protein – hopefully free amino acids floating in your bloodstream. But as activity increases, your body does more of a grab bag and burns more and more proteins.

To spare your muscles from getting eaten during high output activity, a good ratio of carbs to protein is 4:1 (20% protein) mainly in the form of amino acids in your drink mix and complete protein in your breakfast and dinner. If your drink mix doesn't contain amino acids or you're just drinking plain water, eat a small amount of protein throughout the day. Only eat a protein bar if you plan on sitting around for over an hour. Protein requires too much digestion to become available in your blood, something that isn't happening when you are exercising.

> For climbers training hard, I suggest 1.5 grams of protein per kilogram of bodyweight per day, even up to 2 g. per Kg bodyweight if you are really hitting it hard. Consuming 6-20 grams of protein 30 minutes prior to strength training can enhance muscle synthesis. Also, some protein during the day can help with fatigue. Supplementing with BCAAs may also help with fatigue.

MICRONUTRIENTS, VITAMINS, MINERALS & SUPPLEMENTS

Eat Nuts and Vegetables!

Do you want to spend a lot of money to be a human guinea pig for the promise of minor gains, or save some money and just eat more **red, yellow, and orange fruits and vegetables, citrus, dark green leafy vegetables, legumes, healthy fats, and proteins from healthy sources**? For those of us that hate cooking, and don't like vegetables, this section is for you! On a side note for you cooks, some foods are better cooked and others raw (raw food diets can be very unsafe). For example: tomatoes must be cooked to release the lycopene for you raw food fanatics.

Beware! Supplementing with just about anything can give you diarrhea and an upset stomach, completely nullifying any benefit.

Some supplements take a few days or weeks to get used to them, so don't try them just before a climb. For those that are just dying to find that they are deficient in something to explain their medical woes, you can get a micronutrient deficiency test. Sparacell Labs is one company that I am aware of that provides this service, but I am unaware of the quality of their testing or the validity and real world application of their results. I'd personally save my money.

Benefits of any vitamin, mineral, or supplement are listed when they are mentioned. Some fit many different categories and are not repeated. If you are mixing and matching supplements, vitamins, minerals, etc., be sure to realize there may be some crossover in ingredients. For example, sodium citrate contains sodium as well as citrate. Instead of digging out your chemistry textbook for the molecular weight and ratios of atoms (how much sodium is in 500 mg of sodium carbonate??), look at the nutrition label and compare it to the RDA.

Some foods are considered "superfoods", containing high levels of certain nutrients. I don't go into too much detail about specific foods to eat over others, specific diets or menus , that would add another 100 pages and there are better books than this one regarding general diet/meal planning. I did, however, get two requests from climbers to mention **Chia Seeds** because of their high protein, fat, and fiber content.

Multivitamins
Multivitamins have recently come under fire for a couple reasons. One is that they may not do enough to matter since our diet is heavily fortified, and the other is that some may actually do more harm than good. Even one recent studied showed organic food has no more nutrients than regular food. It's always a bummer when something perceived as healthy winds up doing things like increasing the risk of certain types of cancer: like hormone based birth control, soy protein, Vitamin E, and other antioxidants. There are numerous studies that have shown that people who take extra vitamins die significantly earlier from heart disease and cancer!

What to do? Especially when some health professionals (and unprofessionals) suggest mega-doses of certain vitamins and supplements. Vitamin-D comes to mind, but the list is endless. First, if you're going to take a specific supplement, do your research. If you're going to take a multivitamin, don't get a cheap one. I wouldn't recommend talking a multivitamin every day unless you eat garbage. Start taking multivitamins a week or two before and after periods of intense physical and emotional exertion.

Guys without anemia don't need iron in their supplements, and women with normal to heavy menstrual cycles should supplement with a women's specific multivitamin. Extra folic acid is only needed for women about to become pregnant, sorry Luna Bar. Gummy multi's are one of the best ideas in modern times. Who doesn't want a gummy bear before breakfast or before bed? Other good multi's are derived from **"green foods"**. Alive makes a comprehensive multi pill, powder, and juice. Other similar brands include Juice Plus and Nanogreens. There are a million of them and most probably have a ton of unscientific crap in them touting all sorts of claims like making your body more alkaline. But if you are going for a long time without fresh veggies on a climb, these can be better than nothing. Yes, some vitamins can be made more "bioavailable", some aren't very well standardized, and some you don't even digest but poop out in original pill form. I find multi's make me sick to my stomach and cannot take them if I have do any physical activity.

Electrolytes and Minerals
Electrolytes are minerals that carry a charge in solution (ions). They affect blood osmolality, and are major players in cellular function, especially nerve propagation and cellular transport. Some common electrolytes are sodium, potassium, calcium, magnesium, chlorine, zinc, iodine, chromium, bicarbonate, and manganese. Loss of sodium, followed by potassium and magnesium is common in high exertion exercise, hot (sweaty) conditions, or in diarrhea.

Sodium is the main electrolyte and is therefore the main regulator of fluid balance and keeps you from losing water. Water wants to balance the concentration of things, so if one side has more of something, like sodium, than the other, then water will diffuse across a semipermeable barrier to equilibrate things.

Loss of water and electrolytes through sweating has been a theory behind muscle cramping. Although we lose a lot of sodium via sweat, we have a lot of reserves. Table salt makes foods more palatable so bringing salty snacks can help you eat when you don't feel like eating. The addition of sodium to a sports drink is mainly for helping water pass into the blood, not to replace lost sodium levels that we should have in abundance. Regardless, if you sweat heavily or are a very salty sweater you may need to add more sodium to your sports drink.

Supplementing with **potassium** could be effective to prevent cramping. However, some studies have shown this may not be the case. Potassium is a key player in pumping things across cellular membranes, along with its counterpart sodium.

Besides being the key mineral in bone, **calcium** is the main generator of muscle contraction. It is not lost with too much caffeine as some claim. **Vitamin-D** is necessary to make calcium available for use. Vitamin D helps you utilize calcium, and you get it by exposure to sunlight. Hyper-supplementation is all the rage, but again, the evidence isn't there.

Magnesium, unlike calcium, plays a key role in the relaxation of muscles. Magnesium deficiency in athletes is more common than originally believed, and supplementing can aid in relieving muscle cramps. Too much can cause bad diarrhea. Supplementing with magnesium has been shown helpful for those with chronic fatigue, fibromyalgia, and headaches.

Chromium helps enhance the action of insulin.

Chlorine is obtained from table salt (NaCl) and you should be getting more than enough.

Bicarbonate (baking soda) helps maintain blood pH by buffering acids, and is helpful at buffering lactic acid during anaerobic activity and possibly during aerobic activity. Loading can occur 5-6 days prior, and 60-90 minutes prior to activity if it doesn't upset your stomach too badly. Take 140-230 mg per lb. bodyweight with plenty of water. A short term loading can also occur by consuming 140-180 mg per pound 2-3 hours prior to activity. To reduce the GI discomfort, consume several divided doses throughout the day.

Citrate has been shown to offer similar benefits as bicarbonate in the same quantities. Citrate bonded with sodium, potassium, calcium, and magnesium is popular substitute instead bonding with chlorine because it delivers those ions with the additional buffering benefit of citrate instead of chlorine. **Sodium citrate** usually has less gastric distress than bicarbonate. There is no need to use both citrate and bicarbonate, but they can be mixed. In general, chelated minerals are absorbed much better than their inorganic counterparts.

Phosphate also buffers acids and should be taken 3 days prior but not the day of activity. Diarrhea, bloating, and nausea are very common side effects of these acid buffer electrolytes and may be offset by drinking lots of water.

Manganese is a mineral that aids in the support of superoxide dismutase, an antioxidant. Manganese's reported cognitive benefits are shaky. Boron supplementation has been mildly shown to aid in reducing bone loss, increasing testosterone levels, and improving cognitive function.

Zinc helps maintain the thyroid and immune function, and supplementation has been shown to aid in weight loss. Zinc lozenges are slightly effective at reducing the severity of the common cold.

Iodine is added to salt (iodized salt) in developed countries to prevent us from getting thyroid goiters. Too much is toxic to the liver.

Finally, **iron** is necessary for binding oxygen to the hemoglobin in our blood and a regular diet is adequate as most grains and fortified. Women may lose iron in their menstrual cycle and can lightly supplement if periods are heavy. A women at the age of menstruation may require twice the iron intake as men and should be checked for iron levels (and bone density) if menstruating irregularly. People with irritable bowel syndrome may also have a slight iron deficiency. Also those suffering from some types (but not all) of anemia will benefit. Iron deficiencies can has a serious impact on your performance, however, supplementing above the RDA is not recommended for those without a deficiency. Long-term exposure to high altitude may cause a mild iron deficiency.

Unless you want to try out some of the exercise benefits of additional supplementation, a basic diet with an occasional multivitamin should provide you with adequate electrolytes - with the exception of calcium, which requires ingestion of calcium rich foods, or a separate calcium supplement. One gram of calcium is too bulky to mix with regular multivitamins.

> For a calcium supplement high in electrolytes, I would recommend a calcium, magnesium, zinc, and vitamin-D (required to make calcium bioavailable) pill consisting of 1000 mg calcium, 600 mg magnesium, 15 mg zinc, and 600 IU vitamin-D. Take the 2/3rd dose the night before and 1/3rd the morning of a climb. The other trace minerals and electrolytes should be contained in your diet and with a multivitamin.

If you're exercising hard, loss of **electrolytes** in sweat can change the balance of fluid and electrolytes in your body so additionally supplementing electrolytes during exercise with a flavored tablet in your water, fortified sports drink, or pill throughout the day is a good idea. However, the average diet has way beyond the RDA for salt intake, and much is stored inside our cells. Yes, a lot of sodium is excreted via sweating, but our reserves are still high, and there is a reason why we're dumping that salt out. Replacing electrolytes lost in equal amounts is like trying to replace water and fuel lost in equal amounts during exercise – your body can't deal with it during activity. To replace electrolytes fully, you would have to replace the water lost as well. Too much electrolyte replacement can actually induce cramping. The main function of adding salt to a drink it to more it pass more quickly into your bloodstream.

See the section on sports drinks for recommendations on supplementing electrolytes during a climb. As stated a normal diet with the possible addition of a multivitamin and a calcium, magnesium, zinc pill will get you more than you need to fill your reserves.

ANTIOXIDANTS

Antioxidants are categorized as such because they scavenge free radicals that oxidize and damage cells. Different antioxidants have different effects on the body besides just harvesting free radicals and that is the evidence I'll be getting into. Supplementing with antioxidants is supposed to be a good idea because intense exercise produces more free radicals via cellular respiration, and areas with high levels of air pollution. Antioxidants are so hyped-up in marketing, it can be impossible to wade through the next fad: "this antioxidant is equal to eating on million apples!" Recently, some studies have shown that not only can antioxidant supplementation actually increase oxidative damage during exercise, decrease endurance training benefits, and can also increase the risk of some types of cancer! So they fight oxidative stress and cancer, and cause both? Some studies have shown that the oxidative stress caused via exercise increases insulin sensitivity (good) and the supplemental antioxidants may block that effect (bad). And the increased risk of death? First, don't take any more than the RDA of Vitamin A, beta carotene, and Vitamin E as these levels can be toxic.

Vitamin C, ascorbic acid, was the main antioxidant studied in hampering endurance training benefits, although a new article just stated that it had no negative effect! Selenium seem to be safe, and circumstantial evidence suggests green tea and just eating more fruits, vegetables, and other natural sources of the antioxidants mentioned should be just fine. Some antioxidants, like CoQ10 and Vitamin C are taken more for their other benefits than their antioxidant properties. The theory behind why antioxidants can be both bad and good at the same time, dubbed "the antioxidant paradox" is that the free radicals may be useful at destroying bad cells like cancer and germs and that too much may shift the balance in the wrong direction.

Vitamin C has always been championed for its cold-remedy and energy properties. There is actually very little evidence to support that (sorry Emergen-C). However, it is a major playing in the creation of connective tissue, and can help prevent injury and aid in recovery, and is a powerful antioxidant. Too much can cause diarrhea, and you pee out what you don't absorb. It has no effect on your energy.

CoQ10 is an antioxidant that helps enhance the effects of insulin.

Flavonoids are a class of antioxidants that actually may not have antioxidant properties in the body (but do in the lab). However there is good evidence on their anti-cancer properties (although a possible increased risk of leukemia in offspring has been suggested). **Quercetin**, the main ingredient in FRS Energy, is a flavonoid, and is also marketed for producing extra energy. There is no evidence to support that claim.

Grape seed extract contains high levels of various antioxidants. Although no specific exercise performance enhancement is cited, it is excellent as a general antioxidant.

Ginger has very high antioxidant properties, but most people take it for reducing nausea and inflammation due to osteoarthritis.

Alpha lipoic acid (ALA) is another powerful antioxidant, and it may help control blood sugar levels.

Green tea extract is one of those rare supplements that may actually live up to many of its claims (just not to the extent marketing tells you). It has strong antioxidant properties, improves glucose metabolism and may aid in fat loss, and may have prevent some cancers.

Vitamin E has been shown to help with preventing cardiovascular disease, cancer, and cognitive decline.

Selenium has been shown to have some anti-inflammatory properties, and cancer prevention benefits.

Vitamin A and its derivatives (**beta carotene**) are also antioxidants with various biologic functions. They can be very harmful in high doses, so the RDA should be plenty.

Lutein and **lycopene** are also antioxidants that have shown to prevent degenerative eyes conditions.

Resveratrol is an antioxidant found in red wine that is making waves. It can help turn on genes that control the proliferation of cell mitochondria, the powerhouses of our cells. The amount used in mice studies were around thirty times the amount contained in current supplements, so it may be some time before human studies show results.

Superoxide dimutase is a ubiquitous and powerful antioxidant. There is no evidence taking it by mouth is effective, and creams/lotions used for wrinkles may or may not be effective. It is injected to accelerate healing in sports injuries, but the evidence is weak.

There are a billion other antioxidants on the market, like **Acai Berry and Pomegranate**, that need more research before that over-hyped claims are proven to at least some extent.

B-Vitamins

This is a class of vitamin that touts big claims are for stress and energy. B-vitamins are actually fairly helpful in energy production for cellular metabolism. The main B-vitamins are thiamine (B1), riboflavin (B2), niacin (B3), B5 (pantothenic acid), B6 (pyridoxine), B7 (biotin), B9 (folic acid), and B12 (cobalamin).

Thiamine may be helpful for recovering from exercise-induced fatigue.

Niacin helps with fat metabolism and could possibly increase human growth hormone levels, which is why it's very popular with weight lifters and dieters. Too much at once creates a "niacin flush" which is generally safe, but will not help detox your body! It is unknown if the "flush" helps muscles by providing more oxygenated blood. Products like Slo-Niacin time release so there is no flush.

B5 may help remove lactic acid from your system.

Riboflavin, B6, Biotin, and Folic Acid supplementation have shown no direct exercise benefit unless there is a deficiency. Riboflavin is the vitamin that turns your pee bright orange.

B12 supplementation has no effect unless there is a deficiency, so those mega-dose pills and shots will not increase your energy unless you have a deficiency.

Choline is considered a B-vitamin with some possible metabolism and cognitive benefits. Evidence is severely lacking, and high doses are dangerous.

Inositol is another standard ingredient in energy drinks, was once considered a B-Vitamin, and has extremely mild evidence for helping with mental alertness (so it must taste pretty good).

Fiber

There are two types of dietary fiber: **soluble and insoluble fiber.** They help keep your bowel movements regular, help regulate cholesterol levels, and lower the glycemic index of meals. If you aren't pooping regularly, or your stools are always logs, you need more fiber. Climbing food, especially freeze dried food and cheese, is notorious for clogging you up. In fact, if there's anything the average Western diet is deficient in, it's fiber. Fruits and vegies should supply you with plenty of fiber. If you supplement, see what happens before your trip. It is much better to be regular than backed-up on a climb, which can in turn lead to rebound diarrhea. Older adults have less gut motility and require more fiber and water in their diets.

Psyllium is a common soluble fiber used in digestion and lipid management.

Irvingia gabonensis is an herbal supplement high in fiber shown to help with metabolism and fat loss, although more research is needed.

PROBIOTICS

Our intestinal flora is fast becoming a field of legitimate scientific breakthrough. Those little guys in our gut do a lot for us besides just digestion – perhaps more than we think. Eating more **yogurt**, and supplementing with **probiotics** is not a horrible idea. **Prebiotics** can be taken to create a better environment for your new friends. One of the huge new fields in medical research is fecal biology and treating disease via fecal transplants!

KREBS CYCLE SUPPLEMENTS

Many chemicals and byproducts of the carbohydrate metabolism, the Krebs Cycle, are used to try and help athletes gain a competitive edge. Why not skip carbs and go straight to the source of energy: ATP? Because ATP is digested and is not bioavailable. Beware of any product with ATP in it, you might as well eat batteries for their energy (please do not eat batteries).

Citric acid could decrease feelings of fatigue. In a study participants were given citric acid daily. Their subjective scores on perceived fatigue were 20% less tired feeling after intense exercise. Since citric acid is relatively harmless and cheap, it could be a good supplement to fight fatigue.

Pyruvic acid (pyruvate) supplementation has been shown to increase endurance and promote fat utilization by increasing the amount of muscle glycogen available.

Alpha-ketoglutarate bound to the amino acids arginine (AAKG) and ornithine (OKG) supplements are very popular because both have been shown to improve insulin response, buffer ammonia from protein digestion, increase growth hormone, spare protein, and increase nitric oxide (NO) levels. Unfortunately extremely mixed results have been found on their actual effect.

AMINO ACID & PROTEIN SUPPLEMENTS

Some amino acids get burned more quickly than others which is why supplementing with specific amino acids makes sense even though supplementing with a complete protein that contains all the amino acids will eventually supply your body with whatever it needs – just not soon enough in high output situations.

Branched chain amino acids (BCAA's: leucine, isoleucine, and valine) are special because they are metabolized in muscle, not the liver like the other amino acids, so they are more readily available. Some studies have shown that supplementing with BCAA's increases muscle synthesis, decrease wasting, increases release of growth hormone, provides immune support with continued use, and when combined with beta alanine, decreases delayed muscle soreness (DOMS). Supplement pre, during, and post-exercise.

Glutamine is a key amino acid used in times of intense physical stress, and you can run low and start burning muscle bound proteins. Supplement pre, during, and post exercise.

Carnitine supplementation has been shown to be ineffective.

Tyrosine is another non-essential amino acid that has been show to offer some performance enhancement if supplemented. It has been shown to offer improvement during sports that are mentally taxing and require concentration over long periods of time. Evidence of a benefit with supplementation are mixed, but some studies have shown that taking 2 grams just prior to activity can be effective, or dividing does of 0.5 mg/lb. throughout the day.

HMB (beta-hydroxy-beta-methylbutyrate) is a byproduct of the amino acid leucine. Studies have shown it especially helpful to prevent muscle wasting, and helpful with delayed onset muscle soreness (DOMS). It also promotes muscle growth. Supplement pre and during exercise.

Beta-alanine is an amino acid and has been shown effective to improve muscular endurance both aerobically and anaerobically. Supplement before and during exercise.

Arginine is an amino acid that may help stimulate the release of **nitric oxide (NO)**. Nitric oxide relaxes smooth muscle (among other things) and acts as a vasodilator. This may be beneficial to allow pumped muscles to get nutrients and last longer.

Citrulline, an amino acid, is broken down into **malic acid** that may also have some nitric oxide releasing properties. Malic acid has been shown to increase energy with those suffering from chronic fatigue and fibromyalgia. It is unclear if supplementation is beneficial to those in the general population. One theory is that it helps buffer lactic acid. Additional supplementation with magnesium has been shown to have an additive effect with malic acid.

Taurine, an amino acid, is the big random ingredient in energy drinks. It has many physiological functions, and has a few reported benefits for mental alertness and physical performance, but there's better stuff out there.

Creatine is produced from amino acids, and is the king of strength training supplements. It shows benefit in most studies. Creatine is used as fuel in the first stages of muscle contraction — especially during powerful, explosive contractions so it is not as useful for endurance. Most weight trainers have a loading phase, followed by daily supplementation. There is a major downside: water weight gain. The amount of water weight gained may far outweigh any power gains for climbers. The best use for creatine would be specific supplementation for performance on repetitively powerful routes for a short period. Supplementing during the power phase of training could also be beneficial. It also helps with improving the effects of carb loading, and carbs need to be taken with creatine to get it in your muscles. Loading takes about 5-6 days with around 30 g taken per day with about 100 g of carbohydrates to aid in absorption. After the loading phase, you can coast for about 4-5 weeks. To keep up stores you can take 3 g a day for a couple months before reloading.

A study done on **fast protein and slow protein** showed that some types of protein enter the bloodstream quicker (whey) and have a muscle building effect, while others (casein) enters more slowly by stays longer and has a protein sparing effect. Take any protein supplements an hour before exercise and immediately after exercise for the greatest effect. Worrying about taking a fast vs. slow protein is probably a waste of time. Whey protein takes about an hour to enter the bloodstream, so although it is recommended to include protein in your post-workout snack, it is much more important to eat an overall diet rich in protein and to ingest carbs immediately post workout. Perhaps BCAA's would be a better post workout snack. The big downside is the cost. To get your daily dose of protein, it probably isn't necessary to use protein powder, but it can be quicker and easier for pre/post exercise fuel.

IgY antibody proteins (more on antibodies later) are antibodies produced by chickens and some other non-mammals (not by humans). When a chicken is exposed to multiple pathogens the egg supposedly is endowed with a hyperimmune amount of IgY antibody. It has been claimed in advertisements that supplementing with this protein will very significantly improve recovery, decrease maximal heart rate, decrease DOMS, and to a smaller extent increase muscular strength. It has also been suggested that hyperimmunized eggs could help with inflammation and autoimmune disease. Wow! The only evidence I could find were studies done on chickens and guinea pigs or by studies performed or at least subsidized by the manufacturer itself. I hesitate to completely crap all over this product because, who knows, maybe they are on to something. But I don't think I've seen ever seen a product with this little evidence hit the shelves and get marketed towards athletes. With the major claims they are making you would expect this to be worth its weight in gold, discussed on bodybuilding forms to death, and have more than in-house research. The reason I am spending so much time on this particular item is it is heavily marketed towards outdoor athletes.

Adaptogens

Adaptogens are herbal supplements that supposedly help your body cope with physical and mental stress. Evidence is decent, but not overwhelming, except for **cordyceps** which has lacks enough evidence to put on the "do not bother" list for now.

The best-studied adaptogens are: **siberian ginseng (eleutrococcus senticosus), korean ginseng (panax ginseng), rhodiola rosera, and schisandra chinensis**. Rhodiola is quite popular. Supposed effects related to climbing for those listed above are: decreased fatigue and increased energy, improved recovery, glucose metabolism, antioxidant benefits, immune support, and possibly adaptability to high altitude.

Ashwagandha is another supposed adaptogen that had claims from everything from helping with arthritis, inflammation, and anxiety to regulating blood sugar, cortisol and sex hormones. It is commonly used by those with fibromyalgia and chronic fatigue.

Energy and Alertness Supplements

Caffeine is one of the few legal drugs that actually boost exercise performance, along with some other health benefits. Actually, too much caffeine is illegal in many events. Caffeine increases alertness when tired, and spares muscle glycogen. The main problem for climbers and caffeine are the jitters – which do not help with performing controlled delicate movements! Maintaining enough food in the system can help.

To get the full benefit, athletes need to consume between 3-13 mg per kilogram of bodyweight. That is a lot of coffee, and some serious jitters! Caffeine receptors become accustomed to long-term caffeine consumption, so cut down 3 weeks prior to an event so you receive full effect. The water and calcium loss commonly associated with caffeine has been shown to be negligible.

The main, if only energy benefit from energy drinks is caffeine and sugar. Many contain large doses of B-vitamins and other ingredients. If you're going to take an energy drink, I suggest 5-Hour Energy Maximum Strength due to its high caffeine content and small size, or the new gums and dissolvable strips since they are very light weight, and chewing gum wets the whistle.

Other Fat Metabolism, Protein, and Glycogen Sparing Supplements

Two mL of **vinegar (acetic acid)** taken after large meals may help with glycogen repletion by improving insulin sensitivity after exercise. There is no evidence to suggest vinegar helps with exercise induced muscle cramps, but a shot of vinegar can help with heartburn.

Cinnamon extract or raw cinnamon (look for the twig rolled up like a double scroll of parchment) can help reduce blood plasma glucose. Too much is poisonous!

Cissus quadrangularis is an herb that has been shown in some studies to help with weight loss (and bodybuilders use it for gaining muscle). Not enough info is known to consider it effective just yet, however.

Using **5-HTP** for weight loss (from **tryptophan**, the stuff in turkey and milk that makes you sleepy) is possibly dangerous and is not recommended. It is sometimes used for improving mood.

Policosanol is another supplement touted for weight loss and lowering cholesterol. There is no good evidence that it works and has some negative side effects.

Garlic with high allicin levels may help with appetite suppression, but also could increase metabolism rates.

Licorice in the form of **glycyrrhetinic acid** shows promise in regulating blood sugar, adrenal and cortisol function and is one of the more commonly prescribed supplements for those suffering from adrenal fatigue.

OTHER VASODILATORS
Viagra and Cialis: jokes aside, these erectile dysfunction drugs are making their way into the medicine cabinets of professional athletes. The effects on high altitude will be discussed later. Basically they increase blood flow, and may have similar effects as NO supplements – better blood supply to muscles. It's too early to get good results from studies, but expect these to be the new craze.

Beet juice has recently been shown to significantly improve exercise endurance because of its strong NO properties, along with its high levels of antioxidants. Studies have shown taking about 500 mL showed peak results 2-3 hours later. Concentrated shots are also available to reduce GI distress. Remember that beet juice will darken or even turn your urine and stool beet red.

HORMONES AND STEROIDS
Phosphatidylserine (PS) isn't technically a hormone, but it is a phospholipid that has been shown to offer some benefit as an ergogenic aid for athletes although it studied more for its effect on memory and cognition in the elderly. To have any effect you need to take between 600-800 mg per day for 10 days. One of the main benefits for athletes is that it can help regulate cortisol levels following intense activity. Cortisol is a catabolic hormone, one function of which is to break down protein (so it can be build back up). PS has been shown to help combat exercise induced stress, decrease soreness, improve mood and cognition post exercise, and also improve concentration during coordinated activities. It may also increase stamina while performing. It could also be a waste of money – you be the judge!

DHEA is a hormone is taken by athletes for strength gains, and has largely proven ineffective. There is light evidence to support its impact on adrenal fatigue, stress regulation and strength gains on people over 55 due to their reduced natural levels, or people under 55 with pronounced adrenal fatigue (assuming it is a real condition). Supplementation can be dangerous.

Testosterone also decreases with age, and low testosterone levels should be tested. Increasing testosterone levels increases muscle mass and fat loss for sports-related benefits. Too much can lead to a whole host of dangerous or embarrassing health problems. Talk to a doctor!

Natural **testosterone "boosters"** are a billion dollar industry and are an advertising pit of snakes. **Tribulus terrestris** is a common ingredient in testosterone boosters. All I can say is caveat emptor.

Human growth hormone (HGH) is an important hormone for growth and repair, and by the time you're 60 you're running on 25% levels compared to your youth! Exercise and a good night's sleep are a great way to increase levels, as is eating a diet rich in protein. HGH is illegal to inject (and can be very dangerous), and products sold touting it as in ingredient contain doses small enough to be legal. Some say that taken sublingually, over the counter HGH has enough of an effect to be a recovery supplement. The price tag is stiff. Exercising while taking **melatonin**, glutamine, and arginine supposedly help stimulate HGH production. I am not going to discuss illegal anabolic steroids in this section.

Weight Management

Losing weight make a lot of sense for climbers. By dropping a few pounds you have greater strength and endurance. Instead of shaving a few ounces, or even a pound or two off your kit by buying the most expensive gear, think about shaving a few pounds off your body. If you skipped the earlier part of this nutrition chapter, you'll need to go back and read it. There is a lot of information already presented regarding fat metabolism. Please note that nutrition for optimum performance and nutrition for weight loss are two separate entities. You should be planning for one or the other – not both. If planning to lose weight, focus on that and technical skills instead of strength and performance – those are to be trained without any concern for weight loss. Optimizing fat burning vs. glycogen is a goal for both endurance and weight loss, but your planning must differentiate between those goals by focusing on weight loss (really fat loss) and then optimizing your fat burning metabolism for long term energy output.

Body Fat
To see if you even qualify for weight loss, and to measure success, you need to find out what your percent body fat is. Weighing yourself on a scale tells you little useful information. If you are trying to lose weight by exercising, added muscles may show up as no improvement on the bathroom scale. Too little body fat is unhealthy too. Men should shoot for 5-13% body fat and women should aim for 12-22% for optimal performance. Don't try and just aim for the low end of the range, each body requires different levels of fat. According to a recent study, being underweight is just as deadly as being overweight.

When you measure your body fat, you need to use the same method and even the exact same device to keep the numbers consistent. The best test is just looking in a mirror to determine if you are happy with your weight. This is a terrible test for those with dysmorphic body image issues, however! I highly recommend searching out a Bod Pod or Biometrix unit for highly accurate results. Devices that measure bioimpedance vary from good to lousy. The price tag can say a lot. If using a bioimpedance device at home, drink a liter of water upon waking and pee before measuring. Skin fold calipers are cheap and moderately accurate, but it's difficult to do it on yourself. If using calipers, make sure the same person is doing the measurements each time. Taking photos of yourself in your underwear can be excellent visual motivation.

Weight Loss
The goal in weight loss should be to lose excess body fat, not weight. If you change your diet to a healthier one and are getting

plenty of exercise, you should really make your goal to not weigh more and change your body fat percentage, not just to weigh less. Focus on being fit, not fat. If you follow this goal instead of "I want to lose X-amount of fat this month," you will be more likely to succeed and fat will be burned. Your main plan of attack should be to not eat more calories than you need to perform, and to burn a higher percentage of fat. The whole "calories in should be lower than calories burned" works up to a point because as pointed out in the nutrition chapter, you could burn muscle if you aren't getting enough calories and exercising in an anaerobic state. There are very few stored calories as glycogen, and once those stores are depleted your body unfortunately doesn't just start burning 100% fat.

Caloric restriction, low carbs, and exercise are still the key to weight loss. The body turns to fat as the main source of fuel as long as blood sugar levels are adequate and protein will be spared – even if fasting. It takes time to train your body to regulate blood sugar levels when changing your diet (lowering calories and carbs) and increasing your training volume and intensity so start slowly. Expect to be exhausted, starving, irritable, etc. for the first few days or even weeks. This is good, your body is weaning off its addiction to sugar.

Since you need to put in less than you burn and excrete, aim for a 20% caloric restriction. If this means eating 500 less calories a day (if you're eating 2000 calories a day) then the reduction should equate to about 1 pound of weight loss a week. If you want to get specific then do some simple math by figuring out how many pounds of fat you need to lose to achieve your goal. By knowing how much fat weights per calorie (9g/cal), your resting BMR, how much extra energy you expending exercising and doing normal activities, and what your current caloric intake is, then you can make a plan by lowering your calorie intake and / or activity level to a level you can still perform well at.

Fat is stored inside adipose cells, and gaining fat produces more adipose cells. You do not lose the actual cells, but the fat inside of them. This is one reason why it is hard to keep weight off. Adipose cells need energy too, and starving yourself won't selectively kill them. By keeping weight off, the cells do eventually atrophy and die. Because adipose cells need calories too, the more weight you lose, the fewer calories you will need per day.

Exercise

Try and exercise every day – 20 minutes is so much better than nothing. Do not start a new exercise program with guns blazing. This is the easiest way to fail because the new demands will either get you injured, make you too tired to exercise the next day, or take up too much time and you will get overwhelmed.

Don't reward your exercise and climbing by eating more! This is the number one reason why exercise leads to weight loss failure. Plan ahead by getting enough to eat before you hit the gym or the crag, and have your post-exercise glycogen repletion snack immediately afterword. Those calories will not turn into fat: the giant dinner or reward hunger will. Remember that you burn the highest percent fat at rest. However, the more you exercise the more calories you will burn. So even though the percent fat being burned is decreased, the total calories burned becomes increased, and more fat is burned.

Exercising excessively hard will provide diminishing returns, but exercising at too low an intensity will take forever. A good average intensity is at 70-80% of your max heart rate. After you've been at it long enough, you should be able to ride close to the line between aerobic/anaerobic for an hour or two (better) without constantly needing to keep your blood sugar up. Several studies have recently shown that high intense exercise is much more effective at burning fat in the long term than low intensity exercise. Just remember to keep the blood sugar levels up when doing so.

Short bouts of anaerobic exercise are just as good, if not better, weight loss tools as long bouts of lower intensity. You still need to do both. For high intensity exercise you wind up burning muscle glycogen for fuel during exercise, so it is important to eat well at breakfast, before, and during exercise. The fat burning doesn't come as much during this type of exercise, but afterwards. Spread out your anaerobic exercises if you are trying to lose fat because too many in a row (if in a row at all) will lead to failure or injury. Increasing the amount of muscle you put on from this kind of exercise will also help you burn more fat. More muscle = more fat burning engines.

Remember that exercising a body area will not make you lose weight in that area. Sit-ups don't lose belly fat, triceps exercises don't lose arm flab, and leg squeezes don't lose inner thigh fat. Compliment this with endurance bouts of lower intensity exercise. Start well fed, but unlike high intensity exercise, don't consume food (or liquid with fuel in it) during this activity (have some on hand if you are in the hills just in case). You should be mobilizing fat for fuel during this type of exercise and not fully depleting glycogen stores. The first few workouts will be awful, but your body will adapt.

Diet
Keep a food diary and count your calories. If you find that you are eating too many calories, you have identified one of the problems. Cut down on the higher calorie foods and fill up on veggies, and spread your meals out more. Snacking leads to more calories. A bag of carrots and a glass of ice water are a decent snack. The longer you diet and exercise, the easier it becomes to avoid snacks, as you won't be as hungry. Give yourself three weeks of suffering to deal with added hunger, but a general rule of thumb is that hunger and fatigue mean you aren't getting enough calories. Don't take ephedra or other scammy, dangerous, or illegal weight loss pills. They do more harm than good, and the whole point of weight loss is to be healthier so you can climb harder. Only go for some of the supplements listed in the earlier part of this chapter if you have already failed. Do extra research, and try not to take more than one or two supplements at a time.

The stupidest diet I've heard so far is based off of your blood type is called "Eat Right for Your Type". This diet makes me want to invent a whole series of insane diets marketed towards idiots. The Atkins diet is too dangerous on your kidneys and heart and the South Beach Diet is similar but allows veggies but will still lead to dangerous ketosis and failure since no one can stay on it. The Zone Diet (40% carb, 30% protein, 30% fat) will probably lead to fatigue and cheating, and achieving that ratio is really hard to figure out. The Paleo diet is fairly similar to the Zone diet, but less strict on ratios and more focused on quality foods. Many of the recipes and advice from the Zone and Paleo diet are great, but the whole package leaves much to be desired. Eating too much protein is hard on the kidneys. If protein becomes the main nutrient, the body enters ketosis. Fat is metabolized and produces ketone bodies. These ketones are used by the brain and nervous system for fuel since carbohydrates are no longer available.

The Mediterranean diet is one of the better fad diets around as it allows for lots of healthy oils. If you must pick a fad diet, pick the Mediterranean. The popular China Study diet basically states that all animal protein is the source of disease and cancer and touts a raw food, plant-based, vegan style diet. There are some fundamental flaws in this book. But all fad diets really are is sensationalizing a particular aspect of weight loss. By eating healthy whole non-processed foods, limiting calories, not going carb or protein-crazy, and exercising you can throw these diet books in the trash. Buy a current book on (sports) nutrition and you've got your diet book. Eating organic won't give you more nutrients, a fact that was widely assumed but recently debunked. However, organic foods have less hormones and chemicals in them. The more natural and less packaging the better. If can go bad it's good. Instead of wasting money on detox supplements and scams, try fasting, which is free.

What to Eat
Carbs are the evil villain in modern weight loss diets, but you need them to burn fat. Simple carbs are fine during long climbs and after intense exercise to keep glycogen levels high. Foods made with whole grains have a low glycemic index, and should be the bulk of your carbohydrate consumption. Not all food advertised as whole grains are indeed whole grain. Look at the ingredients, and look up the glycemic index and loads online. Healthy oils are good for you, so you should be eating fat. The key is to eat healthy fat, not processed high cholesterol fats.

Low fat diets don't work – it's the calories not the fat. Diets high in protein or protein only diets do help in weight loss. However, too much protein will destroy your kidneys. High protein diets may aggravate kidney and liver problems, increase your risk of cancer if processed (nitrates) or charred/blackened, aggravate coronary artery disease, and increase your calcium loss in urine. Try and eat around a 30% protein diet. Eat chicken and pork with the unhealthy fat trimmed, fish low in mercury, lots of legumes, and nuts (also high in fat). Nuts are extremely calorie dense, so budget accordingly.

Supplementing with protein shakes can make you want to eat more since it isn't as dense as meat products or beans. Remember that more calories consumed than burned are what makes fat. Consuming less carbs and more protein should not be the cornerstone of your diet. Pile on the vegetables! Only eat real food – laboratory food will make you fat. Drink lots of water, especially during your meal. Eating similar meals is a very helpful trick.

What Not To Eat
Avoid **simple sugars and "white" carbs**. These include: all foods with sugar as a main ingredient, most breads, rice, and potatoes. Sugar can be masked in the ingredient list to make it sound more natural. Here are some synonyms: things ending with "-ose", "cane", "malt", "syrup", honey, or "nectar".

Although they contain a lot of vitamins, fruit should be eaten only as a small snack due to their high fructose content. **Fructose** sugars in fruits, candy, and drinks have a very high glycemic index and load and are starting to get blamed for many other health related concerns.

Avoid **alcohol** at all costs, even red wine if possible. Alcohol contains a whopping 7 calories per gram, almost twice that of sugar and carbs. Do not consume any calories in liquid form – including fruit juice. Avoid **fast food, artificial sweeteners, artificial fats, and processed and packaged foods** like the plague. BPA's (the evil chemical that used to be in your Nalgene bottle) just had another study that came out directly relating their use to obesity in children. Don't eat out for lunch. Avoid dairy as much as possible. Wow, that sounds like

225

hell, right? Thankfully there is salvation in the cheat day – described shortly.

Timing
It takes your stomach about 20 minutes to tell your brain that you are full. So chew slowly and take at least 20 minutes to finish a meal, and leave the table when you feel 80% full – not stuffed. Make meal portions smaller, and spoil your appetite by having a pre-meal snack. Exercising large muscle groups for only two minutes immediately before a meal (pull-ups, squats, pushups) will get those calories to muscles instead of turning them into fat much more effectively.

Frequent eating keeps blood sugar high and reduces overall appetite. High intake meals increase insulin and cortisol levels. Cortisol will increase fat storage. Eat right when you wake up, or at least within the first 30 minutes of waking to keep your blood sugar better regulated throughout the day. Get almost all of your carbs at this time (banana, English muffin, oats, whole grain cereal). Insulin sensitivity, or how much insulin your pancreas secretes compared to what you eat, is high in the a.m. so the carbs go straight to your liver and muscles. This primes the pump to start burning fat. Insulin sensitivity is high after exercise too – so be sure to eat your carbs immediately post exercise.

A very recent study showed that skipping breakfast before you exercise would burn more fat. What the study did not show was how much protein from muscle was getting burned instead (and it was only one study), and how this affected the rest of a person's diet and energy levels the rest of the day. This does throw a wrench into the works of eating breakfast and I wish more testing and studies were done before putting this study on the front-page news. If you are going to skip breakfast, you still need to eat enough carbs afterword to replenish the glycogen. Another study from Harvard that followed people for many years also found that skipping breakfast reduced the total calories a person consumed in a day, even if they did eat a little bit extra later on in the day. Your call.

Insulin sensitivity decreases throughout the day, so eat less carbs for lunch and almost no carbs at dinner. Make sure you eat some fat during dinner to keep from getting hungry before bedtime, and to keep from feeling like crap in the morning because you ran out of fuel. Eating your meals earlier than normal can also stop you from binge eating because you are so hungry by the "normal" time. This also front-ends the main bulk of your calories earlier when you will actually digest and metabolize them.

Cheat Day
One day a week, you get to pig out - your cheat day! A cheat day fulfills two important roles. The first is that it quenches intense food cravings for sweets, carbs, alcohol, or whatever you have been avoiding eating and drinking. The other purpose it serves is to keep your body from going into "low power mode". Because you've been changing your diet, and probably cutting down on calories, your body starts to think food supplies are scarce. Eating whatever, and however much as you want one day a week fulfills enough emotional/psychological needs to not cheat during the rest of the week, probably makes you slightly sick of the foods you're avoiding, and keeps your metabolism high. You will gain weight that day, but you will lose it and more the next day. Most of the added cheat day weight is extra water, and most of the extra calories are pooped out. If you find yourself just existing solely for the cheat day you are developing a negative type of reward since you are learning nothing from the process. If this is the case, you can make your cheat day a percentage of your diet

every day by cheating on 10-15% of your healthy diet.

Cold
There are some other tricks you can do to help you lose weight, and many have to do with cold. It makes a lot of sense: the colder you are the more calories you burn. And if you are cold at rest, then you should be burning more fat. Drinking ice water is an excellent start, especially at breakfast. It goes straight to the core, keeps you hydrated, and makes you feel fuller. Taking 15 to 20 minute cold showers before breakfast and at bedtime revs up the metabolism for the meals you are about to eat. Start with hot water to soften the blow. Ice on back of neck after dinner for 20-30 minutes is another great trick – as is a full-on ice bath. Turn the A/C up and the heat down. Being slightly cold is much healthier that being warm anyways. Being slightly chilly (comfortably cool) is the best climbing weather anyways – better friction, more comfortable, and your muscles and metabolism are more efficient. Finally, participating in any winter sports (ice climbing and skiing for climbers) not only gets you cold, it gets you active. What could be better?

Etc.
A recent study found that the three most successful things a person can do to lose weight are to not skip meals, not eat out for lunch, and keep a food journal. Once you make some changes and you haven't gained any more weight, a new realistic goal may be to lose one pound a week. While you're at it, make a doctor's appointment and get your thyroid, testosterone, liver, cortisol, glucose, lipid, and cholesterol levels checked.

Fasting
Fasting is the best embodiment of the saying, "less is more". Fasting advocates claim that fasting can cure everything from asthma, cancer, autoimmune disease, diabetes, cardiovascular disease, obesity, chronic fatigue, leaky gut, depression...you get the idea – any and all lifestyle and 21st century real or imagined syndromes and diseases with the added benefit of life extension. I can't comment on any of these claims, but I'm sure there is some truth behind them. I believe there is enough evidence and theory behind fasting to make it a safe, worthwhile option for those who think it can be beneficial.

You can design all sorts of "fasts" - juice only, protein and veggies only, drink only green tea, whatever. You can also fast for however long you want – part of the day, a day, two to three days, a week, or up to 40 days on nothing at all. It really depends on what you are trying to accomplish. Restricting certain foods makes more of a weight loss-type fast, focusing on healthy foods and supplements makes more of a health fast, and focusing on liquid calories like a juice fast makes more of a gut cleaning fast. These all may or may not produce your intended consequences. However, the only real fast is eating nothing. The other pseudo fasts are fine, including intermittent fasting, as long as you don't overtax your system and get enough calories and nutrients to be able to recover.

Intermittent fasting for weight loss while still being able to function and exercise has you fasting for part of the day and consuming enough carbs during the other part to maintain adequate muscle glycogen, or fasting every other day. Non-exercise days focus more on the fasting part of the day and less on the eating part. One day a week is usually reserved for a 24-hour total fast. Is this safe and effective for weight loss? Maybe. It has to be done and timed perfectly. Too much fasting and you start burning muscle. Too much carb-loading and you spike insulin levels. Screw it up and you'll be a mess. However, there is some evidence that intermittent fasting helps with weight loss and training in a depleted state can cause surges in human growth hormone. Find a trustworthy resource devoted to the topic.

This leaves real fasting to discuss. No food whatsoever except water (might as well drink filtered water as long as you're at it), is in my opinion the only fasting method that is truly worth bothering with unless you are trying to clear out your bowels. Why not just change your diet to a healthy one instead of arbitrarily selecting one type of thing to eat? Total fasting should not be done often. Every 5-10 years more like it unless you really feel the need. Although I'm not admitting to any of the health benefit claims I'm about to list, total fasting would be the only method to get a real detoxification of chemicals, cannibalization of cancer/tumor cells, plaques, etc. (fasting advocates claim your body will autolyze "bad" cells in a fast), decrease of inflammation, and normalization of hormones and pancreatic function. Might as well go for it.

How long? Most sources suggest 10-15 days for most conditions, 14-28 days for very chronic/serious conditions, and more (up to 40 days) for the hard-core. If you fast for more than two weeks please get blood tests to make sure you have adequate electrolyte levels. You should tell your doctor what you're planning. Unfortunately the type of doctor that would tell you "please don't do this" is probably the one who would be best to help supervise your fast!

The first two days expect to feel awful. A good time to start would be Friday morning so you've got the weekend to agonize. By the end of the 2nd day you should start to feel a lot better. Expect weird symptoms to arise besides expected ones like fatigue, diarrhea, headaches, hunger, etc. Go for a walk, do some light stretching. Don't exercise initially, however. After the first 2 or so days you should be able to gauge your ability levels for performing activities. You should be able to work and go to school just fine. Those with high fat reserves may be able to exercise normally, but those with low fat reserves should expect to lay low. If you are exceptionally fatigued or have symptoms that concern you, see your doctor ASAP and/or break your fast.

When your fast is over, slowly introduce how much you eat and what you eat. Some digestive enzymes may have slowed production, so don't eat a hamburger and wash it down with a glass of milk. The more watery your re-introduced foods are, the better. Fruit is perfect. Do some research to plan your first few days to weeks' worth of meals.

Weight Disorders

Eating disorders are definitely more common in climbers compared to the general population. Too little body fat is dangerous, and especially so if below 5% in males and 10% in females. Muscle wasting, hormonal imbalances, bone loss, and mental/emotional problems will occur. Forget about any strength or growth gains. Women tend to get hit harder than men since 10% body fat is twice the levels as is for men to be considered extremely dangerous. The Female Athlete Triad (don't abbreviate it to FAT!) is the term coined for women overtraining and underweight. This includes: loss of the menstrual cycle (amenorrhea), bone loss (osteoporosis), and lack of energy via bulimia or anorexia. There are long-term health consequences for being under fat or undernourished in both men and women.

If you are seriously under your healthy body fat levels you may just not be eating enough (or too much sugar and not enough fats and protein) or may be exercising too much. If changing your diet and scaling back the over-training (you're going to get injured - overtraining will bite you in the butt) and still are underweight, get your hormone levels tested at the doctor. Also, you may have undiagnosed psychological issues that are usually the cause of eating disorders. Unexplained weight loss is a serious medical symptom.

Gaining Weight

For those of you with healthy enough body fat and want to gain some more weight, first ask yourself "WHY!" If you are going on a high altitude expedition, yes, you may want to tack on some extra muscle and fat mass to burn while you wither away up there. Gaining weight for some is like losing weight for others – it seems impossible. The most popular weight gaining diet I've come across since the 1980's training montage of drinking a glass of whole eggs yolks dressed in sweats and bands is **GOMAD**, the Gallon of Milk a Day. Just don't try and drink it all at once, and if you have high cholesterol do something healthier. **MCTs** were suggested earlier as a possible choice for gaining weight. The easiest method to gain weight is to use the opposite math you would in trying to lose weight – eat more calories, especially carbs and protein.

Planning Food and Water

Many climbers, myself included, usually wind up taking their food to the top of (and back down) most climbs, almost as if to show their food around, and only eating the moistest, tastiest treat when just about to bonk. For some reason, climbing slightly hungry just makes some people climb faster. As one partner stated, "who needs to eat when there's worrying to be done?" Although I can't endorse this behavior, I do suggest that eating a big breakfast or a lot of food will also make you really thirsty a couple hours later. Plan for this!

Energy Requirements

Calories provided on nutrition labels are actually kilocalories. For the purposes of this book I will use the term calories (cal) instead of kilocalories.

To find out how many calories you need, you first need to find out how many calories you burn by just being alive. The following equations don't take into account your unique metabolism or lean body mass. Highly muscular individuals numbers may be too low and those with high body fat will be a bit high.
- Men = (Weight in pounds * 6.08) + (Height in inches * 12.1) - (5.7 * Age in years) + 88
- Women = (Weight in pounds x 4.2) + (Height in inches 7.84) - (4.3*Age in years) + 448
- If you know your percent body fat then use this equation: 500 + [10 * (1 - % Body fat) * Weight in pounds]

It's very hard to determine how many additional calories you'll need on top of this, since climbing is generally a combination of bursts of all-out effort, no effort (belaying), and moderate effort. Temperature, metabolism, and how well you deal without eating can affect your caloric needs as well. To give a rough guideline, you expend about 120 to 240 cal (easy to hard) per hour climbing, but extreme effort can go as high a 600 calories per hour. These numbers include your resting metabolism. You can get a rough estimate of how many calories to bring on a trip and on the climb by guessing how much effort you will be putting in. If you count up your dinner and breakfast calories, you can subtract that from the total to get an idea of how many calories to bring with you on the climb itself, assuming you eat breakfast and dinner at home or at camp.

The following is a gross estimate of calorie expenditure. If you'll be cold, go up a level (dressing warm lowers the calories needed).
- **Easy day**: 3,000 calories, or (base calories * 1.75). This could include approaching, a few single pitches, or grade II climb
- **Moderate day**: 4,000 calories, or (base calories * 2). A big approach or a grade III-IV climb. This is roughly the same activity level of a very hard day at work doing manual labor.
- **Hard day**: 4500 calories, or (base calories * 2.25). A typical grade IV-V climb.
- **Brutal day**: 5000-7000 calories, or (base calories * 2.5 to 3.5). This could be a Grade V or above climb done in a day, or a car-to-car 16+ hour day with approach included.

WATER REQUIREMENTS

We can go weeks without food, but only a few days without water. We can absorb 0.75 liters of water an hour, but lose up to over a quart an hour if we're intensely exercising and sweating. It also depends on how hot, cold, dry or humid out it is, what the altitude is, your blood pressure, and your blood osmolality. Not all climbing is exerting energy, and lots of it is down time. We still need a baseline of 1.5 liters for a day of non-exercise. If you're not peeing like you normally do, then you're dehydrated. Being thirsty does not mean you are already very dehydrated, it just means it's time to drink. Thirst is a fairly accurate marker of the need to drink water, not a delayed response to dehydration. You can develop thirst tolerance and adapt to hot, dry, and higher altitude places. Climbers traveling to high and dry climbing areas from the moist lowlands will need to drink more water. Judging your hydration status by the color of your urine can also be misleading sometimes. Use thirst as your gauge unless you are at altitude, are exercising really hard, or suffering from heat exhaustion. In these conditions you must force yourself to hydrate.

Water is really heavy. One liter of water weighs 2.2 pounds (or one kilogram). If you did the math, you would have figured that a big day of hard climbing would mean carrying several pounds of water – something that is just not possible unless you can refill your water supply en route. If that is possible, then drink up and refill. There is no performance benefit to being lighter because you didn't drink as much water as you could have used. Just the opposite in fact. Strength and endurance decrease drastically with dehydration. **Ration your water so you're drinking about 8 oz. every thirty minutes (16 oz. per hour or a liter every two hours) if possible.**

Drinking in small increments is much better than drinking all at once. Use a stopwatch, or pitch count to keep up. Camelbak makes a flow meter that really helps with rationing water, but it snags on everything and the "screw things up" button is too easily pushed. For a long day, bring a minimum of 2 liters (4.4 lbs.), and if it is hot, sunny, or you are unconditioned, bring a minimum of 3 liters (6.6 lbs.). If you are new to climbing in hot, dry, or higher altitude areas, bring an extra 0.5 to 1 liters until your get your systems dialed. If you're camping en route you'll need to add an additional 1.5 liters for breakfast and dinner. Whatever the case, be sure to chug water in the morning and after the climb. Drinking an unreasonable amount of water can dilute the electrolyte balance in your body and cause problems, even death - a condition called hyponatremia. It shouldn't be a concern unless you aren't replenishing your electrolytes (described later). Those who sweat a lot and consume large amounts of plain water are most at risk. If you are a salty sweater or just sweat a lot you may want to consider adding quite a bit more salt to your diet while exercising. Check with your doctor if you are concerned or have high blood pressure before increasing your salt intake. Finally, NSAIDs increase the risk of hyponatremia significantly.

Dehydration is rapidly fixed by drinking more water. However, it does take discipline to continually drink water if you don't feel thirsty, especially after a hard day. Unfortunately the more dehydrated you become, the harder it is to rehydrate and get the water out of your gut and into your blood plasma and cells. Start hydrating at least the night before, but it is better a day before so you don't wake up peeing all night by overdoing it. It can take up to 24 hours of hydration to adequately rehydrate a very dehydrated person. Adding **sodium and some sugar** to your water, like a sports drink, will really aid in rehydrating.

Food Weight

One ounce of fat contains 255 cal, and one ounce of protein or carbohydrate contains 113 calories. If 80% of your calories are from carbs and protein and 20% is from fat, then you can calculate how much your food will weigh. The following totals include breakfast, lunch, and dinner. If you eat your breakfast and/or dinner at the car or camp, your totals will be lower.

The following are just rough estimates of how much food would weight if you packed your energy requirements, and don't include the weight of water inside the food. Add ½ to 1 lbs. of water weight to your totals for non-dried meals. If you're carrying all your water with you, it makes sense that you could choose non-dried foods and just factor that into reducing your water amounts. Too keep the climbing pack weight down, bring along a bunch of extra snack foods to eat back at camp or in the car to make up for deficits (see carb loading below as well).

Pounds per Day
- **Easy day**: 1.5 lbs.
- **Moderate day**: 2 lbs.
- **Hard day**: 2.5 lbs.
- **Brutal day**: 3+ lbs.

Refueling and Rehydrating

You can replace 200-350 calories per hour during exercise due to the osmolality of the food, **or about 4 cal/1 g. of carbs per Kg per hour**. In other words, for the food to go into your bloodstream quickly, it must be around the same tonicity or lower than your blood plasma – **a little less than 5% carbohydrate to water concentration**. You do not want to be routing your energy stores to digestion at this time, which is when the rest of the calories will become available and causes bloating and gastrointestinal (GI) distress. In other words, drink to hydrate and eat to refuel – don't try and combine the two.

Obviously you need water to maintain performance, but you also need to keep your blood glucose high to perform. **To stay hydrated you can't wash an energy gel/chew down with a sports drink. Water is most effectively absorbed if it has the right ratio of electrolytes (mostly sodium) and carbohydrates (glucose and sucrose best), more than plain water alone. If using gels or chews, consume 35 cal (or 9 g) with 8 oz. of plain or electrolyte enhanced water. If using a sports drink a good ratio is about 140 cal (or 35 g) of carbs per liter.** This is obviously not enough calories to fuel you. Keep hydration separate from fueling. You can replace the rest of the calories between hydration.

How many calories depends on how much water you are consuming with carbs. If you are consuming a liter an hour of sports drink, then you could theoretically eat an additional 130-280 extra calories an hour, but in reality shoot for an additional 50-170 calories per hour. **This means a total of**

120-240 calories consumed per hour, counting the sports drink and additional food calories combined. Get in the extra calories if you stop for a while, because otherwise you won't be able to digest the extra calories.

Some sports nutritionists are beginning to recommend eating real food for calories instead of gels and chews. Mixing up all of your food and water at the same time will actually draw water from your system to dilute the soup to a mixture enough that you can actually absorb it. The more solid or "real" the food, the more it needs to be digested, but at the same time, the less it disrupts hydration. Solid food forms a glob, or bolus, and passes into your small intestine for digestion and absorption, and doesn't create an immediate demand for a lot of extra water at once. Unfortunately you will most likely need to eat more calories than you can accompany with the water required to remain at or lower than isotonic unless you carry a lot of water. So the best real world fix is to drink to stay hydrated, and eat real food to fuel with an occasional dose of gel or energy chew to avoid bonking.

Eating **energy gels and chews** provides quick and easy carbs and don't require as much digestion but interfere with hydration, while **solid food** doesn't interfere with hydration as much but can require more digestion and sit heavy for a while. Since you can't really do anything about this, I recommend eating gels and chews when "on the go" or when you start to bonk, and then eat something more solid, like a meat/cheese/veggie/bread **sandwich** when you have a break or are belaying for a while. Don't make a thick drink mix and expect to gain any hydration benefits. It may be an easy way to quickly consume calories, but it will leave you bloated and dehydrated.

Most climbs should focus on eating real food and proper hydration via a 4% carb drink mix with electrolytes, or plain water with an electrolyte tablet and an occasional energy gel/chew. And of course, try and pack the calories and water in as much as you can before the climb.

Extremely fast and long lasting bouts of long term hard activity, like speed climbing or extremely hard-core alpinism should either use **plain water and electrolytes with energy gels or chews, or a 4% drink mix with fewer gels or chews to keep the intake at ½ liter an hour with about 100 cal of carbs per hour.**

Everyone has a different tolerance and can get away with drinking more or less, and can handle higher concentrations of carbs with less water. If you are bonking, eat more. If you are thirsty, drink more. If your stomach is upset, you are consuming too many carbs with your hydration. Eating sugar all day takes its toll, so carry a small amount of fat for crash recovery on high output days. Some like meat sticks, some like chips, while other hard-core types down a shot of olive oil. If your climb is not high output or long, then just eat a normal diet on the climb and don't worry about any of this.

CARB LOADING

It is impossible to eat and carry all the food and water necessary to come out on top on most climbs. To combat this, be sure and eat plenty of food and drink lots of water before a climb. You can also be more systematic about it and "carb load". The problem with carb loading is that it gets your body used to the increased calorie intake, wreaks havoc on your pancreas, liver, and kidneys, and can clog up your bowels something awful. Done once or twice a year it should be fine, and the more easily digestible the food, the better. Concentrated drink mixes and shakes shouldn't clog the system and you'll need more water anyway to aid digestion.

One method of carb loading, known as supercompensation, should not be used. This method had one deplete their glycogen stores to build them up again at a higher volume. This will mess you up. The best and easiest method has you consuming 3.5 to 4.7 grams (14-19 calories) of carbohydrates per pound of bodyweight for 2-3 days prior to activity. This doesn't sounds like much, but it is actually a TON of food, equal to 1 to 1 ¼ packages of spaghetti. Round out the rest of your meals with vegetables, protein, and healthy oils. Don't expend much energy during your loading days.

Glycogen Dumping
As mentioned, supercomensation should not be used to rebuild glycogen stores to achieve higher levels. However, depleting your glycogen by fasting (for the liver depletion) and exercising major muscle groups (for the muscle depletion) to achieve a semi-starved state has been used successfully by extremely top-level climbers. I cannot recommend this for everyone due to the dangers associated with this (there are many), but the physiologic response can be beneficial. First you lose quite a bit of water weight and the benefits are reaped during an extremely important send. The other benefit comes from actually training in this state because levels of growth hormone become elevated. Use at your own risk. Not eating any carbs before exercise for 4-6 weeks, or a shorter period of 3-5 days can help improve fat utilization during exercise as well as making carbohydrates more available for you when depleted with glycogen.

Water Loading (Hyperhydration)
If you've ever wondered if you can "water load", yes you can. The problem with drinking a ton of water before a climb is that you usually just pee it out before you are completely hydrated. You can water load with glycerol, salt, and creatine. Try these out before you actually do it on a climb. Bloating, GI distress, and migraines could make all of this information useless. Furthermore, the added water weight may be more of a performance hindrance than help if it's not available in your blood plasma. Increasing your plasma volume has an added thermoregulatory effect. I would not recommend bringing less water if you do load up, since the whole point is that climbers don't drink enough to begin with on longer climbs. If water is easily accessible or weight is not a concern then it makes more sense to just drink lots of water. Drinking too much water at once will have a rebound effect and you will wind up peeing a lot of it out.

Sodium is the major solute in blood plasma: the more sodium, the more fluid because you're changing the osmolality of your blood. The increase in fluid causes more pressure, which is why people with high blood pressure are encouraged to lay off the salt. Loading with 2000-4000 mg of sodium (consume 8 oz. of water per 1500 mg sodium) depending on bodyweight both the night before and the morning of can boost plasma levels quite a bit (15-20 per cent).

Supplementing with **glycerol** can reduce the rate at which your kidneys pass extra fluid into your bladder and also will generally increase the amount of water in your plasma and cells. It is difficult to find commercially available glycerol supplementation. The dosage and water taken with the dose is critically important: .45-.7 grams/pound diluted with .75-1 oz. water per gram (or a 20% solution). So a 150 lb person would take around 85 g with about 2 1/3rd liters of water! Some sources suggest that this needs to be consumed over the course of an hour, 30 minutes before exercise while others suggest slowly ingesting it throughout the day. Another option (with less data) would be to consume glycerol during exercise instead of the massive amount before using 0.057 g/pound per 450 mL of water. Combining with **creatine** drastically reduces any side effects like headaches due to vasodilation of vessels. Start loading 5 days prior for maximum effect. Glycerol is considered a banned substance in many competitive events. Creatine also helps retain water, but again, the extra water weight in your muscles may be more of a hindrance than a help. Load with creatine and carbs mixed together beginning 5 days prior.

EATING TO RECOVER

You should be constantly eating back at camp to reload the body's glycogen stores that can take up to a day to fully reload after a punishing day. Your body has about 1500-2500 calories stored as glycogen in your liver and muscle (depending on your size), and that needs to be restored. It can take up to four days to restore liver and muscle glycogen levels. This is why it is extremely important to refuel and have full stores before the climb. Constant intake of simple carbohydrates keeps the tank from emptying. Remember, fat cannot be burned during anaerobic activity and during intense exercise (or intense diets) your body starts burning protein as well. If glucose and glycogen stores are depleted, fat consumption drops way down regardless of how much fat you eat. Protein is the new fuel to stoke the fire. Training for long periods at around 75% of your anaerobic threshold will train your body to utilize fat as its main fuel – not just good for losing weight since you have way more fat reserves than carbs. Once carbs are gone, you are screwed until you can eat more carbs. You can starve to death and still be fat.

Once you've tapped into you reserve of stored glycogen, it becomes harder to recover. If you have low body fat, then you may burned some critical fat and protein needed to maintain physiological and mental function. The nervous system only burns carbs, so that crash hits hard. Be sure to continue eating like a pig when you get home if you're skinny to avoid crashing, injury, and muscle wasting.

> After a hard climb or intense exercise consume 2 calories (.5 gram) of carbohydrates for every pound you weigh, 20-25 grams (80-100 cal) of total protein, and 16 oz. of water. For a very heavy day consume around 140 g. (500 cal) of protein to avoid muscle wasting.

Chocolate milk or Ensure are excellent post-exercise meals as they contain carbs, fats, and whey/casein proteins and taste pretty good. Whatever you consume, make sure you at least satisfy the carb requirements immediately after exercise. If the approach is long the day before a climb, don't forget to reload afterwards as well.

Consuming **caffeine** during your post-exercise meal can substantially increase glycogen replacement, up to 66% according to the Journal of Applied Physiology! Don't take an antioxidant near the end of your climb or after training. Antioxidants have been shown to lower endurance training effects in some studies (and of course not in others).

PLANNING WATER
Sport and Electrolyte Drinks

> To make an isotonic (same concentration) or less dense than your blood's osmolality drink mix you'll need about 140-220 calories of carbs per liter. Adding protein in a 4:1 ratio for would then use 112-176 cal of carbs and 28-44 cal of protein or amino acids per liter.

Feel free to skip adding the protein or lower the ratio, there is conflicting information about the efficacy of adding protein or amino acids. However, you will burn the protein as calories regardless. A mixture of glucose and sucrose is best for carbs, and a blend of key amino acids like L-glutamine and BCAAs works well for your protein. Other amino acids with ergogenic effects can be used as well (AAKG, OKG, HMB, beta alanine, arginine). Added protein can make your water a little rank, especially if left around for more than a day if it's hot out. Amino acids don't make your water as nasty.

Adding electrolytes not only helps replace what is lost from sweat, but can also help aid in getting the water into your blood plasma. There is a lot of debate in the amount of different electrolytes you need to replenish during activity, particularly sodium and potassium.

> Here is the general amount you should be ingesting per hour (or ½ liter) to maintain an electrolyte balance in very hot and sweaty conditions during high output with adequate hydration: 350 mg sodium, 100 mg potassium, 20 mg magnesium, 80 mg calcium, 50 IU vitamin-D (to aid in calcium metabolism).

If temps are cool, you won't be sweating a lot, or the day isn't huge, you can get away just fine without supplementation. Electrolytes bonded to citrate (trisodium citrate, potassium citrate, calcium citrate, magnesium citrate) can be more effective than their peers bonded to chloride. Again, these are average amounts – everyone loses different amounts, and it can depend on the conditions outside or how hard you are working – you could need more or less. Since most climbs won't allow you to be drinking ½ liter per hour, don't try to get in the electrolytes without the water. You will just have to suffer and rehydrate and replenish electrolytes before and after the climb. Effects of too many electrolytes can cause muscle spasm/cramps, upset stomach, diarrhea, bloating, and high blood pressure. Before adding all this to your sports drink, look what amounts are contained in the food you will be eating during the climb as well. If you aren't using a sports drink, you can add electrolytes to your plain water, or in the form of **flavored electrolyte tablets** made popular by the company Nuun and other companies (bring back Cola flavor!!!). If you want to add more to your drink, consider vitamin C, B-vitamins, citric acid, malic acid, and caffeine.

Coconut water is all the rage these days as the "perfect" sports drink. The reason is that it contains a ton of potassium and less sugar than say, Gatorade. This may be handy for those on a diet who want a flavorful low cal beverage, but total unnecessary otherwise. Harvesting millions of coconuts for their water seems extraordinarily wasteful. Osmo Nutrition makes the best **commercially produced sports drink** I have found to date, followed by Skratch Labs (not enough sodium).

CHAPTER EIGHT: HEALTH CONCERNS

The information in this chapter is not a substitute for the accurate diagnosis and treatment of a qualified medical practitioner tailored to your individual history and symptoms. This information should be used in conjunction with a qualified practitioner, or for spawning questions to ask your caregiver. A lot of information has already been presented that may be pertinent to you condition or inquiry so I suggest you at least skim through the previous chapters.

FIELD AND TRAVEL MEDICINE

LIFE THREATENING CONDITIONS

Before you venture outside and put you, your partner, or potential rescuers at risk, at least take a first aid and CPR class. Better yet, be responsible and take a Wilderness First Responder (WFR) class. Too many city slickers and gym climbers are heading into the hills have no right to put their partner's lives at risk by not knowing how to handle an emergency. If you are knowledgeable but your partner isn't, then educate them, or make them take a class. If you're initiating someone into backcountry climbing, then it's your responsibility to not only teach them about camping and climbing, but about rescue and first aid. Just because an area is popular like the Hulk or Diamond, and doesn't feel that remote doesn't mean that it isn't. In rescue situations, wilderness means an hour from an ambulance ride. It is also your responsibility to alert your partner of any medical conditions you have that could be relevant (severe allergies, seizures, etc.). This section is not a substitute for a class or dedicated volume on wilderness medicine. This same lecture will be re-hashed in the self-rescue section later.

The big problem with many self-rescue and emergency medicine books/classes is the watering down of important information with useless information. I expect to get torn apart on the following comments. Will you remember acronyms, steps, Venn diagrams, flow-charts, etc., in the field when it actually counts, and will they really help? Are you going to really write a SOAP note when your partner is dying next to you? The harsh reality is that there is very little you can do or feasibly bring with you to help unless you are exceptionally trained in surgery. If an injury was bad enough to kill you, you'll probably die. Your first aid kit, no matter how well stocked, will look like a children's art box at your first day of art school. If an injury doesn't kill your friend, then your primary concern is to keep the victim comfortable and evacuate. Some situations require an understanding of injury consequences. In other words, even if you don't see a bone sticking out or a gaping wound, you at least need to be aware of the high risks involved with head injuries and internal bleeding. If a fall was severe enough, knowing to look for warning signs of more serious injury or playing it safe and pre-evacuating is an important skill. It is important to know when an injury can become serious enough to evac or seek medical attention sooner rather than later instead of just "walking it off".

Here is a small list of what you need to know how to assess, perform, or deal with:
- CPR, Rescue Breathing, and Choking
- Finding a Pulse (including the limbs)
- Asses Pupillary Response
- Shock and Sunstroke
- Severe Bleeding and Burns
- How to Stitch a Wound
- Frostbite and Hypothermia
- Open and Tension Pneumothorax
- Dislocations, Open and Closed Fractures, and when to and when not to apply In-Line Traction
- Lightning Strikes

- Unconsciousness, Concussions, and Changes in Consciousness/Mental Status
- Rattlesnake, Black Widow, and Scorpion Bites
- Anaphylaxis
- Abdominal Pain (severe with no trauma or trauma induced)
- HAPE, HACE, and acute AMS

You need to be able to recognize and deal with symptoms or mechanisms of injury that may not be so noticeable, like:
- Cranial Swelling via Internal Bleeding, Edema, and Concussion
- Airway Obstruction
- Lung Edema
- Internal Bleeding and Appendicitis
- Spine and Spinal Cord Damage
- Ischemia
- Heart Attach, Appendicitis, Gall Stones, Kidney Stones, Hernia
- When to stay with the victim, when to run to a phone or for help, when to assist the victim to get out together, and what injuries the victim should attempt to ambulate on their own

Other Need to Know Information

If the lists mentioned above made you feel unprepared, keep your climbing activities closer to the road and within cell phone range. The rest are some tips on not so obvious stuff you should have learned in your WFR class.

Use a trekking pole, pack stay, or branch to devise a traction splint for a femur fracture. With a harness, water bottle, and some cord you can rig a quick setup. Some authorities do not recommend using mechanical traction like this with a femur fracture – do whatever you need to when far from help. Only pull traction if it alleviates pain and there is no hip or knee joint damage. Traction is required with a compound fracture or dislocation far from help. With any mechanism of injury that could have damaged a spinal cord or broken a vertebrae, immobilize the spine and call for rescue. Clearing the spine for injury requires some medical training so if you aren't trained, you are forgiven for calling in a rescue.

Mild head trauma, especially with loss of consciousness, can be life threatening. Be extra vigilant about monitoring for strange symptoms even if your partner just got a little bump. If they got knocked out evac even if they feel fine afterwards. Concussions can be subtle. Keep the patient upright to reduce cranial pressure and keep your eye on them (don't let them belay you or rappel on their own). Monitor them for 24 hours to see if any symptoms develop – but you do not have to keep them awake when it's time to go to sleep. If you got knocked-out, definitely evacuate. Symptoms of brain injury can last for months.

Multiple concussions have a compound effect and can lead to lifetime neurological problems. Symptoms can include headaches, trouble concentrating, memory problems, emotional imbalance (mood swings, inappropriate emotions, combative behavior), seizures, speech problems, and motor problems (parasthesia, paralysis). These symptoms can all be permanent, leaving you unable to work or lead a normal life. Expect crayons for your next birthday if you don't like wearing helmets.

If you suffered a concussion or traumatic brain injury then problems associated with high altitude can be compounded. Post-concussion syndrome symptoms are the last neurologic symptoms that can last for months to years. Subdural hemorrhages from minor blows to the head can start off completely asymptomatic and leave you in a pine box without any warning. Get thee to a hospital! If you suspect shock and your injured partner says they are fine, be extra vigilant about monitoring their conditions.

CPR probably won't start the heart, it just keeps blood flowing. If there is no possibility of rescue for a long time, do it, but don't exhaust yourself. If the victim doesn't revive within 30 minutes and help in the form of an airlift or defibulator isn't coming, stop CPR. The heart may start on its own if lightning was the cause or take a while if buried by an avalanche or in cold water, so give this victim a lot more time. Hypothermia can severely mask vital signs. An old saying goes, "you're not dead until you are warm and dead".

If there is no breathing, but there is a heartbeat – don't do CPR, but <u>do not stop</u> rescue breathing. Back blows are just as effective as the abdominal thrusts in choking situations – do them first. A camelback tube can be used for an emergency tracheotomy. The incision goes in the indentation below the Adam's apple. Impaled? If it's deeper than skin and muscle leave it in.

Most severe bleeding can be controlled with direct pressure. A tourniquet should only be applied in a situation so dire that losing a limb is no longer a concern. Stick your fingers in the hole or stuff it with cloth – whatever you can do to stop bleeding. A femur or pelvic fracture is a life threatening conditions due to the large amount of blood that can be lost. Knee and hip dislocations are life threatening. Do not relocate the dislocation. Hanging in a harness pools venous blood and can kill you via clots or old coagulated blood.

A cold can turn into pneumonia, which is a life-threatening condition. Pressing firmly on the eyeballs (closed lids!) can help reduce an elevated heart rate (and stop hiccups).

First Aid Kit

Most first aid tools can be fashioned from what you already have on you. Be creative. You can make a traction splint with a few simple items, a breathing tube with a knife and a hydration tube, or a splint from a backpack stay. Big first aid kits just aren't practical unless you are on an extended trip or out of the country. Most injuries can either be dealt with until you get to civilization, or are so disastrous that a first aid kit won't cut it. Bring stuff that you commonly suffer from, be it diarrhea, blisters, headaches, allergies, whatever. Guides and instructors have a lot more liability (and clients have a lot more issues) so their kits are going to be much bigger.

Here is a basic first aid kit you can fit in your climbing pack:
- **Clotting Agent** – Quick Clot is a small vacuum-sealed dressing with clotting agents that can stop severe bleeding, and Celox is clotting granules you pour into the wound and may be more useful. Check the expiration dates.
- **Epi Pen** – If you or your partners are highly allergic to bee stings or anything else. You can develop severe reactions from repeated exposure or from substances you haven't been normally exposed to (rare). Every guide needs to carry one, and it should be in every climber's first aid kit regardless of your experience with bee stings, etc. just in case.
- **Tape** – Athletic and a small roll of Duct Tape. Indispensable.
- **Nu Skin** or **Super Glue** - For minor cuts while cragging.

- **Syproflex** – Weighs nothing and good for closing up large wounds or covering blisters.
- **NSAIDs** and **Vicodin** (or other opiate) – For aches and pains. Morphine-like painkillers may be necessary on longer expedition to subdue the victim as normal prescription and OTC painkillers probably won't do much.
- **Knife** – It's amazing how useful, even lifesaving, a small knife can be. Always have one on you when roped climbing.
- **Phone, Radio,** or **PLB** - I'll spare the lecture for later on, and assume you'll use them for real emergencies or leave them at home if you want to be hard-core. Text messages can sometimes get through when calls can't. Text a friend who can talk to the local SAR. Calling for rescue should be because of possible loss of life or limb. If you can get out on your own (even if it means an extra bivy or two, getting yelled at or work or home) then do it. Suck it up and suffer if you chose to climb in the wilderness. Getting rescued when you could have done so yourself is pathetic.

Depending on the length and location of your adventure, here are some other first aid items to pack or at least have in the car. For huge expeditions far from Western medical care consult an expedition doctor.

- **ACE Wraps** – Sprains and strains.
- **Allergy Medication** – Non-drowsy allergy medications like Claritin D can be lifesavers. Many "colds" are just obnoxiously symptomatic allergies. Even if you don't normally have allergies, traveling to new areas or higher elevations can expose you to new allergens.
- **Aloe Lotion** – Reduce symptoms of sunburn or rashes.
- **Altitude Drugs** – Prevent or reduce symptoms of HAPE, HACE, or AMS (discussed later).
- **Antibiotic Ointment** – Prevent infection, decrease healing time.
- **Anti-Diuretic** – Reducing diarrhea.
- **Antihistamine** – Non-immediate treatment for anaphylaxis, allergies.
- **Birth Control** – You never know!
- **Blister Pads** – Prevent blisters or reduce pain (moleskin, duct-tape, Leukotape, Band-Aid style).
- **Bodyglide** – Prevent blisters and chaffing.
- **Book on First Aid** – On long trips without an expedition doctor or you don't have a WFR instructor in your group.
- **Broad Spectrum Antibiotics** – Cure bacterial infections or disease. Vital on long remote trips. Can upset your gut flora so take some pre/probiotics well.
- **Bug Dope, Permethrin, Citronella Candles, Bug Clothing** – Preventing bites and diseases.
- **Chap Stick** – You'll know you needed it when you forgot it. Sunscreen can work in a pinch.
- **Calamine Lotion, Cortisone Cream** – Rashes.
- **Clove Oil** – For numbing dental problems.
- **Cold and Cough Medication** – Decongestants, expectorants, lozenges.
- **CPR Mask** – Preventing communicable disease during rescue breathing.
- **Dental Emergency Kit** – Ask your dentist. Cavit and Clove oil can help.
- **Eye Kit** – If you need glasses then bring a second pair or extra contacts and lens solution.
- **Eyedrops** - Can also help stop blood loss from minor cuts or a bloody nose or they can help with dry eyes in the field.
- **EMT Shears** – To cut clothing (or rock shoes) off.
- **File or Emory Board** – Reduce calluses to prevent hot spots, blisters, or split tips.
- **Foot Powder and Antiperspirant** – Reduce or absorb sweat in hands, feet, or groin.
- **Hand Salve** – Repair dry or cracked skin (water and oil based).

- **Heartburn/Antacid Tablets** – Rolaids, Pepto, Zantac, Tagamet, etc. Upset tummies are very common reason for bailing when you're scared.
- **Hemorrhoid Cream/Suppository** – Sitting on cold surfaces and straining can cause or irritate these buggers.
- **Hydration Kit** – For heat exhaustion or food poisoning. OTC kit, or ½ tsp. salt and 3 tbs. sugar per liter.
- **Iodine** – Wound cleaning.
- **Latex Glove** – Prevent transmission of communicable diseases from body fluids.
- **Pepto-Bismol, Rolaids,** or **Zantac** – For reducing heartburn or indigestion.
- **Nail Clippers** – Prevent hangnails and ingrown nails, cut flappers.
- **Needle and Thread** – Stitches, subungual hematoma, blisters, splinters, wound debridement (and equipment repair).
- **Safety Pins** – Attaching bandages, splints, and repairing items.
- **SAM Splint** – Splinting sprains, fractures.
- **Soap, Hand Sanitizer, Clorox Wipes, Lysol Spray** – Preventing infection or illness.
- **Sterile Gauze** – Wound cleaning, sterile bandage, wound packing.
- **Sunscreen, Lip Balm, Sun Clothing** – Prevent sunburn.
- **Tecnu** – Poison ivy wash.
- **Thermometer** – For longer trips.
- **Tincture of Benzoin** – Toughen skin on hot spots, helps tape and bandages stick.
- **Tweezers** (or **Tick Remover**) – Ticks, splinters.
- **Vaginal Infection Medication** – Treatments for bladder and yeast infections.
- **Various Bandages** – Sterile bandaging, minor bleeding, preventing infection. Options are Spyroflex, Steri-Strips (butterfly closures), Band-Aids of various sizes, breathable membrane bandage (bad scrapes, burns, puncture wound), Second Skin (burns, blisters).
- **Water Purification** – Wound cleaning, preventing illness.

DISEASES

The CDC is the best online resource to get information on the following information. If you are bitten or suspect and infection that isn't just a cold, explore their website and see a doctor. If traveling abroad, you really need to educate yourself.

Diarrhea

To treat diarrhea you also need to treat the cause. Infection is a common cause, as is a change in diet or medication, as well as anxiety. The gut can be finicky and various nerves and reflexes can cause abnormal bowel movements and diarrhea on climbing trips. Stress, physical activity, and any change in diet are easy triggers – basically your normal climbing trip. It helps to recognize if you are susceptible to these normal triggers so you can plan ahead by finding more agreeable foods, timing your meals and waking hours, or remembering to bring some extra water and TP for the climb. Taking **Immodium** may also be a useful preventive measure, but try this at home in case you get rebound constipation, which can be just a bad for you (and your tent mate).

When you do get the squirts, you must replace the fluids lost with an isotonic solution containing 6 tsp. sugar and ½ tsp. salt, in other words, a **sports drink**. Begin increasing the solidity of food when the diarrhea starts to improve. Hard foods are difficult to digest and will compound the problem. **Oral rehydration salt packets** are available if you are on an extended expedition. If fever and severe cramping aren't accompanying the diarrhea, you can take **anti-motility drugs** like Imodium.

Cryptosporidium diarrhea can last weeks and be carried for about 2 months. You can get symptoms two days to a week after ingestion. Severely painful, explosive diarrhea with vomiting is most likely toxin-related food poisoning and develops rapidly after you ate or drank the organism or its toxin. Many cases are self-limiting to several hours to a day and a high fever may accompany the other symptoms. E. Coli can be severe and cause bloody diarrhea. Unfortunately antibiotics and anti-motility drugs can make it worse. You have to ride this one out and stay hydrated, but bloody stool should be an immediate evac if hemorrhoids, irritable bowel, or dry-cracked skin around the anus are ruled out.

Giardia is probably the most well known cause of water-borne diarrhea for hikers and climbers. Incubation takes one to three weeks so a sudden case is likely to be from something else. Diarrhea is crampy, foul smelling, flatulent, and often explosive. It usually resolves on its own after a month or two, but can continue for months. There is no evidence that states once you get Giardia you are less susceptible to getting it again or it creates immunity. So don't try and get it once to get it over with. It is also highly contagious so you can get it from fecal contamination from your climbing partner. The more giardia cysts you ingest, the higher chance you have of developing symptoms, however. If you are taking a chance by not purifying water, chose a highly renewable source of non-stagnant water (like a snowmelt river or spring upstream from animal life or pooping climbers).

Colds and Flu
There is no cure for the common cold. Any or all drugs and OTC supplements only help to boost the immune system, treat the symptoms, or reduce the severity. It's amazing what we allow as a "scientific" society to treat a cold compared to the scrutiny we place on other questionable medical practices. I tip my hat Rhinovirus. Circumstantial evidence reigns supreme. The most effective things that still only have mild to no evidence on the market are **zinc lozenges, echinacea** (more is better), **Airborne** (because of the echinacea, zinc, and adaptogens I suspect), **Emergan-C** (I think it's mainly a placebo), and chicken soup.

One of the best ways to treat a throat or sinus infection is by gargling with **salt water**, or a saline nasal lavage (snorting salt water or using a Netti Pot). Substituting with Listerine will not help in a nasal lavage (although it does make sense why it would). Rest, proper nutrition, **antihistamines, expectorants, and anti-inflammatories** and **antipyretics** are probably your other best bet. Ingesting silver nitrate or colloidal silver does not work and can have actually negative health effects. For those traveling abroad, it is prudent to get a prescription for a strong **broad-spectrum antibiotic** to treat bacterial infections. The best defense against sickness and infection is repeated hand washing, avoiding contact with your hands to your face (good luck), using hand sanitizer after you poop, and getting a current flu vaccine. Wipe down surfaces with **bleach or Lysol** you contact if they are suspicious. Diluted **iodine** can also work, especially for cleaning wounds.

Skin and Wound Infection
If your wound gets very red around the edges, starts producing lots of puss, or causes red streaks (immediate evac!), you need to go to the hospital to treat the infection. Vigorously scrub and irrigate any injury with clean **soap and water**. Bone ends, burns, and frostbite require cleaning and irrigation, but not so much on the scrubbing. You can get tetanus infections from soil contamination or a puncture would. Get your booster shots.

Insect or Animal Borne Diseases

Although not dangerous except in malaria infested equatorial climates, mosquitos still suck. Clothes are your first line of defense. If you know you'll be near areas of high mosquito concentrations, especially post-snow melt alpine zones as they hatch when standing water develops, then you may want to wear **baggier pants and loose long sleeve shirts** over those tighter climbing pants and tops. A **hat and bandana** help with both sun and bugs, followed by an actual mosquito **head net**. If you get a small non-wire, or non-brimmed head net you'll need a ball cap to keep the netting off your face. Spraying your clothes, socks, and jacket that you'll wear at dawn or dusk temps with **Permethrin** helps a ton. Don't freak out by the "DO NOT SPRAY ON SKIN" warnings. It is not hazardous to you or pets, no matter what your friends who also freak out about fluorinated water say. It really should read, "Does not work on skin" because it is quickly absorbed and metabolized. It does significantly reduce the swarm of bugs around you though! Permethrin is actually an insecticide, not a repellent, but it kills them so quickly it seems like a repellant. Step three in prevention is using a mixed bug dope product containing at least 30% **DEET** in areas of exposed skin. Finally, carry another small bottle, spray stick, or wipe (my favorite) of 100% DEET for extremely bad insects and apply it to their favorite snacking locations. Permethrin or **citronella coils and sticks** that you burn are another extra line of defense, and don't weigh very much. Being careful not to burn down the forest, light a perimeter (accounting for prevailing winds) of mosquito sticks.

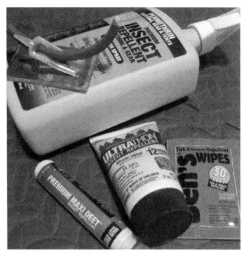

Mosquito coil, permethrin, DEET stick, mixed repellent cream and wipe.

Covering up with baggy clothes is the best defense

Still miserable? You may be in a mosquito zone for whatever reason and moving camp just a few yards could change everything. Hop in your tent, or better yet, use a large hanging **bug tarp** or a take the tarp off a tent that has a mesh interior. Full-on **bug suits** could even be worth the hassle in notoriously awful places like Alaska or the Wind Rivers on a bad day.

Don't tell your partner about this next trick: because mosquitos are drawn to your CO_2 emissions and CO_2 rises, the bugs will attack the person who is higher up. This works pretty well inside netless tarp tents as the vast majority of the mosquitos will be aimlessly buzzing around the tent ceiling and the only exposed skin should be your face. A light piece of cloth over your face and some earplugs should finish the job.

Bites should disappear much quicker if you don't scratch them and set off an inflammation response beyond just the bite. Some people, especially younger kids, are just more prone to developing long lasting itchy bites, or actually naturally attract mosquitos more than others. You can become desensitized to the bites over time. If you are one of the unlucky types, bring along some **anti-itch cream**.

Check to see if the country you are going to has malaria with the CDC and follow their precautions and suggestions. There are no useful vaccines so the key is prevention. There is medication you can take to make you resistant, but some folks react very poorly (go crazy) due to side effects. There are plenty of other diseases to prepare for, so do your homework. West Nile virus is another major one transmitted via mosquito, and it is becoming more common in the United States. Symptoms are flu-like, a red bumpy rash, and an aversion to light. Only about 20% of infected people get symptoms, less than 1% have severe symptoms, and death is uncommon. The thing to worry about mainly is fatigue and mental issues from even mild infections that can last a very long time. Get tested several times if you suspect infection.

Ticks are usually just unsettling more than painful, irritating or dangerous. Nothing develops long lasting bonding like performing a tick check on your partner back at camp. If you get one burrowed in your skin, be careful not to rip its head or mouthparts off when pulling it off. You can use a tick remover or tweezers, but you probably won't have those. Scrub the area with lots of soap and water and monitor the skin for a rash. The old match, nail polish, or Vaseline trick doesn't work – just pull it out. Don't squeeze the tick's body as it can further release disease into your body.

Lyme disease is the most common tick borne infection in the United States. Summer and fall are the more common times to get it. The small deer tick is a common carrier in the Northeast, Midwest, and South while the Western blacklegged tick is more common in the West. These ticks are tiny, and the nymphs that transmit the disease are miniscule. A tick check may not catch these guys, especially in hairy areas. The most easily noticeable symptom is a rash, usually in a bull's eye shape that occurs about a week after a bite. Flu-like symptoms and joint/muscle pain show up around the same time. Get tested! Long-term consequences to the disease can be severe and debilitating joint pain and arthritis, mental and neurological problems, and organ damage.

Dog and wood ticks transmit Rocky Mountain spotted fever, most commonly in late spring and early summer in the Southeastern United States. You develop a high fever about a week post bite and then a red spotted rash on your hands and feet including the palms and soles, and the rash spread and deepens over the body. Hopefully this would clue you in that you have something that is not normal going on! However, some don't get a rash at all. It can be deadly.

Hantavirus is a serious and deadly disease and climbers are at risk. The virus is inhaled from particles of rodent droppings. There is no cure and 38% of cases die. Don't camp in trail shelters, they are mice heaven. 10 cases were recently reported in the camping cabins in Yosemite, another reason to avoid the Village. Luckily, the disease is rare, with less than 600 cases reported from 1993 to 2011. It is more prevalent in the Western United States.

If an animal bites you, then you are at risk for rabies. The best way to determine if you were infected is to dissect the animal's brain. If the animal can't be dissected, any animal bite or scratch should be treated for rabies. Symptoms may take a very long time so get treated regardless. Clean the wound like you are obsessive. Untreated rabies will kill you and the symptoms are unimaginably awful. <u>Once symptoms develop there is just above zero chance you will live. Don't take any chances and get started on treatment ASAP!!!</u>

The best cure for snakebites is **antivenom**, something you may want to carry if you're on your own. Luckily most bites are not a medical emergency. If you suspect venom, however, get your ass to the hospital. Try and get a photo of the snake for the hospital doctor, especially important for the Mojave rattlesnake. Venom extractors are not recommended as they can concentrate the venom in one spot and make it much worse. Pressure bands or even direct pressure may also have the same negative effect. Treat the bite for infection, however. Ice can make the tissue destruction worse so don't use it. Coral Snake bites require a different approach, as do snakes in Australia, Africa, and South America as they inject a neurotoxin. In this case apply direct pressure over the bite with a broad bandage and immobilize the limb after washing the site….and get to a hospital very quickly.

Africanized bees are becoming a problem, and one climber fatality has already occurred in Arizona. These bees aren't more poisonous, but are more aggressive and can swarm and chase you for up to a mile! Other nearby bees get recruited and a swarm of thousands may descend. Don't piss off any bees in the Southwest or California or have fruit smells near you. Dark colors anger bees. If you don't know if you are highly allergic (you can become sensitive later in life), pop 50-100 mg of **Benadryl** ASAP. Get the stinger out to prevent further allergic reaction or infection immediately.

Black widow and brown recluse spiders are the ones to really look out for. A black widow bite isn't usually painful, but the symptoms that follow sure can be. Thankfully the vast majority of bites aren't deadly, but the symptoms can last a couple days. A brown recluse bite may hurt a bit, followed by swelling or a blister, and aching. Over time the bite area dies and ulcerates – about a week. Go to the hospital. Scorpion stings are incredibly painful. Symptoms to follow are pain, and some neurologic symptoms. Some scorpions are just about as bad as a bee sting while others will kill you. Check under the outhouse seat and in woodpiles. Shake out your boots and bag if left in the open. If you want to lay awake all night, shine a UV light around to see how many are out there.

Food Borne
If traveling abroad, or at a real backwater restaurant or grocery store in the States, beware lettuce and other unwashed veggies, ice cubes, anything made with tapwater (including mixed drinks), undercooked meat, unpeeled fruit, dairy, room temperature sauces (including condiments), unrefrigerated sausages, or hot drinks not brought to a boil. Basically, scrutinize everything: how it was prepared, its age, and what the ingredients are and where they came from. I never eat the vegies on a hamburger or a sandwich from low-income areas or mountain-town pubs that employ climbers in the kitchen after getting sick on too many trips. Seriously, restaurants in mountain towns low on tourists don't get inspected often and can employ dirt bags, drifters, or profit hungry owners. Contamination is also likely to have come from your grubby hands, so wash up. If boiling water to treat for fecal contamination, go for a few minutes.

Worms

You can get worms from a variety of sources: water, plant, animal, and insect. However, it is very unlikely to get worms in the United States unless you are eating animals you have hunted. If traveling abroad, check with the CDC and your doctor about medication to help prevent an infection, and follow up if you experience any gastro-intestinal distress – you may have a stowaway.

MINOR INJURIES

Minor Cuts

Cuts, flappers, and gobies all heal quicker in a clean moist anaerobic (no air) environment. Large cuts and puncture wounds require extra cleaning and debridement with **sterile water** (boiled and with **iodine** in the field). Never tape a puncture wound closed, however. Take about three times as long with three times as much water and scrubbing (yes scrubbing) as you think necessary. A **needle and thread** is light and can provide emergency stitching if it will be a long while before the hospital is reached. **Super glue and Nu Skin** can hold together flappers while they heal, and cover scrapes and gobies as well. **Antibiotic ointment** helps prevent infection and also helps provide an air seal over cuts and scrapes. **Granulated sugar** can work in a pinch to prevent infection on minor cuts to prevent infection as well. Large nasty rashes can be helped by wrapping the rash in **plastic wrap** after a good cleaning. If swelling and redness grow around the wound, infection is setting in. If the area starts to streak, get to a hospital as fast as possible. No matter what the wound, thorough cleaning and protection will reduce the chance of infection and decrease healing time. Nu Skin can be a lifesaver, as can packing the wound with chalk and sealing with tape if that's all you've got (and you care more about climbing than infection).

Tape split tips with thin strips of **athletic tape** to protect the split for the rest of the day or trip. The tape will interfere with grip, so take it off before the big send and expect the trip to be over afterwards. Put a ¼" strip of tape over your finger followed by overlapping wraps down your finger down to just above the joint. Secure with a figure 8 wrap at the bottom of the wrap and over the joint. Secure with a few extra wraps.

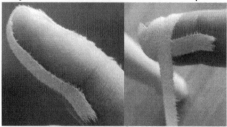

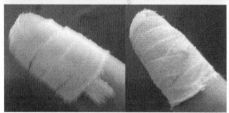

If you get a nasty cut and need stitches, you only have a few hours (about 5) before stitches become too difficult to apply and your wound will take much longer to heal, increase the chance of infection, be super gross, and leave a nasty scar for a long time.

Boils and Abscesses

If you get a boil or abscesses for whatever reason, don't try and lance it or squeeze it in the field, as the risk of further infection is very high. Pad around the area, and apply cortisone creams and antibiotics to reduce the inflammation. If you just have to lance and pop it treat it like an infected puncture wound.

Poison Ivy and Oak

Some folks are deathly allergic while others can bathe in poison ivy. It is a good idea to learn what it looks like so you can avoid contact with your skin or gear. Gear that's been in contact with poison ivy can affect someone allergic to it for long time after the initial contact was made. Some areas are notorious for poison ivy, like the Black Canyon. Long pants and sleeves and a pair of hiking poles or long thin branches forked at the end (please don't rip branches off) can serve as pokers to move leaves out of your way as you move like a ninja through the plants. **Tecnu** is a compound that helps deactivate the poison ivy oils – you can and should wash yourself, clothes and gear with it even if you aren't allergic to protect a significant other or future partners. **Calamine lotion, aloe, and cortisone creams** help with rashes. Serious reactions require heavier doses of steroids. If making a campfire, be sure you aren't burning poison ivy or oak and inhale the oils into your lungs!

Sweating

If sweaty hands or feet (or groin) are a problem, you can use **antiperspirant** besides just in your armpits. You can get little travel sized sprays or bars. Apply about an hour before climbing if using the bar, or right away if it's a liquid or spray. You can also put antiperspirant on your feet to help prevent blisters and cold sweaty feet in the winter.

Chafing and Blisters

Blisters are the most common foot problem for climbs that require a long approach or wearing mountaineering boots. They are also very common injury when jugging, hauling, or climbing rough holds (especially jugs) all day. Friction causes blisters, so the goal is to minimize friction. Calluses cause a great deal of friction, so first try and reduce those. Wet conditions make the skin more fragile and will compound the effects friction. Ultra heavy or overly warm shoes are also blister factories. One person's blister prevention can be another's cause, so prepare for some trial and error. **Thicker socks, liner socks, double layer socks, wool socks, inorganic socks, and foot powder** are good options or may cause blisters. Slippery or rough insoles, too low or too high volume shoes (too tight/loose) can also create blisters. No matter how much you love your boots, if they cause blisters they are worthless.

All the suggestions for dry skin and sweating can prevent blisters and hot spots. Should you pop your blister? It depends on how much it is bothering you and how well you can prevent infection or further irritation. If you decide to drain it, first sterilize your **knife, needle, or clippers** and clean the skin and your hands with soap and water. Make a small hole or incision at the base in an area that won't get rubbed and tear open the blister. Finish the job by covering it with **protective tape or Band-Aids**.

To help prevent blisters and chafing on your feet, groin, butt crack, or wherever before they start, products like **Bodyglide** are available to lubricate hot spots. Bodyglide is excellent as it allows the area to breathe under the lotion. Tiny micro sticks are available to go in the pack. It is difficult to tape over the area if applied once a blister develops, so this stuff is better as a precaution. Thick clothing or double layers can help absorb friction before your skin does.

Duct tape and athletic tape are usually available in the climber's measly first aid kit and can both be used to reduce chafing on the skin. Duct-tape will stick and glide better, but the glue can cause irritation, especially if the area is already inflamed. **Moleskin** provides a lot of protection, but can also fall off quite easily and much better products are available like **Second Skin** and **Spyroflex**. Cutting a doughnut hole out of **molefoam** around a blister can also work, but is not as commonly used. **Leukotape** is stronger, stickier, and offers less friction than athletic tape and could be a better alternative to duct tape, which can also easily fall off with sweating. **Pre-tape spray and tincture of benzoin** can help the padding stay on better. There are some great smooth stretchy and thin **Band-Aid Blister Pads** available that do a pretty good job preventing blisters, hot spots, and stay on. In a pinch use a shiny candy wrapper under whatever tape you have available.

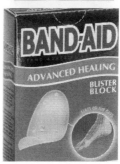

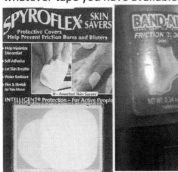

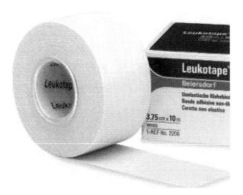

Dry Skin and Calluses

Keeping your hands clean by washing them with soap and water and applying lotion after a day of climbing is key in keeping your hands in use longer and avoiding flappers and painful cuticles. There are tons of **hand salves** out there – some marked directly towards climbers, some for cow udders. **Water-based salves** absorb quickly and **oil-based salves** leave your hands greasy but have a longer lasting effect. Apply the water based first, then the oil-based. Use hand salve after every day of climbing.

Constant bouldering, climbing on rough rock, and dry hands can split the tips or crack the hands. Wearing **belay glove**s when doing anything but climbing is great prevention. Calluses can catch and rupture the skin, so keep them at bay with a **nail file, emory board**, or those **sandpaper sponges** used to refinish paint. Filing down your foot calluses with the above or a **pumice stone** can really help prevent blisters and hot spots.

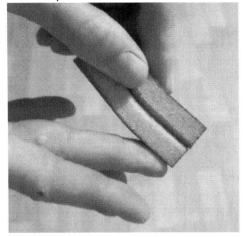

Tincture of benzoin is sticky and stinky, and is sometimes used to get athletic tape to stick. It also toughens the skin. It's probably too messy for your hands, but it really helps to put on blisters and hot spots (coved in tape) to toughen them up.

I don't know who discovered **Antihydral**, but it has swept the bouldering community. Antihydral is a cream with the active ingredient Methenamine (13%). Right now you can only get it from Germany or a foosball Internet website (seriously!) in the states. It is sold to reduce hand and foot sweating, but it also hardens your skin by inhibiting growth of new cells causing callus buildup. Some top climbers call it their secret weapon. It will turn your hands yellow with too much use. Rub a dime-sized dap on your fingertips, middle of your finger, and/or your palms once or twice a day. Do not get it on your joints or they will crack and bleed. File down any excess calluses, and discontinue when your skin turns yellow, or gets to hard or glassy. You can definitely overdo it.

If you are allergic to formaldehyde you shouldn't use it according to the label. Formaldehyde is a controlled substance due to its toxic and carcinogenic effects, so I don't know how you would know if you were allergic to it or not in advance. Methenamine's main prescriptive use is as an oral long-term antibiotic for urinary tract infections. The acidic urea reacts with methenamine and creates some formaldehyde that kills bacteria. Since sweat also contains urea, this must be where the warning comes from. A paper released in 2007 by the <u>European Commission on Health and Consumer Protection by the Scientific Committee on Health and Human Risks</u> entitled "Risk Assessment Report on Methenamine" states a few findings. The most important finding states that it can be detected in placental blood and in mother's milk…so don't use it if you are pregnant or breast-feeding. The paper states that although toxicity and carcinogenic effects were not shown in rats and cosmetic use likely has no toxic or carcinogenic concerns in humans, there still needs to be more research. So unless you are sensitive, pregnant, or allergic, you are probably in the clear.

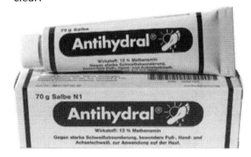

Foot Problems
Athlete's foot and fungal nail Infections can plague a climber's foot. Gross gym floors and showers, dirty climbing shoes, and wet unclean feet can all lead to both conditions. If your nail crumbles when you trim it, you've probably got an infection. The best treatments are **prescription fungicides** taken orally or mixed in with nail polish remover for chronic infections. **OTC fungicide cream** can work for acute or mild infections. Wash and dry your foot and apply it relig-

iously. **Foot powder** is absolute magic to help prevent athlete's foot and sooth nasty feet as long as you wash out your shoes before it turns to foot glue. **Lysol** has a good chance at killing the fungus or bacteria inside your climbing shoes, but do a thorough scrubbing of the inside lining first.

Ingrown nails in the toes can be more painful than a broken bone. You can try and take some pressure off by wedging something soft under the pressure point for a temporary fix, but some foot doctors warn against this as it can increase the chance of infection. You can use tape to wrap around the bottom and sides of your toe to try and spread the skin open next to the nail. This option works well when rock shoes compound the problem. After spreading the skin apart from the nail, wrap another strip of tape around the whole toe to keep things in place. You may need to wrap surrounding toes to prevent chafing from the adjacent tape. Otherwise wait for the nail to grow out enough that it's not pressing into your nail bed if possible, and then trim the nail so it can't happen again. Don't cut the nail too short or curved so it can dive down into the skin. If this doesn't work or isn't possible, you should get the toe numbed up and trimmed by a nurse, doctor, or a really good manicurist. Going one step further (I've done this) is to have a compound applied to the nail bed that permanently kills the cells so the nail won't regrown back, aka **chemical cauterization**.

Hangnails plague climbers, and as stupid of a problem as they sound, they hurt and can bleed like crazy. Wearing belay gloves constantly, trimming your nails and carrying **nail clippers** en route are the best ideas. Keeping your hands clean and hydrated with balms/lotions will reduce the likelihood of getting them.

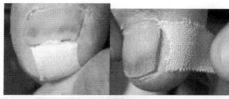
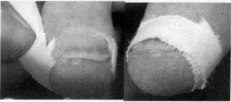

This disgusting individual has a fungal infection from the looks of it. Taping an ingrown nail.

Blood under the nails (subungual hematoma) or nails that have become bruised so bad they're going to fall off also can be exceptionally painful. Next time, careful padding above the toe and meticulous nail trimming can prevent this. **Toecaps** may be necessary if even constant trimming doesn't help. To relieve pressure in the field of a subungual hematoma, you can heat up a thin sharp piece of metal to puncture the nail and relieve the blood. Be aware of infection that can occur from doing minor surgical procedures in the dirt. The sooner you drain the blood before it clots the better chance you have of keeping your toenail.

Eyes
It's easy to get something in your eye – on the trail from a branch, or on the climb from debris or lichen. If you have water that you can spare, irrigating the eye is a good start. A scratched cornea may feel like something is still there even when the particle is removed. Next pull back the eyelid and try and get it out lightly with a wet cloth or cotton swab. Blood in the eye can occur from excessive straining or coughing. Worry about it if it hurts, interferes with vision, or other symptoms occur. Otherwise it will go away. If your partner develops an eye infection, it can spread to you very easily. Be careful if any abscess occurs on or around

the eye, infection can spread to the brain and spinal cord.

Teeth

Thanks to the nerves inside each tooth, dental issues can be trip ending painful ordeals. **Cavit** can also be used to patch a tooth problem and cavity, and it along with **clove oil** can be used to help numb a cavity, lost filling, crown, or sore. You probably won't have either substance on you ever, but if guiding or on a long expedition, you might want to stock some. Ask your dentist for suggestions about other dental emergency suggestions.

ENVIRONMENTAL INJURIES
Altitude

If you're attempting a high altitude climb, don't rely on this book for complete information since it deserves an entire book, or at least a long chapter. These two books are the best: "Altitude Illness: Prevention and Treatment" by Stephen Bezruchka, and "Going Higher: Medicine Man and Mountains" by Charles Houston. A great field reference is "Guidelines for Field Treatment of Altitude Illness (AI), AMS, HACE, HAPE" by Alan Oram, D.O. Another excellent article can be found by searching online for, "Wilderness Medical Society Consensus Guidelines for the Prevention and Treatment of Acute Altitude Illness". Peter Hackett, MD at highaltitudemedicine.org is one of the foremost experts on this subject and has a library of info available. Contact him if in doubt. Please talk to a doctor with experience in dealing with high altitude. The supplements and medication listed are to help guide you. Talk to an expedition doctor before taking any. Many climbers consider using oxygen, diamox, and other drugs cheating. Relying on drugs and oxygen can create a false sense of security and wind up getting you into more trouble than they are intended to solve.

- **Baby Aspirin** helps improve circulation and is helpful for altitude and cold weather. 325 mg of aspirin administered at the onset of a heart attack can also limit the severity.
- **Ibuprofen** may help prevent altitude related acute mountain sickness (AMS), but due to its effects on your stomach with dehydration you need to be careful.
- **Diamox (Acetazolamide)** taken one day before an ascent and two days at altitude may help prevent and treat AMS, high altitude pulmonary edema (HAPE) and less so for high altitude cerebral edema (HACE). Diamox makes blood more acidic and increases respiration to help oxygenate blood. Diamox is a very strong diuretic. It improves blood oxygenation and can help with sleep and breathing problems while sleeping.
- **Viagra** and **Cialis** may improve performance at altitude by relaxing blood vessels in the lungs, and may help prevent or treat HAPE. No studies I know of have been done on their effects at increasing circulation to the hands and feet in cold weather.
- **Nifedipine** dilates blood vessels the lungs and can be used as a treatment for HAPE, but usually only for those who have had it before. Not for prophylactic use.
- **Dexamethasone** is a steroid that reduces brain swelling. It can be used as an emergency treatment for HAPE and HACE while descending. It can prevent AMS but should not be used for this.
- **Ginkgo Biloba** is a common herbal supplement shown to increase circulation to the extremities, which, like aspirin, is useful for cold and altitude. Some studies say it helps, some say it offers no help at all.
- **Garlic** is another common supplement for cold tolerance, but its efficacy is also up for debate as well.

- The company Mountain Might markets a supplement that supposedly improves blood oxygen saturation, oxygen delivery to tissues, and breathing performance that simulates the adaptation that occur from long term exposure to high altitude while remaining at sea level. Their theory is that the antioxidant **N-acetylcysteine (NAC)** will stimulate the production of red blood cells as well as strengthen lung ventilation and that supplementing with **sodium phosphate** will decrease oxygen's affinity to hemoglobin so it will improve oxygen delivery to tissues. They also suggest that supplementing with **iron** and large amounts of **B12** will aid in the utilization of these compounds. Anecdotal evidence suggests some positive results. One study showed that NAC supplementation reduced respiratory muscle fatigue, while another showed that NAC provided hematological adaptations. The amounts of NAC and sodium phosphate per dose were 1600 mg each respectively.

You urinate more at high altitude, and therefore during first few days' blood gets thicker via diuresis. However, it takes 1+ months for your blood to get thicker because you grew more red blood cells. Because of this blood clots can be a problem, so be sure to move around to avoid venous blood pooling. Baby aspirin could possibly help with this. The body deteriorates above about 16-17,000 feet – in other words you don't recover at this altitude, and your cells don't get enough oxygen. To acclimatize properly you should spend roughly one night per 1000 feet above 10,000 feet - perhaps more. Every three days return to the previous altitude to recover and adapt. Climb high, but return to a lower elevation to sleep. The longer you spend at altitude, the better your chances are. A **pulse oximeter** is a useful tool in monitoring your response. There will be a pulse oximeter smartphone app in the near future.

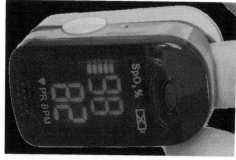

Photo courtesy Brooks Range

AMS can occur at or above 8,000 feet, which is pretty low. Many climbers are caught off guard when they climb in these mid-elevation areas from 8,000-10,000 feet and climb poorly or feel sluggish. If you live at low elevation and plan on climbing a Cascade volcano, or a trip to the Rockies, and wind up bonking don't be surprised. If a climb is very important to you, then spend the time to acclimatize on a nearby non-technical peak. Even those with experience at altitude can have a totally different experience if they spent a lot of time at lower elevations.

More serious conditions like HAPE, or fluid in the lungs, and HACE, or fluid in the brain, generally don't occur below 14,000 feet. If you start developing symptoms (feeling like shit is a good sign), then descend 1-3,000 feet, noting where symptoms first started. If HAPE or HACE is suspected, minimize the victim's effort in descending, administer bottled oxygen, get in a **Gamow Bag**, and take drugs (including diuretics not mentioned in the nutrition chapter). FYI: sleeping pills make you breathe less and can kill you.

Photo courtesy Chinook Medical Gear

If you suffer from migraines, check to see if you have a patent foramen ovale (congenital hole in the heart that can cause migraines), because that could really complicate things at altitude. Get a complete check up by a medical doctor familiar with altitude if you plan on going above 14k because everything wrong with you will be amplified at altitude. You may have to travel to get your check-up from a good doctor. Do this even if you have previous altitude experience. You may vary in your response to altitude each time you travel. A recent cold can also increase your chances to getting mountain sickness, as will prolonged exertion. People who have had Lasik or RK (radial keratotomy) should be fine at altitude, but RK procedures to correct nearsightedness are at risk for blurred vision or a shift towards farsightedness. Talk to your optometrist.

Cold

Frostbite occurs when cells freeze and die. Killing off blood vessels and nerves makes it almost impossible for tissues to regenerate, kind of like getting severe burns. Once frostbitten your scarred tissue becomes much more susceptible to re-injury in the cold. . Frost-nipped (mild frostbite) fingers and toes should be rewarmed without rubbing the tissue or using scalding hot water. Descend before it's too late. Once fingers and toes start to hurt, you don't have much time. **Ibuprofen** is a good choice to treat the pain, and **hand and toewarmers** can stave off the cold for a while.. Frostbite from severe hypothermia should wait for rewarming when at hospital is nearby. Infection and off the scale pain can't be handled in the backcountry. If you can't keep an area rewarmed, do not rewarm it.

Hypothermia is really easy to get. Shivering means you have it. If you suspect it, treat it and descend immediately. You can get hypothermia on a warm day if it's windy or a mild 50-60° day if you aren't moving. Any altered mental status is clear sign. If you can't get extra clothes on, eat sugar and get your metabolism to start warming you.

Besides dying, the worst part of hypothermia is you become stupid and make stupid mistakes. Having a lighter and compact fire starter is a lifesaver during unplanned bivies, as are emergency space blankets. It's a great idea on any climb that you could conceivably epic on to have a kit that only weights a couple ounces containing **firemaking material and a lightweight space blanket**. Sharing body heat, or using your warm stomach or armpit to warm a miserable partner's foot is a great get to know you activity.

Trench foot is a miserable condition that occurs when your feet are wet and cold for an extended period of time. On long trips have at least on **extra pair of socks** buried in your sleeping bag, and maybe even a pair of camp shoes to change into or hike out in if your regular boots and socks get soaked beyond fixing. Heavy waterproof breathable boots sound like they would help prevent this, but in reality they usually get just as wet but take ten times as long to dry. Be vigilant about drying your socks out in your sleeping bag, and changing out of vapor barrier liner socks.

Heat

Most of the injuries that occur from heat are from the sun. Heat exhaustion is very common and can severely impact performance and judgment. The benefits from carrying **extra water** are huge compared to the weight drawbacks are huge on long hot climbs or approaches. Water helps your body thermoregulate, as well as the obvious reasons of water loss via sweating. If your partner is adamant about only carrying a quart on a long climb because "they'll be fine," then be a better climber and sneak an extra quart (or two) in their pack or yours because they will wind up asking to drink your water. An isotonic or hypotonic (more diluted than blood concentrations) **drink mix with some sugar and electrolytes** helps you hydrate way better than normal water because of the osmolality (see the nutrition section).

Once you overheat into your brain, heat stroke develops. You're pretty screwed if this happens on a climb. The only treatment is rapid cooling. Wear **long sleeved clothes** that aren't tight so air can exchange, and a collar or bandana to protect your neck in hot areas. Cotton clothes can be nice as they cool as you sweat into them. If you start getting sick, tired, stupid, or nauseous on a climb because of heat and you find a shady or windy spot, hang out for a bit. Treat heat illnesses like hypothermia – if it's hot and you suspect it, you probably have it. Moving generates heat, so take a solid break. NSAIDs will not help, and they can do a lot of liver or kidney damage because you are obviously dehydrated too.

Sunburns are obviously avoided by proper clothing and re-applying **sunscreen**. On alpine starts, put the sunscreen on in the dark because you'll most likely forget or not want to break the momentum once on the climb. Always have sunscreen squirreled away somewhere on long climbs – in your pack, your pocket, or chalk bag. **NSAIDs** can help with painful sunburns as does ice, and cooling gels like **aloe**. NSAIDs can also be use prophylactically to reduce the severity of sunburns in fair skinned folks. **Spray on sunscreen** is nice to avoid getting your hands greasy, and to get the top of your scalp. Make sure the sunscreen is UVA and UVB rated, and don't bother with anything below SPF 30. Higher SPFs tend to stay on longer, although extra amount of protection offered is negligible above SPF 30.

Make sure to get your ears and back of your legs as those are areas skin cancer can attack. Getting the inside of your nose can prevent inter-nasal burns from water and snow, or very reflective rock. **Lip balm** is a lifesaver in dry, sunny, or high altitude areas. Once your lips get burned or cracked, especially the side of your lips, you'll never forget the lip balm again. Unfortunately your need to re-apply sunscreen every 2-4 hours, something most alpinists never do and craggers rarely do. It is also suggested to use about 2 oz. of sunscreen per application, which borders on ludicrous when compared to what climbers normally apply. If you are a pale while red head then you may want to follow those precautions, otherwise save the slathering for your kids. Protect yourself from melanoma and looking like a leather handbag when you get older.

Protecting your skin during the first 18 years of your life reduces your risk later in life by 75%! Too late for you, but not your kids. There are some concerns about toxic ingredients in some sunscreens, although it would take daily application over decades to reproduce the toxicity on the rat subjects. If you are sensitive or have kids then it may be important. There are some ingredients to possibly avoid, like oxybenzone, an active ingredient, and vitamin A (also called retinyl palmitate), a preservative. It is unclear whether nano particle of zinc or titanium in sunscreen are harmful, but you can get sunscreen with "non-nano" ingredients. The risks of cancer outweighs any risks from sunscreen ingredients by a billion to one. **Zinc and titanium creams** do offer the best protection, as does **covering exposed skin with SPF rated clothing**. All clothing protects from solar radiation to some degree. However, those with very fair skin, high risk factors, or those out in the sun on a constant basis may want to invest in clothing that has a decent SPF rating. Even though you may not get sunburned through your clothing, solar radiation can still damage your skin without the evidence of a sunburn or tan.

Burns from fire or rope burns are extremely prone to infection in the backcountry since you just cooked a little meal for bacteria and killed all of your repair cells. Ice or dip the area in cold water (generally easy to find at camp) for longer than your think: five to twenty minutes. Treat for inflammation and infection immediately. Bandage the area and apply **antibiotic ointment**. Large second degree and any third degree burns require immediate evacuation due to the extremely high risk of infection and permanent loss of function if left untreated. **Second Skin** is a very helpful covering for burns as it cools and doesn't stick.

Your eyeballs can get burned from the sun on water or snow if you don't wear **sunglasses with UVA/UVB lenses**, or if light reflects back into your eye from improper sunglasses. Snow blindness usually doesn't show up until several hours after exposure. Treat the symptoms.

Who to See and How to Be Seen

NMS – I will use the abbreviation NMS for neuromusculoskeletal injuries, which are the most common injuries sustained in climbing. These are injuries involving nerves, muscles, bones, and supporting connective tissues.

SECOND OPINIONS

Get a second opinion from similar practitioners and from practitioners with a slightly different scope and specialization. Some specialists can be myopic and generalists not specialized enough. If a hammer is your only tool, everything starts looking like nails. Recommendations and treatments can vary wildly from practitioner to practitioner. Some are very conservative, will try one thing, wait, and then try another. This is fairly standard practice. However, if there are multiple things going on or unique circumstances then this approach can become slow and frustrating. On the flip side, a "shot-gun" or less conservative approach can become equally costly. Start with the least invasive therapy and most inexpensive options first unless things get worse. But again, I highly recommend getting at least two opinions and stand up for yourself if you think the practitioner is missing something important. Trust your gut. Write everything down you've been concerned about so you don't forget something during your history.

Before you see anyone, make sure they are licensed in your state. Don't go see that weird guy your friend knows at his or her house unless you enjoy wasting your time. No matter who you see, be it therapist, doctor, or surgeon, find someone that specialized in the condition or body part. It is very difficult to specialize in everything. It can be very useful to be co-treated by more than one therapist. Not only is it difficult to specialize in an area, it is also difficult to specialize in a type of treatment. Beware the doctor or therapist that has an answer to everything.

Also keep in mind that the same conditions can be viewed through different lenses or models. For instance, the human body can be viewed from the eyes of a mechanic – your body is made of parts and they all work together somehow, just like a car. Your body can be looked at as a complex system of chemical reactions. It can also be viewed like a computer programmed via DNA and executed via the nervous system.

It can be looked at in biological way, like a how biologist looks at how plants, animals, and cells react to their local and internal environment. You could look at the body through a physical sense, affected by external and internal forces. All of these filters could possibly explain the same condition and successfully treat it.

If you feel that your doctor either doesn't know what he or she is talking about, isn't offering you options, or is reluctant to pursue more conservative, aggressive, or experimental treatments then tell them how much time and money you have been spending on this issue, how extremely important climbing is to you, how this injury is affecting you personally, and to please refer you to someone that will get the job done.

Manual Therapy Practitioners
Chiropractors

Doctors of Chiropractic (DC's) actually receive an education on par with medical doctors as far as the first four years of schooling go, but with a lot more emphasis on NMS conditions than they do in prescriptions and surgical procedures (although they do get some training in both). They are trained as primary care providers, but their scope limits them from prescribing prescription drugs and performing most surgeries. A good chiropractor should be able to diagnose other health problems besides NMS conditions so they can refer to appropriate specialists, or at least treat conservatively through nutritional and lifestyle education.

Unless you need prescription drugs or surgery, a good chiropractor could be a climber's best source of care. However, I want to rant just a bit to help you steer clear of a bad experience. There are many problems with a lot of chiropractors, and these are the ones that give the whole profession a bad name. Some see patients as cash flow and provide as little treatment as possible, but prescribe many many visits.

Some distrust any treatment or theory that isn't "mainstream medical" for whatever grudge they hold ageist the medical establishment. Some ignore current medical knowledge and hang onto an over one hundred year old monocausal theory of disease (bone out of place causes all disease by interfering with the nervous system) with religious fanaticism. Some see all these as a niche to make money by brainwashing and playing to patients' fear to make a lot of money.

Adjusting the skeleton, aka joint manipulation, is only one tool among thousands of manual and physical therapies a chiropractor can do. If all you need is a quick adjustment, then adjusting skill is better than the doctor's intelligence or ethics – that type of chiropractor is more like a Jiffy-Lube when you need an oil change vs. a good mechanic when something is really wrong. Most of the time it's not a one-time fix, but beware of anyone selling you package deals or pre-paid treatments over 6-12 per year. Google any specialized treatments that sound strange. Almost all therapies have a valid theory behind them, but few technique systems have real research behind them (but a lot of marketing to both the doctor and the patient).

Because of the bad chiropractors, the many good ones get a bum rap too. It can be very tempting to go into the practice of high-volume clinics, especially when reimbursement is so difficult. A good chiropractor should be on top of your health concerns, offering solid advice and conservative treatments, while applying the exact same manual therapies as a physical therapist and most likely specializing in joint manipulation therapy. PT's also love joint manipulation, so any discrepancies between the two are the fault of the practitioner, not the profession.

Joint dysfunction is synonymous with "subluxation," but subluxation carries with it the unscientific belief that a misaligned vertebra can cause other health problems and are the root cause of disease. Run, don't walk out of those clinics. However, some good practitioners may present it this way to "dumb it down" for the patient, which can be more than understandable. It's also not a bad idea to get an X-ray of the problem area – all other practitioners do it. But beware the D.C. that uses X-ray as a scare tactic to show how screwed-up you are. See a DC for anything you'd see a PT for, especially for joint manipulation and posture. A referral is not needed. Some states allow DC's, especially those in rural areas, to do blood work, lab tests, minor surgery, prostate and gyno exams, and deliver babies.

Physical Therapists
Most PT's graduating are now DPT's, Doctors of Physical Therapy (PhD-type doctor). They are trained to rehabilitate patients using manual therapy. Many states no longer require a referral to DPT's. PT's do not diagnose in the legal sense of the term (although they can be excellent at it). Look for sports PT's or PT's who work with orthopedic doctors or clinics. Just like chiropractors, some PT's are amazing while others just offer the same routine treatments to everyone. Avoid high volume, franchise-style PT clinics.

Massage Therapists
Massage therapists, or LMT's (licensed massage therapists) use their hands or certain instruments to relax muscles, connective tissue, drain edema, and release fascia among other things. They can be generalists, or perform specialized techniques. Beware of any technique that sounds new age or has a little trademark symbol next to it! Rolfing is a type of deep tissue massage that focuses on muscle fascia. Even though massage therapy requires less education than DC's or PT's, some massage therapists provide more intelligent treatments and are gifted in their technique. Not to be bigoted (your LMT could be a genius – Einstein was a patent clerk after all), but take any diagnostic or home care advice with a grain of salt. I've heard some pretty ridiculous advice and diagnosis. Also, tight muscles and sore spots (trigger points) aren't always a bad thing. Don't let your LMT make you feel bad about your tight "whatever", or make you think you're more screwed up than you actually are.

Athletic Trainers, Coaches, and Personal Trainers
Athletic trainers (ATC), personal trainers, and coaches should all have some certification from a governing agency to be considered. Athletic trainers have a degree, while coaches and personal trainers have certificates from national agencies. You may find one without any certification, but there are too many out there to pick without one if you don't know a good one. Sometimes it takes a fresh set of eyes to help you with technique, training, and weakness. A good one should prove invaluable, but it may be difficult to find one that specializes in climbing. The trainer that comes free with a new gym membership may be excellent and struggling to find work, or just worth the free consultation to humor the gym. Athletic trainers should have at least a bachelor's degree and be certified by NATABOC, personal trainers should be certified by NASM, ACSM, ACE, and NSCA (best), but there are many others. Being certified by a type of exercise (yoga, Pilates, CrossFit, etc.) is great if you're taking a class, but not so great for knowing anything but that type of exercise and no national certification or regulation (especially when it comes to evaluating your health and safety).

Other Manual Therapists
Occupational therapists (OT's) are kind of like physical therapists, but their goal is to get you back to work or to performing ac-

tivities of daily living. They also deal with non-physical conditions that require rehabilitation. Hand therapists may be of special interest to climbers. Both PT's and occupational therapists perform specialized hand therapy (although any practitioner with a basic scope could be an excellent non-certified hand therapist).

There are a lot of other practitioners that perform manual therapy, but I'd avoid the mystical ones that deal with reflexology and energy (unless you're into that sort of thing).

Non-Manual Therapy Practitioners
Allopathic Doctors
Medical and Osteopathic Doctors (M.D.'s and D.O.'s) have pretty much unlimited scope and specialization. Their primary tool is prescribing medication, or performing surgical intervention. Osteopathic doctors are almost identical to MD's, however very few also practice joint manipulation (they were basically chiropractors in the early days). Family doctors (general practitioners) are great for routine physicals, minor medical conditions requiring a prescription or minor surgery, and routine laboratory diagnosis. If you have a complex medical problem, see a specialist in that area. If you have a life-threatening injury – go to the ER! Climbers will most likely visit orthopedic or neurological specialists, the dermatologist for all that sun exposure, or a podiatrist for foot problems. I urge climbers to get a consult from both a manual therapist and an orthopedic/neurological specialist for NMS conditions. However, that can get expensive. If you're not suffering from a serious loss of function, see a manual therapy practitioner first unless you are convinced drugs or surgery is the solution. Don't let the MD or DO boss you around or treat you like an inferior. Big egos are not hard to find in the orthopedic wing at the hospital. If you are debating between an orthopedist vs. a neurologist, see the neurologist. Even if you don't get surgery or a prescription, prepare to spend big bucks on X-rays, MRIs, and office visits for a bottle of ibuprofen you could have picked up at the gas station in a lot of cases.

Nurses and Physician Assistants
Nurses run the gamut from basic bedside caregivers (CNA's), general examination and therapy givers (RN's) to stand-alone primary caregivers (N.P.'s). Along with Physician Assistants (PA's), they are quickly becoming the main caregiver in hospital and private practice setting so more patients have access to care. The big difference between NP's/PA's, and MD's/DO's is the lack of a residency and fellowship (clinical rotations are not the same thing). This goes for DPT's, ND's and DC's as well.

Naturopathic Doctors
Naturopathic Doctors or N.D.'s are trained for primary care, but differ from the allopathic, or the traditional Western medicinal approach. Like chiropractors, you have the vitalists who believe in some sort of innate intelligence, and you have the physicians that combine the science of Western medicine with the use of more natural treatments and prescriptions. If there is a condition you want to try treating without the standard medical regiment, give an ND a try. To call yourself an ND, you must attend an accredited 4-year doctorate college just like MDs, DOs, and DCs. They have excellent educations. There are a few out there without that degree, are not N.D.'s, but have a similar sounding title: run away from those. ND's often use homeopathic solutions to treat their patients. The mechanism of a homeopathic treatment is similar to that of traditional acupuncture, that is, it does not follow a Western-based scientific model. I am very skeptical of homeopathic treatments based on the proposed mechanism at work (sorry).

Acupuncturists

Traditional acupuncture (L.Ac) is an Eastern medicine, and does not follow a Western medical science paradigm. Although I find their theories a bit mystical (but what do I know about our reality), they have been shown to offer relief for pain, and other conditions. Perhaps the needles help short circuit pain pathways gone haywire, help reduce muscle inhibition, and help restore neural pathways. If nothing seems to be working or you're feeling adventurous – give acupuncture a try. The use of needling combined with electrical current is not acupuncture (different principles and described later), and not all use of acupuncture needles is acupuncture (usually trigger point therapy). Make sure your acupuncturist is licensed by ACAOM or NCCAOM. Some practitioners have a degree in another field but are certified to practice acupuncture. Check with your state boards lest you waste your money or walk out with a staph infection or worse.

WHEN TO GO TO THE DOCTOR OR HOSPITAL

When to go to the ER should be painfully obvious. But if you hate hospitals and doctors, or can't afford them here are some not-so-obvious reasons to go. Sometimes really painful or scary symptoms like abdominal pain, blood where it shouldn't be, numbness/tingling, dizziness, fatigue, earaches, chest pain have really benign explanations. It never hurts to get checked out (except your wallet) and better safe than sorry. If a symptom doesn't resolve or get worse, then you should be fairly motivated to get checked out. For those of you with no insurance or high deductibles, nothing is worse than wasting your money for no reason. It isn't out of the question to talk to an expert over the phone or via live chat to see if you really need to be seen.

Reasons to Go
- Moderate to severe ankle sprain: you may have a fracture. Follow up with a 2nd X-ray in two weeks to be sure the first X-ray was accurate. Make an appointment unless it is too painful to deal.
- Deep cuts and punctures, even if you've controlled the bleeding: The risk of infection is high. Go to the ER.
- Trauma to your head, neck, or spine.
- An injury that is not improving or getting worse: you've sucked it up long enough, make an appointment.
- Any chronic symptom, especially unexplained ones: we all feel exhausted, get headaches, and get weird things going on in our bodies: stress is generally the culprit. But we either adapt, the source of stress goes away, and things get better in benign conditions: make an appointment or try and get free advice over the phone.
- An acute symptom that has no explanation: try calling first for some free advice.
- Abdominal pain lasting more than 6 hours: try calling first for some free advice.
- Any illness you are pretty sure needs antibiotics ASAP: try calling first for some free advice.
- Dangerous looking moles and skin lesions: make an appointment or see if you can email a photo.

HISTORY, PHYSICAL, TESTING, DIAGNOSIS, AND TREATMENT

Unless a treatment randomly cures you out of sheer luck or placebo effect, you need an accurate diagnosis to find out what is actually wrong with you. Any good practitioner follows these steps. First a chief complaint history is taken. This should include: location, onset, chronology/timing, severity, modifying factors, associated symptoms, and previous treatments. The great history takers know what specific questions to ask inside those basic questions. You may have pain, but is it only at night? Does it only hurt in certain positions? They use these questions to rule conditions in and out. By the end of the history, they should have a differential list of diagnosis (DDx). There are other important history questions that sometimes need to be asked besides the basic list. Family history of disease and mortality is very important for ruling out genetic conditions. A detailed past health history is extremely useful for relating you current symptoms to past conditions. Everything can be a clue. Finally, a personal history should be taken to rule out environmental and emotional factors. This can include questions about your diet, living conditions, social and love life, mental status, drug intake, activity level, work, life, school, and stresses.

Your ego may get in the way of an accurate diagnosis here. Sometimes we would rather have bad news about something we have no control over than admit the problem lies within. A lot of the non-chief complaint questions are usually check boxes or fill-in-the-blank questionnaires during intake. A good practitioner will actually look at these and ask follow-up questions (and not always believe all of your answers).

After a differential list of diagnosis is created, the practitioner needs to test their hypothesis. This is first done by a physical examination. Usually vitals and basic information are taken such as height, weight, pulse, blood pressure, etc. Next a physical is performed. Depending on your differential, it could be whole body, or it could be regional. Sometimes you'll be asked to fill out a questionnaire that has been developed to help pin down the severity or specifics of certain conditions. There are millions of physical tests that can be done. The practitioner should choose a few that have either a high positive predictive value or negative predictive value (tests that have a mathe-

matically high chance of ruling in or out a condition). Lower predictive value tests are generally done to narrow down towards more specific tests.

For an NMS injury the basic order of testing is: observation (looking at the exposed area), palpation (touching it), a vascular and neurological exam, strength testing, active and passive range of motion (AROM and PROM), orthopedic tests (tests to rule in or out specific conditions), and functional tests (gait, specific movements, etc.). Your practitioner gets bonus points if he or she takes measurements (specific degrees of motion, size of the area, etc.) mainly to use for follow-ups to note improvement. The practitioner should also look at other related body areas to see if they are affected, or contributing to the problem (major bonus points). The more the practitioner tells you what they are doing and why, the better.

One of the most difficult problems in orthopedic medicine and manual therapy and the greatest asset to achieving the most effective treatment is to pinpoint exactly where the pain is coming from. This is much harder than it sounds and imaging won't always help. Some physical therapists and technique instructors love to ham up their report of findings to their patients by stating overly detailed or esoteric descriptions of the injury location when in reality they are just following routine treatment protocols on a general body area.

At this point, if not by the end of the initial history, your diagnosis (Dx) should be in the bag. However, laboratory testing or imaging as a follow-up can really nail the diagnosis. Sometimes these are the only tests required, and sometimes they are useless. Lab tests rule in or out genetic, systemic, or infectious causes – or can provide extra clues. They can also screen for other conditions that may be caused by your initial condition. Imaging (X-ray, MRI, ultrasound, etc.) done by a skilled practitioner can provide instant diagnosis by basically just showing you on film or monitor what's going on inside of you. Imaging can also rule out certain diseases that present with some of your symptoms.

X-rays are the goto choice because they are cheap and visualize bone and hard tissues very well. They do not show soft tissues well. MRI machines visualize an area in thin slices, and are excellent at showing soft tissues. They are very expensive. Imaging is also especially helpful in difficult to diagnose injuries, or chronic complaints. MRI's don't catch everything and a negative MRI should not be the end game of a diagnosis. MRI technology is advancing with different forms like qualitative MRI, 3-D MRI, multi-center MRI, and functional or weight bearing MRI tests.

CT's or CAT scans are also fairly useful. They take many X-ray images to create a 3-D image of an area, and can show a bit more soft tissue than a standard X-ray. Bone scans measure uptake of an injected radioactive substance and can show hard to detect fractures, cancers, and areas of inflammation. Ultrasound can be used as a cheap MRI substitute, but negative tests should follow up with an MRI. There are also many other complex tests that fall between imaging and lab testing. These include muscle EMG and NCV tests that measure nerve propagation in a muscle or nerve, among many other tests. Finally a surgeon could just take a look for him/herself via a scope. Sometimes this is the best way to see what is really going on with the added benefit of surgery on the spot.

Getting an X-ray is kind of a no-brainer (unless you may be or are pregnant). But getting an MRI is a bit tricky – the main reason being the cost of the MRI vs. the treatment options. In other words, if the treatment for the differential list of diagnoses is going to be the same regardless of what an MRI will reveal, then why get one? Good reasons would be to rule surgery in or out, a chronic condition that is not getting better or continuously reoccurring, or to rule out a suspected serious condition. But, if you just have to know and the cost isn't prohibitive, getting an MRI can sometimes give you peace of mind, or cut down on wasted time and treatments.

A great practitioner will tell you that some tests are optional and expensive. Nothing is worse than getting a bill for a test you didn't need, or had recently by another practitioner. There are diminishing returns to too much testing: they may not change the treatment or find false positives or statistical outliers that cloud diagnosis. A course of treatments on an unproven diagnosis may be cheaper with a high probability of success. History should provide a short differential list, an exam should clinch it, and lab tests or imaging should confirm it. Occasionally exploratory surgery is the only way to actually see what's really happening inside you.

After all the history, physical, and testing is complete your practitioner should have pared down their differential list by removing some, and by ordering the list from most likely (which takes the statistical prevalence of your condition into account) to least likely. Now treatment can begin. You should also get some sort of prognosis to give you an idea on the severity, duration, and consequences of your condition. Sometimes a good prognosis cannot be given until some treatment has begun.

Figuring out what treatment to use can be tricky, especially if a diagnosis is not 100% certain. The problem with treating everything with every possible treatment at once is if something makes you better or worse, you won't know what did it. Treatment usually begins with the most cost-effective and most conservative treatment options before progressing to more expensive and dangerous treatments (surgery). However, it is up to you to tell your practitioner what you want. Maybe you're totally sick of rehab not working and you want to take the risks of other treatments like surgery or drugs with side effects. It's also up to you to go back to the practitioner and tell them things are or are not working. Nothing is more frustrating when a patient you saw over a year ago comes back and complains they aren't better from your first and only treatment. Get second opinions, but go back as well. The practitioner may have had a game plan that you weren't aware of. At least call. Doctors have the ability to speak on the phone.

The best treatment should cure what is causing your symptoms, but unfortunately many treatments just help dim down the symptoms. Curing symptoms does not always cure the underlying condition. If an underlying condition is essentially untreatable, the next best treatment should address getting you back to a level of desired function, regardless of the symptoms. It depends on what you desire more. In other words, what's better, lying in bed pain free, or returning to your activity with continued pain? Finally, in regards to treatment options: a great practitioner will tell you of all alternative treatments, risks, and costs. If a practitioner doesn't know what you want out of your visit and treatment, they won't be able to help very much.

Finally, here are some suspect exams I've come across in various chiropractic, massage, and physical therapy offices:
- **Posture stations**: You stand in front of a grid, and the practitioner maps your posture. This can be a very effective general screening tool or a marketing campaign.
- **Muscle or Spinal EMG**: The level of muscle activity is measured by touching electrodes to your skin or down your spine. This test is way too sensitive and unreliable. It can either be done poorly, or be done by someone who wants your money and can easily make the results to make you look like a hypertonic mess of overactive muscles.
- **Applied Kinesiology**: The practitioner uses muscle testing not to test for grades of weakness as done in standard muscles testing, but for highly subjective nuances in the feel of the muscle test usually relating the response to ailments in the spinal column. Some even pair the testing with smelling or tasting substances for nutritional or allergy diagnosis. Rubbish.
- **Postural X-ray**: X-rays are taken to show minute postural problems, often paired with lines and measurement written all over the film. Some are very complicated looking X-ray setups or interpretations, especially on the upper cervical spine. While being able to visual how postural problems affect the spine, or visa-versa isn't a bad thing, but most practitioners use this as a marketing tool or are misinformed about the validity of this type of exam. Hopefully you'll get the marketing vibe. Gross structural problems can be shown on film, but minute rotations or minor incorrect orientations of individual bones or joints are bogus. There are a lot of small genetic variations in the shape of our bones that can be mistaken (or deceived) as a structural problem. Ask for a copy of your films and take them in for a second opinion.
- **Pushing hard on a trigger point** that everyone has or blaming everything on tight muscles.
- **Lab tests** for things you can't test for, don't need to test for, or sent to labs with questionable results. You'll have to research this on your own – ask the name of the lab and test to aid in your research.
- **Anything that shouts B.S.!** Measuring your cranium, looking at your pee, dangling crystals, anything to do with energy, using a device meant for one thing to diagnose another, etc.

NMS Basics

In these following few sections I will try and explain many common injuries that ail climbers and their corresponding treatments. However, many treatments and causes overlap which is why I already presented much of the information in this chapter, and throughout the entire book, including the nutrition section and exercise sections. Rehashing this information for every condition would take hundreds of pages, and I hope that by having explained much and presented the basics of injury and many of the treatments, you can piece together a plan of action. Many conditions can be self-treated in this way. You can also arm yourself with knowledge by being proactive for conditions that require a doctor or therapist. After reading about the type of injury or specific injury, go through the treatment options already listed as most of them can be applied to any body area.

Revisit this chapter, the nutrition chapter, and the exercise chapter (especially the warm-up, antagonist, and stretching sections) to get ideas on how to rehabilitate a particular body area. Besides some new exercises I will present in this chapter, most rehab exercises have already been shown with enough information provided for you to design your own rehab regimen. There are no perfect exercises (or treatments) to rehab an area. The universe did not create specific exercises solely designed to correct or fix an area, so don't get too hung up on finding exact exercises. The point of rehab exercises (and treatments) is to help restore function to a damaged area, and the best (sometimes end stage) exercise is just like the theory behind any exercise for any reason – to mimic the natural function and movement a specific area. As with all the information in this book, I hope you take it upon yourself to use the info I've presented as a guide or stepping stone to do your own independent research. Even the best therapists and doctors in the world will offer different exercises and treatments for the exact same condition with the same results.

Reasons for Injury

To figure out how to fix an injury or to prevent one, it's important to know some basic and common reasons why you get injured. Figuring out the reasons for pain or dysfunction is more complicated than brain surgery for a few reasons. First is that there may be one or more underlying issues, many of which are not directly related to the site of pain or dysfunction. Next is that pain is a multifaceted and poorly understood phenomenon. Finally, we just don't have the technology to pinpoint the anatomic or functional problems occurring. Instead we must rely on very astute observation and there is much subjective and objective variability. The reliability of the patient's response to pain, testing, or history is also severely compromised. In other words: it's a complicated mess.

The most obvious reasons don't need much explanation: direct trauma, disease, genetic conditions, stress, and not taking care of yourself via stress, sleep, and nutrition. Age also plays a part – the older you get the less pliable your tissues are, the more little things add up, and the slower you recover and repair. But figuring out why you got injured when these factors weren't a major player, or if they were, then how to lessen their effects takes a bit of detective work. The three major players are poor technique, genetics, overtraining, and biomechanical imbalances.

Repetitive microtrauma (or stress/overuse) gets blamed a lot for being the cause of many injuries, but it doesn't really explain why one person would get an injury doing the same repetitive task someone else can do forever without complaint. Repetitive stress explains the mechanism of injury, but not the cause. Some common non-climbing repetitive strain producers are looking down at screens and books all day, note taking, sitting for hours, driving, keyboards, mice, texting, large vibrations (like driving machinery or construction), standing on a hard surface for hours, heavy lifting, lifting and twisting, and lifting overhead. Climbing may have tweaked something that you've been damaging through school or work for years.

Technique
Good technique puts your body in a position that creates efficient movement to minimize stress, and act as a buffer to minimize impact just enough to avoid injury. Running is such a good example that even though it's not climbing related, it's worth using for clarification. Running used to be thought of as bad for your knees until fairly recently. The repetitive shock just couldn't be good. But studies have shown that people who run have healthier knee joints on average than those who don't. However, running can injure your knees if you use crappy shoes, don't pay attention to the trail, and have poor technique. It wasn't the running, but how you ran. Same with climbing.

Genes
Sometimes technique isn't an adequate enough buffer to prevent you from getting an injury. The easiest culprit to blame is how your genes developed your structure. I'm not going to discuss extremely rare or bizarre genetic abnormalities – those causing injures should be pretty obvious. But we all have different ratios of arm, leg, and torso length, body mass and strength in one area compared to another, and the shape and length each of our bones can vary from side to side.

Doing day-to-day activities or low stress physical exertion usually doesn't rock the boat, but doing high stress motions can. It usually takes an injury to even notice a structural variance or anomaly. It doesn't even have to be an anomaly, anything that doesn't fit into the "perfect mold" for climbing, even a specific style of climbing can create a weak link in the chain. There are an infinite number of genetic differences that could create or prevent injury in climbing. In some of the specific injury descriptions, I will try and highlight some very common genetic anomalies than are a main culprit for injury of that area. On the flip side, some genetic conditions like some forms of scoliosis look like they would wreak havoc on your body when they wind up only being cosmetic. We are very good at compensating. Long standing genetic conditions and variations in our bodies generally won't create new injuries unless something drastically changes elsewhere in your body, your activity level, or age (usually after 30 years old).

Nutritional and other Chemical Reasons for Injury
Tissues can become damaged by improper nutrition. If you are dehydrated your tissues become less pliable and have a greater chance for injury. Low blood sugar can lead to mistakes in technique that cause injury, or can lead to centralized fatigue. Fatigue can create chemical imbalances that lead to a depressed central nervous system, which creates a downward spiral in health and performance. Overtraining, stress, and fatigue as well as sleep issues can mess up your body's internal repair processes and also increase tissue breakdown from catabolic hormones like cortisol. Stress and overtraining also depress you immune system leading to sickness. Improper nutrition and stress increase generalized inflammation and lead to poor repair and increased injuries. Not eating enough protein will increase the chances of injury and tissue breakdown. Very low body fat decreases natural padding in your joints, decreases key hormone production, and suppresses your nervous system. As we age our bodies

slow down and don't produce the hormones and chemicals that kept us resilient as we once were.

This list could go on and on, but the key points are that chemical changes in your body from poor nutrition, lifestyle, and stress both physical and mental can lead to injury and poor health just as easily as physical forces can. So if you keep getting injured, an injury never heals, or you are always feeling in poor health, take a look at your lifestyle and make some changes. Your body can heal itself better than any treatment or therapy if given the right conditions (to a point obviously).

Biomechanical Imbalances via Movement
Even if you have a perfectly genetically engineered body for climbing, you can still screw it up. These are considered functional versus anatomical since there's nothing structurally wrong, but there is something biomechanically wrong (the parts aren't working together well). I've discussed open and closed chain exercises earlier, and they concept comes into play here as well. Your body at motion is considered a kinetic chain. A motion at one joint effects joints up and down the chain either by moving them or using them for energy absorption.

If an area moves too much or with too much force, something down the line is going to have to absorb that extra energy or move more than it's used to. Likewise if an area isn't moving enough or strong enough, it may cause other areas up and down the chain to compensate more than they were designed to. The weak link in the chain can be where the pain developed but the area that caused the problem, or visa vera.

Distal (farther away) areas usually affect proximal (closer) areas on the same limb, or up the spine from where they attach during closed chain activities. The farther away, the more energy is dispersed and less likely to injure unless the more remote areas also have problems too. In other words foot problems from running (a closed chain activity) should affect your feet, then your knees, then your hips, then your low back, then your neck. But your low back may hurt before your knees if you also have back problems. Areas that have less shock absorption are also more prone to get injured first (so your feet would be less likely to be injured than less forgiving ankles or knees).

Open chain activities are much more likely to injure the area or joint that is performing the main action of movement and spare the other joints and areas of that limb, but can manifest in other areas (especially the spine) if posture and technique is poor in that area. So if you're doing bicep curls – expect to hurt your biceps and maybe even your neck if you are compensating. Compensating for an injury or imbalance can also affect the opposite side. Problems with the spine usually manifest in proximal joints and areas, but weak links far away can be affected. Nerves only affect downstream from the neck, although there are rare cases that nerve pain is felt upstream.

Biomechanical Imbalances via Posture
Posture plays an extremely important role in injury development. I think everyone reading this book can easily grasp the concept that if a body part (especially your spine and lower limbs) is out of whack, then other areas up or down the chain will have to compensate and can become injured themselves. There's more to it than that, however. Your frame is held together by connective tissues and muscles in a way that is designed to reduce stress on your muscles, joints, and connective tissue no thanks to gravity.

It's not just when you're sitting or standing either. Posture is a dynamic shift in the position each of your joints to provide maximum stress reduction during activity. Screw up that posture and joints and areas get stressed more than designed due to compensation. Your joints, bones, and connective tissue have viscoelastic properties. That means they are hard when stressed quickly, and soft when stressed slowly. Glaciers are viscoelastic: they flow smoothly like rivers slowly over time, but when stressed they crack and break. Injuries that push your tissues past their ability to maintain structure should make sense (like breaking a bone). However, you can injure yourself by the slow stress of poor posture over time – known as creep. For example, sitting slouched all day slowly changes your anatomical structure.

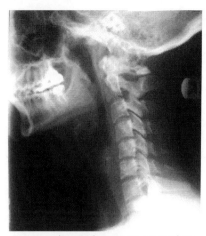

A reversed cervical curve post car accident

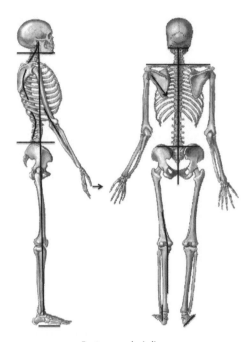

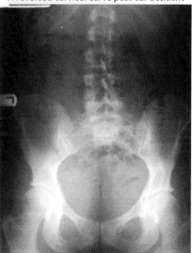

SI issues on left cause the left leg to be higher (see by height of trochanter, ischium, and slight lumbar scoliosis)

Posture analysis lines
Left photo: *head tilted up or down, C-curve in cervical-thoracic-lumbar spine (S-shaped overall), pelvis not tipped, straight line from arm-forearm, palms forward, feet not over pronated/supinated/flat, scapula not winged out. Center line: head not forward, passes through shoulder joint, hip joint, knee joint, ankle.*
Right Photo: *Head not tilted left or right, shoulders and hips even, normal Q-angle at knee, knee not bowed or squinting, ankle not bowed in or out, feet slightly everted, spine straight, torso not rotated. Check leg length when laying down as well.*

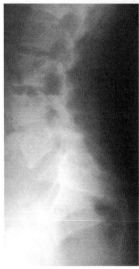

Sacrum is rotated quite a bit forward putting more force on L5/S1 disc and nerve roots.

Biomechanical Imbalances via Shortening and Stretching

Whatever the posture, one side gets stretched out more. When this happens with muscles or the surrounding joints, the muscles become de-activated via sensors in the muscles and joints. The muscles don't always get weaker when used on their own, but when performing with other muscles in a firing pattern (order of muscle activation). They may not fire properly and other nearby muscles must exert more force that shouldn't, and those are the muscles that get injured. Joints and connective tissues that get over-stretched out become weaker, unstable, and more prone to become injured. Hypermobility of a muscle or joint is almost always the pain generator in chronic or overuse injuries. Correcting hypermobility will naturally fix tight or weakened muscles. Tissues become hypermobile from poor posture or technique and fixing this can only really occur by correcting posture or technique over time.

On the flip side, tissues can shorten and become tight due to creep, overuse (hypertonic or over-activated), injury (scar tissue and splinting), or overcompensation. See the section on stretching for more info. This limits range of motion and can cause injury if overstretched during a motion that would normally be safe. Paradoxically, the muscles that cover the joints that get stretched out instinctively protect and splint that joint by becoming tighter. It takes an astute clinician to determine if a tight muscle is protecting a weak area, is tight from already being constantly stretched, or if the tight muscle is from shortening.

Not all tight muscles are pathologic – some people are just tight. Lower cross and upper cross syndrome as well as layered syndrome are terms coined for patterns of tightness and weakness due to poor posture in the upper and lower body. I will talk about specific injuries caused by poor posture later on. Shortened or over-stretched muscles and joints can create postural problems by making another area overcompensate, causing other areas to become overly tight or loose, postural problems, limit range of motion, or exceed normal range of motion. Your body will either adapt or something will give.

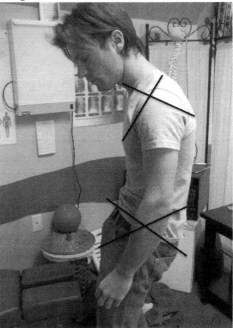

Upper Cross Syndrome: *weak anterior cervicals and posterior rhomboids and lower traps. Tight pectorals and upper traps/suboccipitals.* ***Lower Cross Syndrome:*** *weak abdominals and glut max. Tight hip flexors and back extensors.*

Chronic positions from sitting, sleeping, and standing in one place are major culprits. However, sitting is hands down the worst. Sitting for too long not only leads to a whole host of musculoskeletal problems, it will also kill you. That's right, sitting for prolonged periods shortens your life expectancy. Find a way not to sit or take very frequent breaks. Climbing activities, both active and passive, not only put you in sustained postures that shorten or overstretch tissues, but also over engage certain postural muscles which is why it is vitally important to exercise and train antagonist groups and not over train overdeveloped or shortened muscles.

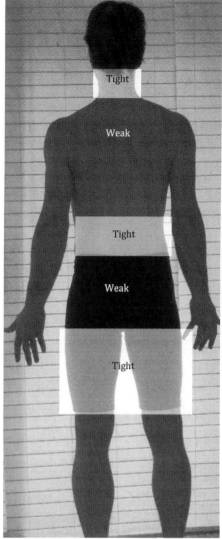

Layered Syndrome: weak and tight layers. The anterior view is opposite: weak neck, abs, quads; tight chest, hip flexors

strength differences from side to side, and the culprit is usually shortening and deactivation due to postural problems. This type of imbalance can create injuries locally or down the line.

The third type of muscle imbalance is when one muscle is much stronger or weaker than the other muscles it works with. If a muscle is much stronger than its antagonist or stabilizer, the antagonist or stabilizer can get injured. If a muscle, especially one of the major large muscles of the body (a prime mover) is overdeveloped from an activity (like climbing), the stabilizer muscles are too weak and can get torn.

For example let's say your lats, delts, and pecs are huge, but your rotator cuff muscles are puny in comparison. Your rotator cuff muscles help with small, fine movements in positioning your arm just where you want it. Your rotator cuff is now like a child trying to take a rabid elephant for a walk. There needs to be a ratio of strength gains between your prime movers, stabilizers, and antagonists or something will be pushed beyond its tensile strength. There is no specific strength ratio for exactly how much stronger a prime mover should be compared to smaller stabilizers. However there are generic rations for gross movements of the limbs.

The ratio between internal rotation and external rotation should be close to 3:2, extension to flexion should be around 5:4, and adduction to abduction is around 2:1.
Orthop Clin North Am. 2000 Apr;31(2):159-76

Overtraining

You can also injure an area by simply applying more force than it can structurally hold. If the muscle is the weak link, it will tear. If a tendon, ligament, or bony attachment is the weak link, it will tear. The quicker the force is applied, the more likely less pliable structures will get torn or broken first (bone,

Biomechanical Imbalances via Muscles

Muscle imbalances can create injuries from seemingly out of nowhere. The first type of muscle imbalance is when the same muscle on one side is stronger or weaker than the other side in the limbs. This generally isn't much of an issue, especially the more distal the imbalance becomes, except that the overdeveloped side has a higher probability of getting injured. Unless a task is totally one side dominant (usually due to handedness), the strength difference is usually small. The second type of muscle imbalance is when core and spinal musculature have ligament, tendon, then muscle), and likewise the slower the force is applied the more likely more pliable structures will get injured (muscle first). Overtraining (or overdoing it while climbing) pushes your muscles, joints, tendons, and ligaments past the point of what they can withstand.

Muscles adapt much more quickly than your connective tissues, and injuries usually occur at the tendinous attachments of muscle to bone, ligaments, and joint structures from overtraining. Constant inflammation further weakens these tissues and also limits range of motion (which increases the likelihood of injury). It can take months to recover from overtraining. Intense training has a negative effect on your immune system and athletes can be more susceptible to getting colds as the while blood cell count drops post-exercise. Eating well, sleeping well, and wearing warm clothes post-exercise can help.

Besides not trying hard enough, the biggest limiting factor for improvement is not resting adequately. Make your training days count and make your rest days count. You could invest in a **heart rate monitor** to chart your resting heart rate in the am, heart rate variability, orthostatic heart rate (change in heart rate from laying to standing), and time it takes to lower heart rate after exertion to see if you have exceeded your training limit. Check out Polar, Suunto, and Garmin for heart rate monitors that have programs for this - Polar being the current best.

Common Inhibited or Weak Muscles
- Deep Neck Flexors (Longus Coli and Rectus Capitus)
- Supraspinatus, and External Rotators (Infraspinatus and Teres Minor)
- Serratus Anterior
- Lower and Middle Traps
- Back Extensors
- Gluts
- Transverse Abs
- Pelvic Floor Muscles
- Vastus Medialis Oblique (VMO) of the Quads
- Intrinsic Foot muscles
- Upper Extremity Extensors (Triceps, Wrist Extensors, Posterior Deltoids)
- Forearm Supinators

Common Overpowered Stabilizer and Antagonists (Weak and Tight)
- Sub-Occipitals
- Scalenes
- Levator Scapula
- Intrinsic spinal musculature
- Rotator Cuff muscles (Supraspinatus, Infraspinatus, Teres Minor, Subscapularis)
- Wrist Extensors and Supinators
- Hip Rotators and Abductors
- Tibialis Anterior

Common Tight Shortened Muscles (Usually Strong)
- SCM and large Posterior and Lateral Cervical Spine muscles
- Upper Traps
- Pectorals
- Lats
- Biceps (and Brachialis)

- Wrist Flexors and Pronators
- Hip Adductors
- Hip Flexors
- Quadratus Lumborum (usually one-sided)
- Hamstring at the Knee
- Rectus Femoris
- Gastroc and Soleus

Common Tight Overstretched Muscles (Weak and Tight)
- Posterior Cervicals (from looking down) or Anterior (from belaying)
- Rotator Cuff
- Rhomboids
- Low Back Extensors
- Quadratus Lumborum (usually one-sided)
- Gluts
- Piriformis
- Hamstrings at the Hip
- Peroneus Longus of the Foot

PAIN PATTERNS

Differentiating types of pain can help you or your practitioner figure out where the pain is coming from. External injuries don't need a lot of clarification since you can actually see the injury. Injuries to tissues such as muscle, tendon, and bone generally show pain in the area and radiate in the same area. Stretching the area or direct compression can cause pain in the site of injury. Depending on the age, location, and severity of the injury the pain can be sharp, dull, throbbing, and stabbing, just to name a few descriptions.

Nerve damage can cause similar feeling pain, but most cases the pain feels more electrical, and sometimes travels along the nerve (down the arm, leg, etc.). Nerve compression can also cause tingling, numbness, weakness, pins and needles, or having the area "fall asleep". Compression of blood vessels can also make an area "fall asleep" but damage to the supported tissues occurs quickly and pain is intense. Almost all cases of tingling and numbness are from nerve compression, not compression of blood vessels. Nerve pain that travels is known as radicular pain and follows a dermatomal (or skin) pattern. Compression of minor nerve pathways, especially around the spine, can cause scleratogenous pain, or referred pain. This type of pain is not easily diagnosed, and can be easily missed in imaging and nerve conduction studies.

Injury to an area will refer pain to another area. Many times myofascial trigger points (MFTP) will develop in muscles. These are painful "knots" in muscles that radiate pain when pressed on. A lot of wasted time and pain can be had treating these trigger points, when they are only symptoms of a problem elsewhere, or a practitioner is actually pressing on a nerve. Joint damage will many times present as a scleratogenous pain pattern because of complex neural pathways. Damage to the structures inside of a joint are usually relieved by stretching or tractioning the joint, while damage to the outside of the joint can be increased by compressing or stretching the joint – depending on which side of the joint capsule is damaged.

Visceral (organ or internal) pain can also radiate, or present in odd scleratogenous-like pain patterns, masking itself as a neuromusculoskeletal type injury. Pain is felt and presented in as many ways as the interpretation of pain varies wildly from person to person. Pain is felt in our brains and not by our tissues, and by the time the signal reaches our conscious interpretation of the signal, it can be anybody's guess as to what the pain actually means. Not all pain means you are injured and vice versa. This can mean you are about to get injured or that pain signals are going haywire somewhere.

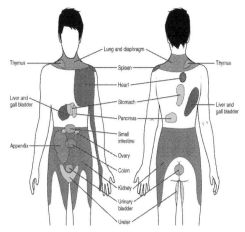

Visceral pain patterns

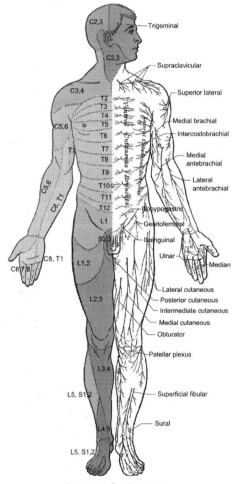

Dermatonal pain patterns

Common Trigger Points. Can be at origin, insertion, or belly. *(Sorry, no photo for the referred pain patterns - use Google).*

- Suboccipital insertion
- Scalenes origin
- SCM origin
- Pec Major and Minor
- Latissimus Dorsi
- Subscapularis (inter-axillary)
- Infraspinatus
- Teres Major & Minor
- Supraspinatus
- Biceps
- Wrist Extensor and Pronator
- Interossei and Lumbricals (especially between the thumb and 1st finger)
- Upper Trap
- Levator Scapula
- Rhomboids
- Rectus Abdominis
- Diaphragm
- Erector Spinae
- Multifidus
- Quadratus Lumborum
- Tensor Fascia Lattea
- Glut Medius and Minimus
- Piriformis
- Hamstring (origin is deep)
- Hip Adductors
- Deep Hip Flexors
- Soleus
- Soles of the Feet

Stages of Injury Repair
Acute and Sub-Acute Phase

New injuries are acute – they just happened. Immediately following a new injury, inflammation occurs. Inflammation is a complex cascade of events your body uses as a way to protect the area and to begin healing.

The acute stage ends with a marked reduction of inflammation. In a normal injury, the acute inflammatory stage lasts a few hours to about three days and up to seven. An injury progresses to the sub-acute phase when the symptoms of the acute stage persist but are decreased in severity. Old injuries can also become flare-ups, an old injury gets re-injured and begins the acute stage once again. Treatment can begin immediately in the acute phase with the PRICED protocol (described later), and some physical modalities can be employed during the sub-acute phase to accelerate healing times.

Inflammation

Normal inflammation is a good thing. Inflammation brings nutrients to heal tissues, and cells to remove waste, debris, and damaged tissue. The byproducts of inflammation are what get the bad press: pain, swelling, and loss of motion. But, without inflammation, your body would not heal. The key to dealing with inflammation is to promote healing and removing the waste (swelling).

Swelling (edema, bruising) is the waste product of the healing process and is removed through the lymphatic system. The lymphatic system is not powered by the heart like the vascular system. It is a passive drainage system that must fight gravity to finally return to the heart and reenter the vascular system. Gravity is one way to get swelling to return to the heart, and this is why elevating an injury while resting is prescribed. But the main engine driving the fluid is muscular contraction.

The paradigm of trying to stop inflammation is wrong. Let inflammation do its thing and promote healing. Help the body flush out the byproducts of inflammation instead. Recommendations to deal with inflammation in this chapter should focus on reducing swelling or dealing with pain if necessary. But, there are times when inflammation itself must be addressed. Very high fevers, compartment syndrome, and preparation for surgery are good examples. Sometime inflammation can run amok, and this is when it needs to be addressed. An area can be stuck in the acute/subacute phase by constant re-injury for so long that a bout of ice and rest are needed to reset the cycle. However, chronic injuries caused by a lack of space and rubbing like, herniations, impingement and some rotator cuff tendinitis may require a bout of aggressive inflammation reduction once chronic to remove the pressure which causes the viscous cycle of inflammation, rubbing, injury, and more inflammation.

As explained later, some injuries just won't respond to any conservative treatments (try them first though), like plantar fasciitis, and may even require a shot of corticosteroids. Start with ice first, then NSAIDS to see if that does the trick for these pesky chronic conditions before going for the needle. Generalized, systemic inflammation though improper diet, stress, fatigue can affect your whole body health and increase your risk of injury. Changes in diet, lifestyle, and taking certain drugs/supplements can address this.

Repair Phase

Once past the acute and sub-acute phase, the repair phase begins. During this phase your body patches up the area quickly. These patch-jobs are known as scar tissue in soft tissues, scabs on the skin, or calluses in bones. Adhesions are scar tissues that bridge two tissues and limit motion between the two. At this point swelling and redness/heat are markedly reduced, range of motion begins to restore somewhat, but pain persists. This phase can take several days from a very minor sprain/strain or cut, to about 8 weeks.

During the repair stage many therapies can be employed. Physical modalities and manual therapies can be used to speed healing, and get a head start on the upcoming remodeling phase to prevent early scar tissue prevention, begin restoring gentle range of motion. Near the middle to end of the repair stage basic stretches, strengthening exercises, and functional/proprioceptive exercises can being if not pushed past the elastic limits of the healing tissue.

Remodeling Phase
Once the structural integrity of the tissue has been restored, your body begins the final remodeling stage. This is the stage where the scar tissues are slowly replaced with normal tissues. Fibers align in their correct orientation to achieve maximum strength, usually in the direction of pull or stress, versus the chaotic weave of scar tissue. The area is re-vascularized and innervated (nerves and vessels grow where they should), and the wound is healed. One of the reasons for pain and tenderness of newly healing tissue (in the repair phase) is that nerves and vessels are either in over or under-abundance, setup like an emergency aid station to the injured area.

Remodeling (or proliferation) phase takes about 3 weeks to a year, unless major neurologic damage or severe trauma (like major burns) has occurred, most function is restored by about one year in most cases – although chance of re-injury is high until fully healed. During this stage one can begin deep manual therapies and full ROM, advanced stretching, strengthening, and proprioceptive/functional re-training exercises. If therapy began early, then therapy in this stage will be drastically easier and shorter. Unfortunately most people don't begin real rehab until this stage, either because they didn't know, or their surgeon or doctor is only good for the scalpel, needle, and thread.

Chronic Phase
Injuries that have been ongoing from months are said to be chronic, usually stuck bouncing between the acute phase and the repair phase. If the cause or aggravating factor hasn't been removed, the injury becomes chronic. Tissues can never fully heal with continued re-injury. Generally acute injuries that are inflammatory in nature get the suffix "-itis". The acronym PRICED outlines the steps to dealing with an acute injury, and is discussed below. Some extremely chronic injuries go on for so long, or get so screwed up in the healing stages that inflammation is absent, yet the symptoms persist. These injuries get the suffix "-osis". This is still a poorly understood condition. These injuries may be more neurological in nature, and some of the tissue may actually become necrotic (dead or dying). Sometimes these long standing chronic injuries need to be stimulated back to the inflammation stage to restart the entire healing process, or the neural pathways need to be re-established or relearned by stimulating nerves in the muscles, tendons, ligaments, and joints and re-training complex movement skills in an affected limb or body area.

<u>**WHEN TO PUSH THROUGH PAIN**</u>
I'm sitting here waffling on how to answer this question as the answer is so subjective and dangerous and the advice "stop if it hurts" is not only good, it's safe. However, sometimes you need to push through the pain to make a breakthrough in healing or training. Starting any new exercise routine creates muscle soreness, and this is also true in rehab. Since the area is weak, simple exercises may feel painful and dangerous,

when it's really just a neurological safeguard. Except under the care of extremely talented therapists, I would call it a safe bet to never push past a pain threshold with an injury (or a non-injury that you are worried is about to become a real injury) unless you can clearly attribute the pain to delayed soreness (DOMS), burning fatigue-type pain, pain from a minor disuse (new exercise or activity), or major disuse of the area (just out of a cast, etc.).

Pushing past the pain does not mean blasting full-steam ahead, but going until it hurts and keeping the intensity there for a short time. Then re-test the area the following time, and going baby-steps a bit farther. The pain should not linger for more than a day or two, and should definitely not intensify after you've stopped for any length of time. If this happens, back off a bit in intensity, or wait a few more days before attempting whatever it is you are trying again. If any pain is sharp or stabbing then you definitely want to stop.

NMS Treatments

Acute Treatment "PRICED"

These are the steps to help begin the healing on a new injury or a flare-up. For almost every injury, the key steps are to stop injuring the area and to help flush out swelling. The ice and drugs steps are only for pain relief if necessary. Avoid re-injury, promote healing, remove waste, and deal with pain if necessary.

PRICED
- **Protect**: The immediate part of protect means padding, splinting, or bandaging the area so it doesn't get infected or injured more – especially important in the field. Once stabilized, protect means not aggravating the area further by using splints, taping, and casts. Protecting also means one further step – stop doing the thing that caused the injury or is making it worse. This could be an activity (climbing), a poor posture, or motion (offwidthing, dynos, etc).
- **Rest**: Along the same lines as the last stages of protect – don't use that injured area. A minor tweak could mean just a few days, a major blow out could mean 6 months. Rest can and should be active if possible. If you injured your hand, you can still use the other arm and the rest of your body. You can begin passive range of motion (ROM), active ROM, light resistance, or light stretching depending on the severity and integrity to the area. Passive rehab modalities can be employed at this time. The more you do earlier in the game, the quicker you'll heal. Too aggressive rehab can re-injure the area, however. Remember that a muscle contraction is what pushes out swelling. The moment the tissue is strong enough to move in a way that doesn't aggravate it, rest for that area should end, and slowly progress towards functional weight bearing activity.
- **Ice**: Ice reduces inflammation and pain. Ice does not help heal an area. In fact, ice inhibits healing by reducing blood flow, and the good parts of inflammation. Too much ice can damage tissue. So why ice? Simple – pain relief or when inflammation must be addressed (reduce swelling rapidly for surgery, compartment syndrome, swelling damages tissues more). Ice can be used to paradoxically bring more blood to an area, called reactive hyperemia. This is an effective therapy for sore tired muscles and chronic injuries. Ice or bags of frozen corn can be applied directly; chemical packs must be buffered via a towel. Ice for 20 minutes, and then wait one hour before re-applying the ice.

- **Compress**: When you injure an area fluids get pumped in via vessels, but fluids also leak in via ruptured cells and osmotic changes. Applying constant pressure with sleeves, bands, and wraps to the injured area reduces swelling by simply pushing the fluid out. You don't want to cut off circulation and injure the area more, however. Snug is a good description for how tight to compress. Massage is an excellent form of compression to push the waste out. Electrical stimulation devices can also be successfully used to use the muscles around an injury to help squeeze out the fluid without moving the area that was injured. If you are severely bleeding compression takes on a whole new level of importance. Apply direct pressure over the wound – but still not so tight that everything below the area gets circulation cut off.
- **Elevate**: If there is going to be a lot of swelling (sprained ankle, fairly serious injury), elevating the area above the level of your heart will help drain the exudative fluid and venous blood out of the area via simple gravity.
- **Drugs**: Check out the nutrition section for drugs that reduce inflammation and pain (ice does both very well).

PROTECTIVE DEVICES AND IMMOBILIZATION

Non-removable casts, splints, and braces and removable protective devices all immobilize an area. **Casts** are used almost exclusively for fractures and avulsions and stay on for about 8 weeks depending on the size, location, and severity of the fracture. **Splints** are used to almost completely limit motion in soft tissue injuries and small fractures and are usually left on for a few days to 8 weeks depending on the size, location, and severity. The reason behind total immobilization is to prevent further injury from movement of the area, and to allow the area to fuse properly. The downside to immobilization is that the area around the healing tissues weakens, atrophies, and adhesions develop making rehabilitation more difficult and prolonged. Some splints provide constant stretching, kind of like braces for your teeth, to realign joints.

Braces comprise between limiting motion for protection and allowing some range of motion either in all directions or only in a limited direction. If an area is transitioning from repair to remodeling, a brace can help the area heal properly by allowing motion but protect it from motions that the area is not yet ready for. Areas with chronic instability or the experience chronic flare-ups sometimes require a brace to allow activity and reduce inflammation and re-injury.

However, braces never allow an area to truly heal and compensation usually occurs, affecting another area or performance negatively. If you wear a brace on a continued basis, or have been prescribed one, then find a therapist that considers braces only a temporary fix.

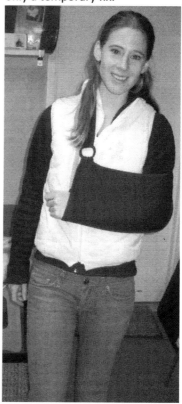

There are certain times when the pros of immobilization outweigh the cons in some cases of chronic joint instability or connective tissue injuries. Loose, hypermobile joints can create pain by altering biomechanics or causing tissues to rub and create inflammation, pain, and tissue damage. Immobilization can cause scar tissue and adhesions to develop. Normally this is a bad thing, but for hypermobile joints this could be bad turned to good. If exercise and other forms of rehab just aren't working on a chronic injury, it may be worth it to try immobilization. The rehab for this type of injury is a fine line between tightening up the joint, and mobilization of the joint to find a happy middle ground. Immobilization of a chronic area combined with icing may also stop low-grade inflammation that has been secretly hindering healing for all this time.

How long to immobilize depends on the severity and chronic nature of the injury. Total immobilization for a couple weeks, or just immobilizing the area when you sleep or perform aggravating activities for several weeks could be the key. There's no equation, but if it seems to help but flares up again, go for a bit longer next time. Injuries to connective tissues require movement for nutrients to reach the area, so on/off immobilization make more sense with these types of injuries. Rehabbing the area after a trial of immobilization is extremely important.

If you wind up with **crutches**, be very careful to not support your weight in your armpit on the crutches. You can develop a neural-crush injury and get two injuries for the price of one. Being wheelchair bound, laid-up in bed, or in crutches sucks. Getting exercise is extremely important during this time. It aids in healing, and helps even more by fighting depression. After a brief bout of doing nothing and feeling sorry for yourself, start exercising and getting out as much as safely allowed.

COMPRESSIVE DEVICES

Some braces, like **tennis elbow braces, ITB straps, or infrapatellar strap**s are designed to take pressure off a tendon that is overly stressed, or rubbing against the area below it. These should not become permanent fixes. **ACE wraps** are almost exclusively used to compress a newly injured area, and mildly limit range of motion. **Coban** is sometimes used to wrap an area that experiences exercise-induced inflammation, but it doesn't work as well as **Spandex sleeves**. **Compression underwear** is also very useful for endurance and recovery as it helps push swelling and inflammatory products produced through exercise out of the area. Some compressive underwear has motion-limiting areas built in to prevent excessive movement, reduce injury, and improve posture – similar to Kinesiotape. The results are subtle, but can be affective.

One company in particular, Thermo Active, makes an amazing compressive device that does dual duty as an ice or hot pack. Each unit is shaped for the desired body area and a pump gently squeezes in all directions. It can be put in the freezer or heated depending on the desired effect.

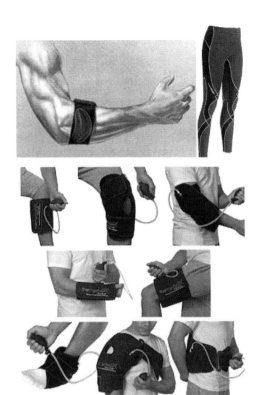

Elbow sleeve, Coban, compression tights, elbow brace, Thermoactive cooling/heating compression

SUPPORTIVE DEVICES

Some areas require protective support because of biomechanical weakness, especially those with weak arches or ankles. Rehabbing these areas is possible, but taping or bracing may be required during times of high impact or exertion. **Taping areas for support** should only be done for support during the desired activity. Cotton **athletic tape** works best in most situations, but a product called **Leukotape** works well in areas that receive high impact because it does not stretch and stays on for a few days. Taping fingers that are rehabbing a pulley or tendon issue is important to prevent further injury, but the goal should be to strengthen the area so tape is no longer necessary. It is difficult for the tendon or pulley to heal properly without stressing it, and too much tape can disrupt the remodeling stage by creating weaker scar tissues. Preventative taping should only be done if you are doing a very dangerous climbing move like dynoing to crimps, or one finger pockets.

Also, preventative taping is useful if training or climbing repetitive high stress moves. But too much taping will prevent the tendon or pulley that should be stressed from getting stronger.

Kinesiotape is a fairly new form of taping invented by a Japanese chiropractor that is designed to aid in swelling, limit specific movements, and provide proprioceptive feedback. There are now several brands of this tape available. Kinesiotape is stretchy in one direction, but becomes stiff at the end range. The glue holding the tape on is applied to the tape in strips, so when applied it bunches up the skin underneath. The theory behind this is that it pulls up on the skin, creating a negative pressure below, allowing accumulated fluids to be sucked out. When applied to joints at specific levels of tautness, the tape can limit dangerous movements at end range, and also serve as a proprioceptive "check," training your body to unlearn dangerous movements. The tape is usually cut (or comes pre-cut) in patterns tracing muscles that create specific movement patterns, or is cut in thin strips to provide lymphatic drainage. There is also a theory that applying the tape from either muscle insertion to origin, or taping in the opposite direction can help activate or deactivate a muscle. I buy the theory, but don't think it really makes any difference. When applying the tape, stretch it so that it becomes tight enough that when the joint nears the end range of movement or at the limit of movement you want to create.

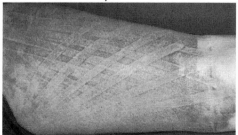

Kinesiotape on a bruise

Tight elastic wraps, aka floss (like Voodoo Floss), are gaining popularity with CrossFitters. Much of the theory is similar to Kinesiotape, but the wraps add an element of compression, a bit more joint stabilization, and even a bit of "pin and stretch" therapy can be added (what they call "flossing"). You can use a bike tube split open if you want. Simply wrap the area up and move the joint. This therapy works well on limbs and on the hips. Bands can also be used for swelling, but wrap them looser towards the heart, move the joint, and take them on and off every few minutes for 15-30 minutes. See stretching section for photos.

Thoracic supports are available in compression shirts with limiting bands across the back and shoulders, and elastic straps are available for wearing over a shirt to help pull your shoulders back and relieving stress on your mid-back. I've never recommended these because simple rehab exercises and quick stretches provide quick relief. But if you're hunched over a computer all day and need to start somewhere, these can provide relief.

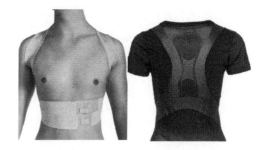

SI belts (sacroiliac) and **trochanter belts** (around your hip joint) are helpful at providing support for those with unstable SI joints, especially pregnant or recently pregnant women. **Lumbar belts and braces** also help with unstable low backs, but not as much as SI belts do with SI joints. SI joints are difficult to tighten, as there are no muscles that cross the SI joint. Low back supports and braces should only be used very temporarily, or for lifting very heavy objects at work. It is extremely important to maintain the use and function of your back muscles – just a little bit of detraining can compound a back injury even further.

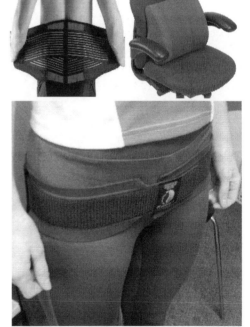

Back brace, back pillow, & SI or trochanter belt.

The same advice goes with **cervical collars** – they should only be used after surgery, a fracture, or for a very short time during the acute phase. Low profile **low back pillows** are excellent, however, because they really just serve as a reminder to sit properly. If you spend a lot of time in your car, or especially in a truck with bench seat, a back pillow can be a lifesaver. Finally, there are several types of special supportive **pillows for your neck** (cutout, rolls, water pillows) to help maintain correct neck posture when sleeping, and special **pillows for under or between your knees** to reduce low back pressure or aid in sleeping while pregnant. Other supportive devices help to correct or assist with anatomic flaws like **foot orthotics and inserts** all the way up to prosthetic limbs.

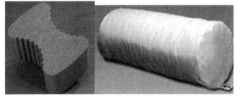

Knee pillow and cervical roll

Physical Modalities

Physical modalities use elemental natural properties to promote healing. They are labeled as such for convention, not because of any mystical belief in elemental forces

Heat

Heating an area increases blood flow and metabolism to carry nutrients away, removes waste, and also makes tissues more supple helping to relax muscles and improve motion. Heat is very useful once past the acute stage, for stiff sore joints and muscles, contracted tissues, and in most arthropathies (inflammatory and non-inflammatory arthritis). The therapeutic temperature range for heat is 104-113° F (40-45 C), but the heat source must usually be hotter than that to achieve the desired tissue temperature. **Hot packs** with protective padding and towels are usually 165-170° F (74-77° C). Treatment time for heat is usually 15-30 minutes. Wet heat penetrates a bit deeper than dry heat.

Hot baths, or hot packs in a hydrocollator do a great job. Dry electric or microwavable hot packs are a good at home therapy if soaking the area is difficult. **Whirlpools and dry baths** of air-circulated sawdust (**fluidotherapy**) also help to rapidly and deeply warm an area. Fluidotherapy, acts like water, but allows for tolerance of much higher temperatures. **Paraffin dips** are extremely helpful in hand arthropathies.

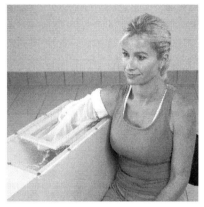

Fluidotherapy

Cold

The basics of icing an area were stated above in the PRICED section. There are some other ways to cool and area besides **ice and chemical ice packs. Soaking** an area in a cold basin of water or bath (cold tap water with some ice cubes) really penetrates deeply. Ice for 20 minutes on and 60 minutes off. **Whole body cryotherapy** using liquid nitrogen is becoming increasingly popular as a way to quickly cool your entire body and helps in speeding recovery between workouts or with injuries. If your gym is lucky enough to have one (or your very rich), try it out.

Although icing is generally used to decrease inflammation and for pain relief, a much better application known as **reactive hyperemia**, or the Lewis Reaction, can be useful in chronic or subacute injuries to increase blood flow to the area. This means blood will flow back to an area as a reaction to short-term cold exposure. To do this only ice for 5-10 min instead of 20. Wait an hour before repeating.

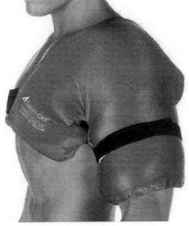

Cold pack fitted for a shoulder injury. Many other body part shaped cold packs are available and work so much better than just a standard pad.

Alternating Hot and Cold
Contrast therapy is extremely effective in rehabbing chronic injuries, or new injuries somewhere in the subacute healing phase and on. The basic principle is to heat, and then cool an area to promote blood flow and to flush out waste. You can use a shower, your faucet, or two tubs/buckets of water. The cold water should be fairly cold: add a few ice cubes to cold tap water. The hot water should not be scalding, but on the hot side of tolerable hot shower. The ratio of hot to cold should be 3:1, ending with cold. A good system is three minutes of hot, and one minute of cold for thirty minutes total.

Plain old heat and contrast therapy are the two best physical therapy modalities you can use to promote healing and repair or even to prevent injuries. Full body contrast therapy feels like you've been born again! For full effect you can to contract and relax the muscle or joint throughout the hot/cold therapy.

Electricity
Electricity can be modulated in many different ways to strengthen muscles, relax muscles, re-train muscles, dull pain, decrease edema, and accelerate healing. Nerves work via electrical impulses (action potentials), and electricity from batteries or wall sockets and be modulated to mimic different types of nerve impulses, usually pain signals and muscle contraction signals.

The most popular form of electric stimulation are portable **TENS** units (transcutaneous electrical nerve stimulation) used to block pain pathways. Although they don't actually fix anything, they can provide relief for chronic or acute pain without the need for opiate pain relievers or muscle relaxers.

The **H-Wave** device may be even more effective than a TENS device for blocking acute or chronic pain and it may also promote healing.

TENS unit

The other most popular form of muscle stim (as made popular by Bruce Lee and subsequent muscle fitness scams) is **Russian Current**. The electrical impulse contracts a muscle, and it is strengthened by resisting the impulse or lengthening the muscle after contraction. It doesn't really work unless you're suffering from pathologic muscle atrophy, or already have made as much strength gains as genetically possible by standard weight training. The Russian stim activates muscle fibers in reverse order than your body normally recruits the muscle, so the results don't translate well into real world strength gains. There may be some benefit in using this device for training explosive power moves (dynoing), but other forms of training are cheaper and more effective. Ab belts and the like do not work. There are fun to play with, however.

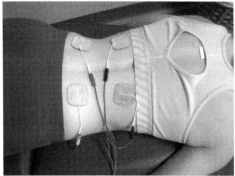

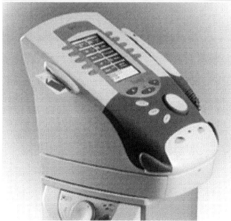

Multifunction E-Stim unit

The most useful form of electrical stimulation for NMS conditions are the **high-volt, SINE, and biphasic** electrical modalities, followed a bit behind by **interferential current**. All of these can be modulated to either block pain, contract a hypertonic muscle until it fatigues and relaxes, or by disrupting the nerve signal from a hypertonic muscle or trigger point to help it relax. The results don't last very long, but they feel amazing and the temporary relaxation or pain reduction can create a window of opportunity for a therapist to perform other therapies.

One of my personal favorites is the combination of **high volt with ultrasound**. The metal ultrasound head acts as the electrical stimulator and is excellent at pinpointing trigger points and inflamed areas.... all the while the ultrasound blasts the area (discussed below).

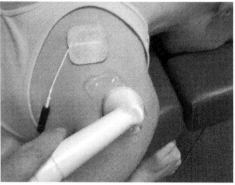

Dry-needling (acupuncture without the philosophical/religious component) with the needles hooked up to an electrical stim machine is another favorite tool for relaxing muscles or destroying trigger points. It can be a bit painful for obvious reasons...but it's a good hurt.

Microcurrent is an electric modality used to aid in healing. This can be done in a clinic or with a take-home device, similar to a TENS unit. The current is sub-sensory (you don't feel it) but the modulation of the electrical current helps tissues heal much much faster, mainly via increasing cellular metabolism to the immediate area. Healing times from cuts, tears, sprains, and strains can be drastically reduced with this neglected therapy. The nice thing about microcurrent is that you can slap on some electrode pads, put the device in your pocket and forget about it.

One newer device, the **InterX**, is gaining fast popularity as multipurpose electrical modality. It uses various waveforms to block pain, relax muscles, re-training muscles, and promote healing at a cellular and neurologic level.

Also new on the scene is **Pulsed Electro-Magnetic Field Therapy (PEMFT)**, also known as **Pulsed Magnetic Resonance Therapy.** Rather than using current, this uses electromagnetic waves to stimulate healing in bone and soft tissue injuries and to help with pain. It has also been used transcranially to help with depression.

The **Marc Pro** device is a new e-stim unit that uses fancy waveforms to help train muscles, aid in muscle recovery, or warm up muscles by neurostimulation. This helps by also flushing out toxins, increasing blood flow, and increasing nitrous oxide levels. It also claims to be used when exercise is not possible to delay regression. It is not meant to be used to build muscles like other bogus devices you see in magazines. In theory it can be used to reduce forearm pump before, during, and after climbing sessions, so if you have access to a portable unit by all means give it a whirl.

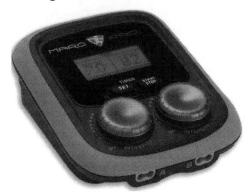

Bone stimulator devices are also fairly new on the scene. They deliver an electrical charge directly to the bone (usually after spinal fusion surgery) or over the skin or cast to speed up the cellular processes to speed up fracture healing. More and more portable devices are being developed.

Electrical stim machines can also be used for **biofeedback** to retrain an atrophied muscle or to relax a hypertonic muscle. A number is displayed representing muscle activation and the patient focuses on contracting or relaxing the area to bring the number displayed up or down. Some other forms of electrical stim help therapists activate nerves and muscles in patients with nerve damage or other debilitating diseases, or make a muscle pump fluid and edema out of an area.

Sound
Ultrasound used in therapeutic frequencies (versus low level diagnostic ultrasound) vibrates a target area very quickly so the area quickly heats up. Ultrasound is basically a heat therapy, but it can penetrate much deeper than any hot pack or bath. In fact the therapist can burn your bone if they aren't paying attention. Ultrasound may be done underwater to reduce the intensity for superficial structures. Ultrasound is a great quick way to heat an area to promote blood flow and loosen tissues. Ultrasound may

also break up scar tissue, calcium deposits, and can push swelling and edema out of an area effectively. It may help with bone spurs. Low frequency ultrasound (30 watt/cm^2) has also been shown to aid in fracture healing. Special units designed for fracture healing are known as **Sonic Accelerated Fracture Healing Systems**.

Extracorporeal Shock Wave Lithotripsy is a hard-core use of therapeutic ultrasound. It can be used to blast kidney stones, but turned down a bit it (using a different device) has been shown useful in treating chronic tendinosis like plantar fasciitis or elbow tendinosis, and for breaking up scar tissue and adhesions in chronic injuries. It can also be used to cause local inflammation to kick-start the repair process. Lower intensity shock wave therapy can be performed with a handheld device, doesn't need to be numbed with local anesthesia, is much cheaper, but may not be as effective as the more powerful units.

Handheld and surgical shock wave devices

Light
Diathermy (basically safe microwave radiation) and **infrared** (heat lamps) are both used to deeply heat and penetrate areas hot packs won't reach. They are especially useful in older patients, and those with chronic arthritis. Don't have any metal on if being treated with diathermy (microwave metal and see what happens). **Ultraviolet** radiation is another form of light therapy, but mainly used as an antimicrobial treatment.

Diathermy unit

L.E.D., cold laser (class III or low level laser), and **high powered laser** (Class IV) therapy are fast becoming very popular therapies to accelerate healing to difficult areas by accelerating metabolism and promote healing. They are extremely helpful in chronic knee, shoulder, or other joint problems that other forms of rehab just won't help, but surgery isn't doing to help much either. Cold and high-powered laser penetrate fairly deep, so it can get inside those joints and promote tissue regrowth and repair. The best units emit constant LED with pulsed variations in intensity-clustered laser.

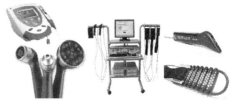

Various laser and infrared devices

Vibration
Vibration is a fairly good therapy used to relax an area, especially large generally tight muscle groups. Some professional **vibration machines** (the G5 in particular) are terrifyingly effective!

Whole body vibration is a fairly new therapy used to strengthen spinal and postural muscles, and may have some general systemic benefits, including bone strengthening. You stand on a vibrating platform and perform exercises.

G5 and whole body vibration

MANUAL THERAPIES

Manual therapy means therapies done by hand. Tools can be used to aid the therapist, and devices can be used to relieve the therapist, but essentially it's all done via human contact.

Massage: Compression and Friction

There are many styles and forms of massage, and I urge you to stay away from new age or trademarked styles. The basic gist of massage is compression and provocation of tissues to improve circulation, relax muscles, aggravate areas to promote healing, or break up scar tissue and adhesions.

Compression of muscles is the most basic form of massage, and it can be performed in various ways and styles. Compression removes blood from the area temporarily, and the resulting ischemia (lack of blood) can cause the muscle to relax. Reactive hyperemia causes blood to rush back in and help heal the area and remove waste products (the dreaded ubiquitous "toxins"). Compression can also inhibit motor reflexes and activation, especially near the attachments. Unless there is injury to the muscle itself, manual therapy at the musculotendinous junction can be a lot more effective

(and painful). These basic forms of massage feel great, and can help overcome oveall tightness. However, unless other therapies, exercises, and lifestyle modifications occur along with a strict regimen of massage (at least twice per week for several weeks), the effects of the massage are only temporary. Overall reduction of stress and its subsequent symptoms can actually be the main benefit of getting a once in a while massage.

There are thousands of **self-massage devices** that utilize compression: from chairs, foam rollers, Theracanes, balls (lacrosse, golf, and softballs are nice) and rollers with spikes and knobs, to climbing specific forearm massagers. Several items have already been shown in the stretching section. Taping two lacrosse balls together creates a nice divot to avoid bony landmarks, like your spine. You can passively press into the tissue you are trying to release, actively roll over the device, or keep the device in one spot actively contract and relax your muscle over it, similar to pin and stretch. Use large deep motions or small oscillating motions over a small space. Self-massage is a cheap, quick, and very effective. Don't do any deep massage before an activity, however. It can cause injury by inhibiting muscles.

Courtesy Arm Relief Massager

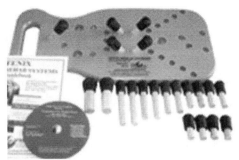

Lay on the nubs for trigger points

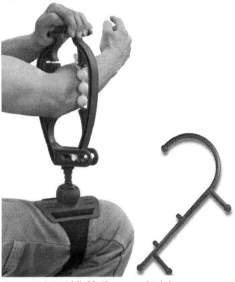

Courtesy Armaid (left), Theracane (right)

Popular foot and trigger point rollers and balls

Trigger point therapy is merely pinpoint compression of tight nodules in the muscles for a brief time. There are several **home care devices** that you can lay on, or press into, to help relieve these painful spots.

Finally, **Active Release Technique** (or the non-trademarked **pin and stretch technique**) combines stretching with compression to provide pain relief and to loosen tight muscles or remove scar tissue and adhesions. There are many subtleties to the technique, but the basics are that shorten the muscle to be worked, pin down the trouble spot, and then lengthen the muscle. It is painful, but effective.

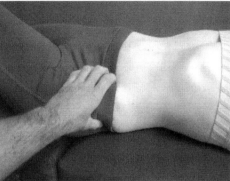

Active release on the psoas – move the leg up and down while squeezing the illiospoas muscle.

Scar tissue is very difficult and painful to remove via massage, but can be done via vigorous **cross-friction techniques** such as by hand (literally rubbing back and forth for about twenty minutes), or with instruments like **Graston Technique, SASTM, or IASTM**. Most friction techniques, like Graston, use a hard tool to literally scrape scar tissues, adhesions, tight muscles, tendons, ligaments, or trigger points. These techniques offer excellent results over a short amount of time (about six sessions). They can lead to some seriously nasty looking bruises over the area, but the bruising is superficial. The scraping can either reduce scar tissue or adhesions, or promote tissue regeneration in tendons and ligaments. Don't confuse the traditional Gua Shua technique with these therapies as Gua Shua is a drastic traditional Chinese therapy whose purpose is to create an extreme amount of inflammation for spiritual reasons.

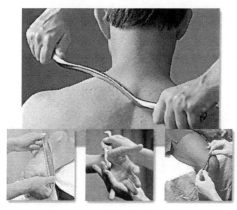

Courtesy Graston Technique

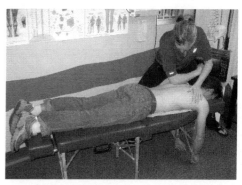

See the stretching chapter for more photos.

Ice massage is an excellent form of friction massage that combines the benefit of cross-friction with the healing powers of ice. Take an ice cube, or peel back a frozen paper cup of ice, and rub it back and forth firmly across the area until the ice melts – for about 15 to twenty minutes.

Other forms of massage use various forms of stretching, compression to reduce edema and lymph, or physical therapy modalities like hot, cold, and vibration. Some forms of massage, like **Rolfing or Kinesis Myofascial Integration (KMI)**, claim to work on fascia. Besides friction techniques, spreading or gliding (**effleurage**) tissues apart by really getting in there can separate fascial layers that are stuck to improve movement along the kinetic chain. This could be helpful in chronic injuries or for postural problems.

Stretching
Traction is passive stretching by separating joints to relieve pressure or stretch the joint capsule. Spinal traction is most commonly used to relieve pressure off of torn or herniated discs. Traction is an excellent treatment for joint damage due to excessive compressive forces, inflammation of the joint, freeing entrapped meniscoid tissues, stretching tight joint capsules, or relieving pressure of nerves and nerve roots.

Spinal decompression machines are extremely expensive, and supposedly target specific joints. I'm a bit leery that this is true, and find less expensive traction machines very effective (although they still cost $20-50 thousand dollars for the clinic to buy). There are basically two protocols for traction: slow steady traction to stretch tissue, and cycled pull/relax traction to help "pump" disc herniations back into place.

Flexion-distraction is a type of spinal traction where the therapist stabilizes the spine with their hand above the area intended for traction, and the bottom of the table is lowered and raised. Traction can also be very effectively performed by the therapist simply pulling on the area, or spreading the joint apart by hand, although it can be very tiring (but way cheaper).

There are many forms of **home traction** for various areas like the wrist, neck, and low back. The best home spinal traction units are made by Saunders and cost around $500 each. I've already mentioned earlier in the exercise section that **gravity boots** can provide traction to the spine and leg, as can very inexpensive store-bought **inversion devices**.

Other forms of traction are **pelvic blocks** that are inserted on the hip crest or trochanter (or both) to slowly rotate the pelvis back into place. Shoes can be used at home by laying on them on the floor. Traction can be applied to the sacrum by lying on a **sacral pillow** and scooting down enough that the friction pulls slowly on the sacrum. The final type of traction device climbers may seek out are **wrist traction** devices. See the stretching section for more info and photos.

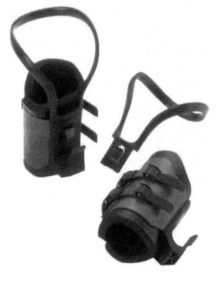

Gravity boots

Passive stretching is identical to traction, except joints aren't separated, but a sustained stretch is still provided with the patient doing nothing. **Night splints** and special socks are used to stretch the foot and lower leg for plantar fasciitis, **toe straps** are used in hallux valgus malformations. Passive stretching is used in restoring a cervical curve by corrective therapy chiropractors. Passive stretching also can be describe as a normal slow steady stretch for 20 seconds to several minutes to stretch tight muscles and joints as mentioned in the stretching section.

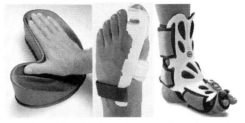

Carpal tunnel and hallux valgus stretches, plantar fasciitis splint

Active Stretching has already been discussed in detail in the stretching section, but again, it is an excellent way to get fast results in chronically tight muscles. Another interesting form of active stretching is called **nerve flossing**. Occasionally nerves become trapped in their sheaths by scar tissue adhesions, resulting in pain or tingling – especially in the nerves in your brachial plexus. Your sciatic nerve is more easily stretched by the active stretching techniques on the hamstring and piriformis. Bring the nerve slowing in and out of tension by performing the following motions to end range and then backing off. Don't go farther than when you feel symptoms, and don't force it. A similar technique can be used for the tendons in your fingers. See the stretching chapter for more info and photos.

Joint Manipulation

Chiropractors and physical therapists both perform joint manipulation as a major therapy, although PT's technically can't legally perform **high velocity-low amplitude** (the crack!) manipulations most states – but they usually do it anyways and just don't bill as such. Again, avoid technique systems with fancy names and protocols – it's usually a marketing scam.

There are **several grades to joint mobilization** – from gently moving of a joint back and forth to the chiropractic crack. Joint mobilization provides several benefits: pain relief via release of natural pain killers (endorphins) and pain-gate mechanisms in the joint and central nervous system (CNS), reduction of a minor dislocation (subluxation), relieves pressure off irritated or compressed joints nerves and discs, restores proper biomechanics by getting an area to move that was stuck or out of place, and milking nutrients into degenerated joints. Any joint in the body, including the almost fused joints in the skull, can be mobilized if proper techniques are used.

Just like any long-term problem and therapy to provide relief, joint manipulation is rarely a one-time fix. Tools are sometimes used to provide the mobilization, from the doorstop looking handheld device known as the Activator, to vibratory units like the Pro-Adjuster, to tables with a drop piece. I've never been convinced that the Activator or jack-hammer device like the Pro-Adjuster delivers enough force to do anything, but **drop tables** are acceptable tools for large difficult joints like the SI or very large patients. I am also wary of manipulation techniques that claim to cure or help with systemic diseases, or techniques that are claimed as a cure-all such as upper-cervical techniques or postural re-alignment systems. There is plenty of anecdotal evidence and a few studies supporting those claims (basically pressure on a nerve or spinal cord can inhibit function to a body system), but not enough to warrant spending thousands of dollars, or using round-about techniques to cure things that have much more valid specific treatments.

Performing self-manipulation can be just as safe and effective as having a chiropractor do it. The problems arise when cracking your own neck, back, or whatever becomes habitual or addictive. Too much of a good thing can lead to chronic joint instability. Also, if you go beyond end range of the joint or try to force a "pop" you can sprain a muscle or ligament, unless you were really forceful – then real damage could result. Getting your neck manipulated is usually very safe. A chiropractor would have to want to break your neck to actually harm you. Usually pain comes from apprehensive resistance, and a small muscle sprain could result. There are a few cases where the vertebral artery in the neck has ruptured following cervical manipulation. Although that's sad, these victims would have stroked out turning their head to change lanes in traffic. Getting your spine, or limbs manipulated won't change you in a fundamental way that will make you require continued care for the rest of your life...that's what crafty sales-doctors are for.

Manipulation under anesthesia is generally reserved for cases post-surgery, like after knee surgery, to restore more range of motion and to break up scar tissue without the patient consciously or subconsciously resisting.

Another type of joint mobilization is to use light to heavy tubing (depending on the joint) to distract a joint into a neutral position while performing an exercise. Kenny Starrett, a popular CrossFit P.T., calls this **"banded flossing"**. The idea is a chronically shortened, overstretched, or pathologic joint will create faulty movement patterns or tissue damage and that by passively placing the joint in a correct position will allow you to either perform an exercise through its full and correct range of motion for better results, or to establish a new pattern to correct old ones.

Continuous Passive Motion (CPM)
This is that dreaded device that passively moves your knee (and other parts) after surgery for hours to reduce scar tissue, lubricate and heal the joints and tissues, and to keep the joint from freezing up. Mostly used after knee surgery.

Movement Therapies
Combining movement with manual therapy and exercise can be the key to unraveling chronic pain patterns brought on by dysfunctional movement patterns. I can't personally endorse any of these as I have not used them - they are just for your reference. The **Vojita Method** combines developmental function movement patterns, like crawling and turning, with other manual therapies to reestablish correct patterns in an adult. The **Primal Reflex Release Technique** is similar but uses developmental reflex arcs (babies have different reflexes than adults). **Feldenkrais** is a method that looks at movement patterns used consciously or subconsciously to correct imbalances. **Neurokinetic Therapy** looks at and retrains compensation patterns in the body by reprograming the motor control in the limbic system. **Positional Release Technique** has the patient placed in various positions that reduce the pain with gentle manual therapies added to address pain syndromes.

There are many other methods, most of which blend various modalities and theories to correct movement dysfunction. Correcting sport specific movement dysfunction or the deeply learned intrinsic patterns could be the final step in fixing an area that always seems to get hurt or is painful.

Muscle Activation Therapies
Many of the manual therapies mentioned also directly influence muscle activation of de-facilitated muscles, but some therapies combine joint positions with manual therapy to help facilitated weakened muscles. The most common technique is **Muscle Activation Technique**.

Drugs

The purpose of most drugs in NMS conditions is to reduce inflammation, relax muscles, aid in repair, or lessen pain due to inflammation or nerve issues. Many medications and some anti-inflammatory medications hinder with the healing process and should only be used through the sub-acute stage if possible. Chronic conditions may require prolonged use of anti-inflammatory medications. Electrical stim machines and ultrasound can be used to deliver pain and anti-inflammation medications, including corticosteroids. This is known as **iontophoresis and phonophoresis** respectively. They are helpful in chronic conditions to get the medication directly to the site of injury, and possibly avoiding some systemic side effects of administering the drugs orally or intravenously. Both can be used to treat pain, inflammation, calcium deposits and bone spurs, among other things.

Prolotherapy is a technique that contains a pharmacological agent (either a natural supplement, saline, or prescription drug) and is injected into a hypermobile joint to cause irritation. The irritation supposedly causes controlled inflammation to active proliferative cells that help regenerate and strengthen the joint. Because hypermobile joints are very difficult to treat, prolotherapy presents as one of the few non-surgical options available to tighten up loose, pain-causing joints. However, its efficacy is still hotly debated.

Platelet-rich therapy injections are another non-surgical (or at least minimally invasive) option for treating painful joints that have become arthritic and degenerated, or for chronic tendinosis. The patient donates blood, which is spun down, and the plasma is collected and serum discarded. What is left is plasma rich in platelets, growth factors, repair cells, and chemical constituents. Some clinics are also including stem cells from marrow biopsies. This is injected into the injured area, and the concentrated healing potion is supposed to regenerate tissue growth to the affected area. This is expensive, but for many, a last resort after failed surgery, an attempt to avoid surgery, or when surgery is no longer an option.

Biopuncture is another form of injection that is supposed to aid in pain and inflammation relief, and to help accelerate or stimulate healing in chronic areas. Biopuncture is simply injecting a painful area with medication. How it differs from tradition medication injections is that the solution injected is in very (actually ultra) low doses of mainly botanical or naturally occurring products. It varies from homeopathy in that homeopathy potions have zero dose of the ingredient (I know!), and the potions are usually not injected. Anyway, the theory is that the substances injected aren't supposed to do the healing, but are there to wake up healing reaction from within the body. Yes, it sounds dumb but it's fairly similar to the basis of prolotherapy, except the injections are into tissues, not joint cavities. Most likely it's not what's injected, but the reaction from the injection.

Painful chronic trigger points are often injected with **lidocaine, cortisone, and or botox** to relieve pain and reduce the local spasm. Artificially oiling your joints by injecting **hyaluronic acid** directly into the joint over 3-5 treatments can really help to reduce pain and stiffness and lasts about 6-8 months. Other slightly more invasive injection procedures are described below under surgery.

Foods to Avoid for Pain and Inflammation
Inflammation in a non-injured area can create a vicious cycle, effectively ceasing repair of an injury, or create whole-body systemic problems. One way to avoid inflammation is to avoid foods that promote creation of inflammatory products. Plants of the nightshade variety can lead to inflammation. These include tomatoes, white potatoes, eggplants, peppers (not black pepper), and tobacco. Foods that cause an individual to have an allergic reaction (low grade to acute) also cause systemic inflammation. Other foods than could promote inflammation are coffee, animal and dairy products (egg whites are ok), and alcohol.

Pharmacologic Pain and Inflammation Drugs
NSAIDs (non-steroidal anti-inflammatory drugs) are almost all over-the-counter (OTC) medications and they aid in pain relief, fever reducing (antipyretic) and reducing inflammation. Higher doses are needed for anti-inflammatory response. Chronic use can affect liver and kidney health, and even mild use can delay or hinder the healing process. NSAIDs include: **aspirin** (not recommended at high doses or long term use due to severe gastrointestinal irritation), **ibuprofen**, and **naproxen**. **Diclofenac and ketoprofen**, along with many others are NSAIDs only available by prescription. Most NSAIDs work on the same basic mechanism, but each requires a different dosage. Some NSAIDs, like ibuprofen, must be taken at higher levels to provide any sort of anti-inflammation benefit. If you are unfortunate enough to need long-term NSAID therapy, you may want to rotate through the different kinds every few months.

Acetaminophen, aka Tylenol, is not an NSAID. It does not relieve inflammation, but is effective for fever and pain. It can be very hard on the liver, and taking it with even a small amount of alcohol can kill you. Short-term effects are pretty safe, however. Combining Tylenol with NSAIDS or even better, anti-inflammatory supplements (below) is a good non-narcotic way to reduce pain and inflammation safely over the short term, as ice good old fashioned ice.

Besides NSAIDs, there are many more prescription pain and inflammation drugs, but with much more powerful (and addictive side-effects) like **COX-2 inhibitors, opiates, synthetic opiates**, and various combinations. **Muscle relaxers** are commonly prescribed for muscle pain. They have their place, but I feel they are over-prescribed. Use your judgment whether the doctor is prescribing them because they will help, or that he or she has a limited toolkit. **Botox** of all things may be an excellent replacement for muscle relaxers, but it is still being tested.

Corticosteroids (cortisone) are extremely powerful and extremely effective prescription drugs that quickly eliminate inflammation. They can be injected or taken orally. They have extreme side effects like severely weakening connective tissues, drastically increasing risks of systemic or local infection, or creating systemic disease like Cushing's disease, high blood pressure, and diabetes. They should be used very sparingly. They can be the magic bullet and totally worth a shot if not contraindicated and a vicious cycle of inflammation is the big thing holding back recovery. However, beware if your doctor goes straight for the needle, or suggests multiple injections.

Some medications are strictly designed for nerve pain, and most are prescribed by your doctor. **Gabapentin** is a common prescription, but keep in mind that it can make your groggy in the morning. Other **antidepressants and anticonvulsants** are also commonly prescribed.

Pain and Inflammation Supplements
Some OTC supplements have been shown quite effective for pain and inflammation. These include (from best evidence to weakest): **capsaicin**, a topical pain relieve derived from cayenne pepper, **SAMe**, very effective but takes almost a month to get working, **white willow bark**, a precursor to aspirin but easier on the stomach, **ginger, boswellia, turmeric** (also as **curcumin**), and **devils claw**. **Ginger** has shown some promise for relieving pain due to osteoarthritis and inflammation. **Limbrel** is a prescription supplement that is more like a natural supplement than an NSAID, COX-2 inhibitor, or narcotic you can try. Too much can be very toxic to the liver, however.

There are many **topical balms** sold for pain relief (especially muscle and joint). The problem is that the ointment needs to pass through a lot of tissue before it gets to its intended target (if at all). Many make you feel better, but no studies have been done to show if they actually do any good. The active ingredient in most balms is **menthol**, which produces a cooling feeling. Biofreeze is incredibly popular, but is hard to get outside of a physical medicine facility. Balms can act as the transmission gel for ultrasound and the active ingredients can be delivered via phonophoresis. Capsaicin is one the most effective topical creams that actually works. Some creams and pain patches contain the NSAID diclofenac (and other ingredients like DMSO) and have also been shown to be effective. Common brands are **Voltaren, Pennsaid, and Flector**.

There are a few OTC supplements that are only for inflammation relief and do not directly relieve pain. These include the **proteolytic enzymes**: **bromelain** (take on an empty stomach), **trypsin**, and **chymotrypsin** and the **flavonoids rutin and quercetin**.

Omega-3 fatty acids like **fish oil** can reduce inflammation over time. **Flaxseed oil** requires too much ingested required in order to be useful. **Evening primrose oil (EPO)** and other forms of **gamma linoleic acid (GLA)** is sometimes used to reduce inflammation, but you need to take a lot since it broken down into more pathways than fish oils. There is insufficient evidence for **D-phenylalanine's (DPA)** effect on inflammation to recommend. **Vitamin B6, magnesium,** and **zinc** are all cofactors for optimal prostaglandin metabolism. B6 used in high doses can help with peripheral neuropathies. Ice is the most effective OTC pain, fever, and inflammation product available.

Osteoarthritis (OA) and Degenerative Joint Disease (DJD) Supplements

Many of the above drugs and supplements are also effective for joint pain due to OA and DJD. The following are specific to joint pain due to a lack of or injury to cartilage and connective tissue containing cartilage, most often manifesting as osteoarthritis or DJD. However, not all injuries to cartilage and joints are due to DJD, it can also be from a trauma, immobilization, or biomechanical stress. Inflammatory arthropathies like rheumatoid arthritis (RA), lupus, ankylosing spondylitis (AS), etc. are systemic, sometimes life-threatening conditions, and are to be treated by a qualified health care provider.

Glucosamine sulfate and **chondroitin sulfate** are extremely popular OTC remedies to help rebuild or support cartilage. You can take either, but be sure to get quality supplements that end in "–sulfate", not "–HCL". Glucosamine HCL is much easier to find on the shelf, but may not have any effect. Relief is not immediate, and it can take several months. You can take it in divided doses or all at once. After a few months, you can take a few weeks off and start again because the drugs stay in your system for quite some time. Both have come under fire recently for possibly being ineffective. If no relief is offered in six months, stop using them – they are cheap and safe.

MSM and **hyaluronic acid** are usually taken in addition to glucosamine or chondroitin. Both have shown to be slightly effective for joint pain. Hyaluronic acid is also occasionally injected into the joint itself. **SAMe** is a chemical the body produces but has been shown to help with arthritis symptoms as well as depression and is recommended. **Avocado-soybean unsaponifiable** have been shown to help protect cartilage via anti-inflammation properties and is also recommended. **Calcium** and **vitamin D** supplementation have already been discussed the bone-loss related aspects of DJD, but of course, I just read a study showing both to be ineffective! **IpriFlavone** is a useful supplement to aid in and maintain bone density. It has been used to aid in boosting metabolism, but there is a big lack of evidence for that.

Tendon Repair Drugs and Supplements

B6 and **vitamin E** are showing a lot of promise in helping treat tendon injuries. **Nitric oxide** has also been shown to be very effective at accelerating healing of tendinopathies. To get to the tendon prescription grade transdermal patches of **glyceryl trinitrate (GTN)** are applied over the area. Sublingual spray and supplementing with **arginine** is less effective.

Tissue Repair Supplements

There is no magic healing pill. Supplements that aid in tissue repair mainly act as supporting enzymes, building blocks to tissue building cells or processes, or antioxidants. A basic list of tissue repair promoting supplements is: **vitamin C, calcium, magnesium, zinc, vitamin-D, vitamin E, B-vitamins, fish oils, selenium, manganese, copper, iron, calcitonin, protein, and amino acid supplements.**

Exercise and Stretches

Most of the rehab exercises are also already listed in the training chapter since many of the rehab exercises should have been pre-hab exercises to being with. New exercises will be presented in the next section of this chapter alongside the condition or area they help with. Besides a quick fix, the one thing people love to get is rehab exercises and stretches – it's something you can do. Rehab exercises serve to re-pattern muscles and strengthen weak/torn or post-surgical muscles. But a lot of times, exercises are not what you need to heal until you've reached the proper stage so re-injury doesn't occur. The order of exercises to do is different that the order presented in the training section. The starting point depends on the severity and progression of healing of the injury.

Exercises aren't just to strengthen or stretch muscles. Rehab exercises and stretches are also meant to re-train your body to correct bad technique, posture, and imbalances (see reasons for injury). Exercise for rehab is the final polish on the recovery and repair of an injury (although it can begin immediately in some cases) and is what will train you to not re-injure yourself again. Although not presented in detail in this book, performing range of motion and body-weight exercises in a swimming pool can be very effective in post-acute or post-surgical rehab.

To remind yourself to do your exercises, set a timer or use an app to ring if you need to do an exercise multiple times, especially stretches.

Surgery

Surgery should be the final line of treatment for pretty much anything wrong with you. Not only is it dangerous and expensive, it can also fail or cause more problems than it fixes. Any good surgeon should tell you this. Obviously there are times when you need surgery, and it's a good idea to get at least two opinions. Sometimes surgery can be a quick enough fix with fairly a good outcome guarantee that months or years of continued rehab just to maintain a level of function just isn't worth it.

Surgery doesn't fix everything either. Obvious tears or tumors are one thing, but spinal surgery and joint repair sometimes just don't work. Become informed on the risks, post-surgical rehab involved, and percentage of positive outcomes for whatever surgery you are considering.

Ask around and find the best surgeon you can – travel if you have to. Surgeons, especially orthopedic surgeons can be total know-it-all divas (but not all!). They are very good at finding fractures, tears, and tumors on film, but often terrible at diagnosing other conditions – especially conditions that require an understanding of physiology and biomechanics. If they can't cut it out, it doesn't show up on film or a nerve study, then you don't have a problem in their view. If this happens to you, consult a neurological surgeon instead or a non-surgical specialist in the area that's bothering you. They may be able to help via drugs or injections, and possible do a minor surgical procedure your orthopod should have done in the first place.

However, if you think you need surgery, try and make your fist appointment with a surgeon, not a specialist that doesn't perform surgery (assuming you've exhausted non-surgical treatments). Why pay to see someone who will either tell you to get surgery not. If you need a springboard for ideas on conservative care vs. surgery then see the specialist first (or a highly recommended therapist). It is very frustrating to spend money for no reason on doctors telling you that you've essentially wasted your time.

Listen to the surgeon's advice regarding healing times and wound care, but don't count on their advice concerning activity modification or rehabilitation as being in your best interest. Go to a highly recommended sports therapist (a good PT or DC) before the surgery for tips on how to be in the best condition possible so recovery is minimal, and then immediately after surgery to begin rehab. Trauma from the surgery itself can prove to be more difficult to rehab than actual area that was repaired!

There are more surgical procedures out there besides opening you up, cutting something out, cleaning up a mess, sewing/stapling/screwing/pinning loose ends together, or creating artificial joints.

Grafting cartilage harvested from another joint in your body is more and more common. Using cadaveric meniscus **allografts** has been around for a while and is still an option. Heat can also be used in arthroscopic surgery to literally shrink-wrap a joint, tendon, or ligament to reduce hypermobility and instability.

However, as technology advances so do surgical procedures to minimize evasiveness and maximize self-healing. Instead of fusing vertebrae, surgeons are starting to use **prosthetic discs** instead. One newer surgical method is **Micro Fracture**, where small fractures are created on the underlying bone to stimulate cartilage regrowth in areas like the knee. Another method is called **Autologous Cartilage Transplantation** where cartilage is harvested, grown, and transplanted back into your joint. **Scaffolds** are starting to be used to patch soft tissues using pig or your own tissues. When scaffolding is combined with the cartilage transplantation described above you get a procedure called **Matrix Induced Autologous Chondrocyte Implantation (MACI)**.

Bone morphogenic proteins (BMP) can be used to enhance fracture and cartilage repair, and hopefully connective tissue injuries in the future. **Hydrogels**, mixtures of bioactive materials and growth factors can be literally spackled into a damaged area to patch and accelerate repair. Radio waves can be used to stimulate repair of fascia and tendons in **Coblation Microtenotomy**, which is a minimally invasive surgical procedure. **Bioabsorbable screws and sutures** use also being used more to reduce problems down the line and also to not have to have another procedure done to remove the objects. However, I was pretty keen on using my titanium pins for ultralight V-threader applications.

Gene and stem cell therapies will no doubt be the wave of the future. Your local hospital probably won't offer any of these procedures any time soon so you may have to travel. The FDA is painfully slow and inefficient at approving many procedures or allowing something approved for the knee to be done in the shoulder for instance. You may have to find a doc willing to go "off label", or go to another country.

Weight Loss, Nutrition, Cardio, Heavy Lifting, and Healthy Living

None of these are direct therapies but can have a profound effect on rehab or prevention. First off, being overweight has a direct biomechanical link to whatever injury you have. Make your injury a wake-up call if weight is an issue for you. Proper nutrition is better than any supplement. Not only does your body make what it needs to fix you when it gets a wide range of nutrients and proteins, but also eating well reduces overall inflammation, which has a huge detrimental effect in the rehab process. Getting in at least a ½ hour of cardio three times a week and 2 days of heavy lifting (more than bodyweight) has a huge effect on your general health – down to the cellular level. Finally all those other bad for you things (you know what they are), especially being stressed-out and unhappy are seriously contributing to becoming injured and slow recovery.

Sketchy Treatments

I've already listed a few borderline treatments, but all of the above-mentioned treatments have good evidence to back them up unless otherwise mentioned. Many treatments may have a reasonable theory behind them, but do not translate into providing a substantial enough outcome. Some are just plain metaphysical.

- Most commercial nutritional supplements and programs (motivation to show up or the placebo effect is what makes most of them work).
- Most detox treatments, especially foot baths
- Anything to do with manipulating or reading energy
- Anything with quantum physics in the description that cost under several million dollars
- Reflexology
- Magnet therapy
- Bio-Identical Hormone Therapy
- Homeopathy - Diluting a substance until no trace of the solute is present

Treatment Plans

Assuming you aren't fixed by your therapist in one shot, you'll have to go back for more care. The stricter you are about following home care advice (ask for it!), the less you have to go back. You actually never have to go back — it's all about how you heal, how fast you want to heal, and what you're willing to live with. After an initial response to treatment therapy including exercises and stretches, there may be a long (1-3 month) period of no improvement — even some flare-ups. After this plateau, if you continue treatment, there is slow continued improvement. Stick with it.

A standard treatment plan for a new injury or a long-standing chronic injury is two to three times per week for a few weeks, once a week for a couple months, then a follow-up visit or two. Figure on about twelve visits if you're optimistic, to twice that if you're a mess. Strict home care and lifestyle modification can cut those numbers in half. Pay your therapist at visit once you think you're feeling better. There may be unfinished business to get an area to fully healed, and you may pay the price ten-fold down the road by not finishing your treatment plan. I would never pre-pay for packages of services, or sign any contracts. Also you usually get what you pay for, so $25 visits are usually crappy care, or a lure to get you to sign a contract for more expensive care.

Some therapists, especially massage therapists and chiropractors, will recommend you come in for general maintenance care to keep you healthy. If you suffered major trauma, or are exposed to repeated trauma (which is usually the case in climbing), and if you can afford it and feel better from treatment, go ahead. There is little evidence, however, that massage or chiropractic adjustments will prevent arthritis of the spine or disease and illness. However microtrauma through work, sport, or lifestyle causes constant stress and poor posture, so preventative care is really about fixing small problems before they become big ones.

QUICK TREATMENT REFERENCE

TREATMENT SUMMARY

Therapies that Protect or Immobilize
- Rest, Activity Modification, Bandaging, Padding, Splinting, Casting, Bracing, Taping, Strapping, Compression, Orthotics, Supports, Pillows, and other types of Immobilization.

Therapies to Reduce Pain
- Ice, Heat, E-stim, Diathermy, Ultrasound, Drugs/Supplements, Injections, Massage, Joint Manipulation, Traction, Exercise/Stretching

Therapies to Reduce Inflammation
- Ice, Ionto/Phonophoresis, Drugs/Supplements, Injections

Therapies to Reduce Swelling
- Elevation, Compressive Devices, Electric Stim, Ultrasound, Massage, Joint Manipulation

Therapies to Reduce Joint Pressure
- Stretching, Traction, Joint Manipulation, Surgery

Therapies that Promote Healing
- Heat, Lewis Icing, Contrast Icing, Diathermy, E-stim, Ultrasound, Laser/LED, Massage, Injections, Surgery, Supplements, Stretching/Exercise

**Therapies that Improve Range of Motion and Reduce Muscle Tension*
- Stretching/Exercise, Heat, Diathermy, Electric Stim, Ultrasound, Dry needling, Biofeedback, Infrared, Vibration, Massage, Injection, Flossing, Traction, Joint Manipulation, Drugs/Supplements, Movement Therapy

Therapies that Stretch Areas
- Traction, Stretching/Exercise, Flossing, Massage, Joint Manipulation

Therapies that Strengthen Muscles and Tendons
- Electric Stim, Biofeedback, Vibration, Exercises/Stretches, Drugs/Supplements, Injections

Therapies that Reduce Scar Tissue and Promote Correct Tissue Remodeling
- Heat, Ultrasound, E-stim, Massage, Stretching/Exercise, Flossing, Surgery, Joint Manipulation, Traction, Movement Therapy, Drugs/Supplements, Injections

Therapies to Stabilize Joints, Ligaments, and Tendons
- Immobilization, Supports, Injections, Exercises, Surgery

Therapies that relax muscles should be carefully examined before applying. Painful tight muscles may be splinting a hypermobile joint or may be tight and painful because they are actually weak. Relaxation followed by activation and/or loading could cause significant damage to the muscle, joint, or tendon. Once out of the inflammation stage, focus on therapies that strengthen or heal.

REHAB BASICS

The basics of rehabbing an injury are as follows:
- **Identify the Cause**
  - ✓ Diagnosis of injured area and cause of injured area
  - ✓ **Stop, Fix, or Remove the thing that's making it worse**
  - ✓ Cease or modify activity, protect the area, drugs, surgery, lifestyle modification, manual therapy
- **Help Remove Swelling**
  - ✓ Flushing out the waste products of inflammation allows more nutrients in, decreases pain, and allows for movement
- **Heal Damaged Tissues**
  - ✓ Promote blood flow, proper nutrition/supplements
  - ✓ Remodel scar tissue
  - ✓ Manual therapy and physical modalities
  - ✓ Movement, exercises, and stretches
- **Restore Range of Motion**
  - ✓ Manual therapy and physical modalities
  - ✓ Exercises and stretches
- **Fix Imbalances**
  - ✓ Exercises and stretches
- **Restore Full Strength**
  - ✓ Exercises

- **Retrain Coordination and Movement Patterns**
✓ Proprioceptive exercises and technique: single joint or multi-joint movement patterns challenged and retrained via instability, biofeedback (a mirror), oscillation (Bodyblade or TheraBand Flex-Bar for example), or drop and catch (dropping a limb and quickly stopping it without support)
✓ Biofeedback on sport specific performance (could be as simple as looking in a mirror or recording video)

ORDER OF EXERCISE PROGRESSION FOR INJURIES
- Passive pain free range of motion movements
- Active pain free range of motion with gravity and bodyweight gradually introduced
- Light active stretching at end range with more focus on the counter resistance than the stretch
- Eccentric contractions with gradual addition of resistance using tubing or light weights, and begin light pain free stretching. Begin with slow, mid-range of motion, then faster mid-range, then slow full range to faster full range.
- Concentric resistance training using tubing progressing to bodyweight or heavier weights (continued throughout the rest of the rehab until full strength is restored) and increased difficulty of eccentric contractions.
- Add isometric holds in various angles while continuing progressively deeper stretches, possibly pushing past pain barriers to restore full range of motion
- Functional movement pattern exercises, plyometric exercises, and proprioceptive exercises to restore correct muscle and movement patterns
- Build endurance tolerance up to normal levels

After these steps you can have at it to regain maximal strength and power.

EXERCISES
- New exercises introduced in the next few sections
- Warm-Up section from aerobic to balance
- Antagonist and Stabilizers section
- Stretching chapter
- Later stage: Intense Core section, Non-Climbing Supplemental Upper and Lower Body section, and some of the strength exercises in the Climbing Specific Exercises section.

NMS INJURIES BY TISSUE TYPE

To narrow down repeating information for every of specific named conditions, I'll begin by describing injuries by the type of injury to various tissues. If you didn't find what you were looking for in the rest of the chapter, it's probably here. Not every treatment will be listed for each condition, but if some treatments are particularly effective, they will be mentioned. Looks at the list of treatments, stretches, or exercises for more ideas.

What Exercises and Treatments Should I Do?

Just like in the training section, there are way too many individual differences between even similar injuries for me to hammer out a specific list of treatments and exercises for each condition. I have already given you the tools by listing all the current available treatments and what they address, and countless exercises and ways to do them. What I have done for you in the following sections is to explain the different structures and types of injury that commonly occur as well as more specific injuries that happen to different areas of the body. Combine this with having read and understood why and how injuries can happen and you should be able to come up with a game plan or add to a plan laid out by a therapist. You may want to reread the first few chapters of the training section along with this chapter to help you sort through the information that best applies to you and your condition.

Bones
Fracture

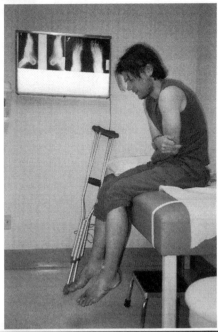

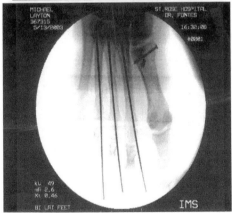

Yours truly after breaking all the metatarsals in both feet

Breaking a bone can sometimes be a mixed blessing. Broken bones follow a fairly predictable healing pattern and timeline, and recovery from a minor break without complications is usually complete. The problem arises when joints and ligaments are also damaged because they take a lot longer to heal completely. It's obviously important to cast, or immobilize a fracture so the bones can join properly. A cartilaginous callus should form around the break in about two weeks. During the next few weeks, new bone replaces the callous. New bone is constantly deposited, and old areas are reabsorbed until the fracture is as good as new. This process of deposition and absorption actually occurs in all of your bones all the time. It takes about five years to completely remodel your entire skeleton. A fracture generally takes 6-12 weeks to stabilize and become able to bear weight.

Bones can develop small hairline or stress fractures than can mimic muscle or joint pain. They usually heal on their own in about a month to three months, but complications can arise if the fracture is made worse by continued stress or activity. The pain may be difficult to pinpoint and may be difficult to reproduce, confounding diagnosis. X-ray may or may not show a fracture, especially if it is very small, or in an area that is difficult to view such as an ankle or wrist. It takes about two weeks for a callus to develop over the fracture, and may not be visible on X-ray until then. Be sure to get a follow-up X-ray after two weeks if it's still on the table as a possible diagnosis.

Avascular necrosis (AVN) can develop in untreated fractures, as can chronic joint instability. AVN occurs when a section of bone is cut off from blood supply and dies. High-risk areas for AVN can be detected with a bone scan, and sometimes a CT. Be extra diligent about possible undiagnosed fractures in ankle and wrist sprains.

There are many different types of fractures. Some only require immobilization to heal, while others require surgery to realign the bone, patch together or remove bone fragments. In most cases, the surrounding soft tissues require more prolonged rehab than the healing of the actual fracture – either due to injury to those tissues, or due to immobilization. Fractures that are close to, or extend into a joint are very susceptible to future arthritis.

Returning the area to optimal function post-fracture healing will decrease the likelihood of developing arthritis (or degenerative joint disease). Some fractures that are stabilized with pins, screws, or plates do not require these implants to remain after the fracture has fully healed. At this point it is just a game of what's worse: minor surgery to remove the implants and the subsequent month or so of inactivity, or dealing with any pain from the implants.

Make sure you are getting at least your RDA of calcium, vitamin C, other minerals and plenty of protein. Don't try to bear weight on the area, or support yourself on the area, even with a cast on. Let your body do its job, and don't make it worse by aggravating the area. As with any injury, staying as active as possible will dramatically increase you healing time, assuming you don't aggravate the injured area.

Once the cast is off, you can go to town on beginning to rehab the area. Begin with slow progression to weight bearing, as the fracture is probably not fully stable. Much of your rehab will be restrengthening, regaining range of motion, and healing the surrounding muscles, joints and ligaments that have atrophied during immobilization or have been injured from the accident or surgery. Make an appointment with a therapist the day your cast comes off.

Avulsion or Rupture

An avulsion or rupture occurs when a tendon (holds muscles to bones) or ligament (holds bones to bones) is stronger than its bony connection, and instead of snapping, it pulls off a section of bone. This usually occurs on the larger muscle groups such as the Biceps tendon of the arm, or Achilles tendon of the lower leg. These can surprisingly heal on their own, but surgical repair can be necessary. Definitely get a consult. Prognosis, treatment, and rehab are very similar to a fracture. However, it is easier to re-injure the area during healing since you've got a large muscle that will be tensioning the area. Also, it is very likely that the tendon, joint, and or muscle have sustained some injury as well.

Follow rehab protocols for those areas as well. Extra diligence is required to ease into weight bearing activity. Chance of re-injury is high which is a bummer because you'll have to be careful for quite some time after everything has healed. Having someone evaluate your technique or for muscular imbalances is a great idea, since unless the tissues in that area was just especially weak (genetics), there is a good chance that you were over-favoring that area.

Dislocation

Dislocations can be chronically annoying problems, or life-threatening injuries. Dislocations in the knee, hip, and spine should never be reduced except in the hospital as major arteries or the spinal cord could become severed or damaged killing or paralyzing you. Dislocations in other areas should only be reduced in the field if the victim has had this happen before and knows what to do, or if it will be a long time before you reach a hospital. In-line traction is the safest and most effective emergency treatment. Dislocations stretch out and weaken the joints, ligaments, and connective tissues holding the joint in place and can become chronically unstable. Scar tissue can develop from one or repeated dislocations. Use rehab to address damaged tissues and scar tissue, as well as rehab to strengthen unstable joints, muscles, tendons, and ligaments.

Bone Bruise

Blunt trauma, even overuse can cause your bone to become bruised, and swelling occurs between the bone and surrounding periosteum. This is almost always just an additional symptom to another injury, but the pain can mimic other conditions or confuse diagnosis. An MRI for a different condition is most likely what will pick up a bone bruise. Treatment for other underlying conditions will most likely resolve the pain from a bone bruise. If a bone bruise is the only thing wrong, rest, reducing inflammation, and minor immobilization are the best treatments.

Spurs, Bunions, and Malformations
Bones can form spurs and bunions due to increased pressure over an area or develop malformations due to genetic anomalies. The problem arises when the extra bone causes inflammation due to pressure or friction on an outside surface (usually shoes), or puts extra pressure on internal tissues such as nerves and tendons. Finally, changes in shape can cause biomechanical problems. I will address common examples in the section that addresses specific, common injuries. Treatment can be as simple as getting a better fitting shoe, to surgically repairing the area. Mobilization of surrounding joints could help minimize the impact of a bone spur. Immediate treatment is usually dealing with inflammation from the pressure or friction.

JOINTS
Joints are tricky because many structures converge here, and issues can be from one or more damaged tissues including tissues inside the joint tissues and tissues that connect to or into the joint, as well as from biomechanical problems relating to movement or aberrant motion (or lack thereof). Joints are surrounded by a capsule made of connective tissue, and contain cartilage that covers the bone, ligaments connecting bones, and a meniscus made of dense connective tissue in some joints for extra protection. The joint is filled with synovial fluid that lubricates the joint and provides nutrients via absorption, as the tissues mentioned do not have direct blood supply.

One good way to rule in joint problems is that compression of a joint is often painful compared to when muscle or tendon injuries are not.

Subluxation and Joint Dysfunction
A subluxation is a minor dislocation where a bone is slightly out of place either due to trauma, one side is being pulled too much, or one side is excessively tight. Some chiropractors use the term to also mean that a joint is not moving properly (too much or too little), and is also defined as joint dysfunction. Any of these causes can create inflammation, edema, pain due to lack of motion (joints that don't move signal pain), referred pain to other areas, nerve pain and nervous system symptoms due to pressure or inflammation, and biomechanical problems locally or elsewhere due to aberrant motion.

Facet syndrome is a common joint injury in the spine due to joint dysfunction. Facets are the articulating surfaces in your vertebrae and can become inflamed. There are many nerve receptors in and near the vertebral facet joints, and the pain can be intense and simulate more complicated problems such as disc or nerve root injury. Facet syndrome can be caused by poor posture, instability, muscle imbalance, or trauma. Treating consists of addressing inflammation, and removing the cause of the pressure. Addressing underlying causes such as posture or imbalance takes time and a smart therapist.

Joints that don't move properly are either stuck in one or more directions or are unstable and move too much in one or more directions. Joints become stiff if structures tighten via disuse or scar tissue from injury, poor posture, or improper biomechanics (one or more weak-links in the chain). Many times a joint will be stuck because one or more joints up or down the line are hypermobile (too loose). Tight joints may also be from splinting of surrounding muscles to protect the joint.

Joint dysfunction is almost always an indirect result of a problem elsewhere or a direct result of an injury to the joint. If nothing seemingly caused the problem, investigation of the underlying cause should take place instead of just treating the immediate area. Stuck joints can be unstuck by stretching, mobilization, manipulation, and by addressing underlying causes. Over treating tight joints can cause more problems than it fixes by making the joint hypermobile and paradoxically creating more tightness by having surrounding tissue splint the joint further. It would take months of overtreatment to create this problem, however, so a few adjustments or therapy sessions probably won't hurt if they are being applied improperly.

Joint instability/hypermobility is very hard to fix. Not only is it more difficult to tighten up a joint than it is to loosen it, as mentioned, unstable/loose joints can present as tight joints due to splinting or inflammation. Joint instability usually presents as chronic pain in the area that gets better with treatment, but reoccurs soon after treatment. Occasionally clicking, popping, or shifting sounds will present – aiding diagnosis. Motion imaging can be done to inspect the joint motion, but is expensive and exposes the patient to excessive doses of radiation unless diagnostic ultrasound is an option. A series of X-rays taken at the end ranges of motion can help determine instability, but many times the instability is too minor to detect on film.

Joints that are excessively tight in one direction can cause the other direction to become too loose, or vice versa. Usually the tight side is treated, hoping that the aberrant motion will normalize. Joints that are loose or unstable can have tight muscles surrounding the area, multiple myofascial trigger points, and referred pain patterns. If in the spine, you may feel the desire to constantly self-adjust (pop) the area. Chronic injury to an area may be the result of an unstable joint.

Treatment involves getting stuck side to move and strengthening the loose side as well as removing any scar tissue. Finding the underlying reason elsewhere in the kinetic chain can be very difficult, but may be necessary to stop the imbalance or compensation that is occurring.

Arthritis
Osteoarthritis (OA) and degenerative joint disease (DJD) are basically synonymous genetic disorders that occur as one ages, usually appearing around middle age but can begin as early as in your mid to late twenties. They are not to be confused with inflammatory arthropathies like rheumatoid arthritis (RA) and lupus, which are more serious conditions usually autoimmune and genetic in nature and should be managed by a rheumatologist.

The joint space between articulating bones begins to decrease, generally due to the destruction of cartilage and grown of bony spurs. The cortical bone (surface of the bone) begins to erode and weaken and can form bone spurs. Fusion of bone and total destruction of the joint can occur in later stages.

The key to treating arthritis is early prevention. Inflammation and trauma are usually what triggers the onset and progression of arthritis, therefor controlling inflammation and rehabbing injuries fully in joint-related injury is very important. Disuse and immobilization will also accelerate arthritis - so keep moving. Remember, it's not motion that causes the problem (motion nourishes and strengthens joints) – it's incorrect motion causing inflammation or damage that's the problem. Repetitive trauma or trauma from a single event can cause arthritis down the line. It may not develop for years, but the chances for developing arthritis in a damaged joint skyrocket.

Non-prescription medications may help. Other prescription meds can help if OTC treatment isn't helping. Some surgeries can be performed to remove spurs, replace the joint (cover it in metal), and stimulate regrowth of cartilage if conservative treatment isn't helping – as well as some newer injection treatment options. Occasionally surgical fusion of the joint is necessary to prevent further irritation.

Arthritis is usually stiff and achy in the morning, or before a solid warm-up, and improves as the day progresses unless aggressive use of the joint causes inflammation. Heat, especially moist heat, is helpful at getting stiff achy joints feeling better, and reducing inflammation when they begin to hurt. Traction can also be helpful sometimes.

Other consequences of arthritis are joint mice, loose bodies of cartilage or bone inside the joint, or calcification of cartilage and connective tissues inside the joint. It is difficult if not impossible to reverse calcification or degeneration of subchondral bone. Occasionally calcified tendons (calcific tendinitis) can be repaired via ultrasound.

Capsulitis and Contracture
Joint capsules can become inflamed, or overly tightened due to scar tissue, immobilization, or posture. Painful or tight joint capsules are difficult to diagnose as symptoms can be confused with sprains/strains to muscle and ligament, tight muscles, or joint dysfunction. Cortisone injections may be necessary to break the inflammation cycle as cold may not reach the joint and drugs won't reach the area due to the poor blood supply. Deep manual therapy and constant end-range stretching or traction may be necessary to loosen up the tight, fibrotic tissue.

Articular Connective Tissue
As mentioned, a meniscus is a thick fibrous cartilaginous connective tissue that covers the surface of several joints, also known as fibrocartilage. The most famous and most injured is the meniscus inside the knee. Another very common structure, the labrum in the shoulder, is very similar to the meniscus.

A meniscus or similar structure can be torn, a flap can develop and get in the way of joint movement, develop microtears, or become bruised, degenerated, or dislocated. Signs and symptoms are deep pain, pain with pressure or certain movements, or catching/clicking/popping with movement. Small tears and bruises often resolve on their own, but can take months of active rest (the joint still needs movement to heal). Surgery to sew up the tear or replacement with cadaver tissues can often become necessary as healing larger tears or degeneration is very difficult. Other commonly injured articular discs are inside the jaw (TMJ), and wrist (triangular fibrocartilage). Meniscoids are smaller menisci in the spine that can literally get pinched and trapped in a joint, causing pain. Relief is usually instant with joint manipulation or traction. Plicae are folds of synovial tissue inside the knee that can become damaged or pinched similar to a meniscus or disc.

Intervertebral discs are generally famous for the herniations they can create. These semi-cartilaginous structures provide shock absorption for the spine and have softer interiors, or nuclei. With enough pressure or degeneration, the nucleus can bulge or fully rupture and compress the spinal cord or nerve roots coming off the spinal cord. The thoracic spine generally doesn't herniate (although degeneration and discogenic pain in the mid back is common), and specifics on neck and low back disc problems will be discussed in greater detail later. Bulges and herniations can and often do resolve on their own, but treatment can help and surgery is sometimes necessary.

It's interesting to note that many people have herniations with absolutely no symptoms, and many people with symptoms of herniations don't actually have them. Think about that before you rush to get surgery. Discs are very pain sensitive, and discs can have micro tears of their annular fibers of varying degrees. Inflammation because of this can mimic a herniation, facet syndrome, or a sprain. Discs usually get injured due to poor posture (too much flexion/creep) combined with a rotatory force and/or forceful loading. Constant vibration can also predispose a disc to injury. When a nerve root becomes compressed or irritated, pain can zing down an arm or leg, followed by numbness or motor weakness. However, pain can be local or radiate in a scleratogenous pattern even if the spinal cord nerve roots aren't involved.

Injuries to articular cartilage not related to DJD or trauma are almost always a result of poor technique, muscle imbalance, and posture.

Bursitis
Sacks of synovial fluid cover several joints in your body to act as protective pillows. These sacks, or bursa can become inflamed from blunt trauma or repetitive pressure. Common areas in climbers are over the elbows, fingers (especially from ice climbing), and over the shoulder. Bursitis is very difficult to treat, again, because there is no direct blood supply to the area. The bursa will get inflamed and swell causing pain, and then take forever to de-swell and heal.

Ice helps, but avoiding re-injury is the best treatment. NSAIDs can help, but not much. Injections may help drain it, and a cortisone shot may offer relief, but generally this treatment is only used in severe or chronic cases. Bursitis from ice climbing can be prevented by using gloves with knuckle padding or using leashless ergo-style tools and by sewing/gluing light kneepads into your bibs.

TENDONS AND LIGAMENTS
Sprain
A sprain is when a ligament becomes stretched and torn. The same thing can happen to a tendon, known as a strain, but the effects are more similar to a strain than a sprain. Sprains and strains are graded by how much the structure has been torn – from micro tears to full ruptures. Interestingly enough, small tears are often much more painful than larger tears, and sometimes complete ruptures are painless. Surgery is sometimes necessary in very large tears and ruptures. Interestingly enough, even full ruptures can heal on their own if fully immobilized for several weeks. Always get a surgical consult, but sometimes conservative management (full bracing) can result in more successful outcomes if the surgery is particularly invasive.

Sprains are usually caused by a single trauma, but repetitive microtrauma can wear down a ligament or tendon over time. Treating for inflammation along with partial to complete immobilization depending on the size of the tear is usually the standard treatment. Once the ligament or tendon is able to bear weight, rehab can begin gradually working range of motion and light stretching, to strengthening the surrounding muscles. Scar tissue can develop and treatments to reduce it are very helpful.

Ligaments can become lax, or overstretched causing joint instability. Either the surrounding structures can be strengthened, or injections and surgery may be necessary of stabilizing surrounding structures isn't good enough. Some people can be so strong, that they can have ruptured ligaments without even knowing it.

Tendinitis, Tendinosis, Tendinovaginitis, & Tendinosynovitis

Tendinitis is probably the most common type of injury that climbers get. Tendinitis is inflammation of tendons, which connect the muscle to the bone. Too much force concentrated over a small area causes microtrauma and therefore inflammation. For climbers, this is generally in the fingers, elbows, shoulders, or knees. Because tendons don't get direct blood supply, recovery and treatment are difficult.

The best treatment is prevention by correct posture and technique, not over-training or pushing yourself too hard, limiting dangerous activities and postures like crimping, dynoing, and offwidths, and exercising antagonists and agonist muscles to spread forces over a broader area. Tendons and ligaments get stronger by constant force (like bone and skin), but take years to adapt to hard climbing. Injury obviously weakens them, and a viscous cycle of re-injury can develop. Tendons can also become loose, or develop scar tissue. Generally, pain occurs when the area is out under load or is compressed.

Once inflammation has been controlled, treat to reduce scar tissue and strengthen the tendon. Cortisone injections can sometimes instantly cure a bout of tendinitis, but is dangerous because the tissue is severely weakened by the injection. The best post-acute treatment is to figure out the cause – usually poor technique, overtraining, and muscular imbalances. Immobilization may be necessary in acute or chronic cases. Tendinitis can be very slow to heal and may take a year to resolve, or at least calm down enough to become manageable if other factors limit healing.

Chronic tendinitis can become tendinosis, and as discussed, this becomes less of an inflammation problem and more of a degeneration and nervous system issue. Stimulating the area via manual therapy, mobilization, or injection may become necessary. Too much strain or impact on tendon makes scar tissue thicken the tendon. The thickened tendon then rubs on the sheath covering the tendon causing tendinovaginitis or synovitis. This friction causes more inflammation, and a vicious cycle begins.

Treatment for this is 1-2 weeks of immobilization, 1-2 weeks of additional rest coupled with NSAIDs, ice, and possibly a cortisone injection. This is a case when you want to stop inflammation because it has created scar tissue that is creating more inflammation. Manual therapies are also effective. Many times the muscles that develop tendinitis are ones that are supposed to stabilize. Therefore progressive eccentric training can be effective for tendinitis and very effective for tendinosis. Practice eccentric exercises daily to 3 times per week doing 3 sets of 10-15 reps that walk the line between pain-free and painful near the end of each set.

MUSCLES
Strain

The big injury to muscles that hasn't been discussed yet is a muscle strain, or pulled/torn muscle. Just like a sprain, strains are graded on the severity of a tear. Muscle strains can hurt quite a bit, but luckily this is because they have an excellent blood supply.

Treat mainly for inflammation and swelling, and rest and protect the sprained muscle. Begin stretching and rehab after the swelling and acute stage has passed. Manual therapy can help speed recovery and remove any scar tissue that may have formed. Pain can last for quite some time after the tissue has heeled in moderate strains when smaller nerves to the area are damaged, or new nerve proliferate into the area. This condition requires more aggressive rehab, and may require you to push through the pain. Electrical stimulation is especially useful in muscle strains, or pain syndromes due to muscle injury. Depending on the severity of the strain, begin exercises and stretches from the most basic to the most functional, especially eccentric training and proprioceptive training. A minor grade I strain heals in about 2-6 weeks, a moderate grade II strain heals in about 6-8 weeks, and a major grade III strain will take 8 weeks to about a year to fully mend.

Bruise
Bruising occurs when a crushing or tearing injury to the muscles causes capillaries and other cells (like muscle cells) to rupture and leak fluid. The fluid has nowhere to go, and it takes time to reabsorb. Most bruises are benign, but some bruises mask larger scale tissue damage. Sometimes the bruise calcifies inside the muscle, a condition known as myositis ossificans. Ice and protection are the best treatment, but Kinesiotape and ultrasound can aid in accelerating recovery.

Deactivation, Shortening, and Tightness
This has also been discussed a few times in much more detail, but to summarize, muscles can be deactivated or defacilitated due to chronic postural over-stretching and nearby joint dysfunction or joint dysfunction near the spinal cord. A posturally over-stretched muscle may feel tight, as could a muscle covering an unstable joint. Active stretching resulting in a muscle "letting go" is a good way to determine if a muscle is tight due to postural or biomechanical reasons, versus muscles that are tight from being shortened. Shortened muscles are generally the result of trauma and scar tissue, or creep due to postural problems or muscle imbalances. Muscles that are over-facilitated and feel tight are generally muscles that get a lot of use and are proportionally too large compared to other agonists or their antagonists.

Cramps
In my opinion, detraining, or not being used to the demands you are placing on the muscle is the most common cause of cramping, especially repeated eccentric and isometric contractions in flexor groups like the calf, biceps, and forearms.

If you really want to prevent cramping, train the muscles predisposed to cramping by overloading them in the way you will be using them. Constant stemming, sloping belays, and ice climbing are common times to get leg cramps. Long all-day face climbs and crack climbs are common times to get forearm and biceps cramps. Jugging, hauling, belaying a stiff toprope, or any constant rope-pulling activity like belaying, hauling, and rope management also are very common times to develop cramps. Train for these situations.

Dehydration (especially via a hangover) is number two on my list of common causes, very closely followed by low blood sugar. Being too hot can also cause cramps via losing the thermoregulatory properties of water and being dehydrated or actual overheating from exercising and outside temps. Muscle contractile proteins can stop working or denature at certain temperatures. See the section on water for more info. Depleting muscle glycogen combined low blood sugar will start to cause muscle breakdown and the metabolic byproducts could also cause cramping. Also, when breathing hard you may not be exhaling enough to CO_2 to buffer the acid build up in your blood. Try overdoing your exhale and taking a large abdominal breath to flush out excess CO_2 and to re-oxygenate the blood.

Electrolyte imbalances have never been proven causes and chances are that you've got plenty of stored electrolytes – just not enough sugar and water in your blood. Not enough magnesium (helps muscle relax), calcium (helps muscles contract – good because it helps weaker muscles) and sodium/potassium (helps nerve propagation) can all predispose you to cramps. If supplementing with electrolytes, make sure you get all of these minerals.

The new supplement making big headlines in treating exercise cramps is **pickle juice**! The science behind this isn't there yet, but major sports teams are already using it as their go-to cramp reliever. It's unclear if it's the high sodium or acetic acid content (or placebo) that is helping. **Acetic acid (vinegar)** is a precursor to acetylcholine, a major neurotransmitter in muscle activation. If cramps are an issue and the other tips haven't helped, you may want to try a small vial.

Fascia
Fascia is the tissue that covers, protects, compartmentalizes, and lubricates muscles, muscle fibers, and even large sections of body area to stabilize and help coordinate movement. Some movement therapists and anatomists have dissected fascial planes that show how structure helps dictate movement and function. Fascia is subject to contracture via postural shortening, and to developing scar tissue and adhesions. Local problems in muscles and joints can occur when the muscle fibers don't glide properly, and can cause global effects because the fascial planes connect multiple areas – so adhesion and restriction in one area can also restrict movement in another area. Reducing tightness and adhesion in muscles or facial planes can help relieve postural and movement problems, relieve pain, and increase range of motion.

Compartment Syndrome
This is a fairly rare but very serious injury that can actually occur from overuse, trauma, and infection. Common areas for climbers are in the forearm, and in the antero-lateral side of the lower leg or calf from running. What happens is that inflammatory products, edema, and swelling from an injury or overuse are not able to drain from an area walled off by connective tissues or other structures. The swelling and pressure cuts off blood and nerve supply. Surgery is necessary and often necessary immediately. Pain and or loss of sensation should get your butt to the ER before you wind up reading this for help in self-diagnosis. Basically if symptoms don't reduce with ice and elevation in a few hours you need to go the hospital.

A more chronic version of this is exercise induced chronic compartment syndrome (EICC), and although serious, it is usually not life and limb threatening. Symptoms are similar but not as severe and go away with rest. Getting continually and abnormally pumped in the forearm is a yellow (not quite red) flag. A surgical fascial release is required.

Rhabdomyolysis
This is a condition that would never have made it into a book like this without thanks to hard-core training modalities – specifically CrossFit. Rhabdo occur when muscle tissue is broken down too quickly or too often from overexertion, and the kidneys begin to fail with the toxic proteins polluting the blood.

NERVES
Nerves take longer to heal than any other tissue. Severely damaged nerves can never heal. Even minor injuries to nerves take at least a couple months to regain normal sensation. Nerves, like any other tissue, can be stretched too far, compressed too much, bruised, and inflamed. Injuries to nerves can

be felt as local pain, numbness, tingling, or shooting pain down a limb.

Nerves conduct information via electrical propagation, and even light pressure can interfere and cause symptoms described above. Muscles innervated by nerves can become victims by becoming weak, deactivated, or paralyzed. Pressure at multiple points along a nerve pathway are more than just additive, they effects become multiplied. This is known as double crush: two minor nerve problems that wouldn't cause problems on their own now cause pain, weakness, or tingling. This can make diagnosis quite difficult if the source of pressure is minimal. As mentioned earlier, nerves can generate local, radicular, referred, and scleratogenous pain.

Traction injuries to nerves from trauma are usually longer lasting due to damage to the nerve or neural sheath. Compression injuries can resolve if the pressure is removed and the nerve was only compressed, not damaged. Nerves can be compressed by swelling and inflammation of surrounding structures, by scar tissue and bone spurs, subluxations, or by disc bulges and herniations. Compression of nerves due to extreme crimping, and jamming can also occur to cutaneous nerves (skin nerves), often resulting in paresthesia, or mild numbness. Tight clothing or equipment can cause this elsewhere. This can take a month to a couple years to fully resolve.

Nerves reside inside a sheath, much like tendons, and adhesions or irritation can occur. Short-term compression of a nerve causes that awful pins and needles feeling, and can also cause an area to go numb, or "fall asleep". Numb limbs or tingling are almost always a result of nerve compression and not compression of an artery or vessel. Cutting off the nerve supply to an area temporarily or intermittently will not damage the affected tissues. Long-term reduction in nerve impulse will cause muscles to weaken and atrophy, however. Even a small amount of pressure on a nerve can result in a marked loss of strength to a muscle. Cold injuries can damage nerves for a long time as well.

Rehabbing nerve injuries begins by treating for inflammation and stopping whatever is causing the problem. Removing the problem usually provides an instant fix unless cell damage to the nerve or nerve sheath has occurred, then you are pretty much limited to rest and waiting with the exception of certain electrical modalities. Do not apply cold to nerve injuries, but around them. Most direct therapies should not be applied directly to nerve injuries. Fix around them and wait for them to heal.

Blood Vessels

Most NMS injuries also wind up injuring surrounding blood vessels (causing swelling, bruising, and inflammation), but specific injuries to blood vessels is fairly uncommon. Injuries to arteries and vessels are usually diseases of age, lifestyle, or genetics. The obvious exception is cuts and punctures from the outside or inside (usually due to fractures and dislocations) that cause bleeding. This is discussed in the First Aid section.

Any injury that damages major vessels, limits circulation or causes ischemia is an immediate trip to the ER. Ischemia means that the blood supply to an area has been cut off due to blockage or compression. Unlike compression of a nerve, compression of a vessel will kill the area that it supplies. Pressure to veins or lymph channels can impede drainage and create swelling – which can in turn cut of arterial flow (causing ischemia). Ischemia is incredibly painful. Ischemic areas can become white, purple, or blue, and will hurt very badly, and may become cold or numb. Numbness without a lack of color to the skin is almost always from nerve compression. Once the blood supply is restored, pins and needles sensation may occur, but again, pain is a predominant symptom (put a rubber band around your finger for a few minutes to find out).

> **AVERAGE HEALING TIMES***
> - Bone – 3 to 4 months
> - Cartilage – 2 to 6 months
> - Ligament – 5 to 12 months
> - Muscle – 1 to 6 months
> - Tendon – 5 to 12 months to regain 90% strength**
>
> *time will depend on many factors
> **may never fully regain complete strength

NMS UPPER BODY CONDITIONS

Even specific conditions have repetitive patterns, causes, and fixes that intermingle with other conditions. I strongly urge you to read as much as possible instead of skipping to the exact point of concern. For example: problems in your feet can cause problems in your knees, etc. In the next few sections I will discuss specific, or named conditions to help you diagnose and treat the area. Many specific injuries are the same injuries to other body parts or tissues, therefore if no specific treatments are listed check with the Injuries by Body Area, and Treatment sections to get ideas. For specific exercise not listed in under an injury, follow the Rehab Progression and Exercise Progression guides and pick out exercises from the first few chapters of the book that target that area and fit the specific protocol.

HEAD AND NECK PAIN
Head and Neck Posture
The muscles, nerves, and joints of the neck are very pain sensitive and most neck pain is a result of postural or muscle imbalance problems that can cause sprains, strains, facet syndrome, or discogenic pain from compression or tearing of discs and nerve roots. The head is very heavy and is constantly supported by the spine and muscles that attempt to keep it perfectly balanced. They are in a constant tug-of-war so your head doesn't just flop to one side, messing up your sense of balance and visual tracking. Changes in this balance can put excessive strain on tissues, causing pain. Constant forward head posture from driving, reading, and staring at various types of computer screens all day long also puts a big strain on the neck. Get a book stand if you're a student or read sitting at a table and make sure your computer monitor is high up enough (it probably is too low if using a laptop). All of these bad postures mess us the normal curve of the neck, which puts extra pressure on the joints, ligaments, and discs. Symptoms can range from neck pain, headaches, sore traps and upper shoulder blades. Problems in the upper thoracic spine and shoulders can also cause neck pain or refer into the neck. Chronic neck issues can also lead to cervical spine instability that will only exacerbate the problems that lead to the unstable neck. Leading with your neck and traps, especially when inappropriately doing ballistic movements while lifting weights, can quickly lead to neck and shoulder issues.

Climbers constantly stretch out the front of their neck, and compress the back of it by belaying. **Prism glasses** are lifesavers and I highly recommend them. Since we spend about a 1/3rd of our life laying down sleeping, one way to prevent neck problems is to improve sleep posture via pillow choice. Basically, you want your neck in the same position sleeping as it is while awake. The best sleep position is on your back, but this just isn't possible unless you really suffer a bit and practice. There are many options out there like rolls, cut outs, memory foam, and water-based pillows.

All treatments are game depending on the nature of the injury, but the best solution is to fix the postural problem or habit causing the neck pain. Too much treatment to neck muscles may result in rebound pain. Retraining correct head posture isn't as simple as trying to maintain perfect posture all day. Forcing perfect neck posture will probably just result in more headaches and neck pain. Strengthen the scapular stabilizers and do neck retraction exercises.

If strengthening areas doesn't fully work, you may need to do some more intense postural re-training. This involves combining cervical traction with passive use of a **neck orthotic**. Traction isn't always necessary, but it sure helps. A neck orthotic is really just a firm wedge you lay on to passively stretch your neck (see stretching chapter). They can be hard to find (check chiropractic and PT suppliers), so a firm roll of paper towels, rolled up bath towel, or lying over the side of the bed may have to do. The key is to have the apex of the wedge tucked tight up against the top of your shoulders and at the very base of your neck. Begin by laying for 5 or so minutes, and work up to twenty minutes.

Finally head weights, which look totally absurd, can help. By placing a small amount of weight on the front of your head, you will reflexively pull your head back and train the weak links automatically. Sitting on a Swiss ball or wobble chair while wearing head weights will help get all the correct muscles fired up. Extension exercises on a Med-X machine if you can find one are very helpful.

I have performed, and been subject to a fairly disconcerting (aka scary) chiropractic cervical traction adjustment. I wouldn't recommend this as the initial go-to treatment, but for some it is the miracle treatment. The chiropractor, using their hands, a towel, seatbelt strap, or a water-ski rope with a neck harness for the grand-daddy adjustment pulls quickly up on the skull releasing pressure off the joints and discs in a vertical direction.

There are some named technique systems for totally retraining spinal posture, specifically CBP and Pettibon practitioners. While the intent is good, many docs use these systems as marketing tools and scare tactics to retain patients. There isn't overwhelming evidence that perfect spinal posture can fix future problems or delay DJD, or that the results will last.

Neurologic Neck Pain
The neck contains all the nerve roots of the nerves that innervate your shoulder to your fingertips. Unexplained pain or neurologic symptoms in the upper extremity should always consider pathology from the discs, facets, and nerve roots of the neck or the brachial plexus (bundle of nerves from the neck to shoulder). Because of the double crush syndrome explained earlier, even minor problems up the line can help compound symptoms distally (toward the fingers). One source of neurologic pain/symptoms from the neck is a genetic abnormality known as a cervical rib. These lucky folks have an extra pair of ribs on their last cervical vertebrae. The problem is that there isn't always enough room for the rib and the brachial plexus of nerves and vessels that should pass unobstructed through the area. Therapy for this is to try and correct posture to allow more room, or unfortunately, surgery. Cervical ribs are usually looked for when patients complain of symptoms that pattern thoracic outlet syndrome (described later).

Disc herniations are fairly uncommon for those under 50, but can happen, especially in traumatic injuries. When a cervical disc bulges into a nerve root, pain, tingling, numbness, or muscle weakness can result down the arm. Excessive inflammation, stenosis (see a specialist), and DJD can mimic symptoms of a disc injury because they occlude the space the nerve roots occupy in the spine. Unlike low back pain, neck surgery is a lot more successful – but a lot more dangerous. The first goal is to reduce swelling and inflammation, then apply any or all therapies that make sense, especially traction, hoping the disc will reduce on its own.

Headaches

Headaches can be from quite a few causes, but muscle tension headaches are the most common. These respond to OTC pain medication, heat, and gentle manual therapy. Climbers are especially susceptible to headaches due to low blood sugar and dehydration. The solution to that should be obvious. Some headaches, migraines for example, are caused by too much blood from overdilating blood vessels. A great treatment for this is an ice pack under the base of the skull and forehead (sometimes a hot/cold combo on the forehead/neck works too). Manual therapy that puts short bursts of fairly firm bilateral pressure over the mastoid process works great, as does laying the sub-occipitals over a pair of curled-up fingers and using the weight of the head for pressure. Spinal manipulation is also a decent therapy to try.

Migraines and other systemic headaches may require meds or OTC supplements. Magnesium seems to help those with migraines. If migraines are chronic, get your heart checked for a patent foramen ovale, a genetic leftover and usually benign small hole in the heart linked to migraines.

Neck Key Movement Test

A good screening tool for neck, upper back, even shoulder problems is to first look for forward head posture. The movement screen is a pass/fail on prone neck retraction. If shaking or chin jutting occurs within 8 seconds, then there are postural or muscular imbalances. See the warm-up section for photos of neck retraction.

MID BACK/CHEST PAIN

Mid back pain is almost always sentinel pain from postural problems in the neck or muscle imbalances in the shoulder, although sprains and strains can occur. Stretch tight muscles, strengthen the neck and shoulder, and fix your posture. Massage and other direct therapies usually just alleviate symptoms temporality. Mild to moderate aerobic activity is very good way to relieve tension. Besides postural problems or issues in your neck and shoulder, joint dysfunction, instability, and facet syndrome can occur here as well. Chronic popping or the need to feel like your mid back needs to pop are signs of instability and you should follow rehab and strengthening advice for the neck and shoulder/scapula.

Rib subluxations and sprains can present as pinpoint extremely painful muscular trigger points along the spine and cause mid back or anterior chest pain. Out of place rib heads usually take a few treatments of joint manipulation before they "stick". Strengthening scapular stabilizers, lats, and rhomboids can help firm up the joint. Rib subluxations, rib sprains to the costochondral joint or costovertebral joint, and MFTPs in the muscles between ribs (intercostal muscles) can create similar pain in chest and sternal area. Anterior rib subluxations are more difficult to reduce, but it is possible.

Sprains, or fractures to the ribs are awful because you can't do much to stabilize the area (no cast). Even minor sprains can take months to become pain free. The best advice is to just be careful. Follow inflammation protocols to help with healing and pain. After a sprain or rib fracture there's a good chance that MFTPs will develop in the intercostal muscles. These MFTPs are also exquisitely painful, can mimic more serious pain from the heart. Kinesiotape is very helpful in thoracic sprains, strains, and fractures to check but not fully limit breathing.

If you have unexplained rib pain, had chickenpox as a child, and you're past your prime, get checked for shingles. GERD (acid reflux) can also cause chest and thoracic pain. Worry about heart attacks if you've got risk factors, have a sudden sense of impending doom (really), or you get referred pain down your arm – especially your right arm.

One final common injury climber's get in their chest is a sternal-clavicular (SC) sprain. The AC joint of the clavicle (see shoulder) is usually the one to go, but sometimes the mechanism of injury (MOI) affects the SC joint. Usually the sprain is just a mild subluxation that can be reduced. Again, the area is very hard to stabilize, so treat for inflammation and protect the area the best you can.

Thoracic Outlet Syndrome (TOS), Shouldergenic Neuropathies, Referred Pain
TOS presents with numbness and tingling in the hands from compression of one or more nerves in the brachial plexus as the nerves pass through the neck and shoulder. Occasionally the radial artery is also compressed. Shoulder impingement syndrome often compounds this syndrome (see shoulder below). Cervical ribs or excessive scar tissue from trauma can be the cause, as could a beaked acromion (a genetic bone spur on your anterior shoulder blade). X-ray should be able to diagnose either abnormality cause easily, but not scar tissue or inflammation from injured tissues in the shoulder or neck. Forward head posture or poor posture may also lead to thoracic outlet syndrome.

MFTPs in the scalenes, SCM muscles of the neck, and MFTPs in the subclavius muscle, pectorals, lats, rhomboids, levator scap, and subscap can mimic numbness and tingling from thoracic outlet syndrome. Orthopedic tests that measure your pulse while you are put in several positions can help rule out a vascular involvement. Nerve conduction tests can be performed to confirm a compressed nerve and aid in locating the area of pressure (ruling in TOS or other areas of nerve pressure along the upper limb). TOS can affect one or all of the nerves that go down into your arm. Depending on what structures are causing the compression, a combination of therapy for cervical posture retraining and shoulder impingement (below) are useful.

Scar tissue and entrapment of nerves can be reduced with various therapies to the shoulder, chest, scapula, armpit, and neck area to loosen muscles and reduce trigger points. Nerve flossing to affected nerves can help reduce entrapment as well. Injuries to the neck, elbow, and wrist can all add to symptoms down the line.

There are other neuropathies to the axillary, musculocutaneus, long thoracic, and suprascapular nerves that can mimic TOS and entrapment/compression of the ulnar and median nerve. If treatment for TOS or common causes fail, explore these other neuropathies. They are fairly uncommon, but can develop from chronic muscle tightness, or from inflammation and scar tissue from a direct or nearby trauma to the neck, trunk, or shoulder. They can also present as chronic and impossible to reduce MFTPs.

SHOULDER PAIN
The Shoulder Joint

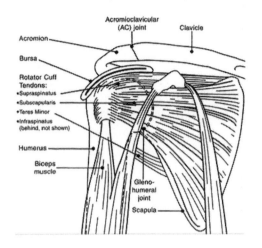

Here are the top reasons for why your shoulder hurts: rotator cuff strain or tendinitis of the supraspinatus, infraspinatus, teres minor, or subscapularis muscle or tendon and impingement of the supraspinatus tendon, bursa, or biceps tendon. A labral tear and arthritis are very common as well. Referred pain from the neck and upper back can also be quite common. There's more, but these are the top culprits. In the acute stage, they may all present with non-specific pain from climbing.

There are several orthopedic and muscle tests that can help determine where the problem is coming from, but X-ray and MRI usually provide definitive diagnosis. MRI is a great option if the pain is severe or chronic enough that surgery sounds like it may be on the table, or if therapy has not been effective because of a misdiagnosis. X-ray should show arthritic changes, but even with degeneration, the pain may be due to another reason. There is often more than one injury going on at once. Resistance in certain ranges of motion points toward a tear or tendinitis (which can go hand in hand with chronic pain).

Pain with compression, especially with clicks, pops, or catching points towards labrum damage. Surgery is often necessary if the labrum is moderately torn. Pain at the upper 1/3rd of arm abduction points towards impingement. Pinpoint pain at where the biceps inserts into the shoulder points towards biceps impingement, tendinitis, or bursitis.

Pay attention to exactly what movements you were doing, and at what times your shoulder hurts. Going in to get your shoulder checked when everything hurts won't help the diagnosis, so unless it's a new injury that needs immediate treatment, de-inflame that shoulder first. Before expensive imaging, rehab is usually a bit of trial and error. Luckily most treatments and exercises overlap. A hard-core PRICED regime is usually necessary – even in old chronic cases.

Impingement occurs when the space between the head of the humerus and the top of the acromion of the scapula decreases, and soft tissues like the rotator cuff, biceps tendon, and bursa gets inflamed or torn in the process. The greater tuberosity of the humerus is generally to blame as it decreases space even more when the arm is abducted above 90°, and compounded by simultaneous externally rotated.

Besides treating for inflammation in a shoulder injury, most therapies mentioned can help reduce inflammation, heal tissues, and reduce scar tissues. Kinesiotape is very useful at checking movements that hurt your shoulder. It has been my experience that the shoulder is too unstable or loose of a joint to suffer from subluxation, so be wary of shoulder joint manipulation (but don't rule it totally out). During shoulder rehab, it is very important that you limit motions that cause pain, especially over the head or external rotation. Immobilizing the shoulder a sling for a couple weeks may be necessary with moderate sprains and labral tears.

Unless the injury is due to trauma, then muscular imbalance, technique, and posture of the neck and shoulders are the heavy hitters. Even if arthritis is causing the impingement, the solution (besides dealing with inflammation) is to address these issues to increase the available space for tissues, and avoid overloading the rotator cuff. While fixing imbalances, you can also rehab the injured tendon or other tissues by progressively healing and strengthening the injured tissue.

Follow the recommendations for dealing with forward head posture, scapular stabilization – including additional exercises for the rhomboids and serratus anterior. Go through shoulder, neck, and upper back exercises looking for weak links and correcting them. After pain has diminished, begin with proprioceptive retraining exercises like the sword and seatbelt – paying extreme attention to keeping those shoulders down and back through the entire range of motion.

Shoulder Instability
Chronically unstable or dislocating shoulders often wind up needing injections or surgery, but that doesn't mean you can't try! The shoulder generally dislocates to the front, or anterior side. The posterior capsule may be extra tight causing extra pressure on the sloppy side. Treatment could involve reducing scar tissue or getting extra tight muscles to relax, especially stretching and working on the posterior capsule. To tighten up the shoulder via exercise, you need to figure out what muscles are weak and allowing the instability (if the joint and ligaments aren't so stretched out that extra muscle bulk won't help). Scapular stabilizer exercises, and exercises that work the rotator cuff are a good place to start. Assuming your pulling and compression generating muscles are strong (enough) since you climb, explore exercises that involve pushing and external rotation.

Immobilizing the shoulder in a sling (no more than 2 weeks) could be a last resort before you hit the knife or needle, but immobilizing the shoulder for too long greatly increases the risk of developing frozen shoulder. Surgery is often indicated for younger folks after their very first dislocation since the likelihood of re-injury skyrockets.

Frozen Shoulder
Frozen shoulders are evil – the more you try and get them to loosen, the more they overreact and seize up. They can also take months to resolve, even with treatment. There are three ways to fix the problem. The first is to do nothing and hope the muscle splinting resolves. The second is to force it free. This aggressive treatment sometimes works, but you need to find a therapist that has had success with this option, or have manipulation under anesthesia performed.

The third option is to slowly try and loosen it up. Begin by treating for inflammation, because it probably froze-up due to trauma. After a few days you can begin heating it. If it gets worse, go back to ice. Manual therapy, ultrasound, and electrical stim may or may not help. Passive, therapist applied, range of motion exercises can be done in a clinic, but doing exercises like wands, circumduction, and wall walks can be done at home (also useful for regaining ROM for post-shoulder surgery).

AC Sprain and Broken Clavicle
The acromial-clavicular (AC) joint is particularly susceptible to separating during a traumatic shoulder injury, and can become chronically unstable. Most AC sprains that fully rupture are left in place without surgery. The best rehab for AC sprains are therapies that aid in healing and reducing scar tissue, and immobilizing the shoulder while the joint heals for 1-3 weeks.

Breaking your clavicle (collar bone) is just an awful experience. The clavicle is like the coat hanger for your upper limbs and supports a lot of weight. Expect prolonged immobilization for a major AC blowout (2-8 weeks in a sling) or a clavicular fracture, but do not push it.

Shoulder Key Movement Patterns
First look at your posture. Is one shoulder much higher than the other, are your shoulders rounded forward? A screening tool for shoulder and scapular imbalance is to have someone watch you with your shirt off from behind. Bend your elbows and abduct (raise) your arms to 90°. There should be symmetrical upward rotation of the scapular and arms. Compensating by elevating a shoulder, or asymmetry in how the scapula and arms move suggest imbalances or restricted movement. Excessive winging of a scapula suggests a weak serratus anterior. The AC and SC joint are both supposed to rotate as your arm is raised over your head. If it is subluxated you may compensate and injure your shoulder, AC /SC joint, or neck. It can be mobilized. The subclavius muscle below the clavicle is commonly tight and full of trigger points.

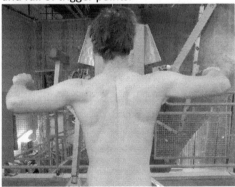

Look how screwed up I am. Left shoulder unable to abduct to 90, left scapula not raising up, left arm externally rotated, left trap lower, and I'm tilted to the side to compensate.

ARM AND FOREARM PAIN
Arm Posture
Stand relaxed with your arms at your side. Palms facing inwards or behind you suggests overly tight chest, shoulder, arm, or forearms muscles.

Arm Sprain/Strain
Spraining a biceps, triceps, or a wrist flexor in the muscle belly or at the elbow is very common. Small tears to complete ruptures of the tendon happen when the load exerted is greater than the tissues can support. The first thing you can blame is bad technique: bad footwork and balance aren't stabilizing some of the weight, or an overly eager dyno. As mentioned, connective tissues don't strengthen as fast as the muscles they support. Apply gains in skill or strength that create extreme forces to joints slowly and carefully, especially as you age.

After the inflammation stage is taken care of (or surgery), begin slow resistance exercises especially focusing on eccentric contractions and strengthening antagonists. Manual therapy and PT therapies that promote healing and reducing scar tissue will help aid in recovery. Kinesiotape or compressive sleeves can be applied for several weeks.

Medial & Lateral Epicondylitis
One of the most common injuries climbers get is epicondylitis, or inflammation of the elbow. Epicondyles are the bony bumps on either side of your elbow. The inside condyle (with palms facing forward) attaches the wrist flexors that flex your wrist and fingers, and inflammation there is called medial epicondylitis or golfer's elbow. The outside condyle attaches your wrist extensors that eccentrically controls and stabilizes your wrist. Inflammation here is called medial epicondylitis or tennis elbow.

Medial epicondylitis is usually due to climbing too much, too hard, or overtraining. The attachment point gets overstressed and becomes inflamed (at the tendon attachment) or the flexor muscles get strained. Although it can become chronic and turn into a tendinosis, this condition usually presents as acute inflammation.

Treatment begins with rest, lying off the crimpers, dynos or forearm intensive climbing, along with a strong bout of inflammation control. Most forms of therapy that promote healing and reduction of scar tissue (if repetitively injured or severely sprained) will help. Extra stretching and warming up will help prevent re-injury. Kinesiotape is effective at limiting motion and helping with swelling and edema. Don't use a strap over the elbow as in lateral epicondylitis, instead place any compressive device at least an inch or two lower. Using a forearm compression strap can help or hinder healing. Try it out when using your forearm, and taper off use as you get better. Some therapists are very anti-elbow brace and they are partially correct. It can hinder healing in some, but can help others.

Lateral Epicondylitis is much more likely to turn into tendinosis and present with chronic pain. The injury has the same etiology as medial epicondylitis, but this time the extensor tendons get over-stressed by being unable to control and check the wrist flexors. The wrist extensors and pronators counter-act the acceleration of the flexors and supinators (prime movers) and will get injured if imbalanced, like a pair of old brakes on the car.

These muscles maintain isometric control when grabbing and pulling down, motions that cause natural flexing and supinating movements – otherwise your hand would flex and turn in instead of staying in one place and exerting power. This is the one injury you can develop over time from belaying someone on toprope! To avoid repetitive strain by eccentrically pulling the stiff rope through your belay device, the using your body and legs to squat down to pull on the rope then stand up and pull the slack in quickly.

Rest and inflammation control efforts must be doubled to prevent this from becoming a lifelong problem, or to get the condition out of a chronic tendinosis. An elbow brace can be employed during the healing phase to take the pressure off the elbow attachment and put the pressure under the brace where injury is less likely. All modes of therapy are fair game, but some have been shown to work better than others.

Friction type massage and ice massage can help stimulate the tendon to begin healing, especially if the injury became extra-chronic and is in tendinosis stage. Injection therapy can help, but is usually done only in chronic injuries that aren't responding to manual therapy and rehab. Manipulation of the elbow has been shown to be very effective. Lack of joint motion can stall the healing process, and improper alignment of the radius and ulna at the humeral articulation can create extra rubbing of the tendon and poor biomechanics. Eccentric pronation and wrist extension exercises help re-train the muscle and strengthen it for the actual job it is designed for while concentric exercises help prevent. TheraBand makes a giant licorice looking device that helps with this exercise, the TheraBand Twist. Eccentrically lowering a dumbbell and pronating with a hammer or ½ a dumbbell are other excellent exercises. You can use tubing to work into heavier weights if the injury is severe enough. Occasionally working radial and ulnar deviation are missing links in elbow rehab, and sometimes weak triceps contribute to the condition. Stretch and massage the flexors while working the other muscles.

Although there's not much you can do about it, a genetic variant in a change in the normal angle formed by your arm and forearm re-route the trajectory of your flexors and extensors, making them more predisposed to rubbing over the condyles. Occasionally the ligament between your radius and ulna (radioulnar ligament) at the elbow can get sprained as well, presenting as epicondylitis. Treatment is very similar, except manual therapy should be targeted at this exquisitely tender spot. Be wary of doc's reaching for the cortisone needle. Short-term reduction in pain and inflammation may be offset in long-term damage to the tissues.

Nerve Pain of the Elbow/Forearm
The ulnar nerve is very exposed when it passes through the elbow. Anyone that has bumped his or her "funny bone" just dinged the ulnar nerve. Injury to the elbow or scar tissue and adhesions to the neural sheath can create pain in the elbow, forearm, or hand along with numbness or tingling. This is known as cubital tunnel syndrome. Manual therapy and nerve flossing can help free up the ulnar nerve. The median nerve (the culprit of carpal tunnel syndrome) can get compressed by the pronator teres muscle in your forearm that helps the biceps pronate the wrist. Tightness, swelling, or contracture of the pronators, pronator teres syndrome, can cause nerve pain, numbness, or tingling in the forearm into the wrist and hand. Carpal tunnel syndrome can sometimes be misdiagnosed when the compression is in the forearm, and climbers are more susceptible for obvious reasons. Pin and stretch therapy works well as does friction type massage on the pronator. Since the ulnar nerve is so exposed at the elbow, aggressive therapy can result in more damage. Don't apply ice directly over the nerve.

WRIST AND HAND PAIN
Wrist pain can be complicated to diagnose since there is a ton of stuff packed into your wrist. First you've got the carpals, tiny wrist bones. Carpals can be fractured, dislocated, or have instability issues. A meniscus-like tissue called triangular fibrocartilage is on the medial side of the wrist and can be torn or sprained. Flexor tendons pass under a bridge of connective tissue called the flexor retinaculum. The flexor tendons can develop tendinitis, or the tendon sheaths can develop tendosynovitis, and the retinaculum can be sprained. Finally, the median nerve passes through the carpal tunnel (exactly what it sounds like) and the ulnar nerve passes through the tunnel of Guyon in the ulnar side of the wrist. These nerves can get compressed or inflamed causing wrist pain, tingling, and numbness.

Fracture of any of the carpals can be fairly serious as avascular necrosis (AVN) can set in since the carpals don't have a great blood supply, especially the scaphoid bone below the thumb, followed by the lunate in the center of the wrist. Get an X-ray and don't rule out fracture until a follow-up X-ray is taken 2 weeks later. If fractured, see an orthopedic surgeon. The hook of the hamate below the thumb is another common site of fracture or avulsion.

The carpals can also become subluxated, can develop wrist instability, or dislocate. Chronic clicking and popping or point tenderness over the wrist are signs of instability. The lunate is the most unstable of all the carpals. Mobilization of subluxing carpals or the distal radial ulnar Joint can restore proper biomechanics, and immobilization or injections can help shore up loose joints. Applying a layer of tape or strapping the wrist can reduce instability during activity. Chronic and severe wrist instability can lead to a whole host of really bad other wrist problems – see an orthopedic surgeon if moderate or worse symptoms appear. Usually the wrist is placed in a cast or splint for 6-8 weeks if not operated on.

If the triangular fibrocartilage on the medial side of the wrist or the flexor retinaculum is damaged, rest and immobilization are the best conservative therapy. You may need to splint for 4-8 weeks. Larger tears may require surgical intervention or injection. Scar tissue may develop and therapies to reduce this are useful. Wrist traction with a device (hard to find) or just by sustained pulling with your other hand can help. Laser and microcurrent are both acceptable option to try and help the cartilage or tendons heal.

The flexor tendons can easily develop tendinitis, especially under the flexor retinaculum. Tendinovaginosis and tendosynovitis also commonly occur in the wrist as the inflamed tissue rubs against the inside of the tendon sheath. Squeaky grinding sounds from flexing your fingers or wrist is a sign that the sheath is also affected. A special type of tendinitis called Dequervain's synovitis commonly develops in the tendon sheath of the extensor pollicis brevis that extends the thumb and the abductor pollicis longus, which abducts the thumb. An excellent test for this is to tuck your thumb into your fist and then ulnar deviate (the opposite of a hitchhiking move). Sharp sudden pain is a positive result. Rest and ice help, as does immobilization with a wrist brace with a thumb spica.

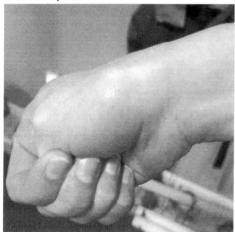

Dequervain's test (above) and wrist brace with thumb spica (below)

Because there isn't a lot of padding in the wrist and it's mostly bone, nerve and tendon, manual or other physical therapies can be difficult or cause more damage than healing. Light friction massage over the wrist or underwater ultrasound can help, as can deeper therapies to the hand and forearm. Cold laser is an excellent choice because it doesn't cause tissue damage.

Nerve Pain in Hands and Fingers

There are several reasons why you would get numb or tingling hands and fingers (TOS, referred pain from other areas, cubital tunnel syndrome, and pronator teres syndrome have been discussed already). Serious reasons could include spinal cord trauma or cervical disc herniations, diabetes, alcoholism, malnutrition, and a lot of other diseases. But specific to climbing would be carpal tunnel and Guyon tunnel syndrome if the source were actually in the wrist. Guyon tunnel syndrome affects the ulnar nerve as it passes through the tunnel of Guyon in the wrist. This is generally a result of direct trauma to the wrist, and is also known as handlebar palsy from injuries due to bike riding. Get an X-ray to rule out fracture, deal with inflammation, and splint the wrist.

Carpal tunnel syndrome is a lot more common. The median nerve becomes compressed as it passes through the carpals. Symptoms are shooting electrical hand and wrist pain with occasional or constant numbness and tingling. The flexor tendons are directly above the median nerve, and injury to them can also create inflammation and pressure on the median nerve. Carpal subluxation and instability can also contribute to decreasing the space inside the carpal tunnel. Repeated, sustained flexion of an unsupported wrist is what gets office dwellers. Surgery for this condition is very common as it is fairly easy and can be done fairly non-invasively to release the nerve.

Conservative treatment should begin with rest and all things anti-inflammatory. A cock-up splint helps for a period of immobilization or activity (like typing – not climbing) with the wrist in partial extension. Wearing the splint at night is quite effective. If you think your computer is a culprit be sure to use a wrist pad below the keyboard and to take frequent breaks. The position of everything from your chair, armrest, mouse, and computer all can contribute to the problem. Seek out ergonomic advice for positioning these items.

Drilling and hand drilling bolts can definitely contribute to the problem for climbers. Pulling down on holds when your wrist is in a flexed or extended position and also pivoting off this position under strain can exacerbate any wrist problems. Try and keep your wrist straight – good advice for general climbing to maintain strength and keep from pumping out. Therapies that promote healing and reduction of scar tissue work well, as does joint manipulation. Although hard to find, wrist traction devices can also help. There are tons of passive stretching devices that help spread the hand open and marketed to help treat carpal tunnel syndrome.

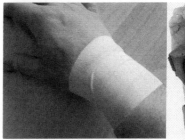

Taping wrist and cock-up splint

Raynaud's phenomenon is another disease that can cause neurological or vascular symptoms in the hand. The main symptoms are unexplained white cold fingers. Women are affected more than men, especially younger women. Raynaud's is a vascular overreaction to cold or stress and can be idiopathic (unknown cause) or due to another more serious disease. Most therapies are drug therapies. Some supplements that have been shown at least mildly effective are ginkgo biloba, fish oil, and arginine (increases nitric oxide). See a rheumatologist if symptoms are severe. Training for cold by cold water immersion or carrying snowballs will make it worse. Ice climbers will suffer the most. Carry gloves or warm socks if you have frequent attacks.

The "screaming barfies" or hot aches occur when cells freeze and re-thaw in your digits. It usually only happens once, as blood supply gets increased to the area to prevent future cell damage. As with Raynaud's, cold training makes matters worse. It does help with tolerance, but long term blood supply is actually reduced which is why old ice climbers have it worse. To avoid the hot aches on lead or following that first pitch, try and get the hot aches on the approach where it's easier to deal with. Better yet, don't get them at all by properly warming up, keeping a loose grip (thick gloves can be counterproductive), and using handwarmers over your wrist. See the section on gloves.

Dupuytren's Contracture

This genetic condition affecting mostly males thickens and contracts the palmar fascia of the hand. It is painless, but over time can debilitate the hands. It's a stretch to include this in this book, but it has affected a few climbers I know. The condition progresses with age. Surgical intervention can help, but the scar tissue from surgery can actually compound the condition, especially if multiple surgeries are performed. There are many treatment options to manage or halt the progression, but see an OT hand specialist. In the meantime, heat therapies can help with range of motion.

Ganglion Cysts

These are actually fairly common, and overuse and inflammation or just bad luck are common causes. These painless nodules grow on tendon sheaths, generally over the extensor tendons of the hand. Do not try and bust these (the old Bible Smack), they will get worse. The best treatment is no treatment, so leave 'em alone unless they become painful or interfere with activity.

FINGER PAIN

Finger Sprain

A strain of a finger pulley is the most common debilitating injury climbers get. The flexor tendons extend up into the fingers, as there are no muscles in the fingers themselves. Because of the length and multiple joints they cross, the tendons need attachment to the bones so that they don't bowstring out, much like a bridge on a guitar. With enough force or irritation, the pulley tears or ruptures. The tendons could be the targets of injury, but the pulleys usually lose out. The ring finger followed by the index finger is the most likely to be injured in a pulley tear. Because of leverage the pulley gets more stress in the closed crimp when the tip of the finger is pointed down, the middle of the finger is parallel to the ground, and the base of the finger is vertical. The A2 pulley on the finger flexor tendon sheath, which is located just below the middle knuckle, is most commonly ruptured of the individual pulleys followed by the A4 pulley, which is located just below the top knuckle.

Symptoms can be just pain and soreness over the base of finger, swelling and increased pain with decreased ROM, bowstringing of the tendon, or the dreaded popping sound of the pulley rupturing completely. Amazingly enough, even a fully ruptured pulley can repair itself without surgery.

Treatment is to immobilize the finger with tape splinting or buddy taping in bad tears, and in all cases then waiting until pain and swelling are gone enough to move your finger without pain – about 1-3 weeks in minor case or 3-5 weeks in moderate/non-surgical cases. Let pain in the active range of motion be your guide. Painful mild tears and moderate tears should progress for two weeks of low resistance exercises, four weeks of only using large hold easy climbing, then four weeks on large holds on steep routes. After this you can ease back into normal climbing. Painful moderate or severe tears can take an additional 8-16 weeks of rehab.

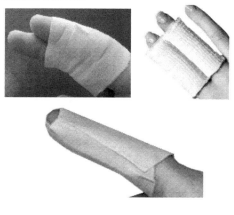

Bowstring Rupture of the A-2 and A-3 Pulley

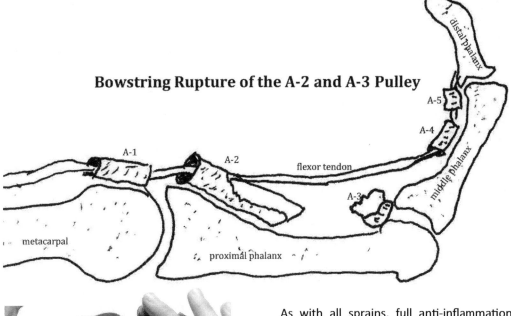

Various finger splinting devices

Most of the time an inexpensive ultrasound Dx can be made without needing an MRI. Mild tears can be painful, but won't need as much rest and rehab as the recommendations given. Go through the steps (immobilize, low resistance ROM, easy climbing, etc.) and use pain as your guide to progress. Still plan on 6-8 weeks of being very careful. The worst case is surgical intervention if there are multiple total ruptures. Expect a return to climbing in 6 months after surgery.

The collateral ligament on the side of your finger joints can also be injured. If they avulse, then surgery is usually needed. If intact the prognosis and treatment is the same as pulley strain. Total time is around 1 week to 6+ months.

As with all sprains, full anti-inflammation protocols should be employed including cold water soaks and contrast therapy. Treatments such as friction massage, laser, and all therapies that promote healing and reduction of scar tissue can be employed. Atomik Pull-up Bombs are great rehab pull-up tools for finger pulley injuries since they don't stress the finger flexors (much).

If you are concerned about injuring a pulley, or have before, it can be helpful to tape for proprioceptive feedback so you don't over-crimp and to tape during high-stress climbing. Taping may be necessary rehab for acute sprains, but taping your pulley doesn't absorb that much force off the pulley. Wean yourself off the tape or tape preventively if you will be climbing something crimpy because it will unfortunately weaken the tendon or prevent repair since it needs load to maintain its strength.

H-Taping
Take a 4" strip of athletic tape and cut it down the middle on both ends, but leaving 1 cm uncut to make an X. Put the middle of the X on the joint to be stabilized and wrap the left (or right) arms of the X below the joint. Flex the joint and tightly wrap the

other arms of the X, but not cutting off circulation. You should be able to flex, but not extend the joint. You can further stabilize the tape by laying down a small, thin strip of tape along the palm side of your finger before wrapping the tape.

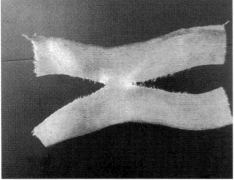

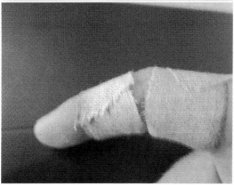

X-Taping
Using a long thin strip of tape, make two wraps just under the first PIP joint, cross under the joint, then two wraps just over the first PIP joint, cross under the joint again with another wrap or two forming an X.

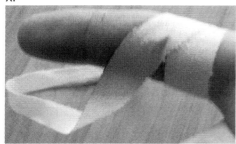

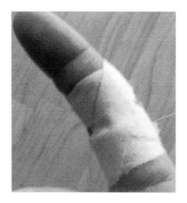

Circular Taping
If the H or X taping isn't helpful then tape tightly just above the A2 pulley with a thin $1/3^{rd}$ inch piece of tape, basically just below the first PIP joint. If you're in a hurry, a few wraps around the first phalanx with medium width tape can do in a pinch, but isn't as supportive.

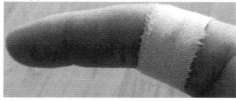

Finger Fracture and Dislocation
Sometimes you can get away with continuing to use a hairline fracture of a finger by buddy taping it to another finger, or splinting it and just not using it if it doesn't get in the way too badly. If not, finger fractures heal very quickly (4-8 weeks) and since there's not a lot of soft tissue around to get damage, you may get off with little to no rehab. Dislocated fingers can be set in the field since risk of bleeding to death with a severed artery is really really low. If a fracture extends into the joint capsule, or you seriously jam the joint, healing and function can be severely comprised. Swelling and acute reduction in ROM should prompt a more thorough investigation.

Other Common Finger Avulsions
Game keeper's thumb or skier's thumb is a common injury when a fall causes the thumb to get bent backwards. The medial

collateral ligament of the thumb gets sprained and can avulse some bone. See an orthopedist if you suspect that a dislocation seriously impacted the joint capsule, or any moderate to severe fracture or sprain to check bony alignment and for joint instability.

Jersey finger is the named condition when you rupture the flexor digitorum profundus tendon off the last distal finger joint. You'll know you've got it if you can make a fist without being able to bend the tip of your affected finger.

NMS Lower Body Conditions

Low Back Pain

Low back pain can be quite an enigma. Most cases have no clear defined MOI or reason that can be directly attributed to the pain. Even MRI's showing a disc bulge or herniation may not be the real reason for the pain. The muscles, joints, ligaments, discs, and nerves in the lower back are very pain sensitive and the pain isn't always localized to one spot that hurts when you push on it. Pinched nerves and strains are usually to blame in non-disc herniation issues but I'll discuss the most common things that can go wrong and reasons why things can go wrong.

Low Back Posture

The joints and discs in your low back must support more than half of your bodyweight. This stress is increased during flexion, and rotation puts the weight on one side. Prolonged flexion from things like sitting or cramped positions like hanging around in a harness all day increases the risk of injury, as does repetitive vibration. The supporting muscles and connective tissues usually do their job at reducing the load or distributing the weight. However, too much force, weight, or poor coordination between muscle groups can overstress the weak link. This is why proprioceptive balance exercises, and working the abs, back extensors, and side-benders are often prescribed for treating or preventing low back injuries. Once a muscle group stops firing in the correct sequence or is substantially weaker than another group you can get immediate low back pain. This is why many people injure their back doing simple activities like brushing their teeth or tying their shoes – no one's paying attention. Bad posture coupled with the theories of creep and muscle de-activation are the base of the iceberg in developing this pain.

Bad posture from your head down to your feet can affect the low back. Some observation signs of poor posture or bad alignment are having one leg shorter than the other when laying down, which is indicative of a pelvic joint or muscle imbalance. Having one leg become shorter than another when lying down is called a functional short leg. This is different from the more rare anatomical short leg where the bones are of different length. When standing, you won't be walking tipped to one side because something will compensate.

Usually the sacroiliac joint gets over-rotated, or a small functional (it goes always lying down) scoliosis (laterally curved spine) may be present usually presenting as high hip or shoulder on one side. The compensation can occur elsewhere like the upper back or neck, but the low back is the closest point of weakness if it's not in tip-top shape. Besides a functional short leg, rotated pelvis, or scoliosis, the low back can compensate by tipping forward or backward (anterior or posterior rotated pelvis) – especially if the abs or back extensors are weak or tight. If a joint in your low back, especially L5, the last vertebra, or the sacrum are stuck in a direction of rotation or isn't moving properly in a certain direction, aka subluxation, then that joint or other joints down the line can send pain signals and create inflammation.

Tight muscles that attach to or affect the low back, especially the hamstrings, piriformis, iliopsoas, leg extensors, and back extensors can wreak biomechanical havoc and severely contribute to low back pain. The same goes for weak or inhibited muscles, especially the gluts, abs, and lateral benders. Remember that tight muscles may be that way because they are being posturally overstretched and actually need some strengthening. The pattern of weak abs and gluts with tight hip flexors and back muscles, called lower cross syndrome, is a common imbalance. The curve in your low back, or lordosis, just like in your neck, gets pulled straight. This ruins the supporting mechanics of the curve and the L5-S1 joint, which contains the last disc in your spine and bears the brunt of most of your weight.

Joint instability in the lumbar spine or SI joints is very common, especially in pregnant women because of the hormone relaxin. Unstable joints in the lumbar area can be splinted with additional muscles strengthening, at least more so than other areas. There are, of course, some genetic abnormalities that may (but usually don't) contribute to poor biomechanics and back pain. Occasionally L5 fuses with the sacrum, or the top of the sacrum becomes a new "6th" lumbar vertebra with an extra smaller disc known as a transitional vertebra. L5 can travel forward (a lot in some instances) because of repetitive stress or genetic variation known as spondylolisthesis. Oddly enough, there isn't a ton of evidence that shows these anomalies directly contribute to low back pain.

Whatever the cause, the effects can cause a sprain or strain in the iliolumbar ligaments, sacroiliac ligaments, sacrotuberous ligaments, the multifidus muscles or other small back stabilizers, the facet joints, and discs. The resulting inflammation or actual pressure can also inflame or compress the spinal nerve roots exiting your spine causing even more pain or neurological symptoms. There's more to get tweaked or smooshed, but those are the most common. Pain in the low back can be intense, and referred or scleratogenous pain traveling into the buttocks or behind the upper leg is quite common. Severe inflammation or compression of the nerve roots or spinal cord from a herniation can cause pain to zing into the leg and foot, and cause numbness, tingling, weakness – even incontinence. Compression of the sciatic nerve, known as sciatica, is usually from an overly tight piriformis muscle and can also cause traveling pain, numbness, and tingling. When your legs fall asleep, it is usually from compression of the sciatic nerve – not your blood vessels.

Most causes of LBP are treated very similarly; the first goal in everything from a herniation to a muscle strain is to reduce the inflammation. Unfortunately hot tubs usually make low back pain feel a lot better initially. Don't do it! When the relief of loosening tight muscles wears off, the pain will come back with a vengeance. The first real goal in a disc herniation is to reduce the neurologic pain from the leg to centralize the pain just in the back itself. The disc can reabsorb the herniation on its own, but in some cases surgery is required. Unfortunately the resurgence of low back pain is extremely high in surgical cases, so most decent surgeons will really push conservative rehab first. A cortisone injection may be necessary if neurological symptoms or pain are extreme, or at least some high-grade pain relievers or muscle relaxers. I'm not saying you have to or should, just that it is common. To help get the disc nucleus or bulge reduced, traction is often employed and is effective. Not everyone with a disc injury will be helped via traction. Sprains and strain to the disc (disc derangement, like in the neck), or other muscles and ligaments may not react so good to being stretched. Other forms of traction like flexion distraction or various exercises may be a more suitable therapy if standard traction makes things worse.

Joint manipulation has been very effective at treating low back pain. Don't expect the miracle adjustment, but it does happen here and there. Any and all therapies are fair game. Electric stim is popular because it feels really good, and can help take the edge of the pain. But be careful when doing anything that causes muscle relaxation. Because the muscles are very pain sensitive, the pain usually reduces substantially. But since the problem is still there, the minute you get off the table the injured area gets all the weight minus the help of your now relaxed muscles. Many patients either collapse in pain immediately or shortly after a relaxing massage, hot pack, or e-stim treatment. Always do some light exercises for the back after any relaxation therapy to get the muscles to wake up and do their job.

The SI joint is really difficult to stabilize because there aren't any muscles that cross the joint. SI joint rehab requires that you fix any imbalances throughout the low back and feet. Bracing with SI or trochanter belts may be necessary. Low back braces are helpful if your job requires dangerous lifting or postures, but prolonged use will only defacilitate stabilizing muscles. Back pillows for the car or office are great if they don't support your back as much as they remind you to sit correctly with a neutral pelvis. Occasionally sitting on a Swiss ball or inflatable disc can help you maintain good posture, and work stabilizing postural muscles as well. Sitting on a wedge shaped cushion can help your low back from slumping.

Always examine your feet and gait if you have problems with low back pain (described below). Your mattress can be a source of low back pain as well. There are no exact rules on what type of mattress to use except that you get what you pay for. Memory foam offers great support, but if you sleep warm you may overheat. Pillow tops over firm mattress act as a sort of memory foam if you can't spend the cash or don't want to overheat. Adjustable firmness or gel mattresses are excellent.

If you need to find a position to get comfortable with very acute LBP, try lying on your back with legs and knees propped up on a chair at 90 each. Lying on your side with a long pillow between your legs can be very helpful. Whatever position you can find to reduce pain or centralize nerve symptoms is the best.

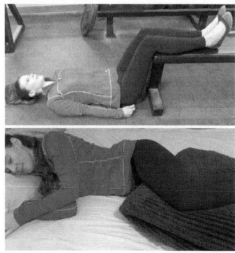

This last photo was the only one my wife enjoyed taking

Flexibility of your low back isn't extremely important because your back should be locked in place with core strength to perform most motions. However, if one side is tighter than the other you can develop problems. Also, low back strength isn't as important as hip strength. Movement should always be initiated by the hips. The low back is a stabilizer, not a mover. Stability, posture, and correct movement patterns are important to maintain a neutral spine during movement or during static loading. Flexion and sitting are the worst things for your low back. Muscle coordination is more important than being strong. In fact, focusing on strength can increase the risk of back injury! If exercising for the low back then doing more reps every day is much better than doing high load exercises three times a week.

Doing a combination of eccentric, proprioceptive, and isometric exercises that work the core – including the abs, transverse abs, back extensors, side benders, and pelvic stabilizers is the best rehab for fixing your back. Focus on the least coordinated and weakest areas. The gluts are almost always de-facilitated and weak with back and hip problems, so training them is critical. Also, stretch tight hip flexors, gluts, hamstrings, and piriformis muscles. For almost every low back exercise, keep the low back locked in a neutral pelvis position with the core engaged. The three best exercises are curl-ups, quadruped, and side-bridges. All stability exercises will help the low back. The Turkish get-up is another fantastic end-stage low back rehab exercise, as are squats, lunges, and side-bending exercises. Focus on low back posture and core activation when climbing and hiking. If doing back extension exercises, scoot back or forward on the weight bench to isolate different sections of muscles. I should also mention that aerobic exercise is just as important of an exercise, if not more, for the low back as repetitive strengthening exercise. Just keep a neutral and stable spine.

Rehabbing the low back requires a lot of core training. The exercises in the lumbar warm-ups, core stability warm-ups, hip warm-ups, intense core (late stage), whole body stretches, hip leg and lumbar stretches, even the balance exercises and some non-climbing supplemental exercises are all good for a full re-training of the low back area. Extension exercises on a Med-X machine if you can find one are very helpful.

Low Back Key Movement Patterns

A postural evaluation should show even level hips and a neutral pelvis.

Do a sit-up maintaining posterior pelvic tilt with your knees bent, arms across your chest, and feet flat on the ground. Do ten reps, and hold the last rep for 30 seconds. Weakness and imbalance are present if shaking occurs, the feet lift up, you lead with your head, if the movement is fluid or rigid (your spine doesn't curl), or your low back arches.

Next lie on your stomach and have someone put his or her hand on your glut, hamstring, and low back. Extend your leg at the hip. Weakness and imbalance are present if the order of muscles firing doesn't occur in this sequence: gluts with hamstrings, opposite side back, then same side back. The neck and shoulders shouldn't tighten up either.

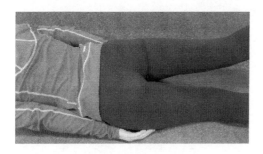

Hip, Thigh, and Groin Pain

The hip is the joint where your leg attaches into your pelvis. Pain in the hip can be coming from a strain, tendinitis, or contracture of the rectus femoris, iliopsoas, tensor fascia lattea (TFL), adductors, piriformis, and hamstring muscles or the joint capsule, as well as bursitis and arthritis. Inner thigh and groin pain at or near the hip at the groin can occur from a strain to the adductors or abdominals, or from a mild to full hernia. Chronically snapping or popping hips with pain can be a common of hip pain. The labrum inside the hip can be torn just like in the shoulder or knee, and AVN can occur as you get older.

The hip joint has quite a bit of range of motion, but is under tremendous pressure from the tightly packed joint and strong muscles that attach. Arthritis is common as the joint space decreases and cartilage wears down. Hip replacements are not uncommon for those as young as those in their 40's. Capsular tightening can be caused from chronic flexion or an imbalance of tight thigh and hip musculature, especially the hip flexors and piriformis. Bursa or inflamed, tight capsules in and near the joint can mimic arthritis, quite like the shoulder joint. Bursa that are on the side of the hip joint can develop trochanteric bursitis, and the bursa in the iliopsoas muscle, and on the ischial tuberosity (butt bone) can also develop bursitis. The bursa usually gets inflamed by friction from tight muscles and tendons. Bursitis, like in the shoulder, can be caused by surrounding microtrauma, not just a direct hit as in elbow (or knee) bursitis.

Hamstring, groin (adductor), quad, and lower abdominal strains are quite common – usually a result of a single traumatic force, but chronically tight muscles from imbalance, poor posture, or problems with foot biomechanics can cause repetitive microstrains over time. Treatment for these is the same a treatment for other strains. Weak side-benders and adductors like the quadratus lumborum or glut medius, along with tight hamstrings, weak quads, and poor foot biomechanics can irritate the side of the hip and knee causing bursitis over the hip, TFL pain, or a painful iliotibial band (ITB). The ITB usually hurts near the outside of the knee, but can hurt all the way up to the hip and TFL muscle it attaches to. Too much ab work or hip flexion (hiking/ slogging, too much Pilates, or driving for hours after climbing) can over time shorten the hip flexors and lower abs, causing pain and can also inhibit the gluts.

The key to fixing areas in the hip is constantly stretching the larger tight muscles, and exercising stabilizers like the gluts, external rotators and adductors of the leg, and the abs or back extensors depending which one is weaker. Fixing problems in the back or foot can directly influencing problems in the hip. Hip traction is wonderful, but also very difficult. If you can find a DC or PT that can effectively mobilize or traction the hip, refer them to your friends.

ITB Syndrome

Pain at the hip, side of the leg, and side of the knee can all be part of iliotibial band syndrome. The ITB is an extremely tough fibrous band that connects your hip to your knee. The TFL muscle, as mentioned, attaches to it. A tight TFL can cause the ITB to rub, or cause pain at the TFL itself. The TFL and rotators of the hip are very similar to the rotator cuff of the shoulder. If overpowered, they will hurt. Fixing imbalances at the hip is a good place to start if the pain is at the TFL or nearby gluteal muscles like the glut medius. Stretching the quads and hip flexors while strengthening the gluts should also help.

Pain in the leg or at the knee is the standard presentation of ITB Syndrome however. The ITB rubs receptively over the condyles at the knee. Most therapy incorrectly focuses on the ITB itself. The ITB is so thick and tough that the idea of actually stretching it is a joke. Stretching to get at the TFL is an option, and does relieve pain. However the TFL is probably not actually tight. The problem is usually due to an imbalance in the hip, or an imbalance between the quads and hamstrings that is pulling incorrectly on the ITB. Stretch both the quads and hams attempting to isolate the tight area. Remember there are three separate hamstring muscles and four quadriceps muscles. You hamstrings may be tight, but they may also be weak. However, the main culprit of weakness in the leg is in the quads, specifically the VMO or vastus medialis oblique. This is the muscle that bulges in the medial side of your quad at the knee when you straighten your leg at the knee.

Problems of foot overpronation can also cause tracking issues at the knee that can cause your ITB to rub. While correcting hip, leg, and foot imbalances, you can do some pain and inflammation relief. The ITB stretch will help, as will rolling over a foam roller with bodyweight. Manual therapy from deep tissue to friction massage can help to address trigger points and adhesions directly over the ITB. Prepare to scream. Ice massage is another great therapy.

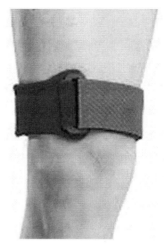

ITB strap

Key Movement Pattern for the Hip
Lie on your side and abduct (raise to the side) your leg and hold five seconds. Imbalance is present if your hike your hip, your foot externally or internally rotates, or your leg swings forward.

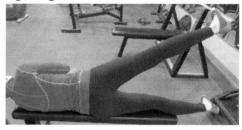

KNEE PAIN
Knee pain is often insidious, it develops gradually and when the pain strikes, it's hard to know what happened. The main pain generators in the knees are the meniscus, the cartilage of the knee and patella (knee cap), the infrapatellar ligament, and the prepatellar ligament. Patellar pain often shows up negative on many tests and imaging and can be frustrating. The meniscus can be bruised, ripped, and torn. Meniscus symptoms are usually pain when loading, sharp pain on or inside the knee, locking of the joint, swelling, and pain with over flexion and extension. Bruising and small tears are usually self-limiting whereas larger tears or degeneration may require surgery. The cartilage inside the knee and under the patella can wear down with arthritis or get

damaged when over stressed, known as chondromalacia patella. Symptoms are similar to meniscal pain, but X-ray and several orthopedic tests can help rule them in and the meniscus out. Folds of synovial tissue, or plica, can also get damaged and inflamed – again mimicking a meniscal lesion. Tendinitis or tendinosis of the infrapatellar tendon is also common. Pain after periods of prolonged sitting or walking downhill is common with chondromalacia patella and infrapatellar tendinitis.

Loading the knee while twisting is a frequent MOI in knee injuries. Walking and running with poor foot or back biomechanics can chronically cause tracking issues. Overpronation is a common foot problem that can lead to knee pain. In climbing, twisting out of the "frog" position can really mess up your knee and your hip. Drop knees can also tear your medial meniscus. Imbalances in the muscles of the leg and hip can cause your knee to rotate too much in a certain direction, as can a weak VMO muscle.

A good knee examination will also look into problems in your low back, hip, and foot – including your gait. Lifting a heavy load with your feet over-rotated, as well as having your knees too far forwards (past your ankles) can put excessive strain to your knees. There are a few anatomical variations that can also affect your knee and create problems that haven't been mentioned. The angle that your lower leg forms at the knee with your upper leg, or Q-angle, can be over and under-pronounced. Women have a larger Q-angle than men. The angle can be genetic, or functional as in over and under-pronated feet. If the angle has your knees too close together (genu varum) then more pressure is on the medial knee, and likewise knees to wide apart (genu valgum) puts extra strain on the outside of the knees. An anatomic or functional short leg can emphasize more weight on one leg than another as well. A more rare condition, genu recurvatum, occurs when the upper and lower leg angle bow inwards. The knee is a common point of compensation for the parts of your lower body, but unfortunately the knee is a very weak link.

The ligaments that keep your knee together often get sprained or ruptured, especially with a traumatic force. The two ligaments on the outside of your knee that commonly get injured are the medial collateral ligament (MCL) and the lateral collateral ligament (LCL). Inside the knee are two ligaments that make it so your lower leg doesn't slide past your upper leg. These are the anterior cruciate ligament (ACL) and posterior cruciate ligament (PCL). Both can rupture, but the ACL is much more common to rupture. Surgery is often necessary to fix these ligaments, but not always. There is a newly discovered ligament in the knee that may also be torn and could be the culprit when ACL surgery doesn't work. Minor tears can be rehabilitated much like any other ligament or tendon can, but recover can take months. Sometimes the knee is super-stabilized by well-developed musculature and other supporting tissue that even a full blow out isn't even noticed.

Your patella can get dislocated or develop serious instability. It can be stabilized with taping and bracing along with strengthening the quads. Chronic patellar instability often requires surgery. Injuries to the prepatellar ligament, aka jumper's knee, and infrapatellar ligament are usually due to tracking issues, quad weakness, or repetitive strain from high impact plyometric activities (like jumping). Arthritic knees should avoid high impact bending activities like heavy or deep squats, running downhill, and although plodding downhill with a heavy pack may be impossible to avoid, at least use trekking poles and go slow. Cycling on a properly adjusted bike can be excellent therapy for most knee conditions.

Therapy is the usual anti-inflammatory, tissue healing, and scar tissue reduction regime as most other areas. Injection therapy is becoming more common to treat knee injuries, and cold laser therapy is helpful because most structures are too deep to directly treat with other "normal" therapies. However, cortisone injections are highly contraindicated in patellar tendinitis because the chance of rupture. Muscle rehab can be slow after surgery, and baby steps from passive range of motion to basic strengthening exercises must be done. Some tracking issues, especially injuries due to infrapatellar tendinitis and chondromalacia patella can be partially resolved by an **infrapatellar strap** (aka **ChoPat**). You can tape the patella to pull it up or medially, but it is an obnoxious and must be done often. Make a little tab with the first layer of tape to pull off of with the next layer.

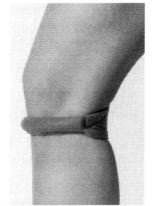

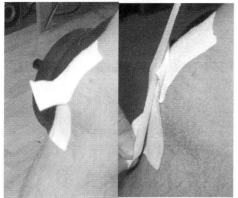

Chopat-style knee brace (above), or taping the patella upwards.

Knee braces aren't as bad for you in the long term as some people say they are. In fact that can actually improve proprioception and generally won't de-train or become a permeant crutch. Run of the mill **neoprene braces** don't offer much protection but can help warm the joint (good post-acute) and offer some proprioceptive protective feedback. **Palumbo or Shields style braces** help with patellar instability. **Unloading style knee braces** are helpful for knee alignment or OA issues. There are lots of other types of knee braces that offer options like lateral stiffness for collateral issues.

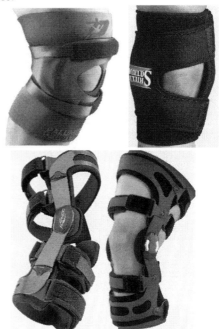

Palumbo, Shields, unloading, and lateral stiffness braces

Exercises that focus on the partial or terminal knee extension, and the VMO for tracking issues should be emphasized, especially concentrically loading and stretching the quads. Wall squats are helpful. The knee joint can be manipulated, including a subluxated patella and head of the fibula at the knee. This is occasionally useful, especially in tracking issues and stiff knees due to degeneration. Try some of the hip warm-ups and core exercises, balance exercises, lower body stabilizer/antagonist exercises, and lower body supplemental exercises.

LOWER LEG PAIN

The most common sources of lower leg pain are shin splints, calf strains, and a stress fracture of the tibia. Both the stress fracture and shin splints can present with anterior lower leg pain, but shin splints go away with rest. The stress fracture is a result of too much impact or poor running technique. Tibial stress fractures are high risk for complications. Prepare for 6-8 weeks of rest and possible casting if it is a high-risk stress fracture. After confirmation with X-ray or a followup X-ray after two weeks, rest and a course of anti-inflammation treatment are usually all that are needed more a non-complicated stress fracture. You should perform an investigation of your shoes and running technique.

A calf strain to the gastrocnemius or soleus has a similar MOI, but weakness and inability of the muscle or tendon to meet the demands placed is more likely. After being treated with modalities that aid in healing and reduction of scar tissue, begin training both concentric and eccentric calf raise-type exercises followed by plyometric training.

There is a bursa inside the two heads of the gastroc behind your knee that can get inflamed or rupture, called a Baker's cyst. If mild, treat like any other bursitis, but if ruptured (it will feel weird) you may want to go a knee specialist and also to see if you may have ruptured a tendon as well.

Shin splints occur from overstressing and inflaming the tibialis anterior muscle or the connective tissue attachments to the tibia. Although its specific action is to dorsiflex (raise) the foot, the tibialis anterior's main function is to eccentrically stabilize the foot during foot strike and toe off, counteracting the gastrocnemius. The peroneus longus can also be a culprit, as it aids in foot pronation during propulsion. If shin splints are becoming chronic, you need to rest for a bit and address the inflammation first. Then begin eccentric training involving lowering your foot and turning it in under resistance. Concentric training may also be useful if the muscles are particularly weak (do the opposite motion). Short foot and balance exercises are also helpful. Overpronation can directly lead to shin splints as can landing on your heel vs. flat or the balls of your feet depending on your preferred new school running technique will increase stress to the anterior leg muscles as more force is generated since the lever is longer and the distance is greater that they must stabilize.

ANKLE PAIN

Sprained ankles are the most common climbing specific lower limb injury. The common MOI's are hiking, bouldering, hitting a ledge/ground or slamming into the cliff during a fall. I suspect alcohol influenced hijinks makes it onto the top reasons as well. The more you sprain your ankle, the weaker and more stretched out the tendons and ligaments get, and the more you are susceptible to spraining it again. Knowing this, it's amazing how many climbers do nothing for chronic ankle sprains. If you can't take more than a few steps on your sprained ankle, definitely get it X-rayed. Chronic pain from an ankle sprain is a warning sign for an undiagnosed fracture. X-rays aren't that expensive, get one after two weeks of pain or immediately if the sprain is bad. Poorly healed fractures can ruin your ankle and lead to surgical, fusion, joint replacement, and arthritis. Rupture of the ligaments near your anklebone, and tearing or avulsion of the tendons that control foot inversion are most commonly injured. Spraining the inside side of your foot in an eversion sprain usually requires a serious force. Go to the hospital in the case of an eversion sprain just to be extra careful.

If you're in the field, find some cold water, ice, or snow to immediately ice your sprained ankle. The more function you can squeeze out of your injured ankle, the quicker it will heal or you'll be able to walk out on it. If you have any **athletic tape** handy, do your best to make a supportive wrap. At home, use all the tricks to get inflammation and swelling down. To tape a sprained ankle make a couple stirrups from the heel to above the ankle. Then make figure 8's in both directions starting from the ankle over the top of the foot, down under the arch, continuing around the heel, then around the ankle. Use extra tape to secure and to dampen any creases or loose ends.

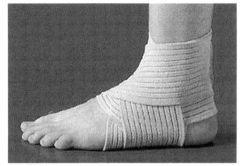
Rock shoe compatible

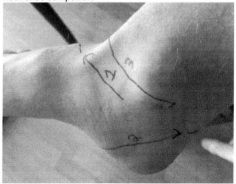
Follow the numbers to tape a sprained ankle

Various ankle braces

Depending on the severity, it may require a week of on/off all day icing. Once the pain and swelling have subsided, beginning range of motion exercises is essential to prevent problems down the road. Progress to easy balance and strengthening exercises. Once stable, progress further to more difficult balance exercises and strengthening of weak areas like plantar flexion and inversion. Reducing scar tissue and getting the tendons or ligaments to heal in proper alignment of force is essential to prevent future injury. Chronically stretched out tendons can heal by more aggressive friction treatments, or injections. When attempting activities that will pre-dispose you to tweaking your ankle again, learn to do a good preventative tape job. You can use other devices to stabilize the ankle, but few will fit inside a pair of climbing shoes. Many runners get their ankles and feet adjusted by chiropractors because biomechanical flaws in the feet can lead to many problems down the line.

Be sure and practice the balance exercises religiously, and visit some of the lower body antagonist/stabilizer exercises.

Posterior Ankle and Heel Pain
Calcaneal bursitis, plantar fasciitis (described later), and Achilles tendinitis can all make the back of your ankle or heel hurt. The Achilles tendon can also rupture, and is pretty obvious when that happens. Poor shoe selection and tight/weak gastrocnemius muscles are usually to blame here. Achilles tendon ruptures sometimes requires surgical repair, or at least casting/bracing. Inflammation treatment, concentric and especially eccentric calf strengthening exercises will help with rehab the area. Strains and tendinitis to the Achilles respond well to friction massage. Do not get a cortisone injection in your Achilles due to the high chance of rupture. Also be very careful when crossing frigid streams. Your Achilles has a very high chance of rupturing

in this activity, and sometimes you can actually hear or feel the creak and moan of the tendon on long crossings with wobbly rocks beneath.

FOOT PAIN

Plantar fasciitis presents as chronic foot or heel pain and is very similar to tendinosis that can occur in medial epicondylitis. The sheet of connective tissue on the bottom of your foot, or plantar fascia, gets inflamed and can go on for months eventually slipping into a necrotic-type degeneration of the tissue. Rest and anti-inflammation therapies help in acute cases or flare-ups. In acute or flare-up scenarios, rest and protection via orthotics and supportive yet shock-absorbing footwear is necessary. Manual therapy and other modalities that promote healing and scar tissue reduction can help, but for many they can be painfully ineffective. That said, they should be the first line of therapy. There are many home-care massage tools available for self-treatment, including ice massage. For tough cases, a **Strassburg sock** or **posterior night splint** may become necessary to really stretch the foot and gastroc. Injection therapies may be helpful in tough cases to reduce inflammation or to regenerate de-generating tissues. Extracorporeal shock wave lithotripsy has also been shown partially successful at treating this. Standard ultrasound would be a weaker version of this therapy. Age and weight can also affect the likelihood of developing this syndrome as degeneration and excess force can weaken the fat pad and shock absorbency of your feet. Check your walking or running technique and footwear or explore new lacing techniques explained in the gear section. Balance exercises and foot exercises can be very helpful as well.

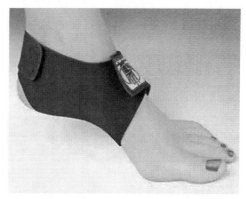
Plantar fasciitis support

Cold roller

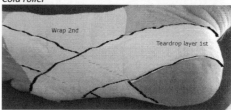
Taping arches (lowdye)

Stress fractures are very common in the smaller, yet extreme weight bearing bones of the feet. Many times you can simply limp through the pain, while other instances, especially stress fractures in the calcaneus and talus bones of the ankle can get worse and require casting or even surgery. Broken toes are fairly benign in the long run, much like broken fingers. Severe pain and swelling of the joint may mean the joint is involved and more attention may be needed besides rest or a splint.

Metatarsalgia, or pain in the metatarsals below the toe joint is often confused with Morton's neuroma, and is usually due to shock or a collapse of the transverse metatarsal arch. A **metatarsal pad** under the ball of the foot and under the toes can help, as can balance exercises.

331

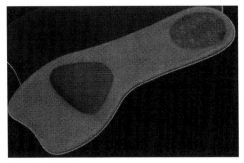
Metatarsal pad

A Morton's neuroma is caused when a nerve between one of your metatarsals gets inflamed. Symptoms are foot pain and sometimes numbness or tingling in the foot and toes. It may even feel like there's a pebble in your shoe. Changing footwear, increasing padding, and anti-inflammation therapies are generally helpful. Sometimes surgery is necessary, and outcomes are generally successful. Alcohol can be injected into the nerve to kill or severely disable it, as can gas injections (**cryogenic neuroblation**), and **radiofrequency cauterization**. You'll probably lose feeling in a toe or two with surgery.

<u>**FOOT ABNORMALITIES**</u>
Pronation is the big buzz-work in gait and for blaming other painful conditions on. Pronation is complex motion of the foot that mainly involves dorsiflexion, abduction, and eversion to propel you foreword, and stabilize and shock absorb force when you land. However, pronation can also describe in the biomechanical shape of your foot at rest. An overpronated foot falls into a pronated position because of muscle and ligament laxity. An overpronated foot offers less shock absorption, and because the motion of pronation is necessary but the foot is already in a pronated position, the force and shock absorption must be compensated for and by other areas. Signs of an anatomically overpronated foot are signs of excessive shoe wear on the inside of the heel, inward bowing of the Achilles tendon when standing, and low arches. Standing on one foot and having the arch disappear is another sign of overpronation.

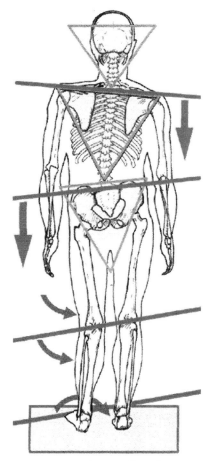
How overpronation can affect other areas

Rigid feet with low arches can mask themselves as overpronated feet, a condition called pes planus, and will not respond well to orthotics to encourage arch support or rigidity and can make things worse. An underpronated or supinated foot generally has a high arch and signs of wear on the outside of the heel. Rigid feet with high arches, called pes cavus, are more akin to a foot that underpronates. Weight bearing foot scans can help show where the pressure is and where it should be. The next best test is to have your gait examined at an expert running shop. These folks do this day in and day out. Although they may not have advanced degrees, they should know their stuff. A podiatrist would be the best next step. See the section on orthotics below.

Underpronated feet usually require footwear that is suppler and shock absorbing, while overpronating feet generally do well with more stable, rigid, corrective type footwear. Foot strengthening exercises from short foot, to balance training, to barefoot running will help strengthen your feet so they can provide their own shock absorption and proper gait biomechanics and wean you off corrective shoes and orthotics. Subluxated foot and ankle joints can mess with proper foot biomechanics as well and lead to overpronation.

Two foot malformations can contribute to overpronation. Forefoot varum is a congenital malformation of the metatarsals and tarsals can leads to an inverted forefoot and overpronation. A **medial forefoot post** in an orthotic can help. Rearfoot varum, or inversion of the calcaneus, is one of the most common anatomical variations that lead to overpronation syndromes. A **medial rearfoot post** in an orthotic may help.

Our hand's ugly cousins seem more predisposed to genetic malformation than most body areas, as well as acquired ones from poor footwear. Bunions and calluses develop for too much pressure or rubbing in one area over time. The most obvious treatment is to get better fitting shoes - even if the shoes causing the problem are the best shoe for rock climbing or a $600 pair of ice or ski boots. Pain severely limits performance. It's amazing what cobblers can do, and spending $5-30 per shoe can be a lot cheaper and easier than getting surgery.

Bunions formed by swelling of the bone or new bone growth can be reduced partially via various aggressive inflammation treatment or possibly ultrasound to break up non-calcified callus material. Temporary padding of a bunion in the field will help it from getting bigger or worse. If you get a pump bump, a bunion on the back of your heel at the Achilles, aka Haglund's deformity, do not use a heel lift for long to treat it as your calf and Achilles will shorten and weaken. Unfortunately bunions usually get worse, not better, and if a certain point of discomfort is reached, surgery may be the only option. You can usually walk out of surgery, but will have to wait weeks before putting the rock shoes back on. Calluses can be taken care of with a **pumice stone**, and should be to prevent blisters and changes in gait.

Hammer toes and claw toes can be congenital, or by looking at many climbers' nasty feet, acquired. Thankfully most cases aren't painful, or painful enough to sacrifice performance by switching to more comfortable shoes. Hallux rigidus, a rigid big toe, is generally caused due to chronic irritation. Joint manipulation may help, but traction, constant stretching, splinting, or most likely surgery as a last resort may be necessary in painful cases. **Rocker bottom soles** are helpful for painful toe problems.

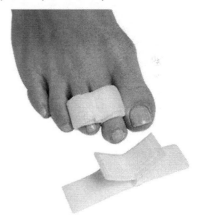

One solution for reducing hammer toes

Hallux valgus can also be acquired, but usually is congenital. This is when your big toe faces in towards your other toes at an odd direction. Pain is usually from the joint that is now poking out – not the actually alignment of the big toe. Tailor's bunions form on the side of the little toe in a similar way. There are some passive stretching options available to help reduce the misalignment, like the Healthy Toe Stretcher, among others.

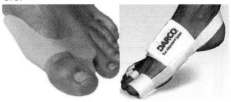

Some solutions for reducing hallux valgus

FOOTWEAR AND ORTHOTICS

As I prophesied in the first edition, **minimal footwear and barefoot shoes** have finally gone mainstream. The concept is that landing on your heels during running creates too much shock to your body and creates an abnormal muscle firing pattern that can lead to a whole host of foot, ankle, leg, knee, back, even neck issues. Midfoot or forefoot (balls of your feet) strike uses your body's natural shock absorption system and promotes a more natural running gait and minimal footwear forces you to run on your feet correctly. Running technique has been described earlier in the Aerobic Training section. Minimal footwear also strengthens your feet because of the lack of support that can help correct foot, ankle, knee, and low back problems mainly from correcting overpronation by strengthening your feet. The short foot and balance exercises in this book will also help. Most fancy running shoes have turned up toes to prevent stubbing, but this interferes with a normal toe-off. Most running shoes also have a higher heel than forefoot for landing on you heel. This makes landing on your mid or forefoot difficult, and will mess with your squat form (wink to CrossFitters). Many minimal shoes champion a 3 mm or less heel rise. I know a prominent podiatrist that runs in Crocs and Converse All Stars (Chuck Taylors), and many many people run in sandals, all of which can be marketed as "barefoot style shoes".

Climbers should have fairly strong feet by using their feet actively during climbing, but not all do. I highly recommend barefoot or minimal running shoes, but remember to follow the recommended break-in period. Barefoot and minimal running can also create as many problems as they attempt to solve. Use them carefully and intelligently.

Extreme overpronators should start with a more rigid shoe and get some miles in and do some active rehab before going "barefoot". Extremely stiff supinators will benefit from the floppy, flexible shoes, but may need more cushioning. Try inserting a **shock absorbing insole and or padded heel cup** if at all possible. If not, go with a minimal shoe that will allow extra cushioning added if you underpronate.

Barefoot and minimal shoe running can cause problems for those with poor form and just don't want to deal with fixing it, those with inflexible feet, are just predisposed to injury, those that don't run that often, or people that run a lot. Thankfully there is backlash to the barefoot revolution. Extra cushioned, yet very lightweight shoes with a more enlightened biomechanical design (less rise, upturn toe, etc.) have started to become popular. Be careful rolling your ankle with these.

Hoka One

If you have other abnormal foot deformities, see a podiatrist. You may need a **wedge or post** placed inside the heel or forefoot (a varus or valgus wedge/post), arch support, or a metatarsal lift. Before seeing a podiatrist, you can save some money and buy over-the-counter **semi-custom orthotics**. Superfeet makes a good pair, and there are some custom moldable varieties. Generally it is best to fit the orthotic to your feet, than your feet to an orthotic, but about 80% of foot problems are solved with an inexpensive semi-custom orthotic than an expensive prescribed one made at a lab. Don't go the middle ground and buy a $300 pair of orthotic made by someone who doesn't absolutely specialize in them, especially if the mold is made from a foot scan.

Orthotics made from a foot scan are much more expensive than store bought ones, but may be no better. If spending the cash, you might as well pay the big bucks to an expert and get a mold taken from a non-weight bearing, neutral mold of your foot. Plaster casts and boxes of foam are the best. Non-weight bearing molds give you biomechanical correction, and are very hard to do-it-yourself. Weight bearing scans and heat moldable orthotics don't correct foot problems – they are accommodating and very useful for certain foot conditions (congenital deformities, spurs, Diabetes, etc.). Also, most orthotics made from foot scans are actually semi-custom. Your foot is matched to one of several pre-made orthotics, not custom made in a lab. Most foot problems are very similar in the general population, so chances are yours are too, so why not save some coin and buy some Superfeet or cheap moldable ones, or inexpensive ones from a scan.

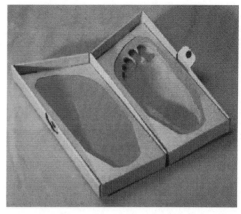

If you are in doubt, get a consultation. You may find that your foot condition can be corrected instead of relying on orthotics as a crutch. They may be helping your feet but weakening other areas in your body.

If you have an anatomical leg length inequality, or a functional one that won't go away with treatment, a **heel lift** may solve many issues for you. There are some quick checks. First lay face down with your head facing straight down. Turning your head may alter the results. Have someone pull both of your legs to straighten you out and have them look at the inside of your anklebones (medial malleolus). One would be higher than the other with a leg length inequality. Next flip over and repeat. Now do a sit-up. If the leg length equalized, then the problem may be in your pelvis. If they switched sides, you may have a leg length inequality and a pelvic problem. One final quick check that I invented is to stand up straight barefooted. Swing one leg back and forth. Now swing the other. Does one foot catch up on the ground?

Leg length inequalities need to be fixed gradually, a few millimeters at a time. If it is severe, you may need an X-ray Scan-O-Gram to measure it exactly. You may also need a **complete lift of the sole** since lifting your heel up too much can cause problems. Work your way up to the desired lift. You may get an unwanted rebound effect and wind up with more pain. If this is the case, decrease the height or don't use a heel lift. A heel lift will raise the femur by the same size as the lift, your sacrum by half that amount, and L5 by ¼ the size of the lift. Also get your feet, knees, hips, pelvis, and low back checked for muscle imbalances and joint dysfunction. There are several heel lifts out there, starting with a simple heel cup from the grocery store or a ridged lift you may need to get from a PT or DC. Get a bunch for all your shoes and tape them securely to your shoe insoles.

Another type of orthotics is **rocker bottom shoes**, also inappropriately marketed as toning shoes. These have a rocker board integrated into the sole of the shoe. They're not a bad idea as they do help training balance, and promote some core work. However, the benefit may or may not be worth the extra money and looks/questions you'll be getting. If you walk around all day at work and you want to splurge – give them a try. They really shine for people with forefoot problems, arthritis, or Diabetes. As with any type of orthotic, if you don't need them they can cause more problems than indented to fix.

I wouldn't make a habit out of taping your arches, but if you need too in order to get your feet strong enough, just tape them for a short time. **Leukotape** works best since it does not stretch. Taping over a sore spot is a good idea to run on while the area heals.

Heel lifts

OTHER SELECTED CONDITIONS

CHECK-UPS

If you haven't had a physical in a while, you probably should now. You can check your own resting heart rate at home, and it can be mildly useful to gauge training progress or signs of overtraining. A high resting heart rate doesn't necessarily mean you are unhealthy or have poor cardiovascular health, it can also be genetic. If you find that you have high blood pressure, stay on top of it and check it regularly. Training may help, but you may need medication. Get your blood checked for the following and follow your doctor's advice: lipids and cholesterol, complete blood count including iron levels, liver enzymes, glucose levels, and hormone levels including testosterone and thyroid. Get a check-up from your dermatologist at some point, it could save your life, especially since climbers tend to be out in the sun for long periods. Don't ignore those men's and women's special health checks. Pap smear, mammogram, and routine gynecologist visits for women of certain ages. Testicle, colonoscopy and prostrate exams for men of certain ages. Ask your primary care physician for when you should begin these routine screenings.

For those suffering from fatigue and or digestive issues check the following: environmental and food allergies, inflammatory conditions such as RA, lupus, and other inflammatory arthropathies, lyme disease (from ticks outdoors), a sleep-study, or adrenal levels (from saliva). Low-level viral infections like mono, or low-grade sinus infections can contribute to a chronic sense of fatigue. General food allergy testing usually only tests for severe allergic reactions.

Check out a naturopath for non-traditional approaches for ailments like chronic fatigue syndrome, irritable bowel syndrome, and fibromyalgia. Visit a nutritionist for advice on healthy eating and weight loss.

A warning: you can spend a lot of money investigating nutritional and naturopathic issues. Each practitioner, book, and Internet search will give you a million different answers. You may find the magic bullet and solve a lifelong health concern, or you may wind up wasting a lot of time and money. My advice is to start simply and make common-sense changes before going down other paths.

OTHER SELECTED CONDITIONS
ALLERGIES AND SENSITIVITIES

True allergies are IgE mediated antibody reactions. They can be mild with cold-like symptoms, or severe causing rashes, hives, or anaphylaxis. They can be caught with a simple skin or blood test at any doctor's office. Another type of allergy ca be described as a low-level allergy or a sensitivity. These are IgG antibody mediated allergies, and they are the source of much pseudoscience and debate. Either type of allergy can cause an immune response and leave you feeling tired, sick, or worse. If, for instance, you are mildly allergic to blueberries and eat them every morning on a backcountry trip with your oats, your performance could suffer. Wheat gluten is the evil villain in food-Nazi land, and I suspect certain people would be upset if they were not allergic to it! There are a few ridiculous tests for food allergies you should avoid, one specifically being Applied Kinesiology which uses muscle strength testing to diagnose allergies.

Allergy testing is very sensitive (it should catch everything), but not too specific (many false positives). There isn't a lot of evidence suggesting IgG tests are valid or reproducible between labs. Food allergy testing can also be done with an ELISA panel or delayed sensitivity test (Cellular Immune Food Reaction Test). Confirm any positives with a food challenge. ALCAT Laboratories is one of the more popular food sensitivity testing labs.

A food challenge is a practical, but subjective test designed to identify food allergies. Remove all suspect foods from your diet for 1-3 weeks. Eat lamb/turkey, rice/potato, any vegies but corn, legumes, and tomatoes, any fruit but citrus, any fats but dairy, corn, or soybean oil if you don't have any suspects. Avoid wheat, corn, citrus, soy, legumes, nuts, animal/fish products, coffee, tea, chocolate, and yeast. Introduce new foods every two days by eating it at least in two separate meals and see what causes a reaction. After 3-6 months of avoiding the offending food, re-challenge suspect foods to see if tolerance has been built.

CHRONIC FATIGUE, CHRONIC PAIN, ADRENAL INSUFFICIENCY, FIBROMYALGIA, AND DEPRESSION

The problem with these syndromes is that we know little about them. We can all relate to anxiety or stress fatigue, but whether this can create an actual chronic syndrome of reduced cortisol levels or not is up for debate. Those suffering from chronic fatigue syndrome and or pain will no doubt know that the problems are real. I believe climbers are more susceptible to developing these syndromes because of the extreme mental and physical stress hard climbs can produce. In fact, a very hard climb can leave one feeling post-climb depression, or with symptoms synonymous with post-traumatic stress disorder (PTSD). As stated, **magnesium, folic acid, malic acid, SAMe, licorice, DHEA** for men, and **progesterone** supplementation for women have been shown to be somewhat effective.

Saliva tests that show reduced sub-clinical levels of cortisol in blood tests have little scientific evidence, as do most supplements containing animal adrenal gland and hypothalamus. Low-level cortisol supplementation to give the adrenals a break has even been stated as a cure. This isn't to say they are bogus, but just that the research isn't there or is looking in the wrong places. You can order your own saliva testing kits without a prescription from many labs. Low levels of neurotransmitters seen with depression have been suggested, and treatment would consist of taking depression medication. **Adaptogens** and vitamins (**vitamin C, E, B-complex, calcium**) that aid in stress may help, but again, there is little evidence. Depression and sleep disorders can be contributing co-factors, but are not always the case.

Some non-medication suggestions are too seriously cut back on stimulants, alcohol, and sugar. One benefit of cutting back on the caffeine is that after about a month, the effects of a cup of coffee (or whatever) will be more pronounced for when you really need it, like at 4 am cold and scared. Improper (meaning not just inadequate, but possibly too much) nutrition, exercise, and sleep as well as allergies should be looked into as possible causes. Get a complete blood count (CBC), get tested for Lyme disease, R.A., lupus, and M.S., check your thyroid and sex hormone levels, and your liver enzymes to rule out other conditions.

Anxiety and depression are very closely related and may be symptoms of the same thing. Talking about more severe forms of depression and mental illnesses are way outside the scope of this book, but many climbers suffer from mental disease. Depression and anxiety can be low level, but no matter the severity, they can both severely affect performance and motivation. Climbing something fun is an excellent treatment, as is exercising on a regular basis. Sticking to a regular schedule, getting plenty of rest and normal sleep (not too much and normal hours), having friends or loved ones close, and having something to look forward to (your next climb) are all great treatments. However, even with the best intentions and surroundings, depression and anxiety can be impossible to break free from without medication. There are some new cleaner drugs on the market. Because there is no real test to determine what drug will work best, you may have to try several, giving each a few weeks trial.

GASTROINTESTINAL PROBLEMS

Irritable bowel syndrome, or as I like to call it, fibromyalgia of the gut, should be investigated if you are having digestion or bowel issues – after more serious conditions like ulcerative colitis, stomach ulcers, and Crohn's disease have been ruled out. You may want to get your colon irrigated, or start taking some **probiotics and prebiotics**. **Ginger and licorice** are other possibly helpful supplements.

If you get the squirts from over-doing it on the supplements or wind up with diarrhea from eating space food, **antispasmodics** slow down your gut so water has more time to absorb before they start pressing against your sphincter. Some, like **Imodium Multi Symptom** also contain a drug to reduce frothing and bubbling in your gut. If you're the type who always seems to get the squirts, test any antispasmodic out at home to see how long it takes, how much you need, and how long it lasts. Bring some along with you. If you are literally pissing out your ass, hydrate with **electrolytes and sugar water**. If it remains you probably are sick or have a food or water borne illness. **Peppermint oil with enteric coating** has been suggested as an effective OTC medication for IBS related GI symptoms.

On the flip side, constipation can make you feel like a ton of bricks. Get your **fiber** in your normal diet and by eating some extra dried fruit. Don't hold it in at night or on the approach. Backed up bowels can create diarrhea later. **Laxatives** work well, but often too well and you may regret taking them later. **Suppository tool softeners** are a bit gentler than laxatives. Constipation and also sitting around in the cold can create hemorrhoids. **Hemorrhoid creams, suppositories, and wipes** will help reduce the pain and inflammation but surgery is necessary to totally rid yourself of these nasty buggers if the get out of control.

If you suffer from GERD or chronic heartburn, or watch TV, you should be all too familiar with the OTC drugs like **Pepcid, Pepto-Bismol, Zantac, Tagamet, and Rolaids/Tums**. Sneak something that works for you in your med kit. **Vinegar** is a lesser-known but very successful remedy for excessive acid. A small shot tells your stomach that it doesn't need to produce anymore acid.

Sleep and Stress

Suggestions for getting good sleep are under the Programming chapter under Rest. For the love of god please try the following drugs out at home before on a climb! **Melatonin** is produced naturally, is quite effective, but most doses are way too high. 1-2 mg should be sufficient. Take it thirty minutes to an hour before you want to fall asleep helps to reset your body clock. It can make you groggy if you take too much (start with ½ mg) and can give you nightmares. Used in conjunction with a **full spectrum light**, like the Philips GoLight, in morning can really help you reset your body's clock. **Valerian root** is an excellent natural sleep aid, but it smells terrible. **Kava kava** and **chamomile tea** are popular herbal remedies, but there is not great evidence for either. Chamomile tea needs to be strong (3 tea bags) to work. Kava has better evidence for helping with anxiety, which may be why it is suggested to aid in sleep. **Tryptophan** (the amino acid in turkey and milk that make you sleepy), **hops**, and **passionflower** are all supplements that can make you sleepy, but dosage and efficacy are lacking.

Diphenhydramine (**Benadryl**) and dimenhydrinate (**Dramamine**) are OTC pills used as sleep aids. Climbers have been using these for years, probably because they are cheap. The sleepiness is really a side effect since Benadryl is an antihistamine and Dramamine is for motion sickness. Morning grog can be fully expected if you take too much (more that ½ to one pill). **Huperzine-A** is a supplement used for memory enhancement, and has been anecdotally suggested to increase your total REM sleep. I'd avoid it. **L-theanine** is an amino acid found in green tea that is able to cross the blood brain barrier. It has been successful shown in studies to help your body cope with stress both physical and mental and to improve mood and cognition by increasing alpha brain waves and helping to regulate dopamine and serotonin levels in your brain. Alcohol is often used to fall asleep, but is a terrible sleep aid. It reduces mental and physical regeneration associated with sleep (especially reducing HGH), and obviously makes you feel like crap then next day. It also acts as a diuretic, dehydrating you for the climb.

Next up on the list are **prescription sleeping pills**. These can cause big trouble, even if taken at proper doses. Don't even think about trying these out the night before a climb or combining them with alcohol. All of these can make you do some very strange things under their influence. I really don't recommend prescription sleeping pills before a big day. Remember, you may need to jolt out of bed in the middle of the night and need to be on your game. If you have chronic insomnia, see a doctor instead of medicating yourself. Melatonin and most of the herbals shouldn't become addictive, but anything can become a habit or dependence – especially when it comes to sleep. **Sonata** works quickly, is least likely to cause hangover (short half-life) but won't keep you asleep. It can still mess you up. **Lunesta** has the second least chance of a hangover, but it still can make you groggy. **Ambien** can make you the groggiest. Everyone reacts differently to each of these prescriptions, so you may have to try a few out. Do this in a safe sleep environment!

UNHEALTHY VICES

Misuse of legal drugs, use of illegal drugs, smoking and tobacco use, and alcohol abuse are obviously negative to health and climbing performance. But climbing is a stressful activity, and sometimes vices can get us through some tough times. This is not a lecture, but just suggestions for those who want to stop or cut back. Climbing can be a self-destructive act, but sometimes that self-destruction avoids other demons faced in the real world. After all is said and done, whatever gets you through the day and up the pitch – your motivations and problems are you own.

Smoking / Tobacco

Quitting smoking can be the most difficult thing a person can ever accomplish. For your partner's sake, don't quit cold turkey on a climbing trip. It may be a tempting time if you plan on being in the backcountry and won't be able to get a fix, but it's a terrible idea for obvious reasons. People have about equal success by going cold turkey, or gradually quitting. The one thing to remember is that it can take many attempts. So don't quit quitting. Immediately get back on the horse (or wagon). Avoid contact with tobacco at all costs. Movies with smokers are the worst. Use a temporary replacement with another, healthier substance to help with the ritualistic habits of having a smoke: **gum, tea, toothpicks**, or whatever. If you're used to going outside, bring a cup of tea outside instead. Chew gum in the car. Also, as described in the mental training chapter, make deals with yourself and follow through.

One alternative to tobacco use that your health care provider may not suggest are **electronic cigarettes**. The FDA has not approved these for a smoking cessation device so they are not regulated...yet. That means you don't know what you are getting or the possible side effects. You could not be getting any nicotine, getting a lethal dose, or inhaling a dirty factory worker's tuberculosis. I haven't heard of anyone getting hurt, but I wanted to warn smokers out there. Now that I've covered my butt, I believe they are one of the best tobacco replacement devices out there. You can even get cartridges that gradually reduce the nicotine delivered. FDA approved nicotine replacement therapies are **patches, gum, lozenges, and inhalers**. Patches will probably fall of when climbing and exercising.

A couple anti-depressants are available to help with smoking cessation: **Wellbutrin** and **Zyban**. Another drug, **Chantix**, helps with reducing hard-hitting cravings. My advice is to arm yourself with as many physical and psychological replacements as possible, and keep quitting over and over and over. If you fall off the wagon, forgive yourself and immediately quit again. Don't give yourself a "break" from quitting. If you find yourself buying a pack, don't plan on finishing it. Run it under water, and throw it out. It can take many many attempts to quit, but you must try to quit immediately after falling off the wagon.

Alcohol

Alcohol is definitely part of the climbing culture, and there is a lot of climbing peer pressure to drink. No one should care if you drink in moderation and aren't driving, but just know that alcohol is detrimental to strength and skill training, and interferes with your rest and regeneration. It's also expensive. Unfortunately many climbers use climbing as an excuse for their alcoholism. Climbers who think they may be alcoholics should consult a doctor for blood tests because many nutrient deficiencies are possible.

Marijuana
Now that pot is legal in some states and legal with a prescription in many more, I can recommend it for those who already partake for a relaxant, sleep-aid, pain reliever, and entertainment. That said, like alcohol, pot can be very unhealthy for your lungs, dull your senses, interfere with performance, and get you or your partner hurt if used in dangerous situations. I do not recommend anyone start, and not using it is probably a good thing (unless you have a physical or mental conditions that a doctor recommends it for).

<u>AGE RELATED CONDITIONS</u>
Many seemingly impossible climbs have been done by people who are bling, missing limbs, paralyzed, are three years old, and 90 years old. Unfortunately this leaves you without many excuses.

<u>KIDS</u>
Climbing is the greatest thing in the world for kids, but training is not. Kids and adolescents can stunt their growth and development by the type of training involved in this book by altering their growth plates, and causing hormonal changes. What kids and adolescents need is skill development, and muscle and cardio training via real world activities and organized sports. In other words kids get exercise through playing and skill development, not by running and weight training. Focus on eating healthy and play – not diets. Kids need to eat plenty, but they can learn to eat too much. If you make them clean their plate, make sure the portions aren't well over their caloric needs. Kids do have a higher caloric need than adults do pound for pound. Under nourishing kids can actually make them obese because their developing bodies won't become as metabolically active. Kids also need plenty of water. They sweat less and don't dissipate heat as well as adults, putting them at higher risk for dehydration and overheating.

Keep the science experiments to yourself and avoid giving kids questionable supplements that screw with metabolism or hormones. Children's' vitamins and milk are safe if standardized and free of additives. A normal ratio of carbs, protein and fats should be supplemented with plenty of fruits and vegetables. Treat sweets like a cheat day – as a positive reward for eating well.

Congenital Malformations and End Plate Injuries
Most NMS problems kids and young adults get (besides broken bones) are due to congenital malformations, or injuries to the growing endplates on their bones. Injury to the growing endplate can cause permanent growth retardation to that bone, or cause AVN if the endplate is avulsed. Be a cheapskate with yourself, but not with your kids. Get them checked after any moderate to major trauma, especially if there is any swelling, intense pain, or reduction in range of motion or function with trauma or if the symptoms seems to come out of nowhere.

Some malformations, like scoliosis, can be managed and possibly reduced by specialists. Treatments involving combinations of bracing, counter weight exercises, proprioceptive exercises, and muscle stimulation have been shown very effective in progressive cases. Scoliosis can be progressive (gets worse) or can be self-limiting and resolve with maturity. Get your kid checked and monitor the progression. Scoliosis in a front to back direction usually resulting in a hyperkyphosis of the thoracic spine is usually caused by Scheuermann's disease, a disorder in calcification of the vertebral endplates.

Kids and young adults (11-20) are susceptible to osteochondrosis, a slow separation of subchondral bone and cartilage in their knee, foot, and elbow from repetitive activities. AVN can occur in both femoral heads, called Legg-Calve-Perthes in children 4-8 years old. Congenital hip dislocation, diagnosed at birth, can lead to problems down the road if not treated properly. Temporary inflammation can occur in the hip joint for no apparent reason, called transient hip synovitis, in children 3-10 years old and can mimic an infection of the joint. The growth plate can avulse or start to slide off the top of the femur at the hip in slipped capital femoral epiphysis for adolescents 10-16 years old. Kids generally grow out of knock-knees, aka genu valgum, but it could be caused by injuries or malformations in the foot, knee, or hip. Coxa vara and coxa valga, decreased or increased femoral angle at the head respectively, can contribute to problems at the knee or hip. Conservative management of symptoms is usually recommended for this. Also the femoral head can be retroverted or anteverted, facing out or in too much at the hip joint. The can lead to anatomic over toeing-in or toeing-out, and a predisposition to instability at the hip. Avulsion of the tibial tuberosity, called Osgood Schlatter's, is common in kids and early teens (8-15), and responds well to conservative care. A similar condition where the calcaneal tuberosity avulses on the heel, called Sever's disease, has a similar self-limiting prognosis. Young children can have their radius dislocate in their elbow and rupture the annular ligament, simply called pulled elbow. Be careful tugging them through the grocery store, and on dynamic climbs. This usually self-resolves.

Getting Old
Skin Cancer
I would say this is the most serious concern for climbers who have had chronic sun exposure. Regular exams by a dermatologist can be lifesaving. The most worrisome and lethal skin cancer is malignant melanoma because it can metastasize and is difficult to detect and occur in non-obvious places. Look for irregular shaped moles, new moles, moles that have undergone any changes in color or size, and moles with dark spots and irregular or jagged edges. Unfortunately some common spots for melanoma are on the soles of the feet and under the nails. The upper back and lower legs are the most common spots, as are any areas that have been sunburned (like the upper back and lower leg). Most basal cell carcinomas, another type of skin cancer, occur on the head and neck and sun exposed areas like the ears and nose.

Basal cell carcinoma can be serious and result in significant damage to the immediate area. It is the most common type of skin cancer and is found mostly on the head and neck. Squamous cell carcinoma is the second most common form of skin cancer and also occurs in sun-exposed areas of the head and neck, but its appearance can be highly variable. It is serious and can metastasize like melanoma. Get any new or growing skin lesion checked out.

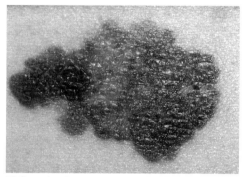
Malignant melanoma

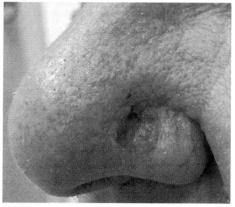
Basil cell carcinoma

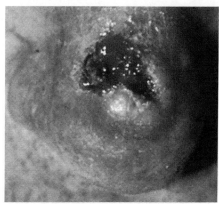
Squamous cell carcinoma. Courtesy NIH/CDC

Genetic Disease

Getting old can mean turning 30 for some health and genetic conditions. Once you turn 30, start to pay attention to odd changes. Some genetic diseases start showing signs now. Besides starting to actually put money in the bank for retirement, also put prevention in the health bank.

50's and Older

Not much happens generally speaking until your start hitting your late 50's to mid-60's. Now you must deal with the increased threat of osteoporosis, cancer, cardiovascular disease, diabetes, and weight gain. Hormone levels like testosterone and estrogen fall, metabolism slows, healing time increases, and things generally start to fall apart. Be sure and eat enough calcium, protein, and healthy foods. Crackers and tomato soup aren't enough! This is the age where most people start taking preventative measures. Do some more research and find out what you can do to prevent cancer, diabetes, and cardiovascular disease – the main killers. Also focus on diets or supplements that aid in recovery, and improving the effects of insulin and spare protein metabolism.

Once you hit your 60's you need heavy resistance weight training if you haven't already. Weight training keeps muscles strong and bones solid for when they really start to get old and things begin to waste. Heavy resistance weight training for seniors is money in the bank. Since tissues are less forgiving, stretching is necessary as well, but the focus is on light stretching, and active range of motion. Heart rates are lower, so cardio can be as simple as going for a thirty-minute walk every day

We are living longer, but as we age longer the burden of disease grows. As we age, arthritis and degenerative joint disease becomes more and more prevalent. Beware of AVN in the hip if you've had trauma to the area or bad arthritis. Connective tissues weaken. Bone weakens, and can develop osteoporosis in some. Spinal stenosis (narrowing of the spinal canal) can cause neurological problem, as can the increased risk of stroke and TIA. Metabolism slows and hormone levels change, making you more predisposed to NMS injuries. Muscles lose strength and endurance.

The list of things to prevent growing old in poor health is simple, and we've heard it all before. Keep an eye on your blood pressure, cholesterol, body fat, and nutrient intake for your heart. Get regular gynecologic exams, mammograms, prostate exams, colonoscopies, skin checks to nip future cancers in the bud, and once a year physicals. Stay active in both cardio and strength building exercises. Avoid stress, injury, and inflammation. Eat well, don't drink too much, or smoke. Keep climbing. The more you move the healthier you stay. Pretty simple advice. I can only hope this is all condescending information to those of you who stayed fit and are crushing it in your 70's, or later!

PREGNANCY

Pregnancy harness courtesy Mountain Momma

Women who are menstruating heavily should supplement with more **iron** than the RDA for women due to the loss in blood, but consult with your doctor for specific amounts. **Folic acid** supplementation is very important before becoming pregnant to aid in neural tube development of the fetus. Supplementation is required before conception. You can also take **prenatal vitamins** for you and your child.

While pregnant, women need to eat slightly more, around 300 extra calories. This is not a good time to diet. Worry about your child over your own self-image issues. Some chemicals pass easily into the child's bloodstream, while others are blocked. Do a thorough amount of research if you put anything in your body besides a regular diet. Avoid seafood high in mercury, undercooked animal products, or unpasteurized dairy.

Your goals will obviously have to change due to your body and new responsibilities. That doesn't mean you need to put your training on hold. Invest in a full-body harness designed for pregnant women that avoids the waist belt, and stick to top roping if you want to be extra safe. This can be an excellent opportunity to re-visit skills, and get a natural way to train with some extra weight! You could also carefully follow pitches, alpine scramble, or boulder low to the ground depending on your ability to not fall far or onto your stomach. Avoid jerky, bouncy, high impact movements, and anything that would cause you to fall or get hit in the abdominal area. Assess risks for your baby, not just for you. Some contraindications to avoid all but light exercise are: pregnancy induced hypertension, history of spontaneous abortion, vaginal bleeding, or pre-term labor.

During the first trimester it's important to not overheat, and armpit temperature should be below 101° F. Also, it's important to keep your heart rate below 140 bmp (can't comfortably carry on a conversation). The 140 bmp is an area of debate for extremely active women, however. Some maintain that if you are extremely fit, staying below that heart rate will lead to too much de-training. It's up to you, but I suggest at least using a perceived exertion scale and try to stay below anything that leaves you totally exhausted. Pregnant women can actually increase their aerobic capacity compared to being non-pregnant if they exercise while pregnant and up to a year after pregnancy!

In the second trimester, weight lifting should be avoided while standing up if you feel dizzy or lightheaded. Avoid lying on your stomach in the second (and obviously 3rd) trimester, and after 20 weeks avoid exercising on your back as well. Avoiding exercising in the supine position is another area of contention for active women. If you must do exercises on your back, keep your knees bent and feet on the floor. Try lying on your side instead. In your third trimester, be careful on trails or terrain that can put you off balance. Finally, unless you already live at high altitude, avoid prolonged activity about 8,000'.

The hormone relaxin loosens joints and tissues, and combined with added weight, injuries to shoulders, elbows and fingers can occur more easily. Sacroiliac joint problems are common because of the looser joints – see a chiropractor or physical therapist to deal with the symptoms and work heavily on the core after you deliver. Swimming and yoga are excellent alternative forms of exercise you can do while pregnant. In fact, because you are going to get looser, now and just after pregnancy are both great times to work on flexibility! The hip flexors, low back, and chest area may get tighter, and the upper back, gluts, abs, and possibly hamstrings may get a little weaker from the change in posture.

Every woman experiences pregnancy in a different way. I've seen women outperform plenty of men well into their 3rd trimester. Listen to your body and coordinate your exercise plans with your doctor or birth councilor. Find one that is experienced treating active, pregnant women. Check out the book, "Exercising through Your Pregnancy" for more information.

PART III: CLIMBING BEYOND THE BASICS

Warning! The following section assumes that you already know what you are doing and can decide for yourself what is and what isn't good advice. The following is not an instructional guide or how to manual. Use this section as a reference to refresh old information, or as springboard for developing your own personal climbing system. Tailor the following information for your own needs. If you want to learn a new skill, buy a book, practice it, and hire a private guide to take you on a low-commitment climb so you have time to learn the skills on your own.

A note on the bias in Part Three: The rest of this book spends a whole lot more time on trad, alpine, big wall, and ice than it does on sport climbing and bouldering. The first two parts of this book can, for the most part, be interchangeably used for any climbing discipline. However, the rest of the book will talk about equipment, backcountry skills, and technical information. It's just a simple fact that sport climbing and bouldering have a lot less to talk about when it comes to these subjects. There is still some good information ahead if bouldering and sport climbing are your main interests, but the main bulk of info is for traditional climbing and backcountry travel.

Chapter Nine: Equipment Planning and Use

Camping, Approach, and Basic Gear

There is a gear checklist included in the appendix as not every single piece of gear will be listed or commented on in this section. Since gear changes, as do the companies that produce it, I will try and make this chapter as general as possible. I will mention certain brands or products as necessary point of reference, and occasionally recommend a particular product or brand. My recommendations may not be current by the time you read this, or you may simply disagree. A lot of info is presented under a specific item of gear rather than in the following chapters.

Ultralight vs. Durable Gear

Climbing epitomizes having the right tool for the right job. Most lifetime climbers have several types of packs, shoes, sleeping bags, tents, protection, etc., for bringing the exact right thing for the climb they intend to do. One of the biggest character building exercises in climbing is just starting out and making do with what you've got. A big decision early on is whether to buy the most expensive, the most durable, or the most ultralight piece of gear. Nowadays, more people are starting with the most ultralight gear. This usually just results in having to replace something (or complaining online that this particular piece of gear sucks), but can wind up in disaster.

Gear today is world's lighter than our forefather's kit, and as long as something is from a respected manufacturer and isn't marketed as a specialty piece, it should be durable and light enough for most forays into the hills. Having something you depend on blow out because you wanted to go super-light isn't worth it. Wait until the climb you want to do depends on that piece of equipment, making or breaking it because of its weight or durability. Then buy it. Much more time can be saved (which is why you would want lighter weight) by not bringing things you don't need, being in shape, and climbing skillfully. Having the lightest weight kit possible is like an Olympic athlete trying to shave seconds off their time. The flip side of this is the common image of the "client" or "gumby" slogging up the trail or mountain with a backbreaking amount of crap. Bringing too much unnecessary kit adds the most weight, but sometimes buying the most durable piece of gear (and usually the most expensive) is also just too much. Sometimes it doesn't matter how durable a piece of gear is if it's cheap to replace or won't take that big of a pounding. It takes time to figure out when to skimp on durability and when not to.

A simple way to go about it is to start with the heaviest item you own. It could be your 5 lb. pack, 8 lb. tent, 1 lb. harness, or whatever. You could save 4 pounds in one fell swoop by upgrading your tent (or downgrading to a tarp), instead of buying a whole new rack of ultralight biners and skinny slings to save just one pound. Knowing what you can suffer through without having a particular item, or how to make do if something fails in the field is a learned skill. Knowing that when it rains, you'll either be in the tent or bailing can save you pounds in pack-covers, rain pants, or heavy Gore-Tex jackets. Knowing that your legs thermoregulate quite well can save you from bringing rain paints and extra leg layers.

Knowing how warm and well you sleep can spare you from bringing that heavy bag and sleeping pad. Not caring that you may get bored at camp, how chlorine tastes, or how palatable or warm your meal is can save pounds in books or journals, water purification kits, and complex cookery. Bring only what you need to be safe enough, warm enough, dry enough, and just hungry enough to get you up the climb and back to the car if you want to keep the pack weight down. Learning to improvise and jury-rig luxuries and to bring enough to be comfortable enough takes time, trial and error. On climbs like multiday technical ridge traverses, every single ounce counts.

Of course this all goes out the window for car camping and cragging. The more the merrier, and the happier you'll be looking forward to cragging that day. A lot of alpine climbs that have mild approaches and bomber weather are basically extended walk-in car camping trips. Treat these trips with enough respect that an accident that requires rescue will take longer, but at the same time, you don't have to pack like you're climbing for a speed ascent of the Eiger. That said, bringing too much, even on short approaches to base camps, can destroy you for the next day

Get a **scale**. If you can, get a hanging one that measures in ounces and pounds, and a tabletop one that measures in ounces and grams. Knowing how much things weight can help you decide what combination of things to bring, what not to bring, and how to divide up group gear. Numbers don't lie, but manufactures do and your guess may surprise you.

METHODS OF TRAVEL

There are ways to get there besides just walking. Four wheel drive cars, trucks, and even **dirt bikes** can save time, but can also really wear on your nerves and shorten the life of your vehicle. See if renting a shorter framed 4x4 like a **Jeep or ATV** is affordable instead of ruining your car. **Bikes** are great to save time, at least on the descent. They are especially useful on closed logging roads or roads too gnarly to drive a low clearance car on. They aren't allowed in wilderness areas. Bikes are also great for stealth camping in crowded camping areas since they are a lot easier to hide than your car. Bring a **bike repair kit** for punctured tubes. Horses and llamas make great backpack carriers on long approaches. Consider hiring a **pack animal** guide for extended base camps with long approaches.

Some climbs require a water-based approach. Nothing is funnier than watching climbers with no canoeing skills navigate their way to Mt. Moran in the Tetons. If your climb requires a **canoe or inflatable boat** to cross a large river or lake, just be sure and wear a **life vest** and watch the crampon and ice ax points. Put your pack in a heavy-duty **trash compacter bag**, or **dry bag** in case you tip over. Klymit makes a very lightweight alpine raft. Stream crossings can require some careful preparation if you don't want to get your boots or shoes soaked. If the water is warm enough, take a pair of **sandals or water shoes** to leave on the other side, or if too cold, bring **plastic bags** to cover your boots.

Courtesy Klymit

Boot packing on firm snow is sometimes faster than **skis or snowshoes**, so don't just blindly strap on skis or snowshoes for no reason. Snowshoes are slower, but a lot safer than skis, although the likelihood of falling through a crevasse or snow bridge is much lower on skis. Snowshoes take zero amount of skill and are lighter to carry over if necessary. You still need **poles** with snowshoes and boot packing.

Skinning up and skiing down is obviously more fun, but if you are carrying a heavy pack and aren't wearing ski boots then expect to fall down a lot and not turn as quickly or smoothly. Wearing **skins** on the way up and down can help poor skiers remain in more control. Apply some **skin wax** for better glide, and carry a **skin repair kit** of some sort in case the tip and tail connectors fail. Tape would work in a pinch. You can arrest a fall with your pole and skis if you get your skis planted perpendicular to the fall. Skis also make great anchors. Watch the rope when skiing - sharp edges can sever the rope. If skiing down in whiteouts or difficult or sketchy terrain, snowplow with the team at a 45-degree angle to each other. **Ski leashes** are pretty necessary compared to **ski brakes** outside the resorts to ensure you get them back, especially in a crevasse fall. In difficult terrain, ski on belay with the rope also clipped to your haul loop to keep you from getting torqued around.

Misery Shoes!

If just using your skis to get around, any crappy pair of skis with AT bindings will do. You can even use a very small pair of skis or **children's skis** if you'll be carrying them, and can probably find them very cheap. If doing more advanced ski mountaineering then **Dynafit bindings** are super light, and the newer compatible boots climb really well. You can also try **split boards** with light step-in crampon compatible boots. There are even a few companies that make hybrid **skishoes** – they look fun. Some companies, like Altai, don't recommend rigid soled boots on their skishoes. Don't forget your skins and poles for these options as well. **Ski crampons** may be helpful for ski mountaineering. If relying on skis you may want to bring a **binding repair kit** if you're a long snowy way from the car. Zip ties, ski straps, duct tape, hose clamps, baling wire, Seam Grip, a ski tool and extra screws are just a few items you could include in the repair kit.

Children's "Snow Pup" skis with universal bindings

Lightweight Dynafit boot courtesy La Sportiva

Ski shoes courtesy HIVE

Ski Shoes. Courtesy Trackers

> Here is a fancy skiing travel time equation called the Munter Method:
> - 1 km (0.63 miles) cross-country = 1 unit. 100 meters elevation (328 feet) = 1 unit.
> - Add up the units and divide by 4 to find the uphill hours, and divide by 10 to find the hours down

Finally you can fly in via **ski plane, boat plane, or helicopter** – or at least to arrange a resupply or pick-up. Some companies will heli you off the summit after a climb.

The legendary John Scurlock and his kit-built ultralight

Backpacks and Ditty Bags

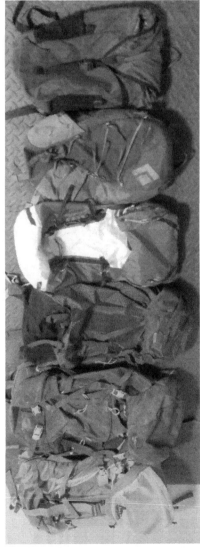

Pack Quiver: 20L Cilogear NWD Worksack, 20L BD Magnum, 30L Mountain Hardware Summit Rocket, 30L MEC Genie, 52L Osprey Variant, 50L Gregory Alpinisto

Fit

Make sure the retailer that you got your pack at has a good return policy if it isn't comfortable or doesn't adapt to your needs. Understanding how to distribute pack weight and to adjust the load straps can usually fix most discomfort. Thin molded hip and shoulder straps may actually be more comfortable than thick foam padded straps for some folks. For those without any hips, a great way to lessen the hip pain is to tie a windbreaker or sweater around your waist and have the buckle ride on top of the knotted shirt. The best part of this trick is that when you stop, you have a layer handy (unless you drenched it with sweat). If your route doesn't require the pack you schlepped in with, pack a smaller frameless 12-30 liter pack as well. The lightest option is to basically use a stuff sack with shoulder straps, followed by a lightweight daypack with a few more bells and whistles.

Courtesy Cilogear (left) & Hyperlite Mountain Gear (right)

Photo courtesy Black Diamond

351

Approach Pack

If a pack's sole purpose is to lug your stuff to the base of a climb or camp, comfort trumps weight. Fortunately you can get a comfy pack in the 3-5 pound range these days. For the speedsters, you can also get a 1 lb fairly large pack with a bivy pad frame. A **45-50-liter pack** should fit up to a week's worth of camping gear, food, and climbing gear if you pack carefully. Mountaineers and skiers that will be carrying the same pack up the hill may want **ski slots, wand pockets** (for wands and pickets), a **shovel flap, ice tool attachments, and crampon pockets or patches**. I recommend a crampon pocket if the crampons will be coming on and off repeatedly. A floating, **removable lid and storm collar** can extend the capacity of your pack. Multiday cold mountaineering objectives could require a **60+ liter pack** with the heavier sleeping bag and tent involved.

Climbing and Approach Pack

If you are climbing a technical route with the same pack you hiked in with, weight and size matter a lot more. You have to decide what will remain in the pack once the climbing equipment has been deployed. Generally these types of climbs require a minimalist packing job (shiver bivy and no comfort items), so all that should remain is a belay jacket, water, food, misc. stuff like a headlamp, and/or a small bivy kit. A **30-liter pack** usually does the trick for 1-2 winter nights, or 2-3 summer nights en route.

Gear loops on the hip belt as well as some of the features listed on the approach pack are nice accessories depending on the type of climbing. **Haul loops** that are sturdy and placed behind the lid and two in front are great for tagging up the pack, or at least for hanging on the anchor. A **rope strap** that wraps completely around the rope is critical. Ropes slide out with straps that just compress over the top of the rope. You can use a sling or two to wrap around the rope and attach it to the front and rear haul loops if the rope doesn't fit inside the pack. Your frame should be fairly minimal, either a single light aluminum stay or a dual-purpose bivy pad frame sheet. The company Klymitt makes an **inflatable frame sheet** for fine tuning suspension and sleeping on that weighs less than a foam counterpart. **Zero frame packs** are excellent if you can pack them carefully using your sleeping pad as the frame in the back.

Make sure your pack climbs well. This means it moves well with you and carries low profile. **Detachable hip belts** can be useful. Even though they are not necessary, some climbers still prefer lids on their climbing pack over lighter and more streamlined **roll top closures**. **Attached lids** are a bit more streamlined than floating lids, but offer less expansion, which are usually not necessary once the climbing kit has been deployed.

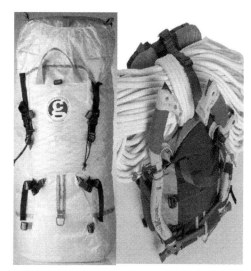

30:30 NWD Worksack & Ropecatch (right). Courtesy Cilogear

Courtesy Klymit. Inflatable pack frame

Day Pack

Big days from the car or camp usually require a small **12-20 liter daypack**. Depending on the temperatures, water availability, length, and difficulty of the climb both climbers may require their own pack, a 12-liter leader's pack and a larger 30-liter follower's pack, or a 30-liter followers pack and no leader pack. The leader could just shove food in their pocket and clip a water bottle or jacket on their harness. A climb with long sections of tight chimneys may require no pack whatsoever (unless dangled off a sling or daisy). The trick is to divide up the weight so that the leader isn't slowed down by too much weight and the follower doesn't get exhausted, but the leader has adequate supplies at the end of the pitch to safely stay warm and refuel if necessary. Tag lines can be worn as a backpack, food and little items can be shoved in pockets, and approach shoes, water bottles, and jackets can be clipped on the harness.

Smaller packs can get tossed in the larger approach pack, or carry as much gear as possible from the car with the rope or whatever's left clipped to the harness and worn on the trail. Featherweight sil-nylon packs that are simply **stuff sacks with strap** are great for their weight, but can last just one climb and access to snacks and other on-the-climb supplies can be a pain to access therefor sacrificing proper fueling or layering. **Sturdier ballistic nylon daypacks** designed for climbing make life easier, but are heavier. The perfect comprise of weight and durability are packs made out of Dyneema, but the cost can be prohibitive. Adding a **thin layer of foam padding** to a minimalist pack can make up for a lot of discomfort.

There's a good chance you'll be using a water bladder hydration system. If your pack doesn't have a **hydration pocket and a sleeve,** make your own hole with a knife and tape. To hold the bladder upright I cut the **keychain clip** that comes in most lids, and rigged it where the hose exits. Add a **tube clip** to your shoulder strap and you're set. A waist belt is nice for the hike, but generally useless on the climb, and can make the pack ride high on the harness and wobble too much while climbing. **Sternum straps** can help keep the pack from falling off during weird moves or falls and not interfere with your harness – but aren't necessary. A sturdy clip-in point is a must, so make sure to reinforce any suspect haul loops. Equalizing a shoulder strap and haul loop with thin rappel webbing or cord not only backs up clip-in points, but serves as backup rappel webbing or a sling for dropping the pack in a chimney situation. Another option that is very handy on daypacks are **stretchy side pockets** to stash topos or a quick bite.

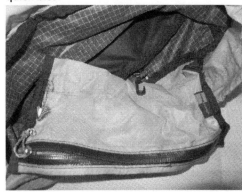

Lightweight ditty and keychain clip (for bladder) rigged inside the opening of a 30L pack.

Haul Bags

Haul bags are essential for multi day big wall fiascos. A burly pack can work in a pinch, but straps and pockets can catch, the pack could rip, and haul bag material reduces friction on slabby hauls. The bigger the haul bag, the bigger the pain. For ridiculous loads it may be better to do two separate hauls. Sometimes two small vertically rigged bags can be more manageable than on giant bag and an on the climb bag can be easier to get food, water, and clothes out of.

As with all things big wall, experience is the only way to know what will work best for you. Dangle your shoes, extra water bottle, and poop tube clipped below the haul bag. How much water you need to bring will usually determine that size haul bag you need. Cut off the top of a 2-liter soda bottle and use it as a **knot protector**. This really helps more for having the knot get caught on lips than it does protecting anything. A **daisy chain** girthed to the haul bag with a **biner, locker, and/or fifi** makes clipping the bag into the anchor a lot easier. Pack what you don't need at the bottom, being aware that water and food can get crushed or explode. Line the inside of the bag with your ground pads first. See the hauling section for more info.

place it in next. All you should have left is your rack, harness, shoes, food, helmet, and rope. Take the big cams off the rack and fill empty space around the stove pot with what fits best, hoping the big cams eventually fit. Lay the rest of your crap on top, helmet last, and close the drawstring shut. Lay your rope and windshirt/sweater on top and secure with the rope strap. Put your sundries and lunch in the lid and figure out where the items you forgot go. If for whatever reason it doesn't all fit, put the large cams, rock shoes, chalkbag, or helmet on the outside. Secure them so they don't bang around. Don't slam your pack off if your helmet is on the outside!

Courtesy Yates

Packing You Pack

Here's an example for a multiday trip with a 40 L approach pack assuming you have normal to light modern gear: Start with your water bladder since once packed, it's impossible to put it in the pocket without completely unpacking. Next put your compressed sleeping bag in the bottom. Now put your foam ground pad on the side of the pack. You should have divided up the group gear based on size and weight evenly. If you got the tent, cram it unpacked around the sides of the sleeping bag and put the poles in vertically. Tent or not, cram the clothes you don't need for the approach in available crevasses. If it could rain, the bag/tent/clothes should have gone in a garbage bag inside the pack. If you got the stove pot find something that will cram inside it - chalkbag, fuel, stove, etc. and

Sleds

Sleds are useful on long easier sieges, or for moving camps on snow. You can make your own sled. Start with a reasonably durable and non-tippy plastic sled from a sporting goods store.

Rigging A Kiddie Sled

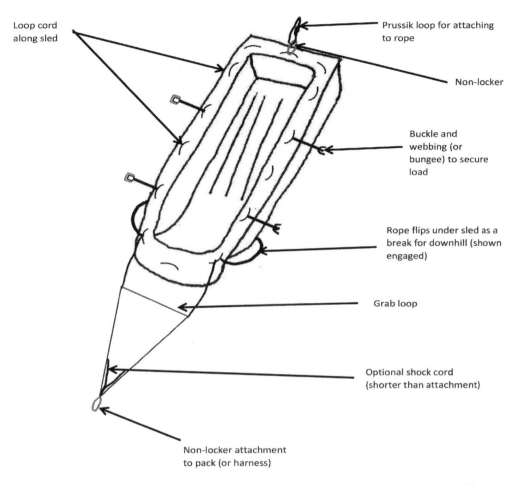

Poop Tubes
Commercial poop tubes are nice, but a **dry-bag** or **PCV pipe** can suffice just as easily. Poop into **grocery store or fruit/veggie plastic bags** or **paper bags** and throw those into **Ziplocs**, or use a **Wag Bag**. Keep some **wet-wipes and hand sanitizer** handy. A pinch of **lime**, the chemical not the fruit, can help with smell.

Pack Covers

Wearing a jacket over your head and pack to keep you and the pack dry.

Pack Covers are almost entirely useless extra weight for most climbing trips since most packs are fairly water resistant, and your important gear that can't get wet should be watertight via **stuff sacks** or a **garbage bag**. Your gear is only exposed during the approach, and if it's going to rain that much why are you still out? Bring a pack cover for extended trips with a high chance of rain with very long approaches that you intend to stick out rain or shine. Your pack will still probably get wet. During rainy approaches rain shells are sometimes too warm to wear while slogging. Rig your rain jacket up over your pack and head.

Stuff Sacks

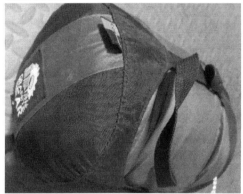

Fast and light long distance backpackers frown on stuff sacks, but that kinda goes out the window when you're lugging several pounds of nylon and metal they aren't. Stuff sacks and **compression sacks** help keep food and clothes dry, sundries together, and everything from getting covered in dirt when you're unpacking. This is where super light sil-nylon shines. Still, **grocery store plastic bags, Ziplocs, and garbage bags** are way cheaper and still just as light. Sleeping bags should get a commercially made sil-nylon compression sack since bags take up a lot of room. Tents don't need a stuff sack, and are great for filling gaps and voids around gear. **Crampon bags, ice ax covers**, and the like are totally useless except on the airplane or duffel bag. Post office **priority mail envelopes** made out of woven material and plastic do a great job and weigh nothing. It doesn't take much imagination to create **spike protectors** from what you already have at home.

Food bags can easily be a grocery store plastic bag for a one or two night trip. In bear or rodent country you may need to (legally) bring along a **bear container**. There is no good way to pack these awful containers, so try your best and plan on needing a larger pack. You could rig something up with tape and cord to hang from your pack, but make sure it doesn't swing around!

Ursack makes a bear-proof sack and inner liners that don't leak smells. Ursacks aren't officially allowed in many areas that legally require a bear container, but they still are a much friendlier way to pack your food and smellables. Just using the **inner liners** on a normal non-bear country trip could be nice if you are prone to rodent and raven plundering attacks. There are also lighter and more packable chainmail style food bags that work well, but aren't legal where bear containers are required.

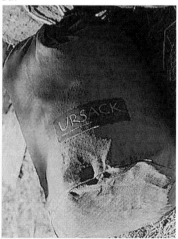

When traveling you'll want **duffel bags** with strong enough material to withstand pointy metal objects and a good zipper to withstand a crammed full bag. **Ski bags** are necessary if traveling with skis. Get oversized ski bags so you can pack in as much stuff as possible to avoid paying for extra bag charges.

Poles

Trekking poles are excellent on long approaches and can be used for setting up a light tarp shelter at camp. They are an extra pain if they require a carry-over. Cheap poles are available at Wal-Mart and Target, but nice light 3-section poles are worth the price if you have to carry-over or are skiing. There are many slick options.

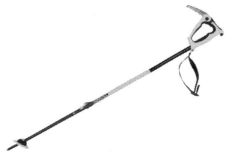

Condor with retractable pick and fit over any pole. Courtesy Grivel

Combo poles and ice axes for self-arresting are really nice on non-technical terrain like glaciers and snowfields. Black Diamond makes a pole with a pick, the **Whippet**, and a few companies make an ice ax with a telescoping bottom pole. You could tape your ax to your pole, but I've never seen it done. The main drawback for a ski pole ax is that the pick gets in the way when it is not useful, and can be dangerous during alpine stumbles. You can self-arrest with ski poles, many ski mountaineers do it. Trekking poles make great stick clips, double as tent poles, can repair a broken tent pole, be used as a splint, to self-arrest with, and have many other uses around camp like hanging food. If you're ski mountaineering or setting up shelter with trekking poles you may want to bring a **pole splint and duct tape** for broken poles, or tape something rigid to it like a stick, pack stay, or nut tool.

Sleeping Systems

Finding the perfect sleeping system for a climb is an art. Sure car camping or plush base camping just requires a warm enough bag and sturdy tent, but carrying your bivy system on a climb requires more thought.

Fill: Down or Synthetic

First consider the insulation: down or synthetic. Down is perfect for most one to two night expeditions because of its warmth to weight ratio, but consider a synthetic bag if the weather is questionable, you're on a bigwall, or in winter conditions if there's a chance the bag can get wet and not dry out. New types of **waterproof down** have only recently come out and not enough testing has been done to say if this down will indeed be

Courtesy Stubai

as good as synthetic insulation in wet environments or low-breathability situation. If you are very careful and conditions inside the shelter don't become tropical, a down bag should work.

No matter what insulation you use, getting it wet is miserable. Down isn't as bad as the marketing media would have you think. Down does become pretty useless when wet, but it takes a few days for this to happen unless it's exposed to a lot of water – simply protecting the bag (or jacket) can offset this if you're careful. If you spill water on a down bag (or jacket) the shell should repel the water. It takes pressure from compressing the down into water to really get it wet, or constant humidity from sweat evaporating or from humid conditions. Sleeping out in the rain will probably get you through one night, and sleeping in a humid tent or bivy sack will probably get you through two nights. Layering properly should keep your jacket dry. Why wear a down garment if you are sweating or if it is raining? If snow or humidity starts to dampen the down (or synthetic for that matter) and you have more than a day left, dry it inside the tent and lay it over your torso to help push the moisture out.

Bottom line, if you think you can get away with down then do so. If you think conditions will get it wet and your trip depends on it, then go with synthetic. Wet multiday winter trips and big walls should go with synthetic. One to three day trips (depending on conditions) can go with down although at the end of day two or three it may be a bit soggy and weigh more.

Staying Warm and Asleep
Knowing how warm or cold you sleep is also important to bring the lightest bag you can safely sleep in with enough energy and will to climb the next day. Wearing all of your clothes, brewing a **hot water bottle**, and eating a calorically dense meal of fats and carbs just before bed will help you stay warm – at least until those cold pre-dawn hours. Hand-warmers may add some warmth. Another trick is if you build a fire (emergency fire starters are a good item in the kit) and heat some rocks to put in your bag. You'll need to wrap them in something like foil from your stove's windscreen or a freeze-dried food pouch. **Sleeping pills** can also help you ride out some discomfort if they are appropriately safe to take.

It's almost negligent to give recommendations on temperature ranges to suggest for summer, winter, or shoulder season trips. Two similarly sized people can have drastically different warmth needs when they sleep. Any given day could affect how cold you sleep, as can the humidity, type of shelter, and companion next to you. A bad nights sleep will affect your performance much worse than carrying an extra few ounces or even pounds. However, if it won't kill you or jeopardize your trip, see what you can get away with, experiment with a lighter bag. I find that I am cold no matter what around 4am and was able to start bringing lighter bags once I discovered it didn't matter how warm my bag was.

Where to Sleep
Your dry bivy spot may be a lake if it starts to rain. Avoid sleeping in a low spot where water will drain or collect. The more porous your sleep surface, the better chance you have that water won't pool around you. Fine-grained porous surfaces like sand and dirt may not be able to absorb water quickly enough, however. Rock slabs are great if they allow for the water to run off quickly and not collect in a depression. Caves work as long as the entrance doesn't slope inward or your feet dangle out the lip.

Obviously be aware of sleeping in a possible avalanche path (look at a map if it is dark out), or right below a wall subject to rock fall (look around for meteors). Try and anticipate wind direction either by the forecast, or know that cooling air rushes downhill and down valley. It may be worth the extra time spent constructing a wind block out of snow or rocks (scatter the rocks in the morning). Areas very protected by winds are more subject to bugs, as are areas near stagnant water. Before you stop for the night in a buggy area, scout around for an area of low bug concentration (it may only be a few yards away) over the most scenic spot.

No Sleeping Bag

The best way to stay warm without the weight is to just climb through the night, maybe napping the next day if time allows. The old saying, "if you bring bivy gear you will bivy" isn't necessarily true with the new possibilities of bringing a sub 2 pound bivy kits these days. If there's a strong possibility of a bivy and conditions would kill or really sap your strength, then err on the safe side and bring enough to endure a semi-horrible night. If warm(ish) summer nights allow more room for error, an open bivy – or as I call it "alpen-waiting" – could be on the menu. Make sure to let loved ones know of this possibility so you don't get accidentally rescued. A **super-light space blanket or VBL** is worth the extra weight to stash in your pack for any climb that has a remote chance of bivy on the climb or descent. SOL makes some very light emergency bivies, including a breathable one. It's a hard decision whether to keep climbing or descending, or to bivy. If you think you can stay on route by going up and have a good headlamp, or going down even off route will at least get you out of the elements or put you in a better spot than you are now – then keep going. You never know what the weather will do during the night or next day. Don't keep going if you don't think you have the gear or skills to push on without getting hurt or putting yourself in a situation that you can't reverse. However, just because there is an absence of light doesn't mean you have to stop.

Breathable space blanket courtesy SOL

Another compromise is to bring a **bothy bag**. These very light floorless and frameless tents are designed to be supported by the counterweight of two climbers, or with the use of poles. Bothy bags are great to wait out a storm during the day. You can make your own with some sil-nylon and a sewing machine (Seam Grip the seams). Take a 10' by 5' rectangle of sil-nylon and fold it in half. Take another section of 5' by 1.5' sil-nylon, fold it in half, and cut it into two triangles that you stitch together to make the sides. A bit more complex, but not too hard, is to sew on two tunnel vents to provide circulation. Keep the shelter up by you and your partner leaning against the inside walls, suspending it from an anchor above (add tie in loops), using two crossed poles in the center inside the bag, or two pairs of poles inside the bag at both ends. You can use a **tent fly or sil-tarp** tent as a makeshift bothy in a pinch.

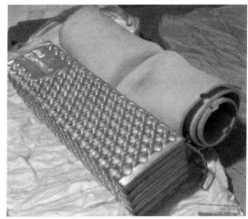
Z-Rest and hardman pad

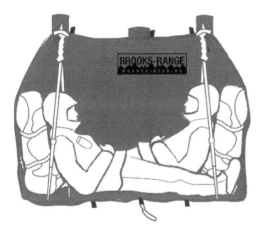
Courtesy Brooks Range

Sleeping Bags and Pads

Courtesy Klymit

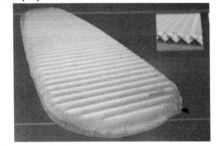
Thermarest Neoair

Unsheltered bivies with an **ultralight down or synthetic bag** and using the rope, backpack (crawl inside), and/or bivy pad frame works well in the summer with a solid forecast. Adding a light closed-cell foam pad like a **Z-Rest or thin 1/8-3/8" Ensolite "hardman pad"** adds little weight and a lot more comfort. Be sure to reinforce a hole and tie a keeper loop to your pad to keep it on the wall. **Water resistant sleeping bag covers**, space blankets, or even wrapping up in a light sil-nylon tent fly or tarp can make a light rain or windy night tolerable and increase the bag's warmth. **Half bags** and a belay jacket weight less than a bag plus a jacket you're already carrying. **Quilt-style sleeping bags** are becoming the insulation of choice with many fast and light backpackers. Less material because of the lack of zipper and hood save quite a bit of weight, and they can be modified for hot nights as a blanket, cold nights as a sleeping bag, and can be shared.

Quilt-style bag. Courtesy Katabatic

Half bag and parka. Courtesy Nunatak.

Some bags have **no bottom insulation** with a sleeve to insert a sleeping pad. In theory these save weight, but in practice are uncomfortable and a quilt may serve you better. No-bottom bags are great for **layering bags** by using a down bag on the inside and bottomless synthetic on top. Layering bags with the down on the inside is a decent modular system and water vapor should push into the synthetic over bag.

Epic fabric sleeping bag cover

Hoods are overrated on sleeping bags unless you sleep on your back, except for cold conditions. For more warmth or comfort, start with a better ground pad. Don't breath into your bag if you're a side-sleeper or you'll soak the bag. **Wider spooning bags** designed for two climbers, a slightly larger quilt, or a single bag that has a **triangle shaped nylon extender** (gotta make it yourself) save a ton of weight. They are a great option for your significant other, and a warm secret between you and your buddy.

V-shaped bag extender. Courtesy Wayne Wallace

Easy approaches and basecamps allow for **warmer/heavier bags**. Go for warmth and comfort if you don't have to carry your bag when climbing. General mountaineering climbing where you're schlepping big loads and slogging up the slope also demand a slightly heavier bag and synthetic insulation unless you are extremely careful. The difference between a top quality 32° down bag and 0° synthetic bag is only a small percentage of your total pack weight in those situations. Once the temps drop in higher altitude or winter expeditions, down or a down/synthetic combo makes sense once again. One fun trick is to draw a chess, checkers, backgammon, etc. board on your sleeping pad or backpack pad.

Besides the light ghetto options described above, there are a few **very light inflatable pads** out there that either use cut-out airspaces, foil, or both to trap and reflect heat. Check out the company Balloonbed for an interesting lightweight sleeping pad. Bring a small section of **repair tape and a small tube of Seam Grip** when they inevitably pop. Double up on closed-cell foam pads and inflatable pads when it gets really cold. **Luxury pads** are amazing, but get really heavy. Some **insulated pads** contain synthetic or down insulation for added comfort and warmth. These are only useful at basecamp, but they are awesome. Don't get a down pad if you will wind up moving camp and have to inflate the pad multiple times per trip as the down will get too damp from your breath. Bring a warmer bag instead of a bulky pad on a bivy. If using a corrugated foam pad, be aware that snow likes to get trapped in the ridges.

Vapor Barrier Liners (VBL) and Over Bags

Another solution for maximizing your warmth is a vapor barrier liner (VBL). A VBL can really increase your bag's warmth, by about 20° F, but there are major drawbacks.

The trapped warm air can soak your clothes, but wearing the bag sans outer layers immediately reduces your warmth because you've got fewer clothes on. You can try and lay your jacket over the VBL between you and your bag, but unless you lay motionless, it may fall off to a spot that won't offer much insulation. You can also get **vapor barrier clothes** so you can put your other layers on over the VBL suit. This solves many problems of a VBL bag, and you may want to consider this for multi night trips. The huge downside to this system is that you have to strip to your long underwear at night and in the morning – a very unpleasant experience. The major upside is the huge increase in warmth for the weight of a VBL suit. A VBL works best in really cold conditions where you're not going to be perspiring enough to matter much, or using it on the outside of your bag like a space blanket (or use a space blanket as your VBL) for a one-night only bivy assuming your bag will get wet and you'll be unable to dry it. A synthetic bag is a safer bet here, but is heavier.

You may be able to get away with using a lightweight synthetic insulated over bag with your down bag inside of it if worried about getting your down bag wet. Your perspiration will heat out of the inner down and condense on the outside layer of your synthetic over bag. You will probably wind up saving more weight by just using a full synthetic bag, but if perspiration or condensation are going to be big issues, a synthetic over bag with or without a bottom can be useful. Synthetic sleeping bag liners do add warmth, but for the weight, a warmer rated bag will do more.

If you are planning on an open bivy, be aware of the dew point (see weather section). If there's a chance of a dewy night, a lightweight breathable water resistant bag cover is worth the weight. **Waterproof-breathable bivy sacks** are an option for winter climbs and big walls to protect your bag from snow, rain, and wind if ledge space is sparse. Otherwise there are lighter shelter options for two. Waterproof breathable shells on sleeping bag won't do much and are only useful for protecting from interior condensation or a high dew point. They will increase heat retention, but will also increase water retention. These only work in very cold climates or for open bivies. A light bag cover will dry quicker, cost you less, and make your bag more useful when you don't need it. If you are just using a bag for basecamp in very cold weather, then these shells are nice and will dry out in the tent during the day. Water resistant shells are a pretty good compromise between breathability and carrying the extra weight of a light bag cover. Of course a hybrid bag with down on the inside, synthetic on the outside, and a superlight semi-waterproof shell with breathable reflective dots would be nice for open bivies or humid tents, but no one makes this.

Single Wall Tents and Tarps

Black Diamond Betalight tarp tent

There are single wall tents and tarps available that offer more space and comfort that weight less than two bivy sacks if pitching space allows. First consider a tarp-style tent. **Tarps and tarp-tents** are more spacious and lighter than even sil-nylon single wall tents, and can withstand some pretty intense storms. Some, like the Black Diamond Beta Light have additional floors and mosquito netting that when added, still weigh as much as a sil-nylon tent. Condensation is less of an issue with tarps. They also make excellent cook tents, and tops for dug-out snow pits. They are not as warm or sturdy as a tent, and do require you to bring one or two trekking poles.

Black Diamond First Light

Single wall tents are best applied on technical alpine climbs where shelter is required for survival. **Non-waterproof single wall sil-nylon** alpine tents are a compromise in that they are much lighter and offer somewhat better ventilation than waterproof-breathable style single wall tents. The non-waterproof tents are best used on alpine routes where snow easily sheds, and rainstorms are generally short enough to not soak through. Some of these single wall tents don't have guy lines on the sidewalls of the tents, causing the tent to bow in during windy conditions. You can bar tack a sling to the side of the tent. Be sure to Seam Grip it. You can sew the sling so part of it goes inside the tent for clipping into. Beefier **waterproof single wall tents** offer superior storm protection and are less likely to fail in winds, but are extremely expensive and a bit heavier. If for some reason you are using any type of single wall tent in non-stormy conditions or protected location, you can crisscross trekking poles, protecting the fabric with a helmet to save weight instead of using the poles provided (assuming you're bringing trekking poles). Brooks-Range offers tents that can utilize your avalanche probe and/or trekking poles instead of the provided poles to save weight. Most single wall tents don't have a **vestibule** to save weight, so cooking needs to be done inside or outside in good weather. You can get a vestibule add-in on some, but the whole point is to save weight and deal.

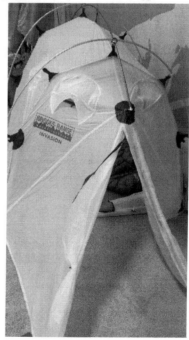

This tent can be pitched with ski poles and a probe

Firstlight tent pitched with ski poles. Courtesy Josh Kaplan

Double Wall and Base Camp Tents

The best tent to bring for any extended stay at a base camp, or in harsh conditions is a **double wall expedition style tent** because single wall tents are not only cramped, they are less secure and get wet with condensation eventually. They also have a **vestibule**, which is a very nice luxury. Double wall tents are much heavier, however. **Bug tents and large tarp or dome-style cook tents** are also great base camp luxuries.

Portaledges

If hauling, you have the option to haul up a portaledge. The obvious downside to these are the extra weight and bulk for hauling. The up side is that you can bivy whenever and wherever you want. Even on routes with multiple ledges like the Nose, a portaledge can give you a leg up when crowds fill available ledges. Also, you have a ledge to belay on whenever you want. You will need a **rainfly** for your ledge if there's even a chance of getting pinned down because bailing would be too dangerous in bad weather. If you don't bring a fly, you should definitely bring a **bivy sack**.

Courtesy Runoutcustoms

In fact, bringing a bivy or light over bag for your bag inside a rainfly in wet/humid conditions may also be necessary as it can become a wet mess inside a fly. If the fly doesn't attach securely below the ledge, you must rig something to keep updrafts and rain from getting inside the fly from below. Rigging a **tent pole** around the inside of the fly can help push the fly out, increasing room and keeping the wet inside of the fly from getting you wet. Water can creep in from your tie-in by following the rope into your bag. Tie in with some slack, tie a knot, and weight it so it is below your level and the water will drip off of that point. If you plan on standing on a portaledge for belays and the angle is steep enough without roofs, you can keep the ledge setup attached to the rope above the haul bag, flying it like a flag. Clip the top and bottom of one side of the ledge to the rope. Only do this on pitches that overhang top to bottom unless you want to trash the ledge, however.

Courtesy Black Diamond

Courtesy Grivel. K2 Makes a similar produt.

It can be a nightmare sleeping on sloping ledges without a portaledge, and getting the right amount of tie-in slack. Leave some slack for moving around and use an ascender to fine tune the length. Think carefully about where the haulbags and portaledge will be oriented when setting up your anchor for the night. Moving things around after the fact can make the last hours or seconds of daylight nasty. Practice this on a cliff with very heavy bags and a ledge to get an idea.

Cheap climbers have been known to rig a hammock, pool deck lounger, or PVC pipe as their ledge. Do that at your own risk!

Caves and Igloos

Other shelter options are rock caves under boulders or talus fields and digging snow caves. Rock caves may flood or be infested with rodents, bats, or bugs so do a little inspecting before you fall asleep. A good **sturdy shovel** is indispensable in making snow shelters, and part of a standard avalanche rescue kit or big mountain bivy kit. You can buy small plastic scooping blades, or **ice-ax attachments**, but only when weight trumps everything else – even speed because a shovel will cut the time drastically. A snow saw can also be helpful.

Digging a snow cave requires a slope to dig into. Test the integrity before both of you go inside to sleep. You want your sleeping chamber higher than the entrance hole to increase warmth and decrease drafts, but good luck actually accomplishing this. Poke a hole in the top to avoid suffocating. Use your poles and probes or pack stays if you have either to gauge the thickness of the walls. Digging generates a lot of warmth, which can be good, and can get you overheated and soaked. Make sure you've got your shell on, and de-layer underneath when you get warm.

If you have the time and space, you can make a ghetto igloo, or Quincy. Pile up a bunch of snow and pack it down. Wait a while for the snow pile to settle, and dig down for the entrance (to prevent drafts and heat loss) and then up and in, hollowing out enough space for you to sleep. Poke a hole in the top to ventilate noxious emissions from your breath and stove. Do some structural integrity provocations to the outside before you hop inside in case you get buried from a weak structure. A crappier version of this would be to dig a trench in the snow and cover it with a tarp, or if the snow is solid, make an A-Frame roof with snow blocks. Crevasses and moats can be very useful snow shelters as well.

Misc. Tent Info

Ground cloths are a lot like gaiters in most scenarios, they are redundant and can make things soggier. If your tent floor can't handle it or keep water out, get a new tent. They also don't allow water to percolate into the ground and can act as a funnel to collect more water. The best use would be sleeping out on an inflatable mattress to avoid popping it. A superlight emergency bivy can do double duty by protecting your pad, and crawling into if it rains.

You may want to bring along a **small tent repair kit** on longer trips with a pole splint, fabric repair tape, zipper repair or some safety pins. Spray your tent zippers with silicone spray at home to prevent problems, or to aid in frozen zippers and zipper clogged with dirt from desert areas. For multi night winter tent camping, a lightweight **broom** is useful to sweep out snow, and a **sponge** is indispensable for removing water and spills.

There are usually plenty of rocks lying around to get away with not bringing **tent stakes**. Sticks from deadfall also work. In winter, snow stakes, and buried extra stuff sacks are helpful for multi night stays. If you are moving camp or climbing with your camp in your pack, pickets, **deadmen**, and ice axes can be used. You can buy ultralight titanium stakes, but again, rocks and sticks are free.

Pay attention to prevailing winds, avalanche slopes, water drainage paths, trampling meadows, and ant colonies when pitching camp. Use a smartphone app or an inclinometer to figure out where to put your head. Establish where you both will be using the toilet, and practice leave no trace and bear country camping ethics.

Cooking Systems

Besides the extra food, cook systems are the 2nd heaviest item to add to your pack for a bivy after your sleep system, and this provides the climber with yet another simple item to totally geek out over. You need fuel, a container to heat, and a stove or something to hold the fuel.

Stove Purpose
The most basic need for a cook system is to melt snow for water. Do not forget that you need a little water to prime the pot for snow. Dumping snow onto a hot pot will burn the dirt and minerals in the snow and make your water taste awful. You will also waste fuel because the fluffy snow has very little heat capacity. A slurry has the best concentration of snow and water, so be patient.

If melting snow isn't an issue, the only other reason to bring a cook kit besides comfort would be to save water weight by bringing dried food. This only saves weight if you can find water en route. Otherwise water in pre-cooked food or food that doesn't need cooking is just as good and weighs just the same as water you carried with you to add to dried food. Most dried food compared to food that doesn't require cooking requires a lot more water than what is contained in the "fresh" food so you can't compare the two. How much water is in a dinner and breakfast's worth of bars and dried fruit (assuming that's what is replacing your dried meals)? I don't know, but you can guess. A "normal" lightweight alpine stove setup that would heat enough water for two dinners and one breakfast for two (or more depending on temps) weighs about ½ liter of water. So after one bivy, a stove probably makes up its own weight – again only if you can find water en route. The other drawback to stoves is that they add time and are prone to failure. The plus side to bringing a stove when you don't necessarily need one is that you will probably get more hydrated from a wetter dinner, and from more palatable hot drinks at night and in the morning. Also, a morning without hot coffee isn't much of a morning.

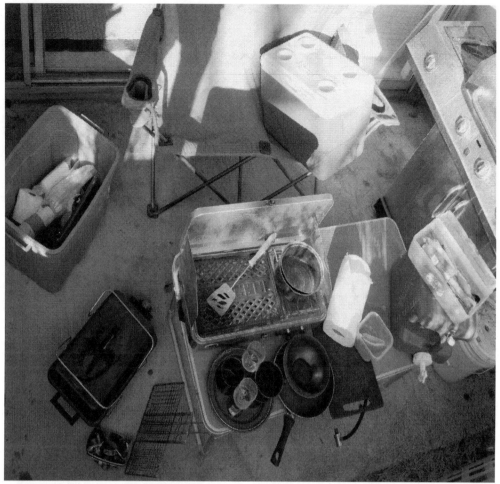

Car camping kitchen (optional BBQ grill lower left)

Car Camping Stoves

Coleman propane oven with 2-burners on top

There are basically six types of stove options useful for climbers. I'll describe them from heaviest to lightest. The heaviest, if car camping, is a propane or gas powered "Coleman" **double burner stove**. The best car camping stove I've ever used is a combo **grill/one burner unit**. Instead of being creative with a fry pan or pot every night, just slap on some meat and veggies on the gas grill. **Cheap gas grills** offer more space than a combo unit, however.

High Efficiency Stoves

Car camping aside, the heaviest stove you would actually pack are **Jetboil and Reactor** stoves. These super heat efficient units boil water in the blink of an eye, and wind up saving weight on gas

after several days of backpacking. I, and many others, have attempted to graph exactly how many liters of water you would need to boil in order for these units to save enough weight on fuel to offset the total weight. The reality is, it doesn't matter. The first reason why it doesn't matter is that you never want to cut it so close that you unexpectedly run out of fuel. Also changing temps, wind, and pressure create too many variables. But the real reason why you should bring this type of stove over another would be because the climb you are on requires quick snow melting or boiling time, durability, extra wind protection, and ease of use.

Inverted canister stove. Courtesy of Jetboil.

Jetboils shine on approaches and at camp for pure ease of use, and Reactors shine on long snow/ice climbs that require melting water. The extra weight of a Reactor should be worth it to you for speed, safety, and comfort. Weight savings due to efficiency over time should be a bonus, but again, with leftover fuel, savings will probably be offset. If you plan on cooking inside your tent, or hanging your stove, these are by far your best option. Making your own hanging stove is pretty easy with some thin cable, a punch, and a swage. Jetboil and MSR both make **hanging kits**. Making your own should be simple enough, just try it out first. Jetboil just came out with a new stove, the Joule, that inverts the gas canister and shines in cold weather along with the Reactor (but is heavier).

Liquid Fuel Stoves

Liquid gas stoves are the next heaviest stoves. Granted that after a few days the savings in weight from not bringing multiple fuel canisters will make them lighter in the long run, but the stoves themselves are heavier than the gas canister-style option. These liquid gas backpacking stoves are probably the least useful stove for climbing, but they do have their place. To begin with, you can adjust the flame a lot easier. This allows you to be more creative in your cooking, either car camping or on long trips where the extra weight of both the stove and cookware is worth it for sanity. If you don't mind messing around with priming the stove, and dealing with clogged lines, they are the lightest option for week-long trips.

Gas canisters are difficult to get on international expeditions, and most liquid fuel stoves allow for multiple forms of fuel to be used. You can't fly with gas canisters, even trips to somewhere moderately cultured could be frustrating when you can't find a store that's open or nearby that sells gas canisters, although many standard grocery stores, sporting goods stores, and Wal-Mart type stores now stock gas canisters. Liquid gas is cheaper and on extended base camp sessions, it's easier and cheaper to just have a jug or two of liquid gas outside the tent. Finally, gas canisters won't work in very cold conditions if canisters won't de-condense into vapor.

Some liquid gas stoves are better designed for adjustability and fuel savings for general cooking and boiling, like the **MSR Whisperlite**. Some are designed for efficiency at high output for melting snow, like the **MSR XGK**. There are **hybrid stoves that accept both liquid and compressed gas**, and allow compressed gas to work in cold conditions by inverting the canister and vaporizing the liquid by pre-heating near the flame. By inverting the canister with a blended fuel, the propane portion will float on top, and help push the fuel below out. These are useful cold climbs where you want to use canister fuel for cooking in the tent. Inverting canister fuel on a stove not designed for this, or making your own adaptor is a very bad idea. You may get the liquid compassed fuel to come out, but it won't be an efficient flame because there is no preheating mechanism or regulation. You will more likely burn yourself or tent with a giant uncontrolled fireball. Cooking inside the tent during storms should be only done in a vestibule with gas stoves to prevent burning your bags from flare-ups and to allow for ventilation. If you are doing a winter climb and are in doubt whether to bring a canister or liquid fuel stove, err on something like a liquid fuel XGK.

Whiperlight with inverted canister and liquid fuel options

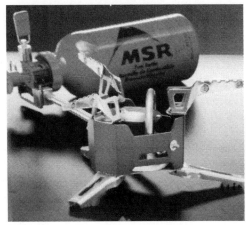

XGK

Liquid Fuel
The most efficient and cleanest burning fuel is **"white gas"** specifically sold for camping stoves and found in most camping and sporting goods stores. This is the fuel to get. Unfortunately it can be hard to find this fuel in a pinch or out of the country. Your stove may have (and should if you're out of the country) the option to burn **unleaded gas, diesel, or kerosene**. Unleaded gas should be your first choice if white gas is unavailable. If you can, get environmental unleaded gas meant for lawnmowers as it has fewer additives that can be harmful to breathe. Kerosene should be next on the list. It requires more priming and will clog up your stove much more than gas will. Only use diesel if you have no other choice. Before you go on an international trip, do your research to find out what kind of fuel you need to ask for and where you can get it. Try it out before hitting the trail.

> A general rule of thumb for how much liquid white gas to bring is 8 oz. per person per day if melting snow and cooking meals, and even less, like around 4 oz. if you are only melting snow into palatable water or only boiling or heating liquid water.

Canister Stoves
Lightweight canister stoves are the lightest short-term efficient stoves you can use. Many models weight sub three ounces, not including the canister. Some even have regulators

to control output in cold temps to increase efficiency. Because of the ease of use, lack of clogging issues compared to liquid fuel, and safety from flare-ups and less CO2 output, they should be the goto stove for most short trips and warmer alpine climbs. Depending on the size of the fuel canister and pot you bring, your entire cook kit can weigh less than a pound. Canister stove setups can actually wind up being lighter than liquid fuel stoves (or close) on longer trips so don't assume you need a liquid fuel stove on a long trip.

Canister Fuel
Canisters have some combo of n-butane, isobutene, and propane in them. The various types of compressed fuel need to be vaporized, but they all stop vaporizing and remain liquid (thus trapped) at different cold temperatures. n-Butane remains liquid at 31° F, isobutane at 11° F, and propane at -43° F. The colder the fuel can still vaporize, the more pressure the fuel is under, and the thicker/heavier the canister needs to be. The weight of the actual difference in fuel type is not important. The act of vaporizing these liquids is a change of state of matter and requires energy, which is acquired by the change of the liquid going from a high to a low-pressure system. This makes your canister cold, thus lowering the temperature of the liquid below the outside temperature. Let's say it is 30° out: the n-butane isn't going to vaporize, but just sits useless in the canister.

Now it's 10° and only the propane is working. Add to this the additional drop in temperatures from the change in state of liquid to gas, and now it can be a lot warmer outside than 31° before the n-butane becomes useless. So why not just get 100% propane? There's always something. The lower the vapor temps, the more pressure the gas exerts, the thicker metal you need to keep it contained. Also, increased altitude actually helps with your cartridge because of the increased pressure differential, but with increased altitude comes decreased temps. Don't forget that the higher you are, the boiling point may lower but cooking time of non-instant foods will increase drastically (why are you cooking food that requires cook time?). Once a certain altitude is reached your stove could be pumping out so much fuel that the flame can't be controlled. Beware.

In the order of butane, isobutene, and propane the current fuel blends available right now are: Primus (70/10/20), MSR (0/80/20), SnowPeak (0/85/15), JetBoil's unpublished blend is estimated at (0/70-80/20-30), and off-brand or camping oriented canisters generally have a ratio of (70/0/30) percent ratios. To pick the best, I'd suggest finding how much gas is inside the can of a few of the highest propane level brands, and weigh the can. The lightest gas per ounce with the highest concentration of propane is the best for cold, and the lightest with the highest concentration of butane is best for warm weather.

> For trips when you are melting snow and making instant food, figure on about 250 mL or 8 oz. of fuel for a team of two per day. You could get away with the same volume of fuel for a week in the summer (or none at all!). I plan on 2 oz. for two per day in the summer if just eating instant and being careful about wasting fuel and 4 oz. if it is cold and windy but not melting snow. It all depends on your stove and pot system, temperature, wind, altitude, snow vs. liquid water source, how much cooking you do, etc. The only real way to know is to practice. If you depend on the stove for melting water do not be conservative. MSR suggests 2 oz. for a team of two per day in the summer (sounds about right), and 16 oz. per day for a team of two in winter (sounds a bit much).

If you can keep the canister warm, then outside temps can be reckoned with. To get your canister to work more efficiently (or at all) you may need to warm it to offset the cooling through vaporization effects. Here are some various tricks. Setting it in a pool of water, even an inch, will help disperse the cold into the water. Freshen the water as it cools or freezes. Keep the canister insulated from the ground on a **small cutout piece of foam padding**. Keep the canister warm in your jacket or sleeping. Use some chemical **handwarmers** on it. The best, but not-so-safe method is to create a **copper wire heat exchanger**. Your stove can explode with this setup. Really, it can. Take a 1/8" diameter copper wire flattened with a hammer, put both ends in contact with flame and wrap the remainder of wire around canister. You can wrap some foam padding in aluminum foil and wrapping this over the wire/canister to prevent yourself or gear from getting burnt from the wire. Check regularly to make sure it's not getting too hot so your canister blows up.

Copper wire heat exchanger. Courtesy, Monte Lamb

Some international climbing areas like Patagonia or Nepal have rigged setups to refill a cartridge stove. Don't try this without knowing what you are doing!

Stove Accessories

If you have a liquid gas stove, you must know how to completely dissemble the stove and clean it and the fuel pump when it clogs with carbon or dirt. Bring the **repair kit** that came with it that contains a little inorganic oil (spit only works for so long), some extra gaskets for the pump, a wrench (some spoons have wrench cut-outs), and an additional jet. Electronic, or **Piezo igniters** built into stoves are handy but should not be relied on. Think of them as a backup for losing your lighter instead of the opposite. **Mini lighters** are an essential, so carry at least two (one stashed away safely somewhere). Industrial Revolution makes a powerful **flint and steel** that weighs nothing (½ oz.) and is a great backup lighter called the Light My Fire Steel Mini.

Commercial **windscreens** are burly, but replaceable with a couple layers of aluminum foil in most cases. If you plan on walking out with gas still in the stove (just a night stay), you can get away without one if you can get the stove out of the wind. **Bulky heat exchangers** made to go over pots on non-Jet Boil/Reactor stoves are mostly worthless because you should have brought a Jetboil or Reactor. Use them when you are using a Whisperlight or XGK at a basecamp when weight isn't important and you want to save some fuel. They do make up their weight after a time, but it's not worth risking bringing less fuel based on an iffy calculation.

Tiny fuel cartridges can tip over when a big pot is on top of them. JetBoil makes a very light **base support** that snaps onto the bottom of various sized canisters. I believe the weight is worth not spilling. A small cutout piece of closed cell foam to put under your canister is also worth the weight in the winter. It can also serve as a scalding guard for placing your hot pot of water on. Sleeping pads, backpacks, and shovel blades work too, but not as well or as safely.

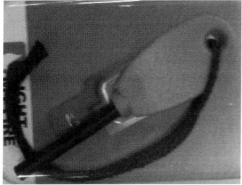

Light My Fire mini flint and steel

Back: aluminum foil windscreen. Middle: cat-food stove, Esbit titanium/Fosters stove, Soto canister stove, MSR Reactor. Front: MSR spoon with stove cleaning attachments, Edelrid spoon/fork, pot grips, GSI measuring cup, Fossil origami bowl (on top of cup)

Minimalist Stove Options

One of the lightest options, and I'm talking ounces for the whole setup, are **ESBIT and alcohol stoves**. Both can use extremely lightweight (sub one ounce) stoves to heat or boil water. Alcohol is a bit heavier than ESBIT tablets, but provides a cleaner and more stable flame. Luckily alcohol can be stored in lightweight plastic containers unlike white gas. Alcohol stoves are a great alternative to white gas or canister stove on short trips. Both types of stove do not perform well at all in windy cold conditions, are not hot or efficient enough for melting snow, and take much longer to heat water than gas. You can buy very light alcohol stoves, or just make your own by punching, holes around the top of a **can of cat food**. In the summer plan on boiling about 12 oz. of water per oz. of alcohol, or 5 oz. per person per day. Factoring in the weight of your stove and fuel containers, alcohol is a much lighter alternative for a few days.

ESBIT tablets weight about ½ ounce each. ESBIT tablets smell awful when they burn, and take a lot of time to heat up a liter of water, but are the lightest commercial fuel available. You can use the cat-food setup for the tablet, but use a paper clip to balance the tablet on so it can get air. The pot can't sit directly on top, so use some baling wire to rig a support to allow air flow below the pot. Better yet, there are sub 1 oz. **titanium ESBIT stands** available. The standard bear trap style ESBIT stoves commonly sold for emergency camping or car kits are too heavy to make the ESBIT a viable heat source. Two tablets are generally plenty to get a liter of water hot enough for two 12 oz. coffees or to heat a freeze-dried meal in decent conditions. ESBIT stoves are the lightest choice for a day or two if you have the time to wait for the water to heat.

An alcohol stove with a titanium pot and wind screen is safe and efficient enough to be a viable option for longer summer trips with a liquid water supply. ESBIT stoves aren't hot or reliable enough compared to the weight savings of alcohol, take too long, and smell like crap. However, an ESBIT setup with a titanium base and the **beer can pot** (described later) only weighs two ounces, essentially nothing. A long climb with a miserable bivy can be turned into smiles and sunshine when you can make a hot cup of coffee or hot meal without anyone bitching about the extra weight if you have a little extra time. Also, ESBIT tablets make excellent fire starters for emergencies.

The lightest possible option is a **campfire**. The drawbacks are reliability (you're out of luck if you planned on it and it rained or there's no wood available), safety (don't burn down the forest), legality (many areas don't allow fires), and leave no trace ethics (although you can make a small fire with minimal impact). Careful getting the pot out of the fire! Still, if you're going ultralight and are a campfire wiz, why not? There are some stoves, like the **Biolite**, that run on biomass (pine needles, pine cones, etc.), and have a small built in fan to magically burn a small amount of fuel with minimal effort. Some even use the heat energy to charge USB powered devices! Unfortunately they weight just enough to make other lightweight stoves a better choice for shorter trips. A cartridge stove and a large 250 gram fuel cartridge which supplies about 5 days of fuel for two in summer weighs the same as a Biolite stove. If you are extremely carbon-footprint conscious, the Biolite stove has much less impact. If you can get fuel, a Biolite stove is the lightest option over a longer period of time.

If you want to geek out over stove and fuel weight options based on the length of your trip check out: howardjohnson.name/Backpacking/Stove/Stoves.htm for a calculator. I can't guarantee its accuracy. Weight is the least important factor, however. Bring the stove and fuel that best suits your needs and conditions and the weight issue will take care of itself.

Biolite stove

Pots

Figuring out the perfect pot and eating bowl/cup setup not only can save weight, but also save pack space as these items are pretty bulky. Aluminum is heavier than titanium, but transfers heat into the pan better than titanium. If you plan on melting a lot of snow, go with an **aluminum pot** for the sake of speed. Nitpicking on where weight savings come into play over time is made moot by the fact that it's better to go with what works better. The bigger the aluminum pot, the faster and more efficient large amounts of snow melting are. A **2-3 liter** pot works great at camp, a **1 liter pot** is perfect for long climbs where you'll be melting snow en route, and a **1.5 liter aluminum pot** for longer (multi night) climbs. Unless you plan on gourmet cooking, **titanium pots (.75-1 liter)** are the way to go for summer trips. Reactor and Jetboils already come with an aluminum pot, but JetBoil offers a titanium option.

A 16 oz. Heineken beer can with the top cut off fits alcohol and ESBIT stoves perfectly and is still lighter than even a **500 ml titanium pot**. Fosters beer cans are too tall and narrow to have enough surface area for the flame, unless you live in Utah and can't find a Heineken for the life of you. You can use a punch and some baling wire to make a little handle, and put a wrap or two of fireproof tape around the can to insulate your hand, and use a small sheet of aluminum foil for the lid. These additions still weigh less than a titanium pot for your ghetto 2 oz. ultralight setup. Don't expect much, but if just heating water for coffee or a free-dried meal, this works in good conditions.

Eating Container Logistics
Mentally go through where your food is going to be cooked (in the pot, bowl, in the packaging), and in what order it will be consumed to avoid bringing too much cookware and to avoid juggling the order in which you cook, eat, and drink. If both you and your partner eat the same thing and don't have a hot drink, plan on having the hot drink after finishing your meal, or only plan on having a hot drink, then you can get away with a single titanium pot. A **1-liter pot** should suffice if you share a freeze-dried meal with a follow-up non-cook snack, or if waiting for the other to finish **another 500 mL titanium pot** will work.

Things get tricky at breakfast when you want a coffee and oatmeal, don't want to share a pot to eat and drink out of, or need two pots for whatever reason. A neat trick to solve the breakfast/coffee conundrum is to use **two titanium pots** of similar volume, but different shapes so they can nest. One pot can be placed upside-down on the other, replacing the need for a lid, and acting as a heat exchanger! Usually just the oatmeal needs the lid, as the upside-down pot now becomes the coffee vessel and doesn't need a lid since it doesn't need to get hot enough.

Stacking two titanium pots. *Courtesy Wayne Wallace*

A titanium pot weighs just as much as a bowl, mug, or measuring cup – all common backpacking eating and drinking vessels. If you're being gas conscious, a lid really helps with heating efficiency. A **square of tinfoil** does the same job and is much lighter. Don't bother with a lid in the summer if you've got plenty of gas except for straining purposes or to keep pine needles and bugs out of your pot. If you aren't sharing, then you'll need at least one other container.

Foldable **origami bowls** are one of the lightest and best backcountry eating containers, much more so than silicone collapsible bowls. Once unsnapped, they are super easy to clean, and are useful for scooping snow for melt water. They take up zero pack space (put them flat inside your hydration pocket), and essentially weighs nothing. They don't work so well for holding hot drinks, and if your pot is in use or nasty from food, you'll need a hot water vessel. The **foil bags** that come with freeze-dried meals can be reused for breakfast or the next freeze-dried meal for further weight savings. Red-sauce meals linger into the next a bit more, but you can save some weight/bulk by only bringing one package, and repacking other freeze dried dinners into lighter Ziplocs.

A **water bottle** (preferably a hard Nalgene-style, but a 1-liter Gatorade bottle shouldn't kill you) can work for your hot drink. A **cut off bottom to a plastic 1-2 liter drink bottle, or cut off bottom to a collapsible Platypus water bottle** is also a great food and hot drink container. GSI makes a **measuring cup** that is nice for longer trips when you don't feel like sharing food and split with your partner every meal.

Spoons and sporks are fairly necessary to eat hot meals, and light plastic or titanium options negate any reason not to bring one for weight reasons. **Fast food plastic spoons** are virtually weightless and free. Just be sure to pack them somewhere you won't break them, like under your pack lid. When you or your partner inevitably forgets their utensil, it's time to get creative. Hunger is a good source of creative inspiration, so I'll leave it to you to figure this one out. Finally, **pot grips**, or spondonicles for you Aussies, can be incredibly useful. You can remove the handles off of your cookware if using pot grips to save weight. I always forget pot grips and have managed just fine with carefully pinching the pot with my jacket sleeve, or with folded garbage wrappers for years and only one minor jacket melt, partially thanks to sensation loss due to too finger jamming and ice climbing. If you've got pliers then you're set.

WATER
Water on the Go
One way to pack less water is to fill up on approaches in springs, streams, or lakes instead of carrying water for the entire day. Bringing a stove will hydrate you on long winter climbs. You may want to consider bringing an **alpine straw** or use your camelback tube to suck water from seeps on rock or ice. Trickles can be difficult to fill bottles and bladders so use other gear to get creative to construct a funnel. If you can't figure it out, you could always just use your mouth to spit water back into a container.

Purifying Water
You usually don' have to purify clean looking water. Most sickness is from dirty hands. If you don't trust the water the lightest weight options are **chlorine tablets** (chlorine dioxide to be exact) and **iodine tablets**. Iodine purifies more quickly but doesn't kill as much as chlorine, especially organisms with a shell, like cryptosporidium. The colder the water, the longer it takes. Most chlorine tablets say you need to wait four hours. This is conservative estimate. Most nasty's are killed when the pill dissolves. Small bottles of **two-part chlorine solution** like Aquamuira are quick and effective, but harder to come by and are slightly heavier. A broken bottle leaking onto your gear may affect the integrity of the nylon in your kit. Although the bottles say they have a quicker kill time, the pills are the exact same thing. The longer you wait, the less you need to use. The sooner you need to drink, the more you should use.

When used over long periods of time, iodine tablets can harm your liver and taste horrible (the taste eliminator tablets help) and iodine doesn't kill crypto. Go with chlorine tablets. In real nasty conditions or in sketchy 3rd world countries you'll want some extra protection. **Steri pens** that use UV light or electricity (to create chlorine ions) to kill microbes are the quickest solution, but check your batteries. It is hard to tell if your pen is working, and it won't kill larger organisms. If you are conceded. double it up with something else.

The **MIOX** system creates chlorine ions in the water via an electrical charge and salt. MIOX is discontinued, but Potable Aqua recently introduced a similar system. It is extremely effective and fairly lightweight. Run of the mill **water filters with activated charcoal and micropore filter pumps** take forever and are bulky, but are the only thing that filters particulate matter out as well. This can be useful when filling up from sources contaminated with heavy and toxic minerals or gross stagnant pools. There are squeeze bottles with an attachable filter for immediate filtration, but are fairly bulky. A new product, Lifestraw is essentially a high powered filter inside a straw. It may be a bit annoying on a climb, but it is handy in a pinch. Bringing water to a rolling boil takes care of almost everything, but you waste gas and time. For most alpine climbs in the unpolluted areas, chlorine tablets are the best, cheapest, and lightest option.

Aquamira, Squeeze filter, chlorine tabs, iodine, SteriPen

Water Bladders

Water bladders with drink hoses are the best way to have constant easy access to water, but do have drawbacks. The biggest drawbacks are leaks from a punctured bladder, bad connectors, or losing a bite valve. Accidents are common. It's also harder to judge how much water you have left with a water bladder, and harder to drink big gulps of water. Drinking several ounces at once is more effective that tiny sips all day. Camelback makes a **flow meter** to help you know how much water you've had, or to help you ration water. The button is easily pushed, and I haven't had much luck with using mine (plus it's bulky and catches on everything). It could be a good idea if you can use it well and you need to plan or ration water. If you really need to plan your water and food consumption, use a **stopwatch or timer**. I find that I never drink enough water with a hydration system, and my partners always drink too much (and winds up asking for my water).

Having a hose flop around and interfere with climbing is extremely annoying, and angled bite valves have a habit of catching on everything. If your pack doesn't have a shoulder strap clip, buy a simple clip with no moving parts. A **bite valve** should have an **on/off switch** to avoid accidental leaks by setting your pack down on top of the bite valve, or leaning into the rock. You just need to remember to switch your valve to off. A good backup is to have a **bite-valve protector** that slips on and off the bite valve and is backed up to the hose with a thin cord. This added level of security is great, and it also protects the valve from getting dirty. The hose can get really gross and lined with black mildew after a lot of use and improper drying. **Hose cleaners and brushes** are available. Drink mix can really contribute to the problem. Rinse your bladder out with soap and water, blow out any extra water from the hose, and hang it dry. An empty table paper towel holder works well to put the bladder over to help it dry. A boot drier is even better assuming the intake isn't dusty.

If you absolutely depend on the water you're bringing, bring a **water bladder patch kit**. Soft rubbery bladders, or more rugged Dromedary bags don't seem to leak nearly as often as the stiffer food grade plastic models. Do not expect much life out of plastic water bladders; they will leak from wear and cracks. Soft water bottles without tubes that hold around a quart with a drinking spout have become rather popular, and for good reason: they weigh little and pack nicely. However, every single one I've ever used from any company has leaked after a short time due to the plastic nature – except for smaller but awkward **MSR Dromedary bags**. If you are using a Dromedary bag, tape down the spout (it is useless for anything but showering) and attach some cord from the small cap to the large cap with glue and tape to avoid the inevitable loss.

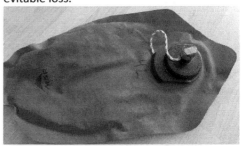
Dromedary with keeper cord

Simple hose clip & flow meter with straight bite valve

Platypus Wine Container

Before committing to using your bladder, stress the bladder by squeezing it hard and torqueing on the hose connection to check for leaks. Some Seam Grip around the hose connection can add some insurance. Some bladders have hoses that can disconnect from the bladder. These are great since if the hose pulls off the valve keeps it from instantly draining into your pack. Some models do leak at the **disconnector valve**, so really put your bladder through the works. The other nice thing about a disconnector valve is not having to re-thread your tube through your pack when refilling it.

One of many soft 1-liter bottles

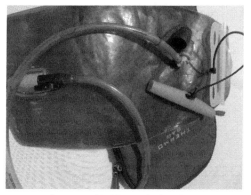
Deuter soft 100 oz. bladder with detachable hose, bite protector, and insulated soft case.

Water bladders pack down way better than bottles. The best place for a water bladder with a drinking tube is vertically hung in the back of your pack. With minimally padded packs, the bladder adds some comfort from cams and biners poking you in the back. If you don't have a pouch it's not a big deal. To keep the bag upright so drains properly, most packs have a tiny **little clip** you can use. If not, rig your own with some cord and a knot, or pilfer the plastic key holder in the lids of some packs. Because water bladders pack down to the size of the volume you are carrying, 100 oz. bladders make a lot of sense.

Key holder to hold up bladder

It's hot out and your bladder is right next to your back you could heat the water up with your body making it less palatable. You can get **bladder insulators** that help in really hot weather. If filling up at home, use ice cubes. Try freezing your water bottle if it'll be really hot, or are hauling them up a multiday wall. **Insulated tubes** don't do a thing in the winter. To be on the safe side, don't use drinking tubes with water bladders when it's cold out. Instead use water bottle parkas and Nalgene-style bottles. Start with hot water, and don't fill the bottle completely. Drink mix with salt will decrease the freezing point. If you're not using mix, add a **dash of salt** - you won't mind the taste. A little air left at top by not filling the bottle completely will keep the water sloshing a bit more and reduce the chance of it freezing. A thermos does the best job, but is much heavier. Save the thermos for cragging.

If you are hiking in to an area without any water and plan on spending a night or two, you'll need to slog in a lot of extra water. The best containers to use are MSR Dromedaries (up to 10 L). Overestimate the amount you'll need if the only drawback is a heavy pack on the hike. If on a climb, you'll want to try and get it exact. Big wall climbers love to rig **2 liter soda bottles** for their haul bags by wrapping them in duct tape and adding a clip-off loop. Unfortunately these take up a lot of haul bag space. Dromedary bags are way better (not the Dromlite). If using 2L soda bottles, skip the duct tape - it does nothing. If you have a basecamp, you can pack a **black Dromedary or garbage bag** without residue on it with snow to get a head start on melting water when you return.

Water Bottles
Regular water bottles with secure lids are generally more pleasant to drink from, don't leak, and are easier to eyeball and ration how much water you've got left. I have stopped using a bladder except on long approaches. **Nalgene-style or aluminum bottles** are the most secure, but you can't easily judge amounts in an aluminum bottle. Don't clip the lid on either. Nalgene lids are barely attached, and the ridged nature of aluminum bottles allow for the lid to get slowly torqued off. **Gatorade-style bottles** are actually pretty secure (I've had some for years!), are lighter, and much much cheaper. Nalgene's are best for hot drinks, especially combined with an **insulated water bottle holder**. If climbing

without a pack, or the leader wants to have some water on hand, rig a Gatorade bottle with webbing or a sling and duct tape and clip it to your harness. Water bottles also act as a great coffee cup if you forgot to pack one.

Thermos and insulated Nalgene cover

Food
Camping and Cragging

You can eat whatever you want when the car is nearby. A **campfire** or a **propane stove with a grill** attached can really open up your menu options. Keeping things fresh or from getting water logged in the cooler can be an issue. **Dry ice, frozen water bottles, or cooler dividers** (gotta make your own) helps to keep things dry. Ziploc bags do little to keep the water out over time. Since weight isn't an issue car camping, go for **real food** instead of instant dinners, breakfasts, and "wrapper" lunches.

Eat plenty of **fruits and vegies, meats, cheeses, nuts, and oils. Fresh eggs, hash browns, pancakes** (they make spray pancakes now!), **pre-cooked bacon** (bake it in the oven 350 for 30 min), **corn beef hash, Grape Nuts, fruit, and yogurt** are all great long lasting breakfast items. **Fresh pastries and confections** from the bakery with a **banana** are great for quick breakfasts. **Stir-fries and curries** are great ways to get meats and vegies in you without too much mess. An all-time favorite of mine is to line tin foil with bacon, and stuff the foil with potatoes, onion, carrots to serve alongside a grilled meat (or mix everything with hamburger). Add **olive oil** to anything you're frying. Healthy **chips and a few beers** for desert of course. **Big ol' sandwiches** with avocados, cheese, sprouts, fresh bread, deli meats, tomatoes, and spread do the trick to keep you fed for most of the day. Supplement with **nuts, trail mix, fruit, jerky, and chocolate**. I usually bring **non-sports drink mix,** like generic Kool-aid, in a gallon jug for cragging so I drink plenty of water with some extra calories. Even the most discriminating 'foodie' can't say no to a **Coke** on a hot day. **Thermoses** are awesome at crags and base of ice climbs. Fill one with **soup** if you never eat solid food ice climbing. Although more coffee may sound nice in the morning, it gets gross on the climb. Try **cocoa or tea** (although the bags usually erupt) instead.

Alpine Trips

Watch with alarm on pack strap

Make sure your partner is up to speed on the whole food and water thing. If he or she isn't eating right and bails, it doesn't matter if you were. Take the time to eat and drink, your performance depends on it. Set an **alarm** if you need to. If you're not bringing a pack, stuff bars in your pockets. Some items require water to wash down, and some items are more difficult to eat or take too much time to eat on route. Unless you've got a lunch break factored in to the day with time to spare, bring food that you can shove in your mouth and that you enjoy eating. Even pre-made sandwiches can stay in the pack all day if you're moving too fast or belays suck so bad you don't even want to bother opening the pack. Toss a **high calorie emergency bar** that contains fat into the bottom of your pack for maintaining through an epic or unplanned bivy.

The optimum food weight to ensure you'll be getting enough to eat is around 2 lb. per person per day. If going ultralight, then plan on bringing about 1.5 lbs. per person per day. These weights assume you're bringing concentrated food items like bars and dehydrated dinners. Plan out how many calories you need per meal and where they are coming from (fat, carb, protein, sports drink). See the section on energy requirements. Reading labels and using scales while packing food for important trips is important.

Bring whatever you want, the following are only suggestions. Just because REI doesn't sell it doesn't mean you can't bring it. Be creative! I'm always finding new favorites at the grocery store by looking at nutrition labels for calorie content. Trader Joes, Asian, and European markets always have the best snacks. Add whatever supplements and vitamins to your breakfast, lunch and dinner menu you think you want in from this section. **Little pill containers** found in camping stores work well, as does using a small bit of tin foil. For long trips, try and plan in some sort of whole grain, fruit, and veggie, even if it's just **freeze dried veggie drink supplements, dried fruit, and a health bar**.

The legendary Meat-ton

Osmo pre-load, Osmo drink mix, N.O-Xplode, Nuun, Hot apple cider, 5-hour energy, Miso soup, Tea, Hot Cocoa, Caffeine strips, Starbucks Via, Instant chai

Breakfast

Start off the day with fats and carbs, and some protein. If you are going to be doing something cardio intense, skip the fat. If you aren't a big breakfast type or must hit it right when you wake, eat at least 400 calories and ½ liter of liquid to get the system going. The more you eat for breakfast, the less you'll need on route. If climbing at altitude, eat the bulk of your food at breakfast instead of dinner. Eating a large dinner at altitude will interfere with sleep.

If you plan on making a cocktail of supplements, powders, etc., just make sure you can choke it down and not suffer stomach issues. If you can, drink a liter to fully hydrate. I drink a liter of coffee. If you drink too much at once you'll just wind up peeing it out.

Hot drinks (like coffee!) are a good way to get your fluids, caffeinate, and give yourself a few more moments of sanity. Here are some suggestions: **Starbucks Via coffee packets** (alpine gold), **hot cocoa, powdered chai, powdered apple cider, tea, and hot Jell-O. Miso** is another excellent hot drink and has a lot of salt. It's a better dinner beverage though. If you're in a hurry, gulp down a **cold sports drink**.

Oatmeal (5 minute steel-cut oats are good) with some **powdered milk, brown sugar, almonds, and blueberries** (pre-mixed) is a pretty standard breakfast, but you may want to top it off with something that has some fat and protein. **Grits, multigrain hot cereal, Grape Nuts and powdered milk, pre-cooked bacon, hard-boiled eggs**, or just some calorically and carb/fat/protein mixed **bars** are decent choices. NIDO makes the best powdered milk because it has fat and taste real. Try the Mexican section in the grocery store to find it. Probars or Raw Revolution bars with some dried fruit are choice quick eats, although there are many other gut-bomb high calorie energy bars out there as well. Hostess-style fruit pies pack a calorie wallop, but are obviously full of crap.

My all-time favorite is a bottle of Ensure Clinical Nutrition and a macaroon cookie (any pastry will do) or hard-boiled egg. **Ensure** has 350 calories, 11 grams of fat, 13 grams of protein, tons of vitamins, and tastes decent. It also makes a good recovery drink or on route pick-me-up and takes about two seconds to drink. Just consider the water weight into the water you bring. It can also give you rebound diarrhea on an empty stomach. I eat my 400 calorie cookie on the slog up to the base. You could figure out your own perfect **smoothie** or try to use **powdered breakfast drinks or protein powder** and add stuff (gross). There are many options for **breakfast bars & cook-**

ies, or you can also make your own. Keep your eyes peeled when doing your regular shopping to sniff out fun things to eat instead of the regular old instant oatmeal. Beware of freeze dried instant breakfasts. Most are super gross, and many require a skillet so read the directions.

If you don't have time for breakfast, shove something simple in your pocket and munch it on the approach slope or first few belays, but do not start the day developing a caloric deficit. If you are simply training before breakfast be sure to get 200-300 calories worth of carbs to keep you going until you're done.

For cold winter climbs or before a big demanding alpine climb try and get in a greasy spoon breakfast – really pack in those calories. This **lumberjack breakfast** will serve as your base calories and a light breakfast just won't cut it. If you are already out in the wild, then try to at least increase the amount of oatmeal you'll choke down that morning. A greasy breakfast will get burned, but loading with carbs followed by proteins is still more important. A breakfast of roughly 1/3rd protein content can help with insulin spikes and fatigue during the day.

Lunch

Lunch is a misnomer, what you should be doing is constantly snacking from breakfast to bedtime. Eating nothing but carbs with a small amount of protein and fats is one thing on high-output climbs, but as omnivores, we crave various types of food and our bodies operate better with **"real" food**. So if a climb isn't too intense, bring some real food. You can even trick yourself on intense climbs by bringing different kinds of **high-energy snacks/candy** instead of just **GU packets**. On approaches you can bring whatever your heart desires, and you should be eating and drinking (instead of the standard hike there as fast as possible mad dash) in order to retain stores for the climb ahead. **Taffy and hard candies** are nice for sucking on while hiking, and **trail mixes** are a good source of carbs fats and protein. Trail mixes don't work so well on a climb (guaranteed to stay in the pack), but are also good for snacking around camp.

Camp snacks are great ways to eat those extra calories, so bring some tasty "fun foods". Remember that on the climb you don't really need much protein, so **protein bars and protein "Shot Rocks"** are best served at dinner. Some good "real foods" to bring on any climb but a speed assault are: big ass **sandwiches (bread or bagels), tortillas and peanut butter, cheese, salami, pepperoni, landjeager** (amazing), **smoked salmon** (bears!), **cookies and confections/pastries, and whole fruit** (the extra weight is water which so need, nullifying the extra weight). **Nuts** (almonds especially the sea salt and olive oil variety, or the sesame almonds from Trader Joes) like **pistachios, almonds, and macadamia nuts** are excellent. **Peanuts** are a bit acidic but are cheap, salty, easy and delicious. Don't forget the good **chocolate** if it isn't too hot. I consider a giant meat and cheese sandwich the quintessential climbing lunch, and you don't have to sit down and eat it all at once. Supplement the sandwich with an **apple** and chocolate bar.

Canadian Landjaeger

Migrating into the world of not-so-real food but still not astronaut-grade are **candy bars** (Snickers is still the king), **granola bars** (chewy dipped bars), **trail mix and nut bars** (like Kind Bars), **chocolate dipped nuts and raisins, regular raisins, dried fruit** (Philippine **mangos** rock as do **apricots** – both for taste but also for potassium), **fruit leather** (Sun Ripe Fruit bars are killer), **sesame snaps, halva** (great and tons of energy from fat and carbs), **fruit chews, licorice, gummies, and cream cheese packets** (eat 'em like GU). In the summer candy bars and chocolate don't work so well.

For the hard climbs where you just need to shove pure energy into your mouth, nothing beats **GU** or GU-like products. The big problem with GU is that it's messy and gross. Thankfully someone invented **energy chews** (Chomps, Cliff Blocks, Sharkies, Sport Beans, Honey Stinger etc.). Another player on the market are **energy waffles** made by Honey Stinger and are pretty good and calorie rich. **Powerbars and Cliff bars** are the major players for solid food energy bars. Just avoid the protein rich ones for the climb. There are a billion other bars on the market, and most of them are good but expensive, but not a lot better than real food you can get at a bakery or make at home. Save the expensive energy food expense for chewy GU-type gummies, regular GU, and a quality sports drink. Again, even if you are going full-on GU, bring some fatty snacks to avoid bonking, a little protein, and some real food to satisfy cravings and normalize your gut. At least one or two solid food items like chewy granola bars keep your stomach from growling. One more nice aspect of real food is that it keeps you regular.

You don't need to survive on GU packets and sugar on long climbs. Sugary energy food is definitely useful to get a quick boost on any type of climb, but too much sugar too quickly could cause an insulin spike and resulting crash. Gels and chews are for when it's all go go go. We are designed to eat real food, and many top-level climbers and endurance athletes simply eat normal food. A big alpine sandwich may be a much better choice than twenty GU packets. Uli Steck brought a block of cheese to supplement Gu packs on his most recent Pilot d'or winning climb on Annapurna If living off GU during the climb, be sure to have plenty of real food for dinner.

Take 5 bar, Sunripe fruit bar, Sesame Snaps, Chewy granola bar, Snickers, Shot Rocks, Pistachios, Cheese, Chocolates, Carmel Waffels, HiChew, Kind Bar, Pro Bar, Yogurt Almonds, Oreos, Granola Bar, Apple, Gu Chomps, Honey Stinger Waffle, Raw Revolution bar, Trail mix bar, Peanuts, Tuna packet

Find out what works for you and your climbing style.

A **"crash kit"** can be a nice thing to have on a long climb to avoid bonking and cramping. If you bonk or cramp, first **eat a sugary carb-rich quick to digest snack and drink more water**. **Caffeine** is a next good choice when bonking. **Aspirin** is a good on-the-climb pill for headaches due to its blood thinning effects. Ibuprofen and naproxen also work, but naproxen (Aleve) requires that you are hydrated. **Oily fatty snacks and a little protein** may help pep you up after a bit. **Electrolytes** and fancy chemicals may help too, but odds are you need sugar and water. Also bring an emergency high calorie bar for epics (Pemmican Bar, Raw Revolution, ProBar). Here are some other suggestions for a crash kit to avoid bonking, cramping, and feeling like crap: **5-hour Energy Maximum Strength, caffeine pill, caffeine gum or dissolvable strips, Starbucks single serve shot, Red-Bull, recovery drink (Ensure), olive oil shot, oily snack (Raw Revolution, Halva), meat stick, extra energy gel (usually does the trick), electrolyte pills (Salt Stick Plus), small vial of pickle juice, and/or a small vial of pre-mixed pump and fatigue cocktail of any or all of the vitamins and supplements mentioned earlier. N.O.-Explode** is a decent combo of many supplements mentioned. The caffeinated version has a lot of caffeine in it – go with the caffeine free version.

Post Climb/Pre-Dinner

Remember your glycogen and protein replenishment window only lasts a short time after a climb. Have a recovery snack immediately. Get the right amounts of carb, protein, and water in your system quickly. Keep snacking until dinner. Plan ahead and have something hearty to devour if returning back to the car, like another sandwich.

Dinner

Dinner should be a carbohydrate-based meal with generous amounts of additional fats and protein. The dinner the night before a trip should be considered a form of last minute carb loading but with a little extra focus on fat and protein compared to a typical carb-load meal. On route, dinner can just be a continuation of snacking from breakfast through lunch if you planned your food well and actually ate it - it doesn't have to be an actual "meal." Just be sure you're getting enough of each type of calorie and you rehydrate as much as you can stomach. This type of snacking meal avoids the need for a stove if you aren't melting water. Good dinner snacks are **salami and cheese** with some **Triscuts** (oily) or **French bread** followed by some **protein type bar or nuts**, and another **energy bar**. The more you eat, the better you'll recover and perform the next day, and the warmer you'll sleep. So if you do need a big meal, then down a **vial of olive oil**, or drench your dinner in it for extra fat. Non-caffeinated hot drinks, like **Miso**, will help you stay hydrated by actually wanting to drink something.

Most climbers using a stove will make some type of **freeze-dried dinner**. Check the calories on the package, some offer a surprising low amount. You only need one foil pouch per trip, so repackage your meals and re-use the foil for the next meal. You can add more calories and nutrients by adding **foil packed tuna** and olive oil. Don't forget a packet of **hot sauce** you borrowed from the gas station or fast food taco joint. The deli at a large supermarket is a great place to get free condiments and silverware too. Get your hands on the new MRE, the First Strike Ration (FSR) that have less packaging and has a full days nutrients and calories. Some **chips** have a ton of calories (check Cheetos out!), but aren't what you'd consider healthy. For the sake of a climb, don't worry about it. Just eat what tastes good, has calories, and the right amount of carbs/fats/proteins. Eat salad when you get home.

Instant mashed potatoes, couscous, or instant soups also make lightweight bases for adding **cheese, meats, oils, and spices** to. Instant rice doesn't offer much in the way of calories or nutrition. Tic Tack containers make pretty good little **spice containers** (and pill bottles).

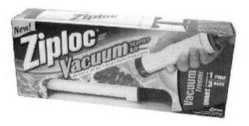

Take a trip down the pasta and ethnic isle at the store, you may find some instant or semi-instant dinner a hair better (and probably cheaper) than freeze dried meals. European, International, and Oriental Markets can yield many tasty alternatives. **Baked sweet potatoes and hard-boiled eggs** weight a bit, but again, you'll be using the water for good use. If you're just packing into a base camp, think of better, healthier, more real food to bring. Ziploc makes a $5 **vacuum pump** that attaches to corresponding special Ziploc bags. Shrink-wrap some yummy leftovers from home, tape up the air hole and folded over zipper, then boil in bag yourself a decent meal (be sure to cook it thoroughly if spoilage is an issue). If there's a grocery store or restaurant on the way, stop and shrink-wrap something from the deli or restaurant. Are you camped near a lake? Get a permit and bring your **fishing pole, fry pan, and some onion, garlic, and oil**! After dinner, start snacking and drinking some more. Bringing a **small frying pan, butter, and popcorn** to a basecamp makes a fun popcorn movie night.

Alcohol
Alcohol is obviously a bad idea if you want to stay hydrated, fully recover, and avoid hangovers the next day. But for those who don't care about those reasons, nothing says "Miller Time" like getting back to camp and hanging out. **Hard alcohols** pack way better than **wine or beer**, but the truly dedicated climber doesn't mind the weight of some cans of beer and will stash them in the river or lake. Check out **Pat's Backcountry Beverages** for a kit they make to rehydrate & re-carbonate their craftsman beer concentrate. Powdered alcohol has recently made the news, so expect something commercially available one of these days too.

If repackaging hard alcohol or wine, don't put it in a regular plastic container. It will leach plastic chemicals out. My buddy brought 80-proof vodka in a regular Platypus and we nearly died choking down what tasted like a tire fire. Use **Platypus wine containers**. If you really want to impress your tent mate, bring **sake** in a Nalgene bottle and stick it in your boiling water while making dinner or tea. For big-wall cocktails, a **Rehydritta** (lime Gatorade, water, salt, and tequila) is a classic. Some climbers feel that a mid-afternoon **Pabst Blue Ribbon and a Red Bull** can get them up anything, or at least out of the mid-day slump. I obviously can't endorse this (or any dangerous or unhealthy tips presented in this book), but climbing is 90% mental so do whatever works for you.

Caching Food
Caching food makes sense to lower your pack weight on long traverses, epic approaches, extended wilderness trips without resupply possibility, or if you bail and plan on returning. Either do short missions on days off to do your caching, or carry in a huge load and cache along the way for your return. Unfortunately animals and weather wind up getting into your cache unless you are extremely diligent about burying it. A large pile of rocks means nothing to mice, water, or insects.

Ursack food bags are helpful at reducing food smells and weight nothing, and ammo cans and bear containers are fortresses but only add to more weight and bulk. Make your cached food the highly packaged astronaut food to further limit attracting critters.

My only useful advice is to go to the 10th degree when caching food and don't rely on it 100 percent. If caching non-food items like fuel, then don't expect other people to leave your stash alone. If caching water, hide it well. Leave a note in a baggie along with your name and the expected date to deter would-be thieves.

If you come across cached water that is obviously not going to be used by the party who left it, you should be safe to drink it as long as there wasn't any drink mix in the water. Musky tasting water is most likely algae and mold. Give it a sip and let the taste be your gauge. If you have purification they by all means use it. But if the water looks clear, doesn't taste like death, then you should be fine to drink it without getting sick.

At the Car
Keep a supply of **post-climbing food (and beer)** in the car to keep from crashing and aiding in recovery for the long drive home when all the stores and restaurants are closed because it's late or Sunday. The deli or Trader Joes is a great place to prepare a pst-climb feast. Bring a **cooler** if your car will be cooking in the sun all day. Even having **something to make coffee with** is a great idea back at the

car to keep you awake and alive for the drive home. Add a **change of clothes and shoes** the car will feel like Christmas morning.

MAKE YOUR OWN

Making your own version of commercially available climbing food is fun and inexpensive only if it actually tastes good, you make full use of the ingredients, and don't screw it up. Making your own can wind up costing more and tasting worse than buying commercially made items. I admit that I just buy the commercially made stuff on sale, online, or in bulk. Taste matters more to me. REI sells food items at 20% off if you buy in bulk.

Makes Your Own Sports Drink

First re-read the section on sports drinks to determine what you want to get out of your beverage. Some ideas for ingredients: honey, brown rice syrup, maltodextrin, glucose, sucrose, salt, baking soda, lemon juice, apple cider vinegar, blended mango, whey protein or amino acid liquid, coconut water. Extra potassium can be obtained from Morton's Lite Salt or salt substitutes. Supplement by adding any other commercial supplements. If you want to be cheap just use diluted generic Kool-Aid or powdered Gatorade. If you find that buying commercial sports drinks becomes a big enough expense to make your own you can just mix table sugar (sucrose) and dextrose powder (glucose) together very cheaply. Beer supply stores are good places for many of these ingredients. Aim for about 35 g of sugar per liter. Add some table salt and you're done. Adding other ingredients (like flavoring) is up to you, but just be aware that the more you add the more it will cost, and the grosser it will get. Like all edible do it yourself substitutes for commercially made sports food, you can wind up wasting a lot of money making disgusting concoctions when in the long run a manufactured item (they perfected the processing) may wind up being much cheaper and tastier. If I were to add anything to this simple recipe, it would be flavored electrolyte tablets. If you add these then don't add additional salt.

Make Your Own Energy Gel and Chews

- ✓ 100 mL glucose
- ✓ 50 mL sucrose
- ✓ 100 mL water
- ✓ Pinch of citric acid (brew store or lemon juice)
- ✓ Flavor extract
- ✓ Drop of gin (optional)
- ✓ Gelatin (optional - contains protein)
- ✓ Oil (olive, macadamia – optional)
- ✓ Pectin (optional)
- ✓ Other ergogenic aids, proteins, vitamins, and minerals
- ✓ Brown rice syrup (optional)

Gradually heat the water and add the sugars, then the rest. Stir until lumps are gone. If your flavoring isn't alcohol based, add a drop of gin. Package in squeeze tube found at sporting goods stores. Add flavorless gelatin to the mix with a little pectin and oil to make energy chews (remember Jell-O Jigglers?). You could also just put some brown rice syrup in a tube and call it good.

Make Your Own High Calorie Bar

This is basically a glorified Rice Krispy Treat. If you need amounts, loosely follow a Rice Krispy Treat recipe. Go to Whole Foods or other fancy store and substitute whatever high calorie/glycemic index (like granola) cereal you feel like. You can use marshmallow for taste and perfect consistency, or try and use some form of brown rice syrup or honey and add some maltodextrin or other sugar to keep it sticky. Butter works great, but you can use olive or flax seed oil instead. You can add all sorts of stuff, so be creative. Some ideas are: coconut flakes, chocolate chips, nuts, powdered milk, nut butters, whey protein, and dried fruit. It all depends on how gross you want them to be! Be sure to jump up and down on them to squeeze the extra air out of your bars! Honestly, any baked goodie you make with higher glycemic index sugars, and healthy oils will work. My new cold weather calorie bombs are buckeyes (peanut butter and condensed milk dipped in chocolate).

> **Make Your Own Fruit or Vegetable Roll-Up**
> These are easy! Puree some fruit and or veggies, spread it over waxed paper, and put it in an oven over low heat or a food dehydrator. Add a little honey or brown rice syrup to make it sweeter, a splash of coconut oil for texture, and a drop of lemon juice, and a little ascorbic acid (vitamin C) to keep it fresh. Some fruits and veggies don't dry well or mix together well, and need to be mixed with a large concentration of apple puree. You can just dry sliced fruit for little fruit snacks instead of the roll-up for an even easier snack. For the easiest version, just pre-slice/peel or pit your favorite fruit and veggie and put it in a baggie and sprinkle some lemon juice or ascorbic acid powder on them. The extra weight is compensation for the extra water that you need anyway. Just before this book went to press I found a book called, "Power Hungry: The Ultimate Energy Bar Cookbook" by Camilla Saulsbury. Her recipes are way better – get this book!

NAVIGATION AND COMMUNICATION

Binoculars and Scopes

Mini monocular

Binoculars, a good pair that is, are super handy for scoping complex routes from afar, especially when doing a first ascent. **Cameras** take such good pictures these days that you'll need a really nice pair of binocs or a **spotting scope** to make bringing them along worth it. Most first ascents just use a photo or figure it out on route, but if the rock is really slabby and featureless, high powered binocs or a scope could help you create an imaginative line you would dare attempting while on the wall. They are also fun for looking at mountains at camp for most uses.

Cameras

Even though climbers are migrating towards taking pictures with their **smartphones**, nothing beats a quality camera for documenting the trip or zooming in on a route to scope it clearer. For those that bring larger models than a point and shoot, you probably already know the deal. If you're not familiar with a **larger digital SLR** and are planning on bringing one for the first time, ask your photographer friends and expect it to be a bulky time-consuming mess. For those of you sane enough to just bring a **small point and shoot** be sure your **camera case** is bomber enough to withstand dirt, getting crushed in chimneys and offwidths, and will stay clipped to your harness.

For heightened security use a lightweight locker to clip the case to your gear loop (and lock it), and clip a superlight wiregate to the camera leash (protruding out of the case) and to the locker. When you want to take a photo, open the case, unclip the biner, and take the photo. Also the little **springy leash** that comes with some Metolius nut tools is a perfect solution. **Hard shell plastic and aluminum cases** are available for added protection of both smartphones and cameras, and in my experience of trashing countless cameras, worth it. Check out the Alpinist Camera Case or Otterbox cases for cameras and phones. **GoPro** helmet camcorders can make some cool (or obnoxious) videos, but they also can be set to take a photo at set intervals, a little known, yet very cool feature. Don't forget an **extra battery and memory card** for longer or super cold trips.

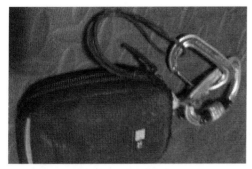

Camera case on a locker with non-locker on strap

Compass and Altimeter

Electronic compasses that come with altimeter watches or smartphones are useful, but they are subject to a lot of error. Be sure to calibrate your electronic compass often. Electronic compasses are fine when the chances of getting lost are slim. But a **small no frills standard compass** is much more reliable, and you'll be glad you had one when you get turned around and you're not trusting your electronic one. The most you need from a compass is a needle that points North. A **rotating bezel with grid lines and degrees markings**, not just cardinal directions, is a very useful when using a map to triangulate. **Mirrors** greatly aid in sighting exact degree measurements, and **adjustable declination** settings are very nice in intensive navigation situations.

An **altimeter watch** that has been recently calibrated is also an extremely useful tool. Make your wrist altimeter watch standard fare on most alpine trips, and just toss your compass into your normal pack or small emergency kit for all non-cragging trips. Calibrate your altimeter at as many known locations as possible to keep it accurate if barometric changes mess with the actual elevation. At least calibrate it on the summit, and at camp or trailhead. Having an altimeter that you can easily track your elevation without the same fears is also incredibly handy for judging time, distance, and navigation. Standard altimeter watches also gauge barometric pressure, and incredibly useful weather forecasting tool. Some smartphones are now incorporating barometers, humidity, and temperature sensors. Only climbers would be excited about this.

GPS

Handheld GPS units, watches, and smartphones with built in GPS and mapping software are fantastic at pinpointing your exact location and marking waypoints. The big problem with a GPS unit is it can run out of batteries, and more commonly, won't get a signal in thick forest or cloud cover – just when you need it. Don't forget to **download maps** for the area you'll be going before heading out. If your phone or GPS has a lot of memory, download as many maps as possible for when you inevitably forget to plan ahead. To keep your smartphone from running out of batteries, put it on airplane mode so it's not constantly searching for a cell signal. Some smartphones turn off the GPS when put on airplane mode. There are some apps that fix this issue, like Backcountry Navigator on Android phones.

Bring an **extra battery or external charger** (of varying capacity) to keep your phone alive. The main advantage of handheld GPS units is they are a bit more powerful at finding satellites, and don't run out of batteries nearly as quickly. Learn how to mark waypoints, and do so at important areas. The option to track your progress on the map is a great feature, but quickly drains batteries. You should be able manually enter known coordinates, and import and export waypoints to your computer for easier planning at home. Besides pinpointing your location, a great thing about GPS units is the ability to get to a predetermined coordinate for locating a route, and to cache locations for finding you camp or navigating a glacier in a whiteout. If there's a remote chance of getting lost, bring a **map and compass** and use other electronic options as backups.

Maps and Topos

Google Earth and Bing maps are excellent tools to scope approaches, descents, routes, camps, etc. at home. Take the time to fly around an area, and print out some photos to take with you. Printing out **topo maps** from an online source makes it easy to bring a map tailored to your area. USGS paper maps are excellent for navigating terrain, but may not be current on man-made structures like trails, roads, and dwellings. Specialty maps for popular regions are usually the best to bring since they are more current, and you can identify distant peaks for your enjoyment. No matter what map you bring, be sure that the detail level is zoomed in enough that contour lines are a useful distance apart (and that there are contour lines with enough elevations listed to be of any help), the map area is large enough to use distant peaks to aid in navigation, and there's a legend stating contour intervals, distance, direction, and declination. There are many online topo maps, but many require a purchase. The best tools available to date are mappingsupport.com and hillmap.com.

Take a photo of the route topo, including the drawing or overlay, description, approach, and descent info with both climbers' cameras (in case one breaks) if you don't feel like tearing pages out of your guidebook or couldn't Xerox one. Also take a photo of the climb itself so you can zoom in to help with route finding or descents. Some topos provide minimal or incorrect beta, so go online and research the route. Write in comments from other people that you find helpful, but remember that many people on the Internet are idiots and liars. Sometimes too much or too specific beta can get you so locked in looking for something that you miss it. Be especially wary of subjective or overly detailed descriptions. "Look for the rock that looks like an elephant" may totally screw you up when to you, it looks nothing like an elephant. Also be wary of gear beta for climbs that show a section of a particular size, but don't suggest bringing that size. The author or Internet troll may be sandbagging you.

Another thing to be extra cautious of are people who say, "you can rap it with a single 70" or something similar. Even super detailed guidebook topos for popular trade routes are just plain wrong sometimes. Don't follow their advice unless there is at least one second opinion confirming this. I've been astounded at how off some suggestions have been. If something sounds weird, do not trust it. Topos get trashed in your pocket on long routes, and if you fold them, don't put the crease over important information. Print off at least **two copies, and laminate** with packing tape if you can. Keep approach, climb, and descent topos in separate locations so you won't lose everything at once. Following a topo too closely without using your intuition can get you off route. Pretend like you are the first ascensionist – where would you go or what would you do? Mountain Project offers an offline app for you smartphone to access route info on the go. It is helpful to download the area and the photos before you lose cell reception. Rakkup is a newer app that offers turn-by-turn GPS coordinates to the base of routes at some popular climbing areas.

Wands

Wands are really great for marking routes around difficult crevasse navigation, leaving a trail in case of a whiteout (or during a whiteout), marking a camp perimeter, and marking caches. Put neon flagging tape or reflective duct tape on bamboo rods are found in the garden department. Marking info on the tape with a **Sharpie** can be useful. If you plant a wand, don't litter, pull it out. In a whiteout, plant wands every rope length (25 wands per mile if using a full 60 m rope). Take bearings between wands, especially if placing them far apart.

Wind and Temperature

Smartphones even have wind gauges (via the microphone) but I'm assuming they don't do real wind gauges justice. I can't imagine a real need for a **wind gauge**, but hey, I'm trying to be thorough. A **zipper thermometer** is worth the weight and always right if on something external (like a zipper, duh).

Watches and Alarms

Another gadget smartphones are replacing is a watch with an alarm, but a **regular wristwatch** still has its place (if you can find one). Knowing what time it is without worrying about draining your battery or dropping your phone will keep you on track or alert you that it may be time to go down. Smartphones don't make the greatest alarms because you need to have them on for the alarm to go off unless you're lucky enough to have one that turns on the alarm in low power mode or when completely off. Missing an alarm could mean not climbing anything. **Small travel alarms** are still useful so you actually hear the alarm and don't waste your phone battery. If your watch has an alarm, make sure you can hear it. Since wearing a watch on your wrist is pretty disastrous on most climbs, put it on your pack strap or tear off the band and attach the watch with some thin nylon cord. The little pin won't bear much weight, so back it up with some tape and glue. The cord helps you from losing the watch, especially if in your pocket. Having access to a watch, especially one with a timer and stopwatch is a great way to speed things up by timing pitches, transitions, rests, etc., and to time when to eat and drink. Clip it to the top of the tent and have it dangle over your face so you can be sure to hear the alarm.

As long as we're talking sleep, bring **earplugs** if your partner snores, or you don't know if your partner snores. They are worth their weight in gold. If you snore, bring a fresh pair for your partner who probably didn't bring any. Make sure everyone and everything is on the correct time zone.

Lighting

One of the biggest reasons for an epic is the lack of a (decent) headlamp. **Tiny micro headlamps** are so small and light there is no excuse for not stashing one in your pack, pocket, or chalkbag. Reaching for your headlamp should be as automatic as reaching for your harness when packing up. Micro headlamps may get you out of a pinch, but can be worthless when you really need some light to adequately navigate. If a climb has an approach or descent, or is long enough that getting caught out at night would prove epic, pack a **good headlamp**.

Headlamp technology has come a long way in the past decade, and you can get really powerful torches with spot beams that don't weight a ton. A headlamp with a **spot beam of high lumens** (160 or more) is invaluable for continuing to climb at night so you might as well skip the midrange models and get one of the best. Headlamps with **external pouches** to keep batteries warm and provide extra power are only really necessary on big cold climbs. Bring **extra batteries**! It's unbelievable how long your headlamp will work for until the time comes when you really need it and it dies. Better yet, put new batteries in it before any big climb and bring extras. It is worth the weight.

As for batteries, get the best lithium ones you can find. Lithium batteries last longer in the cold or heat, and are much lighter. Energizer Ultimate Lithium is best one to date. Headlamps that have rechargeable batteries are extremely handy. Charge it at home or in the truck and never have your headlamp battery die an early death again because you didn't replace the batteries. Some rechargeable battery can be swapped out with regular batteries, a great feature on route.

Little tent lanterns are nice for around camp to cook and read so you can save your headlamp and not have to shine it in your partners face constantly. **Large lanterns** are extra nice for car camping, and with LED models you don't have to replace mantles and broken glass after every trip, or burn your hand on the little knob on top. LED lanterns made by camping companies are a lot cheaper than ones made by climbing gear manufacturers.

Communication Devices

Figuring out a system of rope tugs is the simplest method of communicating with your partner, but unfortunately it rarely works. If a pitch is really long, it's windy, you're near a river or highway you should hammer something out before heading up. If you're belaying the leader and can't hear, just keep belaying out rope until it comes tight on you. Wait a couple minutes while taking down the belay, staying clipped into a single piece with the rope. While clipped, move up a couple feet and see if the rope stays pulled up, then unclip and assume you're on belay.

If you're the leader and it's hard to communicate, don't yell anything that could be misconstrued as "off-belay" when you're still climbing like "I'm okay". When secure at the new anchor, try yelling "belay off" or "secure"

instead of "off belay" - it's more distinct. As the belayer, don't take the leader off if you're not fully confident. Again, just pay out the rope until you're out. Assume you're simul-climbing until the rope is acting like you're on belay. **Whistles** are way better than rope tugs and don't weigh a thing (especially if you can whistle without one). They are also helpful for initiating a rescue. Many backpack sternum straps incorporate a whistle.

Walkie-talkies aren't as useful as one would think. For one they are hard to attach to your harness without breaking them, accidentally turning them off, accidentally switching channels, or actually being able to hear anything. Nice expensive models may work better than the fairly inexpensive Talkabout-style walkies, but how much information do you really need to convey? Whistles are unmistakable. A common newbie mistake is not yelling loud enough. Don't be shy.

Sternum strap whistle (took me years to notice this)

There are several ways to communicate with the outside world. **VHF/UHF radios** can be found very cheaply, and are very convenient and powerful communication devices. Technically you need a license to use them, but can get away without one in an emergency. **Satellite phones** or expensive radios provided by an air service (helpful in Alaska) are pretty bomber methods of communication – they're just expensive, heavy, and overkill for anything but an expedition with air support or frequencies monitored by a basecamp or authorities. Areas where you'll want sat phones or radios should be obvious because the air service, expedition, or agency you register with will let you know and most likely let you rent them. Expect sat-phone technology to improve in both cost and weight, however.

Delorme and SPOT both offer autonomous satellite communication units, and units you can hook up to your smartphone that offer satellite communication stating an SOS, checking in with loved ones, and communicating your location. Checking in with an "I'm Ok" message is really useful in avoiding a rescue, but when you actually need help, it's really important to be able to have two-way communication. The models that attach to smartphones can also let you send and receive customizable texts, which really helps with establishing a two-way communication. Both devices require a pricey monthly subscription so you can't just pay for it at the store and when you need to use it unfortunately. Do a lot of consumer research on this type of device, there are a lot of complaints about some of the models.

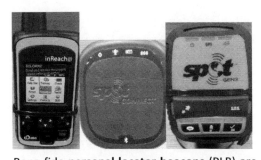

Bona-fide **personal locator beacons** (PLB) are a bit heavier and a lot more expensive (~$500) but are a lot more reliable and powerful (compared to the many complaints about the DeLorme and Spot), especially in bad weather. Some models allow you to send an "I'm Ok" message to loved ones (again a great way to avoid an unnecessary rescue), and some newer models will actually send/receive texts. Besides working better, standard PLBs usually don't require a subscription so it's a one-time cost. Some fancy new units that offer two-way communication with a subscription are starting to come out, however. Most climber's scoff at bringing something like these on a trip, but most climbers haven't been in a rescue situation that requires them. PLBs get a bad name because of the idiots that use them like a taxi service. Just don't be one of these types and use it only when you have to. If you get one that pairs with a smartphone, bring a backup power source for your phone.

Regular **old flip-phones** are great because they don't drain batteries like smartphones and some models can get a signal much better. They are also harder to break. Some carriers also offer better service in some parts of the country, so it's helpful if you and your partner have different carriers (like Verizon and AT&T). If you aren't getting service, you may be able to sneak a text message out if you wait long enough or just get lucky. If your phone isn't off or at least on airplane mode your battery will drain very quickly while it constantly tries to get a signal.

Smartphones are awesome backcountry tools. You can watch movies, listen to music and podcasts, and play video games in the tent or suffering an unplanned bivy. Some phones take great photos, and most record good movies so you can leave the bulky camera at home. You can download apps that store topo maps offline, turning your phone into a GPS (with all the functionality and more of a handheld GPS). Some phones have a barometer to aid in forecasting, a humidity sensor, and outside temperature sensor. Most phones have built in compasses (be sure to calibrate them). You can even get flashlight apps if you don't mind draining your battery. There are apps to measure height and distance, inclinometer apps (for avalanche forecasting and making sure your tent/truck is level), weather apps, avy forecast apps, pulse oximeters, heart rate apps, wind speed sensors, peak finders, naturalist identifiers (flower/animal etc.), and a Mountain Project App for route beta right at the crag. On the road you can find cheap gas, hotels, constantly check email, post your Facebook status, make a wireless hotspot, and not get so lost finding hard to find trailheads. Google Earth allows you to fly around a new area, scoping descents, approaches, and even new routes. Hopefully someone makes an avalanche beacon app, a satellite phone option, and a walkie-talkie option.

If watching movies in the tent, **bring a headphone splitter (and two headphones)** or **portable speakers** to save on battery life so you both can hear over the wind or water. A shoe makes a good stand, as does a paper clip bent in a clever position. If your phone is slippery, make a secure strap by attaching some cord to its accessory case, or duct taping a strap to the back of the phone.

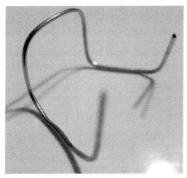
Paper clip phone stand

It won't be long before these devices replace every gadget, hopefully they have a climbing lobby at the R&D labs. This book can even be downloaded onto your phone if you forget how to do something in the field (assuming I figured out how to do that). If for some reason you still have an **IPod**, bring it and earphones for tunes instead of your smartphone to save batteries.

If you can't use electronics to get a signal for outside communication, you can always try good old-fashioned **signal mirrors**, the mirror on your compass, fires (don't start a forest fire), or stamp large messages in the snow or use branches. Some climbers have even been known to bring a flare or smoke signal to signal for a rescue!

Recharging Batteries

The big drawback (besides not getting a signal in most climbing areas...at least for now) for smartphones is battery life. If your phone allows you to swap out batteries, get an extra (or more for expeditions) or a **small pocket charger**. Check the milliamps on the chargers, you'll need at least 1700 mA for a recharge. Keep the phone on airplane mode, standby and/or turn off the GPS and wireless to save juice. Once you drain a battery pack, **solar power** starts becoming weight worthy. Small hand sized units take forever to charge and disseminate the power to a device. Larger panels work a lot better and you can get kits that charge AAA or AA batteries, or recharge your battery pack. Goal Zero is a good company to check out for solar power needs. Biolite stoves may or may not be useful for recharging. Several companies are developing other ways to charge electronic devices using your cook stove. Test 'em out. If you are car camping and want to charge stuff without draining your car battery, get a **portable car battery jumper** that has a usb and cigarette lighter adaptor. These units are incredibly cheap and hold a serious charge when compared to hip, trendy slim little iPhone chargers.

FIRE STARTING

It is a very good idea to pack a **tiny lighter**, or at least some waterproof matches en route, even if you aren't bringing a stove. A little lighter doesn't weight anything, and being able to create fire is an amazing human invention that could turn a shitty night into an endurable one, or could save your life or help you get rescued. Even a little bit of **fire starter** is a smart thing to bring (still weighs nothing). Dryer lint and a little wax, steel wool, or a small ESBIT tablet wrapped in tinfoil is good insurance to have as fire starter. **Fire starter gel** is only useful when you utterly fail as an outdoorsman/woman when making a campfire near the car. Use your stove if you've got extra gas to really get it going in bad conditions.

Leave no Trace and Hygiene
Pooping

Nothing is more helpful than being regular at 4 am if you're an alpinist. However, the urge may not be there and doesn't kick in until you've got your harness on and are a couple pitches up. The rest of the day becomes an ordeal. Don't hold it in at night to create ammunition for the morning, you could dry out and get backed-up. **Stool softener suppositories** taken at bedtime may help kick-start things off. Try at home first! **Oral stool softeners** have too many GI side effects, besides nothing says alpine like putting something in your butt. **Bulking agents like Metamucil** may also help. Stress and anxiety and lack of sleep are very common causes of morning constipation and daytime diarrhea so if you notice this is a recurring thing on climbs, you can prepare better. Chewable **fiber gummies** taken regularly can be a great preventive measure.

There's a reason **toilet paper** squares are called mountain money. You can get tightly rolled TP that burns very quickly (but isn't too soft on the anus) at most camping stores. **Napkins** stolen from gas stations are the choice among top dirt-bags, and Fred Beckey. However, you can find natural items to wipe with like leaves, moss, clean smooth rocks, etc. if you prefer to stick to a Leave No Trace ethic.

Keep your TP and a tiny lighter in a small Ziploc bag. **WAG Bags**, like freeze dried dinners, usually have a lot of extra wrapping you can get rid of to save some weight. **Ziplocs, grocery store bags, and bulk food bags** are stinky but lighter alternatives to WAG bags, but do not biodegrade. If you plan on packing out your turd, a dry bag can save the day, or just offend everyone on the hike out by putting it in a grocery store bag on the outside of your pack. When packing up your turd, close your poop bag securely! Before dropping the kids off, think about how you'll close the bag and how you'll deal with splatter. Poo smell only intensifies as the day rolls on, and any accidental "exposure" can make belays a gag-suppressing experience.

Methods for pooping on a wall when you plan to have been discussed slightly under haul bags. If you have to poop on the wall and don't have a container, and the route gets at least some traffic, please try and hold it! I know climbers that are so conscious of others, that they've taped the thighs on their pants up, and crapped their pants on purpose. If you have a free stuff sack or Ziploc, use that. If they are too small empty your pack lid and poop in it or in a piece of clothing like your hat! Better yet, take the time in the morning to stimulate a bowel movement. Don't hold in a "maybe" before it's too late.

Around camp and on the trail, bury your feces well away from any water source and burn or pack out your toilet paper without starting a fire. A **lightweight plastic trowel** avoids pooping under rocks, and a big **army surplus trowel** is great for the car. If the ground is too shallow for digging a hole, look for some rocks you can lift up and poop under. This method is by far less than ideal. Bring some WAG bags or at least some extra light plastic bags of some sort and pack your poop out in fragile environments. The Elephant's Perch in the Sawtooths, the base of the Diamond, and the Incredible Hulk are good examples of places you should probably pack out your poop. There isn't a rock that's not covering a turd for miles. Smearing your turd thinly over a flat rock to get dried and later scatter to the four winds is a dated method, and not an option.

Throwing a garbage bag full of turds on a glacier may sound like it will never see the light of day, but there's no way of knowing how popular an area may become in the future. It's a judgment call in this situation, but just be mindful of future consequences to you actions. Instead of using a garbage bag, use a **plastic composting bag** that will biodegrade.

Peeing

I don't know how girls can stand wearing a harness or snowsuit and not have a piss-adaptor like a **Freshette**, aka "Modular Man" or "Shenis". Pack a few **wet wipes** and put it in a **little mesh stuff sack** on the back of your harness to allow for air drying after use.

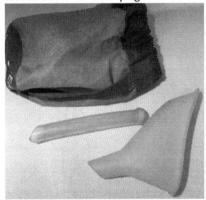

Freshette

Holding your pee while you (don't) sleep is a bad idea. Just get up and get it over with. The whole idea that you lose heat or whatever the logic is to hold you pee is plain stupid. Waking up to go pee can also be a good alarm clock, so drink a lot of water before you sleep. This will also get you hydrated for the next day. If you wake up, go pee, look at the clock and if you have to get up in an hour or less, you may as well just get up and have a nice head start on the day. If it's too cold or stormy to get out of the tent, use a **piss bottle**. Any old bottle with an opening large enough for your junk will do as long as there's no danger of overfilling it! **Collapsible wide mouth bottles** work great. There are tons of stories about pee bottle mishaps, so it's not as easy as it sounds. I'm surprised climbing tents don't have waterproof glory holes. Some tents used to have a square on the bottom of the tent you could undo and poop under the tent. That must have been something, and it obviously didn't catch on.

Pee is sterile, but try not and do it into a water source. Pissing all over a climb isn't unavoidable. Carry a piss bottle and dump it somewhere out of the way. If you've ever been on the Nose, you know how it can add up. If you are so thirsty that you are considering drinking your own urine (as a friend of mine did once), think about how thick and nasty your urine is going to be if you're that thirsty. Throwing up afterwards will waste more water.

Showers

Taking a shower can provide instant recovery and clear out those thoughts of home, even if you weren't really complaining about being dirty. Local pools, rec centers, gyms, YMCAs, and (ugh!) even truck stops provide showers. Expensive campgrounds you're probably not staying at will allow you to use their shower for a fee. Most guidebooks offer shower suggestions. You can buy a **solar shower** that heats up water throughout the day, and you can spruce it up a bit by adding some water you heated on the stove. In the alpine, **MSR Dromedary Bags** actually have a use for that minuscule trickle spout, and make great alpine shower stations.

Use **biodegradable soap** that's easy on the water and soil. Most camping stores have biodegradable concentrated camp soaps. If the container is too big, transfer it into a smaller vial. You can also buy **dried leaves of soap** designed for backcountry use and ultra-light hikers. You can also take a vegetable peeler to a bar of soap. My favorite is Dr. Bronner's, mainly because I like to read the label. You can also sponge bath with a **bandana or lightweight pack towel**, but this puts the soap directly into the water source or makes you use your cook pot which is gross. It may be okay in a large volume or fast moving river, but certainly not in an alpine water source you'll be drinking from.

Leaves of body and laundry soap

If you are taking a rest day or spending a lot of time in the backcountry or dirt camping, showers and laundry are worth the extra effort and minimal extra weight, as you'll wash out all of the "I want to go home" dirt off.

Sanitation

Pack towel, Clorox wipes, wet wipes, concentrated soap, hand sanitizer, soap leaves, toilet paper, mini-Lysol, Q-tips, WAG bag

I mentioned that the number one cause of water born contaminants is actually from your nasty hands. Wash your hands with **soap** and water after pooping or after snotting all over them all day. If soap and water are out of the question (like on a wall), use a small vial of **hand sanitizer** or a **travel package of Clorox or Lysol Wipes**. The wipes kill more than alcohol based hand sanitizer and help wipe off grime. **Wet-wipes** are alpine gold for finishing the job of scratchy camping TP, doing a quick wet-wipe "shower," and keeping your lady parts fresh after peeing. A few extra ounces of sanitation supplies won't end your trip or even slow you down, but getting sick will.

Cleaning your teeth after they feel like you've grown a rug in your mouth can be a chore for some, while others seem to count the hours until they can brush their teeth once again, and do it for like 10 minutes. A **regular or travel-sized toothbrush and a travel-sized tube of toothpaste** doesn't weight much. Travel toothbrushes can create some mess if you're an idiot like me. Brush your teeth far from camp in case of bears, and nowhere near a water source. Spray, don't spit the waste out so you don't concentrate the paste in any one location. Several **alpine-style toothbrushes** have come out in recent years. While probably not the intended market, ounce-counting climbers may benefit from light finger covers that have some dried paste and bristles, or super tiny brushes with a dot of dried paste on the inside. Don't forget the **floss**! Nothing can drive you crazy like a stuck piece of food you can't get out, and not a piece of floss for miles. You can even find **alpine-style floss packets**.

Luxury Items

Finally, let's talk luxury items at the crag. Why not mock a climb with a long approach, or take advantage of roadside cragging with a nice foldable **camp chair, foldable camp**

couch, hammock, portable propane heater, hot thermos of cocoa, or a small cooler full of cold beer and fresh lunches. You can always tell the alpinists at roadside crag with their skinny slings, rope backpack, and nasty bars. Come on, climb civilized. Pack your **tablet, laptop, Frisbee, good book, journal, portable speakers, deck of cards, or portable chess set**. Bring a **full on camp kitchen** for making more than just quesadillas on your Jetboil.

Portable propane heater

CLOTHING

Bringing just the right amount of clothes is also an art. Too much and your climbing will suffer from too much weight or overheating, or your hike in will be even more exhausting. Too little and you can freeze, get soaked, or be uncomfortable enough to want to go home because you're too hot, too cold, or too dirty.

First of all, don't believe the marketing hype. Every season a new "revolutionary" material is advertised and not much changes. This isn't always the case, but don't get suckered or made to feel bad for using an inferior product. Unless you are a product tester, get free gear, or can afford to live on the cutting edge, wait for the masses and the gears of capitalism to turn out what really works. A few ingenious products and ideas get stamped out by lack of demand or word of mouth, but they'll turn up again if the really do make a difference.

MATERIALS AND USE

Cotton, the most common material in clothing, is excellent at keeping you cool in hot weather, and is useless in wet and cold conditions. Cotton t-shirts, socks, and pants (especially canvas pants) are perfectly acceptable low-tech options for dry conditions if you plan on beating your clothes up. **Wool** (merino) and **synthetic** garments can also be worn in hot weather if the weave is light enough, however they are best used when getting soaked is an option since they (depending on the weave) can stay warm when wet, and nylon dries especially fast. Wool is a better thermoregulator and more durable than cotton, but heavier. It is replacing many previous synthetic only applications. Synthetics are the old (in a modern sense) standby fabric. Synthetic fabrics can be spun, woven, coated, or tweaked in a billion different ways to improve on waterproofness, wind resistance, breathability, insulation, and drying ability. **Down** and synthetic insulation have the same pros and cons as they do in choosing a sleeping bag fill. As far as clothing purposes go, down really only trumps synthetic in very cold climates as an outer jacket or suit, or as fashionable sweaters while cragging. **Primaloft** still remains one of the best synthetic insulation at the time of this writing. Some heavier types of synthetic insulation, like **Thinsulate**, are preferred over down or fluffy synthetics in areas that receive a lot of compression: mainly in gloves, socks, and boots.

No matter what the insulation, a wet garment is miserable and there is no such thing as warm when wet. Down clothing usually gets wet from evaporating sweat when moving or sleeping, outside humidity, or from wet ice climbs. There is no reason to be wearing down if it is raining.

When selecting a down piece, the higher the fill power, the warmer it will be for the weight unless it is being actively compressed somehow. Besides fit and features, the outer material weight and baffling of said piece will determine how light and how warm a jacket or bag really will be. Material choice will reduce the weight of a piece more than the fill of the down, and how the piece is baffled to distribute the insulation will put the insulation to its best use. Superlight outer material isn't always the best choice, and too much or improper baffling/quilting can create cold spots and add unnecessary weight. If two pieces look similar in fabric and weight, but one is more expensive, chances are the more expensive piece has been more carefully baffled and will be warmer. How much insulation is added, or the fill weight, is an often overlooked but an extremely important detail. Companies can trick consumers into buying "the lightest jacket ever made," when in reality it's because there's barely any insulation in it!

Another exciting development at the time of this writing are the advances in **waterproof down**, higher down fill power, and warmer/lighter synthetic insulation materials. Unfortunately not enough real-world testing has been done to determine just how waterproof these new down products are, or just how much fill power begins to diminish on returns. One pro that synthetic insulation still has is that tears in the fabric don't leak precious insulation. Advances in synthetic insulation are on par with advances in down insulation. More breathable insulation is being made that can vent heat while in use, but retain heat (with a shell) when you're not moving, while other companies are creating more "down-like" insulation.

Battery powered clothing is probably the wave of the future and some garments do exist from reputable companies. Unfortunately either no one can afford them, or they don't work, because I've heard nothing about their performance, which is too bad because the weight and space savings would really make them amazing. Many other materials and ideas have been developed to increase warmth without added insulation but absolutely nothing has caught on yet. Focus has been on using lighter fabrics and better insulating material. More focus should be on reducing radiant heat loss, improving thermoregulation, and use of electricity, solar, and movements to generate, store, and redistribute heat and moisture.

Shell materials can get confusing as the line between an inner and outer shell gets blurred with fabric advances. There are several gradients between fully waterproof or windproof and fully breathable that includes both the kind of material and the weight/thickness of the material itself. **Waterproof breathable** Gore-Tex-like fabrics took a big step forward in recent years, coming closer to the holy grail of fully waterproof windproof and breathable. **Cuben fabric**, basically woven or unwoven Dyneema, has become popular in making ultralight yet extremely strong and durable tents, tarps, and packs. It has begun to make its way into clothing options as well, mainly as an extremely lightweight waterproof and windproof layer for ultralight hikers. New waterproof breathable Cuben jackets have recently emerged and may be very useful to climbers. Cuben has normally been reserved for creating light packs, sacks, and shelters. Insulated jackets and fleece jackets used to be only for belay parkas or mid-layers, but new materials, and more importantly, new designs, have produced garments that are worn for both insulation and activity.

A few years back **softshells** revolutionized the outdoor clothing system by providing excellent breathability with fairly good water resistance (and looked sharp). When I use the term softshell, I am referring to stretch woven garments with or without bonded fleece. The problem with softshells is that they can be too heavy for the amount of insulation and protection they provide, and can get soaking wet because of the Spandex in the blend. Softshells still have their place for aerobic pursuits where you won't be out for long enough to need to stay totally dry like skiing, rock climbing in cold weather, and relatively dry ice climbs. But with the advances in more breathable shell membranes and lightweight insulated jackets, softshells are becoming unnecessarily heavy sponges.

Each layer should do the best job it was designed for with the least amount of weight. Now, insulated jackets with a hard face with or without a Gore-Tex style shell, and venting options make a lot more sense for certain situations. One problem with hardshells, or any light or tearable outer fabric is ruining them on ice, rock, or mixed climbs when dragging the fabric across abrasive rock – especially when chimneying or offwidthing. This is probably the biggest difference of opinion there is between other friends and me. At least know that Gore-tex-like shells are way more breathable than they used to be and that softshells will absorb water given enough exposure.

Windstopper fabric has never made a lot of sense for climbers, as it is usually too heavy, doesn't breathe well enough, and why not just have a real waterproof shell for the same weight/breathability, or a super light wind jacket shell. Windstopper shines in fleece gloves. New fleece materials are using windstopper fabrics in key areas only, or are using semi-wind resistant fleece material.

As I just hinted at, the next iteration of shell material are uber-light **water resistant shells** (wind jackets), usually made from some type of **silicone impregnated nylon**, like the material used in some lightweight non-waterproof tents and tarps. These micro shells are very tightly woven and provide obvious wind protection over insulating layers, and shed light rain and snow very well. They are great alternatives for shells in climbing situations where snow will be what gets you wet, when a rainstorm will be short, quick, escapable, or endurable, and when the wind picks up on a summer rock climb. Super lightweight fully **waterproof non-breathable** rain jackets and pants are also making a comeback. The theory behind these are that if it rains you won't be exerting effort since you'll be staying put waiting it out, and a thin layer of plastic still works better than any fancy membrane. Pick a lightweight water resistant shell for when you'll be moving fast and would overheat with a waterproof shell. For start and stop activity a waterproof shell offers more insurance, and many models only weight an ounce or two more than a windshirt.

Leather still reigns supreme as a grippy, durable, supple, and breathable material for shoes and gloves. There are plenty of synthetic alternative that work just as well, but they just aren't as durable or fit as well as quality leather. Many forms of leather exist from Nubuck, to pigskin, to Pittard's. Price pretty much dictates the quality. Be sure to clean and condition your leather items regularly to keep them longer.

Heat Loss
Body Regions
In order to decide how to dress, it's important to understand how we lose, and generate heat. The fact that we lose a high percentage of heat through our heads is a myth. We lose heat at the same rate via any exposed area of skin. Those of us that still have hair will lose less heat through our head as we do our face and hands because less skin is exposed. In fact, we lose most of our heat via breathing warm air out and cold air in. But unfortunately we have to be practical. Covering up our face (except in very cold climates) would impede our performance via not breathing enough, soaking everything with our moisture, and being incredibly uncomfortable. We do, however, perceive cold more and sweat less in certain areas, which is where the myth probably perpetuated. So why do we focus on our torso if this is the case? One big reason is that bulky clothing on our legs, arms, and feet would severely limit performance. Another reason is that some areas of the body are working harder than others and are producing more heat.

Our legs and arms don't get as cold because they are moving and produce lots of heat. Our torsos don't move as much and therefor don't produce as much heat, and the torso also has the most surface area. If everything is moving, then most likely your face, hands, and toes will be the coldest as they don't have as many muscles to generate heat. In other words, all areas lose heat at the same rate, areas with more surface area lose the most heat, and areas with large active muscles produce more heat. The best way to stay warm is to cover and insulate all the areas that are the most exposed and not actively producing heat. If nothing is moving, then cover everything (a sleeping bag). Knowing this, you could realize that donning a pair of light insulated pants could make you warmer than donning multiple jackets because less heat would be lost overall.

Evaporation
Heat is lost via evaporative cooling, either from sweat turning into vapor or getting wet. On fast and light missions, or hard work in cold weather, sweat will be your enemy. Just like in the gas lecture in the stove section, when water changes from a liquid to a gas, the resulting change of state takes energy from the system and makes you colder. Insulating layers over a wicking layer help by taking the moisture and distributing it over a large surface and moving the evaporation even further from the skin, reducing the cooling effect of evaporation. If your undershirt and inner insulating layers are too efficient in areas that get really sweaty, your layer could be working against you in cold weather. This is one reason wool is a great next to skin layer – it has a good ratio of absorbance to wicking. To further combat this, your clothing should be layered from low loft to high loft. Wearing a fleece over your undershirt will still allow you to dry by pushing the moisture away from your skin and into an outer insulating layer, but buffers the rate at which moisture passes into loftier layers, and hopefully dries as it reaches the outside air. Thicker undershirts in winter also buffer the heat loss via evaporative cooling.

Most fabrics are marketed towards sweating in warm temps. In hot climates you want to be cooled by this evaporative cooling loss. Mesh undershirts and pants worn with mid-layer are another idea, and many winter climbers love these. There is enough material to move moisture, but the spaces between (the mesh) trap warm air and help to insulate at almost no weight cost.

If you aren't sweating hard, or it's not freezing cold, this won't be a huge issue. But getting sweaty in cold weather really makes dealing with evaporative cooling difficult. Non-breathable shells will impede the desired anti-cooling effect by trapping the moisture in, but you'll freeze when you stop moving. Really sweaty areas that don't breathe well, like your back and waist against your backpack and harness may benefit from a vapor barrier to inhibit evaporative cooling since the moisture can't go anywhere no matter what you are wearing underneath. Some cold weather alpinists suggest wearing a tightly woven windshirt over the undershirt to act as a semi permeable vapor barrier – moisture will eventually escape and dry, but greatly buffering the heat loss via rapid evaporation.

Mid-layer synthetic insulating pieces of roughly ~60g density Primaloft or similar insulation are lightly shelled on the inside enough to not need this inner VBL, and are tightly shelled on the outside enough to wear as an outer shell in dry conditions. Temps and conditions, metabolism, and how much you sweat are variable enough that only trial and error will dictate how you deal with evaporative heat loss.

Conduction
Heat is also lost via conduction. If you touch something colder than you, you warm it and it cools you. The more conductive a material, the more of an effect this will have. Air isn't very conductive, so as long as the other types of heat loss are accounted for and your clothes aren't made of conductive material (I hope not), then it just being cold outside won't steal your heat very quickly. Air isn't thick so cold air is easily converted to warm air with little loss on your end. Rock, ice, and snow aren't extremely conductive, but they are dense and therefore have a lot of surface or stored heat capacity (or lack thereof) to steal your warmth. Luckily not much surface area on your body besides your hands, toes, or feet touches the rock or ice so effects are fairly local. Doing it all day will have an effect, which is why insulating the bottoms of your feet in winter is crucial. And of course lying down to sleep without insulation to reduce conductive cooling can have a huge impact.

Besides ground pads, gloves, and footwear, not much thought needs to go into avoiding conductive heat loss while climbing; except of course when it rains. Water is extremely conductive which is why getting wet versus getting snowed on makes you instantly cold and why a rain shell is critical for staying warm in wet weather. Water takes a lot longer to heat than air, which is why non-absorbent insulation is superior to absorbent cotton. Add evaporative heat loss, and water is the worst heat offender!

Radiation
Although the sun provides us with all of our external natural heat via radiation, it is very difficult to keep our own heat around via radiation because clothing liners that reflect heat can also limit breathability. Some companies are attempting to solve this problem by making **reflective-breathable membranes**. If a company can find the perfect balance between added weight, added warmth, and breathability, this will revolutionize outerwear. Space blankets are perfect examples of radiant heat reflectors in outdoor gear (they also reduce evaporative heat loss at a cost). Many ice and mountaineering boots incorporate reflective liners.

Convection
Convection, or the movement of gas (air), is the final form of heat loss (besides running out of calories to burn), and is the biggest concern for staying warm. Although cold air conduction chips away at your insulations'

retained warmth, what really pulls the heat out is the movement of warm air out of your layers. This can be due to the breathability of the fabric, allowing a free exchange of cold and hot air, or physically compressing the warm air out. High loft garments trap a lot of air and warm it up. Low loft garments don't trap as much air, but lose less due to compression. In other words, you're not warming the material, you're warming the trapped air. If a garment were able to keep the warm air trapped forever (by limiting breathability), a light garment would be just as good as a heavy one (minus conduction) which is why wetsuits work - only water (very high conduction) is substituted for air. The problem with us delicate humans is that too much of a good thing leads to overheating and that is almost as bad as freezing! So the goal is to find the balance between trapping enough dead air in, while letting just enough out and cold air in.

The more active you are while wearing a piece, the more breathable you want your insulation to be, assuming it isn't so cold out that conductive heat loss starts to become a real issue. Highly breathable insulating layers are perfect for climbers if used properly. Instead of taking layers on and off, you can climb in an appropriately thick or thin insulating layer without overheating because it is lost via convection, and when you stop climbing you either put on a lightweight wind-shirt if it's not too cold out, or a thicker wind resistant insulating layer on top of what you've got on. Not too hot, not too warm.

Because your legs don't sweat as much or feel as cold or hot as other areas (to a point), you can get away with wearing a less breathable pant so when you do stop, you don't lose the heat as quickly. This would be the end of the issue if that pesky thing called wind, second only to water in terms of elemental heat loss, didn't come into play. Wind essentially amplifies conductive heat loss based on the temperature, and convective heat loss based on the speed. Climbing in a breathable piece loses all value in high or cold winds. Simply adding a light wind layer will solve the convection issue, but if it is also very cold, a thicker shell is necessary to combat the conductive loss as well. Luckily we have seasons versus utter chaos, so we can predict what to wear based on the time of year and weather forecast.

CLOTHING CHOICES BY BODY AREA
HEAD

Wool and synthetics both work well for your **warm hat**, took, or beanie, but fleece doesn't shrink and feels a little nicer. If you're really trying to save weight then get a down or Primaloft hat. Blackrock Gear and Outdoor Research make lightweight **down hats**. A warm hat is an essential piece of gear for all climbing pursuits except very warm days or if you have a hoodie pullover mid-layer. Still, if a climb makes its way into the night, a hat stashed in the pack is worth the extra two ounces. Lighter weight hats (or **helmet liners**) are useful enough for most summer alpine pursuits, and for high output winter pursuits where taking your hat on and off multiple times under a helmet is a pain. Use a jacket with a **hood** for extra insulation in those cases. For cold days and camping out in the cold, a normal **ski hat** is good enough. Save the **super-thick hats** for cold ski descents and zipping around on a snow machine.

Windstopper seems like a good hat material, but you will probably overheat and if the membrane covers your ears makes you deaf, especially in the wind. Headbands and earmuffs are fairly useless unless it is quite cold and you are running or climbing very fast and only want to protect your ears. **Balaclavas** are very useful multipurpose hats. They protect your neck and face and head, and can be folded up into a hat when you don't need the extra protection. A silk weight balaclava is a good summer alpine hat alternative as well. Hooded jackets and shirts are great to provide insulation in place of or in addition to a warm hat, to protect your neck and ears against the sun, or to keep snow from falling down your shirt. Beware of wearing too many hooded garments, however! Cutting a silk weight balaclava and sewing it into your main outer layer for winter climbing is a great way to prevent spindrift shivers and to minimize overheating. Tube style neck warmers, called **neck gaiters**, aren't usually necessary unless it's brutally cold and windy, or you're skiing and not producing much heat. **Face-masks** are essential in very cold conditions to protect your exposed face. Check out the **Cold Avenger facemask** that warms and humidifies cold air. A lot of water is lost at altitude due to the dry air via respiration.

Balaclava, face mask, neck gaiter, down hat, wool hat

Silkweight balaclava sewn into collar for a spindrift hood. Black Diamond makes a lightweight balaclava.

Ball caps with a cloth neck protector are great in the summer for both sun and bug protection. A **bandana** serves the same purpose and can be worn under a helmet sans ball cap or visor if you don't like a brim getting in your way. **Buffs**, or multifunction headbands that can be worn various ways are great for long hair or sun protection. **Visors** work ok for shading your face a bit, but really are more for looks than anything. Sun damage to your scalp can help you go bald, burn your scalp, and increase your risk for hidden skin cancer. Spray some sunscreen on your head if this is an issue, although the chemicals may increase chances of balding (as does bug dope). You can also get brimmed helmets and visors that attach to helmets for reducing glare in the summer, but make tight chimneys a total pain.

Eyes

If you wear **prescription glasses** you've hopefully got your system dialed for climbing and backcountry camping. Bring an **eyeglass repair kit if necessary**. **Contacts** can be a chore, but are choice for wearing sunglasses and goggles over.

Sunglasses are essential in the snow. Wraparounds should do the job, but if you're in extreme environments you may want to get a pair of quality **glacier glasses**. Using a little **nose protector** may look dumb, but could be a lifesaver if you'll be in sunny snowy terrain for more than a couple days, or you could apply **zinc oxide** like lifeguards do.

Your call, not everyone uses them. **Polarized glasses** help reduce glare in the snow, but are really more helpful in the water and are not really needed. If you can't see your digital camera screen, it's because you're wearing polarized glasses. Real glass lenses protect your eyes pretty well from UV rays. When getting plastic lenses, try and get ones that block 100% UVA and UVB rays. You may not experience effects any time soon, but constant exposure to UV rays can accelerate retinal degeneration.

Sometimes sunglasses make route finding more difficult, especially in shadowed corners. Orange **tinted lenses** (and yellow after that) help protect your eyes but allow you to see a little more clearly. Beware that the color of your cams may change with tinted colored glasses! If it's not super bright out, but you'll be climbing choss or sandy rock, **safety glasses** can really help (like in the Fisher Towers). I found a yellow tinted pair of safety protective glasses that filter 100% UVA/B at a Wal-Mart optometrist for $2. If you always break, lose, or scratch your expensive glasses, there are decent cheapies out there. Glasses with **interchangeable lenses** are handy for switching between dark, clear, and colored lenses. If you can't wear contacts, invest in prescription sunglasses and treat them better than a newborn baby, or wear the senior citizens option over your glasses. For a cheap, light, packable backup pair of sunglasses, get a pair of those **flimsy plastic glasses** you get after an optometrist appointment.

There are also **goggles** made to fit over eyeglasses that aren't as ridiculous looking the AARP sponsored sunglasses that fit over glasses. In whiteouts, snowstorms, and freezing winds, nothing lets you see as well as goggles. They also offer good protection for ice climbing. The big issue with goggles is fogging. The easiest solution is to get an expensive pair that is designed to reduce fogging. Pre-treat them with **anti-fog solution**, and maybe even bring a **fog wipe packet** stuffed in a pocket. Have a chamois handy to wipe them off. Your wet snotty glove or greasy fingers will only make it worse.

If you're a particularly violent ice climber, or don't want to look like you've been in a bar fight, you can get a **helmet face protector**. You can make your own by copying the Petzl face shield or just winging it by cutting up plastic like PET2 type plastic. There are even some wire cage-style face protectors. These have never really caught on, however.

Belay Specs, glacier glasses, goggles, Beko nose protector, orange tinted sunglasses

Courtesy Petzl

Prism belay glasses are the latest craze at the gym and the crag. They make you look insane, but allow you to belay the leader without constantly craning your neck backwards. I strongly recommend these to everyone, not just those with current neck pain. Many small businesses are producing these and reducing the cost.

TORSO

UPPERS: *Big down puffy jacket, 80g/m synthetic jacket, three 60g/m synthetic jackets, down vest, Driclime windshirt, canvas shirt, Goretex Proshell jacket, ultralight waterproof shell, softshell jacket, hooded hybrid windblock/standard fleece sweater, R1 fleece sweater, wool baselayer, synthetic baselayer, one-piece baselayer, cotton t-shirt, flannel shirt.*

Figuring out what to wear for your torso layer is the trickiest body part to outfit on a climb. Carry your layer clipped to your harness inside a **small stuff sack** with a hat, or inside its own pocket if you're leading without a pack, or expect to get chilly at the belay. One trick you can use if your layer doesn't stuff into its own pocket is to stuff it inside one of the arms and sew in a little bungee cord clip-off loop at an appropriate spot.

Base Layers
Without worry of getting and staying wet from sweat or rain, nothing beats a **cotton t-shirt, lightweight ventilated nylon long-sleeve shirt, tank top, or sports bra**. Try out that sports bra before you commit to a long climb just in case it chafes. Both a **silk weight nylon or wool (short or long-sleeved) base layer undershirt**, or a **button-down style nylon loose fitting shirt** both dry quickly and stay warmer when wet or sweaty. Long sleeve shirts provide more sun, bug, and abrasion protection and don't add too much extra warmth. In winter wear a long sleeve silk weight to **medium weight long underwear top**. Wool is a nice fabric for this application.

Mid-layers
Your mid-layer should provide adequate insulation for belays in warm weather, or climbing/approaching in during cold weather. In winter, you want it warm enough while climbing, but no so warm you need to take it off. If your mid-layer is your final piece, it should offer at least some wind and light rain protection. If layering over, focus on lightweight outer material and good breathability for the mid-layer. In summer, depending on temps and winds, this layer can anything from nothing, to a **light fleece, light insulated jacket or vest** (~60 g. insulation or down if you are careful), **wind-shirt with or without a lining, a lightweight rain jacket**, or a combination of all of the above. **Vests** provide the best heat to weight ratio, but you may want an **ultralight wind-shirt** to put over it. Fleece sweaters provide great abrasion resistance and breathe better than anything if it's cold enough to need to climb in a layer. Light insulated jackets are the best do-it-all piece providing insulation and some wind and rain resistance. Hooded pieces reduce the need to bring a hat. If you don't think you'll get cold, but want a minimal piece of protection just in case, a super light windbreaker or rain jacket is a good call if afternoon showers are common or mild winds are forecasted.

Burly rain jackets, aka **hardshells**, aren't very useful in summertime pursuits, unless very specific conditions require one. Hopefully you'll know. Rain jackets are being made that are almost as light as uber-light wind-shirts nowadays. If you're deciding between the two, you may want to err on the side of better storm protection. Pit zips are for backpacking in the rain and are useless in summer or wintertime climbs. If you overheat, unzip your jacket. If you and your partner are moving very fast, an uber-light wind-shirt may be a better bet. Insanely light and **cheap rain slickers and ponchos** are available in most convenience stores, and **garbage bags** are basically free. These options may actually weigh less than an expensive super-light fancy rain jacket. The big drawbacks to these are that durability and fit may not provide superb rain protection. However, if you usually don't bring a rain jacket as part of your summer kit, these make a great addition to the bottom of your pack. Unless you and your partner are very fast and confident, bring some form of rain protection on longer routes. **Cagoules**, knee length rain jackets, suck for climbing but are the ticket for approaching in the rain.

In the colder shoulder seasons the same advice for summer goes fall and spring, with maybe a few changes. **Wind shirts with lining**, like the Marmot Driclime Wind Shirt, provide slightly more insulation than just a simple wind-shirt alone. If it's brisk while climbing, **softshell jackets** are sometimes a good choice. Both options achieve the same goal. In fact, the celebrated Marmot Dri-Clime Wind-shirt is considered the original softshell piece. Consider a similar jacket (lined wind-shirt) instead of a heavier softshell, although a softshell is much more durable. **Hybrid fleece** with strategically placed wind panels or insulation are generally more comfortable to climb in, but usually require an additional layer if windy, like a light wind-shirt. Light **canvas shirts** (hard to find but awesome) and old **flannel shirts** are great climbing outer climbing layers in dry weather as they add great abrasion resistance and have some wind blocking properties.

Winter mid-layers should focus on warmth with a light wind resistant shell built in. Depending on the temps, you can wear a light or **mid-weight fleece, light synthetic ~60 g jacket, vest**, or all of the above. You can also have your mid-layer be a quasi-shell by using a **wind-shirt or softshell jacket** if you won't be using a waterproof shell. The moment you take off a softshell jacket to climb in the layer underneath is the moment when you invalidated the purpose of bringing a softshell jacket so make sure you dial your setup so you don't overheat when moving. You can also use your lightweight insulated jacket as your climbing outer (pure fleece will probably attract too much snow/water).

There are several **hybrid fleece/wind, insulation/wind, and insulation/fleece** combinations becoming available. These pieces are all meant to provide insulation and wind protection while venting enough heat to be able to climb in. The point is to save weight by reducing redundant shell material and decrease on/off layering hassles, but they fit in a very narrow window of temperatures and conditions. They are amazing when used properly, but they require a lot of thought and knowledge of your personal temperature zones, and how fast you generally move (and your partner). Miss the mark and you'll be cold. Overshoot it by bringing layers they were intended to replace and you added more weight and should have brought one of each instead.

Outer-layer
In most cases, just a mid-layer is enough in the summer. Chillier locations may require a fleece as the mid-layer and a **lightweight synthetic or down jacket or vest** as your outer-layer, even adding a **light rain jacket or wind-shirt**. If wearing a **hardshell** as a protective outer-layer, you will want a final insulating outer-layer for belays or bivies that goes over the shell. Shoulder seasons and warmer winter days can facilitate the

need for a **lightweight belay jacket** (~80-100 g synthetic insulation or down) to be thrown on over your mid-layer at belays. Even warmer belay jackets (big puffies) may be necessary on colder days or climbs with a bivy. Choose synthetic if you plan on bivying (or until dry down shows its merit). **Big puffy jackets** are also great for cold weather cragging since you don't need to worry about the extra weight, and for epic belay sessions in the shoulder seasons. If you and your partner are following pitches quickly and swapping leads, consider only bring one big puffy to share.

If the climbing is wet enough, long enough (you'll get wet on long days), or cold enough (see conductive heat loss) to warrant a hardshell as your climbing outer, consider **softshells** for short duration and hardshells for longer duration. As stated, hardshells are becoming more and more breathable, making softshell jackets less attractive. You will still want a belay jacket to go over the shell. If your climbing **mid-layer has a burly face** to it, like a climbing version of a ski jacket, you may be able to skip a shell completely assuming the climb isn't dripping wet, you aren't dealing with a lot of snow wallowing or digging, and it isn't super windy. For warmer winter climbs you may choose to just climb in your long underwear and shell, tossing on a belay jacket at the end of your pitch. This only works if your shell is highly breathable. **Hybrid waterproof-softshell jackets** and standard softshells are good shells in this situation. What you ultimately are trying to avoid is having a layer sitting in your pack the whole climb.

Optional Uppers
Waterproof-breathable insulated jackets are generally too heavy and get wet from the inside on winter routes. However, they do have a niche on committing summer or shoulder season routes where if it rained you would also be wearing a warm jacket under a shell and the option to just suck it up and get wet would have dire consequences.

Umbrellas are kick-ass rain and sun shelters, and can be used as one of your trekking poles if the handle telescopes. Like poles, they don't climb very well. If you are pretty sure it's going to rain, or are climbing a hot route in direct sunlight, these can be worth the weight.

LEGS

Goretex bibs, softshell salopette, softshell pants, insulated pants, fleece pants, synthetic baselayer

Lightweight cotton pants, zip-off nylon pants, lightweight softshell cargo pants, midweight softshell pants, heavy canvas pants, stretchy Coolmax jeans, nylon shorts, silkweight boxers

Most people's legs can withstand a much larger temperature gradient than their torso area because of the heat generated by the large muscles and they are less cold sensitive for whatever reason. In other words, legs don't overheat or get cold as easily (but they lose heat just as much as anywhere else). This is good news since you need to stop and take your harness off to change leg layers unless donning a pair of **zip-on puffy over-pants** at belays, similar to a belay jacket. Do not underestimate the power of leg insulation to keep you warm when you are standing still or sleeping. If you can easily don a pair of puffy pants on climbs with cold belays you will be very happy.

In the summer, **silk-weight underpants** are gold. Even though going **freestyle** can be liberating, a pair of underpants is nice for alpine accidents. Guys can (or more accurately, will) usually keep the same pair going for many days. Over that, **shorts** are your call if you can manage to not sunburn or scrape your legs up on the rock or bushes. Many climbs have nasty leg scraping bushes on the approach, climb, and descent. **Zip-off pant legs** are a solid compromise. Looser **quick drying nylon hiking pants** with minimal Spandex are generally perfect for everything from cragging to alpine rock climbs. **Wind pants** (or cheap nylon **track pants**) are very popular with lightweight backpackers, but may not work so well on the climb itself since they offer very little friction.

Softshell pants have been extremely popular because they stretch, look sexy, and supposedly offer some snow and rain protection. A **mid-weight pair** for cooler climbs is a better choice than light loose nylon pants just for the thicker face to protect from wind, but softshell pants soak up water and don't dry well because of the Spandex material. Consider a **thicker nylon pant**. **Leg pockets** are sweet for stashing topos, lip balm, etc. I'd hate to be the one to stop the trend, but **yoga and running tights** aren't a great alpine option and can feel pretty warm in the sun. They do move great, and are perfect on cooler summer days, or thicker ones on warmer days. **Harder face slightly thicker cold weather tights** are a better alpine choice if you must climb in fashionable sexy style. **Canvas pants or burly jeans**, like Carharts or some of the newer cotton/synthetic stretchy jeans are excellent dry weather climbing pants.

Lightweight long underwear leggings are occasionally useful in the summer to help you sleep warmer, take the edge of cold mornings, or add a layer if a climb is going to be chilly all day – especially in the shoulder seasons. Taking them off on the climb is a real pain if you overheat, as is carrying a useless layer. If I consider bringing leggings, I will usually just bring a slightly thicker pair of pants instead, or overpants if I'm being a wuss. It really depends on if you are a cold-legged person or not. You could wear zip-off pants with the long underwear underneath and risk looking like a tool. Shorts over polypro for their own sake make no sense in layering or fashion.

Rain pants are almost never necessary in non-snowy conditions unless you are on a committing big wall, or you decide to climb in the rain all day for some reason. Legs don't get as wet and usually dry pretty quickly. Long rainy approaches through the bush may necessitate a pair of light non-waterproof track pants to wear on the approach while you keep your regular pants in your pack. If you do feel the need for actual rain pants, get the lightest waterproof breathable pair you can find. **Coated nylon rain pants** (and jackets) which aren't breathable but totally waterproof are useful for big wall sieges. These are available at gas stations, sporting good store, fishing stores, and Camp USA makes an actual quality coated jacket and pant.

In the winter start with a **mid-weight pair of wool or synthetic pair of long underwear**. You probably don't need underpants under the long underwear. **One-piece long underwear suits** are great as they eliminate gaps and untucking. The zipper could bite, or cause frostnip on your junk, so wear underpants, and make sure the zipper goes under the crotch for pooping. If it's not insanely cold and you have **lightly insulated softshell bibs or pants**, you can stop here. **Polartec Powershield** is an excellent pant fabric in winter. **Waterproof breathable shells** don't insulate, so you may want to tack on a pair of **expedition weight leggings** over the base layer. Add the expedition weight leggings to your softshell pants if it's really cold. Softshell materials are more useful for legs shells than as for jacket shells because legs can tolerate a little moisture build up and also dry quicker because the shell material is closer to your skin due to less layers and your legs generate a lot of heat to aid in drying. Softshell pants also handle crampon slices a bit better (and cheaper) than hardshells. However, when in doubt, go with a waterproof breathable fabric or hybrid.

Suspender-style bibs are useful for some added protection over your chest if you have your jacket off, and chest pockets offer a warm and safe place to stash things since hand pockets either aren't there or are too hard to access. Gloves can also be stashed directly behind the chest fabric to help warm and dry them. **Salopettes**, aka overalls, are just like bibs, but the shell material (usually softshell) extends broadly over the shoulders and chest. They climb a bit better, are a bit more comfortable than suspender-style bibs, and offer a bit more protection for layers underneath if your jacket is off. **Regular pants** and pants with **suspenders** don't offer the extra protection or pocket space as bibs. The main drawback to pants is that your shirt can become un-tucked, exposing your waist to snow and just being uncomfortable. Suspenders keep your pants up when approaching without your harness on. Pants offer better ventilation since there is less fabric, are easier to de-layer shirts and sweaters, and using the bathroom is easier. Any style of pants that goes over your shoulders will require taking off your jacket and harness to poop, so I highly recommend **through the crotch zippers** to avoid this. Peeing is a major problem for girls without crotch zippers, so at least carry a pee funnel.

One-piece shells aren't very common anymore. They don't offer as good layering options (you can never take the jacket off), are really expensive, and you're out of luck if the top or bottom wears out before the other. If you find your knees and butt get cold (or knees get banged up) from kneeling or sitting, try s**ewing or gluing thin closed cell foam** into your pants to add an extra protective layer. You will sweat more in those areas, however.

Lightweight foam knee pads and butt pads sewn into pants. Girdle fabric makes an excellent and tough fabric for a pocket to slide the padding in and out of (and works well for side-pockets on packs).

Zip-on insulated overpants, usually synthetic, may be necessary for climbs with extra-cold bivies, or for comfort hanging around camp. There aren't many times when you would actually climb with them except high altitude expeditions during which you would more likely want heavier down pants, or a full-on down suit. As mentioned, it could be more useful to don insulated pants at the belay than it would be to layer with a second jacket.

KNEES

Kneepads are useful in rock climbing, ice climbing, and tele-skiing. If you're going to a cave or severely overhanging area, especially a limestone area, you probably want a **sticky rubber kneepad**. They not only help with grip on kneebars, they protect your knee. Commercially available rubber pads are available, but aren't commonly sold in most shops. You can make your own by sewing a slab of sticky rubber onto a knee brace. Make sure the pad rides high on your thigh or it will slip off, but make sure you can still bend your knee.

Pads used for aid climbing can be fairly burly if not a lot of free climbing will be done in them, however they many people, including myself, find them annoying and lame. If you're using a **pad for knee protection** in chimneys and offwidths, make sure the pad is soft enough to fully flex your knee, offers enough friction between your knee and the pad, and between the pad and the rock if worn over your pants. Hard-shelled pads are trouble because the plastic tends to skid off the rock and the pad tends to travel, but work well for tele-skiing. A good model uses a thin elastic sleeve in back so you can bend your knee, a soft-flexible foam or gel-like padding in front than will mold to the rock, and are wide enough that they won't rotate around to the back or ride up or down. Soccer kneepads are a good option. Mild knee padding is also helpful for ice climbers. Glue a thin foam pad inside your shell. Don't do this for rock routes, your knees will sweat causing you to grease off.

Hands
Fingerless belay gloves are nice for climbs that involve a lot of rope work and jugging

lines, or to protect your hands during rappelling or belaying. Some climbers swear that always wearing belay gloves when not climbing will really help extend the life of your hands for long trips or climbs. **Fingered belay gloves** are more useful for intense aid climbing, jugging, or hauling to protect your nails, fingertips, and cuticles. Making your own is incredibly easy. For a compromise, just cut the tips off the thumb on index finger.

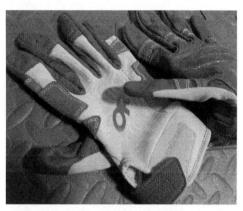

Really cold rock climbs may require you to climb in gloves. Hand jamming may be accomplished in a full glove, but most face holds and finger jams require fingerless gloves. **Tight fitting leather gloves** work better than **sticky mechanic gloves** found in gas station or Home Depot. Try taping **handwarmers** to your wrist, or stash one in your chalk bag to help keep your hands warm instead of using gloves. Warming your whole body up before a pitch by some of the techniques described in the hot aches section can help stave off hot aches.

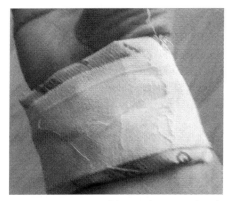

In summer, a **pair of liner gloves** or leather belay gloves are usually all that's necessary for crossing snow or glaciers. **Lightly insulated water resistant shelled gloves**, aka spring gloves, are usually good enough for longer summer snow climbs. **Windstopper gloves** are nice for cold winter approaches.

On winter climbs, the glove selection becomes increasingly complex. Poor technique from over gripping and not shaking out makes for cold hands. A warm core will make for warm hands. Wet hands makes for cold hands. In fact, overly warm gloves will make you sweat and create even colder hands. This is one reason why expert ice climbers wear **lighter weight dexterous gloves**. Difficult screw and rock gear placements also require more dexterity on hard leads. **Ice gloves** can get wet regardless if they have a waterproof breathable laminate in soaking conditions, and the membrane will make you sweat and make your hands even colder. Even a pair of **fleece windstopper gloves** (with or without an overshell) can be warm enough for cold leads, and they dry out much faster than **shelled gloves and gloves with a waterproof membrane**.

A cheap light dexterous glove not only can keep you warm, they are cheap enough to bring several pairs. In very wet conditions you could use a **close fitting waterproof/breathable shell** to glove over the fleece. Outdry and Hyrda gloves seem to offer the best waterproof breathable membrane for a shelled glove right now. One of my favorite all-winter gloves for pretty much anything but leading ice are those made by Flylow or Kinco.

Belay glove courtesy Flylow

You should always carry two pairs of gloves on short routes, and possibly more on longer routes. Some top-level climbers bring three or four pairs up a climb. **A little stuff sack** to contain your gloves isn't a bad idea. Gloves are light, and changing temps can make having just the right pair easier for you on lead, and wet gloves suck. Keep a pair close to your torso to pre-warm them, or to help dry them out if soaked. Your gloves may not dry overnight. Your hands put out a lot of heat so wear them to bed to help them dry.

The popularity of leashless ice tools has lessened the demand for **knuckle padding** on ice gloves, but they still remain a good choice for chronic knuckle bashers. Adding a **liner glove** inside your lead glove can add a bit of warmth, but more dexterity is lost compared to just using a slightly warmer glove. A **good lead glove** for all but extremely cold leads should have leather or synthetic grippy palms and tips with a light layer of interior fleece on the palm side. The backside should have thicker synthetic insulation. The gloves should fit perfectly, with no extra room in the fingertips to trap in carabineer gates or interfere with gear placement. They should be just warm enough to keep your hands cool so they don't sweat. Don't go off of how warm your hands are for those painful hot aches on the first pitch. If your hands aren't warm enough by the end of the second pitch of the day and your hands are dry, then you needed a warmer pair. It is a hard lesson to learn that a lighter glove can sometimes be warmer because the extra thickness also causes you to pump out and not get fresh blood into your hands more.

Once it gets too cold for a nice dexterous pair of gloves, move on to thicker gloves with a **ski glove thickness**, but with Primaloft-type insulation. These are a good thickness of glove for slogging up cold mountaineering climbs as well. If it's brutally cold, you will need **Primaloft mittens** to keep your fingers from getting frostbite. Hopefully you won't be leading anything very technically demanding, but you can still swing your tool and fumble in a screw. On mountaineering trips that require very warm gloves or mittens, do wear some medium weight liner gloves as you will need to perform tasks without your warmer gloves on. **Modular waterproof-breathable Gore-Tex style overmits** are usually overkill except on long cold mountaineering trips. Mittens are warmer than gloves because your fingers are exposed to less surface area to the cold. Handwarmers are fantastic to stick in your gloves at a belay, or on the back of your hand or around your wrist (warms the blood for the whole hand at the source) for cold pitches. They are also good to put inside your wet used pair in case you'll need those gloves again. Some handwarmers are too big and **foot warmers** offer a bit more compact warmth. Only get the shake and warm style without the stickum. The old ember burning cases are just too bulky (if you can even find them anymore).

Dry tool gloves are considerably thinner and offer less (or no) insulation because of the precision involved, and sweating will make things that much more difficult. If your hands warm up after a pitch or climb, they make nice belay and rappel gloves. If your hands will get cold from belaying, use the warmer ski thickness gloves or mittens (and handwarmers). **Electric gloves** are slowly entering the sport, but like their jacket and boot counterparts, there hasn't been enough feedback to recommend them just yet.

Bald Eagle, Punisher ice glove, thicker shelled glove and mitten, cheap mechanic glove, liner glove, Windstopper liner, waterproof spring glove. Standard Windstopper fleece glove not shown.

Gloves are one of the most expensive pieces of gear for the size you can buy. As long as it is warm enough and fits well there's no reason to avoid cheap pairs that work. Some gloves are almost as long lived as their name brand counterparts that cost $1/10^{th}$ the price, making it easier to bring three or four pair along for the climb instead of suffering with just one. Home improvement superstores and truck stops provide a wonderland of gloves. Try them out before using them on a committing climb. Gloves advertised with extra grippy palms may not prove true in cold and wet conditions. The non-waterproof Thinsulate version of Bald Eagle Mechanics Gloves are perfect for climbing in, and the leather Fly Low glove is a dream for belaying. Both of these may possibly be the best gloves I have ever used and they cost as cheap as $10 and $30 respectively. **Baseball, golf and bike gloves** (with fingers) are great drytool gloves.

Tape Gloves

The most common gloves used in non-winter climbing are tape gloves. The better your technique the less tape you'll need, but there will be a point where you will really want them. Granite climbing doesn't require crack gloves as much as desert climbing because jamming is usually less sustained. This isn't always the case, and some granite areas are very rough on the hands. The easiest form of crack gloves are pre-made ones, commonly referred to as **Hand Jammies** (actually a name brand). There are varying degrees of quality to pre-made crack gloves, Occun produces the best pair so far, followed by Singing Rock. You can also make your own by painting over your own light tape job with **Stealth Rubber paint**. Depending on how well you made your own (it is a difficult and messy task), they can be excellent re-usable gloves for all but super tight jams. I've also heard of climbers using **bike tube rubber** to design their own. The downside on pre-made gloves is that they are still bulkier than a good tape job. They are useful for beginners, mildly tight to off hands, or for a short section when tape gloves would be overkill. They are also nice for climbing gym cracks. Some climbers go so far as to double up a tight pair and a medium pair of pre-made gloves for fist and off hands. Once the grade gets stiff, a regular tape job works a lot better.

Tape gloves with Stealth Paint & Occun crack gloves

You may want to add a spritz or two of Mueller **Pre-Tape** (M Tac, Adherent, and Stickum) if your hands sweat, you'll be jamming all day long, you are reusing a pair, or your tape sucks. The older the tape the sticker it is. Also, **Mueller Euro Tape** is much stickier than the U.S. version. Shaving your hands and wrist may be helpful if you have very hairy hands. Nothing besides **cloth athletic tape works** for taping. I've tried everything and actually prefer the thin cheap stuff and a spritz of pre-tape for thin cracks.

To make tape gloves for most climbs (or sustained wide hands to tight hands - Red to Blue Camalot) apply one to three over-lapping layers of tape over your knuckles and down to the middle of the back of your hand. The less tape (or none) here, the more precise and tighter you can jam. Just a quick wrap around your hand one or two times covering the upper ½-1/3rd of your hand could be enough for a pitch or two. Next put a strip around your little finger from your wrist and back to your wrist. Do the same with your index finger. If you want the least amount of tape, only do those two fingers and make sure to spread the tape out to cover as much skin as possible. You can get your thumb, middle and ring fingers. Whatever finger you finish with, continue by securing the ends of all the wraps by going around your wrist 1-3 times. Be careful not to wrap your fingers or wrist too tight. Start over if you do. If you tape your thumb, you may need to hit your thumb knuckle from two angles to completely protect it and keep the tape from rolling down (good for cupped hands and fists). If you need boxing gloves for wider cracks, add more base layers, thumb wraps, and finger wraps. This method of taping keeps your palm tape-free.

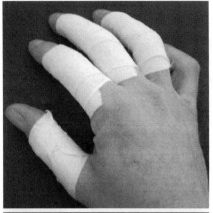

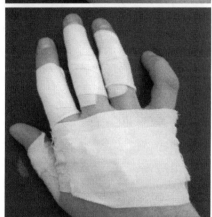

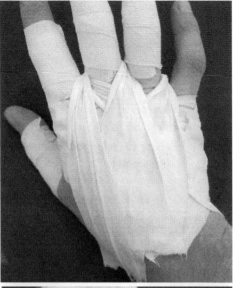

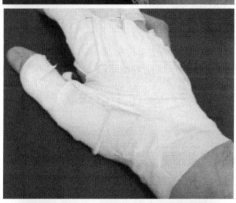

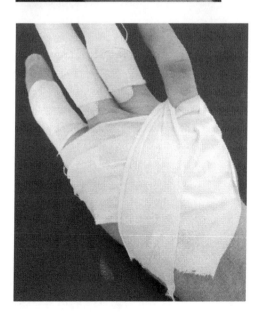

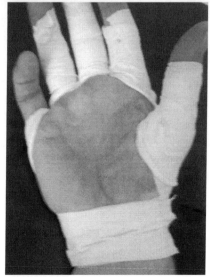

Tape glove steps with finger taping that leaves the palm free and exposed (a good thing)

Tape your fingers in an ergonomically flexed position before making your tape gloves to prevent the tape rolling off. Tape your middle knuckle over your thumb for wide cracks, your thumb and first three fingers to the last knuckle for ringlocks, and the first two fingers for off-finger jams. You can either buy thinner tape, or tear your standard tape in the center for fingers. Tape your ankles for cracks wider than fists. Continue taping up to your pant cuff and even up to your forearm and elbow if the offwidth is burly enough. You can also continue taping from your wrist up your forearm for the hellish offwidths. Taping over the elbow joint can be very painful. Try using a **compression sleeve or thin neoprene elbow brace** instead for offwidths.

FEET

No matter what type of shoe or boot you have, Seam Grip the crap out of threads and areas that may delaminate before you use the shoe to prolong the life out of your shoe.

Synthetic bootie, leather ice boot, plastic ice boot, high top sticky rubber (5.10 Guide), low top (Guide Tennie), technical approach (Ganda), ultralight approach (Cruzer), Merril barefoot shoe, hemp slipper, sticky rubber flip-flop (Evolv).

Summer Footwear

The simplest and lightest approach shoes are **sandals, flip-flops, slippers, boat shoes (Sanuks), and minimalist running shoes (barefoot shoes)**. These also make great **camp shoes**, and are light enough to sneak in the pack if you need to wear sturdier shoes on the hike. If your rock shoes are extra painful, these also make good shoes to slip into during belays or descents. Some of these flimsier type shoes have decent traction, you may even decide to **resole them with sticky dot rubber** if possible.

Some amazing feats of approaching and technical climbing have been done in the skimpiest of footwear, including **taping or strapping crampons over the top of sandals and sneakers**. It takes some finesse to master good proprioception and foot awareness, and have strong enough feet to feel comfortable tackling sketchy or long approaches in a pair of quasi-shoes but the payoff (if you don't destroy your feet) is huge in comfort and weight/bulk savings. If wearing barefoot shoes or flip flops at camp and the bugs come out or it gets cold, you'll want to have brought **fingered socks** as well. Iniji is the most prominent, if only brand. Another really light camp option is to tape or rubber band the **insoles** from your regular shoes over your feet or socks for padding around camp. Light **neoprene ballet slippers** are ridiculously light (1.5 oz.), make good camp shoes, to switch into during belays to give your feet a break, and can cover your climbing shoes if approaching or descending in them. Needless to say, I'm a fan. Nufoot makes a cheap pair. **Karate slippers and Toms** are another great choice.

A step up in protection from the suggestions above are your standard **sticky rubber approach shoes**. There are many brands and styles from high top boots to minimalist barefoot versions. **Sticky dot rubber** generally works best, **treaded sticky rubber** works best for easy scrambling, snow, and trails, but not as well for techy moves. Five Ten makes the best approach shoe rubber, hands down. The major drawbacks of regular approach shoes are durability. Most don't make it past a year. **Seam Grip** all the seams, and resoling the sticky rubber can extend their life. Getting approach shoes wet drastically reduces their lifespan. Look for shoes with minimal seams or bonded areas that look like they'll come apart or delaminate easily. **Barge Cement** works well to patch together split seams and soles. You can make your own approach shoes if you can find a dirt-cheap pair of tennis shoes that can be resoled with sticky rubber.

If your feet or ankles are in just miserable shape, you may need to use a pair of nice **running or hiking shoes** that fit your feet better. There are so many styles of approach shoes these days you should be able to find a pair that works without resorting to a clunky pair of hiking boots. Gore-Tex or other membranes sound like a good idea, but any amount of water protection will ultimately fail and take that much longer to dry out. Also shoes with waterproof breathable membranes don't breathe as well, creating a warm moist environment for blisters to develop. Depending on how well your feet can deal, try bringing the lowest volume, lightest weight pair of shoes for the approach as possible. Long bushwhacks with glacier crossings and snow climbing may require a burlier shoe than your standard shoe, but many great climbers just use your standard approach shoe. See that your toes don't jam into the tip of the shoe, and the heel doesn't dig into your ankle. When in doubt, go a ½ size up and lace them tighter.

Lightweight summer mountaineering boots

Long stretches of aid climbing in ladders can require a shoe with a stiffer sole, a raised heel (too keep from slipping off the steps), and **more ruggedly built especially in the toe**. However, it is far more efficient to wear rock shoes while aiding in order to bust occasional free moves.

Thick, medium, and thin Merino, Coolmax double dock, fingered sock, light Schoeller gaiter, light nylon gaiter.

Cotton socks are just fine for dry climbs, assuming it won't be cold enough for your feet to get too cold. If that's the case, or cotton socks give you blisters, then use **synthetic or wool socks**. Different feet develop blisters based on different sock choices. Thick warm socks may require a **liner** if they give you a blister, or see if you can just use some light thin socks. If you don't get blisters, thinner and cooler **mesh or light weave socks** dry quickly. **Double layer socks** (one pair with two built in layers) may work great for you, or create too much sliding and create blisters. The same thing goes for liner socks – they can solve or create blisters. For ice and snow approaches with approach shoes, it's a good idea to bring a

medium weight pair of hiking socks. Individually toed socks may help with some foot or toe problems if you can stand wearing them, and work well with flip-flops at camp. For multiday trips, always stash a pair of **sleeping socks** inside your bag to give your feet some needed dry time. Pack at least a **second pair of socks** for the hike out. Fresh socks are amazing things and don't weight very much, so bring extras.

Zem Ninja shoes

Once on the climb you can either put your shoes in a single follower's pack, shoes in your own pack, or clip them to your harness. If you're a size 6 and your partner is a size 14, you may want to suggest carrying your own shoes! Clipping shoes to the back of your harness is usually the best way to carry them with small packs and harder climbing. To keep the shoes from taking up too much space, put them toe to heel and wrap them in athletic tape (or a **rubber band** if you've got one). The shoe that doesn't get clipped in the heel (because they're facing opposite) needs to use the laces to backup into the clipping point. If you are lucky enough to have the **same shoe size as your partner**, some situations could allow for only needing one pair of rock shoes and once pair of approach shoes.

The next step-up from approach shoes are **lightweight leather mountaineering boots**. These usually don't weigh much, but are fairly bulky. They usually have a heel welt but no toe bail, and accept strap-on or crampons with a heel bail and front harness. These are good boots for summer glacier climbs or warm weather alpine ice climbs where a standard ice boot may be too warm and heavy. They may be useful for long alpine scramble or ridges if you have weaker feet, or for short glacier/ice crossings if you aren't comfortable using strap-on crampons over tennis shoes. Be sure to break this type of boot in because they are especially blister-prone.

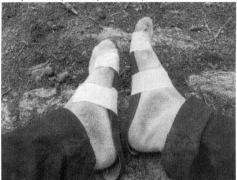

Cheap camp insole shoes

Winter Footwear

Olympus Mons high-altitude boot courtesy La Sportiva. Phantom Guide courtesy Scarpa.

Spantik double ice boot

Ice climbers and mountaineers have a lot of expensive options to choose from. Once you decide on the type of boot you need, make your next decision completely based on how they fit – not what the "best" boot is. You will lose a lot more technical precision with mangled feet in the year's most hyped boot than you will with an "out of date" pair that fits perfectly. It can be very difficult to find a local shop with enough selection and a good return policy. If you know just what to get, please visit the local climbing shop. Otherwise, waste some shipping dollars and find the perfect pair online. Make sure you can completely wiggle your toes and there are no pressure points over any of your toes on top or the sides. Slam your foot hard into a concrete wall and make sure your big toenail won't get compacted by doing this all day long. Fit your toe box first, then worry about the heel. Of course you don't want to slide up and down in the heel for blister and precision sake, but you can add a **heel insert** to take up some volume or try lacing tighter. If you can't get it to fit, move on to another pair – don't make your feet fit. Even plastic boots take time to break in, so bring your old pair on a trip just in case. Don't break in a new pair on a big climb! Spend at least three full days of slogging up something wet before committing (this is where a good return policy comes into play).

Light leather or synthetic ice boots with step-in compatible welts are generally the lightest, most precise, and least warm ice boot. If you get a pair that fits and have a warm sock, lightweight ice boots should work even in very cold conditions. Be sure and Seam Grip all the seams, clean them when dirty, and apply **leather conditioner**. **Gore-Tex membranes** are acceptable in these boots since you really don't want to get your feet wet, drying time is huge no matter what, and the membrane acts as a mild vapor barrier. **Fruit boots** are an even lighter, more flexible, less insulated boot with a permanently attached crampon. They are not cheap, and you have to carry them to the crag. If you are on a budget, making your own by taking a pair of monopoint crampons apart and bolting them carefully on can save a bundle if you already own an extra boot and crampon.

If a climb you're doing requires long stretches of technical rock climbing in extremely cold conditions with little to no ice, I recommend wearing crampons regardless. Leather boots with sticky rubber soles still don't climb as well as a precise crampon point. Switching in and out of crampons is a chore, and drytooling grades has proven that very difficult routes can be climbed much more efficiently with ice tools and crampons than without. If the rock is dry, you could climb with **socks and a larger sized rock shoe** and fingerless gloves. **Insulated rock shoes** are very hard to find, but again, climbing with crampons and tools has proven to be the way to go if you have experience drytooling.

Soft plastic double boots are a good choice for easy mountaineering. They are usually more comfortable than leather boots, are warmer, and are useful for spending the night since you can take the liner out of the shell for inside the tent. When technical climbs require a warmer boot, the ability to dry the boot out at night, and a higher margin of error and safety for frostbite, a quality pair of **double leather boots or firm plastic boots** are in order. Double leather/synthetic boots have improved so much in the last decade that they can be used on all but the harshest (coldest) routes. For a frigid 1-2 bivy climb, a longer warmer backcountry trip, or a really really cold day climb double leathers are perfect. Super-warm **high altitude double boots** are available for extremely cold or high altitude trips. You can add **overboots** (cover the entire boot including the sole) for extreme conditions as well. You must wear crampons at all times when wearing overboots. **Supergaiters,** insulated gaiters that add some extra warmth over the top of the boot but not under, aren't as common because boot technology has made them mostly unnecessary. Supergaiters and overboots can be used to increase the warmth of your lighter boots, but fitting crampons can be a real challenge. It's a better idea to upgrade to a warmer boot. For technical climbing in plastic boots, be sure to buy a pair that uses heat moldable liners so you can size a shell as small as possible. **Ski boots** can be horrible to climb in, but somewhat comfy pairs can be found if skiing well on the approach trumps what you'll actually be climbing. There has been a recent surge of very light alpine ski boots that are ridiculously light and climb pretty darn well.

Supergaiter

Overboots

Thick merino wool socks are usually the way to go for cold weather footwear, and a good pair can help increase the warmth of your boot. A major source of heat loss in boots occurs in the sole of the boot. You can really help this situation by **insulating the bottom of the boot**. You can do it yourself by cutting out a piece of firm closed cell foam, covering it in tin foil, and placing it under your insole. You must size the boot accordingly for this. Some custom foot beds offer winter insulation like the Superfeet **merino wool insoles**, and can be swapped out for the ones that came with your boot. There are some **electric heated foot beds** on the market, but not enough testing by climbers has been done to determine if they actually work well.

Vapor barrier socks, or plain old bread bags are fairly useful for very cold weather climbing. Put on a liner sock, then the VBL, and your wool sock over the bag. Shake and warm **toe warmers** are also an option, but may interfere too much during technical climbing or approaching. Add them to your boot as a last resort. Overheating and water from snow/ice inside the boot can make for some chilly feet as the day draws to a close. If this could be an issue, change your socks before frostbite sets in, don't just wait for camp. Applying antiperspirant to your feet before a climb could really help if your feet sweat and then get cold. Don't use the old cayenne pepper trick, it will cause more problems than you know what to do with and it doesn't really work. Be sure and trim those toenails, especially the big toenail for ice and winter climbs. Compacted toenails are trip-ending epics.

Camp booties are wonderful luxury items at basecamp. Only get **synthetic booties with smooth soles**. Down booties get sopping wet quite easily, and tread will trap snow and soak through the sole.

Gaiters

The only function gaiters should have is to keep snow from getting inside your boots. If your pants adequately cover your boot, you may not even need them. Many high end pants have **grommets you can use to add an instep cord**. Deep snow may push your pant leg up and then necessitate gaiters. If your pants cover your boots, snow conditions aren't wallowing, or the trip is short or warm enough, you may not need them. The big problem with gaiters is that they further inhibit water vapor from leaving your shoes. Adjusting laces for ice leads becomes more difficult, and a well-laced boot may be sacrificed because getting at the laces covered by crampons and gaiters proved to be too big of a chore. Gaiters can cause overheating (especially in the summer) which causes blisters. **Thin softshell** material is usually all you need from a gaiter to keep snow out and minimize breathability issues.

Using gaiters to protect the fabric of your pants only makes sense if your pants are expensive Gore-Tex type material and the gaiters are cheaper softshell. Even so, crampon rips in Gore-Tex pants are easily fixed with repair tape, and lower legs are not a place where you really need a bombproof storm shell. It makes no sense to layer **Gore-Tex gaiters** over Gore-Tex pants. Using gaiters to protect from scree in the summer is also overkill, just take your shoe off and dump out the rocks. **Summer gaiters** to protect from snowfields will probably just keep your shoes and socks from drying, unless you are wearing waterproof footwear for long glacier slogs. Get gaiters with Hypalon straps that go under your foot, nylon will get destroyed quickly.

Lacing System

There's more than one way to lace your boots. The laces that come with most boots, shoes, and rockshoes are too thin to last. Get a set of **round polyester laces as thick as will fit**. Separate the different sections of your shoe, like your toes, midfoot, heel, and calf with a locking knot to apply different tension to each area. A locking knot is just a simple overhand knot with one extra pass around. Check out this great video for some lacing techniques:
http://youtu.be/SOE28brAcEc

Moldable Liners

Many double boots offer **custom moldable liners**, which are highly recommended. You can mold heat moldable liners yourself, but I highly recommend doing it at a ski shop. Moldable liners can be refitted several times, so if you didn't get it right the first time, try again. Before you mold the liner, fit the shell to your socked foot to make sure you're buying the right size. Two fingers should be able to slip between your foot and the shell. The shell can be stretched, but consider buying a brand that fits and doesn't require stretching. Any boot can be stretched, so don't suck it up and wear a boot that has tight spots, you'll wind up crippled on the descent or with permanent bunions. To mold the liner you must prep your foot with a toecap. The toecap ensures that your toes have adequate wiggle room. You can make your own toecap by cutting and taping a thin closed cell foam pad around your big and 2nd toe, and around your pinky and 2nd to last toe like a sleeve. Next cut a strip and tape it across the tops of all your toes. If you have areas that have spurs, bunions, or are prone to pinching, tape padding over those areas as well. Slip a liner sock over your toecap and then the thickest socks you plan on wearing. Heat the moldable liner according to the manufacturer's specifications. When it's done, slide your footbed inside the liner, and put the liner on. Spaying the inside of the boot with silicone can help you get into the boot, but either way, when putting your foot into the shell, be very careful to not create any creases. Lace the boot up tight, and hang out for 10 – 30 minutes. If you don't plan on having any serious foot issues and want a tighter fit, still make a toe cap, but use a medium thickness sock instead and don't tighten the boot as much.

You can also stretch the outside of a plastic shell. Line the shell with a turkey basting plastic bag and fill it with boiling water. After 20 minutes, put the liner and your feet in. I have also considered buying a pair of mannequin feet a half size bigger than my foot to do the dirty work!

Rock Shoes

Big comfy slipper, Muira lace, hightop Grandstone, Mythos, Mocassym

No matter what shoe you get for what purpose, get a pair that fits. Excruciating pain will subtract several grades in performance. Bear in mind that most shoes, especially leather, will stretch out – up to about two U.S. sizes in some cases. Some shoes take a few days, while other more aggressive shoes take a month or two. For example, if you want a precise pair of **leather uppers** and you wear an U.S. 11 you may want to suffer with a size 9 or even an 8! If you get a **synthetic** shoe with a lot of rubber and want a comfort shoe for easy climbing then you may just get a size 11 or 10.5. Having experience with a company's sizing can have a huge impact on what size to get. Have a **backup pair** during the break-in process for long routes or important sends, but try and deal with the discomfort as much as possible to break the new ones in. One way to speed up this process is to get your shoes wet and wear them around the house until they dry a few times. Shoes that are purchased as mildly uncomfortable can turn into sloppy oversized shoes if they are prone to stretching. If the liner that has the size written on it doesn't look too durable, or will rub off, write the size in Sharpie under the tongue so when it comes time to buy a new pair you know exactly what to get.

Stiff or board lasted shoes tend to edge well, and make cracks and standing on sharp ledges more comfortable. They are less sensitive than more malleable **unlasted or unlined** shoes, don't smear as well, and won't fit in thin cracks as well. They can also dig into your heels. Heavier folks usually fare much better in this type of all-day or generic crack shoe because their extra weight allows the shoe to deform to the rock (and helps them stick). Stiff shoes can also create more pressure/pain points. These shoes can come with **high-tops** to protect your ankles from wide cracks, and extra padding to protect from foot jamming. A Czech company, Saltic, makes an **ankle protector** that fits inside rockshoes as well. Cutting off your socks at the arch is a cheap alternative.

TC Pro

Softer unlined all day shoes are a lot stickier, especially for lightweight climbers, more sensitive than stiffer all-day shoe, and tend to perform better on slabs (if the soles are in relatively good shape) and thin cracks. They offer less comfort and support (unless stiff shoes are uncomfortable for you) and lose extremely precise edging capabilities after the rubber has rounded out in the toes. They also tend to stretch a lot.

The final type of shoe (and with the most models out there) are **aggressive slip lasted face climbing shoes**. These shoes are usually stiff in the toebox to help with edging. Most have an aggressive **asymmetrical last**, meaning the toes are wrangled towards the big toe to focus the power there. Some have slight, to extremely **downturned toes** to aid in using the toes to pull into the rock. Usually the more downturned or asymmetry, the more painful, but more precise the shoe. **Rubber over the toebox** helps with toe hooking and jamming, and **rubber on the heel** aids in heel hooking. The more specialized the shoe, the poorer it will perform on everything and better it will perform for it specific intended use. Many trad climbers use a face climbing shoe because the trad cruxes involve more face-type footwork and less foot jamming.

Lace-ups tend to be more all-around in terms of stiffness and fit, **Velcro** tends to be more performance oriented, stiffer, and aggressive for steep overhangs, and **slippers** tend to be softer and tighter. For trad climbers, lace ups can get pretty chewed in cracks, including the eyelets. If this is a constant problem, use some pliers to remove the metal eyelets, which is usually where the abrasion takes place, and replace the laces with thicker ones. Velcro closures open up in hand to fist sized cracks and cause pain. Slippers, especially when fit relatively loose, excel in thin cracks but hurt like crazy over the top of the toes. Many thin crack masters will stand on their toes to keep them flat before a hard send. Softer flatter slippers also work very well on slippery rock, like cobblestone, as more surface area and pressure can be exerted over a broad area. It can help to paint the surface of slippers with Stealth Rubber paint or something else to protect the fabric over the toes, tape your toes, or wear a **toe sock cap** (the other end of the sock you cut up for ankle protection).

The final choice you have is the type of rubber. **Thinner rubber** works well on thin cracks and slabs for better fit and precision, but doesn't last as long obviously. **Thicker rubber** lasts longer, is more comfortable to stand on, and will edge better (but with less precision). As for the brand, lab tests have shown that they all are about as sticky. However, that's not the opinion of most climbers. Stealth C4 is by far the most requested rubber for all applications. If your shoes don't come with the rubber you want, you can always resole them later.

Prepare for when it's time to resole your shoes. Some popular resoling companies have a 6-8 week turnaround time! Don't wait for the shoe to blow out before sending them in, they may not be repairable or it may cost you much more to fix them. Usually just the front half of the shoe needs resoling. Just like foot specialists look at running shoes to diagnose foot problems, you can diagnose technique problems by the longevity and wear of your shoes. No matter who you send your shoe to, do your research. Some companies are run by climbers in desperate need of an income source. A poor job will either delaminate, or change the shape of your toebox – ruining your shoe. A normal resole with shipping costs around $30-45 bucks. If you need to make temporary repairs, **Barge Cement mixed with Stealth Rubber Paint** works really well. Paint the rubber on heavy abrasion areas on your shoe to extend their life, which also aids in purchase over that area. You can resole a shoe yourself using **resole kits**. I strongly urge you to not do this unless you are a good craftsman and have the proper tools.

Before heading up a route, be sure your shoes are clean. Spit shining the soles by getting them wet (with spit) and vigorously rubbing the soles together not only cleans the soles, but also removes oxidized rubber that won't be nearly as sticky. Hard cores will bring a small square of **AstroTurf** for shoeing up at the base.

Drying, Cleaning, and Repairing Clothes and Gear

Wet clothes in the morning are not only a major bummer, they can be dangerous. If your bag is warm enough, wearing the clothes will dry them the quickest. The next best option is to lay the wet garments flat on top of your sleeping pad and under your sleeping bag. If they just need a little warmth, put them in the bottom of your sleeping bag. **Hot water bottles and handwarmers** can help dry wet gloves, socks, and boots. Double boots are great because you can leave the shells in the vestibule, upside down outside, or near the front of the inside of the tent, and either wear the liners in the bag, or keep them warm at the bottom of your bag. On the climb, make sure to immediately stuff your climbing gloves inside your bibs (or as close to your chest as possible making sure they don't fall out) before putting on belay gloves. Pre-place activated handwarmers in your belay gloves, and swap them into your wet climbing gloves before stuffing them in your bibs (or have multiple handwarmers).

It can be difficult to keep things dry on winter trips, even if they are based out of from huts, hostels, or hotels. The first thing you should do after the climb is to focus on drying your clothes, and gear. Bring **parachute cord** on these trips to string up around your room so you and your partner aren't cramming everything on top of the hotel heater. Packing a plug-in **glove and boot drier** for the room or car is fully worth it to avoid the hotel room sauna. In the summer, a **mesh stuff sack** can be indispensable for drying clothes on the climb or hike.

There are two camps on cleaning your gear. One states that washing your gear will make them fall apart. The dirt is holding everything together, glue can delaminate, and seams will blow. The other believes that dirt wears down your gear and cleaning will keep lasting longer. Durable water repellent (DWR) treatments on the outside of synthetic clothing do the brunt of the work on waterproof shells and water resistant jackets. If water doesn't roll off or soaks into the outer fabric, then the garment won't breathe or will soak through if it wasn't fully waterproof. Outdoor companies insist that you gently wash your garments and dry at a high heat to redistribute the coating. If the DWR finally wears off, you can buy expensive **DWR spray**. Do not use wash-in waterproofing, it will ruin the performance of your clothing. It won't make the whole garment water resistant – once the exterior is permeated, it will get wet. The same goes with wash in down-proofing as it will reduce loft, and silicone-based waterproof spray reduces breathability compared to DWR spray. The key to not ruining your gear by washing it is to use cold water and **gentle detergent**. You can be safe and use an expensive tech wash, or just use Woolite (I can't fully guarantee Woolite). The new product, Never Wet, looked like a miracle treatment. However, it is totally useless.

Down garments and bags occasionally need to be washed to get rid of smell and restore their loft. This should be done very rarely as repeated washing will remove the natural oils on the down feathers that improve loft. A good rule of thumb when to wash a down item is when you think, "I really need to wash this". Only use techy down wash recommended by outdoor companies. Turn the bag or jacket inside out and place it in a very large front loading washing machine, or do it by hand in a bucket, using only cold water and gentle settings or hand agitation. Run a full cycle of plain water after the soap cycle is completed. Be very careful about pulling the bag out. It will be heavy with water and can tear the delicate inner baffles. Squeeze out (gently) as much water as possible and put it in the drier on low heat. Don't add tennis balls to reduce clumping – if the bag is dry there won't be any clumping. Plan on waiting a very long time at the laundromat for the bag to dry.

Use a front-loading washing machine, or the gentle cycle on your top loading. You can be extra careful and wash things in a bathtub or a plastic storage bin. I am paranoid and run a full hot water cycle of just water before washing anything expensive or load bearing. Air dry anything wool or spandex enriched, but put your shells with DWR in the dryer on hot. Don't use drier sheets!

If your gear is still stinky, use **Myrazyme** to deal with the odor. Rock shoes require a healthy dose of **Lysol** to kill the fungus growing inside. Some folks even put their rock shoes in the wash with reported good results. As mentioned, leather garments should get cleaned and conditioned to keep them from drying, loosing suppleness and water resistance, and cracking. You can get **liquid or wax based leather conditioning** products, but wax seems to do a better long-term job. You may want to find **spray that adds UV protection**, and this can be fairly useful if you spend a ton of time in your tent and want to keep it for a long time, especially at altitude. Don't spray your ropes and slings with anything.

This brings me to washing you rope. I'm in the don't wash camp, mainly because I usually retire my rope before it is so dirty I'm considering washing it (or it becomes a gym rope), and also because they always seem to fatten and fuzz up, and probably lose some DWR properties. If you must wash your rope, use a commercial rope wash detergent or nothing at all, and make sure the washing machine didn't have any harsh detergent residue left over. A **mesh laundry bag** will help keep your rope from developing an impossible snarl from the process. Don't dry it! And do not even think about using warm water or a drier on anything Dyneema. You can still find Nickwax Rope Proof in some places, meant to re-waterproof your rope. This is a low-grade version of the much higher-tech DWR processes added to your rope when it was manufactured. In other words, it is probably a waste of money. Other wash-in rope treatments have been taken off the market due to toxicity.

As long as you're washing your body in the alpine, you may as well wash your base layers and socks. Use the same **biodegradable soap** used for the shower tips, or you can buy special **dried leaves of biodegradable laundry soap**. It's really hard to not contaminate the water supply when washing your clothes. Use your cook pot to agitate the clothes (gross!), and the alpine shower to rinse them away from the water source. If it's warm enough, put the wrung out damp clothes back on to dry them. If you brought a change of clothes, then you can air dry them. Be careful of winds blowing dirt or causing the clothes to drop on the ground and get dirty again. Sun facing rocks and tent flys make quick drying surfaces.

Fabric Repair

Although **duct tape** is the repair material of choice for things around the house, **Gorilla Tape** is superior in about every way. Old duct tape is stickier than new, like athletic tape. But both are heavier and won't stay put compared to fabric repair tape on material. **Fabric repair tape** is perfect for mending holes and tears on anything from jackets, to tents, to sleeping bags, to waterproof jackets. If you really want it to stay put, coat the area with **Seam Grip** after you've applied the patch. **Gore-Tex patches** only make sense if repairing a large hole without using Seam Grip. Seam Gripping over a Gore-Tex patch or applying Gore-Tex over Gore-Tex will kill breathability so just go with cheaper and lighter repair tape in most cases. You can also find **Cuben fiber repair tape**. There aren't many fabric repair jobs that can't be fixed with the tape and glue method. Store used Seam Grip in the freezer so it doesn't harden and become difficult to reuse.

Barge Cement, Seam Grip, fabric and Goretex repair tape.

For more cosmetic repairs a **needle and thread or iron on patches** (applied on the inside) do the job. **Dental floss** makes a very durable thread. A spool of dental floss taken out of the case and **medium gauge needle** weigh nothing and can save the day. Repairs to tears in load bearing areas will require stronger stitching and a burlier needle. The **Speedy Stitcher** does a wonderful job penetrating tough fabric and the waxed thread it comes with is pretty strong, especially when coating in Seam Grip afterword. Busted laces are easily solved with **4 mm accessory cord**. If you're in the woods, steal from unnecessary items, like from your pack drawstring.

General Climbing Gear

Marking Gear

Keeping track of your gear between you and your partner can be difficult. **Nail polish** lasts a while and doesn't catch like tape. Paint the nail polish on low wear areas. Marking your initials on slings and webbing with a **Sharpie** probably won't damage much, but it's your call. Engraving is probably ok too, but it would worry me enough to avoid it. However, printing out **stickers** that have your name and phone is an excellent way to play on people's conscience to give you your stuck cams back. Asking for your gear back is only acceptable if you had an accident, major epic, or lost a serious amount of gear. Asking for a cam on the Internet back that you left while bailing, got stuck, or forgot is lame. Don't put someone in a position to relinquish their booty and make a trip to the post office for your failure or ineptitude.

Helmets

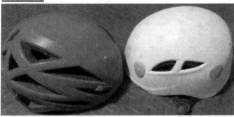

The current trend is to make helmets lighter so people actually wear them. This trend can be misleading to consumers, suggesting that **ultralight helmets** will give them the same level of security as **heavier models**. While new materials and architecture have increased strength and subsequently lowered weight, ultralight helmets are by no means as strong or safe as their heavier modern counterparts. Helmets are designed to protect your skull mostly from falling objects, and the current UIAA standard is to protect your from an 11 pound object falling from 2 meters that transmits 8 kN or less of force to the head (which could easily give you a concussion or spinal fracture). The current CE standard is 10 kN. Tests to the side, front, and read and also puncture tests use even less weight from an even shorter height. Testing results compiled from: Climbing Magazine Aug 2013 (317).

Depending on the size, shape, and durability of the helmet, some helmets may not offer much protection from a front, rear, or side impact - something that can easily occur in a swinging or upside-down fall. Considering the severe consequences of even a minor concussion (or worse), it is crazy to not wear a helmet. Accidents are never expected and can occur at the most benign crags or climbs - even to the belayer or while bouldering. John Sherman in his book "Better Bouldering" simply stated that he couldn't find a good reason not to wear a helmet. Due to the horrible consequences, which death may not even be the worst of those, it really doesn't make any sense to not wear one. If a redpoint or onsight would go much smoother without a helmet for whatever reason, or navigating a tight squeeze chimney, then the risk vs. reward ratio may be enough to not wear one (which is understandable - climbing is a risk/reward sport). But not wearing one because it makes you look cooler (better be wearing jeans and no shirt with a beanie) or it weighs too much on a moderate route is pretty stupid and puts others at risk as well as ruins the lives of loved ones or those who witnessed your accident.

Wear your helmet correctly. Not only will you look like a moron, you'll be exposing your head to more surface area or transmitting forces inappropriately if you do get hit. DO NOT STORE ANYTHING UNDER YOUR HELMET! This is less of a concern as most helmets these days don't have a hollow space under the webbing, but the force of impact would transfer directly into your skull. Remember getting hit on the little button on top of your baseball cap when you were a kid? Very soft items still reduce the helmet's impact strength, and firmer items will break your skull.

It has been suggested that by offering a false sense of security by wearing a helmet climbers may take greater risks. I don't know about you, but that argument seems absurd. That said, know the protective limits of your helmet. Helmets won't save your life in disastrous falls or from large falling debris, but they may reduce your risk or severity of injury in moderately dangerous falls or smaller falling objects. Helmet technology to improve protection is limited due to market demands. Future helmets could incorporate dual density foam or other technology to absorb and reduce impact or offer complex designs to prevent the brain from rotating or slamming into the skull, which is what happens in a concussion. If one person forgets a helmet, it is difficult to decide who should wear it. If the climbing is difficult, the leader should wear it to protect from upside-down and pendulum falls. If the rock is suspect then the belayer should wear it. If ice climbing, climbing below a party, or a multipitch route with suspect rock then go home. Wear a freaking helmet. A good test to see if a helmet is appropriate would be to explain to someone you care about why you chose not to wear one after an accident.

Reasons to Wear a Helmet
- Any ice, snow, or alpine climb – goes without saying
- Rock and icefall – rockfall can happen at the cleanest most popular cliffs at any time for any reason from above the leader to onto the belayer. Reasons for icefall should be extremely obvious.
- Dropped gear from above – again, obvious.
- Upside-down falls – how confident are you that you won't flip and hit your head?
- Pendulum falls – even a low short fall can slam your head into the arête next to you.
- Bouldering – if you don't have good spotters or are going to do a move that may cause you to smack you head on the ground then wear a helmet. Falls from bouldering are hard enough to kill or disable you.
- Banging your head – standing up into a protrusion or roof sucks.
- Getting injured sucks - being paralyzed or mentally challenged is a lot less cool than your fashion sense.
- Respect - for loved ones, friends, rescuers, and people who don't want to see or deal with a bloody mess that could have been avoided.

Reasons to Not Wear a Helmet
- Squeeze chimney – you usually can take the helmet off and trail it behind you.
- Out of danger – The odds are low enough that getting hit is negligible.

Bad Reasons to Not wear a Helmet
- Ego - not cool, no one else wearing one, better climber not wearing one, impress friends, narcissism
- Too hot – get a vented lightweight helmet
- Won't protect from disastrous falls – The odds are stacked you'll get killed by rockfall or small lead falls by banging your head than taking the monster whip of death. Keep the odds in your favor. No a helmet won't save you from everything. Neither do seatbelts, but they save lives.
- Leads to riskier behavior – when have you ever based a decision to go for it based of the fact that you have a helmet? If you have, please exit the gene pool.
- Interferes with your redpoint/onsight: This is a valid reason until something bad happens.

HARNESSES

All-around harnesses made today are all fairly light, packable and comfortable and can be used on pretty much any type of climbing without a lot of compromise. One of the best harness features out there are the **"supersafe" models** made by Metolius in which every single thing on the harness could hold a moderate fall. This is an especially useful feature on routes you need to clip a tag line to (clip it anywhere) or if a gear loop ripped off spilling all of your gear (it happens). **Large front gear loops** are always a great feature, and it's amazing how many models out there have tiny ones. **Rear gear loops** are useful in almost every type of climbing and don't add any weight, as are **haul loops** in the back. Even sport climbers need to bring a rappel device or haul a 2nd line for a long pitch. If your harness only has front loop it is easy to add rear loops with some 3-4 mm cord. Duct or electrical tape could be used to stiffen the loops if need be.

Adding rear gear loops to a harness without them

Aid climbers might even want to make a **2nd lower hanging gear loop** to create more clipping room and organization. Adding a haul loop is a bit more difficult. Poking a small hole in the fabric of the harness to accomplish this is probably a bad idea, so use your own judgment. Some light harnesses have a small plastic tab in back that is not full strength so be careful not to shock-load this with your tag line, especially if you fall. One solution may be to use some 9/16" webbing to tie around the entire back of the harness, but this may prove to be uncomfortable.

Self-locking, or **speed buckles** that don't require you to double back your harness are amazingly handy, and much safer. Feeding the buckle back with frozen hands on an ice climb is no fun. **Double-back buckles** are very useful when wearing a bulky winter outfit, big boots, and crampons so you can remove the harness without a balancing/contortion act. **Adjustable leg loops** aren't as useful as one would think – unless your thigh width is seriously out of whack with the waist size of the harness. The main reason for adjustable legs is for added layers. But how thick are these layers really going to be? **Non-adjustable leg loops** have several inches of give, so if you're wearing inches of insulation odds are you'll be wearing a different harness. Adjustable leg loops can make it easier to drop trough and poop without taking the whole harness off, but it can still be done with non-adjustable legs. It is also handy for pooping if the elastic keeping the legs up can be easily removed while wearing the harness, although they have an annoying tendency to come off.

Ice climbers and mountaineers, like sport climbers, don't need thick bulky harnesses because of the extra layers of clothing to pad under the harness. Also, a **thinner harness** will dry more quickly. Harnesses marketed for ice climbing really only has one additional feature that is useful: **ice clipper slots**. Some allow for a normal carabineer, others only allow for the larger plastic ice clippers. Lefties beware, most ice harnesses put two slots on the right side, and only one on the left. The one on the left is usually farther back as well.

Plastic ice clippers can and do break – sending your much needed protection down the hill. Large opening keylock carabineers (bent or wiregate) make great durable ice screw clippers. If your harness doesn't have the slots (or they are on the wrong side), the solution is incredibly simple. Clip the biner to your gear loop and wrap it in electrical tape. The tape is non-structural, it only stiffens the biner for easy clipping. Coldthistle used to make **aluminum ice clippers** for those who distrust plastic models. There are other methods and devices out there, but nothing as simple and easy as a **biner-style ice clipper**. The Petzl and Grivel **panpipe ice screw holders** are not a bad system for racking ice screws either. They haven't caught on, but work very well.

Photo courtesy Grivel

Alpine **diaper-style harnesses** used to be the lightest way to go, but were no fun to hang in. Luckily there are many full-strength harnesses out there much lighter than those old harnesses for objectives where you don't plan on falling on hanging. The main drawback of these harnesses is the lack of gear loops. Either add your own, use a gear sling for everything, or use a pack that has gear loops on the waist belt. Camp, Mammut, Arcteryx, and Edelrid all make several **ultralight harnesses** geared towards ski mountaineering and sport climbing. Ultralight harnesses have extremely low durability so save them for when it counts and check them often for wear. Making your own harness from webbing or a cordalette would only be slightly heavier (and a lot cheaper), and using the rope to make your harness would be the lightest (and strongest) possible option. These are good things to know how to make in a pinch, regardless of speed ascents.

Photo courtesy CAMP USA

Courtesy Black Diamond

> To make your own harness: Five feet from the end of the rope or whatever you're using, tie an overhand loop big enough for your thigh. Six inches past that, make another loop for your other thigh. Step into both loops. Wrap the long side of the rope around your waist two to three times. Wrap the short end (tail) around your waist. Connect the loose end backed-up bowline. An easier, but less secure version would be to use approximately 12 feet of webbing (or a 12 foot loop of rope secured on a bight). Put the loop behind you, around your waist, and under your crotch. Connect all three loops (the two around your waist and the one under your crotch) with a locker.

Method One

You can get pants, shorts, and skirts with an **integrated pant harness**. These may or may not be more comfortable than wearing both, and may offer some weight savings. Their best application may be for ski mountaineering when getting in a harness could be a real chore, alpine climbs to save on weight, or going from work to the gym/crag on Casual Fridays.

Photos courtesy Mammut

The last major style of harnesses are **big wall harnesses**. Just because you're aid climbing does not mean you should be using a big wall harness. They are really heavy, and unless you are using them to their full capacity (you have pounds of gear clipped to you), they are less comfortable even if they do have a lot of padding – just like an over-padded backpack hip belt. Gear intense routes like major direct aid climbs and bolting jobs are nice to have a more burly harness.

Method two

Big wall harness. Courtesy Yates

Some wall harnesses have **two belay loops**, and this can be really handy to sort out daisy chains, belay, and hauling systems. Worn belay loops are usually the first noticeable thing that should get you thinking about retiring your harnesses. You don't need to back up your belay loop, just check it every so often. It is acceptable to girth hitch a daisy chain to your belay loop, but change the location on the loop often to not create a specific wear point, or tie off the girth with an overhand knot. Girth a daisy to both tie-in points if you want to be extra safe.

Petzl Omni Biner (best solution)

Tying off a girth hitch

Belay loops help orient your belay biner in the correct direction, but a lot of attention has been devoted towards creating belay carabineers that limit cross loading rotation. Here's a tip to not only backup your belay loop (not that you need to), but to keep your belay biner from becoming cross-loaded so you don't need a fancy yet annoying cross-load reducing belay biner. Make a closed loop of narrow (9/16"-ish) webbing by following around the inside of your belay loop and tape it in several spots to the belay loop to keep it on. Instead of covering the whole thing in tape, leave gaps that you can tightly slip your belay biner through.

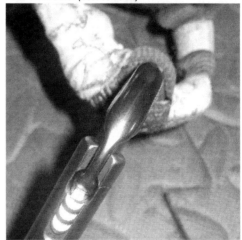
Crossload-proofing belay loop

Chest harnesses are very useful when solo climbing with a device that won't catch an upside-down fall (pretty much everything but a Silent Partner or clove hitch). They are occasionally handy aid climbing or mountaineering with a huge pack, but full-strength double gear slings usually do the job. You can make your own (a real one is a lot more comfortable) by twisting a long sling or girth-hitching two slings together and passing your arms through the holes. To make it a little more secure, you can make a knot with a bight (or use a clove-hitch) on the breast of each side to clip the biner through. Make sure the chest harness is snug so you won't fall out of it.

Kids and pregnant women will both want a **full-body harness** to keep the weight off the fetus, and kids can fall out of a regular harnesses quite easily.

On Your Harness

For multipitch climbs, rappelling, or to deal with unforeseen issues on shorter climbs, you'll want a few things on your harness besides a **belay device and locking carabineer**. The first thing you should ALWAYS have on your harness is a **knife**. Just get a super tiny one, or even a **mini multi-tool**. It's impossible to predict when you need to cut a stuck rope – it can be an issue on any type of climb, and a rescue situation could occur on a simple cragging route. Knives are helpful to cut rappel tat (tat means any type of cord/webbing to rap off of), for freeing ropes stuck above or below, cutting through impossibly stuck knots, fixing things, and first aid situations. Rocks can be used to chop stuck ropes, but they aren't always around. It's actually frightening how easy it is to chop your rope with a loose rock. Attach some durable cord to your knife, and hitch it to your back gear loop or harness so you never forget it. Make sure it can't accidentally open. Nothing is worse than realizing that your knife has been open during a climb.

Daisy chains are another very common item always on the harness. Using one is totally a matter of preference, some folks hate them. The new style of interlocked closed loops, otherwise known as a **personal anchor system (PAS)** is the best choice compared to the older sewn flat loop kind of daisy. These PAS are full strength, rated anchor systems, and can also be used to equalize an anchor. Another type of tether gaining popularity, especially in Europe, are short sewn lengths of full strength climbing rope with one or two clipping ends. Beal makes one called the **Dynaclip**. These are primarily used in multipitch sport climbs or at the anchor on single pitch climbs. Clipping in directly with this system is the safest method of tethering into the anchor without additionally tying in with the lead rope.

Metolius PAS

435

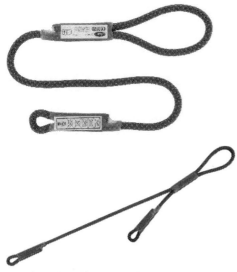

Dynaclip and Double courtesy Bluewater

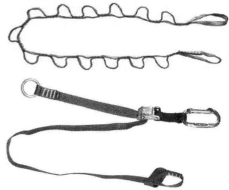

Standard flat loop & adjustable daisy. Courtesy Yates

Adjustable daisy chains are useful on steep aid climbs and will be discussed in detail later. On non-aid climbs, daisy chains add weight and bulk and are less safe compared to tying into the anchor with the rope.

The most common use of a daisy is to attach to an anchor during a rappel. Haters can use slings from the rack girthed onto their belay loop, or two sets of quickdraws: one set for each bolt. If you are using a **flat-looped daisy** then have your main locker at the end of the daisy. If you need to shorten it up, use a second biner to clip to the main biner, or your belay loop. NEVER clip the main biner to another loop – if the bar tacks rip (they do so at very low loads) the main biner will be attached to nothing. See the video "Daisy Chain Dangers" by Black Diamond on the Internet.

Depending on how prepared you want to be it is never a bad idea to have a **bail biner** or **quick link (mallion)**, some **extra tat**, and a **micro ascender** (Tibloc, Microtraxion/ Rollnlock, prusik) on the back of your harness. The extra 2-3 ounces are worth their weight for easy bailing, rigging quick rappels, jugging a rope, and various other self-rescue scenarios. **Two spare carabineers** per partner are always incredibly useful, from setting up an anchor, to running out of quickdraws on a sport pitch, or spare biners on big walls. I find the **DMM Revolver biners** to be worth the extra weight for busting out when rope drag is an issue, reducing the impact force on a sketchy piece (described later), and using in an emergency haul system at the anchor.

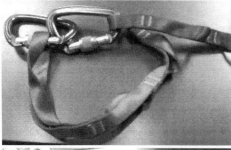

Adjusting a flat-looped daisy with a second locker at the top clip or from your belay loop.

1/4" quick-link and 1/2" tat, bail biner with autoblock cord, knife/multitool, Microtraxion = 3 ounces.

A **cordalette, webolette, or extra slings** are essential in setting up an equalized anchor in addition to using the lead rope. Extra slings are quick, but could be needed on the next pitch and are more difficult to equalize. Webolettes are quick and easy to equalize, but can't be cannibalized as easily as a cordalette for rappelling. Tying your own by knotting both ends of a 7mm length of nylon, aka a **snake cord**, will make a much weaker version (around 7kN per arm after knotting) unless you double it up by clipping both ends to the first piece. **Pre-sewn cordalettes made of Dyneema**, are strong, nice and compact, but also can't be cannibalized as easily for rappelling. If you do cannibalize Dyneema for rappelling, remember that it won't hold a knot very well. Eighteen to twenty-two foot 6-7 mm nylon cordalettes tied with a double fisherman knot are a very good comprise. They take a bit more effort to unfurl and re-coil, but are cheap for cutting up on rappels, cheap for replacing often, bite the rope well if used for ascending a line, are great for rigging aiders and ascenders, and can equalize several pieces.

Nylon cordalettes also stretch and absorb more force in the anchor and are significantly stronger than Dyneema or Technora cord when absorbing a dynamic fall onto the anchor. If you prefer to have the cord untied and to join them later with an overhand knot instead of a double fishermans, make sure you have plenty of tail, and you'll probably want to tie two knots. **Technora cord**, a variation of Kevlar, can be used for cordalette material because of the extremely high tensile strength and thinner diameter (usually around 5-6 mm). I don't recommend this for anchor material (or really anything) because not only is it extremely hard to cannibalize for rapping (just try cutting it), it offers no dynamic properties, and the strength is drastically reduced with knots and sharp bends. It can be used as a pull-cord, but better options exist. **Mammut Pro cord** is one of the best choices because it's essentially the same as regular nylon cord, but the sheath is woven on and is a bit stronger (and has a pretty nice hand). It is more expensive, so if you eat up your cordalettes, it may not be your favorite.

To bundle up a cordalette, double or triple loop it up and tie a big fig-8 knot in the middle. You can also double it up and then twist it around, just like you would rack a double length runner. Either way, clip all the loops together. There are fancier and better-looking ways, but take more time. Anchor building and materials will be discussed in more detail later.

Another great thing to have on your harness at all times is a **small loop of 6 mm nylon cord** for backing up rappels or busting out for emergency prusiking. Using the cord in an autoblock fashion is the preferred method of a rappel backup. It takes a bit of trial and error to get the perfect sized loop. The **Sterling Hollow Block** is an excellent pre-sewn and low profile autoblock sling. You can wrap your loop of cord several times around your leg loop, the back of your gear loop, or knot it up and clip it to something. Just make sure it's easy to get on or off so you actually use it on rappel.

Dyneema, nylon, rabbit runner, & snake cord anchors

Chalk

There are a few types of climbing chalk out there. Light **powdery chalk** feels great, but in strong winds it blows right out of your bag. Blocky **clumpy chalk** takes a little work to break down, but lasts a lot longer. Gymnastic chalk is usually cheaper, but usually doesn't have drying agents that climbing chalk has in it. **Chalk balls** last the longest and don't spill, but require more effort to chalk hands on difficult climbs and don't coat your hands as much as loose chalk. **Eco chalk** is darker and doesn't markup routes as much. It may or may not perform as well. **Scented chalk** is even available!

Another option is **liquid chalk**. Liquid chalk is basically chalk dissolved in alcohol. It's really nice as a pre-coat on hot/sweaty days and for routes that you don't want a chalk bag on due to weight or for a quick send. Liquid chalk also helps get rid of sunscreen on your hands. I highly recommend just making your own since it's really cheap and easy. All you need to do is dissolve chalk in isopropyl alcohol (get the highest concentration you can find) until you get a cake batter consistency. You can add unscented liquid antiperspirant to it, along with any other drying agent, or skin hardener or conditioner (like Antihydral or Benzoin). Put some in a rinsed out shampoo, mouthwash, or other **travel bottle** for the crag or alpine climb. If going sans chalk bag, just put it in your pocket or make a tie-off. This is a great lightweight option for alpine climbing. Chalk isn't just for rock climbers. Ines Papert used chalk to improve grip on her ice tools to go on to win the women's 2013 Ouray Ice Comp in the sub-freezing mixed competition.

Keep in mind the consequences of chalking up routes. It's pretty embarrassing to see an outdoor climbing area coated in white, and I'm amazed that it hasn't become more of a problem. Chalk can get you off-route too. Blindly going for chalked holds can get you to commit to a sucker hold. Tick marks (putting a dash of chalk on important feet or holds) are also a problem. Don't be a jerk, clean up your tick marks. Another type of chemical grip aid seriously frowned upon is Rosin. It permanently sticks to rock and creates awful greasy holds over time. If you see someone using it, knock it out of their hand and chase them away with a stick. Many liquid chalk manufactures add rosin or other grip additives. Since the chalk dries only leaving a thin coat on your hands, it's probably not a problem...probably. Edelweiss makes liquid rosin called **Stick It** and Mueller makes several products that may or may not be damaging to the rock. Adding some to your liquid chalk concoction could improve your formula, or it may harm the rock.

Liquid chalked-up hand

Chalk Bags can either be clipped to your harness, tied around your waist with thin webbing and an overhand knot, or with a belt. A belt can become unclipped and fall off, especially wriggling around in chimneys and offwidths. Tat and biner options can be multiuse, mainly for bailing. Keeping a **hook** in your chalk bag is an old sport trick for aiding or leaving on a runout face climb. I highly recommend removing your clip-belt and using some 5 mm cord instead. Just use a simple overhand to secure the bag.

There are three basic types of chalk bag. The **ultralight** alpine kind that isn't very durable, the standard **stiff brimmed** sport type for easy dipping, and the **bucket** for bouldering. Chalk bags, especially bags with **pockets,** are great places to stash little important items like **nail clippers, a small headlamp, lighter, pain killers, topo, vices, and a role of tape through the belt**. Keep in mind that some chalk may migrate into the pocket, hard items tend to wear holes in the fabric, and zippers get ruined from abrasion. Keep your knife on your harness in case you forget your chalk bag.

Zipper pocket chalkbag with tat belt, tape, lip balm, nail clippers, lighter, med kit, floss, mini headlamp, and firestarter.

Brushes are very useful for boulders or sport-o's working a route to remove greasy chalk off crimps and slopers. A **toothbrush** and climbing brush fit in that little loop on your chalk bag. **Larger brushes and extendable poles** may be necessary to get big areas or out of reach spots. **Stiff wire brushes** and **horse brushes** are great for cleaning choss and dust off of new routes.

Courtesy Moses

BELAY/RAPPEL DEVICES

The two lightest belay/rappel devices out there are a **body belay** and a **Munter hitch**. These don't work so well belaying difficult climbing, but they weigh nothing minus the weight of a locker with a Munter. Body belays can be very secure if the belay has a good stance and are really useful for quick easy but exposed pitches. A body rappel, aka the **Dulfersitz**, is not safe, horribly uncomfortable, and how do you have a rope but no harness and biner? There's no reason to not use a Munter hitch or carabineer brake (described later) instead. A Munter is ultra-useful if you drop or forget your belay device or want to go as light as possible, but takes a bit of getting used to. It's a really good skill to tie it one handed. Clip the rope through a biner, grab the brake strand (not going to the load) thumbs down, turn your palm up, and clip it in. If you need more friction, wrap the brake strand around the locker one more time for the **super Munter**.

You can also use another locking carabineer to construct an **auto-locking Munter**, just like a Reverso or similar device. This can also be useful to construct a quick way to jug a rope with the auto-locking Munter attached to your belay loop and a foot prusik on the rope above. The big problem with an auto-locking Munter is that it is extremely difficult to release under load and should only be used on very easy terrain where the climber will not need to be lowered or have slack paid out.

Use a larger locking pear biner for the Munter and a smaller locking pear biner for the lock mechanism with the gate facing in. The **lock mechanism biner** should be small enough to pass through the larger biner. To set it up clip the smaller lock mechanism biner to the load strand and through the strand coming out behind the Munter biner, making sure the gate faces toward the rock. You can also clip a draw from the lock biner to your belay loop to keep it from getting trapped and to pull smoother.

To release the load first tie off the brake strand to serve as a backup and get both hands free. Unclip the load strand from the lock biner. If your lock biner is small enough to pass through the Munter locker you should be able to push it through the Munter biner and it will come free. It won't be clipped to anything so don't drop it when you get it loose. Munters are way more useful and less gear intensive than a carabineer brake bar for rappelling.

Simple Munter

One-handed Munter (good to know along with one-handed clove hitch)

"True" one-handed Munter. Great for wearing big gloves. Takes a bit of practice, but worth it on expeditions.

Super Munter

Locking Munter

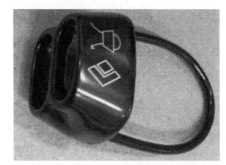
Black Diamond ATC

Mammut Alpine Smart, DMM Bugette, Kong GiGi, Petzl Reverso 4, Petzl GriGri 2

Simple belay devices, like the **ATC**, are extremely light and worth the weight. There are even lighter tubular belay devices meant only for skinny ropes, like the **DMM Bugette** or the heavier but even skinnier rope rated **Edelrid Micro Jul**. Single rope tubular belay devices that only have one hole for the rope are useful for the gym, or cragging situations where you don't need to rappel. If you are using super skinny ropes, check the diameter range of your device before heading out.

As of this moment, the lightest most useful belay devices are double rope tubular belay devices that can belay a leader with one or two ropes quite smoothly, and also can be used in self-locking mode, aka guide-mode, for belaying up the follower(s). You can clip these devices in guide-mode to your harness for ascending a rope, but it is not smooth in any way. The Petzl Reverso is the most commonly used type of this belay device, closely followed by the Black Diamond ATC Guide. For convention's sake, these types of belay devices will be referred to as **Reverso's, plaquettes,** or guide-mode. Simple tubular devices will be referred to as ATC's.

Belay devices that can automatically lock when catching a leader fall add an extra element of safety and are getting lighter and getting more useful on longer climbs. There are several models, but the most recognized and used device is the **Petzl GriGri**.

441

Nothing inspires confidence like knowing that your partner won't drop you because he/she screwed up, assuming they are using the device properly. The nice thing about the GriGri is how smooth and burly it is, and is now light enough to consider bringing on longer climbs. The GriGri can be used to belay a leader, one follower, rappel (described later), rope-solo (described later), ascend a rope (described later), and haul (later). The major downside of the GriGri is that it won't accept two ropes or very skinny ropes (but skinnier than the old GriGri). Other disadvantages are that it is still heavy in comparison, an inexperienced belayer will "short rope" you on desperate clips, it's possible to feed the rope the wrong way (and it happens quite often so check your belayer), and it doesn't slip.

Wait, doesn't slip? Belay devices that do not auto-lock let a small amount of rope slip through during a leader fall and this lessens the force exerted on the protection that's catching the fall by a couple kN's. This is usually good thing. One way to offset the hard catch of a GriGri effectively is to use your body to give a bit more of a dynamic belay by jumping a bit. You need to tie in to the anchor at the perfect length on multi-pitch climbs to keep you from falling off the anchor or going too far up. There are other auto-locking belay devices like the GriGri and it is a matter of personal preference, but they are much less safe in other "not recommended" setups like short-fixing and rope-soloing. These devices are the **Eddy and Cinch**. Don't use a GriGri or other auto-locking devices with icy ropes. With all that said, the GriGri is extremely useful in all types of climbing (except for double rope or icy belaying) and is worth its weight on everything from sport climbing to glacier travel to aid climbing to multipitch alpine climbing. Special uses for the GriGri will be scattered through the rest of the book.

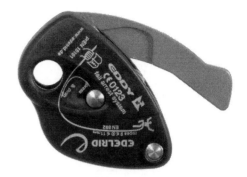
Eddy, courtesy Edelrid

Trango Cinch

There is a new generation of auto or **semi-autolocking belay devices** that allow two ropes instead of the single rope devices like the GriGri. Mammut makes the **Alpine Smart**, Edelrid makes the **Micro and Mega Jul**, and Climbing Technology makes the **Alpine Up**. Besides the ability to add an extra level of safety to belaying a leader on twin/half ropes and belaying two followers with assisted braking, the other major benefit is the added safety on rappelling on two ropes with an auto-locking backup. Ascending a pair of stuck lines is also made easier by just yarding up the lines, pulling in the slack, and resting on the device (not the most energy efficient method, but pretty quick). These devices are not a fully autolocking device like the GriGri, but assisted locking. What this means is they automatically lock in case you let go, but there is some slippage and the locking isn't foolproof. This is great news for reducing impact forces on falls. The devices can be trusted for letting go while belaying a follower off the anchor, or on rappel assuming there won't be any shock-loading going on. I have tried to use these in place of a GriGri for the "frog-style" variation of ascending a rope (described later), and do not recommended it at all. I've also completely disobeyed the manufacture's recommendations and used the Smart to rope-solo a wall in Zion. All I can say is that it would probably work in a fall (I tested it multiple times with a backup), but the uncertainty kinda ruined my enjoyment. I have even heard of climbers using a Reverso in guide-mode as their solo device.

These devices can be setup in a non-autolocking mode for belay or rappel, and feed smoothly. However, even with practice, these devices are less smooth feeding out rope while belaying and jerky on rappels. The Edelrid Jul is by far the lighter and more compact of the units available. These devices are much safer to use on icy ropes than a GriGri, and are the only locking devices one can use on double ropes. They do it all, but comprise slightly on performance because of this. I can only assume more devices or changes to current devices will appear on the market and perfect on current designs, just as what has occurred with a seemingly simple standard tube-style belay device. Some will love them, some will hate them.

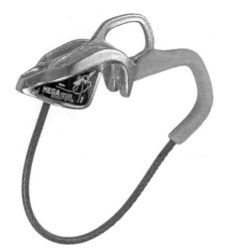

Mega Jul. Courtesy Edelrid

Alpine Up. Courtesy Climbing Technologies

There are many other types of rappel devices, but their main uses are for rescue, rigging, and possibly caving. The once common **figure-8 device** is useless to 99.9% of climbers, the .01 percent being climbers on 11 mm frozen lines. The only other useful device out there for climbers is the **Kong GiGi** belay plate. Its main use is to bring up a follower(s), and it does this better than any other device. It can also be used to ascend a line and rappel, even lead belay, just not well (described below). The main reason to use it is to save time at the belay if you're swapping leads. The second gets to the belay and doesn't need to clip in (saving time) because they are auto-locked by the GiGi. The slack coming out of the GiGi can be used to put the new leader on belay. When the new leader is ready to go, they simply unclip the GiGi and take it with them. No wasted time compared to switching a Reverso from belaying a 2nd to belaying the leader when swapping leads.

To belay a leader with the GiGi, clip one round hole to your belay loop and put a bight of rope through one of the slots so the loop comes up toward the sky. Put two lockers through the loop, and belay. It can also be used to rappel using the same setup. Use one locker for thick ropes and two for thin rope rappels. It can be used to lower in this setup as well, but clipped to the anchor and not the harness. Use a prusik knot on the brake hand for a backup.

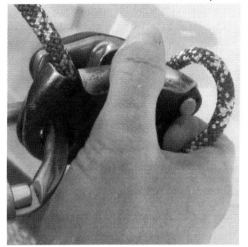

How to hold a GriGri.

CARABINEERS
Lockers

Unless you want to live dangerously and go seriously light, a good locking biner is essential for your belay device. This biner gets a lot of use, so if you get an ultralight locker, constantly check for wear grooves for retirement. **Auto-locking biners** are excellent choices for added safety as forgetting to screw the gate shut isn't uncommon (and some gates unscrew themselves easily). They are a bit heavier and can freeze up in icy conditions or stick in when sand gets in them. The Black Diamond **Magnatron** biner attempts to solve this problem by its unique auto-locking mechanism. Belay biners with **added cross-loading protection** are becoming quite popular, although I've never heard of an accident that's occurred from a cross-loaded belay biner. They do add a level of safety from cross loading, but the extra steps adds to fumbling a belay device and accidentally dropping it (see alternative solutions under the harness section). If belaying a 2nd in guide-mode you will need a 2nd biner to hang the device off the anchor. This actually doesn't have to be a locking carabineer if you're out, but it is much safer and highly recommended.

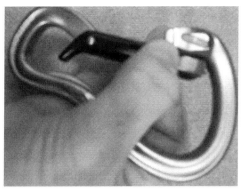

Black Diamond Magnatron Gridlock. Lots of extra clips to attach belay device to your harness with this one.

Top to Bottom: Trango Superfly, Edelrid Slider, Petzl Attache 3D, Camp autolocking

If you're using a daisy chain, you'll need a locker for this too. A **keylock nose locker** works the best to avoid catching of the loops. If using a pilfered sling from the rack, just use the two non-lockers that were on it. Lockers are not necessary to attach to individual anchor points, but generally the master point also gets a locker to anchor yourself with the rope. Use a **larger pear-shaped HMS locker** for this and keep your anchor material bundled to it. The **Eldelrid Strike Slider** is a very useful locker for daisy chains and GriGri's because the biner can rotate completely around through a bolt or the GriGri. Grivel has recently developed a twin gate carabiner than is safer than a standard locker and supposedly just as easy to use as a standard biner.

Master point biner

Depending on your climb, how light you want to go, or how much hauling/jugging etc. you'll need more or less lockers of varying weight and strength. For fast and light climbs, two ultralight lockers for belaying and anchoring can be enough, and for walls you can never seem to bring enough.

Non-Lockers

Petzl Spirit, Wild Country Helium, Black Diamond Oz, CAMP Nano

Very small **ultralight wiregate** biners, like the Camp Nano or Edelrid 19g, are great for things like hanging your pack, clipping your camera, and as spare harness biners. Using them on your rack or slings will really save weight, but there are downsides. First, they aren't as durable and are more likely to break – so check them often. If your rack is substantial, your gear can get really compressed and difficult to access. The clipping area is very small and removing them off your rack and harness, or clipping the rope through them can be a chore, especially with glove or twin ropes. Micro biners also make great bail biners.

Wider diameter, but still **lightweight, keylock wiregate biners**, like the Wild Country Helium, are still quite light but help keep gear from becoming a cluster on your rack. Keylock-style biners are excellent for snag-free deployment. One exception for wanting a **notched nose** on your biner is on your nuts to help prevent them from all falling off the biner.

Wiregates are better than **barrel gates** in almost every way, especially now that wiregates are manufactured in keylock models. They are generally stronger, lighter, better in icy conditions, have less gate flutter (accidental gate opening from vibration), and open beers. So why get a barrel gate? The action on clipping the rope is still smoother in some barrel gates, and has a little longer lifetime of snappy clipping. The rope clipping end can also be made into a bent gate to further aid in getting the rope in there. Bent gate barrel-style biners are great for desperate sport clips, and are very hard to mistake with the bolt side biner on quickdraws. They also make nice ice screw racking biners. **Oval shaped biners** aren't as useful for your aid ladders as normal biners.

As mentioned before, **DMM Revolver** biners, the only integrated pulley-biner, are great for reducing rope drag, improvising a haul, and reducing impact force on your gear. They will increase your fall length as will any force reducing system - not by much, but enough if you are concerned about decking. Revolvers help in two ways. First, they transfer the force off the top piece and onto the belayer by reducing friction. Second, they reduce rope drag so more rope is available to stretch and absorb more force off the entire system.

Mad Rock makes the **Trigger Wire**, a biner with a small, light, innocuous lever that keeps the biner gate open until it snaps closed when clipping. Its stick clip use is described later, but it does make for some pretty quick clips on bolts and ropes, especially compared to some other pretty silly auto-clipping biners out there, like the Kong Frog. It's also nice for clipping reachy fixed gear on aid climbs.

Every season, go through and look for rough spots and cracks in your biners. They do break. More than one climber has been killed because the rope was cut from a rough carabineer. To avoid this, be extra vigilant about checking biners left on sport routes. Also, don't swap out the biner used to clip bolts with the biner used to clip the rope as the bolt biner has a higher chance of developing rough spots on it. Mark the bolt clipping side (the loose biner) of your sport draws and don't swap that biner with the rope side (the stiff biner). A good marking scheme would be blue for bolt and red for rope.

Ropes

Most climbers want the lightest possible rope setup, but weight should really be determined between two comparable ropes not the type of rope. There is no single best system and every option discussed has a perfect time and place for implementation. The first things to consider when buying a rope are the diameter and the impact force ratings. Actually, grams per meter is a better judge of the rope's mass than diameter, but for simplicity, I will just be using diameter. The more mass per meter (from now on referred to larger diameter), the less likely the rope is to fail or to get damaged, and the longer it should last. Besides being heavier, thicker ropes absorb less energy (less stretchy), and therefor generate higher impact forces on your gear. The flip side to this is that you won't fall as far. There are many other factors to look at when choosing a rope, usually when comparing two similar ropes such as dry treatment, number of falls held (your rope isn't going to break but may wear sooner), static elongation and dynamic elongation (usually a factor of impact force and diameter), middle marking, length, and a few other factors.

Single Ropes

For top-roping, jugging lines, chossy climbs, or rock with particularly sharp edges, larger diameter ropes of **10+ mm** will hold up a lot longer but will be heavier and have higher impact forces. Medium diameter **9.6-9.8 mm** ropes are a good size if they will get a lot of use cragging or get a lot of abrasion from dirt and sand but you still want something somewhat light, springy, and that offers some extra cut protection. Small diameter ropes around **9.4 mm** are excellent for moderate use trad, ice, and sport climbs. They are light for the approach, and offer low impact ratings for suspect gear. They don't last as long, but usually long enough for their intended use. Ultralight single very small diameter ropes of **8.7 to 9.1 mm** (and getting thinner) are perfect for the hard send where you want minimal weight, lightweight alpine climbs with long approaches, but stretch a lot, won't last very long, and are more susceptible to cutting and damage.

Double Ropes

The next step down in diameter are half ropes and twin ropes. **Half ropes (7.8-8.8 mm)** are usually thicker and are meant to be clipped separately. **Twins ropes (6.9-8.2 mm)** are clipped together. The obvious benefit from these are redundancy in the system – if one rope fails you are still attached to another and more so with twin ropes. This benefit is huge. In fact, using two ropes allows you to place pro over a wider area with less use of long slings, say two parallel cracks, without the associated rope drag or dangerous angles of pull on the gear – essentially equalizing two pieces. You can clip a high piece without the added danger of having more rope out. Also, the impact forces are quite low upping the safety margin (minus the extra stretch in ground/ledge falls).

Half ropes do weigh more than twins, but their advantage is that by clipping ropes independently, you can minimize rope drag (assuming you don't cross them up). Half ropes are great for a team of three, wandering routes, using as an ultralight single line or doubled up, and can be used to haul and jug. Glacier travel is commonly done on a half rope, and is generally acceptable to use it as a single line for this purpose. You will need skinnier prusiks or use more wraps - so plan ahead. Don't clip half ropes into the same piece – the combined impact force is too large and your gear could pull or break.

Twin ropes have an advantage over half ropes in that they are thinner, thus lighter and lower impact force, and there is redundancy for every clip. They are great for easier routes you need to make double rope raps off of and ice climbing. A single twin can also be safely used doubled up, great for fast and light climbs with shorter cruxes, but is not as safe to use as an ultralight single line although many a climber has done this. Don't make the mistake of getting both ropes the same color.

One drawback of using a two-rope system is that two thin ropes are heavier and harder to manage than any single rope. If you have to carry a pull-cord for rappelling if using a single rope, twin ropes may or may not come out lighter in the long run. Belaying a leader on a difficult climb is much more difficult with double ropes, especially controlling the amount of slack between ropes or when the leader calls "take". The leader could also take a larger fall because of stretch and extra slack in the system. Keeping the ropes in order is also no fun on hanging belays, or sloping ledges. Bring double ropes when the leader doesn't expect to take or hang often, no jugging is expected (unless you are fearless), or when redundancy outweighs any disadvantages in rope management. There are very few climbs that wander so badly that even proper sling placement, a little bit of rope drag, and a shorter pitch with a single line is still inadequate. Another issue with double lines is that they are much more expensive together than a single line, and if one gets damaged both become useless. Double ropes are ultimately safer by providing redundancy and force reduction.

Use half ropes for climbs that aren't at your limit (you don't plan on falling or taking very much) where either impact force reduction and/or a 2nd rope backup is highly desirable, or use a single half rope for glacier travel or doubled up for ridges, simulclimbing, and easy alpine climbs. Use twins for multipitch ice and moderate alpine climbs that require two ropes to get off where the weight of twins is lighter than a single rope and pull cord – or if a lot of simulclimbing/soloing will occur so one person doesn't wind up carrying the weight of a tag line. Double ropes are also quicker to setup for a rappel since both ropes are usually out and ready to go, don't get as stuck as easily as a light pull cord, and can be used to lead on no matter if the other one gets stuck.

Impact Force
After you figured out what diameter to get, narrow down your selection by looking at the impact force published with the rope specs. The higher the impact force the less the rope absorbs the force of a fall and the

more force will be felt by your top piece of gear, climber, and belayer. The published number of falls held and elongation of the rope (and possibly the durability) are more a factor of the diameter and impact force. So a rope with a low impact force will stretch more and hold less falls than a rope with a higher impact force.

So why not just buy a rope with the lowest impact force? It depends on what you want. For leads on sketchy gear and the possibility of an anchor fall, you'll want this. But you also may want a thicker rope for abrasion, durability, and cut protection as well. For leads with ground or ledge fall potential you might not want the stretchiest rope. It's doubtful you'll buy a rope specifically for a ground fall project, but many sport climbs have ground fall zones (usually around the 2nd clip). A softer catch means you fall father, and besides hitting the ground, it can be annoying on overhanging routes or jugging and hauling a line. Durability is also compromised with skinnier or stretchier ropes but can be offset by a quality sheath and coating.

The published number of falls held doesn't mean that your rope is going to break after that published number of falls, as these are lab tested disastrous falls in succession. Use this number to compare two ropes with similar specs that you desire. Ropes are no longer rated on their ability to survive the chop on a small diameter edge fall. The odds of a rope of any diameter getting the full chop are low, but it happens. Ropes don't break, they cut.

Length
The length of rope is also obviously important. The longer the rope, the more gear you need, the heavier things get (added weight of extra rope and gear), the farther your partner is from earshot, the more rope you need to pull up (if you didn't climb the whole length), and the higher the chance of your rope is getting stuck on a longer rappel. For two people, a **30 m** rope can be adequate for glacier travel, short belayed pitches on a mostly soloable climb, or simulclimbing. Shy away from **50 m** ropes unless you know that the area you're climbing in is set up for 50 meter pitches (then it's perfect). If you don't know, then **60 meter** ropes are still the best all-around size. With a few exceptions, most climbs with established anchors for leading or toproping are setup for 60 meter ropes. That said, **70 meter** ropes are incredibly useful. Many single pitch climbs and rappels that would require two ropes with a 60 are doable with a 70 m. On long routes, you also have more rope to chop off and use as rappel anchors, assuming the raps are set for 60 m. You can also shave off time by leading 70 meter pitches on easier climbs, and the odds of linking pitches increases. Ice climbing really lends itself to 70 meter ropes. If you plan on climbing a 70 m pitch, you need 70 meters of gear.

Get a 70 m if you think you can save time by linking pitches, or you want some wiggle room on the possibility of only needing one rope. Some routes and rappels are setup for 70 meter ropes only, but they are hopefully published with that information. Otherwise, you should be able to assume 60 meters will be adequate, although when in doubt get a 70 meter. The weight of hiking in the weight of an extra few meters can usually be offset in time and energy unless the climbing is difficult enough that you really doubt you'd push a 70 meter (even a 60 meter) lead and no significant gain can be made on the rappel.

The next size up is an **80 m** rope. For multipitch climbing an 80 m rope is just too long for almost every situation. However, there are many single pitch climbs that an 80 meter rope is the perfect size to not have to bring a 2nd rope up with you to lower off. Also, there are some multipitch climbs that an 80 meter rope can link into one huge pitch. There are some long climbs where you won't be doing 80 m pitches, but the rappels are between 35-40 meters. Finally, if fixing a route to jug the next day, an 80 m rope gets you that much higher. These are obviously all highly specific situations mean to shave off time or weight – all of which could be done with shorter rope and a 2nd line.

Rope Treatments
Ropes with **dry treatment** are essential in snow and ice situations. Not only are icy lines dangerous as they can become impossible to deal with, wet ropes (and nylon slings) are significantly weaker – 40-70% weaker depending on the treatment and level of saturation. Even little wetness can have some impact on the strength. Dry ropes are good insurance on long rock climbs in case an unexpected shower comes along. Wet ropes are also incredibly heavy. There are various methods and degrees of dry treatment and it's hard to tell by what the company says considering they all claim to be the best. Quality and degree of treatment is usually reflected in the price – the only reason to not get a dry treated rope. Some companies add additional treatments to their ropes to reduce abrasion and damage due to heat. I can't say with any scientific certainty, but the more a rope is treated, the more durable it seems.

One of the better treatments in terms of durability out there is **Teflon coating**, however there may be other better treatments. Predicting the durability of a rope is nearly impossible without experience with a company or opinions of others. I've had extremely expensive ropes go caput after a very short time, and have had fairly inexpensive ropes last much longer than expected. Two cheap ropes will last longer than one expensive rope with fancy treatments if performance isn't much of an issue. It should be noted that rope makers can get a lower quality batch of imported nylon and your option of that rope/company could be skewed based off of that particular batch.

Sheath
How a rope feels, or handles, can be helpful in selecting what you want. Soft supple ropes are easier to belay with and don't tangle as much, but they are harder to clip and may not last as long. Firmer cords are great for hard clips and could last longer, but tangle and twist and need more attention during the belay. They also don't pay out of a GriGri as smoothly. Few ropes are made with a single pick (look at the weave and you'll see two parallel "double pick" strands or one single pick). However, single pick ropes do last a bit longer and handle quite well. They are more expensive. The sheath thickness will also determine the ropes feel and durability. Thicker sheaths are more durable and safer, but heavier and not as stretchy. There are some new rope technologies emerging that change the thickness of the sheath near the end of the rope (to help you not rap off the ends), and some technologies that bond the sheath to the core drastically improving the cut resistance and durability.

Rope Marking
The final important factor in selecting a rope is how the middle is marked. **Bi-weave** pattered ropes are great because the middle mark never wears off. They are more expensive, and if one side stretches out more than the other or if you had to cut some rope off, the system becomes useless. A **big black mark** in the center is the most obvious, but wears off frustratingly quickly. Opinions differ on how safe it is to use a Sharpie to remark the rope, so buy a special rope marker if that makes you feel safer. Marking the last 5-10 meters (15-30 feet) using thinner marking stripes on each end of the rope is also very helpful to help you gauge how much rope is left, and to avoid

rapping of the ends. Metolius Monster ropes actually sews in bright orange **fluffy thread** into the rope's center, making the center unmistakable. The threads do wear off over time, but not completely. They do not interfere with belaying, but you can feel the center slide by, aiding in yelling "half rope". I have heard of climbers weaving bright thread or dental floss in and out of the sheath pick, but the possibility of the thread catching on a rappel has scared me off from trying this idea. No matter what system you choose, marking the middle of your rope can save time and save your life.

Metolius Monster middle marker

Companies put **plastic identification markers** on the very ends of the rope. I highly recommend taking these off. They do help you find the ends for coiling or tying in (a bit too late for avoiding rapping off the ends), or for remembering the rope specs. However, they can get stuck in the anchor or on an edge while rappelling. When they do get stuck, it is absolutely amazing how much weight they can support. It can be impossible to pull the rope if they hang up on something. This happens often enough to seriously think about removing them. I've heard stories about climbers jugging stuck lines to only find in horror that they were jugging only off the taped end stuck on a rock crystal. Never ever use tape to mark the middle of the rope. There's a 99% probability it will get jammed in the belay device or stuck in the anchor on rappel.

Haul and Tag Lines

Haul lines are **static ropes** that do not stretch and are designed to drag up haul bags, although sometimes you'll want to use a dynamic rope (not that bad to haul really) in case you need to lead on it. They and are between **8 and 11 mm**. The thicker the haul line, the easier it is to pull and the less likely it is that your line will be severed or break, but will really suck if you do any free climbing if it's too thick. If you are simply hand hauling the line with a light load, you could use a rope skinnier than 8 mm, but it may not work well with a ratcheting pulley.

Tag lines are usually skinnier cords (**5-7 mm**) that are useful in tagging up more gear to the leader on a gear intensive pitch or to send up a drill. You can only be less than half a rope up before the tag line can be guaranteed to be sent back down to the belayer for reloading. Consider having your tag line longer than the lead line. This can help you when leading past the halfway point to tag gear, and give you extra slack for lower-out and pendulums. A 3rd **rope** can serve to lengthen a tag line past halfway, or as an additional lower-out line for the haul bag to avoid having your bag swing and crash all over the wall.

Pull Cords

If you are climbing a route on a single line that requires a second rope to get off, you'll need a pull cord. The lighter and skinnier the pull cord, the more risk you are taking. If you can get away with making rappels with a single line, or are establishing a new rap route, then go for rapping with just one rope even if that means more raps. Stuck ropes almost always occur when pulling two ropes. Weight aside, the best pull cord would be a second lead line. Besides not owning a pull cord, there are two scenarios where this makes sense. The first is on a single pitch route you want to lower off and toprope longer than half of your lead line. Using a **second lead line** is safer than using a pull-cord in terms of its strength and usability with a belay device. Using a pull cord is possible in this scenario if the 2nd belay device can handle its diameter and the climber doesn't shock load by dynoing or penduluming all over the place. Not safe, but it is commonly done. Another reason to use a second lead line would be on climbs that have an extremely high probability of getting your rope stuck or on very windy days. If only one rope comes down, you can be sure that you can lead on it. Finally, routes that require fixing multiple ropes necessitate a second lead line (or burly static line).

The next lighter option is to bring around an **8 mm twin or half rope** as the pull cord. This is lighter than another single line, less likely to tangle and hang up than a very skinny line, and you could still lead on it in a pinch. A **static haul line** is another option, but considering it weighs the same or more as a half/twin rope of the same diameter, you may as well use a viable lead rope instead. The extra stretch in dynamic ropes is also useful in long rappels.

A **true pull-cord** is a skinny line not meant to bear weight. Its only function (besides tagging gear) is to retrieve your lead line in a double rope rappel. The setup for this will be described later. Tag lines are usually between **5 to 8 mm** and have a small amount of dynamic elongation, but you certainly cannot lead on them with any degree of safety (better than nothing however). The advantage of **skinny pull cords** can be offset by the amazing snarls they can create and can get stuck on everything. Most pull cords are 50-70 meter lengths of nylon, the same cord you use to make a prusik with. Considering the lead line will stretch more, it could be prudent to make your pull cord a few meters longer than the lead line. Some pull cords can be bought with **5 mm Technora**, the same stuff in "**Tech Cord**" used in high strength cordalettes and cord used to sling hexes, Big-Bros, and other chocks without sewn slings. You can find long lengths of this stuff in rescue websites or from Sterling. There is certainly an added level of cut resistance in using Tech cord and the 5 mm

diameter offers some weight savings. These Technora ropes can be very expensive. Mammut **Pro Cord** is all nylon, but the sheath is woven to the core. This allows you to get away with a slightly skinnier pull cord, and helps reduce sheath slippage – something that will happen (and is a bit unnerving) when rapping on a regular nylon pull-cord. Again, it's still pretty expensive.

Pro Cord and Tech Cord. Courtesy Mammut and New England Ropes/Maxim

There are times when you would want the pull-cord to be pretty strong and bear full weight safely. This is usually when there is a high probability of one of the two ropes getting stuck and you want to pull the lead line instead of the pull-cord or don't want to chance a bulky backup knot and biner to catch on something. Two of the best options for a pull cord besides a lightweight twin rope that compromise strength and weight are the **Imlay 6 mm pull cord** and the **Esprit 6 mm Alpine Personal Escape Rope**. Both are tightly woven, strong, and don't absorb much water - with the Imlay being polyester and the Esprit being nylon. The polyester rope offers very little stretch, something very helpful when trying to pull the rope down, and is fairly supple and easy to pack. It's pretty cheap to boot. The Esprit cord (you must call the company and won't find the rope on their website) is quite strong and is fairly dynamic.

Although I (and the company I'm sure) do not recommend it, several high level alpinists have used it as their lead rope (don't fall!) and rappel line. The rope is light, but it is extremely stiff. You would think that it wouldn't feed well through a rappel device, but it does so just fine. The major benefit of it being so stiff and tightly woven is that it doesn't get stuck easily, it's very light, and strong enough to bear full weight. It also doesn't blow around in high winds, a huge bonus. There are major drawbacks. The first is that it's very expensive. The other drawback is that since it is so stiff, it is hard to lay flat in a pack (doable, but annoying), tied as a backpack coil it cuts in your shoulders and doesn't climb well on you, and it doesn't stack very well at belay ledges. The pros outweigh the cons for when they count, but it's definitely a specialty piece.

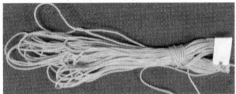

6mm Imlay Pull Cord

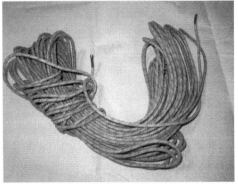

Esprit Alpine Personal Escape Rope

After you figure out what type of pull cord to get, you must decide on the length (remember to add a little extra if the pull cord is static). A **65 m** is usually perfect, even if the lead line is **70 meters** since you can probably fudge the difference by moving the knot and getting a 65 meter rappel which should be adequate in almost all situations. A 70-75 m pull cord can certainly be useful, but remember that you wind up climbing with the cord in your pack in many scenarios. If your foreseeable raps will occur in 100 meter lengths, a 50-55 m pull cord will save weight, but having that extra 10 meter of rope to use is always useful (an-

other reason to make your pull cord slightly longer).

As mentioned, your pull cord will be in your follower's pack in many situations. You can trail the pull cord, but as they are generally lighter and affected by the wind, it is safer to keep it in the pack (unless you are in the habit of dropping backpacks). The cord could also hitch itself around a rock or branch, or a snarl could get caught in a crack without anyone to tend to it. Also, the leader is pulling the full weight of the pull cord the entire time. If the cord is larger than 8 mm, you probably will wind up trailing the cord.

To fix any stuck trail cord issues, the leader should be pulling the cord up and stacking it before bring up the belayer, then flipping it or switching the end the biner is attached to. This is especially annoying at hanging belays or belays with tiny ledges to stand on, and adds time. If there are parties below, a pull cord dangling in their faces all day will not make you any friends. The obvious issues with carrying the pull cord in the belayer's pack are weight, extra bulk in chimneys, and logistical issues if both climbers have packs and the rope is in one of them. If you don't have a pack, the follower should wear the pull cord in backpack fashion, being extra careful not to drop it when switching leads and the rope.

Rope Care
Unless your rope company advertises that the rope is ready to climb on, you must deal with undoing the factory coil. Just dumping the rope on the ground will create at least an hour's worth of untangling, and it will probably take more than a few climbs to finally unsnarl the rope completely. Put the circular coil through both arms, and spool the free end off by turning the coil with both arms. Go slow and deal with stray loops and the like without desperately just saying screw it and dumping it out. If you

actually managed to uncoil the thing without incident, pull the rope tightly through your hand end-to-end several times to get as many coils and snarls out as possible.

The correct way to unspool a new rope out of the package.

Besides the manufacture's recommendations on the rope's shelf life and amount of use, it's time to retire your rope when you feel flat spots, it starts to feel strangely stiff, any signs of damage to the sheath, and any exposure to abundant sunlight (you left it sitting in the sun for a couple weeks), or exposure to corrosive chemicals (any acid, especially battery acid). Basically, retire it when you start to think, "I should I retire this". If your partner's rope looks sketchy, make them lead the first pitch and scrutinize it while belaying them.

Commercial rope protectors are worth their minimal weight if fixing pitches. Get the kind that roll onto the rope and stay put without any additional aid. Washing ropes has been discussed in the equipment care section.

Really the only way a rope (or sling, harness, etc.) will break vs. getting cut is if it has been exposed to chemicals, especially acids. Even fumes from battery acid can damage a rope or other nylon products (harnesses, slings) enough to cause it to fail under moderate loads. So if you are storing gear in the trunk of your car, think about what's been back there. There have been two recently reported cases of a rope breaking and a harness breaking under moderate loads (bodyweight or small falls) that the owner of the gear had absolutely no recollection of the gear being exposed to any chemicals. Upon analysis of the broken fibers, it appears that sulfuric acid (a component of battery acid) had been exposed to the nylon fibers. Scary stuff!

Carrying the Rope

Rope bags and tarps are useful in keeping them out of the dirt. I find them to be annoying, hard to pack, and wind up getting the rope dirtier by packing dirt that made its way onto the tarp. If you're the type that doesn't find themselves retiring their rope due to core shorts and overuse well before dirt becomes a problem, then a rope bag and an occasional wash will prolong its use. Rope bags are somewhat useful for sorting gear (dirt in cams is a way bigger issue). A **tote bag**, like the ones you get at IKEA for less than a dollar, make good rope bags and cam holders for cam intense crags, or for a severely ghetto cragging "pack."

Rope buckets, or large stuff sacks you've stiffened the brim with something at home are handy on walls where rope management is going to be a major issue, or stacking the rope for rope-soloing. The **Metolius Rope Hook** is mildly useful and smaller/lighter than a rope bucket.

Metolius Rope Hook

Coiling the rope over your anchor tether and then putting it in a shoulder sling clipped to itself (or use the rope instead of the sling) at an anchor point works almost as well and weighs almost nothing. The rope can also be stacked on top of packs and haul bags, in etrier steps, or just draped over your tether (belaying from this is difficult).

Coiling the rope in a backpack coil is standard fare for the alpine, or the non-ropebag user. It's obviously helpful for carrying the rope without a pack, but also lays nicely on top of the backpack. Rope straps on the tops of packs are enormously useful. Never carry a pull cord draped over a pack on a multipitch climb without backing it up to something on the pack, it will easily slide off. Better yet, stuff it in the bottom of the pack so it doesn't get in the way of things you may need en route. Coiling the rope in circular loops (the mountaineer or Swiss coil) also lies nicely on top of the pack, but it can create tangles. Save the mountaineer coil for simulclimbing or glacier travel in a Kiwi coil fashion (described later). For some reason, keeping a rope in backpack fashion from unknotting around your waist always seems to be a problem. You can use all sorts of fancy knots and tricks like a sheet-bend, but the quickest and most secure way is to adjust the tightness with a single overhand (the first part of tying your shoelaces) and then tie a simple double overhand knot like you would for an EDK on rappel.

SLINGS AND DRAWS
Nylon and Dyneema
It's been mentioned a few times already, but this is probably the best place to talk about using **nylon** vs. **Dyneema** (**Spectra, Dynex**, etc.). The pros of nylon is that it offers some dynamic properties that can reduce impact forces, it's easier to visually tell when you need to replace it, and it can hold a knot. The pros of Dyneema is that it is very strong for its weight allowing for very light skinny slings, doesn't absorb water (good for ice climbing), sits better when slinging rock horns because it's narrower, has better abrasion and cut resistance, and has superior resistance to UV damage and chemical exposure (except acids) compared to nylon. The downsides are that it degrades easily in heat, doesn't hold a knot, doesn't have any dynamic properties (may as well be a steel cable), and is difficult to tell when it's time to be retired. One gear manufacture that works extensively with Dyneema told me that even Dyneema slings left in a hot car in the summer (around 150° F) should be thrown out.

There have been some worries about the loss in strength in Dyneema slings after a lot of hard use due to damage via repeated bending cycles. It seems that after a year or two of regular use, Dyneema slings lose enough strength to cause concern. The flex life of nylon is substantially better than Dyneema. However, Dyneema slings have been around for quite some time now and I haven't heard of any accidents from a Dyneema sling failing any more than a nylon sling in a non-knotted situation. Never ever use a Dyneema sling to hold a knot – even one for bodyweight on a rappel, and especially not to girth hitch to anything. Use carabineers to connect multiple Dyneema slings, or basket hitch them instead of girth hitching. The friction of the knot tightening down quickly with a fall can easily melt the sling. Tying a fig-8 in a long doubled/tripled up Dyneema runner to create a power point on equalized gear is ok, however.

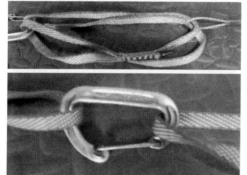

Basket hitch and carabiner connection

For sport draws, Dyneema offers a very light draw for hard sends. The downside to this is that they are really hard to grab when chickening out. Big thick beefy nylon draws are long lasting, durable, and fun to grab, but do weight quite a bit more when added up. I'm all for Dyneema slings on winter routes or saving weight on hard sends or lightweight missions, but replace your Dyneema slings after a year of constant use, two years of moderate use, or immediately after a burly alpine trip. But because of the element of the unknown condition of a Dyneema sling (especially your partners),

higher turnover in replacing them, and no dynamic properties I still greatly prefer nylon slings. It should be noted that slings advertised as Dyneema (Spectra or Dynex) do contain a mix of nylon in the weave. However, a few companies make a **nylon/ Dyneema blend** sling with a much higher ratio of nylon. Edelrid makes a skinny sewn or open length of webbing, called **Tech Web**, consisting of a Dyneema core with a nylon sheath over it so you can tie it, although they are not much lighter than similar nylon slings. These make good hex, big bro, and replacement slings for cams. Metolius, Trango, and Bluewater make a hybrid sling. Dyneema alone shouldn't be used as the sewn sling on cams or other rock protection or as a rappel backup friction knot as it may find its way back onto the rack. I realize that several companies do use Dyneema as their cam sling material, but the pros/cons of Dyneema aside, the fact remains that climbers are very lazy about getting their gear re-slung. Another poor application of Dyneema is use in daisy chains and as anchor building material. Although you should never shock-load a daisy, the additional force reduction of nylon adds a margin of protection, including improving marginal anchors. Lightweight alpine trips would seem to facilitate the use of Dyneema anchor cord, but the probability of cutting up your cord for descending is very high and you can't do that with Dyneema. PAS with burly hybrid nylon/ Dyneema blends should be fine, however.

Shoulder Slings and Quickdraws

The two most common slings used are **shoulder length sewn runners (60 cm) and quickdraws (12 cm/18+ cm)**, and both are useful at the sport crag and the alpine. Quickdraws generally come in two lengths: long and short. The shorty's are by far the most common. Longer quickdraws are useful on overhangs and roof pitches to reduce drag and swings into the wall. If the short draw causes the bolt biner to cross-load, use a longer draw. Longer draws are also handy when a shorter draw biner lays over the rock poorly. Rack your biners facing opposite or the same direction on your draws as it's pure preference, but do them all the same way. Most prefer the biners facing the same direction.

Remember to only use the same biner to clip the bolt to avoid roughing it up and severing your rope. The stiff end of the quickdraw clips the rope while the loose end clips the bolt. This makes the rope easier to clip, and lessens the chance of the bolt side levering off the bolt. Make sure to orient the lower biner away from the direction you are climbing to avoid cross-loading the biner and unclipping yourself, aka back-clipping. The rope coming up to the biner should be under the biner, not over it. It's a good idea to bring one more draw than you think necessary on an unknown sport climb. Not only could you misjudge the clips, the extra biner can be used to clip in direct to a biner to give your belayer relief when you de-pump, or in the anchor if you forgot to bring anchor draws or a daisy. It's ok to use two draws as the anchor in a standard bolted anchor for lowering and top-roping. The odds of both becoming unclipped are extremely low. If you feel the need, bring two shoulder slings with a regular biner and locker on each to up the safety, and possibly extended the anchor if needed. DMM Revolver biners make excellent toprope biners. Please don't lower or TR direct through chains (unless there are hook-style cold shuts), it shortens the lifespan of the chains making more work and cost to the great folks that volunteer their time and money to replace anchors.

Sewn shoulder length slings are meat and potatoes of tradsters and alpinists. You can make your own **tied runners** (cheaper and great if you need to create multiple makeshift rappels) with 9/16" tubular webbing or Edelrid Tech Web. To save weight, you can

just put one biner per shoulder sling, but on harder climbs it's still pretty common to double up every shoulder sling with two biners clipped to your harness and not extend very many, but use them as quickdraws. Removing a one biner sling off your shoulder is hard when cruxing. Even though the fall would only be two feet farther when extended sounds trivial on paper, extending slings looks mighty long on hard leads. Draws in this case would be a better choice, but it's nice to have wiggle room. The other drawback to having some slings with one biner and some doubled with two is that it can create a messy rack once the pitch has been cleaned, making the transition slower, and you'll inevitably wind up with a binerless sling at some point on your lead. Benefits of weight savings for one biner per sling are often offset by the added time. Deciding what slings/biner and quickdraw combination to bring depends on the route and you and your partner's personal preference. Sometimes a few redundant biners are worth the weight savings in time saved, sometimes not.

Shoulder sling doubled, lightweight wiregate draw, ergonomic sport draw, rabbit runner

Load limiter and shoulder sling with a DMM Revolver on the rope clipping end.

Some climbers put **rubber caps, aka Strings**, or rubber bands used on some quickdraws to stiffen the rope clipping side on their doubled shoulder slings. This is a horrible idea. It makes extending the sling a lot easier to screw-up as you need to unclip the correct biner. More importantly, if you screw up how you unfurl it, you can completely detach the biner from the sling. Check out the Petzl website on their String, or this video at:
http://vimeo.com/4138205 to see how this can happen. This can also happen on longer open looped quickdraws, but not many climbers use those anymore. At least one person has died from this easy mistake.

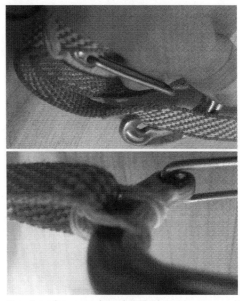

Securing a long open loop draw with a string can result in only the rubber part being loaded.

It's good practice to get over the fear of falling an extra two feet by extending a shoulder length runner. If the extra two feet could result in hitting a ledge and you are pulling a hard move, fine keep it short. If you think you'll need to hang on the gear then just clip in direct with a draw. But most of the time an extra two feet won't make any difference and the odds of a piece pulling and reduction of rope drag are significantly decreased by extending runners. On straight up and down cracks, placing at least a quickdraw on your gear is still a very good idea. You'll only fall an extra foot, but you'd fall a lot farther if your cam or nut pulls from rotation by being clipped too short. The forces on your cams will be much more in line with the way you placed them and the likelihood of a cam pulling is still lowered substantially. It's always a good idea on sport routes to carry a couple to a few shoulder length runners for when the carabineer sits over a lip or bulge in the rock to prevent the rope biner from breaking, or for when the climb jogs to the side or over a small roof to help prevent the bolt biner from pivoting and snapping (see next two photos).

in very handy as you normally never have enough.

If you run out of draws and desperately need more you can use nuts as long as you can push the nut down the wire and clip a biner on each end. If you need a longer sling, attach multiple nuts together. Don't forget your **gear sling**, it's probably rated to hold a fall. If you know you won't need certain cams, you can use their slings – attaching multiple cam slings together if necessary. Check and see if you have climbing spec tat on your chalk belt, pack, or squirreled away somewhere on your harness.

Double Length Runners
Double length shoulder slings and rabbit runners (an open sling with sewn loops at each end) are sometimes nice on wandering routes (although you could just clip two slings together). They can also double as short cordalettes for the anchor. **Rabbit runners** are great for slinging natural pro (icicles, trees, horns, etc.), equalizing two pieces of sketchy gear, and are easily deployed if clipped around your neck and shoulders with a single keylock biner. Most routes don't require them, but on an unknown wandering routes or ice climb, they are handy to bring at least one along.

Racking a rabbit runner

How many slings and draws you bring depends on the climb. For a standard difficult trad alpine climb, 12-14 slings and draws is a solid number – more if you plan on placing a lot of nuts, using slings in the anchor, and the route wanders. The harder the climbing, the more you may want to substitute quickdraws for shoulder slings. Aid pitches need more – 15 to 20 – depending on how hard the aid is and how many pieces you think you'll leave in vs. backcleaning. Bringing an extra shoulder length sling or two is never a bad idea, they come

Load Limiters (Screamers)
Screamers (made by Yates) and load limiters are slings that are bunched up and bar tacked together lightly enough that the stitching rips under load (around 1.5-2.5 kN). The stitching rips and absorbs force (2-8 kN) lessening the impact on the piece it is clipped to. These are fantastic to have on climbs where a piece or more may not be so bomber like aid climbing, ice climbing, or difficult/poorly protected trad routes. There are occasional rumors that they don't work, or worse, actually increase the impact force. This is simply untrue. It's not a bad idea to carry one or more instead of a quickdraw on an unknown climb, sketchy climb, or on a soft rock route. When combined with a DMM Revolver at the clipping end (among other tricks to reduce forces), you can really lessen the force applied to the piece. Load limiters can also be used on anchor pieces or points, especially useful for rope-soloing. Yates makes several types of load limiters for ice, aid, long Screamers, and shorty Screamers.

The **Ice Screamer** allows you to tie-off screws that don't go in all the way, but you should still clip the hanger with another sling to the rope as well. Also, Ice Screamers hang fairly low and it's easy to get your crampon caught when kicking your foot back. In fact, any low hanging loop (long draws, cordalettes, daisy chains etc.) can be dangerous because of this reason. **Aid Screamers** offer several clipping options for getting high on a piece, activate at low loads (1.5 kN), and aren't as strong (7 kN). They should only be used on really sketchy placements. Most other screamer and load limiters activate at around 2 kN and reduce the load by 3-4 kN. The new **Yates Zipper** activates at 2 kN, but can reduce the load by 4-8 kN, but you will fall farther. Remember that most load reducing tricks increase your fall length. There are pros and cons to everything. Load limiters should be a failsafe for a piece you don't want to fall on,

so the odds of falling onto one are pretty low. There's no reason why you shouldn't switch all of your ice climbing quickdraws out for screamers using the logic that they should be used on pieces you don't want to fall on, and you never ever want to fall on ice.

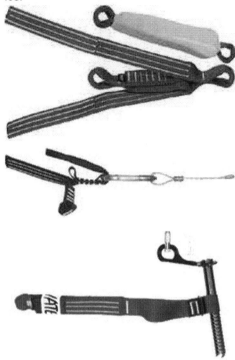

Zipper, Aid, & Ice Screamers. Courtesy Yates.

There are other load limiters out there. E-climb makes the **Dissip**, a "rechargeable" load limiter that you can thread a sling through. The company does not have activation or load reduction forces published unfortunately. If for some reason you can't justify bringing a short screamer with you, you could sneak a Dissip along and place a sling through it when you need it. I haven't used it, but placing the sling in it can't be easy to do quickly on lead, but I mention it as an option. Kong makes a load limiter called the **KISA** that can be setup to activate anywhere from 1.5 kN to 5 kN. It is like the Dissip, but you use a pre-cut length of 9-11 mm rope with a stopper knot instead of a normal sling. It can be used to clip pro on lead, but its best application would be used in a rope-solo anchor set to activate at a higher impact force.

Shorty screamers and Zipper Screamers are the most useful, however, with the ice being moderately useful (better to switch to a shorter screw and use a normal screamer), and aid being a good choice for extra sketchy placements. If you're thinking, "why not just clip a screamer to your harness and rope?" you must remember that the climber, belayer, and piece all receive different loads on a fall. A sketchy piece most likely will have popped before your personal screamer would have activated. I suppose it couldn't hurt, but it probably won't help. Using a screamer on a daisy chain also makes little sense, as you should NEVER be falling onto your daisy – use the damn rope. It could make some sense if you are soloing and are "daisying" past cruxes, but you would want to use combined nylon shoulder slings instead of a daisy.

Dissip and Kisa. Courtesy E-Climb and Kong

Stick Clips
Stick clips allow you to clip draws to fixed gear out of reach. The most basic stick clip is a **branch** (don't pull branches off trees!) and a quickdraw taped to it. Other non-commercial stick clips can be made from **backpack stays, tent poles** (usually too bendy), **avalanche probes** (they work great!), and **painter's poles**. **Tape** the top biner open and tape the spine of the biner to the pole. Old pitons may require a very narrow biner, or a bight of sling to pass through (a very tricky stick clipping scenario). Clip the lead rope to the bottom draw and feed slack out while you attempt to clip. A taped-open biner isn't safe to fall on, so this method is usually reserved for pulling up on the rope to the clip in direct. Either take the tape off the gate, or try and swap draws if stick clipping again from that piece. A **commercially made stick clip attachment** holds the gate up until clipped, and the gate snaps closed when you pull down on the pole. This is safer and easier if attempting to free climb up and past that bolt. You could rig your own with a spring loaded **wood clamp** or keep the gate open with a **rubber band** or loose piece of tape attached to the pole so they break/rip when you pull the pole.

Mad Rock makes the **Trigger Wire** biner with a very light mechanism to keep the gate open that snaps closed when clipped, and Kong makes the Frog. Both are designed for quickly clipping a bolt or rope while sport climbing, but make nice stick clip biners. The Frog is total overkill and probably won't be seen on anyone's harness. A **short stick clip** for just out of reach clips (useful in aid climbing) can be easily made by stiffening a quickdraw with duct tape and taping the gate open (or break the gate off for a committed piece), or taping a draw to the end of a wall hammer.

Mad Rock Trigger Wire on a stiff draw with an avalanche probe with tape.

Tat
If you plan on doing a lot of rappelling using your own tat, you can save weight by tying your own slings with ½" **webbing**. This diameter isn't the safest and you should con-

sider using **9/16" webbing**. Knotted slings are not as strong as sewn slings. If you aren't making your own slings or plan on salvaging your cordalette and have the choice between using ½" tubular webbing or **5 mm nylon accessory cord** for bail tat, use cord. It is 30% lighter, 20% stronger, is much easier to cut and tie knots, knots slip less, and can fit in smaller holes and wedge behind flakes and cracks easier, and is way cheaper. Half-inch tubular webbing is still excellent for slinging hooks and making tie-offs, but can be hard to find.

Petzl Basic and Croll

Petzl Protraxion

BIG WALL GEAR

Not all big wall gear means you're aid climbing, although many walls have an aid pitch or two.

Ascenders

(shown elsewhere: Petzl Ascender, Tibloc, and Microtraxion)

Petzl Microcender, Ushba Basic

Rollinlock. Courtesy Climbtech

 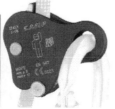

Wild Country Ropeman & Lift (courtesy CAMP)

Block Roll (courtesy Kong), Ushba Hogwaller, Wallhauler (courtesy Rock Exotica)

There are a lot of things you can use to ascend the rope. Any rope gripping knot or device should work, but some are better than other in terms of efficiency or weight. For short sections or unplanned jugging, you can usually rig something from what gear you already have. For most jugging situations, nothing beats a **toothed handled ascender** for the upper clamp, aka a Jumar or jug. A good ascender has an ergonomic handle made for the left and right hand, and you should be able to disengage the clamp comfortably with your thumb from the grip position. The ascender should have a hole in the bottom to clip your daisy and aider to, and a hole above the clamp for clipping on overhangs and roofs. Another of the same ascender is the best choice for standard jugging, and a clamp that slides and locks easily like the Petzl **Microtraxion** or Climb Tech **Rollnlock** work well for the "frog-style" method, as does a **GriGri**. For the latter, "frog" method, a Petzl **Microcender** is another good choice because it has no teeth and can be removed from the rope while still being clipped in. Other great options are **toothless models** from Camp and Ushba (out of business).

If you can't tie backup knots on the rope (because it's fixed, or would pull the rope away from the next person to ascend the line), and you are using two handled ascenders, then it's really nice to have a backup third rope clamp as the odds of three ascenders failing are really low. The Microtraxion/Rollnlock and Microcender work very well for this. A **Tibloc** isn't a great backup mainly because it won't slide great until well up the rope unless you find the perfect biner. A **GriGri** won't slide on its own, but will work. Clip the backup ascender to your belay loop under the other two ascenders. If you have to do a lower out or clean a roof, or get both Jumars above a piece, the 3rd backup may get in the way which is why the Microcender is nice because it stays clipped to you.

There are some speed ascenders out there that strap right to your wrists and feet. I haven't used them or seen anyone use them, even in speed climbing movies so I can only assume they aren't safe or effective for big walls. Other ascenders are **basic ascenders without a handle, knots (prusik, Bachman, Klemheist, Autoblock, locking Munter, garda hitch), Ropemen, autolocking belay devices like the GriGri, semi autolocking belay devices, and plaquettes**.

Hauling Devices
For lengthy hauls you may want a climbing rated **swivel** to save your rope from tangles, especially when hauling up slabby terrain. Most of the time, even on slabs, you will be fine without one. Attach the swivel to the bag and the rope. To save biners, you could just tie the rope to the swivel with a figure-8 or double bowline and clip the swivel to the bag with a locker. You may want to back the swivel up by tying into the bag with the extra tail end of the rope.

When solo climbing, you can attach a **fifi hook** to the haul bag. This helps to do because the bag may get stuck before rapping down and this can save you some trips, as well as aid in lifting the bag off the belay since it's hard to do without shock loading the system from below. **Lower out lines** are necessary if there isn't enough rope left from the lead to get the bag in line with the haul. A newbie mistake is to forget that the bag needs a lower out and the leader pulls in too much slack when fixing the jug line. Communicate this!

If you are doing anything more than tagging up a small pack, you'll want a haul system. You can make one with any rope clamp knot or device, but seriously think about get a ratcheting pulley. The **Petzl Microtraxion and Rollnlock** are amazingly light, can haul a very heavy load, and do so very well. They also great for toprope-soloing, jugging, and rescue. For huge multiday routes get a **Protraxion or Kong Block Roll**. The older model of the Protraxion has broken on some folks, but it is most likely user error by either cross-loading it or not clipping a biner in the bottom hole. For most 1-3 night walls, you only really need to use a 1:1 system, that is just pull the rope through the Microtraxion/Rollnlock using your body, aider, and or ascender. It is debatable if you really even need to attach your main non-moving ratchet to the anchor with a locker, or if a strong non-locking biner is just fine. To add mechanical advantage but slow down the process, you can construct haul systems of varying mechanical advantage by adding more rope clamps and pulleys. The better the pulley and rope clamp the easier things will be. If going light but still want a 3:1, use two **DMM Revolver** biners and a Tibloc in addition to the Microtraxion/Rollnlock. Practice at home or on the first pitch to see if you can get away with a 1:1. Specifics on setting up haul systems, and more info on types of ascenders will be described later.

Fifi Hooks and Daisies

Daisy chains are useful in aid climbing because they allow you to keep your ladder and gear attached to something in case the piece blows, and the multiple clip loops aid in fifi hooking or clipping in short quickly although you can also just clip into your ladder. They are incredibly useful maintaining balance while jugging, even though they are not meant to bear much more than body weight. PAS are a more durable and safer alternative. Save the light **flat looped daisies** for the haul bag. There is no reason to fall unless your piece blows while aiding and if the piece blows your daisy won't be doing much but falling with you. Hopefully you have the rope, not another daisy clipped into the lower piece you're falling on. If using daisies while aiding (it's much quicker not to on easy aid) you will probably want two – one for each ladder or pair of ladders or for each ascender. If just using a one ascender system or just one ladder, you only need one daisy. If you don't plan on using daisy chains because the aid is easy but encounter a short difficult section of gear placements just make sure you clip something into your aider in case the gear blows. To do this, pull up about 5' of tag line for extra wiggle room and clip it to the aider or use your daisy.

Adjustable daisies are really nice for quickly finding the perfect length, and for hoisting yourself up to a piece while staying in balance. They are extremely useful on very steep or overhanging terrain. You can even place a fifi on the end of one or both adjustable daisies. Adjustable daisies can slow you down by getting tangled (like any daisy would), and loosening them or forgetting to loosen them can be a chore after a while. They are also rated much lower than even traditional daisy chains because of the sliding buckle. Usually the kN rating means the force at which the daisy will slip, not break. Metolius makes the user-friendliest loosening system, but unfortunately the pulling end is attached to the daisy, making for a giant annoying loop. Un-attaching the pull strand by getting rid of the D-link attachment and putting something that will jam in the buckle (like bar tacking on a rappel ring) is not recommended by Metolius.

The standard use for a **fifi hook** is to hook into your daisy, ladder, or gear to stay in balance. You can get away with a quickdraw, but the design of a well-made fifi makes it pretty secure, quick, and light. The proper length of the loop is around 8 inches before you girth hitch it to your belay loop.

Use some ½" webbing or 6 mm cord and girth hitch it to your belay loop. Occasionally it will be too short or too long, for instance if the gear is set deep like in chimneys and flared grooves. Use a quickdraw instead, or if this happens a lot, have a second fifi on a different size cord. If the cord is too long you can always wrap the fifi around the gear and fifi back into your belay loop. There are **adjustable fifi** hooks that allow you to add some accessory cord through a couple holes in the fifi. This may work better for you instead of two fifis. This style of fifi is also handy for maintaining balance while high stepping on very steep terrain. Attach **cord to the top hole** in the fifi to help you yank it off gear or for tagging. If you aren't tagging heavy loads, 3-4 mm cord will do. Use 5-6 mm cord for heavy loads. This loop can also be clipped off to your harness to get the fifi out of the way when climbing or following.

Clipping a fifi back on itself. Fifi rigged for tagging.

Adjustable fifi courtesy Kong

The **Petzl fifi** is designed specifically for tagging gear and solo hauling because it engages more if pulled accidentally from below and not from the top. The top of the Petzl fifi should be used with a quick link to have this feature function properly.

Courtesy Petzl.

Some people use a fifi to protect for a rest when ice climbing by fifi'ing into their ice tool. You can also use a fifi to set up the one of the world's sketchiest rappels, and this will be described later.

Ladders

Ladders, aka **etriers and aiders**, are almost essential aid climbing gear. You can make your own in a pinch or for a route with very short aid sections by tying up a cordalette or girth hitching slings together, but beware the wear and tear on your slings. **Lightweight 3-4 step alpine aiders or pocket aiders** are really nice for short aid sections, speed climbing, and walls with only minimal aid pitches like the Nose or Half Dome. They should have a **grab loop** and allow for decent high stepping. The ability to quickly hide the aiders in the pocket so they don't snag during free climbing is unbelievably useful and the pocket doesn't get in the way too much. For some reason the flap is on the bottom of some models so they fall out regardless! Add some Velcro or button closures to fix this silly shortcoming.

5+ step aiders are useful for overhangs so you're not struggling to high step when transition into the lower step. **Offset stepped aiders** are helpful because they allow you to more ergonomically alternate feet while walking up. But somehow they twist and get all crazy compared to vertical ladder aiders, or **Russian aiders,** and also get stuck in cracks way easier. If your aiders don't have a grab loop at the top, tie one in. The grab loop can also be used for extreme high-stepping (less scary than not reaching a piece). Add a **small loop of 1/2" - 9/16" webbing** for attaching useful gear if the normal clip-in loop is small. **Heavier aiders** are meant for intensive aid, and a much more comfortable and easy to access steps. If you do a wall that is mostly aid, get a nice big beefy set as you won't be carrying them. These are **ladder style** and have a **spreader bar** on the top to help you get your feet in and out.

Adjustable aiders seem like a great idea, but if things get crossed up (and this happens pretty much every five feet while aid climbing), and it takes forever to get your feet in and out of them. I'd stay clear unless you have things dialed, then they could be faster. For lightweight aiding you just need two aiders, or just stand in **slings**. Three aiders are handier than two if weight isn't a high priority because having a **floating aider** (no daisy attached) can be a real nice to keep your center of gravity by using an aider on each foot. **Four aiders** are useful on overhanging terrain when you always want the stability of two, but are very rarely ever needed. If using three (best), then you will need to stand on just one aider while transitioning to your new placement.

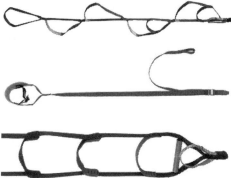

Staggered, adjustable, and ladder-style etriers. Courtesy Yates.

Pocket Aider. Courtesy Metolius.

Hammers

A good wall hammer isn't cheap. You can get a **very nice wooden** one from Black Diamond, or a **lighter metal** one from several companies. You'll want a **holster** (or place to clip it off) and a **long leash attached to a shoulder sling** so you can just drop it when you're done banging or taking a break. A slightly **chiseled nose** helps in head placements and prying out pins, and a hole in the nose offers a good place to clip your funkness device. A **funkness device** is a static piece of Dyneema or a swaged cable. Besides driving pins, heads, drilling bolts, and funking gear out, hammers are useful for tapping on the rock to judge stability. You can use a **cheap hardware store hammer** and duct tape a Dyneema leash on it for climbs that you just plan on hammering a few pins in. Get only the best hammer for hand drilling and intense nailing. **Crowbars** are very handy for prying off old bolts and levering off death blocks if cleaning up old routes or putting up new routes.

Funkness. Courtesy Moses

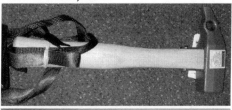

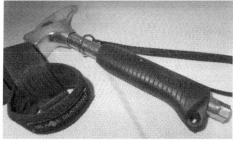

Belay Seat

A **boson's chair, or belay seat** is almost always unnecessary – file this under the suck it up category. The times when you really want one are usually in 20/20 hindsight. But, if you know a pitch just has a hands down miserable hanging belay and takes forever for the leader to finish the pitch, you'll be glad you had it. Small pocket nylon seats are available, but don't add much in the way of comfort. If you're bringing one, might as well bring a solid platform, either from a commercial vendor (hard to find), or make one yourself using plywood and attach cam buckles with webbing to adjust the length. 99 times out of 100 you'll have a portaledge when you'll actually really want one of these seats.

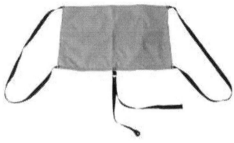
Belay seat. Courtesy Yates

Bosun's Chair. Courtesy Black Diamond

ICE AND SNOW GEAR

Ice Axes

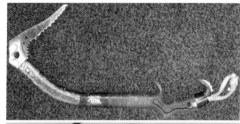

Petzl Nomic, Petzl Ergo, Black Diamond Cobra, X Blade (courtesy Grivel) technical ice tools

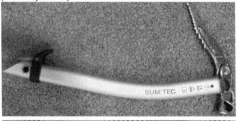

Petzl Sum'Tech & Camp Corsa axes

Ice axes are reserved for general mountaineering. These **straight or mildly bent axes are longer** than water ice tools for assisting with stability walking up or across steep slopes and for plunging into snow for upwards progress or anchors. **Water ice tools that aren't leashless-style** tools can be substituted for a mountaineering ax if performance on technical water ice trumps mountaineering usefulness. The straighter shafted the ax, the easier it is to plunge the tool for steep snow, rig snow belays with the ax, chop large sections of ice and snow, and hammer in pickets and pitons. **Very light axes** exist for weight savings, but their performance and durability are greatly sacrificed – especially on hard/brittle ice. They also are not fully strength rated for belaying and torquing on. These are good just in case axes to assist in arresting a fall and aiding in getting up a steep snow slope. Get a **burlier ax** if you plan on doing a lot of chopping and swinging. To check the strength rating on your ax or pick see if it is B or T rated. B rated means it is tested to 200 Kg and T is tested to 400 kg.

The picks on mountaineering axes are different from the reverse curved pick on a water-ice tool. They curve downward in a **C-curve** and self-arrest and grip snow much better than reverse curve picks. **Straight picks** like the Alaska Pick from Black Diamond are a great comprise between a reverse curve and C-curved mountaineering pick. They work great on mixed snow/ice/rock pitches, like the majority of conditions found on climbs in Alaska. They offer better holding power in snow, and require less overall effort on low angled ice. These straight picks are meant to go on water-ice tools. Tools like the Cobra with Alaska picks are a good comprise between classic ice axes and technical ice tools for technical mountaineering routes. One way to reduce the weight on a big alpine route is to have the leader use a high-tech modern technical ice tool and let the follower use a light-weight technical ax for following. **Adzes** are usually only found on mountaineering axes these days, although putting an adz on one of your ice tools may be useful on big routes that involve clearing a lot of snow off the ice and rock, and digging snow pits and platforms. Don't bother with **spike and adze guards** except when traveling. Cardboard and duct tape do a great job and cost a fraction of commercially available products.

Black Diamond Alaska Pick

Ice Tools

For pure water ice and mixed climbing (not much snow climbing) there is really only one type of tool to get – a **leashless ice tool**. Save the non-leashless grip ice tools for technical mountaineering. The more aggressively bent the tool, the better it will clear bulges and allow for better a better angle of grip on overhanging terrain. However, **radically bent tools** are less efficient on steep to low angled ice. Save the radically bent tools for mixed terrain, and for severely overhanging or extremely featured ice. The ergonomic handled grip makes every hold a jug versus a pinch, making leashless climbing a safer and less pumpy exploit. Climbing leashless allows you to place screws without the extra mayhem involved in getting out of your leashes, and move between tools or tool positions naturally. Circulation isn't cut off from a leash choking your wrist, and you can shake out as much as you like. People can usually climb a full grade harder in leashless tools. Leashless tools have several grabbing options for getting high on the tool for mixed, technical ice, or just plain old moving faster.

There are a lot of very interesting tool designs out there these days that involve one-piece designs. Check out E-climbs, Camp/Cassin, and Grivel for some cool designs (compared to Petzl and Black Diamond who make the most popular ice tools). Just don't buy the most sophisticated looking thing out there just because, unless you can afford to buy a lot of tools and test them. Ask around and have your friends let you try theirs. Look at photos of the pros and see what they are using (assuming they aren't using a tool because they are sponsored). In the end, it's really a poor musician who blames their instrument (but you don't see professional musicians playing on junk either).

Also beware of tools with **integrated picks**. That's a lot of money to spend on a one-use pick. **Spikes** are extremely useful on the bottom of your tool shaft to avoid slipping when you use your tool in cane position, but interfere with full rotation of the tool when you swing. **Head weights** help with the follow-through on your swing into pure ice and usually make the tool perfectly balanced. The tradeoff is a heavier tool for mixed climbing, or alpine climbs with thin or minimal ice. You should be able to remove the head weights.

Almost all technical ice tools do not have adz's and many don't even have **hammers**. Hammering pitons is really a chore when the tool is bent the wrong way, but a hammer is essential on non-bolted mixed alpine routes. Coldthistle used to modify tools by adding a hammer, along with a lot of other really cool modifications. Another option is to bring along a short **3rd tool with a hammer**. If the ice is hard enough and you've got to place pins, a 3rd tool is really handy. Plus if you lose a tool or break a pick on lead, you've got a backup. It's actually pretty difficult to find a perfect 3rd tool. Simond used to make the "Fox", a straight shafted extremely light children's ice tool with a great technical pick and a burl hammer. If you can't find the one you want with a hammer, you could send it to an expert welder. Honestly, just bringing a **cheap wooden hardware store hammer** is the easiest solution and weighs barely anything.

Simond Fox

Leashes do allow you to hang from a tool while totally pumped, but the ability to shake out completely nullifies that argument. Also the fact that you should never climb ice until so pumped you're gonna fall out of your tools. The first thing you should do when you get leashless tools is to make sure you can clip in to the bottom of the tool if pumped. Some spike holes are too small for a biner, so add a very **small loop of thin webbing or cord** that won't get in the way of anything. Non-locking biners can easily lever out if clipped directly to a spike hole.

To avoid dropping tools, climbers found a comprise between leashes and leashless by using **umbilicals**. These stretchy tethers aren't supposed to be weight bearing, but usually hold a small fall. For reference, the Black Diamond Spinner Leash can hold about 2kN. Umbilicals are useful on longer routes when retrieving a dropped tool would be impossible or climb ending. They are annoying, and can hang up under little icicles. Practice clipping your rope to avoid trapping the umbilical. One way to quickly free a tangle is to clip your umbilical to your belay loop with a non-locking biner instead of girth hitching it. This allows you to quickly unclip and pull the tangle through. Just beware that the biner may unclip itself unknowingly.

Black Diamond and a homemade umbilical

Courtesy Blue Ice

Android Leash

Many umbilicals employ a swivel to avoid tangles when switching tools or crossing through. You can make your own full-strength versions by bunching up some 1/2" webbing, sliding shock cord through, clipping biners to the ends and a small swivel to the base (optional and check the load bearing of the swivel). Make sure you can get full extension on the tools and the shock cord isn't so tight every swing becomes resistance band exercise. Blue Ice makes a wonderful umbilical. If you are doing a route that makes sense to still use leashes, the **Black Diamond Android Leashes** allow you to switch back and forth very quickly. Some tools need some **grip tape** wrapped around the shaft to increase purchase and offset some cold conduction. Petzl makes a good grip tape, but Scotch makes a great tape too: the 228 moisture sealing electrical tape.

There are a few types of **reversed curve picks** out there. **Thinner ice picks** excel at pure ice, but are weaker (can break) and sometimes go in a bit too well and can be a pain to remove. I've had to fashion a funkness device on lead to extract an impossible to remove tool with an ice pick on it! You may want to file down the first tooth and blunt the other teeth if extraction becomes a real problem. **Mixed picks** have a lot burlier teeth and are thicker. Some have teeth all the way up to where the pick meets the tool. And of course there are picks in the middle of the two. One really burly pick was made by Black Diamond, the **Aermet Pick**, fashioned from an extremely strong alloy. They only cost $75 each! They aren't made commercially anymore, but Coldthistle may have some if still in operation. They are very strong, and because of that, can also be made thinner. Add an extra half hour of sharpening time to these.

Back in the day climbers had to modify their picks from the factory designs. Now you can get **picks designed for ice, mixed, and general purpose** as companies have caught on. If you feel your picks need some extra tweaking you can still use a file to modify them. To get really good penetration in the ice, file down or bevel the teeth on the top two to three inches of your picks and lower the profile of the pick. This will also aid in pick extraction. The tradeoff is less purchase if hooking ice or most mixed routes and a weaker pick, so use these picks for pure ice climbs that have ice at least a few inches thick. You can keep or add a hook on the first tooth to still have some hooking power.

The more you file down and sharpen your pick, the better it will penetrate and remove from the ice with less effort, but the weaker the pick will be.

If climbing very different mediums in different locations around the country or world, you will want at least a couple types of picks: **one for pure ice and one for mixed or bullet hard ice**. The more bevel on the teeth, the easier they are to remove. The deeper the teeth, the more purchase but the harder they will be to remove. More often than not you will want the teeth with a moderate bevel and depth. The first tooth is the one you will want to deepen, bevel less, and increase the angle on for thin hooking and mixed climbing. If you can get a stock "ice" or "mixed" pick, most likely they will perform for their intended use just fine. If not, taper and bevel the pick for pure ice, work on the first tooth for mixed and difficult hooking, and for **very thin ice and cracks** file your pick down to a knife (but don't expect it to last).

No matter what type of climbing you are doing, you want the picks to be as sharp as possible. A **big bastard file** works well for shaping the pick, and **smaller chainsaw files** puts on the finishing touches. Sharpen your picks after every climb to keep them from becoming so blunted that restoring them to the original shape becomes impossible. Just sharpening the tip of the pick isn't enough maintenance. Eventually your pick will be a misshapen stub with a pointy end. Work on getting the pick back to how it looked from the factory, meaning filing down the top of the pick as well as working on the teeth below. Even bringing a file on a long route is a very good idea. Hopefully you know not to use a grinder, as this could lose the temper on the metal and significantly weaken them via heat. A long beefy file works best for returning the picks to their proper shape, smaller files help fine tune, and **rounded files** help with the teeth. Keep the front pick angle low so the pick is pointy, and sharpen the spine of the pick to aid in penetration. Mixed climbers may want to go so far as to individually sharpening each tooth on their picks.

Where to put your tool can be a problem while placing a piece of rock gear (no ice to leave the tool in) or when just using one tool. Ice tools clip really nicely into ice screw biners on the harness – unless they are full of ice screws. You can stick another one on each side specifically for your tools, or use a biner on one of your slings temporarily. Unless you've tested the security, don't slide the tool through your gear loop, especially if it's a hammer or no-hammer or ax tool. It can easily slide out. You can use a holster, but considering the most of your climbing is done with tools in the hand or in the pack, holsters make little sense except for 3rd tools. When mixed climbing, the task of clipping and unclipping your tool can be too much. At this stage of the game, you will just rest the tool, pick facing back, over your other shoulder. A better option, is to put the pick of the tool not in use between the thumb and index finder of the hand holding onto the other tool. Putting the tool in your mouth works well too. I've often considered placing Velcro strips on the breast of my jacket and shaft of the tool (too expensive to play with...you try). Maybe magnets? It's still a new sport, there will be plenty of products I'm sure.

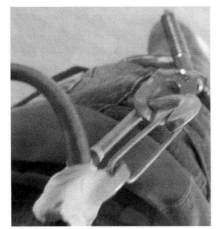

Taping biner to gear loop to rack screws

Crampons

Grivel Airtech strap-on, Black Diamond Sabertooth, Petzl Dart

Camp XLC Nanotech

Black Diamond Cyborg

Black Diamond semi-automatic crampon

Before I mention any specifics about crampons, let me offer this suggestion: put your harness on before your crampons, and put both on before the final approach slope below the climb. It's amazing how steep the base of a route can be and how dangerous it is to try and get into your kit on a steep slope.

No matter what crampon you buy, make sure they fit your boot. It's amazing how many incompatible combinations there are. You can make them fit with some monkeying around and brute force with a hammer, but having a crampon come off on lead is one of the more horrifying experiences you can have – and losing a crampon can be deadly. If you hear rattling around, your crampon is probably about to come off. And however obvious this sounds, fit the crampons to your boot before you get to the route, especially if you need a wrench or something to adjust them.

For summer snow and sketching across steep ice in your tennis shoes, **strap on crampons** are the best way to go. **Lightweight aluminum crampons** can be found that only weight a pound or less. These are perfect for snow and very short ice approaches (very painful on the toes), but aren't built to last. Don't get crampons without front points, and slip on snow traction cleats weight more than ultralight ones with front points. Camp makes a very light model with steel front points to add some durability and safety for speed mountaineering. For easy mountaineering trips in boots without a heel welt, get a **more durable pair of strap-on crampons**. Many mountaineering boots only allow for a rear heel bail and a harness for the front of the boot. These are to be paired with **semi-automatic crampons** that are half step-in half strap on. If you can strap them on tight enough, you can use them for regular water-ice climbing.

All high tech ice boots will accept **step-in or automatic crampons**. You can get **rigid or semi-flexible** crampons, although the trend is certainly going with flexible crampons as boots become more and more like a big pair of rock shoes. The theory behind rigid crampon was stability for hard ice climbing, but became more or less obsolete as boots got softer and ice climbers started climbing with better technique. You'll only want a stiff crampon for lower angled hard ice to help with efficiency and fatigue.

The crampon should fit with a firm snap and the frame fit a hair smaller than the sole of the boot in the back, and the base of the front points exactly at the end of the toe. The sole should have no gaps between the crampon frame and the sole. If not, they don't fit. Try again, or expect them to come off on lead. You should call the crampon company first, and then see if you can get free parts from other crampon companies to mix and match parts for a perfect fit. The front wire should wrap around and contact the majority of the toe bail area. Hammer the bail into place if your boot is really small or narrow. Some front bails offer a loop that you can wrap the strap though for added security. If your crampons don't have a front bail strap make sure the front welt isn't extremely worn or file the welt in better, get the boots resoled, or get a new pair of boots. The rear bail should at least have an ankle strap to minimize crampon loss.

You have several front point options. Flat **horizontal front points** are usually reserved for snow climbing and mountaineering. The flat blades have more surface area and therefor don't slice through snow as easily

as vertically oriented points. **Vertical points** shear through snow easier, but displace less ice for pure ice climbing. They are sharper and also fit into little pockets and rock divots better for mixed climbing. That said, horizontal points edge on mixed terrain better and are more stable on slushy, weirdly bonded, or bullet hard ice that will shatter no matter what you're using. In other words, well-made technical horizontal point crampons can be amazing on mixed and ice in the right conditions. But if you had to choose only one for ice or mixed, I'd still go with vertical points.

Some crampons allow you to **offset the two front points** (usually you make the big toe point the long one) to focus more power on the big toe just like in rock shoes, and also for better precision on highly featured ice. **Monopoints** are usually the most desirable in mixed climbing to focus all the weight in one precise spot. They work great in plastic ice for easy in, easy out climbing, but may not make full contact with the ice in highly featured or extremely kicked out ice. **Replaceable front points** can make a crampon last for decades, and usually allow you to offset them or make monopoints out of them. **Offset monopoints** can offer some advantage for mixed climbing or highly featured ice. Fixed front points provide a lighter crampon and transfer energy a bit better, useful in hard sends. By the time you need to replace them, a newer better model has probably arrived.

A good feature on any crampon are **aggressive secondary points**. These add more purchase on the ice, and act as a kind of a tripod for monopoints. Some crampons have extra points or a hole where a **screw** can be added right in the center of the crampon for stability standing on big cauliflowers or ice slopers.

Heel spurs are still frowned upon for mixed ice, and are useless on easier water ice climbs because most crampons have a **rake** (backwards facing tertiary point) that can be used for wrapping a leg around a pillar, etc. However, unless you are in a competition or are trying to break a record, no one should care if you use heel spurs or not, it's up to you. Make your own cheap heel spur by drilling a hole in the back of your crampon and put a bolt sticking out the back.

Most crampons come with **anti-balling plates**. These are lifesavers in sticky snow conditions and don't really affect the performance of a crampon or add significant weight. You can make your own using milk jug plastic (or really any semi durable plastic), or with some duct tape and cardboard. If whacking snow off your crampons with a carbon fiber ice tool like the Cobra, keep in mind that you can poke holes in it. Use the middle of the head of your tool instead. Never glissade with crampons! Take the time to take them off, but beware the first few cramponless steps - especially if you're standing on a frozen riverbed on top!

Crampons are easier to sharpen than ice picks, but you still need to stay on top of it so you don't deform the front points so badly that matching the original angle is impossible. You're in luck if your crampons have replaceable points. Just like picks, try and match the original slope angle and bevel the top on both sides. Sharpening the other points usually just takes a few strokes of the file to keep them pointy, spending a little more time on the secondary points.

Miscellaneous Ice Gear

Shovels were discussed already, and **beacons, probes, and other avalanche gear** will be described in the avalanche section. Be sure to have an **extra pick and a tool to adjust your pick and crampons** (if they need them). It's also a good idea to have a **small file** handy to sharpen points and screws en route. Petzl came out with a **portable ice screw sharpener** which is a godsend. You can fit a **knife, small chainsaw file, tool wrench, spare pick, V-threader,** and one v-thread worth of **cord** on a small biner on the back of your harness.

Bail biner with small file, tat, knife, v-threader, pick

Petzl ice screw sharpener, courtesy Petzl

ROCK AND ICE PROTECTION

HOW MUCH PRO?

When racking up for a climb it's always hard to decide what and how much pro to bring. Less gear means less weight and clutter, and more gear means a higher margin of safety. Sometimes a pitch will go quicker with a little extra gear because less time is wasted debating whether to use up a piece and what size to give up. Guidebooks, beta, and being able to scope the route obviously help. Beta from online sources can't always

473

be trusted. When someone says something like, "You don't need the #4" or "Link pitches x and y," take it with a grain of salt. They may be a way better climber, didn't see a good placement option that actually does exist, have actually placed that size, followed the pitch and decided it wasn't necessary, or they may not have ever climbed it. Anytime I read a comment like that, I usually bring the size mentioned that apparently wasn't needed and was glad I did. If you know the general size of the crux, bring one or more extras in that range so you aren't hoarding a particular piece that would be very useful in places besides the crux. Take the time to know an area or guidebook nuances (is the guidebook author a sandbagger?), and bring extra until you feel more confident. Some areas tend towards wideness, while some areas tend towards nuts and small cams.

STANDARD RACK

Since there are many versions of the same type of protection, picking the best piece for you will always be a compromise. The lightest of a particular piece of gear probably isn't the most durable or functional. The piece with the greatest range or adaptability is probably slightly heavier and may not fit in certain special situations. A specialty piece may have no use on a normal route.

A **generic rack** for a moderate to difficult climb is usually a set of small to medium nuts, a single tiny cam in the tips range (blue alien), and doubles from there up to hand size (gold Camalot), with another single wide hand and maybe a fist size. Of course that's just a generic rack suggestion. For **long difficult climbs** a standard rack usually means a set of 6-10 nuts from two up from the smallest offset brassie to one down from the biggest, doubling up on the biggest of the brassies up to the small/mid-size standard nuts. Cams are usually a single set of .3-.5" (black and blue Alien), doubles of small cams from 0.6"-1" (green, yellow, red Alien), doubles of 1.25"-2.5" (0.5 Camalot to 3.0 Camalot), and depending on the rock singles or doubles from there up (the 3.0 Camalot size may not be necessary either). Again, different areas and rock types, and your lead head will alter what a standard rack means. On **first ascents** it can be a good idea to bring two pieces covering 3.5" - 5.5" (4.0 and 5.0 Camalot) just in case an offwidth appears, plus a small selection of pitons and tricams.

Obviously your rack totally depends on the climb and could resemble nothing like the "standard rack". Triple up (or more) on crux sizes or if a crack is a continuous size. Multipitch desert routes can create monster racks, especially if each pitch has a different but unchanging size.

RACKING

Racking on a gear sling versus your harness gear loops is generally a matter of preference. Racking on your harness avoids the yard sale of gear cluttering around you while climbing and may make you feel a bit more streamlined. It is certainly in vogue with the cool kids to rack on your harness. If your gear loops are big enough, you know where everything is both by memory and touch, and you're able to not only find your gear but to also get to it, then racking on your harness makes sense. Same sized desert cracks, ice climbing, and climbs where you've got the protection sequence wired lend themselves to racking on your harness.

Racking on a **simple gear sling** (usually just a nylon shoulder sling) is helpful if you don't have a dialed harness system, you've got a lot of different sized gear, you want quick visual access to your pro, or access to the gear with either hand. Too much gear on a shoulder sling can wind up bunching together and make removing a piece difficult. One way to deal with this is to clip the nuts and largest sizes to your harness.

The best gear sling for a free climb is just a **sewn nylon shoulder length sling**. **Padded gear slings** inevitably creep around, making you constantly adjust it, or attempt to unclip a piece through inches of padding. If your partner sweats like crazy, nothing is more disgusting than putting his/her sweat drenched padded sling on when you swap leads. **Multi-loop gear slings** attempt to solve the clutter issues, but for most part they just make things worse. It's all personal preference so try a few different ways. **Double gear slings** for big-wall aid climbing are really helpful for managing giant racks. It's a matter of style how you organize it, just have a system to speed up finding your gear quickly. Be sure and adjust the loops so they don't hang too low. I actually prefer two crisscrossed shoulder slings to a standard double gear loop. There are some fancy **double slings that double as a chest harness**, or have a small backpack compartment in the back. Bringing **two gear slings**, one for each climber, isn't a bad idea and weighs nothing. Transitions could be slowed if you wind up transferring the leaders extra gear onto your sling if he/she didn't place a ton of gear, however.

You wind up with a lot of extra biners by racking each cam per biner and every sling with two. For most climbers this is a necessary evil on moderate to difficult climbs just for the time saved fumbling around. If you're going with a lot of single biner'd runners and start doubling up cams on a single biner, you may find yourself with a lack of biners to clip. To save space on the rack, you can clip cams onto each other, and doubled biners/draws in groups of two or three. Doubling, even tripling up cams on a single biner saves weight and consolidates the rack for easy climbs or lightweight missions, but make sure you've got enough draws with two biners. What biner you use on your cam can make getting a cam off your sling/harness easier, lighten up the rack, and consolidate the rack. Too light of a biner will make a black hole of cams and make unclipping the cams very frustrating. Keylock wiregate biners are the best for racking cams.

Multiloop and big wall gear slings, courtesy Metolius Climbing

Clipping draws or cams in stacks to save space

When racking gear while following and cleaning a pitch, try and organize as you go – it will really speed up transitions. A good method is to clip cams to biners on other cam biners to consolidate if you're not wearing a gear sling. If a shoulder sling was deployed on the pitch, you can use that as your gear sling when you get to it. Try and redouble up the shoulder slings as you clean, or at least separate the cams and nuts from the slings. Nuts are hard to keep track of when they are left on the draw or sling placed with them. If you can, take the nut off the sling and clip the nut to a cam biner. You will most likely notice the nut while re-racking cams than you would with slings. If a section is desperate, just pull the piece and have a yard sale of gear on the rope above your knot, then tidy up at a rest.

A big no-no is to start mixing and matching biners on slings and cams. You did a good job when after a climb is completed, the cams and slings have their original biners. Otherwise a downward spiral of cams with two biners, slings with no biners, doubled up cams, etc., starts happening. When it's your turn to lead, rack how you like instead of just dealing with a mobile of gear on a sling. Check your partner's harness thoroughly, they may have a much needed cam or nut squirreled away under their cordalette.

One final racking tip is for extremely hard sends with the gear dialed in. Cams or biner'd nuts already have draws in place and are attached to your harness with tape, magnets, Velcro…whatever works for extremely quick deployment that will stay on relatively securely for the pitch.

<u>Fixed Gear</u>
Finding a piece of fixed gear in a hard section is like a surprise birthday present. But you should always be suspect of fixed gear. There are plenty of stories about pulling a bolt or piton out by hand on a route that gets hundreds of ascents a year. Like any decision to protect a climb, if you see a fixed piece and decide to run it out to the fixed piece, think about what would happen if that fixed piece pulled or is a piece of junk. If there's a chance the fixed piece may not hold a fall, put a piece in beforehand to back it up if possible. Never trust a fixed piton, no matter how often the route gets climbed. Back it up if you can. There is no way to determine the strength of a fixed piton. The only way for the follower to know what gear is fixed and what was placed without yelling is to mark your gear.

Occasionally you'll run into hangerless bolts, or rivets, usually on aid routes. This is done to save time, weight, and money (and possibly visual impact) – especially on bolt ladders. **Rivet hangers** are the most secure way to clip a stud. You only really need two if you're back-cleaning, but for long rivet ladders you'll want to leave a few to keep things safe. Tie a little **keeper cord** to the hanger to not drop them, especially while cleaning them. Moses rivet hangers come in 3/8" and 5/16" sizes, the latter being more useful since you can use it on ¼" studs (but not as securely as a 3/8"). If you are worried about prying the bolt out with a bent style hanger, use wire rivet hangers (faster too), or use the wire on a nut.

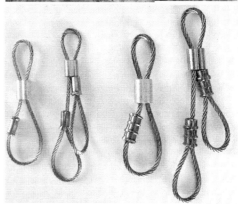

Rivet hangers. Courtesy Moses

<u>Natural Rock Pro</u>
You always get bonus points for slinging natural protection. Solid trees, rock horns, chicken heads, bucket handles, large stable blocks (use your cordalette), and chockstones are the most common choices, so

keep on the lookout. The most common method for slinging natural pro is to girth hitch it. The problem with girth hitching slings (especially Dyneema) is that the force of a fall can cause a ton of heat from the friction of the webbing tightening against itself. One way to remedy this is to use a basket hitch, simply draping the sling over (instead of through itself). You may need to then clip the ends of the basket hitch with another sling, or use a double length runner to get enough extension. If you're running too low on slings, either use your cordalette, or try and orient the girth hitch so the sling minimally tightens – impossible if the diameter of the object is very small. On objects that can allow a sling to fall off, like a chicken head, you can use clove hitch it if possible, or use a slipknot to add some tension. You may need to clip a heavy object, like some pro you don't need, to keep the sling in place. **Knotted slings** are an extreme example of using natural protection. Unless you're climbing in an area that forbids nuts and cams, you probably will never use them. However, knowing that they are an option may save your ass when you are out of gear on lead or rappel. One Czech company, www.Orbworks.cz, has developed a **webbing-based chock**.

Girth, clove, & slipkot on chickenhead. The slipknot is best in this situation.

Basket hitch around "natural pro"

Girth on left puts resistance on the sling (bad)

Slotting a loose rock in a constriction can serve as a make your own chockstone in desperate times. Some folks make custom sized **wood blocks** to protect a wide crack on a specific section. Some have even gone so far as to make a giant wooden cam to protect a very large offwidth. Even carabineers and belay devices have been jammed in cracks for pro in desperate times!

Knotted sling as pro.

NUTS

Metolius Ultralight Nuts with Mad Rock nut tool, Wild Country Ultralight Rocks, DMM Peanuts

Nuts are the soul of trad climbing. Being able to place nuts instead of cams, especially in hard terrain, is the single best thing you can do to advance you gear placement abilities. Beginners usually are pretty good at placing nuts because they're on easier terrain and it's fun to practice. Once people get into the 5.9 to easy 5.11 range, nuts sort of become a lost art, replaced by cams. But harder climbs rely heavily on crafty nut placements and the knowledge that they will hold a fall. If you find yourself only placing cams and feeling like harder climbs all seem runout – it's time to relearn to place and fall on nuts. The better you get at finding nut placements, the smaller your rack will get. Limestone routes don't accept nut placements nearly as well as granite, or even many sandstone climbs. Consider bringing pins and/or tricams instead, and maybe a couple of the biggest nuts.

Any decent company that makes your run of the mill nut will generally do just fine. Wild Country and Metolius both make very durable **ultralight nuts**, which is nice because most ultralight gear doesn't last very long. The best specialty nuts in the larger sizes are the DMM aluminum **offset nuts**. These excel in pin scars and funky placement, and work excellent in your standard placements as well. The downside to the larger offsets is that they can get stuck very easily and you can expect to lose one or two a year. I find this to be worth the price of their performance. However in straightforward trad climbs with normal cracks or easier alpine climbs, I'll bring a normal set of less expensive nuts (DMMs are expensive and sad to leave as bail gear).

Smaller nuts (RP's) are where offsets really shine. The smaller offsets, made by several companies, are usually made of brass or other softer metal to allow the nut to deform slightly reducing the impact force. The DMM **offset brass micronuts** are usually the goto small nut, however DMM **Peanuts** can sometimes be the perfect piece. The three smallest size of brass nuts usually stay at home, along with the largest two sizes of standard nuts, except on specific routes or rock types. Larger nuts, although useful, can often be replaced with a cam. If you wind up bringing a large selection of nuts, put the micros on a small wiregate and the larger sizes on another medium sized **nosed (non-keylock) biner**.

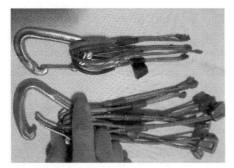

DMM Offset Nuts on a keynose biner and micros on a separate mini biner.

Placing nuts requires good visualization of how a fall will pull on the nuts so you don't pull them out, or worse, zipper the climb. Know when to place long slings, or even when you may need to place two nuts in opposition or with active tension between the two. One of the best reasons to oppose nuts is to keep the top nut in place to prevent a zipper. Use a clove hitch on each nut so you don't create the American death triangle, which increases the force substantially.

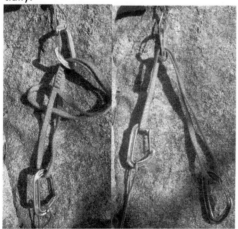

*One way to sling **opposing nuts**. Put a loop through the upper nut and pass it between the strands. Pass the loop back up through the upper biner.*

Clove hitches to avoid the exponentially loading the nuts (ignore direction of pull - it was insanely windy!)

If your first piece or two are nuts, expect them to pop once you've climbed higher, and only needed to protect the opening moves (assuming they aren't needed to prevent a zipper). **Stacking nuts**, like stacking pitons, comes from necessity, but you need to remember it's an option to actually wind up using it. Hammering nuts into place, aka **nut heading**, is acceptable on non-classic winter alpine routes.

If you're bringing nuts, bring a **nut tool**. Just bringing one doesn't help the leader get a poorly placed nut out on lead, and it's inevitable that you'll forget to swap it out at the belay. Most nut tools nowadays have an integrated clip to directly attach it to the harness. There aren't any downsides to this design. If it doesn't you'll have to give it its own biner.

Photo courtesy Metolius Climbing

If you find yourself dropping nut tools, then a **keeper cord or spring leash** is advisable. Most likely that's overkill. Some nut tools have an integrated knife, wrench to tighten bolts, or a wide striking surface to help clean nasty pieces. I haven't seen one with all three, but that would be pretty sweet. Nut tools are super useful for cleaning dirt out of cracks on first accents, eating your dinner because you forgot your spoon, opening beers, and cleaning stuck cams. If you're on a route with an ice tool, you can probably leave the nut tool at home.

Before simply using the attached sling or draw as a **funkness** to pop the nut out, look and see how it was placed. Jerking nuts out may wind up fixing them. Likewise, I've jerked nuts out easily that a partner took an eternity to try and carefully extract to no avail. It can either be an art or a lucky guess to clean stubborn nuts. Unless you have a hammer or a loose rock handy, not much on your kit works well to strike on your nut tool. It may be worth leaving it instead of damaging your cams by pounding on stuck nuts with them.

TRICAMS

Tricams still have their place in the modern climbing world. They fit when nothing else will, especially weird pockets, and some areas just seem to call for them. One of the great things about tricams is that a set of normal sizes (**black to brown**) weighs about as much as a single cam. And because they can fit where nuts can't, they offer a much cheaper alternative to leaving bail gear than a cam. Bringing a set of tricams on a difficult climb where your rack is already huge but you still think you may need additional pro can allow you to climb a little faster and safer by placing more gear, or have backups sizes for the belay. If you're on an easy climb, a set of nuts and tricams can get you up safely with a very light rack. They do take a little longer to place, sometimes require two hands, and if set well they are really difficult to remove. The most useful tricams are the pink, red, and brown, and unless a truly specific placement exists, they become much less useful beyond the #3 size. Also, the smaller **black and white sizes** can be incredibly useful. To stiffen up tricams, wrap the floppy part of the sling in duct tape. This helps you place them one handed a lot better. New tapered Camp tricams are pre-stiffened and can be placed like nuts more easily.

Russian titanium tricam found after 30 years on a second ascent

HEXES

Nothing says old school like a hex. Sadly they serve very little purpose in rock climbing as cams are just so much better. If you become a hex placing expert, then sure, they are lighter than cams and you get bonus points all around. Hexes shine on alpine ice and mixed routes because they work in icy and wet cracks where cams won't, they are light, and you won't give a second thought to bailing off one or welding one in with your hammer on lead. The smaller sizes aren't as useful at the mid to larger ones. The smaller sizes can be replaced with nuts and pins. Practice placing hexes before sticking them on your rack.

PINS

Even though many climbs are now going clean, pitons still have their place. Most (not all) established aid routes that require nailing have an equipment list that lets you know what to bring. It takes years of experience, or several hard walls to know what selection of pins to bring on an unknown aid wall. Fortunately there's enough clean gear out there that the vast majority of walls requiring nailing only require thin pitons and hooks. There aren't many placements beyond thin nailing, hooking, and heading where you need Z-pitons, sawed off angles, and the like where you can't get in a cam or other clean protection.

Black Diamond Bugaboo, Angle, RP, Lost Arrow

Z-piton. Courtesy Grivel

Besides aid climbing, there are two opportunities to bring pins of various sizes that you can bash away. You have the right on a first ascent to hammer in pitons and other fixed gear. Is it the best style? No. But bringing a small selection of pins is not a bad idea. Subsequent climbers can dial in the perfect clean rack. You need one or **two**

hammers (two if you want the pitons back) unless your pitons are only hand-placeable (still considered clean if done this way). Because new climbs could have a lot of dirt choked cracks and vegetation, a short straight-shafted ice tool with a hammer **(3rd tool or children's ax)** works very well. Or you could use a hammer and nut tool. The other venue where pitons are fairly common is mixed climbing where cracks are usually pretty thin, or icy – a great place for a piton. Most long alpine winter/mixed routes are totally fair game to whack away since the rock quality is usually low and a summer route would get negative stars. However, you may be ruining a climb in more popular mixed areas. Think before you hammer away. **Titanium versions** of some pitons are available and are a great option if you want to save weight and don't place a ton of pins (more quickly ruined). Try and avoid using soft iron pitons. They are cheaper, but not nearly as strong – especially if you leave the pin for others.

Ushba titanium pitons (R.I.P.)

To place a piton, you should be able to slide about a 1/3rd of it into the crack, and hear an increasingly pitch ringing as you whack it in all the way. If the crack bottoms out, or opens up in back, the ringing will turn to a thud or the piton won't move or drive way too easily. The ringing sound doesn't always correlate with the placement. Sometimes the pin just thuds in and sometimes the pin can be driven further. Drive the piton in as far as you can regardless of the sound if you require the most secure placement possible or are leaving it. Pressure and surface area are what hold pins in place. The only real reason to not pound a pin in as far as possible is if you want to get it out and it's good enough, or if the crack opens up in back.

Stacked bong anchor on the FA of Broken Tooth, AK. Courtesy Curt Haire.

If you have to clip the pin off short, be sure to clip a **keeper sling** to the hole and rope in case the **tie off** slides off. Not all biners fit in piton holes, so check first. This is usually more of a problem with old fixed pitons. To remove a pin, knock it side to side and see if that does the job. If that doesn't work, you need a funkness device. Turn your head out of the way when jerking out pins.

Assuming you'll be placing nuts and cams when you can but need some bomber gear in icy, dirty, or thin cracks, there are some pitons the work better than others. **Beaks** like the **Moses Tomahawk** and **Black Diamond Pecke**r are valuable in thin cracks and

are much more useful than **knifeblades** (KB) or **RURPS**, however RURPS are still great in roofs and horizontals. **Bugaboos** are the best next size up for thin crack protection. **Lost Arrows** (LA) are still useful in the baby sizes, especially for hand placing in blown out pin scars, but cams work well instead of using larger sizes. **Universal piton**s, essentially a LA with an offset biner hole, can be useful in weird rock like limestone. **Pointed LA's**, filed or commercial, can be helpful on winter mixed routes. **Angles** are pretty much replaced by cams, but when a cam or nut placement is crappy, nothing beats hammering in one of these. The baby sizes are more useful for winter climbs, while sawed angles are also useful for hand placement in blown out scars. Angles also stack great with **Z-pitons**.

Photo Courtesy Clint Cummins

Tomahwak

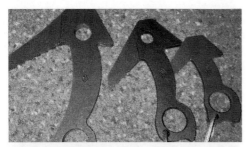
Black Diamond Peckers

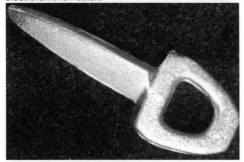
Universal Pin

Old Crack N Ups

Courtesy DMM. Bulldog

Icepider - *goes into holes left by ice tools for pro. Courtesy E-climbs*

Warthog, courtesy Needlesports

For an alpine rock climb where you think you'll need pins bring more or less of the following: **2-3 beaks small to large (Moses/ Pecker), #1 & #2 Angle, and 2-3 longer Bugaboos**. For winter, tack on a medium followed by a larger ice hook.

Most piton modifications are to saw off the end of the pin for less leverage in shallow placements. Other modifications are adding notches in the pin with a file to add bite in super soft rock like the Fisher Towers. **Notching the pins** while smoothing the sides helps for tying off pitons so the slings don't slide off. Most sawed off pins remove the first $1/3^{rd}$ of the piton, commonly on angles and Z-pitons. **Sawed off pins** fit shallow pin scars when longer pins won't. Past modifying pins, you delve into the realms of **stacking pitons**. The more common stacks include angles and Z-pitons because you can place smaller angles in the holes, or sliding knifeblades in with a pin if you don't have the proper size. Be creative.

Ice hooks like the **Black Diamond Specter** or **DMM Bulldog** are another choice for iced cracks due to the extremely aggressive teeth and large clearance, but the beak is usually way too long for most cracks (but nice for turf). Originally marketed as an ice piton, most climbers only dare use them in cracks or frozen turf. Aid climbers enjoy these large ice beaks on rock climbs as well. **Warthogs** are another type of ice piton, and are very useful for driving into frozen turf and dirt. The last resort in pitons for ice climbers are the **picks on your tools**. Whether it's a spare pick on a lead or removing one of your pick in use on a descent, keep this in mind as a last resort.

For piton intensive aid climbs, you may want a selection of **tie-offs and hero loops** (bigger tie-offs) to accommodate the various sized pins and fixed gear. You will want a tie-off for just about every piton placement on an aid climb, assuming you're not driving them to the hilt (for aiding, not freeing). Girth hitches, slipknots, and clove hitches all have their place to tie-off pins. Longer tie-offs, or hero loops, can be used to stand in or clip large pins like with bongs. 9/16" webbing cut in 4" and 8" loops works well. Some piton intense climbs require a few hundred loops. You can make keeper cords with thin cord to keep the piton from falling out, or just girth the tie-offs through the piton hole and clip to the rope.

It looks like you'd want to clip a keeper sling (but the loop is actually girthed through a hole in the head so it won't fall out). Courtesy Moses

Pitons are usually the only gear that causes gear to pop on expanding flakes, although really loose flakes are another story! To work around an expanding flake, clip your daisy into the pin you are driving so if the piece you are standing on pops, you stay put. Staying low in your aiders also puts less torque on a piece that's causing the flake to expand. If you aren't worried about the flake breaking, you can use and oversize pin and overdrive it to keep the flake expanded for higher placements. You could also place a nut below the over-driven piton if you need the piton back.

Broken fixed pitons can still be usable by hooking them, stacking inside them, or hammering a beak between the pin and the rock. If a piton has a hole too small to clip, either put a sling in it, or stick a big nut through the hole.

Hooks

Cam hooks are really great little gadgets. They allow an aid climber to quickly cam up a crack without sacrificing cams, and are quickly back-cleaned. There are several sizes, with the most useful size for aid climbing is the wide size made by Moses. You can file down the end to a sharper point to aid in gripping the rock, but it isn't that necessary. Cam hooks tear up soft rock like sandstone, so it's pretty frowned upon except in granite. They take little training, and are a lot more confidence inspiring than other types of hooks described below. Cam hooks are must for aiding quickly through thin cracks.

Cam hook, Bathook, Grappling Hook

Camhook. Courtesy Moses

The best hooks for minimal hooking, or a just in case piece, are the **Black Diamond Talon** because of the three hooking options available, and the **Black Diamond Grappling Hook** for garden variety hooking. The **Black Diamond Cliffhanger** would be a good third hook. **Larger hooks** are great for clearing bulges and hooking flat ledges. **Smaller hooks** tend to either slide off, or torque out if there is any sort of bulge. **Bat hooks** are used to hook bolt holes. Don't actually make bat hook holes, placing a hangerless stud scars the rock less and is safer. You need to sling your hooks. Use 4 or 5 mm cord over flat webbing for longevity and added strength.

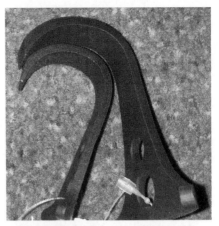

Black Diamond Grappling Hook & Cliffhanger

Logan Hook. Courtesy Moses

*Pika **Ibis Hook***

You may choose to file your hook to aid in biting and catching on nubbins. You can file the hook to a sharp point, bevel the edges for a knife-edge, or file it to resemble the tip of an ice pick. Shortening or flattening a hook helps with stability on flat edges. **Blue Tack** and even duct tape is sometimes used to help seat hooks

HEADS

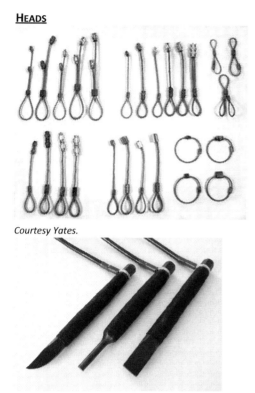

Courtesy Yates.

Chisels and punches. Courtesy Moses

Many aid lines have old fixed **copper or aluminum heads**. Aluminum heads are a bit stickier, better for softer rock or bigger placements, but are much less durable than copperheads. **Circle heads** work better in horizontal placements. You want to lightly bounce test fixed heads first. If the clip loop has blown, you can girth hitch with a small diameter cord (2-3 mm) above the swage and clip off to that. If the swage is blown you'll need to use a beak to hook or hammer into it.

To actually place one you need a corner or a small crack that a cam or tricam won't fit in. You may have to pre-mold the head before placing it and clean the rock as well. Tap it in with the pointy end of your hammer, or if it doesn't have one, use a **5/8" chisel**. Paste the top, bottom, then middle with the hammer or chisel. Finish pasting the head into place with a **center punch** or the **tip of a lost arrow piton**. Don't test the head too hard – you'll rip it or break the cable. Heads can also be snuck in behind thin expanding flakes, trapping them inside as pro. You can also create **equalizeable copperheads** by swaging two heads on the ends of a cable and lightly swaging the middle of the cable together so the cable can slide and equalize the two heads. Testing head placements is somewhat of a Catch-22 because you weaken the head by testing it, or the cable can pull out of the head before the head pulls out of the wall. Don't use a funkness, but test with a few slightly more than bodyweight tugs instead.

CAMS

Nothing gets opinions raging like talking about cam preference. Cams are the single most useful and bomber piece of climbing protection ever made. When selecting a cam there are several factors and trade-offs, but you get what you pay for so don't buy cheap cams.

Cam Angle and Range

Cams with wide expansion range are usually the best all-around cams. Cams with less expansion range because of a smaller cam angle, like most **single axle** cams exert more outwards force and are therefore stronger, but can be trickier to place with less room for error, and you need more cams to make a set. However, with more sizes, they will sometimes fit better than cams with a lot of range.

Link Cams offer an incredible expansion range, and are great "oh sh!t" pieces, on easy alpine climbs where you only need a few cams, or to save for unknown sized anchor cracks. They are also nice to have when a pitch is very difficult and cam intensive and your rack is already hefty. The links can and do break. This happens when they are not placed in the direction of pull during a fall. The cam rotates down, and if one or more of the lobes gets caught on something in the crack, then a lateral shearing force is applied to the lobe and the links are not

Link Cam, Totem Cam, C4, Offset Mastercam, Mastercam, TCU, C3, and Ballnut

designed to bend sideways. They also have a very high tendency to get stuck, especially when maxed out. To properly place a Link Cam, orient in the direction of pull whether it is in a horizontal or vertical crack. Always use an extended shoulder sling to offset any errors in placement, and to limit any sideways pull, which can also break the links. With all that said, Link Cams are a godsend on gear intensive pitches and routes, especially on routes with natural anchors or when doubling up or more is needed for many sizes for the entire route, but not each individual pitch. Even if you aren't using Links, always set your cam in the direction of the fall force to ensure it doesn't pop out, break the cam or the rock, or get fixed.

A couple cams with large expansion ranges entered the market not too long ago by tweaking with lobe orientation, one of which is no longer made (Trango), while the **Metolius Super Cam** is still available. Super Cams are very handy pieces of gear in the hands and larger range when you want to pair down the rack, or aren't sure of the terrain ahead. Just because a cam has great range doesn't mean you can bring fewer cams, however. Bring the amount you plan on placing to adequately protect the pitch.

When using cams for ice climbing, be sure that the cam works in winter conditions. Some cams freeze and are useless in cold/wet conditions. No cam will work if the lobes are contacting ice or frozen moss. Just because it cams and stays with a tug doesn't mean it won't shear out with the force of a fall. Make sure there is a constriction below and there are cam stops when placing in icy cracks.

Metolius Supercam

Cam Features

Double stem cams may be lighter, but are less flexible and could walk more easily than single stem cams. **Thick lobed cams** offer lots of surface area and holding power for soft rock, but are heavier and harder to place in tight placements. **Narrow cams lobes**, and **three cam units (TCU's)** place great in pin scars or tight spots, but offer less holding power. They also fit better in pockets, like limestone. Narrow lobed cams, especially the larger sizes, tend to walk and rotate. Some cams have normal width heads, but the overall width is small, the best of both worlds. Some small cams, mainly the **Fixe Aliens**, use softer metal. Judging by the fact that most companies don't use softer metal on their small cams, softer metal probably doesn't do much. However, it sure feels like it will stay put. Most cams, especially small ones, are super flexible. However, the **Black Diamond C3** and any double stem cam are not flexible in a vertical direction. The theory is that the stiffer stem will twist and actually help the cam hold by the additional twisting camming action. Whether this is true, or the additional leverage will offset any additional camming action is debatable – it really depends on how well you placed it.

Fixe Aliens

Cams are either single axle (most) or **double axle** (**Camalots**). The benefits of a double axle design are larger expansion range, and that the cams equally retract which helps with stuck units and cam lobe inversion. To prevent cam lobe inversion, most single axle cams use **cam stops** to prevent this. Cams with stops or double axles can be placed like nuts. **Black Diamond X4** micro cams use an innovative stacked axle design to fit a double axle into a small unit. **Totem Cams** use a unique single axle design that provides light weight and an expansion range similar to double axle designs, and also has greater holding power in flared cracks. Many climbers scoff at the Totem cams until they actually use them. Then they become their goto piece.

X4 Cam

Most cams have **wire triggers**, but some newer cams use **Kevlar cord**, while Totem cams hybridizes the trigger and the stem. There was some trial and error with the first couple productions on Kevlar wire giving them a bad name, but don't let this deter you. Wire triggers are easier to fix with repair kits, or **weed wacker wire** for cam first aid on trips (the wires are not weight bearing). If using wire, start with **#19 gauge wire** and go down from there. Aliens are harder to fix. Try using a **safety pin**.

Photo courtesy Blake Herrington

Thumb loops are very desirable features on a cam. They not only place great, they provide an additional clipping location for aid climbing or setting up belays. Black diamond decided that too much force is applied in one spot to just use a standard sewn sling or Dyneema, which is one reason they still use nylon. They also added an additional **reinforced loop** to remedy the problem. Most other companies that use thumb loops did not find this to be a big enough issue to double up the loop or to use pure nylon instead of Dyneema.

Many companies are using 12 mm nylon/Dyneema blend sewn **cam slings**, which is great. Black Diamond uses 14 mm nylon except on the X4's, which use Dynex. This isn't a bad thing since as you recall, nylon offers some dynamic force reduction and is easier to tell when to replace. A few companies are using skinny Dyneema sewn slings. Some folks love this. I think it's a terrible idea mainly because you should get those cams re-slung every year or so, and not knowing the condition of the sling just freaks me out. Sending cams out to be re-slung is never fun, but necessary. With nylon or hybrid slings, ship them out for re-slinging when you start to think, "maybe I should re-sling these", when they start looking faded and chewed, or it's been a few years. Scrutinize your partner's cams and slings. Other sling features are **extendable slings**. Doubled up they are as long as a normal cam sling, but extended they are about the same length as a quickdraw clipped to them. This is a great idea to save weight by bringing less slings, and to just have the option available right there in front of you. However, correctly unclipping and re-clipping the sling to extend it can be a real pain, especially on a hard lead - enough so that most climbers don't like it. On easier alpine routes where want to go fast and light they are great!

Dragon Cam with narrow lobes, double axle range, and extendable Dyneema sling. Courtesy DMM

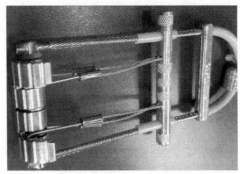

Metolius **Fat Cam** for soft rock

Most find it quicker to just slap a draw on the cam and can deal with the weight of an extra draw. Maybe if everyone switched and fought through the learning curve we'd all embrace the extendable sling. Unless you're piss-poor, get your cams **re-slung** with sewn slings. Using webbing and a water knot isn't as strong and winds up being pretty bulky. Some climbers basket hitch a Dyneema sling and keep it there with a biner or tape. This can be acceptable unless only one side of the sling gets clipped by accident!

Offsets cams are the final type of cam option available. Offsets are typically used in pin scars and are very route specific. However, offset cams work exceptionally well in area that have jagged, non-uniform cracks, and flaring cracks. Some areas have route specific recommendations or are at least known for having pin scars (like Yosemite), but trying bringing some to areas that contain bottoming, flaring, or jagged cracks. Totem cams work very well in flaring cracks, pin scars, pockets, and aid climbs where you can only get one set of lobes in by their ingenious design of being able to just clip one side to load those lobes.

Offset Basic Cam. Courtesy Totem

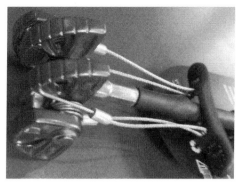

Wild Country Helium Friend

Sizing

Even with overlapping sizes, there are some gaps that only sometimes you need a cam made by another company to fill in the gaps. This is only ever a problem in perfectly parallel cracks, like in Indian Creek. If you plan on spending a lot of time in the Creek and have mostly Black Diamond cams, fill in the gaps with either Metolius or Wild Country. Most small cams overlap enough when going smaller than a #0.75 Camalot.

There are gaps in a few Black Diamond C4 sizes. A #2 Friend or #5 black Metolius fits between a #0.75 and #1 Camalot and this can be a noticeable gap in hard desert splitters. A #2.5 Friend or #6 green Metolius fits between a #1 and #2 Camalot but this is not a very common size to have an issue with as most people cruise this size. A #3 Friend or #7 Metolius fits between a #2 and #3 Camalot, but again most people can cruise this size. An old style #3.5 Black Diamond Camalot, a #4 Friend, or #10 Metolius fits between the new #3 and #4 Camalot which is the second most common gap to fill. Finally, a #3 green Big Bro or #9 Valley Giant fills in the gap between a #6 Camalot and a #4 Blue Big Bro even if the published size charts say different. Check out Supertopo's or Clyde Sole's Cam Conversion charts (find it online) as well as this handy online tool: http://estk.github.io/camvis/. Print them out and stuff them in your guidebooks that use cams or sizing you don't have memorized.

Super tiny cams, like the last couple sizes of **Wild Country Zeros** or a #000 Metolius TCU and Black Diamond C3 are not meant for falling on. The nice thing about insanely small cams is that they don't weight anything. On first ascents, climbs with notorious runouts, and some aid climbs, it's nice to have a biner with a couple super-micro cams and/or ball nuts if you're not hammering in knifeblades.

Finger sized micro cams, green to red Aliens or blue to orange Mastercams for example, are indispensable on most climbs, and it doesn't hurt to bring extra on unknown difficult climbs, as they don't weight much. In terms of crux size, the #0.5, #0.75, and #4+ Black Diamond Camalots are generally the hardest pure crack sizes bigger than tips, so you may want extra of those if there's a pure jamming crux in those sizes. Once past the red Alien size, it's advisable to switch to standard, non-micro cam models. The larger sizes of micro cams are usually too floppy and heavy when compared to other normal cams.

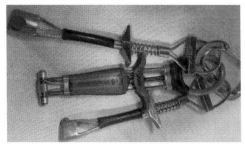

Oh sh*t lightweight biner of micro gear. Two ball nuts, and a #000 X4 on a Camp Nano biner weighs nothing.

The **Black Diamond #6 C4** is currently the largest cam you can buy over the counter. Black Diamond redid their cam sizes a while back, but not long enough ago that all guidebooks and online beta has been corrected. This is especially important if a route description says to bring a #5 Camalot as the old number five is much bigger than the new. An old and new #4 can be interchangeable since the new #4 has a larger range, and it's pretty obvious when a guide mentions a 3.5 or 4.5 since those are obviously the old size. Past the #6 Camalot you will need to start using Big Bros or Valley Giants. **Valley Giants** are custom made giant cams. The two most common sizes are the #9 (the most useful) and the #12. The #15 does exist. Valley Giants are much heavier than **Big Bros**, but are a hell of a lot easier to place and slide up. Unless you do a lot of wide climbing and have no trouble placing a Big Bro, I recommend dealing with the extra weight of a Valley Giant on hard wide crack. If the wide crack is fairly easy, then you can take the time to figure out a Big Bro. Kong reintroduced a wide cam, the **Gypsy**, which was in use years ago under a different name and brand. Most climbers think it's garbage, but you may like it. To keep your big cams low profile, place a stick between the holes in the cam lobes.

Maybe you'll like it, the Gypsy. Courtesy Kong.

Training weight: Big Bro, #6 Camalots, #9 Valley Giant

Consolidating a big cam

Some climbers pair their largest cam they are willing to bring with a **block of wood to stack** with the cam for aiding (or sketchy free climbing). The block must be at least as wide as the cam lobe and have a rough surface. The wood should have a hole and loop to attach to the cam so it doesn't drop on your partner's head when it inevitably fails.

Stuck Cams

Usually a cam is stuck because you aren't removing it in the direction it was placed. Yell up and ask if that doesn't create more confusion than it will solve. Try being gentle and take the time to visualize the cams placement and exit. Don't get over excited if one set of lobes loosens and try to yank it out. Be gentle. On overcammed units you need to pull back on both sides of the trigger while pushing the cam in the other direction. Nut cables can work in conjunction with a nut tool to fiddle with the lobes or trigger. Try putting a sling around both arms of the trigger. If that doesn't work, try pulling back on the trigger and slamming the cam with something. This may free it or get it stuck even more. If you are on sandstone, use some water to loosen it up. No water? Try peeing on it. Don' do this on popular splitters, someone will get it out (you just won' see it again).

Cam Repair and Maintenance

Slow or sticky action, or grinding means it's time to clean and lube your cams. It's astounding how dirty they get. Be very careful about exposing the sling to chemicals when cleaning your cams. A good time to do the hardcore cleaning is just before sending your cams in to get re-slung so you can avoid ruining the sling. If you think your sling has been compromised, do you and your partner a favor and cut it off and send it in. Even exposure to fumes of heavy solvents and acids will totally compromise your sling. Metolius makes a commercial **cam cleaner**, but hot soap and water and a stiff brush (trim the bristles on an **old toothbrush**) does a pretty good job. But even cam cleaner doesn't always do a great job on the dirtiest cams. You could bust out a pressure washer and some heavy-duty solvent/detergent. Compressed air cans do nothing. Once clean, you need to lube the cam. Again, don't get a single drop on your sling. If the lube runs dirty, you didn't clean it well enough. Actually, **cam lube** is the best cam cleaner, but it's expensive. Metolius makes a good cam lube, but silicone or waxed based chain lube like Greased Lightning works just as well. **T9 oil** is the absolute best. Oil based lubes like WD40 will only attract more dirt. After you oil the cam, be sure to wipe the heads of the cams clean of all lube and let them dry.

Big Bros

Big Bros were invented by the late great Craig Leubben to protect the widest cracks. They are light, and can protect some really wide cracks (up to 18.5 inches). They have a high learning curve, and sometimes even that goes out the window when you actually need to place one on lead. Placing your first Big Bro on lead when you really need it is one of the more character building experiences you can have on lead. You can get them in smaller sizes than the big boys. The smaller ones are lighter than cams, but the weight savings are lost on convenience. Still, they are an option if you're trying to go as light as possible but you will be in the vast minority. One of the most common errors in placing Big Bros is not tightening the collar down after placement BEFORE tug testing it.

Slider Nuts

Slider Nuts, aka Loweballs or Camp Ball Nuts, are great thin crack gear. They are useful for clean ascents, and also mixed climbing because they have quite a bit of surface area in comparison to a similar sized micro cam (also making them stronger than similar sized cams). If set well, they can become extremely difficult to remove. The best sizes are the smallest to about 11 mm (the first three sizes), slightly overlapping with a #00 Mastercam or black Alien. Because these are so light, many climbers have the first three on a small biner on their harness at all times. To clean them, play around with the non-sliding piece and not the ball/trigger. Once it starts to wiggle, pull back the trigger. For aid climbing, a mixture of Ball Nuts and small flexible three and four cam units are the ticket, but if you truly want to put the odds in your favor for the gear to hold an actual fall, use the slider nuts (just don't expect to get them back out).

CRASH PADS AND SHIELDS

While not designed to hold falls, boulderers need protection too. It can be really demotivating and scary to really try when bouldering if you're out by yourself with a single pad. If you only have one pad, try and figure out where you'll mostly likely fall at the crux. If the crux is low, place the pad where a fall would be the most disastrous. If you have a friend, they can do double duty moving the pad and spotting. If you really want to succeed, you'll probably need more pads, larger pads, and a group of friends. **Bouldering shields** are fairly new, but are helpful to protect the spotter and soften the blow to the faller. If you get a folding pad, get one with fabric over the fold instead of one with just a crevasse to sprain your ankle in. Pads with flaps at the bottom are nice to burrito up your gear without it falling out. Falling between two pads will result in a sprained ankle, so if this in unavoidable, place another **smaller pad** on top of the gap. Check out "Better Bouldering" by John Sherman for excellent details on using pads and spotting.

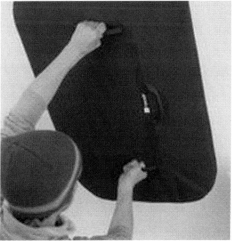

Bouldering shield. Courtesy Metolius Climbing

NATURAL ICE GEAR

Ice and snow lend themselves nicely to natural anchors since you can mold the medium. For ice climbers, **trees and icicles** are the most commonly used natural anchors. A big thick icicle, quickly slung, is way faster than placing a screw and often overlooked. **Ice and snow bollards** can be unbelievably strong, and are also often overlooked as rappel options. If using a snow bollard, be careful if slinging it with a skinny rope. 1" webbing works best. Make it as big as you can. **Frozen rocks** can act as a bollard if you chip out a better groove around the rock. Just about anything can be a super strong **deadman** if buried deep enough or in strong snow. Get creative – bury your pack and clip it off. A **boot-ax belay** can be used in belaying easy pitches, or you can just sit on a vertically buried ice tool and belay off your harness in a solid stance. Belaying of ice tools is another option (clip to the tools, don't belay directly from them) for reaching belays where nothing else works. That said an ice tool would easily break if fallen on.

V-threads are fantastic anchors using the natural medium of ice and can be extremely strong in good ice. Black Diamond makes a **v-thread template**, and although often scoffed at, it works every time.

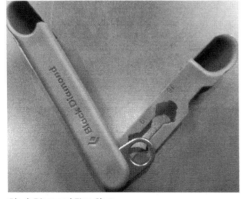

Black Diamond First Shot

If you're worried about your screw stash on lead, making v-threads can get you up a pitch or create a belay with enough screws to spare. If you have a choice, a vertically oriented v-thread is stronger than a horizontally oriented one.

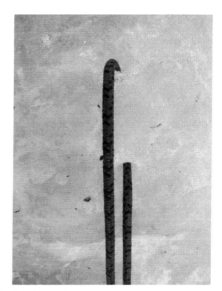

Vertical V-thread

You can thread **5-7 mm nylon cord** or webbing through the holes for bailing, or a long sling on lead. Many people are switching to just feeding the rope through the holes on rappel to minimize trash left on route. If the rope or holes are wet, they could freeze in place and make your rope impossible to pull in rare situations. Have the first person down do a test pull, and immediately start pulling or moving the rope when the last person is down. Backup the v-thread with a screw and remove it on the last one down, or equalize two v-threads.

A **v-threader tool** is really helpful (or piece of clothes hanger or baling wire), but if you lose it you can do it without one. Feed a loop of sling into a hole and make sure the end of the loop is open and big enough to get a rope through. You need a small amount of overlap in the holes so when you feed the rope in the other hole, enough tail passes through the sling. After the rope is fed through the sling, start twisting the sling until you're sure the end of the rope is fully pinched. Now pull the sling hard and quick and the end of the rope (or cord) should come with it. If you have a nut on you with a big enough loop, it can be used similarly.

Using a sling as a v-threader tool. Works every time.

PICKETS

Pickets are indispensable snow protection while traveling on a snowy glacier, or protecting steep snow. A good way to rack pickets is either in a wand pocket or inside your pack with the sling clipped to your shoulder strap. This keeps the picket from tripping you up clipped to your harness, and grabbing the sling and yanking the picket out like an arrow in a quiver allows for quick deployment. A well-placed picket in very firm snow is really bomber, and can sometimes be the only thing keeping you on the mountain.

Some very interesting testing following a fatality has changed the way you should be placing pickets. Even if snow conditions are perfect for a picket, the picket could still fail by bending or popping out of the snow. Honestly, there is really only one type of picket you should be using due to its shape offering much more strength: **V-shaped pickets with a cable attachment**. And how to place them? A mid-clip attachment. Let me explain.

Pickets clipped at the top push against the snow on top, but the bottom part will lever backwards. Also, clipping at the top bends the picket and it can buckle and fail. Upright placed pickets compared to T-slotted pickets are almost always stronger, even in poor snow conditions. Depth trumps width by a big amount. Drilled holes also weaken pickets severely. Wire is the absolute best attachment, especially pre-installed wire. Girthing slings and clipping biners greatly weakens the picket, and can also cause the picket to rotate off axis and pop out. The cable should be 2 times the length of the picket.

To place a mid-clip picket you want to minimize it lifting out and maximize it driving down when loaded. To do this you want to actually tilt it back 15-45° relative to the slope. The weaker the snow, the more angle. Point the open end of the V towards the load in poor snow, and it doesn't matter in hard snow. Always try and pack down the snow to make it harder and to fill in any trenches left. If the snow is too hard to get a mid-clip, then clip nearer the top. Point the V towards the load in a top clip. When belaying off a picket, be sure to stand back about 5 feet to minimize the picket lifting out. In extreme situations, sit on it. *Info on mid-clip pickets taken from "Snow Anchors" by Don Bogie and the NZMSC Snow and Avalanche Committee, NZ LandSAR Technical Rescue subcommittee.*

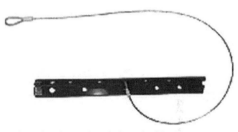
V-shaped picket with mid-clipped cable. Courtesy Yates

Your ice tools or skis can act as makeshift pickets in both of these orientations in a pinch. Many alpine climbs don't take screws, and a picket could be the most reliable thing holding you to the mountain on long snow pitches. How many you bring is hugely dependent on how much of the route is snow and how comfortable you are at running out steep snow. Most high end climbers do not bring pickets because climbing steep snow is comparable to soloing easy rock.

FLUKES

Snow flukes are generally not commonly used snow protection on difficult climbs (except for one on the harness for extended glacier travel). Either the snow is good enough for a picket (stronger and easier to place than a fluke), or it's soft enough that wasting time with a fluke would be better spent continuing up for a better piece of pro. Flukes are small enough to carry on the harness, and since you need to be down on the ground to place one they make good initial quick anchors during a self-arrest for a crevasse victim. Brooks Range makes an excellent snow fluke. They make nice tent anchors, so if you're bivying en route, you may want to bring one or two.

ICE SCREWS

It's debatable who makes the best ice screw, but initial bite in teeth design, ease of getting it started in the head design, ease of screwing it in all the way, ease of clearing surrounding ice, and rackability are the characteristics to look for. For example, the **Grivel Helix** is easier to get started because of the huge palm sized handle but is bulky on the rack and ice must be excavated to clear the head. The **Grivel 360** is also easier to get started because you can get your whole hand over the head (but less torque from the small head) and the lever design allows for minimal ice clearing. They do not rack well (but worth it). **Coffee grinder handles**, like the **Black Diamond Express and Petzl screws** allows for extremely rapid screw placement once seated, and rack very well. There are some screws that already have a **sling attached for clipping** the screw while placing it in case you fall during placement. E-climbs produces a screw with **replaceable teeth** to ensure a fresh bite, and Petzl makes a new screw with an **aluminum body and stainless steel teeth** for weight savings.

Black Diamond Express, Grivel Helix & 360

Petzl screws

Petzl aluminum screw

Replaceable ice screw tips. Courtesy E-climb

Regardless of what screw is the best, I do recommend having at least one screw on the rack like the Helix or 360 that you can place in desperate times when screws won't bite or there's too much ice to clear. Drive-in piton screws, **Snargs**, are just about useless with modern screws. They usually take two hands, aren't as strong, and take forever to clean. They are handy to place in a really tight spot that would take a serious amount of cleaning and are good to bail off of. **Russian titanium screws** (the cheap ones with the red cap) place miserably, but are light and are good bail screws. Almost no one uses **conduit** for bailing anymore, but if the ice is so crappy that nothing else will do don't tell anyone I suggested it. Remember, when the ice melts, you just littered.

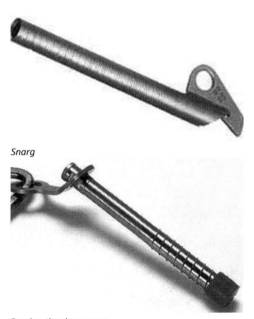

Snarg

Russian titanium screw

Screws come in a few sizes: **stubby (~10 cm), short (~13 cm), standard (~17 cm), and long (~22 cm)**. Stubbies are really useful in thin conditions and can be very secure – certainly more secure than tying off a longer screw. Short screws are choice for placing in good ice when you want to move quickly, or are getting pumped, and if the ice is good they are just as solid. Standard length screws (13-17 cm) are what most people use on standard ice pitches for the extra security and when the pump clock allows for placement. If the ice isn't great, the extra length allows for some added security, but a good 10 cm screw can be just as strong as a 22 cm screw in good ice. Long screws (22 cm) aren't used that much, especially on alpine routes where the ice doesn't get that thick. If a 17 cm screw is sketchy, then you're probably not going to get any extra safety with a 22 cm. Since a lot of ice isn't that thick, the chances of hitting rock and ruining the screw goes up with a long screw. In fact, longer screws can be dangerous because if they take longer to place and if any screw is sticking out the placement is much weaker.

Screws generally fail by the tube collapsing or the hanger shearing off unless this ice is just total garbage. There's nothing wrong with placing a long screw on lead if you can, it feels great to have one of those clipped below you. Long screws are great for belays and making V-threads, but standard length screws are also perfectly acceptable. If top-roping off ice screws, check them after each lap if radiant heat has loosened them.

Many alpine mixed snow, rock, and ice routes, even hard ones, only require 2-6 screws if the ice is too thin, you can get the majority of your gear in the rock, or it's just really runout. The more solid the ice, the more screws you should bring. Bring at least two for each anchor if natural or rock anchors don't exist. Easy, plastic pure ice routes may only require a handful of screws for the lead, while long pumpy routes could make you place 10 or more screws. Don't let peer pressure or ego bait you into bringing fewer screws than you'll need – they aren't that heavy. Running out of screws or running it out to save gear on ice is stupid and unnecessary. If you are down to your last two screws, put in a belay instead of running it out to the next belay location if it's much farther than a standard spacing between placements. Learn to place screws with both hands, it isn't that hard, and creates twice as many placement options.

The most common mistakes while placing screws are not clearing enough ice, and trying to place overhead. When judging where to put a screw, visualize yourself at waist level at that point. If you don't and pick a point overhead, you may have misjudged you run-out comfort level and wind up trying to place the screw overhead to avoid climbing higher. So find your spot and climb up to it. Placing overhead is not only more mechanically difficult to get the screw in, thus pumpier, it also increase you fall distance if you blow the clip. Clear as much ice as you need to create a flat plane to clear the screw hanger. Clearing the screw as you place it increases your chances of damaging or knocking the screw out, and possibly knocking the ice tool you've let go of out. You may have to do some serious excavating if you find a crappy layer of ice, or to knock out a highly featured area.

One of the hardest parts of leading is finding screws in funky, featured ice. You have to guess where good ice may exist behind icicles and cauliflowers and then go to town on the area. After the area is clear, pick out a solid starter hole, and use your hip to help press and drive the screw until it securely bites. If your screw has a lever/grinder handle, use that after the screw is engaged and secure. Drive it all the way in, clearing more ice as needed. If you encounter a bad layer during placement you either need to start over somewhere else, or put the effort in to excavate further. If your screw contacts rock before it's fully driven place a shorter screw before giving up and using a **tie-off**. If you do use a tie-off, be sure to clip a sling to the hanger and rope in case the tie-off falls off.

If the ice is good, screws fail by collapsing and buckling. If the ice is bad, the extra leverage could break the ice. What actually holds you in a fall are the screw threads. In fact, a perfect screw placement orients the screw 10° up, not down into the ice so the screw acts like a lever. That's in a perfect world, so just do your best and at least try and get it level 90°. If you placed a screw, you know it is total crap and are getting too pumped to place another, clip it and back yourself up to a well-driven ice tool before calling "take" in case it blows. Placing screws in hard or crappy ice is usually a lot pumpier than actually climbing, which is another reason why ice climbing is pretty dangerous.

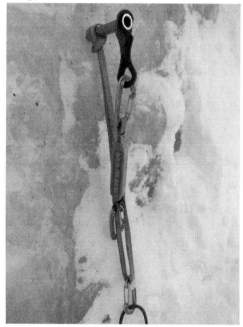
Backing up a tie-off (screamer is unnecessary here)

Try never to run it out, even on easy ice, past the point of a ground fall - keeping in mind how stretchy skinny ropes are. Many top climbers have died or been injured from run-outs on easy terrain. There comes a time in an ice climbers lead career where continuing to run it out becomes a safer option to get to the top or easier terrain because stopping to place a screw (or you're out of screws) could cause a fall just as deadly as falling even higher, and you'd rather save the gas for the top than messing with a screw. I can't condone getting into this situation because the climber should have placed more gear, down-climbed, or backed off earlier, but it happens.

To back yourself up in order to place a screw while pumped silly, first get as bomber of a stick with a tool as possible. If possible (it could cause the tool to blow and you'll fall), hammer the tool in further with your other tool. Clip a quickdraw to the bottom spike of the tool (or loop you added) and clip the rope into this. The rope offers way more dynamic force reduction than clipping direct to your harness or daisy chain. Be sure you're below the tool/draw so if you fall, less force will be applied to the tool.

Clipping off to the tool with the rope and a draw.

Use your free tool to clear out the ice for a screw placement and to make a starter hole. You can now drive your free tool in solid in a spot where you can hang on while placing the screw, and have to option of also clipping this tool, or equalizing it with the other. Once the screw is placed, quickly move the quickdraw from your tool to the ice screw. A much quicker but much less safe option is to quickly set a good tool placement and drape the lead rope over the top of the tool, but depending on how sharp the tops your picks are will determine how sketchy this action is. Some climbers pre-rig a fifi hook on their belay loop to quickly rest on their tool.

Placing a screw straight down is sometimes your only option, and if the surrounding ice is good and you get it down to the hanger, you'll be fine. Sometime an area is just a bunch of pillars or icicles too sketchy to drive a screw into. One option is to chop the pillar out until a platform is made big enough for a screw to be placed straight down in the much more solid base. Placing a screw in a previous leader's screw hole is probably ok, especially if the hole has narrowed a bit from freeze-thaw. Making a fresh hole in good ice is much safer since more pressure will be on the threads, but using an old hole in good ice is still better than placing a new hole in bad ice, falling, or running it out. One of the more ridiculous things you can do with a screw is to punch a hole between two solid pillars and slot the screw in sideways. If it's all you got, then something's better than nothing.

Racking was discussed in the harness section, but just remember that you can still rack on a gear sling – especially if you only have a few screws and an assortment of rock gear. They may be easier to reach when leaning back on really steep terrain. If your screws fill your available and easily accessible gear loop, put slings and draws on a shoulder sling instead.

Keeping your screws sharp, dry, and free of ice on route will ensure better bite on cruxy placements. Make sure your follower cleans all ice out of the screw by whacking the hanger (not the teeth!) on the ice, blowing, or poking with a V-threader. Once uncleaned ice re-crystalizes in the screw from melt/freeze (especially in cold temps), it can be impossible to clean it. A screw filled with ice is almost useless because it's so difficult to place. Transport your screws to and from the climb in the **mesh and plastic cap and thread protectors**, in a commercially made **ice screw carrier**, or inside a bag that doesn't allow them to rattle. The caps and covers are a pain to keep track of when racking at the base (stuff them in your belay jacket inner pocket), but worth it. Replace the caps and covers back at your pack, and remove them to dry the screws the minute you get back to your home or motel.

Spraying your screws with **lubricant** (and picks/crampons) before and after a climb can really extend their life and make them easier to place. If the threads start to corrode it's probably time to retire the screw, or place it in your bail gear bin (mark it somehow). Inspect the teeth for bumps and wear marks. Minor imperfections can be filed gently down with a **small rounded chainsaw file**, or you can use the **Petzl ice screw sharpener tool**. Compare the screw to an undamaged one as a template for sharpening. Sharpening services are provided in the appendix.

THE 3 TO 25 ESSENTIALS

This list doesn't include obvious items like a rope, harness, shoes, gear, etc.

Essentials on you at all times
- Helmet
- Knife
- Something to make a friction knot on the rope (Sterling hollow block)
- Knowledge of car key location and someone not on climb who knows your plans.

In the Pack or on ground if single ½ rope pitch unless you're across the street from the ER:
- Tape
- Phone/PLB
- Quick Clot or Celox
- Epi pen (if applicable)

Very Important: could be seriously screwed depending on the climb and conditions
- Backup glasses/contacts if you are truly blind without them
- Headlamp with full battery or spares
- Navigation equipment (map, compass, barometer-based altimeter watch) if darkness or getting lost is a possibility or dangerous
- Something warmer than just a t-shirt – at least a light Wind-Shirt clipped to harness and/or:
- Rain Jacket and/or:
- Tarp/space blanket and/or:
- Lighter

Almost Essentials (you'll live but suffer)
- Sunscreen
- Sunglasses (if snow for sure)
- Tampons/pads
- Painkiller
- Toilet paper with tiny lighter
- Enough food with a high calorie bar hidden away for when you run out of food
- Enough water
- Water purification tablets

Not Really Essential, but Nice to Have Handy
- Lip balm
- Nail clippers

In the daypack: Sunglasses, Toilet Paper, Sunscreen, Liquid Chalk, First Aid Kit (in pocket shower case), Phone/Camera, Headlamp.

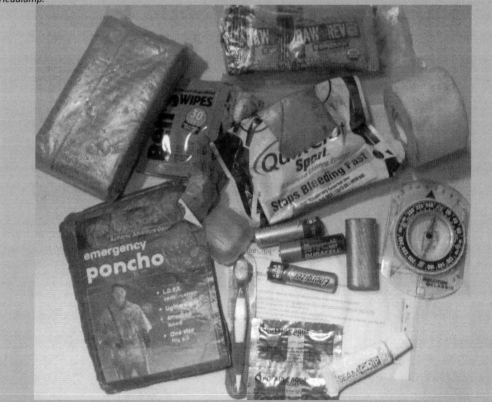

Climb Dependent: Space Blanket, Insect Wipes, Quick Clot, Emergency Food, Tape, Cheap Poncho, ESBIT tablet, Ear Plugs, Spare Headlamp Batteries, Duct Tape, Compass, Micro Toothbrush, Chlorine Drops, Seam Grip, Blister Pad, plus Zippered Chalk Bag Contents shown earlier.

See the gear checklist in the appendix for a full run down of what else you may find "necessary."

Bolts and Anchors

Bolts are permanent structures and should be placed as such. This section will discuss how to install bolts and anchors well. See the ethics section regarding impact. If you ever hear yourself say or think, "someone should fix this anchor or bolt," that someone could be you. The American Safe Climbing Association (ASCA) does an amazing job updating old bolts on popular climbs, but they are a non-profit organization made up of folks who invest their own time and money and they can't update them all. Clipping a bunch of free bolts and anchors and then complaining about them is kind of absurd. Do not skimp on quality and safety when placing bolts.

> If you can't afford bolts and anchors that meet modern standards, don't place them. If you haven't placed bolts before and are considering putting up a new route, or replacing old bolts and anchors please get input from someone who is experienced and input from the local climbing community and the ASCA.

TYPES OF BOLTS

There are two basic kinds of bolts used in modern climbing: **glue-in and expansion bolts**.

Expansion Bolts

Expansion bolts are the most commonly used bolt in the United States. There are a few types of modern expansion bolts: **Sleeve 5-piece, Wedge, and 3-piece removable bolts**. You can get **stainless steel or zinc plated**. Zinc plated bolts are cheaper and a bit more flexible, but weather poorly compared to stainless steel. In my opinion, you should always get stainless steel so you put something in that lasts. No matter what, use the same type of metal on your hanger. If you don't, galvanic corrosion will eat away between the two different types of metal. Stainless steel comes in varying grades of quality; higher numbers (like 316) are better and have less iron content that lower numbers. If the area is wet, get the best quality stainless steel available. Unfortunately, the lock nut on stainless steel bolts likes to loosen over time. Add a drop of **Lock-Tight** to keep the nut on, but easily tightened or loosened if needed. **If you can't afford the best materials then don't bolt it**.

Sleeve style bolts are almost always the **Power's 5-piece Power Bolt**. They used to be called **Rawl**, but Powers bought them out. These are the best 5-piece bolts. The advantage of the Power Bolt is holding power in softer rock compared to other expansion bolts. The disadvantage of this style bolt is that it is more susceptible to corrosion and it is very hard to remove and replace. If the rock isn't soft enough for a glue-in, but it isn't bomber granite, you can use a Power Bolt with confidence. However, consider placing a bigger diameter and longer removable Triplex bolt if you think it will need replacing after some time. Power Bolts are difficult if not impossible to place with one hand and it will help you to pre-place the hanger on the unit beforehand. The nose cone must be unscrewed a bit before you hammer it into the hole. The **washer** that comes with these bolts is necessary. A note on washers: never use stacked washers to fill the gap between the hanger and the nut on a crappy bolt job. Pull the bolt and do it right. Stacking washers only encourages corrosion.

Bad: stacked washers to attach chain. Courtesy Kurt Hicks and the Washington Anchor Replacement Project.

Wedge-style bolts are also very common bolts and are excellent choices in hard quality stone. They are less susceptible to corrosion and are by far the easiest bolts to place. You can place shorter wedge bolts in good hard rock. These bolts are also extremely difficult to remove. For softer rock you can get wedge bolts that have **two wedges** on them for more holding power. Good companies that make wedge bolts are **Fixe and Hilti**. Ramset produces "Redheads" that can be very good, but I suggest you go with top quality from Hilti or Fixe. Never buy bolts not specifically sold for rock climbing anchors.

Fixe Triplex

5-piece Powers Bolt

Legacy Bolt. Courtesy Climbtech

Fixe Double Wedge

Fixe has developed the **Triplex Bolt**, a 3-piece wedge style bolt that can be easily removed with just a hammer. These should be your bolt of choice on anything but low quality rock requiring a glue-in. Climb Tech has almost finished developing a similar removable bolt called the **Legacy Bolt** and it looks like it is even more easily removed than the Triplex and could be the best bolt out there.

Glue-Ins
If placed poorly or if inappropriate materials/modifications are made, glue-ins are dangerous and ruin the rock. This is not for beginners and the information provided should be for brushing up after proper instruction with someone that knows what they are doing. That said, glue-in bolts are the strongest, least corrosion prone, and longest lived bolts you can place – if done correctly. They are excellent choice in soft or porous rock, wet climates, or when you want your bolt to last lifetimes. Occasionally glue-ins won't provide adequate holding power in very soft rock, and a huge expansion bolt is still necessary (still better than a drilled piton). Glue-ins cannot be replaced without at least a minimum of rock scarring since the hole can never be reused. They also take longer to install and require more expensive bolts and glue. Unlike expansion bolts that are always under stress, glue-ins are only stressed when weighted.

Many **glue capsules** don't provide enough glue for the hole and you need to use a **caulking gun**. The glue takes a full day to cure, making it impossible to bolt on lead for more than one bolt a day. Eyebolts must be totally flush with the rock so there is no chance a fall would twist or torque the bolt, and the welded bond should point up. Glue-in bolts should be clean and scrubbed well with soap and water to remove any factory oils. Most older glue-ins were made at home or modified and required notching to properly prepare. Enough companies make glue-in bolts now that there is no reason not to use climbing manufactured glue-in bolts.

There are three kinds of glue-in: **eyebolts, wave bolts, and staples**. Eyebolts are the most common and have a straight shaft on them. Wave bolts combine glue-in strength with expansion strength, however many experts believe that one compromises the other and if you're going to use a glue-in, go all the way. Staples have two shafts requiring two separate holes to be drilled. They are cheaper and require smaller holes to drill, but can break the rock between the staples and the hole distances must be exact. Go with an eyebolt until wavebolts prove themselves to be superior (which they should).

Only use glue capsules or **injection Epoxy glue** provided by reputable manufactures like Ramset, Hilti, and Powers. **Capsules** break and mix in the hole, and the mixing must be done by spinning the bolt with your drill at full speed. You will need an **adaptor** to fit the bolt in the drill. Hilti sells one. A **caulking gun** is easier and cheaper, but messy. Only use capsules if you have the knowledge and experience to use them. With a caulking gun, fill the hole halfway and place a thin strip on the bolt. Insert and twist the bolt until the glue globs out. Wipe off excess and use it to seal the rest of the hole around the bolt. You may need to use duct tape to keep the bolt in while the glue cures on overhangs. Some suggest that you should drill at a slight angle, around 15°, so the bolt can also use a bit of leverage to its strength. Check the manufactures specifications for the size of the hole you need to drill. Too small and you won't have enough glue in the hole. Do not forget that your holes must be spotlessly clean. This is extremely important. Also, never ever combine glue with an expansion bolt. This severely compromises the expansion properties of the bolt, making it useless. Finally, never use caulking, sealant, or rubber to prevent water from getting in. This will quickly crack and reduce the area of contact between parts, a big no-no.

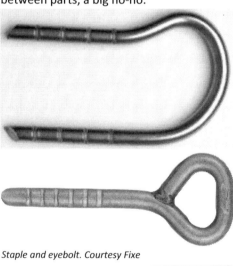

Staple and eyebolt. Courtesy Fixe

Wavebolt. Courtesy Climbtech

In marine environments or mineral heavy rock like seeping limestone where corrosion is a major issue, please use **titanium glue-**

ins. Ushba made a quality titanium bolt, but is out of business. Only use stainless steel glue-ins everywhere else.

Ushba Tortuga

Sketchy Bolts

Drilled angles and machine bolts are a thing of the past and no longer necessary. A well placed expansion bolt or glue-in of adequate length and diameter is better than a **drilled piton** in the desert, and considering the time and effort it takes to drill a hole large enough to fix a piton, a piton costs more than a bolt and is heavier than one, it should come as a relief. Drilled angles that are placed well are still pretty bomber, but they won't hold much (if at all) of an outwards pull because so little of the pin actually makes contact with the rock. They also corrode due to the type of metal they are made with, and water can seep in. You could add glue, but why not just place an actual glue-in if going through all that trouble? **Machine bolts**, like the kind used to connect a couple of 2x4's, offer very little pull-out strength and have a much shorter life span. **Button heads, Z-Macs, ¼ inchers,** and the other relics found on classic climbs amazingly still hold whippers, but should be trusted about as sketchy as they look. They do have their place on some first ascents and emergency bolt kits for their lightweight and easier drilling. Some sketchy looking bolts are in fact still bomber, and some great looking bolts are time bombs. People can only judge the bolt by its outward appearance. So make sure your bolts are beefy, in solid rock, and look good so we don't have to guess. **If you are concerned about bolt quality, take the time to remove and replace a few to see what is really going on beneath the surface.**

Drilled piton

Machine bolt

Zamac

Removable Bolts and Hangerless Studs

Removable bolts by ClimbTech (the camming device, not the Legacy or Triplex) and not placing a hanger on a bolt are acceptable methods of creating bolt ladders or protecting a blank section on a first ascent. **Studs** do impact the rock more, but are certainly easier to find on future ascents. Removable bolts sound like a wonderful option since you would only need one or two and not have to deal with anything more than just drilling a hole. However, the smallest diameter removable bolt made currently is ½", and drilling a ½" hole is a lot more challenging than drilling a ¼-3/8" hole and hammering in a stud or inserting a **#2**

505

or **#3 copperhead** for aiding or dicey free moves. Until smaller units are made, they aren't very attractive alternatives. Totem is currently working on a 3/8" (10 mm) removable bolt.

Removable Bolt. Courtesy Climbtech

Size and Length
Whatever bolt you choose, the diameter and length will depend on the type of rock you are drilling. In soft rock the minimum size should be **3/8" (10 mm) by 3"**, but going bigger with a **½ inch** bolt is a safer option. Any bigger and you should consider switching to a glue-in. In hard rock the minimum size should be **3/8" by 2 ¼"**. Using a larger diameter or length bolt than the minimum recommendations is highly encouraged. Longer expansion bolts do not offer more pull out strength, so go up in diameter then in length. Don't be a cheapskate. Some rock has a very hard exterior only. This "dinner plate" rock, like in Frenchman's Coulee in Washington needs a much longer bolt to avoid the outer layer from coming off with the bolt.

HARDWARE
Power Drills
There are two kinds of power drills: gas and battery powered. **Gas drills** greatly extended how many holes you can drill, but are much heavier and more expensive. Almost no one uses gas drills, but they can have their place. **Electric drills** use rechargeable **lithium-ion batteries**. Use up a battery on a practice rock to see how many holes your battery (and bit) can drill. Don't forget to charge your batteries at the car with a charger (**A/C inverter**) or back at home! You can re-wire your drill to accept external battery packs. Check out Fish Gear's website on how to do this.

Battery powered drill

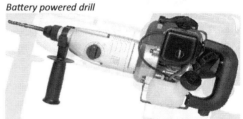

Gas drill

You want your drill to accept **SDS drill bits**, which are the modern standard bit attachment. **Hammer drills** are substantially better than regular drills as they add some jackhammer motion to the drilling process. Smaller voltage electric drills won't provide enough power or torque to drill in hard rock. Don't expect them to last, you'll lose money by buying a new drill and many bits after a very short time. A **36-volt rock hammer drill** is a good choice.

Bits

SDS bits come in 6" lengths, long enough for modern bolt lengths. Get **carbide tipped bits** if you want them to last more than a couple holes. Use can use a **file** to try and keep your bits sharp, but doing this offers diminishing returns rather quickly. If you aren't gaining any depth when drilling, chances are your bit is dull. A hole that is too tight from an overused bit can cause spinners because the wedge is not engaging the rock and expanding. Dull and used up bits are a very common cause of spinners and difficult to place bolts. Because you want the hole you drill to be deep enough (actually slightly deeper), wrap a **strip of tape on your bits** according to the length of bolt you are using so you know when to stop drilling. If drilling a hole for a wedge bolt, consider going ½" deeper so you can pound it in if you can't remove it.

Hangers

Some bolts come with hangers, some don't. Get quality hangers from a climbing gear distributor. You may be tempted to use cheap but light old **Leeper hangers** in the alpine - don't. As mentioned, use the same metal on your hangers and you are on your bolts – hopefully stainless steel. Finally, use the same diameter hole on your hanger as the bolt you are placing.

Leeper hanger. Courtesy Kurt Hicks and the Washington Anchor Replacement Project

Hammer

Discussed earlier in this chapter.

Wrench

Don't forget to pack a wrench that fits the nut on your bolts! Tie off the closed end of the wrench with some cord so you don't lose it. I highly recommend using a **torque wrench** when placing a new type of bolt. Tightening a bolt is what causes it to expand and over-tightening will cause it to fail or break. Some bolts, like Powers 3/8" stainless require only 12 foot pounds (easy to over tighten) while some require 45 pounds of pressure. Using a torque wrench will teach you how that feels.

Torque wrench

Blow Tube and Brush

Dirty holes make crappy bolts, so a wire test tube brush and a blow tube or a bulb are essential for cleaning your hole after you finished drilling. Tape on a length of cord to your tube and tie off your brush.

Bulb, wrench, & brush

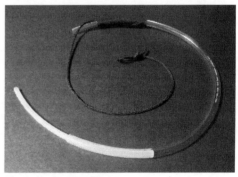

Blow tube. Courtesy Moses

Carrying Cases

An empty **chalk bag** works well to carry your extra bolts, bits, and hangers. Attach **leashes** to your wrench and hammer. Your hammer could tuck in a gear loop if there's room and it won't fall out, but an **ice tool holster** tied to your harness or chalk bag works much better. The hammer leash should be attached to a shoulder sling so you can easily grab it and drop it. The drill should also have a shoulder sling, and if

507

possible, a padded protective sleeve surrounding it.

Glasses
Drilling and cleaning creates sharp little rock splinters you don't want in your eyeball. Wear glasses.

Glue
Only **epoxy** sold for glue-in rock climbing anchors will do. If using a caulking gun you will need a **spiral mixing tip**. If using a capsule you may need two per hole and an adaptor to attach the bolt to the drill so you can spin it in the hole at high speed. Bring a **rag** for your mess.

Mixing Tip

PLACING BOLTS

The Basics
These are the basic steps to place an expansion bolt:
- Consider the ethics of the area and what impact your actions will have and your bolting skills
- Find a suitable location and test the integrity of the rock
- Drill and clean the hole
- Insert the bolt and hanger
- Hammer the bolt in and orient the hanger
- Tighten the nut

These are the basic steps to place a glue-in bolt:
- Consider the ethics of the area and what impact your actions will have and your bolting skills
- Find a suitable location and test the integrity of the rock
- Drill and clean the bejesus out of the hole
- Add glue and spin the bolt in the hole with the drill if a capsule is used, or by hand if using a caulking gun.
- Wait a day or two for the glue to cure.

Location
The first thing you want to do is to get an idea of the general location of where the bolt will go. You want that first bolt to be high enough to be useful, but low enough to protect the anchor and prevent ankle-breaking ground falls. The location of the second bolt is crucial because ground falls are very possible here and the consequences of a fall are much higher. If there is easy terrain just above the first bolt, it is very tempting to run it out. Consider consequences and who will be climbing your route before running it out on easy terrain. All subsequent bolts should at least allow for protection against ground falls. Consider who will be climbing this route to determine bolt spacing. Not all climbs need to be spooky test pieces.

The next thing you want to figure out after determining spacing is to place the bolt in the line of the climbing to keep the route contrivance level down. This can be a challenge if bolting on rappel. Climb the route on toprope and tick your bolt locations with chalk. You want the bolt to be placed at a location where clipping can be done from a good hold to minimize missed clips, which can be disastrous falls. Take into account where the rope will be in the clipping location. Some poorly placed bolts have the climber in a dangerous stance that could result in a bad (like upside-down) fall if the clip is blown. If the climb dances back and forth, but is essentially a straight line to the anchor, bolt location can be problematic to avoid rope drag and sideways, ankle spraining, or upside-down inducing falls.

Look for edges and lips when establishing a location for a bolt. Put a standard size quickdraw over the spot and see if the biner lies over features that could snap the carabineer. Large changes in the surface of the rock texture can also cause the bolt hanger to not contact the rock completely. Put the hanger against the rock to see how it will lay. Other concerns are: will your bolt placements pin the rope under flakes, horns, tufas, over sharp edges, etc., or will the placement create rope drag?

Placing the bolt just before and after cruxes are generally the best locations, unless the crux is long and sustained. Placing before allows for shorter less scary falls and after provides psychological relief. This also includes the location of the anchor location. Placing the anchor at a crux clip contrives route a bit by making the anchor clip a crux, not the features of the rock.

If there is natural gear on your climb, it is ultimately your call whether to bolt or to leave that clip open for using natural protection. Expect complaints from both the sport-o's and the tradsters. If other routes nearby use gear you'll probably want to leave that bolt out. If your climb is the only one in the area with a gear placement then you should probably bolt it. If you leave the bolt out then please test the gear placement by taking a solid whipper, and make sure you make it clear that this route needs gear. If the gear required is esoteric (like a tricam, micronut, slidernut, or tiny tcu) but bomber, you probably should bolt it. Please don't place pitons, especially in soft rock. There is no way to test their integrity from corrosion and freeze/thaw action and a piton scars the rock more than a bolt. If you can't get gear in the piton crack, place a bolt. Pitons are just as visible as bolts and unless you are the one placing them, they add nothing to the experience to future climbers. A fixed piton does not make a climb more trad or adventurous.

You want to place the bolts in solid rock. Tap the rock with your hammer in various spots of good rock to get the feel of what solid rock should feel like and test a fairly large area around your intended placement. If the resistance of your bit suddenly lessens when drilling, you should really reconsider the location. Your route may require substantial cleaning with your hammer and a crowbar. This is a good place to note that you should quarantine the areas below your drilling to avoid killing people below you. You may need your belayer on the ground directing traffic. If drilling in soft rock and using big bomber bolts, you still should place more bolts than you normally would on hard stone.

Drilling
Hold the drill perpendicular to the rock, not the ground. If you have difficulty getting the hole started at a completely perpendicular level, look for small concave indentations instead of convex micro bulges. You may need to rotate the drill around to establish a small starter crater in really hard rock. Once you've gotten the hole started, hold the drill firmly enough to apply pressure, but loose enough to engage the jackhammer motion of the drill. You may need to move the bit in and out (or change bits) in very hard rock. Pulling the bit completely out and blowing out the dust helps the bit grind into the rock, and not spin in place over the dust. If your hole is taking a strangely long time, your bit is probably dull. Drill just past the length of the bolt you plan to install by ¼ to a ½ inch. Pre-taping your bits saves the headache of pulling a hammered in bolt and re-drilling.

Cleaning
Cleaning the hole completely is extremely important. Do not skimp on this small, but important detail. Dust and debris will create spinners, and also your bolt will be supported by dust, not rock. A bulb, straw, or length of aquarium tubing works well. Look away, there will be a lot of dust. Protective glasses when drilling are very helpful to protect against dust and rock splinters. After the hole is blown clean, insert a wired brush to scrub it clean and re-blow out with the tube. A **test tube brush** works great. Also clean up the dust splatter away from

the drilling area. If using glue-in bolts, be extremely aggressive in your cleaning.

Installing the Bolt
Before putting the bolt in, take any tape off the bolt and slightly expand a sleeved expansion bolt. Make sure the hanger and washer are slid over the stud before placing it in the hole. The washer goes between the nut and the hanger. Wedge bolts do not use washers. Screw the nut on the outside of the bolt to the near the end, just tightened enough to not strike the nut with the hammer. Striking the nut can damage the threads. Hand place the bolt into the hole, and then tap it in with the hammer. Before the last few strikes, loosen the nut so it is almost at the end of the threads and finish hammering it in. If you didn't drill deep enough too much thread will be exposed and you did a bad job. Pull the bolt and drill deeper. Once flush, make sure the hanger is oriented in the direction of pull. Usually this means letting the hanger orient loosely in a plumb line with gravity. Now tighten the nut with your wrench until tight. Tight means more than finger tight, but not so tight you shear off the head. Use a torque wrench for your first few placements on a new type of bolt.

If the bolt rotates or the hanger spins, you did a bad job. The causes may be too tight or loose of a hole (check your bit size), you didn't clean well, or the rock inside the hole is too soft and you need a bigger bolt or the rock is unsafe. A dull or overused bit can create too small of a hole, which can cause the bolt to buckle or bend when hammering it in. There is a chance the cone just isn't engaging for some reason. Try using a funkness device and jerking the bolt a few times and try re-tightening. If this doesn't work, pull the bolt and drill with a new bit, larger bolt (and bit) or find a section of better rock.

After you have cleaned the hole extraordinarily well for a glue-in, fill the hole halfway with glue and coat one side of the bolt with glue like toothpaste on a brush. If using a capsule, stick it in like a suppository, and shove the bolt in to break the vial. Now spin the bolt at high speed with a drill attachment if using a capsule or turn the bolt by hand a few times if you used a caulking gun. Clean up your mess and use some drippings to seal the hole completely. Make sure the welded side of an eyebolt is face up.

Drilling on Lead
Drilling on lead can be a real challenge. Running it out to good stances usually doesn't make a very fun route for others. Being a good aid climber is helpful. Many bolts have been drilled on lead off A4 placements or just hanging off one arm! Carry some hooks, pins, small gear, and aiders to hang on and stand in. Make sure the drill and all of your equipment is tied off.

To avoid climbing with the drill, you have a few options if you brought a tag line. You could just tag it up and lower it down for each bolt, but this could become tedious. After a half rope length is out, this becomes much more difficult because the belayer won't be able to pull the drill back down. The tag line could run up through a pulley or just a biner on the leader's harness and the belayer could pulley the drill up to the leader. This keeps the weight of the haul line off the leader as well. This only works for the first ½ rope length. After a half pitch the leader could leave the drill fifi hooked onto the last bolt placed to tag it back up, just like the description on leaving a pack fifi'd to a piece.

Overhanging Terrain
Drilling overhangs on lead or rappel is probably the hardest type of drilling logistically. In order to stay close to the rock you

need to drill bolts at least each body length. One solution if aid or gear solutions aren't available is to use removable bolts. This still requires many holes drilled, but at least the amount of bolts placed can be minimized. You can mix some rock dust with epoxy to fill in the holes when you are done to minimize impact.

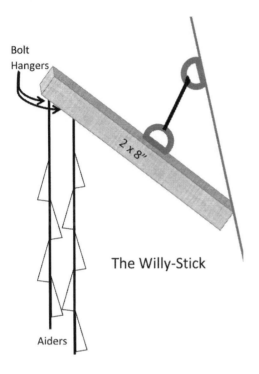

The Willy-Stick

You can also try the **Willy-Stick** method, invented by Maple Canyon climber Bill Boyle. While not the safest method, but certainly the most ingenious and least impactful method, the Willy-Stick allows for better spacing of bolts with no extra drilling. To make a Willy-Stick get a very solid 6' length of 2x4" framing lumber and place three bolts in it. The first two are placed 2" and 8" down from the top on one side of the board, and the third bolt is placed 3 ½' from the top and on the other side of the board. To use the stick, the center bolt is clipped to the last bolt and the upper two bolts (facing out) are used to clip aiders and to tether into. The stick acts as a big lever in this configuration, with the bottom of the board pressing into the rock and the center bolt as the fulcrum. The lever action doesn't work if you lean to far forward and the result is a terrifying fall dubbed the "windshield wiper".

Hand Drilling and Emergency Bolt Kits

Hand drilling is a necessary art in the wilderness where power drills are illegal, and probably too heavy anyway. You will want to practice hand drilling on the rock you intend to bolt to not only figure out how to do it, but to determine how long it will take to make a suitable hole. Please practice on rocks that no one would ever notice, not the boulders around your campsite. This is a great way to earn new respect for first ascensionists who hand drilled on lead in difficult terrain.

Commercial hand drills accept SDS bits as well, and have an ergonomic handle, and striking surface. Everything is exactly the same, bolts, bits, hangers, etc., except the fact that you must provide the muscle power to drill the hole. **Emergency bolt kits** are useful on first ascents where you don't want to drill, but they may wind up being needed. They are also useful for climbing obscure forgotten routes where fixed gear may no longer be reliable, or for bailing on a blank unknown face. **Smaller diameter bits and bolts** are acceptable here as the bolts you are drilling should be for "oh shit" moments to avoid death and injury, not for the masses to whip on! Don't forget you still need a hammer, wrench, and blow tube. If using the bolt solely for an aid move you can forgo the hanger. Hangers aren't that heavy, so it doesn't make much sense to save weight on hangers for free-climbing moves, anchors, or rappelling. The follower could back-clean the hangers to minimize the amount.

If **removable bolts** are offered in smaller sizes, they could be useful in the emergency kit. Some options are to place **¼ bolts, Fixe Button Heads, hangerless studs**, back clean **Triplex or Legacy bolts**, or insert a **copperhead** into the hole to act as a cam of sorts. No matter what you do, please do not bathook! A final option would be to use the Petzl self-drilling 8 mm bolt, the **Chevilles Autoforce, with the Perfo SPE drill** (or the **ADP adaptor** for a hand drill). The Petzl self-drilling bolt system is sketchy to say the least since you've only got a ¼" inch bolt in a 1 inch (3 cm) hole, but is one of the lightest systems for emergency bolting available.

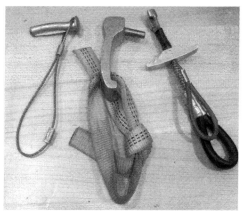

*River hanger with buttonhead, bolt hook, **bolt cam**, old version of removable bolt*

To help with hand drilling, make sure you have new high quality sharp bits. Hold the drill very loosely in your hand and perpendicular to the rock. Frequent light taps are more effective than Thor-like strikes. Hit the drill between, not during turns. You can also break the bit by holding and striking too hard. Rock splinters can fly, so either protect your eyes with glasses or look away. With each tap rotate the bit ¼ turn in the direction that the bit spirals, usually clockwise. Try and drill the hole as uniformly as possible. A starter hole, much like placing an ice screw, can help getting the hole going and in a uniform, perpendicular direction. Clear the dust so you aren't spinning the bit against dust instead of the rock. Be patient!

BOLTED ANCHORS
Build your anchors to last with bigger bolts and **durable hangers, chains, or rings**. The rules are the same as placing protection bolts, but extra scrutiny should be employed. This is definitely not a place to be frugal with your time and money. Don't cut corners on placing or replacing anchors. Use **½" expansion bolts, or big burly glue-ins**. If the rock is quite soft, place three. Anchor bolts really need to be in solid rock, hopefully for obvious reasons. Occasionally this means putting the anchor in an obnoxious location. If it's way off to the side, you may need to put a directional bolt in before the anchor, use more chain to extend the an-

Self drilling bolt and drill courtesy Petzl

1/4" buttonhead courtesy Fixe

chor, or place the anchor lower. If the rock at the nice ledge is "almost" good enough but not quite, put a bolt (or more) the good ledge to stabilize the belayer if the good anchor is a reasonable distance away. Anchor bolts should be placed at least 6" apart to account for minute variations in rock quality.

Vertically oriented anchors are stronger than side-by side anchors. However, if the rock is good, placing bolts side by side makes for easier rope management, especially on big walls where anchors will be used to jug, fix, and haul. Three or more bolts should be placed on routes with jugging and hauling. The closer the bolts are, the less force is applied, but the more the quality of the surrounding rock quality comes into question. One compromise to improve anchor strength and rope management is to diagonally stagger the bolts. Bolted anchors on multipitch climbs not used for rappelling do not need to be equalized with chain or equipped with special hangers. Anchors bolted for rappelling or single pitch climbs do.

3 Basic Anchor Set-Ups

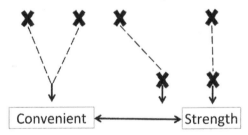

Pay extra attention to where your rap anchors are placed. Your anchor should allow for a clean pull, avoiding knot jamming lips, trees, rock horns, choss, rope-eating chimneys and cracks, etc. If there is a section of steep blank wall to the side of the route, consider making the rappel route separate from the climb. Consider making the rappels 30 meters instead of double rope. Not only will climbers enjoy not bringing that extra rope, rappels will be quicker and cleaner with just one rope.

You have a few options deciding what type of rappel anchor to choose from. The easiest and lightest are rappel **hangers with large smooth lips** followed by **hangers that have rings pre-installed**. The drawbacks of these are that if they become worn, you need to completely replace the hangers. From a climber's standpoint, these anchors can twist ropes and be difficult to pull since the angle of pull will have a sharp bend if the next rappel isn't in a plumb line straight down. They also offer less room to tether into and feed the rope through. **Cold shuts** are an extremely simple, quick, and safe (no untying from the rope) top anchors on single pitch routes. The big drawback on these is expense. They are (or at least should be) very beefy and should last a very long time. Open cold-shuts are cheaper, but aren't as safe. They are safe enough, however.

To extend the rappel or lower point down from the bolts you will need to use **chain**. Chain is nice because if can be replaced without replacing the bolts or hangers. But just because this is true doesn't mean you should skimp on the quality of the chain. Like it or not, people will be top-roping directly through the chain. Even strict rappelling will cut into the chain. Add rust from the elements and enough time and your cheap chain will need to be replaced. The problem is that you may not be around at the time when they need to be replaced and climbers don't roll into crags with a bunch of chain, so your anchor just becomes a time bomb.

Use at least **3/8" high-grade chain**, and for single pitch use even **heavier steel chain**. Lowering through the anchors at crags shouldn't be a crime because you were too cheap. Use at least two links of chain per bolt. To attach the chain you will want to use **beefy quick links.** Make sure the chain is equalized in the direction of pull for rappelling and lowering. The rope can be fed directly through the chains if the bolts are side by side, or a combination of chain on the upper bolt and beefy quick link on the lower. Using burly quick links at the end of the chain will make replacing worn sections very easy.

Equalizing the chain with a **burly stainless steel coated rap rings** is even better for improving the longevity of the rap point and aiding in a smooth pull as two separate points can kink the rope. The lower bolt could be a bolt with a permanent rap bolt equalized with chain to the bolt above it. **Steel carabineers** are quite strong and burly, but are generally heavier and more expensive than equally strong ring and quick link counterparts. Unless you will be coming back with supplies to refurbish your anchors, do not equalize bolts with webbing, rope, and carabineers. This is just asking for disaster. There are only two outcomes and both are bad. The first is that at some point the anchor will fail and kill someone, the second is a mess of tat and trash that future climbers will add as time goes on. Rockfall and constant use can weaken carabineers compared to using much beefier attachments. Webbing and rope will also start to cut into their attachments.

REPLACING BOLTS AND ANCHORS

Being a good samaritan and replacing old bolts and anchors is a sure way to make friends and contribute to the climbing community. Chopping bolts, adding more bolts, replacing a piton with a bolt, or bolt with a piton could put you on the hot seat. When the decision has been made to remove an old bolt your first priority is to minimize damage to the rock removing it. First try to pull the bolt completely out with a funkness device or length of chain (common with Powers bolts). An option with 1/4" bolts is to make a **tuning fork out of a #4 Lost Arrow** piton to get behind and pry it out. You may need to work up to the LA with a knifeblade to get started. Contact the ASCA for a pre-made tuning fork piton if you can't make your own.

If this doesn't work, a little help from a **crowbar** may be in order, but your chances of bending and just shearing off the head increase. If it won't come out, use a hammer and chisel to hammer it farther in or to shear the bolt off. The blade of a piton can also work to shear it off. If the bolt pulls you may need to use pliers to pull out the sleeve and then try and unscrew the rest. If you couldn't clear the hole, patch it up with **rock dust mixed with epoxy** and drill a new hole. If you got the bolt out, then use the existing hole. I highly recommend using a larger diameter bolt and re-drilling inside the old hole. Your drill or hand drill may jam up a bit by catching inside the smaller hole. If this is the case, drill backward for a bit, and then try going in again.

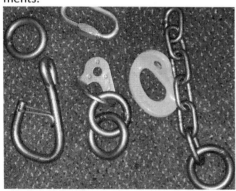

Photo courtesy Clint Cummins

Before removing any bolt, check out what type of bolt your are dealing with and ask around to find out the best strategy for that exact type of bolt. Many crafty techniques are always being developed. Unless you are confident you won't damage the rock, either have someone else do the work, or worst case, then chop the bolt, hammer it in, patch the hole, and drill a new hole so you don't damage the rock more with good intentions.

Chapter Ten: Backcountry & Climbing Skills

Backcountry Travel

Navigation

GPS units, smartphones, detailed directions, and trails all make getting around in the backcountry a lot easier. But the time may come when you either get lost, directions don't add up, or you need to travel off trail. Knowing how to navigate with a map and compass, or using natural clues can save your butt from getting rescued or finding the car days later. You should be able to logic your way through orienting with a map to the compass, compass to the map, etc., by just understanding a few basic principles described below.

Magnetic and True North

Maps are oriented to True North (the top of the map) and your compass needle points to Magnetic North. The difference between Magnetic and True North is the declination. Add declinations that lay East of 0° to your bearing to get True North, and subtract when West of 0° (0° being the Midwestern United States). To ballpark it:

- Denali adds about 27°
- Seattle adds around 20°
- Utah adds around 15°
- Chicago is around 0°
- New York subtracts about 15°.

Set the declination for triangulating or following a compass bearing when obtaining exact positions with a map and compass count. Adjustable declination compasses really help. Align the compass needle with the declination arrow, not the orienteering arrow. Declination changes over time, sometimes drastically. Your 1965 topo map may not have accurate numbers. Also, where you bought your compass matters. The needle is also pulled down by the Magnetic North and compasses are made to offset this to a certain amount. But if you got your compass in Alaska and brought it to Patagonia, it may not work.

Triangulation
A line drawn in the direction of two (or more) known locations will cross at your location. If all the lines intersect, you did well. Typically three measurements are taken and you fall inside the triangle created. This is triangulation. If there's a significantly large triangle created between three measurements, retake your measurements or use more known objects. The more lines you draw, the more accurate your position will be. Pre-existing natural known lines on the map (trails, ridgelines, elevation contours, rivers, and roads) only need one other known bearing line drawn to intersect your exact location. So if you see a mountain you know, sight a bearing on it, adjust for declination, and draw a line on the map from that mountain in the direction of that bearing. The farther away something is, the more inaccurate your reading will be. If you know where you are on the map, but want to I.D. an unknown peak ahead, take a bearing on the peak, place a corner of the compass on the map at your location, and rotate the compass until the needle is boxed. The compass will be pointing at that object.

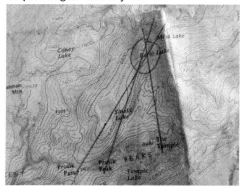

Orienteering
The easiest way to orient yourself is to point the map in the direction of True North and look around. Sometimes you need to follow a bearing to navigate a whiteout, dense forest, or desert. You can also take a bearing from the map to aid in navigating. Line the compass between you and the location you're trying to get to. Turn the compass bezel so the internal lines are parallel to the North - South lines on the map. The reading is your heading, assuming you have to compass pointed to, not away from your destination! This also works in reverse.

Compasses with sighting mirrors, or augmented reality apps on smartphones help pinpoint exact bearings. Entering information into a GPS and letting it navigate for you is a lot more accurate if you have the correct coordinates, and also the sky is clear enough to get a satellite fix.

To stay in a straight line while following a bearing (dead reckoning), sight objects along the way, and take back bearings between your chosen identifiable objects (boulders, rocks, big trees) as well to stay on route. In whiteouts, use your rope and partner to create straight lines to take bearings off of. If you just followed a compass bearing without doing this, you'd probably be way off.

If you are trying to hit a spot on a road, river, trail, etc., it is really hard to hit it exactly. When you hit the road do you go left or right? Compensate by purposely aiming off, so that when you do hit the road, you definitely know that the car is in the opposite direction you aimed off of.

Whiteouts
Flat light makes skiing an unpredictable roller coaster, and whiteouts ruin the day. Goggles help immensely with visibility in both situations. Toss a snowball ahead to gauge the slope. Use the rope and your partner to dead reckon off of, being extra anal retentive about keeping an accurate bearing. Marking key points with a GPS can really save you a lot of trouble, but your GPS may not catch a signal in a whiteout. Wands are good backups, especially if you placed them while taking bearings. Bring a Sharpie or **grease pencil** and record the bearings on the wand.

Lost Without a Map and Compass
If you don't have a compass and get turned around there are some tricks. The sun rises in the East, sets in the West, and is in the South at mid-day, although this isn't too accurate in the heart of summer or winter and in far latitudes. If there are no stars you can use, then use the moon as a rough guide by knowing the simple fact that the moon is lit by the sun shining on it and knowing what direction the sun rises and sets. A moon that rises before or during sunset is in the East and a moon that rises after midnight will be in the Eest. You can roughly find South with a crescent moon by drawing a line from both horns down to the horizon. Also, a half-moon lit up on the left is waning and lit up on the right is waxing (becoming full).

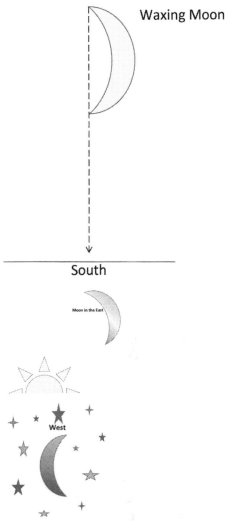

Moonrise at sunset is to the East, moonrise after midnight is to the West

In the day, look where the shadows are, or where snow still lingers in the summer. In the forest there are fewer branches and more moss on the North sides of trees, and ant mounds and spider webs are usually on the South side of trees. You can also put a stick in the ground and mark its shadow. Wait 15 minutes and mark the new shadow the same distance out. Draw a line between the two marks. The line pointing to the first mark is West.

517

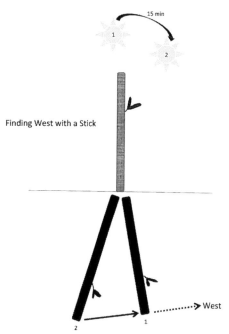

Finding West with a Stick

laris is also the end of the handle of the Little Dipper. In the Southern Hemisphere, draw line along long beam of the Southern Cross and another line from the two "pointer stars" just below the cross to find True South, or go down five times the length of the beam. Everything else gets reversed for the Southern Hemisphere.

If you get lost, waiting in one place is probably not going to be the best advice unless you are desperate and out of resources. Get out on your own. The number one best thing to do is to suck it up and go back uphill. Being lazy and continuing on can just make matters worse and you'll have to go twice the distance later. Retrace your steps to the last known and correct location. If that's not an option, find a high point and look around. Unless you know for sure that by going the way you are going you will hit a road, trail, or river that can lead you somewhere, go back uphill and start over. If you think you need a rescue, go to a place where you will be expected to be (like the summit), or to an open or high point where you can signal for help using fire, bright clothing, and something reflective.

You can also use your watch or pretend your digital watch has an hour hand (you need to remember what an analog watch looks like). Point the hour hand toward the sun. South is half way between the hour hand and 12.

If my ceiling fan was the sun then Southern would be towards 1:30

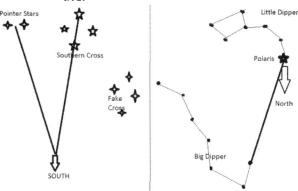

At night you can measure the distance between last two stars in the Big Dipper (the bottom of the pan on the non-handle side to the top of the pan) and go five times that distance to find the North Star, Polaris. Po-

Trust your instruments over your instincts. If you are unsure about where you are and the map makes it look like you've only gone ½ mile or are in the wrong drainage, you probably have.

APPROACHING

Sometimes it's fun to blast in and out to your climb car-to-car style, especially if the approach is an uphill grind, or less than four hours. Camping can be a lot more fun, but you can't spray about your car-to-car effort then. Sometimes camping makes getting up in the morning, especially when it's cold, less attractive than just blasting from the car. I find my more memorable trips involve camping or a bivy. However, climbs done car-to-car are usually more successful. Less can go wrong unless you screw up the approach, and motivation/psyche is usually higher going car-to-car.

A fit person hikes an average of 3 mph on flat trail or open timber, and uphill at about 2500 feet per hour regardless of mileage. So, if a section is three miles long and gains 2500 feet, it should still just take about two hours. Intense bushwhacking or snow wallowing takes around ½ mile per hour regardless of elevation gain. Your pack weight and fitness will ultimately determine how fast your go. A heavy pack (30+ lbs) should only slow you down a little bit. Add an extra 1-2 hours per day if packs are very heavy. Untrained individuals can take far longer.

Hiking out should take 2/3rd the time to hike in, or if it's all downhill, then about ½ the time. It usually takes one or two approaches at the start of the season to hit a fast pace.

When you're hiking in, set a fast pace to start. An all-day pace is just that, it is slow and takes all day. You don't want to completely waste yourself, but you will most likely be using different muscle groups during the climb. The first hour is always the worst. I usually start hiking as fast as I can until I start to sweat. I then back off just a hair. Stopping slows down momentum, so keep some water and snacks in your pockets to avoid bonking before the climb even starts.

You should be wearing just enough to stay warm. In the summer, this usually means just wearing a t-shirt and in all but the coldest conditions, a wind-shirt. Overheating and stopping frequently to relayer adds a lot of time to the day. But stop and fix any hot spots and deal with any gear issues immediately. Take your breaks before the uphill slog and you'll go faster. Take your breaks either every 1.5 hours, or every 3000 feet and set goals like "I will stop for a second when I reach that tree" or "when my altimeter hits 6000 feet". Stop for only enough time to eat a snack and fix whatever it is you need to fix.

If the approach is the only thing planned for the day, then take your sweet time to ensure proper nutrition, hydration, and recovery for the climb the next day. Hide your watch so you're not constantly checking how long you've been hiking on how much altitude you've gained unless you need it for navigation.

Have your water handy, preferably in a hydration system with a drinking hose. If you know there will be water available on the approach, consider your options. It's lighter to carry less, but it also takes time to fill up, not to mention the loss of momentum and psych you get by stopping all the time. If there will be water about 2 hours into the approach, carry 1-2 liters and chug so you can stay well hydrated and refill at the water source. If the only water is less than 2 hours into the approach, stopping to fill can be a waste of time and energy and will lug the extra water instead of stopping.

An I-pod or smartphone with music will help speed up the hike and to possibly provide a marching beat, but make sure your lonely partner has one too. If you don't have one and your partner does – do not let them tell you what they are listening to! Bring trekking poles if you can stash them at the base of the climb for return pickup, or if you are camping and can just leave them at camp. If you don't like them, try to get used to them because they make you go faster.

RIVER AND LAKE CROSSINGS

River crossings can be the most dangerous part of a climb, especially in the spring and early summer during snowmelt off. A crossing you were able to pull off in the morning may be wiped clean by the end of the day from the sun's heat on the upper snowpack.

Bringing a **fixed line** to leave is probably a case of 20/20 hindsight, but something to consider.

Split up and decide on a meeting time. Each person should walk up or downstream for as long as you're willing to sacrifice time before pulling the plug on the climb, looking for crossings on logs, rocks, or a wide section safe enough to cross. When crossing a log you may want to wear crampons if you've got them. **Crampons** can even be helpful just fording a slippery bottomed river.

Take your pack straps off in case you fall in. Ditching your pack can save your life. You may want to use the rope to setup a line to shuttle packs. It's hard to say if falling in a swift river would be escapable on a belay, so belaying your partner across will most likely just drown them. If you fall in, swim like hell and set a ferry angle to the other side. You should also consider wearing your **helmet**.

Be careful with spraining your ankle or snapping your Achilles tendon while crossing frigid cold water. If you think there may be a crossing, bring a cheap pair of **tennis shoes or sandals with decent straps (flip flop**s are ok in shallower slower water). Locking arms, especially with a larger group, is a fairly common way to cross rivers, like in Alaska.

In winter, crossing frozen rivers and lakes can be really dangerous because moving water doesn't freeze or freeze as thick. If the river is shallow enough to survive breaking through, wear **plastic bags** over your ice boots for when you step in. Snow over frozen lakes and rivers, especially near the shore, may be floating on top of sloppy ice slush. Wet ice boots usually end the day. If the river is deep or you aren't sure the lake is frozen, don't chance it. Walk around or find a good crossing.

WILDERNESS SURVIVAL

If you are climbing in remote locations, you will be heavily relying on what you brought with you. You can survive 30 days with no food, but only 2-3 days without water. Basic wilderness survival skills are not only handy; they are extremely satisfying to engage in.

Nothing says self-sufficient like living (or surviving at the least) off the land. When that mortgage, job, insurance policy, retirement plan, etc. gets the better of you (or the apocalypse occurs) you can always relax and know that if it really hits the fan, you can still survive. I urge you to read a book or take a class in wilderness survival. Urban survival is another set of skills that could also prove really handy (yes, I'm getting ridiculously off topic here).

If you're into survival, knowing how to start a fire with a bow can be a lifesaving skill that you have a 0.000001% chance of actually using. Make a bow and loop its string around a stick. Hold the top of the stick with a rock with a divot in it. Spin the stick on top of a dry nest of tinder. You can do this without a bow and just using your hands.

Bow and Hand Fire Drill

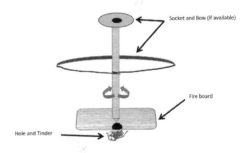

Crafty climbers can figure out how to use batteries and headlamp wire, or lenses and sunlight to get a fire going. Most climbers are ingenious enough to figure out how to craft a shelter via natural crevasses or making a simple lean-to. The basic way to obtain water from the air, moist earth, or a pot of salt water is to trap the air with some plastic, use the sun to heat the water into vapor, and collect the condensation.

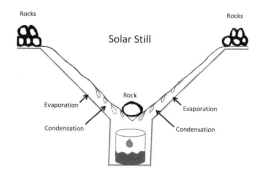

Solar Still

Learning about edible plants & insects, and trapping animals & fish are really fun and interesting skills to have but probably only useful for insanely remote expeditions or the apocalypse since you can survive for weeks without food and it's probably better to be super hungry than to die of poisoning. There is a system called the Universal Edibility Test and it is something like a skin allergy test and food challenge by smelling, then slowly testing the plant on skin then on mucous membrane, followed by slowing tasting and ingesting specific parts of the plant over the course of many hours. The Boy Scout berry rule (which may or may not kill you) is: never eat white or cream colored berries, red berries have 50/50 chance of being edible, and blue/black berries are about 90% edible.

BEAR, MOOSE, MOUNTAIN LION, & GOAT

These animals are very dangerous and bears and lions eat people. Keeping yourself and your camp-spot bear-proof means keeping food smells at a minimum. Cook, camp, and use the toilet in different locations. Hang your food, keep smellables in bear boxes and smell-reducing bags, and don't keep anything smelly in your tent. If you spilled food on your clothes, you're taking chances by wearing them to bed. When hiking, make your presence known by making noise so you don't surprise a bear or moose.

If you encounter a grizzly (brown bear), don't make eye contact and back away slowly. Make yourself seem bigger, but don't provoke it! If it charges, deploy your **bear spray** (certified bear pepper spray) if you have it handy. Stand your ground and appear larger than you really are. Do not run or try and fight...yet. There's a good chance a charge will be a bluff. If it wasn't a bluff, fight back. If you can't fight back (or are pretty sure that isn't going to work), protect yourself by curling up to protect your guts and covering your head and neck with your arms. Don't get up until the bear is gone, it will attack again. Black bears can be frightened off much more easily than grizzlies, so act big and yell. Just don't run.

Moose are actually more dangerous than grizzly bears and are more prone to attack. Back away, etc., but if one charges, try and get behind a tree. If you can't, curl up as in the bear attack. Mountain lions are trying to hunt and kill you. If you see one making eye contact - do not run. Make yourself seem big and fierce. Just don't crouch down. If you think you're being stalked, do the same while seeking shelter and protecting your neck. If attacked fight back. The best prevention is to never travel alone in lion terrain. Goats can occasionally charge if you get too close. They love salt, so don't pee where you'll be hanging out or belaying. If leaving your gear at the base, it is always a good idea to hang your pack!

WEATHER

Nothing can screw up plans, ruin a climb, and put you in danger like the weather. Having plan B's (or more) can keep you climbing when the area you want to go is bad since you've brought a different set of gear and guidebooks. Be creative. Sunny South facing routes or overhanging areas can be warm or dry during improbable forecasts. Or use a bad weather day to practice climbing in poor conditions on easier climbs, aid climbing, or dry tooling.

BEFORE YOU GO
Planning ahead can save you time, money, and failure. If you've got planned vacation time, a partner, and plane tickets you may be committed regardless of weather. Don't make the mistake that has cost many their lives by going regardless. This is especially

true on mountains like Mt. Rainier and Hood. Get travel insurance, or change your plans to sport climbing. Rent a car at the airport and head South. If your destination is on soft sandstone and it just poured or will rain, don't go! Climbing on soft rock after a heavy rain is dangerous and ruins the climbs for others.

We live in a great age where we can check the weather for just about anywhere with relative accuracy. Understanding how forecasts relate to different areas is a learned skill. For example, a 30% chance of rain in the PNW or greater can be a different story to a 30% forecast in a non-mountainous area. It also depends on the season. A percent chance could mean it may sprinkle for a few minutes, a quick and heavy mountain shower in the afternoon with lightning, or it could mean it will rain for thirty percent of the day. The more digging and asking around about local weather patterns during a particular season, the better.

The first thing you should do, and up until you no longer have cell service is to check the weather. NOAA at **weather.gov** has the largest infrastructure and should have the most accurate forecasts, but every weather site uses their own algorithms. Check a few sites. **Climbingweather.com** is a handy website and app because it links climbing areas to the NOAA pinpoint forecast. **Windguru.cz** and **Weatherspark.com** are powerful websites. They allow you to check tons of variables and backdated forecasts. Read the text forecast on NOAA to get an idea of what is happening in your area. Keep a climbing journal to go back and extrapolate conditions based off your previous experiences. **Weather Underground** and Weather Spark websites both have backdated weather conditions to help you out. **Weather.com and Accuweather** with have long-range forecasts. These won't be very accurate, as it is almost impossible to guess more than 4-5 days out at best. Accu-weather has extremely optimistic forecasts. **Weatherbug** is another site and app that has fairly accurate forecasts.

Weather.gov (NOAA) has many useful feature other sites (besides Weatherspark and Windguru) do not have. The forecast discussion can give you a high level overview of what's going on with the weather in the area you are in. On the map, you can click for a pinpoint forecast for a specific location. You can look at radar and satellite imagery as well as animations to see an overview of where the weather systems are and where they are going. NOAA has two very useful maps you may want to check out. The QPF (quantitative precipitation forecast) shows how much expected precipitation there will be, and the PQPF (probabilistic precipitation forecast) shows a map of the expected chance of rain.

When checking the weather you want to look for trends. A nice day at the start or end of a storm could wind up bad if the system moves in fast or leaves slowly. If the forecast has been the same for a couple days and could go either way, look at weather cams to see if it's raining or sunny. The days with similar forecasts will most likely have similar conditions. Look at the radar images to see how widespread a system is. If it's patchy, you may be ok. The animation will show if it's growing or moving on. Highs and lows will help you figure out if it will only be warm for a few hours in the afternoon, or warm all day. You can find out what time the high will be and the temps throughout the days as well on websites like Weatherspark or Windguru.

Knowing the aspect of the climb could help you match the highs with when the sun will be on the route (up in the East, down in the Wast, and in the South for most of the day). Check the probability of precipitation in the NOAA pinpoint map for where the climb is, and also check the high points, lowlands, and in the direction the storm or prevailing winds are coming from to get a good idea to see what's coming and going on in nearby areas. You can also check when the precipitation plans on coming, the rate at which it may fall, and how much is expected. The dew point is something to check if sleeping out. If the dew point drops to the night's lows, you may get frost or soaked with dew. Dew point correlates the humidity with the temperature air moisture will condensate at. The higher the dew point the more humid it is. Check the percentage of cloud cover to see if you'll be in the shade of clouds or in the sun.

Look at sunrise and sunsets as well as dawn and dusk (when it starts to get light and when it's actually dark) to plan how much daylight you've got. The sun lingers a lot longer in the summer than it does in the winter. Moon stats can also be helpful. Knowing when a full moon will be facing your climb and when it will be up can make night climbing a more attractive option. Prevailing wind speed, gusts, and direction are important things to know as well. What looks like a nice day could be a disaster in high winds, but your climb may be protected if it faces away. Weatherspark and Windguru show all of these factors, and many apps on smartphones show at least some of these.

A lot of wasted days can occur if you let a chance of rain keep you from climbing. Many big climbs have been done with a horrible forecast and looming cloud and the climbers stayed dry. Go for it if your desire is high enough and you think you can escape with nothing worse than soggy gear, a few nuts and slings, and a smile on your face from at least trying.

Pressure and Temperature Gradient Impact on Weather
Low-pressure systems generally mean weather is moving in. Cold low fronts usually bring arctic cold moving in, and warm cold fronts usually mean snow. Warm high-pressure systems bring in nice weather and cold high-pressure systems will bring in a storm. If there is a slow change in temperatures, systems will generally linger. An unstable air mass means it is cold up high and warm down low (warm air rises). A stable air mass means that the difference between upper and lower temps is gradual or that it's warm up high and cold down low and could mean an inversion. Warm up high and down low is stable, as is cold down low and up high - until the ground heats up, and then it becomes unstable. Cold low-pressure systems can be quite stable as there's no warm air to rise. Either way in good weather, rapid changes are bad and slow or no change is good. The more unstable or rapid of a change in pressures and temps the bigger the storm that's coming.

Decoding Vague Forecast Descriptions
- **Cloudy**: 90-100% cloud cover
- **Mostly Cloudy**: 70-80% cloud cover
- **Partly Cloudy**: 30-60% cloud cover
- **Mostly/Partly Sunny**: 10-30% cloud cover
- **Sunny**: 0-10% cloud cover
- **Clear**: No cloud cover or at night
- **Fair**: Good weather with less than 40% cloud cover

- **Showers**: Intermittent or brief rain
- **Rain**: Steady rain for hours
- **Snow Flurries**: Light Snow with not much or any accumulation
- **Show Showers**: Snow likely, will start and stop, with accumulation
- **Snow**: Steady snowfall
- **Rain or Thunderstorms**: Probability of precipitation is 75%

- **Brisk, Breeze, or Blustery**: 15-25 mph wind
- **Windy or Very Windy**: 25-40 mph Wind
- **High Winds**: over 40 mph

IN THE FIELD
Forecasting in the field is an educated guessing game, and every range and season are different. Some areas are famous for thunderstorms around 2 pm during even a bluebird day, like the Rockies. Some areas are famous for long periods of rain and low pressure followed by long periods of sun and high pressure, like the Cascades. Start your predictions with by learning local trends. Most of the information given here regarding weather direction is for the mid-latitudes of North America.

Barometer or Altimeter Forecasting
One way to tell what the weather may do objectively is by checking the barometer or an altimeter based off a barometer (not a GPS). You need a baseline, and that means staying at one altitude for at least a few hours. Leave your barometer in one place, preferably outside, and wait for it to stabilize. If you have a known altitude, reset the altimeter to match. That way if you're climbing, you can tell if the barometer is rising or falling even if you're gaining altitude. You have to know your official altitude to make any accurate predictions, so this is more useful for predicting weather at camp or on the summit. The changes in barometric pressure and altitude have an inverse relationship. A rising barometer or decrease in altitude means high pressure (usually good), and a falling barometer or increase in altitude means low pressure is coming (usually bad).

Normal changes in pressure increase in the mid-latitudes around 10 am and 10 pm (around 0.04 Hb), and pressure decreases normally the opposite amounts at 4 am and 4 pm. This change doesn't happen in upper latitudes like Alaska or lower latitudes, and changes could be double those amounts near the Equator. Barometric changes are less reliable in Alaska or the Equator because both areas have permanent low-pressure systems. Above 14,000 feet changes are more subtle, so add extra caution if barometric changes do occur.

> **Barometric Change Predictions**
> - Changes in -0.04 to -0.07 Hg (inches in pressure) or +40 to 70 feet (in altitude) in a three hour period mean that changes in weather could develop slowly.
>
> - Changes in -0.06 to -0.08 Hg or 60-80 feet in three hours means that significant changes in weather can be expected. Winds can be high 20 mph up to 40 mph.
>
> - Changes greater than -0.08 Hg or 80 feet in less than three hours is bad news and winds can be very high and weather is coming in fast and furious.
>
> - Greater changes in -0.20 to -0.40 Hg or +200-400 feet, but over 12-24 hours means the weather could change slowly.
>
> - If the change is greater than -0.40 Hg or +400 inches in 12-24 hours then significant weather change could come in rapidly.

Cloud, Temperature, and Barometric Predictions
The easiest clues when used with barometric readings are if the barometer is falling and clouds are thickening. Then you should expect rain in the next 12-36 hours. If the clouds are breaking and the barometer is rising, then weather is improving.

Using the barometer with weather clues like changes in temperature can help increase the accuracy of your predictions. If the barometer is falling and the temps are rising, a Southerly storm is coming and it could last for days. If the barometer is rising and it's getting cooler out as well as a wind shift to the North then a cold front is most likely passing and high pressure is moving in. If the base level of the clouds begin to rise and it's getting warm, or the barometer is rising for more than 12 hours, a warm front is most likely passing and a high pressure system is moving in. If the barometer is rising and it's getting nicer out, then you can be pretty confident that it will be nice out.

Wind Predictions

Predicting and planning for wind is just as important as planning for rain or snow. High winds not only make life unbearable, they can cause hypothermia, make you climb horribly, and cause horrific rope management issues especially when rappelling. Wind force increases exponentially with wind speed. In other words, 40 mph winds are four times stronger than 20 mph winds! If you are looking at a weather map that shows isobars, or lines of pressure gradients, you can expect high winds at tightly packed lines.

Winds are excellent predictors of weather. Any increase in wind speed or change in direction usually means worsening weather and colder temps. Wind occurs when air from a high pressure system is moving into a low pressure system. This also happens during changes in temperature (because changes in temperature affect pressure), especially in valleys. Valley air warmed by the sun rises and cool nighttime air sinks. This creates morning and evening updrafts on walls, and creates cold sinks in valley floors. A climb only a couple hundred feet above the frigid valley floor could have reasonable temps. This also means that if possible, bivy on a slope above a valley to keep from freezing your ass off.

Warm winds can sweep a range of snow and ice in a very short amount of time, called Chinook or Föhn winds. This occurs when a moist air mass rises, cools, and deposits on the windward side of a range, known as Orographic precipitation. Then this air mass warms as it lowers, an adiabatic process, and pulls moisture as it lowers on the leeward side. Temperatures can rise on leeward slopes significantly. If a strong storm is forecasted for the West side and you'll be climbing on the East side, you may want to think about the possibility of a Chinook killing the ice or snow. You can expect a Chinook if you are on the leeward side of a range, usually the East side, and there are high winds with precipitation at the crest.

Bora winds are the opposite of a Chinook, and are caused by quickly sinking cold air from snowy ranges or glaciers. Expect these cold winds down valley or at the mouths of canyons in late afternoon or evening. Mountain cirques can affect wind in strange ways too. Storms can be made to circle, over and over again and you may get hit by the same rain cloud twice or more! If it rain, clears, rains, clears, you may be in a circulating systems that can take several days to pass.

In the Northern Hemisphere a shift of winds towards a more easterly direction usually means a low pressure system is developing, and precipitation is possible - especially if the barometer is also falling. When the West wind shifts from a Southern to more Northerly or pure Western direction, this can mean high pressure and drying, but precipitation could also likely on the windward side as the front enters.

The "calm before the storm" saying is true. If it is blustery and cloudy out and all of a sudden things get quiet, you better find shelter because you're going to get hammered. If it's calm out and you notice things like low hanging campfire smoke or an increase in the amount of bugs outside, you can expect rain.

You can also use the wind in the lower 48 to determine if a high or low pressure system is coming. Stand with your back to the wind. If you are facing North, then a storm is moving towards you. Facing South and the storm is moving away. If facing the wind, the low pressure will be to your right. This occurs because wind moves in such a way from high to low pressure due to the direction the Earth spins, known as the Coriolis Effect. The reverse is true in the Southern Hemisphere. This also determines the direction water spins as it goes down the drain.

Cloud Predictions
Some obvious cloud clues that weather is coming are thickening dark clouds to the West (or direction of the storm movement) and lenticulars forming over the mountains. Yes, you can get lucky and miss a localized storm, but it takes years of experience to take that risk. Thickening clouds and lenticulars means that a warm front is moving in and you should expect to get weather in about 12-24 hours or immediately if you're actually in the lenticular. Predictions get a bit hazy if there's a lenticular but no other clouds in the area. Again, if you're in the lenticular, you'll be in bad weather, but surrounding areas may get a mix of sun and rain, no weather, or a storm is sneaking in you can't see just yet.

Lenticulars aside, if clouds are becoming more organized and lowering, rain should be expected. If you don't see any high clouds anymore and the lower clouds begin to break, you can expect good weather and an ending storm. If you don't see any clouds develop in the afternoon at all, good weather should last. The earlier clouds build, the earlier you can expect a shower.

Knowing what different clouds mean is very important in predicting the weather. Nimbus isn't a shape, but just means a cloud that will produce precipitation. Add the word nimbus (plus or minus a few other letters) to any cloud to call it a rain cloud.

Lenticulars were already mentioned and are king of the obvious. There are many other types of clouds and combinations than mentioned here.

Stratus clouds are uniform layers of low altitude clouds, the kind you see in the grey days of a Pacific Northwest winter. Stratus clouds are essentially thick above ground fog. Stratus clouds are usually stable, meaning they are they to stay for a while. If it's raining, expect more. If they are there and it's not raining, you may be ok. Altostratus clouds, or high level status, that begin to lower (stratus) are very good indicators that storms are less than 12 hours away. You should start planning an exit strategy. Nimbostratus clouds look like a boiling cauldron, and mean wet and possible long lasting weather.

Altostratus. Courtesy NOAA

Stratus

Cumulus. Courtesy NOAA

Nimbostratus. Courtesy NOAA

Stratocumulus

Altocumulus. Courtesy NOAA

Cumulus clouds are the puffy cotton balls you stare at on lazy summer afternoons. Cumulus clouds are unstable, meaning they may come and go without incident, or they could coalesce or get bigger and storm. If cumulus clouds are separate and stay white all day you should be ok. If they start to get dark with flat bases, or an anvil shape, you may want to find shelter if they're coming your way. High-level cumulus, or altocumulus, which look like a quilt spread across the sky, usually mean stable but warmer humid weather. This can also mean afternoon thunderstorms. Stratocumulus clouds, a cross between the two types, are low puffy grey clouds that have blue sky between them. This usually means it will by dry, especially if the daytime and nighttime temperature differences are only a few degrees.

Cirrus clouds are the high wispy clouds that can look like horsetails or can spread out over miles. Cirrus clouds are oft cited as the "weather's coming" cloud to look out for. Actually, mild cirrus clouds means that you've got fair weather in the immediate future. They can mean that a change (good or bad) is coming within 24 hours. By the direction of streaks, you can get a pretty good idea where they are moving and where a front is coming from and use that information to make predictions based on temperature changes and direction. Cirrocumulus formations aren't usually a bad sign and can mean that you've probably got fair, but cold weather for the near future (except in the tropics which could mean hurricanes). Cirrus clouds that coalesce and turn to a mixed cirrostratus or altostratus is a meaningful (bad) sign and may mean rain within 12-36 hours, especially if coming from the Northwest. Expect a wet warm front.

Cirrostratus. Courtesy NOAA

Two variations of cirrus. Courtesy NOAA

Cirrocumulus. Courtesy NOAA

Fog can create some difficult weather decisions and navigating issues. Valley fog forms overnight during stable high pressure and calm winds when the air is moist and dew point is reached. So thick valley fog usually means that it's clear in the hills (if you can find the climb). Things get weird when fog develops in the mountains instead of the valley. This usually happens after a very recent rain or snowstorm when humid low air gets blown uphill. It can stick around until pressure changes, usually in the evening or by morning. If temps don't change, the pressure won't change, and the fog can stick. Dew or frost in the morning with no fog or a morning fog that burns off quickly are excellent good weather signs.

Sun and Moon Predictions

Brocken Spectre

The "red sky at night" proverb is only true in the mid-latitudes of the U.S. where prevailing winds blow from West to East. Only pay attention to the red color of the clouds, not the haze in the air. You also should only pay attention to the clouds looking away from the sunset (to the East). "Red sky at night, climbers delight," means the front is moving away and you may have good weather for the next 12-24 hours. "Red sky in the morning, climbers take warning" (base of the clouds to the West, or away from sunrise are red), means bad weather is coming. Halos developing around the sun or moon are reflections off high ice crystals and mean that high clouds and moisture is increasing and a warm front is on the way. Hazy halos are worse than halos in clear skies, as are thicker halos.

Time of Day Prediction

High, dry, inland mountainous areas like the Colorado Rockies often get thunderstorms and heavy rain in the mid-afternoon, generally around 2 pm. You can expect this almost like clockwork during monsoonal patterns when it does this every day. They usually last from a few minutes to a little over an hour. Short notice showers and thunderstorms usually mean that the storm will be very brief, but intense. If a lot of notice is given, you can expect longer lasting precipitation. Rain in the early hours can often mean that the storm will pass when it warms up – as in the phrase, "Rain before 7, dry before 11". If it fogs up or the moon and stars get murky you can expect bad weather the next day. Likewise if it is foggy or dewy in the morning you can expect a bluebird day.

Snow Predictions

Predicting snowfall is the same as predicting rain, but predicting how much and the density of the snow is a bit more useful. The warmer it is the denser and more likely it will snow more – at or just below freezing.

Lightning and Storms

When a storm hits, the heaviest precipitation rate, usually towards the end of the storm, the storm could pass in around 3-12 hours. Lightening usually precedes heavy rain, so you need to be most careful at the beginning of a storm. The more lightning you get, the heavier the precipitation or stronger the storm will be. The darker the clouds the more the chance and amount of lightning is possible. Lightning is no joke, and if you are exposed, begin preparations. First, ditch all of your metal. Get out of exposed locations like mountaintops, ridges, and shallow caves or overhangs. Crouch to minimize contact with anything but the rubber on your shoes on a nonconducting surface like your rope, pack (ditch the metal), or ground pad. If you're totally in the open, lightning may (weak evidence here) have a hard time hitting a moving object. Better to cower on a nonconducting surface. If you need a solid visual on the power of lightning, check out the ranger station in the Grand Tetons where they have melted carabineers and gear on display from a tragedy that took the lives of several climbers hit by lightning.

> To gauge how far away lightning is in miles divide the elapsed time between lightning and thunder by 5.

Temperature and Altitude

Air temperature is affected by altitude, and the higher you are the colder it is - unless an inversion is occurring. Inversions occur when cold dense valley air lingers and warm air from weak fronts or daytime warming sits on top. Pollution can act as a lid on the lower cold air. Cities that lay in valleys can be a disgusting smog trap during inversions. Ice climbers should rejoice as inversions helps climbs grow like weeds. Without any other external factors, air cools by approximately 3.6° F every 1000 feet or 2° C every 300 meters.

> If climbers want to get a handle where the freezing level is, use these equations:
> - Elevation in feet + 1000 x [(temperature in Fahrenheit at current elevation – 32) divided by 3.6]
> - Elevation in meters + [(temp in Celsius at current elevation x 300) divided by 2]

Avalanche Safety

If you are traveling, skiing, or climbing in avalanche terrain (there is a slope with snow on it) and don't have avalanche training, this section is no substitute for taking a class and reading a book devoted to the subject. This section is only for a quick reference. Avalanches are no joke and kill even the most experienced climbers on the easiest climbs. AAIRE provides the best classes in the U.S. and "Staying Alive in Avalanche Terrain" by Bruce Tremper is the most useful book on the subject in terms of practicality. Like any other rescue situation, it's imperative that your partner is up to speed if YOU want to be rescued too.

Understanding Snowpack

Shallow snow means high avalanche hazard. This may sound counterintuitive, and size does matter in large slabs, but less snow means weak snow and avalanche fatalities are common in the early season. Here's what happens: the snow insulates the ground creating a huge temperature gradient between the colder air and warmer ground. This turns the snow into loose unconsolidated unbonded coarse sugar called faceted snow (sometimes referred to as hoar). What keeps snow from falling down slopes is gravity (less than 33° it usually can just sit there and more than 45° it falls before it can accumulate) and the energy stored in the bonds between crystals. If there aren't bonds, then the snow will roll down the hill (an avalanche). If another storm deposits snow onto the faceted snow, you've got a nasty sliding layer and very dangerous conditions. When enough well bonded snow accumulates to average the deeper faceted snow into the total pack, conditions stabilize. So more depth in a well-bonded snowpack = good.

One meter of solid surface snow is usually safe unless conditions are horrible, and over three meters of solid snow is generally quite safe. If temperature gradients continue, a layered snowpack of well bonded slab with layers of faceted snow develops, creating the dreaded slab avalanche. The thicker and deeper the slab relative to the amount of weak layers the better. Towards the end of the season, warm temperatures create a reverse temperate gradient, and slabs can weaken. After enough warm weather, things re-equilibrate and stabilize, creating the stable spring snowpack. In the spring slab avalanches occur during warming, and after stabilization, sloughing avalanches and wet slides can occur from the upper snowpack destabilizing.

Predicting Avalanche Conditions
The Big Three Variable Factors

Check the avalanche forecast until the last possible opportunity before you head out. This should be a no brainer, but the issue is what you do with the information. Most accidents occur when a party is informed but makes choices in conflict with the information they know. Just like you'll constantly look for signs of rain when the forecast says 30% chance of rain, you should be constantly evaluating risk for avalanches when the forecast states the probability of avalanche.

The most basic signs are:
- Avalanche forecast
- Signs of avalanche activity (red light!)
- Weather forecast or observation of any rapid changes in increasing temperature, snowfall, and wind.

Burn this into your brain. Make a **notecard** you look at every time you make a decision. Signs of avalanche activity are: seeing an avalanche, new and old slide paths, no trees, and hearing cracking and whumps, seeing cracks and sheers and rollerballs of snow.

Rapid warming quickly weakens bonds that hold everything together. If the sun comes out, rethink your position. This is especially true during inversions. It may be baking up high while you shiver in the valley unaware of the dangers cooking above. When an inversion leaves the valley, so should you. Snow and ice that's been super stable for days or weeks due to the inversion are now warming up for the first time. The usually dangerous N and E facing slopes are usually so cold that nothing triggers them, but S and E facing slopes get cooked. Frost on the windshield in the morning is a good sign that an inversion is occurring. Inversions like to form surface facets at lower elevations. Lower elevations have less snow depth. Shallow snow is unstable and surface facets will become an unstable layer. Beware low elevation snow, especially when an inversion leaves or is loaded with more snow. In the spring the safer S and W facing slope are now the dangerous ones.

Wind and snowfall increase the load and chance of a slide. Wind can transport massive amounts of snow in a very short period of time and should not be understated. Wind will move snow if blowing 10 mph or more, but the most snow is transported at speeds of 15-80 mph. Most snow is moved during the initial first couple hours. Active or very recent snowfall should be a no brainer.

Rain also quickly weakens snow, as does snowmelt from the sun as bonds are quickly destroyed. These are common causes of slides in late spring and early summer. Layers aren't overloaded, but weakened. A rain or sun crust can act as a great sliding layer as well. However, if the not-yet-formed crust is still wet and sticky during a new

533

snowfall then a solid bond can be created and a sliding layer avoided. Luckily wet snow regains strength quickly, either overnight if it's cold or after a day of settling.

Slope Angle

The next big one on the decision tree, if not the most important, is the slope angle of what you'll be on, what's just below you, and what's above you. **The red zones are 33°- 45° slopes, 38° being the magic number.** You could have all best or worst avy conditions imaginable, but without a slope you won't get avalanches. Get good at using an inclinometer or phone app to gauge a slope by looking up it or down it. It's better to gauge a slope before getting on it than on the slope itself. To test the angle of the slope you're on lay your ski pole down and put your inclinometer on the pole.

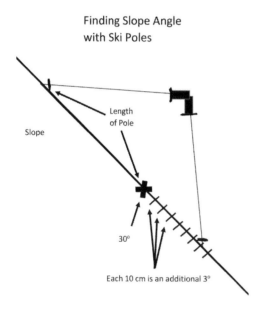

Finding Slope Angle with Ski Poles

Each 10 cm is an additional 3°

To find slope angle with only ski poles first lay a pole down the slope and mark the ends of the pole in the snow, the downhill mark being 30°. Now hold both pole handles together (same size poles) and tip them downhill. One pole pivots at the uphill mark while the other pole dangles. When the dangling pole hits touches the snow mark that spot and measure from where the pole hit to the 30° mark. Every 10 cm downhill from the mark is an additional 3°. Use your probe or a 10 cm ice screw to measure.

Aspect

No less important, but more variable are Northeast facing slopes which are the coldest and least likely to settle, leeward slopes where more snow is quickly accumulated, convex slopes which are less stable with more stored potential energy, and cornices below or above you. Leeward slopes aren't always on a face, they can be on sides of ridges too – don't forget that.

Terrain

Look for other terrain clues. Trees and ridges could be safer than open terrain, concave slopes may be safer than convex, anchors like boulder fields could be safer than grassy slopes. Ice climbs make wonderful sliding layers and funnels. Beware of trigger points, or the weak point in a slope's stored energy. Tree and boulder wells, especially the downhill sides of trees at snow/timber transition zones, as well as where snow starts to get shallow like ridge tops or spur ridges may look like the safest place but can often be the avalanche button and the most dangerous place to be. These usually trigger deeper faceted snow avalanches. The tops of convex slopes or the crest of a concave slope could be the weak link that pulls you down with an avalanche instead of being buried from above. Even being fairly far back from a cornice could be the weak energy point that sends you over the cliff. Take a look at what's below you. Terrain traps like trees and cliffs can kill you just as easily as being suffocated by burial.

For many reasons, hearing about climbers and skiers getting killed in their tents just makes your stomach turn at the helplessness of the situation. Please pay attention to what's above you when setting camp. Run-out angles are used to judge how far an avalanche will run based on the height of a similar slide and the distance it ran based on snow conditions. To make a rule of thumb, be at least 2-3 times the distance away (horizontally) as tall as the starting point of a possible avalanche could be. Let's say you look at a map or gauge that an avalanche would start 2000' above the base of the peak. That means you should be hiking and camping 4-6,000' horizontally away from the start of where a slide would start, or about a mile. If you can't see above you, maps become lifesaving tools when planning approaches or campsites.

Ice climbers are a bit too lax about avalanches. Good places for avalanches to occur are on snow steps between pitches, shallow snow on lower elevation approach slopes, or slabs at higher elevations, descents when the snow has warmed-up, bowels above the climb, and trigger points where the snowpack gets shallow as you near the top or the base of the route. Know what's above you. Also, know what aspect your climb is going to be on and what the weather is going to do. A climb could be safe until the sun hits it and loosens snow, the wind picks up and rapidly loads slopes, or large unknown ice hangers above you like seracs, cornices, and ice daggers melt or break. Your attention should be focused on avy terrain on ice climb approaches and descents, not the climb ahead or the car below.

Snowpack and Stability Tests
Digging pits and testing the snow to get a mini view of what's going on inside the snowpack is a valuable activity and is especially useful when you don't have an avy forecast. Avalanche tests confirm hazards to help understand the current avy forecasts, they don't determine them.

Dig a snow pit in as close to replicating the elevation and aspect to what you're going to be on, under, or above. The slope angle does not have to be the same. Red lights should be sounding if you find and large changes in snowpack during the first three feet, and if the snow slides when digging the pit or with minimal provocation. But snowpack can vary drastically in pinpoint location, so the more pits you dig, the better decisions you can make.

On the go tests are done to learn about near surface layers, crusts, and old/new snow interfaces. A pole test is easiest test you can do, and can be repeated hundreds of times. Just plunge your pole (ice ax, or probe) into the snow and feel for layers. You can also easily test slopes on the go by jumping on small test slopes. If you're skiing, quickly skiing across suspect slopes, or cutting the slope, is a good idea. Spread out if you can, (and never go first)! Step above your tracks and see how the snow collapses.

The next step in evaluation is to stop and dig a pit on a similar aspect and elevation if possible (but not crucial). You can get big clues if things slide just digging the pit. Use your hand to feel for layers, and if in a hurry, use your shovel to pry behind the pit you dug. If you really want to check the snow stability for sliding layers and weak layers, do some more substantial testing. Besides the pretty much too complicated to be of any use Rutschblock test, and not as realistic shovel-shear test, the compression test is the most commonly known and used snow pit test and is very useful. All test must be done three times to confirm accuracy.

The Compression Test tests for how easily layers can slide, but does not test for the stored energy, or propagation potential of a snowpack. Before doing this or the other tests, do a visual inspection and tactile inspection to understand what layers are present. Isolate a snow column on all sides in your pit the size of a shovel blade. Put the blade on top of the column and 10 times each tap from the wrist, elbow, and shoulder (each body part should be using more force). Snow stability is judged by how easily the column failed based on how hard you tapped. The more easily it breaks the less stable.

Another good test is the Propagation Test and is done as a Compression Test follow-up. Start by isolating a 3 foot deep (90 cm into the slope) by 1 foot wide (30 cm) column. Plant your probe 3 feet into the pit, and use a **knotted cord** around the probe to cut the appropriate length. You could also attach a saw to your probe to cut. Next use your snow saw to cut into the weak layer until you get fracture propagation. If you get propagation by cutting into less than half of the column, then that slope is unsafe.

The Extended Column Test (ECT) is probably the best test because it evaluates how easily a slide can occur like the Compression Test, and also the potential that a slide will propagate like the Propagation Test. Make a column just like the Propagation one, but go in 1 foot (30 cm) and across 3 feet (90 cm) instead. Instead of cutting the weak layer, use your shovel to begin tapping like the compression test until you get a fracture. If you get a fracture, look to see if it propagated across the column. This is a pass/fail only test. If you get propagation, then go home if your test slope is a fairly accurate representation of the slope you intended to be on. If you pass, you could still be in danger or be totally safe – just like any other test result.

Extended Column Testing from the elbow. Courtesy Jonathon Spitzer

Extended Column Test excavation. Courtesy Kurt Hicks

EQUIPMENT

Not only do you need to bring the right equipment, you need to know how to use it, and remember how to use it. Basic avalanche equipment is a **shovel, beacon, probe**, and a partner.

You're pretty much out of luck if you don't have a shovel. Good luck using your hands or an ice ax. Don't skimp on the shovel to save weight. Moving a lot of snow and doing it fast requires a good shovel. Practice digging. Start on the downhill side and dig horizontally towards the victim. Make the hole bigger than you think. Standing on top of the victim and digging straight down only make things worse.

Probes help you rapidly pinpoint a victim's location, and they should be around 240 cm. Any deeper than that and you're better off digging down and re-probing. Probes are also useful for digging pits and rigging stick-clips.

Probe, shovel, beacon, Avalung, compass with inclinometer & sighting mirror.

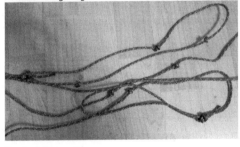

Knotted 4mm cord.

Beacons are only useful if you know how to use them, practice often, they are turned on, and the searchers aren't on transmit mode. Finding multiple victims is harder than you think. Get a beacon that can identify multiple burials and know how to use it. Smaller in-bounds beacons are nice and small, but their range sucks. Get the best beacon you can and make sure your partner has a good one. Digital beacons drastically speed things up, so maybe it's time to retire your old analog one. Beacons that switch back to transmit after a period of motionlessness are excellent as the odds of getting hit twice go up compared to not getting hit by an avalanche at all. Keep fresh batteries and perform a beacon check before leaving the car. Beacon practice makes a good rest day activity. Unless you are a total absolute idiot, do not assume that a beacon will protect or save you from an avalanche and go for it just because you have one. 4G cell phones will interfere with your beacon, analog or digital. Put your phone on airplane mode.

Black Diamond **Avalungs** are incredibly helpful at prolonging survival time if you don't get killed during the ride. You need to put the tube in your mouth before the snow sets, so have it on the ready and practice quickly getting it in your mouth, otherwise it is worthless. **Airbags** are a relatively new technology, but have shown amazing results. By making you a larger object, the airbag keeps you on top better (like a bag of settled potato chips). Unfortunately airbags are probably a bit too heavy to pack on a climb, but may be useful on the approach. If your regular pack stays on, it will help you stay near the surface. If you've got a helmet, wear it in avy terrain. Trauma during the ride is just as likely to kill you as suffocating.

Have a **compass with an inclinometer**, or an **augmented reality app** on your phone handy to constantly gauge slope angle and aspect. A **mirror** on the compass helps you sight the slope and look at the needle at the same time. A phone app allows both simultaneously. If conditions are unchanged, then slope and aspect are the biggest variables and needs to be constantly determined.

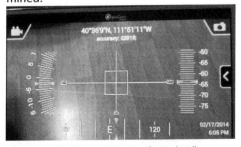

Augmented Reality App (GeoCam for Android)

Snow saws speed up digging pits and are helpful in building walls or digging snow caves. A **breadknife** or a **$5 folding bush saw** (useful in treed approaches) are equally good snow saws. A knotted piece of 4 mm cord is also really useful for cutting samples inside pits.

Travel

Slopes steep enough to enjoy climbing are usually too steep to avalanche – but they can slough and spindrift with enough snow to feel like an avalanche. Pay attention to the sun and heating trends at upper elevations for upper bowels to naturally slide. You can pick safe travel lines by avoiding slopes and bowls by finding mini ridges and protected terrain and in the micro-topography of the mountain (beware of trigger points in the safe zones in shallow faceted snow). If crossing a suspect slope, go one at a time either unroped or on an anchored belay – not running belays or simul-soloing. Going first is much more dangerous. The following climbers need to be well out of the slide zone so they can initiate a rescue, and not get side-swept away. Never go above someone when switching back and descending. If you are on skis, quickly ski across and cut the slope one at a time to a safer ridge where you can re-ascend.

If Caught

If you see or hear an avalanche coming, try and get out of the path. Most likely this is impossible, but a fortunate few have escaped. If climbing, duck under overhangs, press yourself up against the cliff, and get ready. You may have moment brief enough to beef up the anchor, slam in a piece, tie the belayed climber off - anything to stay attached and keep the belay on If caught. Fighting and swimming may help, but is probably impossible. Prepare for the snow to set like concrete rapidly. Make a breathing space over your mouth and nose with your hand, and get the Avalung in your mouth. If you've got an airbag, pull the ripcord. Try and shoot an arm or leg up (hard to tell what's up) so someone may see it.

If you survive or are out of the way, try and watch the victim to aid in finding them. Look for any signs: clothes, equipment, blood, a body part sticking out of the snow. The clock is ticking before the victim loses air and consciousness. You may find a victim, but not knowing CPR and rescue breathing could make your efforts in vain. Don't go for help, every second counts. Go for help after you find your partner and deal with the ABCs.

Finding the victim gets a lot of attention when practicing avalanche skills. Digging a victim out can be just as challenging and requires practice. Leave your probe in place when you've located the victim and look at the depth. Just start digging if they are less that 1.5 meters deep. If buried more than that (4-5 feet) then begin digging 1 meter downhill of the probe. Dig one and a half times (1.5x) the probe depth shown, and dig into the slope towards the probe to move less snow. When digging down plunge the shovel straight down as this could collapse air pockets. Dig horizontally, into the slope, up to the victim. Avoid the temptation to narrow the width of your digging as you progress towards the probe. The moment you reach the victim, make finding and uncovering the airway the priority.

Deciding Avalanche Risk
- Avalanche and weather forecast
- Signs of recent avalanche activity
- Rapid changes in wind, temperature, and precipitation
- Slope angle
- Slope aspect and elevation
- Terrain
- Testing
- Experience, instinct, and desire

DON'T BE AN IDIOT! TAKE AN AVALANCHE COURSE AND READ A DEDICATED BOOK IF PARTICIPATING IN SNOW OR ICE ACTIVITIES.

SNOW TRAVEL

Crevasse rescue will be detailed in the Jugging and Hauling sections. If you are on bare ice, do not rope up. If someone falls in, there is no way to hold the fall. Luckily crevasses aren't hidden on bare ice glaciers. Never be roped up without having running protection on technical terrain or above steep slopes/cliffs. Many tragedies have occurred.

ROPE TEAM SYSTEMS

Most climbers looking to do a difficult route will be in a team of two, possibly three. To set up the rope and gear for traveling in crevassed terrain you'll need to figure out how much space between climbers, and **pre-rigged prusiks** for climbing or hauling out of crevasses. To gauge how much rope and where to tie in, first get an idea of how big crevasses are where you'll be going. If a crevasse is 50 feet across and you tie in 45 feet apart then both climbers could fall in. However, the more rope you have out the less you have to work with for rescue. In general, a team of two should by 30 meters apart, subtracting 5 meters per additional climber. Using a 30 meter rope for a team of two is adequate, but you won't have much to work with especially if a loop needs to be dropped down. Don't forget that with thinner ropes your prusik needs to be thinner (5 mm) or you'll need to put more wraps on it with your prusik.

To set up the ropes, have both end climbers tie into the end, then take in coils and finish by passing a bight through the coils and clipping to a locker on your belay loop, or after passing the bight through the coils, pass it through your belay loop and tie it off to the rope going towards the other climber. This is called a Kiwi coil and allows for extra rope to pay out if more distance is needed. The middle climbers tie in equal distances by clipping a locker to a butterfly or overhand with a slipknot finish. The extra coils can be worn over the shoulder or put in the pack.

Kiwi Coil

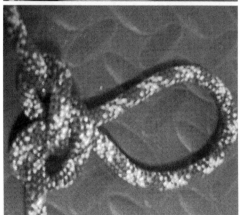

Tying a butterfly knot

You can choose to put stopper knots on the rope to jam in a crevasse lip which aid in stopping a fall or takes weight off self-arresting climber by tying overhand on bights or butterfly knots starting 10 feet out, then every three feet. This makes ascending the rope or hauling more difficult because the knots must be untied or passed unless you can drop a loop, but it is worth it. They do and have worked and with a team of two you should use this system as both people in a crevasse is way worse than dealing with knots to haul someone out

For the rest of the kit you'll want to have your prusiks on the rope and ready to go. Tie the **chest prusik** onto the rope above (in front) of the **foot prusik** if using a standard chest and foot prusik system, aka the Texas Kick. Clip the chest prusik to your belay loop with a locker, and daisy chain up the longer foot prusik. Clip the shortened foot prusik somewhere handy so you can use it to clip off to a snow anchor after a self-arrest from a team member's crevasse fall. If you are using a toothed ascender, don't have them on the rope because a fall could cut the rope. Keep them attached to whatever slings they go with and ready to deploy. The middle person(s) may want to hedge their bets on put one of each prusik on either side of them. A **chest harness** (just a doubled sling) with a non-locker is really helpful in staying upright during a fall, and a **pack leash** and non-locker allows you to ditch the pack when you fall in. Don't use **ax leashes** unless dropping an ax jeopardizes safety. Padded ax heads are also hard to hold - just use a thicker glove or put some tape over the metal.

If you are using a **GriGri**, and I highly recommend giving this system a try, put the GriGri on the rope and your belay loop. Put a prusik above the GriGri. That prusik does not need to be clipped off, but within reach accounting for rope stretch. Also, have a tether and some long slings handy to rig up the foot stirrups that attach to the prusik. There are many benefits to the GriGri system, one being that it acts as a ratcheting pulley on the anchor when rescuing. It also makes jugging out easier, quick transitions to belaying out rope, and lowering is always breeze.

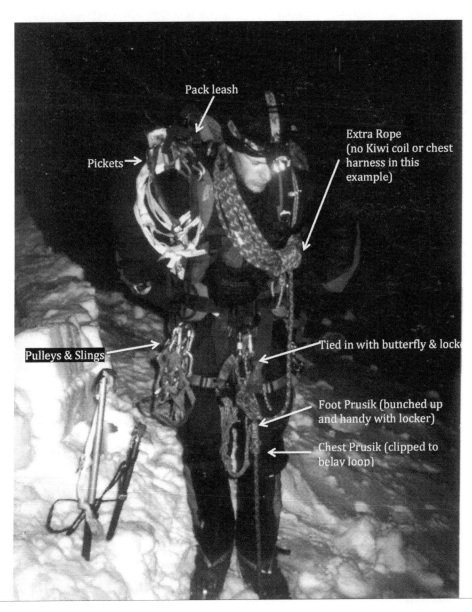

There are many variations on jugging a rope so see that section to see what works best for the climb you'll be doing. Hauling a climber out is really hard without pulleys, so bring two per climber. **Real pulleys** are better, but if just traveling to access a hard climb, you may want to improvise with **DMM Revolvers or Microtraxions/Rollnlocks** No matter what system you'll be using, having at least one prusik on the rope is essential in transferring the load during a self-arrest to an anchor. Keep any snow anchors handy for turning a self-arrest into an anchor, like a picket and fluke. Always have your ice ax at the ready to arrest a fall..

The leader should have a **probe or long ski pole** with no basket handy for probing around crevasses and snow bridges. Remember to keep the rope taught at all times. This can be tricky when end-running crevasses, especially with multiple people on the team. Backing up and moving quickly may be necessary to pull slack out of a traversing leader or middle member. Jumping is sometimes necessary. Snow bridges are always a highlight of the day. Probe the crap out of it, and belay across it with an anchor on each side. It may be ok in the morning, but fully sketchy on the way down.

When traveling on the rope team it is important to keep the rope on the correct side when traveling on a slope, and when switching back. You want the rope on the uphill side so if you fall, you aren't flipped over. This requires coordination when turning a corner on switchback. This is especially important for the middle person(s) as they will be stepping over the rope at awkward moments. Simple commands like, "switching!" are helpful if the leader is moving to fast to stay coordinated and have enough rope and space to do the switch. If clipped to the rope on a team on a running belay with gear along the way to pass, or climbing a fixed rope, you want to use the "magic clip" to avoid being unclipped momentarily when passing pro and avoid the extra time, clutter, and weight of using two sets of tethers. Simply clip the rope past the anchor with the rope still in the strand you are already clipped to with your biner. This magically frees your from the previous side of the rope. Try it out!

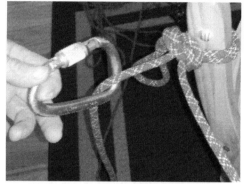

Magic Clip: about to reach the anchor on the right.

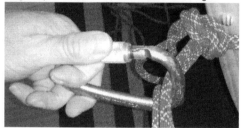

Both strands are clipped and you are free from the left side of the anchor and clipped to the right (hard to show).

MOATS, BERGSCHRUNDS, AND CORNICES

Bergschrunds, moats, cornices, and transitioning onto the rock from snow are probably the most dangerous sections of snow travel, but they can make good bivi sites if you have a tarp. Many casual steps across onto the rock from snow have turned to looks of total horror when the leader realizes the drop below. Always always always be on heads-up mode when getting near moats – even if it looks like the snow reaches right up to the rock. When going from rock to steep snow, it can be a good idea to grab a bunch of rocks so you can bury and rap from them.

One of the most difficult parts of climb is climbing down into a moat, stemming between the ice and rock, and getting onto the rock safely. Leaving something up top as a toprope could save the day, and you can probably fetch it on the way back. Bringing one crappy pound-in or titanium ice screw on a rock climb with a snow/glacier approach is prudent.

Many alpine rock starts require climbing a steep ice or snow slope in the cold morning. Padding up suncups in approach shoes and using a rock, ski pole, nut tool, or large cam for an ax is one way of doing this. Better yet, bring a pair of strap on crampons and light ax each. You may need the ax for pounding pins, and the crampons and ax for getting back down. If the descent takes you to a lower angled slope, you expect the snow to soften enough to not need equipment, or can rappel past the steep section then the ax and crampons will be bulky dead weight on the rock climb. You could share a pair of crampons (I'm never doing that again), or have one person lead up with a single pair of crampons and an ax and belay the other climber up (or lower them back down on the rope). If you're feeling lucky, you could chuck the ax and crampons off once you've reached the rock, assuming you can easily retrieve them when you're done. Saving weight by using crampons without frontpoints, and using rocks etc. for self-arresting isn't worth the risk – they barely work. Really smart climbers will have remembered to bring a pair of lightweight gloves for all of this. I have never remembered.

Besides posing impending doom above you all day long, cornices add the extra difficulty of getting past them. Usually the snow near or in cornices will be extra awful and traversing a bit could be worth the extra time. Climbing up and over them is probably going to be the crux of the day if you decide to do this. Of course you can travel through them. Burrowing through a cornice and topping out from inside the mountain is an experience you'll never forget.

If you think this is a possibility, bring a **tool with an adz** and even consider a **shovel** because this takes a long time. A picket or two is a good idea in case it or you fall off. You'll want your belay to be out of the way and bomber in case the cornice collapses during excavation. Prepare to get soaked and hot, and then freeze your ass of on top. Put your belay jacket in your pack and the hood of your shell under your helmet.

Once on top of a mountain, you can still die from a cornice. Trigger points could be a lot farther back than you think. Proceed with extreme caution. On knife edged ridges, put in running belay protection in case you both get blown off the top. Have material to ascend the rope handy if you do wind up dangling off the summit ridge.

CAMP

If camping on a glacier, probe the entire campsite and mark the perimeter with wands. Familiarity lets your guard down, and there may be a crevasse lurking below your camp. Probe out to the toilet area as well. Make large wind blocks for your tent and toilet pit from cut snow blocks and bolster the sides with piled snow.

A **plastic compost bag** in a pit usually serves as the group toilet. Place it downwind and have a spare in case of splatters. Bury your food (and wand it) to keep ravens from destroying your stash. You can melt water by placing snow in a large 10 L black Dromedary bag or a garbage bag (can be stinky) during the day to save on gas. Solar chargers are nice to replenish the batteries on your toys during the day as well. Some work much better than others, so test them out first. A **4-season tarp** over a dug out kitchen makes a nice group kitchen. Cook in your vestibule with the vent open if you're doing it in your tent. Have plenty of **books, games, music, movies,** and **fun food** for extended base camp delays or at least one item to keep you occupied at higher camps. Don't forget any **vices like tobacco or other smokeables, liquor, and a backup coffee supply.**

Maximizing Success

This section will discuss some strategies for climbing more successfully, including some specific examples for different climbing disciplines. Please see the Skills and Mental Training Chapters for a lot more information on the following topics.

Finding Rests

Redpointing routes is a great way to find unobvious rests on seemingly sustained routes. After a while you may find patterns to finding secret rests and be able to apply them to your onsight attempts. If you know that a pumpy sustained section is coming that is best climbed fast and fresh, don't just zip past your best holds. Milk them, shaking out one arm at a time in a straight arm lock off for as long as it takes to feel as fresh as you're going to get. If one arm is going to get flamed much more than the other, finish shaking out with that arm if your rest position doesn't allow a full rest.

Finding a semi-rest by flagging and dropping onto the heel To find rests on hard terrain, find a hold that you can at least match on, or two holds that are good enough to hang on for a short time. Finding a good foothold can be even more effective if the handholds are just too thin. Sink down into the foothold by bending your knee and hip, sitting as low on your heel as possible. Flag the other leg, and position your arm(s), torso, or even head to find a point of balance. Press your chest into the wall. By finding this balance stance you may able to take enough weight off your arms to be able to shake out.

On steep and overhanging terrain, actively pull with your toes to pull your weight over your legs and off your arms. Underclinging can help you position your weight over your feet. If you can undercling with a knee (a kneebar), or any other body part than your fingers (like your thigh, head and chin), then you can help avoid flaming out your arms even more.

Finding stems on a face (or really anywhere) can also get the weight onto your legs and off your arms by applying side pressure on the holds with your feet, or by pulling in with both feet. Heel hooks and toe cams are extremely effective. You don't just have to heel hook holds above your feet. Try hooking holds to your side, or around arêtes. Back-stepping offers a half stem. Drop knees can offer a similar rest as sinking into your heel as just described. Down-climbing out of a crux or tricky sequence back to a rest can help you onsight a climb by trying out sequences. Let your belayer know you're down-climbing so they don't take your weight by accident.

Don't let fear and the desire to be done with it overcome your need to milk rests to their full potential.

Using Holds More Effectively
Grabbing and pulling is certainly the fastest and easiest way to climb through tough sections, but to fight the pump you'll have to be a bit more creative. If a route is really crimpy, start with open crimps for as long as possible before switching to full crimps. If you can sneak a thumb under a hold, a thumbercling, you can take some of the pressure off your fingers. Start a pitch by using weaker fingers on thinner holds and gripping lightly, like grabbing with your pinky through middle before switching to your index middle and ring fingers. With pockets, use the weaker digits first while you still can. If you can hold onto something by using a wrist wrap, elbow wrap, open hand/palm, or even a jam then do so even if that's not the most secure way to hang on to it. Grab onto holds as lightly as possible maintaining the lowest level of security on the hold as possible. Grab as lightly as possible however long it takes to move your feet or other hand (or bumping the same hand) to a better hold, or from hold to hold increasing your grip as the need for security increases. Grabbing lightly is also very important when the rock quality is suspect.

If a hold is poor and you don't see a way around it, don't waste time and energy trying to make it better. The hold sucks; accept it and move past it quickly or down-climb to a better hold and regain your composure until you can fire past it.

Using your feet to grab the rock like your hands or to find balance points to provide mini rests is probably more important than how you use your hands. You wouldn't just press your palm into a nice incut hold after a pumpy section, you would grab it and use the incuts as an advantage. Do the same with your feet.

Moving Efficiently
Climbing quickly and even dynamically lessens the time spent on a pitch, on difficult holds, and can keep you ahead of the pump clock. Turn your brain off and climb quickly through the cruxes. Fire through big moves. If a pitch is sustained, climb at a constant speed, use holds as effectively as possible, and start looking for rests when you notice the pump coming. The lowest part of the route should be climbed as quickly and dynamically as possible. Climbing past clips, even skipping ones if it's safe, to find better clipping stances will save a ton of energy than struggling to clip the bolt, pulling up unnecessary slack (more dangerous than climbing up to the clip) and then struggling to clip the draw. Clipping or placing pro too high can also trick you into feeling more run-out than you really are because climb-

ing up to the clipped pro feels like you are climbing above it. By the time your waist actually reaches the bolt or pro, you feel like your ten feet out already. A good trick on the first clip is to place the rope over your shoulder. This also helps orient the rope out of your feet.

Rope over the shoulder for the first clip

Sewing it up also saps strength, especially if placing gear in the midst of a crux or pumpy section. The only way to overcome this fear is to practice falling. Doubling gear placements and gunning for rests can help you feel more secure if you are worried about the consequences of a piece blowing. Not trusting gear or falling, or not using your rack inefficiently by placing the wrong pieces at the wrong times or not using nuts will also train you to start bringing too much gear which will also slow you down and pump you out. If you overprotect and don't bring enough gear you may slow yourself down or pump out by all of a sudden finding yourself in bad situations. Over-chalking saps strength, so break the habit. Use liquid chalk at the start of a pitch, put some antiperspirant on your hands, or quickly wipe your palms on your pant leg.

Climbing calmly also helps reduce the pump by not wasting energy engaging unnecessary muscles. Relax your face, breathe calmly, and make your movements delicate and deliberate with relaxed arms and hands. Act like things are casual. When you need to gun it, don't second-guess yourself or movements. Go for it or rest until you are calm enough to fire through. Don't let fear or overexcitement slow you down on the sections you need to motor on.

MOVING AND MAINTAINING YOUR BASE OF SUPPORT

One of the keys to reaching a difficult hold, and avoiding the pump is to move your base of support via the above moves: X-position, frog position, backstep, drop-knee, inside flag, outside flag, and twistlock.

Press your hips in or push them out to establish stability on walls of varying steepness from slab to overhanging, or on odd features like corners, roofs, and arêtes.

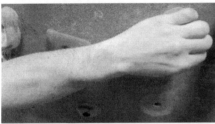

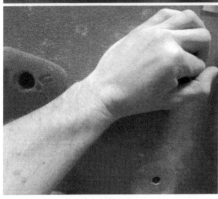

Keeping your forearm at 90° to the direction of the handhold or parallel to the crack when jamming. Note how fingers peel off when arm is turned out of position with the hold.

Applying maximum foot pressure on holds instead of passively resting them there is essential for almost all climbing. Push in rather than down on greasy footholds. Use the inside edge of your toe parallel to the hold and get the most surface area and stability possible. However, on steep routes using the outside edge will aid in balance as you twistlock and flag. Asymmetric shoes will help.

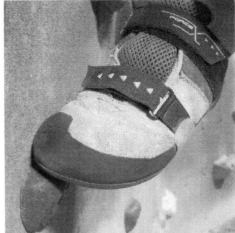

Just like with the hand/arms, placing your foot to cover maximum surface area keeps you from slipping off small slopey holds.

Grip and pull with your feet like you do with your hands. Place your feet inside holds and on holds, then grip with your toes and by flexing your foot. Try camming your toe in pockets and cracks on face climbs. This is one of the best ways to relieve your arms and get balanced on climbs.

Work on your timing when pushing with your feet. Firing with your arms before your feet will limit your power, reach, and pump you out.

PLANNING YOUR PITCHES

First decide if today is a performance day, a day you want to start figuring out some difficult routes, or just a fun day to blow off some steam. If you plan on crushing, don't pump yourself out on your warm-ups. Spend the morning doing easier routes or more difficult climbs you can climb without getting pumped. It takes experience to figure out how many warm-ups and what type of warm-ups to do to prime yourself for the send. A good method is to climb one route that doesn't give you a pump, another one or two routes that gives you about a 30% pump, and then one or two that pump out at about a 60% pump.

Generally you'll want to climb until one number grade below your project. If the wall doesn't offer much in the way of warm-ups you'll have to improvise by bouldering or just climbing a few bolts up. Now take a long rest. Eat lunch, walk around or do a light jog, and don't spend too much time belaying to get a total arm rest. If you get flash-pumped, take a solid break and do some warm-up exercises. The time of day is also important. You may find that you climb a lot better in the morning, afternoon, or even at the end of the day. A climb may be too hot or too cold to do at a particular time of the day as well. Cold weather helps with friction, but frozen hands and feet add a few grades to the climb. You may even need to save super hard slab or sloper climbs for a wintertime send. Plan for this. If you have multiple projects or pitches you want to send, try and order them to avoid pumping out at particular areas first. Start with technique intensive climbs to least technique intense climbs and from fingery climbs to bicep and shoulder intense climbs since large muscles tire out slower than smaller muscles.

REDPOINT AND ONSIGHTING
Redpointing Strategies
Visualizing is a commonly talked about strategy to redpoint climbs. Mentally rehearsing a climb in as much detail as possible wires your brain to learn the moves so when the time comes to perform, you aren't thinking, you're doing. To be able to visualize you need to be paying attention when working a route or you'll always be baffled or out of sequence.

To work a route, divide it up in sections. Your first attempt could be a bolt-to-bolt or gear-to-gear attempt. Clip in directly to each bolt, rest, figure out the moves in your head and see what happens. Don't work moves still clipped in direct, do it on the rope to avoid high factor falls onto the gear and to trust the rope. Your second attempt may still be bolt-to-bolt, or you may get a clip or two further. Lower back down to your last rest and try to get farther than where you last hung. This is where you should start taking some falls. Taking a fall or two (or more) on purpose can help get the pre-fall jitters out of the way.

By working a route in this way you should be really good at the lower sections compared to the upper sections. Working a route top-down is an excellent way to become familiar with the upper terrain where you're the most tired. If you've got the top dialed and are fresh and cruising on the bottom section you may be able to finally get it. The last area that may need work are the transitions between sections that stop you. Work the points on the route you find yourself taking or falling by starting below them instead of at them or just before them.

If cruxes are really hard you can try to to-prope through them with some weight off by a very tight belay, or using a power spot while bouldering (spotter pushes up on you). On baffling cruxes it is helpful to have practiced skills so you can reach into your bag of tricks. Mentally go through all the moves you could try, and try them however crazy. Top roping the crap out of a pitch for a headpoint or redpoint is a great way to deal with scary pitches. If a section is run out and you will be relying on one piece of gear to save your life, use locking biners on the gear and rope or double up on biners. Biners do fail, so it wouldn't hurt to be redundant in this situation. If it's a trad placement always use a long runner on mustn't fail pieces. See if you can cram in another piece of gear above, below, or if the crack is deep enough, place gear on top of each other.

Stick clipping, rodeo clipping, and leaving draws can help with redpoints on sport climbs. You can even bring the stick clip up with you for hard clips when working the route. To keep the rope in the first bolt after pulling the rope, clip the rope to your harness between the 1st and 2nd bolt while being lowered. Rodeo clipping is trying to clip the rope into a pre-placed quickdraw (must be overhanging to work) by twirling a bight like a lasso from the ground.

Put your foot above the tie-in knot...

By clipping into the rope here, the rope will remain through the lower quickdraw for another attempt.

Ticking holds can help, but be very sure to clean them off when you're done with the climb for the day. To get back on steep routes you can either jug, boing (bounce and have the belay pull in slack), or get a foot around the rope above you and pull yourself up while standing on the rope.

...and stand up. Grab a hold or the draw for the belayer to pull in the slack (or if too far and your gear is good, just let go and have the belayer pull in slack while you fall to get higher for the next go around).

Onsight Strategies
Before getting on an unknown route you really want to onsight, take the time to look

at the route. It's understandable to just want to hop on it without thinking to maintain your psyche or to avoid getting psyched out. But you can save yourself a lot of grief by fully scoping the route. The first step is to look at the guidebook if you have one. Scope the route from below, far away, and off to the sides. Binoculars are a great way to really scope a route. Even looking at it by climbing another route right next to it, looking down from the top, or even climbing a tree are acceptable onsight tools. Rappelling the route, asking advice, or watching someone else will really help, but this comes pretty close to the line between flashing (no beta) and onsighting a route if that matters to you. Look for chalk marks and tick marks, rests, good holds, bad holds, sucker holds, and hidden holds that don't climb directly in line with the bolts.

Make sure you are warmed up, actively stretch, and try to keep your breathing and heart rate down. Eat some sugar and have some water even if you're too psyched to bother. Clean your shoes giving them a good spit shine and rub them together to expose better rubber. Take a few minutes to just sit and chill in a quiet spot and visualize yourself sending it, climbing strong, fast, and fearless.

Once on the route you have to commit, don't fool yourself or succumb to fear and bad habits. You have to quench your fear of falling, climb through cruxes quickly, judge your pace, find rests if you need them, clip past bolts, and don't climb bolt-to-bolt or with the anchor as a goal. Don't just let go or take when you're pumped, climb until you fall. Don't forget that you can downclimb and still get an onsight if you get surprised by a bad hold or bad/no gear. Climb back down to a good spot or last available good gear, put in more gear and or shake out, then fire the blank or hard section.

Trad climbers should spend time sport climbing or top-roping to more safely find out how pumped they can really get before they really will fall. Pretend like you are on toprope. If you could TR this pitch without falling then you should be able to onsight it. If you're bouldering, increase your padding and get more spotters to ease your mind so you can focus on the moves.

Moving Fast
The best way to climb fast is to climb fast. Not Dan Osmand fast, but at a smooth non-stop speed. Conquering your fear of falling helps immensely. Standing around on lead doing nothing, however obvious that sounds, is worthless. Watching inexperienced parties just standing around doing nothing for literally hours is always a mesmerizing experience. The next best piece of advice is to work on speeding up your transitions. Knowing what to do and what to anticipate will make you move faster, as will confidence from mileage and success. Print out complicated things on a handy note card, like how to follow a pendulum, rig a haul, or a crevasse rescue if it's your first time or you're rusty. It's amazing how you can forget when you are tired or scared.

SPECIFIC DISCIPLINE STRATEGIES
Crack Technique
Just like using holds effectively, climbing a certain crack size the right way will less the pump on steep and unchanging sided cracks. Below is a list of crack sizes in order from small to wide. Taping suggestions are for those learning the size. The more experience you get, the less you will want to tape.

Hand and Body Parallel Cracks
Thumbs up jams are more restful, but are less secure. Thumbs up jams allow for alternating the leading hand (crossing over). Thumbs down jams are more secure due to the extra torque that occurs. Either way, torque your hand up or down, and bring

your elbow down and in line with the crack. Sometimes it can actually be helpful to have your elbow stick out on very difficult thumbs up jams, however. Alternating thumbs up and down jams by crossing over or shuffling can be an efficient way to climb faster and compromise stability. Double thumbs down jams lend more easily to shuffling vs. crossing over. There is no hard and fast rule, however. If you get stuck, change your hand position. I added common Camalot and Alien sizes for a men's medium sized hand.

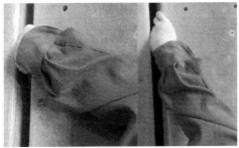

Elbow out (insecure) vs in (secure)

Tips
Partial laybacking and smearing. Trim your cuticles for this and tight fingers. Green and smaller alien.

Tight Fingers
Combo of tips and tight locks. Pinkie in first may be the only thing possible for smaller quasi-jams, and index in for wider (and easier to cam). Green-Yellow Alien.

Fingers
Perfect! Thumbs up on leading hand. Shuffle or cross through with lower hand thumbs up or down. Yellow-Grey Alien.

Off-Fingers (Rattily Fingers)
These are like little offwidths for your fingers and are just about the hardest size to master. Put your fingers in thumbs down possibly stacking your fingers adding your thumb if needed) as far as you can, sticking your elbow straight out, then torque your elbow down. Stack your fingers. Place your thumb on the outside of the crack to press in while your fingers twist or thumb cam by pressing your thumb into one side of the crack and fingers on the other. Rand smear with your shoe or try and get some toe in the crack, keep your hands and feet high, and climb very very fast. You may want to tape your first two to three fingers and your thumb joint. Thin slippers work well, but edging shoes could also be the ticket depending on the lip of the crack. Tape your middle finger through thumb. Depending on the pain levels, you may need more than one coat of tape. Painkillers may be in order! Purple Camalot.

Super Tight Hands or Super Loose Fingers (Ringlocks)
These are similar to off fingers, but a little wider. Tape your first three fingers and your thumb knuckle with one or more wraps. Start by placing your thumb in the crack (thumb up) and then stack your index finger (and possibly your middle) over the nail of the thumb followed by stacking the other fingers in the crack above the thumb. Keep your hand high, and shuffle. Only cross through if you can muster the strength. Try and get a little toe jam and torque hard. Keep your feet close and high using opposing pressure (frog position). Your lower hand may be able to sneak into a thin hand jam to save some strength. Painkillers may be in order! Green Camalot.

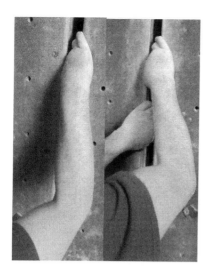

Tight Hands
Use a light tape job over your knuckles. Top hand thumbs down, bottom hand thumbs up and shuffle. The key is using thin, flat-toed slippers with a small amount of protection over the toes (sticky rubber, Seam Grip) and really stuffing those hands in good before you toque on them. Red Camalot.

Hands
Heaven! Standard tape job or hand jammies for this and above. Overgripping (or over camming) will tire you out, use as little strength as necessary to keep you from falling (good advice for everything actually). Gold Camalot.

Off-Hand (Cups)
Still not too bad. Tape a little thicker, including your thumb. Cup your hands to make them bigger. Blue Camalot.

Fists
Keep your thumb in front (and knuckle out of the way) of your fist for standard jams, and place your thumb outside your fist for wider fists (ouch, tape your thumb)! Tape well, including possibly your forearm and ankle. These take practice to feel secure on, kind of like trusting your feet for the first time on a slab. These should not be too bad once you get the hang of it. Palms up and palms down are just like thumbs up and down. Shuffling with the top palm down and bottom palm up help with insecure sections.

Off-Fists (Butterfly)
Cross your arm and place your hands back-to-back palms out. Tape your forearm, even up to your elbow depending on the depth for the rest of the sizes. The feet are usually the crux on this size. Grey Camalot.

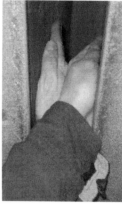

Fist Stacks
As the crack gets bigger, start combining things. Experiment with crossing or not crossing arms, and if crossed, then experiment with which hand is on the top of the cross. As the crack widens, go from a vertical fist/hand to a horizontal fist/hand. Double fist stack are really insecure, and at this point you can probably get in an arm bar. Grey Camalot and bigger.

Photo courtesy Zac Robinson

Chicken Wing and Arm Bar

Wear a tough shirt, or tape your elbows. A sticky rubber elbow sleeve can help. These are disastrous positions for your shoulders. You can cam elbows up or elbows down, but you probably will want them down for the most part to push off of to gain upwards momentum. Chicken wings are better for rests, and arm bars are better for gaining upwards progress or when chicken wings won't fit. The other arm Gaston's on the lip of the crack. Big gear.

Chicken Wing. Photo copyright Cathy Pierce/Dave Elder

Arm bar

Feet

Feet, even in thin cracks, are generally placed in sideways (pinky toe down), and torquing the knee in line with the crack. If the crack gets to thin, the feet will need to use face holds or smearing on the outside of the crack. When faced with excruciating or thin foot jamming, practice finding anything to use as a foothold, like the corner of the crack. In all cases, look for even the smallest constrictions or pods to sink your hands and feet. Thin or tight jamming requires flat thin slippers or softer lace-ups. Cover the top of the foot with Stealth Paint or Seam Grip. You may need to tape over your toe knuckles to deal with the pain. Having someone stand on your toes to flatten them before the pitch can actually help. Use stiffer or thicker edging shoes for when the crack gets wider (hand jams and above), or for mixed crack/face climbing. High tops help protect the inevitable ankle scraping that occurs in wide cracks.

Stealth Paint and taping over toes. *Cutting off half a sock to keep over the toes is another option.*

Smear

Too small to jam your pinky toe. Still keep the pinky toe down, and find inconsistencies in the crack, or if one side of the crack juts out a little more. Look for anything with the non-smearing foot to help on the outside wall. Press like hell.

Toe Jam

Work that pinkie toe into the crack. The thinner and softer the shoe the better. Horribly painful.

Foot Jam

As you work your toes in, the crack becomes a foot jam

Foot Cam

Tape your ankles. When you can no longer get a foot jam, turn your foot in and/or up at an angle to increase its width. Continue to try to jam, but increase the rotational torque and/or upwards or downwards slant of your foot. See Leavittation.

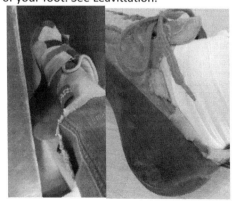

Off-Foot Cam

Tape your ankles. This is just awful. Your foot cam becomes worthless and it is too small for a heel-toe or knee jam. You have two solutions. One is to wear your approach shoes which is usually the best solution. The other is to employ every other possible foot maneuver you can to cheat by trying to find something, anything on the face, inside the crack, or the lip of the crack.

Heel-Toe

This can be pretty secure. Use your outside foot whenever possible.

T-Stacks

Stacking your feet in a "T" position sucks. Maybe just for a quick rest. Try instead to force a heel toe or shove your leg in harder.

Calf Jam, Knee, Thigh-Bar/Jam

Tape up your limb – ankles to calf, or wear a compression sleeve. Tape your pant opening onto your leg. As the crack widens, get more and more leg in there! Torqueing the foot on the leg attached to the jam will help a lot. Usually it's pretty hard to get both limbs in, so the other leg generally smears, finds holds on the face or lip, or it cams the toe on the outside of the crack.

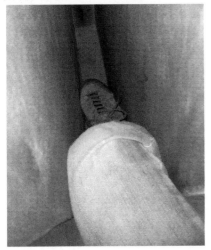

Butt Jam
Don't wear your nice pants. Once you can get your butt in there, things get easy again.

Difficult Hand and Foot Combinations
Flaring Cracks
Just like the offset cams needed to protect these nasty's, you need to have your hand jam two separate sizes at the same time. Really paste your hand in there, and adopt the most productive jam possible with the outer part of your hand. You must torque more sideways then down the wider the angle of flare. Feet should smear and torque. Have some painkillers handy as you turn your hands and feet into human copperheads.

Leavittation
This is a way to ascend difficult off-widths that require stacked hands, but are too wide for a decent foot to jam. You usually start with a knee jam (can be calf, thigh, etc.) as high as possible that is torqueing hard to keep you in. The other leg/foot has the top of toe cammed on the outside face/lip of the crack. Cam and torque and engage your abs (they are doing a lot of the work here). The upper foot cam (knee or whatever) is torqueing hard and the bottom foot is torqueing/pressing to help stabilize. Now work your stacked hands higher while levering off the outside foot and pushing with jammed knee. Gastoning and side pulling off the lip helps you reset your hands. Do not expect to gain much height or to climb quickly. Endure. There is an excellent video by Leavitt himself posted on Vimeo.com. Yosemite and Indian Creek have some good cracks to try this technique out.

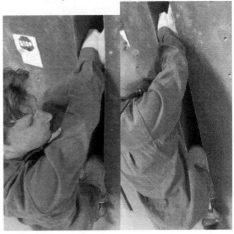

Inversion
To get around off-width roofs you will sometimes need to invert your foot above head! Abs of steel are required. To get upside-down, you can kick-over using momentum gained by using your abs. Depending on the steepness and width you can get a calf lock, or heel/toe cam. To gain altitude, either shuffle your hands up, or pivot out of the invert. To do this you again use your abs, possibly pawing on the outside of the crack, to re-establish a hand-stack. The benefits of going upside-down are to use more powerful legs and abs to take weight off the shaky hands and arms, and to get a more secure heel/toe lock to move from. If you can't gain progress or your stacks aren't doing it for you, try inversion. Once past the initial weirdness of the notion, it can be the best way up. There are many climbs in Indian Creek, Mt Woodrow, and Vedauwoo where you can try this out.

Photo courtesy TJ Brumme

Photo courtesy Russ Walling

Sidewinder

Tape everything or wear some heavy clothes. This is a technique used inside hard squeeze chimneys where feet are too wide for heel-toe and T-stacks aren't working. One trick is to use the "sidewinder" technique of getting into a sideways position (head slightly higher than feet). Press with your elbows, knees, palms, butt, and soles of your shoes. Chicken-wing, cam your hip and butt, and knee bar simultaneously. To move up, worm your way loosening, tightening, and camming with your chicken-wing, hip/butt, and knee bar. Craig Luebben invented this one on the climb, you guessed it, Sidewinder.

Sidewinder technique

Worm and Shoulder Scrunch

Soft kneepads are very nice, and you probably will want to tape your ankles and elbows. Tight chimneys that allow a bit more movement than the "sidewinder" can be ascended by worming your way up, inch by inch. Chest cams done by breathing in and relaxing out of the cam are helpful. Steck-Salathe anyone?

Chimney

Kneepads are useful and tape your elbows. Counter pressure between the soles of your shoes, knees, back, and arms (chicken-wing through palming) are the name of the game. Once the chimney widens, turn sideways and stem/palm. Epinephrine anyone?

Body Stem
I actually fell out of one of these and faceplanted canyoneering as a teenager. Once you can no longer stem sideways, you must invert. Ament's chimney in the Black Canyon has a section you can test your skills on.

Placing Gear
Certain crack sizes can present some problems for trad climbers. As mentioned, placing gear in cruxes will pump you out. Look for rests and fire between them, doubling up on gear instead of constantly placing it, if necessary. Placing gear in thin cracks can fill up the space needed to jam or fingerlock, or it can have the draw hang over needed holds, pinching your fingers. Place your gear low after climbing through a section, or set the gear deep and jam in front of the gear. Don't set your nuts too much if you want them back or want to do the route quickly. As mentioned, doubling up on placements then gunning to a rest or next logical spot is not only more energy efficient, but it also keeps you paying attention to the climbing instead getting gear tunnel vision.

Offwidths and Chimneys
You can attach a long sling or daisy to your belay loop and attach a large cam if you need to slide the cam up for a long ways, especially if leapfrogging large cams. This is one instance where clipping directly into the rope can complicate things because rope drag on the upper cam can make it hard to push the cam, and z-clipping becomes even more likely. Just make sure you don't take a fall onto the cams if clipped directly to them. If you don't weight the cams, it still counts as a send.

Just because the guidebook says so or the crack just looks like it, it doesn't mean you won't find a nut or smaller cam placement somewhere. Leapfrogging cams up a long pitch of the same size may be necessary if that's all you got. This usually occurs with wider cracks since you can easily carry four or more of the smaller sizes, hand cracks are easier to run it out. If you have cams of the same size, you can leapfrog those cams until you reach a point on the pitch that you can start leaving one cam at a time behind to adequately protect the pitch. If placements are anything but bomber, you may even need to leapfrog three cams at a time (staying clipping or tethered into two at a time instead of just one) so you're not just relying on one cam for a long ways. Leapfrogging takes a lot of energy, so if in doubt, bring additional gear.

If you plan on leaving your cam and going for it, place the final cam before you get too pumped. If you're not inspired to go for it and continue leapfrogging, then you will wind up in the ironic situation of being at the anchor with both cams needed to protect the pitch and a lot of air below you!

You might need to ditch the pack, your helmet, chalk bag, or anything else on your harness inside squeeze chimneys. You can hang your gear off your harness with a long sling, use another rope with a fifi to get it back, or haul it separately. Put your gear sling over your neck and in front of you and make sure the rope is between your legs so it doesn't get trapped or pinched in a place you can't reach. Chalk bags with buckles can get unclipped so use tat to tie in an overhand so it doesn't get pulled off. Rotate the chalk bag in front of you. Before becoming horribly stuck, move other gear around on your harness. You may need to clip your approach shoes on your front gear loops, or put your camera somewhere it won't get smashed.

Choss
If you're privileged enough to only have climbed on clean, immaculate routes, then there are a few things to know if you wind

up climbing on choss. As a partner once said about climbing choss, "I love it, everything can be a jug!" You really want a helmet on you and your partner. Consider bailing if you don't have helmets. Choss can be controlled by distrusting every hand and foothold, however big. Look for fractures around large objects, even ledges and large pillars. Push in and down, like you are trying to keep the holds on the wall rather than prying them off. Your partner and the rope are the main target in choss. You are usually safer than the belayer unless you fall and the gear blows out or you sever the rope. Double ropes are perfect for this terrain. Besides watching out for what you grab, kick, or stand on, look out for what the rope may knock off. Rope drag from pinning the rope away from sketchy blocks may be better than having it in harm's way. Your belayer needs to be well to the side. If this is not an option, do short pitches to minimize impact. When you are descending down loose terrain you either want to be right on top of your partner to limit acceleration impact, or let one person go first and have them turn a corner and out of the way before you go.

Big Walls
Visualize and plan out your gear for walls that require jugging, hauling, and aiding well in advance. This will save you weight by not bringing too much, and save you trouble by realizing that you need a lot more lockers, etc. (don't skimp on lockers and slings on walls, they vanish). Figure out how many biners, lockers, slings, jugs, aiders, GriGri's, ratchets, pulleys, anchor slings, ropes, etc. that you need on paper. Toss in a few extra slings and biners. Knowing exactly what gear to swap at the belay saves hours. The leader may not need any jugs for example, or he/she may need at least one for setting up a 3:1 haul system. You must remember to trade out that extra jug during changeovers for example. Forgetting to give the leader the haul line or tag line can be disastrous. The leader may need to start out with two anchor slings complete with two free biners each and a locker on the first pitch before swapping leads. If there's a lot of crap, put it on a notecard and look at it during changeovers.

Ice & Mixed
Mileage, especially top-roping and headpointing, is the best way to improve your ice climbing. Listen to and feel your sticks and practicing climbing as efficiently as possible. Look for gear and practice placing it. Comfortably placing gear and knowing where to get it, trusting sticks and your crampons, and climbing quickly are all you need to lead hard ice. Leading hard ice is all about being efficient. The less you swing and time spent on lead, the easier a pitch will feel.

Never put gear in thin pillars or columns that could break or snap off. Pillars can snap off in very cold weather, farther up than you think. If a pillar is very thin, hook and use small taps with your tool.

Stem as much as possible, and incorporate as much rock movement to get weight off your arms and to find balance. Learn to match, and use higher grips. Don't overgrip, and be sure to shake out! Use natural features on the ice with your crampons. Don't just kick steps all the way up. And of course keep those heels down. Placing gear at waist level on steep terrain becomes a vital skill.

Getting good at climbing in a T-pattern vs. climbing in a splayed out X-pattern is a critical skill in climbing efficiently. Get a good placement as high as you can with one tool, usually slightly off to the side. Kick up to your tool weighting your feet, not your arms, while pulling your lower tool in a smooth motion.

X Position – should've moved up on that left tool before swinging the right tool.

T Position (bring feet up to right tool and stand before placing left tool higher).

Even with a pack full of clothes, staying warm ice climbing can be difficult and counterintuitive. Food fuels the furnace and it can be a real chore to stop and eat on an ice climb. You may not feel hungry or want to stop and eat due to cold or anxiety. Stuff your pockets with snacks that you really enjoy, not astronaut food. This mean gummies, candy, and fatty snacks. Make hot sweet tea or cocoa in your Nalgene – even hot soup. Throw the nutrition chapter out the window, especially if you are dieting. Eat a greasy spoon breakfast before you head out. The cold will seep in long before you feel the need to eat or drink so make it

a priority and an easy one to accomplish by planning ahead. Long belays get cold no matter what, but this doesn't mean you should just stand there looking up. Keep moving at the belay, and don't wait to do so until you get cold. Do squats, leg kicks and raises, windmills, and shoulder shrugs. It is easier to stay warm than to get warm so keep on top of it.

The Swing

To swing a tool you need a relaxed grip to let the tool do the work and to allow it to rotate down at the end of the swing. Your wrist should be straight, not flexed – a very common mistake. This not only pumps your forearm, but reduces circulation. Your fingers should wrap around the outside of the tool, not the front, with the pinky and ring finger more bent than your middle and index. The swing is initiated with your torso and lats, not your shoulder. When the tool accelerates forwards let your elbow extend, don't try and clench your biceps. When your arm is extended at the elbow past 90° the momentum of the tool and gravity carries the tool forward. The power of your swing comes from your core, lats, and pecs. Your triceps now engage here in one quick "turbo boost" to speed up the final arc of the swing. Just before contact, your radial deviators give the tool one final flick, like you would throw a playing card or Chinese throwing star.

During this final flick, the ice tool rotates around the pinky on the grip rest. A chokehold on the tool won't allow this important final rotation - you almost want to let go. Big spikes on the bottom of your tools also limit this rotation. Imagine there's no ice to swing in and you are going to huck your tool like an ax tossing contest. Without the follow through (important in every other swinging sport) your swing and your performance will suffer. You aren't chopping wood, the shape of your tool and pick aren't designed for a chopping motion, and this is how most beginners attempt to swing. You have to tighten your grip and reduce your fluidity when hooking or mixed climbing, just like you would change from a drive to a chip to a putt in golf. Practice getting good first swings, sticks, and minimizing repeatedly kicking into the same place with your crampons. Small frequent kicks to gain upward momentum helps minimize effort and ice displacement. Pre-tapping your intended placement will help with accuracy and won't pump you out any more.

How to grip the tool and how to let it rotate

Bulges

Clearing bulges is one of the more difficult movements in ice climbing. Remember to save a good screw just before a top-out. The ice is often terrible or non-existent when the climb transitions from steep to flat, and there's a good chance you've ran it out a bit to here. Many accidents happen at this transition so be safe. To clear a bulge or go from steep to flat, keep your knees bent and your arms straight. Keep your weight over your crampons and take small steps. Do not lean forward as this will disengage your crampons. If fishing around for a hook under powder snow over rock on top, resist the temptation to commit to any hook that stops your pick. Test it well and keep constant pressure in line with your tool as you top out to avoid levering your pick off. You will be psyched on that screw you placed just below the lip.

Hooking Ice

Know when to hook and when to hammer away. Hooking is much faster and less strenuous, but it takes knowledge when to trust it and when to get a stick. Hook when you are at or just above gear and swing when you start to run it out. Learn to swing well before you start hooking. A solid tug on the tool is similar to testing an aid placement. If it holds a tug then it (should) hold you, especially if you're weighting your crampons and other tool. On thin ice and mixed, stacking pick placements (placing one pick on top of the other) can help you get higher without displacing as much ice.

Mixed Holds

When mixed climbing on sketchy holds and moving off them, pretend like there's a hot cup of coffee balanced on the pick (from Will Gadd). When hooking, always place constant downward pressure. On slopers, angle the pick perpendicular to the greatest surface area and apply counter pressure with your lower body. When pick camming, you want to apply constant sideways pressure. Moving your hand up the tool or getting high on a tool in an insecure hook or cam can pop you off in an instant so maintain body tension and pressure while moving smoothly. Learn how to maintain this pressure while positioning the rest of your body or other tool to balance and continue upwards motion. After you've learned to maintain your hold you can start applying more complicated rock climbing-type maneuvers. You ice tool is a much better hold than just about any rock grip and the temptation to switch to using your hands means you may need more practice.

Knowing how to stash your tool when placing gear is critical. Each has its own set of advantages and disadvantages.

Pinching the pick between your thumb and tool you are hanging on (my favorite), over the shoulder (least secure), in a holster (needs to fit snug - especially if the tool is hammerless), clipped to a biner/ice clipper (most secure). Some high end climbers will wrap tape in their favorite spot to hold the tool in their mouth.

BEFORE YOU GO

The big trip enders are partners (see mental training chapter), gear issues (see gear chapter), and weather (see weather chapter). The number one trip ender is yourself.

Prepare for plan B – D, possibly stashing some **extra kit in your car.** Picking out the perfect superlight rope and rack setup with minimal bivy gear, etc., won't help much if you wind up changing plans to cragging at a campground instead. Research your climb by actually reading everything about the approach, climb, and descent before you go. Check the weather on multiple weather sites and don't use wishful thinking if it looks bad. Sometimes you get away with an inaccurate forecast, but most times you don't. Decide whether it's worth the chance and not climbing anything, or changing plans. Having too much psych for one particular route can squander your actual climbing time and keep you from progressing as a climber. If there's a chance that your route has a massive line-up on it, be sure to bring some other route topos and even some special gear if those routes require it. If you plan on doing a trip and are blasting from school/work, a stressful day, or have a very long car ride don't expect to perform well. Try and get a rest day or just do the hike in. If you do climb hard the next day, expect to crash at some point - if it's a long trip this can ruin it.

Try and foresee all that can go wrong and preplan for it. For example, every climbing trip usually requires total reliance on your car working properly as most climbs don't have public transportation to trailheads. Many a climb has been ruined because of car troubles, or not having the proper equipment handy to fix minor problems.

Forgetting basic equipment is another common trip ender. You can get away without many forgotten items or replace them on the road, but forgetting major non-replaceable items can waste a lot of gas and time. Checking at the trailhead at 6 am is pretty useless when you don't have a rope. Check at home and call your partner to check with them while retailers are still open the day before. Your alpine start may have to wait until 10 am if the gear shop has closed for the day if neither of you have a fuel canister, for example. Another comforting bit of knowledge is knowing that your partner's gear isn't sketchy or inadequate for your needs. Nothing is worse than saying "you bring the rack and I'll bring the rope" and your partner pulls out a rack of off-brand cams with slings that need serious replacing. If you really like your setup, bring it along when you meet-up to divvy up gear in case you don't like your partner's setup. You can always leave it in the car. Double check that you both have necessary first aid and safety gear, and a repair kit for items you fully rely on to complete the climb. If you weren't on top of repairing and replenishing items in your kit, make sure you take care of it before you go.

Remember your first aid and self-rescue basics, and if the climb requires advanced techniques be sure to practice on the ground. Quiz your partner on these to make sure he/she is also up to speed. If you suspect they aren't, spend a day practicing or even teaching. If you head up a big wall without doing this, I can almost guarantee failure or very long belays.

Finally, take care of even minor body issues and health concerns that can inflate into trip-enders. Things usually don't get better, so take the time to fix or prevent whatever could seriously bother you.

CHAPTER ELEVEN: TECHNICAL SYSTEMS

ANCHORS

When you fall you are accelerating, causing an increase in the force you will generate on your gear or anchor. When you hit your gear, your force must be less than the force the piece is rated to and the quality of the placement. If it is not, your gear will blow. What happens next is a common misconception. Sometimes force is not removed from the system by that piece blowing. Distance between gear, holding power of the gear, and the amount of time the gear holds you for are all variables.

One major variable is impulse (kilonewton-seconds), or how long that piece held for. The longer a piece of gear absorbs your force, the less you will continue to build force and velocity as you continue to fall further. The next piece could receive a similar, smaller hit, or even greater hit depending on how many kilonewton seconds the original piece held for. If the piece that blew didn't absorb much, you continue accelerating, and your velocity and force could be greater by the time your reach your next piece. So don't think that shaky piece will slow you down.

The rope will regain a lot (but not all) of its elastic properties quickly between pieces, but knot tightening, which absorbs quite a bit of force, will not be a factor after the first piece blows. So if the next piece is the same or worse – it will probably rip. The farther it is between placements the faster you'll be going due to acceleration, and the more force you'll hit the following piece of gear. This is the dreaded zipper effect. So sew it up, or better yet, equalize and combine strengths of marginal placements.

Besides rope and sling stretch, slip from your belay device (little to none with a Gri-Gri), a dynamic belay, reduced friction via rope management pulleys, and screamers among other things will absorb quite a bit of force. Knot tightening on the lead ropes (and all systems) helps reduce impact force quite a bit. Loosen knots, or switch rope ends and re-tie.

Anchor Forces

Anchor material made from nylon will stretch a bit and absorb some force, Dyneema will not. If a direct fall occurs onto the anchor – the same zipper effect can occur. Three pieces rated individually less than the force applied by the falling leader will all pull either by the rating of the gear itself or by its placement. If there isn't good equalization, the piece that takes the initial weight would blow, then the next, and the next. Horizontal anchors in poor rock or placements are at the highest risk. Equalization of your anchor is more important when the gear is bad, and with good anchors it is important to emphasize redundancy. Take the time to create an equalized anchor using the systems described later.

It is nice to know that you rarely, or ever, hear of entire anchors failing. Just keep in mind that the rope is a useful tool in creating an anchor because it absorbs way more force than cord and slings, and is way stronger. Don't use crappy gear for anchors. If that's not a reality, then your body should be the object absorbing the force before the gear. Unequalized anchors and anchors with extension are only as good as the best piece. Perfect equalization is difficult. Protect the anchor by getting in bomber gear ASAP. Screamers can even find their way into anchor or first piece. This is a good reason to tie into the anchor with the rope, have a piece to oppose the force of you being lifted up very far (especially if the anchor mainly protects a downwards pull), and to have the leader put a good piece in right off the belay, not just clipping a piece off the anchor. You can even use the rope itself to equalize your anchor.

Sling and Rope Strength

I mentioned that nylon absorbs force via stretch, and Dyneema (Spectra/Dynex) does not. Even a short static fall (like clipped in direct to a bolt) can generate huge forces, and it's very possible break a sling rated to 22 kN. DMM did some tests with nylon and Dyneema slings by subjecting them to factor 1 falls (up half the length of the sling) and factor 2 falls (extended at the full length of the sling). The Dyneema slings broke on the 3rd factor 1 fall, nylon did not. The Dyneema slings broke on the first factor 2 fall, the nylon survived all three drops. Knotting the slings drastically reduced the slings strength. None of the slings survived a single knotted factor 2 fall, however the nylon did survive a knotted factor 1 fall (Dyneema didn't). This situation is very important when clipping in direct and working moves above the bolt vs. using the rope. Never climb above gear attached to a sling, daisy, or even a PAS. I'll repeat: DO NOT FALL DIRECTLY ONTO A SLING, DAISY, or PAS. Another common scenario would be shock loading a daisy chain at the anchor, or shock loading the anchor itself. One more reason to tie directly into the anchor with the rope. It keeps the anchor from getting shock loaded, and your daisy chain from being shock loaded. Use your tether as a backup and for balance. See the gear chapter for more information on using Dyneema vs. nylon slings.

Your 22 kN cordalette isn't 22 kN by the time you've made your anchor. Doubling up cord and slings (two strands coming off a piece) almost doubles its strength. It is a bit less than double since the tight bend over the biner weakens the cord. Knots really reduce the strength of the cord, however. The following information comes from a 2001 Seattle Mountaineers article and the numbers may not be completely accurate, but they do show a trend. Super strong Technora (tech cord) loses 60% of its strength when knotted, and sewn Dyneema cords lose half (48%) of their strength (also according to Mammut). Breaking strength of a Dyneema cord is around 22 kN, so doubling it makes it 44 kN – but the knot brings them back down to 22 kN minus sharp bends, and much more if other knots are on the gear. 7 mm Nylon cord only loses 8% of its 12 kN strength in comparison, so when doubled then knotted total strength is about 20 kN. - pretty close to Dyneema and Technora. Clove hitches on your pieces reduce the strength even more, as does repeated bending over time or by going over biners, wrapping, etc. Technora loose a ton of strength when repeatedly flexed – up to 45% additional loss – kind of pointless if you ask me. Spectra loses much strength with repeated flexing (no published number) and nylon loses almost none.

6-7 mm nylon cordalettes are extremely useful because you can cannibalize them for rappelling, and offer some dynamic properties for anchors. I would only use Dyneema, web-o-lettes, or fancy low bulk/high strength anchor systems for scenarios where there is little to no chance of shock-loading the anchor and extra slings are not required for bailing.

Building Anchors
Your anchor should be the most solid section between you and the next belay. Regardless of how you setup anchors, having bomber gear takes priority over everything.

Poor Anchor Spot
If you can't build a good anchor, seriously consider down-climbing to a better crack system and deal with a hanging belay, or simulclimb to a better spot – both options are much safer. If a great ledge has bad cracks you could climb a bit higher, place a few bomber pieces, and lower back down to the ledge, belaying through the anchor above you. The worst case scenario is having to belay your partner up with a miserable anchor, or worse, have them jug off your body. If a pre-existing anchor is equalized with tat, back it up with at least one of your own slings or rope.

Good Anchors
Two bolt anchors in good rock are bomber, and it is acceptable to clip in to one bolt and belay off the other bolt as long as you use a runner to connect them if they aren't already with chain. Equalizing bolts is a good habit, but if your anchor material is knotted and winds up being rated less than a single bolt (usually around 22 kN each when placed well) you just made the system weaker! A good set up for belaying off two bolts would be to at least tie in to one of the bolts with a rope. In gear intense climbs using two bomber pieces is also acceptable instead of the standard three pieces.

Vertically equalized pieces (one above the other) are stronger than horizontally equalized pieces. The closer horizontal pieces are to each other, the stronger they are as the angle between them is decreased. However, the closer pieces are, the more the solid nature of the rock or ice comes into question. If a chunk breaks, you're in trouble. This is especially important when creating ice anchors. However, horizontally spread out anchors are usually easier to deal with rope and anchor management, especially when hauling on big walls.

Putting in a bomber piece, tethering into it, and yelling off belay before working on the rest of the anchor saves time. It's better to have one solid piece in quickly than to take forever figuring out the perfect belay, especially if you are low on gear. You obviously want a safe anchor, but forces are not going to be as high belaying a follower than protecting a leader on an anchor fall. So you may want to wait to make the perfect anchor when the follower comes up with the gear you really need to finish the anchor. When leading up and you start to slow down because your gear is dwindling, you're tired, or you're not sure about the next section ahead it could be a lot faster for you to just make a belay if you're quick on your transitions. Doing this can make leading the rest of the pitch much faster than taking forever getting to the intended belay spot. Don't forget about terrain anchors for quick belays. Moats, the down side of a slope, giant boulders, incut ledges, etc., all make for great quick belays just off your harness. Make sure that if the next pitch is technical there will be pro very soon on the next lead. See if you can use those nuts and tricams to put in the anchor, or at least cams that aren't as important on the next pitch, so you can give the leader the gift of an extra cam that fits.

Using the Rope

The rope is your strongest, lightest, and stretchiest method of anchoring in. The only major downside is that it makes escaping the belay or establishing transitions for self-rescue more difficult, but this is a pretty weak argument. You can use your rope as a cordalette by equalizing the slack and tying a master point and then tying in tight into the master point. Cloving in direct to each piece works only when your gear is bomber. If a piece isn't bomber, then equalize it to the other, and clip into the sling you used to equalize instead of a single piece.

Cloving each piece with the rope

Equalizing three pieces with the rope

Standard Setups

Never just clip in with a daisy. If attaching directly to the anchor with a tether (even a PAS), you must be certain that there is no way that the leader could take a fall directly onto the anchor or take a high factor fall and pull you off the anchor very forcibly.

565

Things get more serious if belaying the follower off your harness or redirecting through the anchor. Now you should also use the rope and be tied in tight, facing the direction of pull. When tying into the master point of an equalized anchor, it's a good idea to also tie in to the best piece with the rope as a backup.

Using slings or **cordalettes** to connect anchor points helps to equalize or prevent extension. It's better to equalize two pieces than three at a time and attach everything at same point, as it's almost impossible to create a 3+ piece anchor with no extension and perfect equalization. When all is said and done, it is most important that the anchor is equalized in the direction of pull a leader would take falling onto the anchor. Cordalettes work best with two bomber pieces when the direction of pull can be anticipated easily. One arm of a cordalette will always be shorter than another arm and the short arm will receive more of the load. This is why it is better to have multiple sets of two piece equalized anchors connected together than several pieces equalized on a cordalette. Because the short arm receives the bulk (sometimes all) of the load, failure of each arm of the cordalette could be successive – so the pieces are more redundant than equalized. Nylon stretches so the load is shared more evenly. Not the case with Dyneema or Tech cords!

To make a good 3+ piece anchor that deals with equalization and extension issues you have several options. With relatively decent gear placements it is better to worry about extension than equalization between all three pieces. As stated, it's almost impossible to equalize three pieces without creating extension. Using a cordalette in all three pieces by pulling the strands equally and tying a master point is probably the most common method, but is far from perfect because it requires you to perfectly estimate the direction of pull. Even then, equalization is far from perfect, and there will be an inch or so of extension on at least one piece.

Standard 3-piece cordalette

You can equalize two pieces with clove hitches on each piece or by tying a master point between the two. Put in a third piece and use another sling to add it to the system. Get it tight using cloves or wraps. Now you have two independent systems equalized against the middle piece. This 3rd piece can be placed as the first piece of pro for the next pitch, or can be removed to give to the leader if a bomber piece can be placed immediately off the belay since it is an independent – as long as the other two pieces are bomber.

Two pieces equalized with a third piece added in

If you put in more than three pieces, combine equalized sets of two, limiting extension by getting things tight using wraps or clove hitches.

Two independent sets of two connect at master point. I used clove hitches on the left to get the length right.

Some climbers tie the ends of their cordalette into figure 8's on a bight, aka a **snake cord**. To safely use a snake cord, clip both fig-8's on a bight into the same piece of gear instead of one end to separate pieces.

Snake Cord setup so each piece uses two arms

Sliding X's do a great job with equalization, but create large amounts of extension. With really crappy gear, it's much better to worry about equalization than to worry about extension in the system. A sliding X creates great equalization, but allows for an incredible amount of extension. If equalizing three pieces, be sure to twist both loops coming down! You can tie extension limiting knots that won't interfere with equalization in sliding X scenarios. The closer the knot, the less equalization (bad) but less extension (good). Sliding X's are great to use on lead to equalize questionable pieces.

Three piece sliding-X

Sliding X with extension limiting knots

If you have a lot of cord left you can tie a big overhand on a bight on one of the arms. This shortens the length of the cordalette. If you do it on the arm of a bomber piece, you can clip into the bight with for an added backup.

One arm shortened and used to belay off of.

Equalettes and ACRs

One solution to manage the comprise between extension and equalization when making anchors with a cordalette is the **equalette**. To make an equalette, get a length of cord about 20' long and tie the ends with double fisherman's knots. Tie two overhand limiter knots ten inches apart in the middle, trying to keep the double fisherman's knot just slightly to the side of one of the limiter knots.

Pre-tied equalette

For a two piece anchor, connect each arm piece-to-piece. The master point is between the two limiter knots. It is much safer to clip in to both strands with two lockers, one on each strand. If just clipping one, put a twist in one strand like a sliding-X. This creates an equalized system with minimal extension.

Using two lockers (L) and one with a twist (R)

For a three piece anchor, clip one arm to a piece of gear and use clove hitches to connect the other two pieces so that everything has equal tension. For four pieces, use clove hitches on everything. You will note that any cloved piece will only have one strand of cord coming off of it. For the ultimate in safety you can double up the equalette, nicknamed the "quad". Double up the cord before tying the limiter knots. By constructing the equalette or quad at home you will be able to quickly deploy it and create good anchors without any added time.

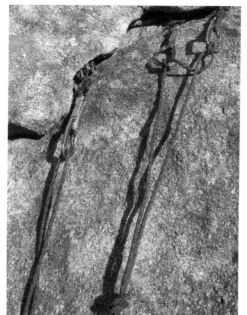

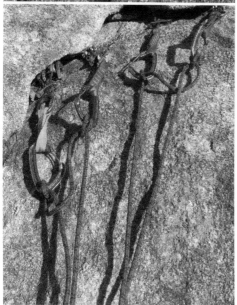

Three piece (above) and four piece anchor with equalette.

The **Trango Alpine Equalizer and the Alpine Cock Ring (ACR)** both attempt to equalize multiple pieces evenly by using a sliding ring or rap ring. The whole point of the ACR and the Trango is that friction is greatly reduced to further increase equalization compared to using just cord or slings. Pieces do become equalized quite well with both systems, more so with the Trango. The ACR is a lot cheaper to make, the nylon cord provides some added dynamic properties, and it can be cannibalized for other uses (the ring doesn't get much in the way). The Trango system slides better, thus equalizing better. Like cordalettes you can tie extension-limiting knots, shorten it by tying a big overhand on a bight on one arm, belay of a piece by tying both strands in an overhand, or clove pieces like the equalette. Not all strands of each arm of the system will be weighted if cloves are added, but all pieces will be loaded on at least one strand of each arm.

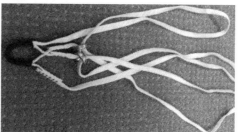

Trango Alpine Equalizer

To make an ACR feed one end of your cord through the rap ring as shown, and tie both ends with a double fishermans. To use it, clip the two outer pieces like you would a normal cordalette. Bring the ring down to the center and clip the ring and the free strand with a locker. For three pieces, pull the loop on the ring up to the third piece. Clip into the master point go through the ring AND the free strand. Attach yourself to the locker and even clove the rope to the best piece for extra security. To tie off something like a tree, just use it like a normal cordalette, but with the ring in the system. Pilfer the ring for a smooth rap, and the cord for tat!

Attaching the ring. A bigger ring allows the fishermans knot to pass through easier.

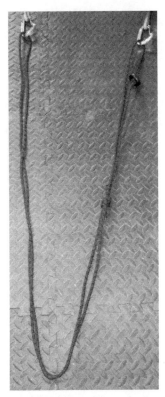

Attach to two pieces, then slide so the ring is at the bottom.

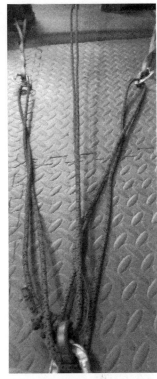

Clip a third piece by pulling a loop through the ring to the piece.

Clipping the master point through the ring and free strand.

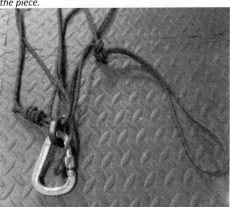

To reduce extension and shorten the anchor tie off one strand of one arm.

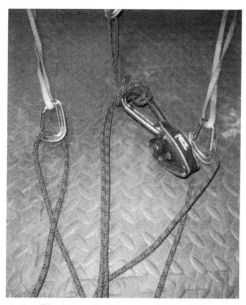

Or tie off both strands of an arm to belay off of.

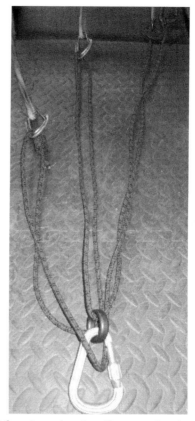

With four pieces, clove them like an equalette (on right)

Tie extension limiting knots to reduce extension

Use like a normal cordalette to wrap around a large object

Most of the anchor nit picking only comes into play if the leader takes a high factor fall directly onto the anchor (usually solved by a single good initial placement) or when belaying the second off the anchor and he/she somehow takes a big whip. You should employ dynamic belays, belay off your harness, and be tied tight to the anchor with the rope if you don't trust the anchor and an anchor fall is likely. This could also happen if you are belaying very poorly or they aren't paying attention to the speed of the rope coming up and they fall, or if pulling a difficult move (like an overhang) and repeatedly falling with little rope left between them and the anchor and you don't have enough time to pull in the slack. I had a very heavy climber do this and I watched in horror as he nearly broke my anchor. Using load limiters on the pro itself and/or at the master point can help limit forces on the anchor, as does belaying directly off your harness.

Fixing the Rope to an Anchor

If you are fixing a line for the follower to jug and or to haul here are the steps. Make the haul anchor and jugging anchor independent if at all possible. Pull in the haul line (allowing enough slack for the lower out if necessary) and pull up the slack of the lead/jugging line, leaving enough slack – especially if the beginning of the pitch traverses. Clip the lead line into the master point with a fig-8 on a bight with a beefy locker. If worried about knot tightening and one piece is absolutely bomber, you can pull a little more slack past the fig-8 and clove it to that bomber piece since a weighted clove is much easier to untie. Fix both lines, and yell "Line is fixed". Now you can chill or haul. Don't yell line is fixed until both the jug and haul line are ready to take a load.

Tying In

The figure-8 follow through is the best knot to tie into the rope with for most climbers. A bowline with a Yosemite finish or rewoven bowline unties much easier than a figure-8 when fallen on hard or repeatedly, and sport climbers may want to use it. However, you should be very familiar with a bowline tie-in. Even an unfinished figure-8 follow through is difficult to come undone, while a messed-up bowline is deadly. Although you and your partner should always check each other's knots and harnesses before climbing, a great place to triple check is while clipping the first piece of gear because the consequences of falling are the same regardless before you clip if starting on the ground.

BELAYING

BELAYING THE FOLLOWER(S)

After you are safe and in the anchor, your first order of business is to first yell "off belay," or "secure". Pull up the lead line and put it on a Reverso off the anchor or tie off the brake strand if belaying off your harness, and yell "on belay". This should take moments and it will give the follower time and safety to strip the anchor and get ready. If trailing another line, pull that line up before pulling up the lead rope, or put it in your belay device and just pull it up with the follower to save time. Get what you need (clothes, food, water, take off shoes) handy. Flake it nicely on a ledge, your tether, a folded sling, or what have you. All of this should go quickly – every minute of down time adds up with multiple pitches. While belaying, organize any gear leftovers to hand off for the next pitch. By belaying on a Reverso you can eat, drink, and fiddle with stuff instead of wasting time doing them while the follower waits for you. Belay the second tight. Not only will they appreciate this, but also they will climb much faster.

You have three options on how to belay the follower up. The first option is to belay directly off your harness. This is the best option when your anchor isn't very safe, or if the anchor is below your waist in a very unideal situation. If belaying off your harness, your body will be taking the weight of the follower if he/she slips or weights the rope - so be prepared. Get a good stance and keep them tight. Stay oriented in the correct direction of pull between you and the anchor and be attached snugly to the anchor (assuming it's at least good enough to hold body weight) to prevent shock loading the anchor and getting pulled off your stance. Another option is to belay off your harness, but redirect the follower's side of the rope through the anchor. This helps the lead belayer maintain an ergonomic position to pull in slack, and to aid in not getting knocked off balance. The big problem with this method is that the anchor will receive twice the weight of the follower when the follower weights the rope. This method is only recommended if the anchor is bomber.

The third, and best possible way to belay the follower is to belay directly off the anchor with a Reverso-type belay device (including a GiGi, Munter, and GriGri). If the anchor is too far from your belay stance you can put your belay device on bight of rope coming off the anchor master point. This can be done without a guide mode belay device but with the advances in belay plate functionality, there is little reason not to have a lightweight belay plate that can belay a 2nd in guide-mode. The biner used to hang the device from the master point (or a high totally bomber piece) could be a non-locking biner as the device won't be moving around at all. However, a locker is a far safer choice, so if you have one then use it. Another benefit of belaying off the anchor is it makes escaping the belay and lowering much simpler. It's important to know how to lower a follower in guide mode. See the section on lowering for instructions on this. Belaying off a GriGri or Munter hitch makes lowering a breeze. Be careful if you are belaying two followers on two different sized ropes with a device in guide mode. The thinner rope has a tendency to slip. Keep the follower tight so they feel comfortable quickly following the pitch, unless there is a large poorly protected traverse where you could pull them off their feet.

Belaying directly off the rope

A great system to speed up transitions is to belay the leader on a GriGri or Reverso-type device with the leader bringing up the follower up on their Reverso, similar to the GiGi scenario mentioned in the Gear section. The follower stays on the Reverso during the transition so they don't even have to bother clipping in, gives the GriGri (or other device) to the belayer (the person who just lead that pitch if swapping leads) and grabs the Reverso off the anchor when he/she takes off to lead the next pitch. If just bringing one Reverso and one GriGri, then on rappel, the person with the GriGri goes down first with the line fixed. The line is unfixed for the other climber to rap on both strands with the Reverso. This is one of the smoothest, lightest, and fastest systems. Who said GriGris are too heavy to bring in the alpine?

BELAYING THE LEADER

Behind every good leader is great belayer. A leader should be focused on the lead, not the belay.

> **Here is a list of common belay errors:**
> - Not paying attention to the leader
> - Not paying attention to coils and twists in the rope
> - Not paying out enough slack for a clip – short roping the leader
> - Not taking in slack after a clip or too much slack in the belay
> - Not knowing how to properly use a GriGri. See the Petzl website for the best way to hold one for paying out slack while keeping the brake hand engaged.
>
> **Not holding a fall, not keeping the hand on the brake, or dropping the leader are inexcusable mistakes. Accept criticism about your belay, and hold back the anger when the leader is being a little princess until the end of the pitch.**

The first order of business is to make sure you are in a good spot. Will you get pulled off a stance, have the leader fall on your head, get hit by ice or rock fall, trip up the leader with the rope or flip him/her upside-down during the beginning of the route? Is the rope stacked well and lying on the brake hand side? Are you tight on the anchor so if the leader falls, you can stand your ground? Take the time to make your location safe and hassle free. Fixing issues while belaying takes your attention away from your belay duties. If on the ground, give the leader a spot if he/she needs one before they clip the first bolt or placement. If the leader screwed something up, tell them unless breaking their attention would be worse. Be encouraging, but don't break the leader's concentration. Some people like a constant stream of encouragement, most don't. Try not to yell anything unnecessary to the leader especially if communication is difficult. It's hard not to yell, "WTF are you doing?" after 30 minutes of an unmoving rope. Unless your partner is narcoleptic, they haven't forgotten they are climbing or have fallen asleep. Eat, drink, and put on layers while belaying to keep energy levels up, but be ready for action.

Let the leader know when they've climbed halfway and have 10 meters left. If the climb is multipitch, start taking down the anchor (assuming there's enough good gear that a lead fall won't zipper to the anchor and you are in a hurry) and stay tethered into the best piece when the leader is setting up the belay or it looks like you'll be simulclimbing. If there's a situation where you aren't positive the leader is off belay, keep paying out rope as it is taken up until it's gone. Test to see if you are on belay by climbing up a few feet and see if the rope comes tight. If getting the belay device off in time isn't going to happen, just leave it on and climb.

There will be times when belaying the leader requires a dynamic belay or the ability to reel in slack quickly. If the leader pulls up rope and blows a clip, or could deck from a fall then pulling in slack quickly is a must. Be extra attentive at the dreaded 2nd clip, the most common spot for a leader to ground fall. Running back is a lot quicker than pulling the rope in by hand. Placing a piece very near to the ground helps the belayer pull slack in quickly without too much extra rope out. Some run-out climbs may require the belayer to literally jump off a boulder, platform, or even a ledge. Be sure the rope is clipped through the master point of the anchor if the belayer needs to simul-whip with the leader.

To avoid short roping the leader or to keep the slack levels to a minimum it is very helpful to use your body to give or take slack in addition to paying out or pulling in rope. A squat or step back can pull in some slack after the leader clips and pulled out too much rope or is climbing up to a clip over his/her head. If the leader needs slack quicker than you can pay it out or a snarl comes out of nowhere, a quick step or two forward while paying out rope can provide that extra slack to avoid short roping the leader.

A dynamic belay provides the opposite effect as taking in slack. Giving slack during a fall reduces the force of a fall due to more rope stretch, but increases the length of the fall and the fall factor. Here is a way to lessen the fall factor by using more rope: If the leader is looking at a high factor fall onto the anchor, the belay may want to lower him/herself down below the anchor to a small ledge or just tied off to a piece to provide more rope out to decrease the fall factor.

Make sure the leader took the time to put in a bomber piece immediately off the belay, even if the initial moves were easy. More commonly, the belayer uses his/her body to give a little during the fall, or even a small jump forward. Good methods of giving a dynamic belay or "soft catch" are crouching down (if expecting the fall) and then standing up, walking forward a step, or placing a foot on a stable rock so you naturally stand up onto it during a catch. The belay must time these moves just right so the belay is absorbing some of the force and not just giving out more rope. Providing a dynamic belay or "soft catch" is very important when a leader falls on an overhanging route and may swing and smack into the wall. Falls are more comfortable, and ankles can be spared during many lead falls by giving a nice soft catch...unless of course the leader is looking at a ground or ledge fall.

Dynamic belays are also handy on soft rock or onto suspect gear to lessen the force onto the protection. Remember that Gri-Gri's and some other automatic belay devices provide much harder catches than tube-style belay plates. If you are significantly lighter than the leader you'll want to be tethered in tight to something below you. However, if you plan on giving a dynamic belay, you may want some slack in the system – enough for the soft catch but not so much you get pull off a ledge or hurt yourself.

Top Rope Belay with Two Joined Ropes
When the situation arises that you want to toprope a pitch longer than half a rope, you will have to join both ropes and pass the knot. If one rope is significantly skinnier than the lead rope and you must use it (not recommended), be sure to set the ropes up so the main lead line is being used the most before switching to or from the skinny line to reduce the danger. This means the climber is tied into the lead line and the belayer begins belaying on the skinny line.

To pass the knot the belayer will need two belay devices or will need to use a munter on the first rope. A few feet before the knot comes to the belay device when belaying the climber, the belayer should take a couple of steps backward. When the knot is at the device, the belayer needs to tie off the device and tell the climber to stop. A mule knot is the quickest and safest method so it can be released under load if the climber cannot hold on during the changeover. Once the device is tied off the belayer takes a step or two forwards to get slack, attaches the new device, and continues belaying.

While lowering, the belayer must communicate to the climber to take weight off by holding onto the wall so they can remove the device, step back quickly and undo the mule knot to transfer the weight back onto the original device with minimal slack.

If the climber cannot take weight during the knot pass it can be very difficult to remove the rope from the belay device on the lower belay device, or put the new belay device on during the ascent. To solve this issue the belayer must have a prusik available. The prusik is put on the loaded rope and clipped to the belayer's belay loop, sliding the prusik until weighted and enough slack is available to change devices. Tie a backup knot if you only have one device when the prusik is loaded and you are switching the device to the new side of the rope.

Fixed Point Belay

If there is a chance that the leader is going to fall with an enormous amount of force, as in a factor 1-2 fall, it has been suggested to belay the leader off of a fixed point belay. If the leader falls before clipping the first piece or runs it out and whips early into the lead, the leader can generate so much force that the belayer would not be able to hold onto the belay device, or would get injured from being quickly pulled of his/her stance or thrown into the anchor or rock. This is particularly dangerous if the leader clipped the anchor (see clipping the anchor under the leading section). Even if the leader didn't clip the anchor, the belayer can still be violently yanked up in a lead fall onto gear, or violently yanked down if the leader had not clipped any gear yet. Belaying directly off a single, backed-up anchor piece can actually be safer than belaying off the harness in high factor fall scenarios. According to a summary of the May 2005 IFMGA Technical Commission Meeting, real life testing has shown that because of rope stretch, even a dreaded factor 2 fall does not generate forces greater than 5 kN on the anchor and 2-2.5 kN on the belayer! It should be noted that 2 kN is still a lot of force and could easily seriously injury a human body and more than enough to cause an ATC style belay device to slip a lot (like several feet). This should be convincing evidence to wear gloves when belaying! This puts concerns to rest that a single anchor point (backed-up of course) would be insufficient to rely on to provide a belay or hold a fall. Using a fixed anchor point removes the belayer from the system and the belayer would not get hurt, or drop the leader in a high factor fall.

The fixed anchor point must have a solid upward resisting pull, or have a piece equalized to it from below that resists an upwards pull. The upward resistance piece doesn't have to be super-bomber as the force applied to it would be low (but high enough to mess up a person). The other anchor pieces are tied to the fixed point to back it up. The belay device isn't attached directly to the fixed piece, but rather on something like a doubled sling no longer than 10 cm long so it is still within reach when it rises up when the leader falls. A Munter is a great belay device for this setup because the locking motion is applied in a motion opposite an ATC. If using an ATC you need to redirect the brake strand by clipping it through a biner right next to the locker the ATC is clipped to. A GriGri will also work.

Clipping the belay device to the master point in a traditionally equalized cordalette anchor is a bad idea because it not only allows much more movement of the belay device, but catching a forceful fall can actually cause the belayer to be slammed hard horizontally into the wall. Another solution has been offered to reduce fall factors and protect the belayer by having the leader clip off the anchor and the belayer lower down below the anchor (and clipped of to something) to increase the amount of rope out in the system and avoid getting pulled into the anchor. Of course high factor falls are rare, but when they do happen, most people are totally unaware of how hard it is to hold such a fall and how brutal it can be on the belayer.

LEADING

AVOIDING ANCHOR/LEDGE/LARGE FALLS

When leading, don't forget how important your first two pieces are. The first piece not only reduces the chances of a high factor fall onto the anchor, it should provide an outward pull to minimize the outwards pull onto high pieces to avoid zippering your gear. It should also be bomber if climbing above the anchor on a multipitch route. Don't skip placing gear if it's easy ground of sketchy gear. If it's sketchy, put a screamer on your shaky pro (and use the other tricks to minimize impact). If the start of the pitch involves a traverse, then your first piece won't have a straight down pull after you place a 2nd piece. Either make that piece have a sideways and upwards pull as well, put a long sling on it, or backclean until the rope runs in a more upward direction. This will also provide a better toprope for the follower. Ground or ledge fall potential is high at the second clip or piece.

Clipping the anchor as the leader's first piece of gear may sound like the safest thing to do, but you should be aware of the dangers of doing this. If the leader falls before getting in another piece of gear the fall factor and the force applied to the belayer will be huge. The belayer can get violently slammed into the wall and may lose grip on the belay from rope slippage, putting their hands up for self-protection, or have their grip pulled off if their body gets twisted around. If this doesn't happen, the belay device will get sucked into the biner the rope is clipped off to. This could damage the rope or drop the leader, or the belayer's fingers could get seriously messed up. Don't forget that the anchor receives twice this force in this type of fall (with no rope to absorb it) – the force of the leader falling and the force of the belayer resisting. As mentioned, a fixed anchor point will solve this issue, but may be awkward to belay with that setup. You can always change from a fixed anchor point to a normal off the harness belay after the high factor fall danger is minimized.

At any ground or ledge fall clips, don't be tempted to clip from below the gear. Clipping from the waist at the piece is actually safer since there will be a few feet less rope out (the rope coming back down to the leader). Long slings can be scary, but they reduce zippering gear and rope drag. Make sure the gear you place is oriented in the direction of a fall. The more rope drag, the less functioning rope is out to absorb the fall, and the fall factor is greatly increased on your last piece. Drag can increase the force on your last piece by up to three times. DMM Revolvers help in minimizing drag and decreasing forces on your gear. If a biner is lying over an edge, use a longer sling. Don't girth hitch another sling, but use the basket hitch instead. Looping webbing over a nut cable is stronger than even girth hitching two nuts together. Another way to deal with rope drag that may or may not increase your risk is to clip a Microtraxion/Rollnlock to a piece and pull as much slack as needed.

Running it out can be fun, but anything can happen so be sure to put enough gear in to avoid ground falls. Doubling placements essentially makes each piece redundant. Just because a piece protects a ground fall doesn't mean you won't deck if it blows. Also, don't skip the chance for a good placement (assuming you're not in a splitter crack the entire time). Better to sacrifice a piece in a great placement, and then screw around making something fit ten feet higher. A longer fall onto a bomber piece is way safer than a shorter fall onto a questionable piece. If you are headpointing a pitch, test a runout by tossing a pack to see where it lands and add an extra 10%. If a large swinging fall is likely, you can have another belayer stand way off to the side with a second line to pull you hard when you fall.

In this gym-simulated situation to obtain a photo, the leader is looking at a big pendulum fall onto the clip on the right. Another rope is attached on the left to mitigate the pendulum fall.

PROTECTING ROOFS & TRAPPING THE ROPE

Roofs present more problems than just strength or technique: they are notorious for pinning your rope. What can happen is the rope will push cams deeper into the crack, trap your rope and fix your cam. Even if the rope slides fine, a fall or take by the leader or follower could be what finally pins the rope. The best way to prevent this is to backclean and leapfrog your gear to a point, possibly way past the roof where your rope won't get pinned. If this is unsafe it may be a very good idea to belay soon afterwards. Another good trick is to lead on two ropes: tied into one, and clipped to lockers with the other. At the edge of the roof, clip a long sling and anchor the rope with lockers to the last piece, leaving it there. Clip the other rope through this sling as well and continue up. The belayer must securely tie off the belay device on the first rope, and belay on another device for the second rope. Finally, you could put the rope behind the cams. This may or may not work, and if the follower is jugging, they will not be able to clean the gear and be in big trouble.

Trapping your rope can happen anywhere the rope runs through a constriction. Try getting some slack from the belay and flicking the rope. The belayer should do the same. Both the leader and belayer pulling tight at the same time may pop the rope upwards. Whatever you do, don't be too forceful and cut your rope. If downclimbing is safe and easy enough, then tie in backup knots often as the belayer won't be able to pull in any additional slack. The only next option would be for the leader to prusik down or the belayer to prusik up. Either way, the leader should make an anchor and fix the rope. If the leader is lucky enough they have slack to rappel, then great. Don't chance it if there's just barely enough slack because the leader could get trapped on their rappel device and be truly screwed. The belayer will have the easiest time jugging up because they will have slack to work with for jugging up with a GriGri or other easier method and be able to zip back down to the belay vs. jugging back up again.

PROTECTING THE FOLLOWER

To make the follower happy, try not to bury cams and overset nuts when you're gripped unless you want to lose your gear. If you need to slam something in because you're that gripped, better to hang and take the time to place another piece of the gear correctly and backclean the jammed-in piece. Don't flip biners over, especially if the 2nd winds up jugging – this makes unclipping a total pain in the ass. If a pitch has a traverse, don't forget about the follower and protect it well. Sometimes a crux occurs before an easy climbing that traverses. After you pull the crux, put one more piece in so the follower isn't looking at a pendulum in the midst of the crux. Sometimes backcleaning gear can protect the follower more by keeping the rope more straight up and down. It all depends on the length of the traverse and where the climb goes after the traverse.

A **second rope** or tag line is a great way to help protect a long poorly protected traverse. Trail both ends of the tag line through a fairly solid fixed piece left at the original anchor and pull the tag line tight. The leader could use a Munter or garda hitch to pull with to really get the line tight, finishing the knot with a mule backup. The follower is then belayed on the lead rope going through whatever gear was left on lead, using the taught tag line as a backup from a big swing if he/she falls. If you only had one rope and wanted to fix it tightly doubled through the original anchor, the follower would not be able to be belayed over by the leader, instead trusting their lives to a taught lead line and the anchors attached. Those anchors had better be incredibly bomber. If using a tag line, then the leader could also belay the follower with that so he/she could still protect traverse while the tag line provides a more straight up and down belay.

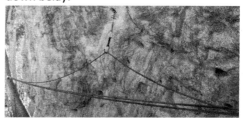

2nd rope is pulled tight on this sketchy traverse with only one piece the lead rope is clipped to. See drawing at bottom of page also.

If the pitch will be too hard for the follower, be nice and leave long slings clipped to plenty of gear so they can French-free their way through. This is a lot easier than yelling directions on how to rig an ascension system on prusiks. Flag fixed gear that your follower may not know was already there and fixed. If you can yell it clearly while clipping it, do so. If the fixed piece is out of earshot while being belayed, it may be in earshot while belaying them up. Don't yell anything unnecessary down while leading. Best case is that your belayer thinks there's a problem and belays you better, worst case is they take you off belay. "I'm ok!" sounds a lot like off belay. If there's nothing the belayer can do about whatever you're trying to communicate, keep it to yourself. For important commands, like "Off/On belay," yell super loudly and reply with a loud "thank you" for confirmation (or use whistles) to save time waiting to decide whether to yell again or not.

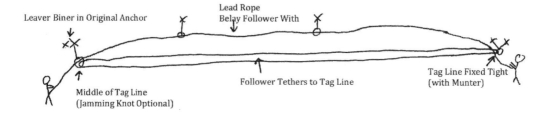

DITCHING A LEAD PACK

If you're on lead and need to ditch the pack because it's too heavy or too hard to climb with (like an offwidth or chimney situation), you can **fifi** hook the pack to a piece of gear and attached to the tag line via a strong enough cord tied to the top fifi pull-hole. You'll need to pull up enough extra slack on the tag line. If it gets stuck, the follower can help it along. If the leader doesn't have a fifi, he or she will have to wait for the follower to unclip it. The follower or leader can also clip a long sling or daisy chain to the pack to pull it behind them when trying to climb squeeze chimneys.

AIDING

The term aid climbing conjures up a mess of complicated systems for those who haven't participated in the activity. All aiding climbing is really is standing, pulling, or resting on gear. Some super obsessive climbers even consider hanging belays to add an A0 grade to the route! Some other terms used are interchangeable: Etrier=Aider=Ladder, Daisy=Tether=PAS, and Ascender=Jumar=Jug (noun, not the verb 'to jug').

French-Free and Pre-Clipping

Apologies to French climbers, the name just stuck! This is the simplest, fastest, but most tiring form of aid climbing. All you do is grab a piece of gear instead of the rock. This tactic works well on routes that have a small section over your head but you still want to get up it, or on short bolt ladders. Clipping in direct by using a draw or sling on your belay loop allows you to rest on the gear without pissing off the belayer. Extending the sling allows for active tension to clip a higher piece within reach. Just don't fall onto your tether since this creates huge fall factors.

The next step to gain extra height would be to clip a shoulder length sling to the piece of gear and stand in it. In this situation you definitely don't want to be clipped into the gear with a tether – use the rope. You may need to use two slings for each foot to offer more balance, or tie the slings in half to gain a little more reach. If this allows you to reach the hold, just start climbing. If you need to use another piece of gear you can clip it with the rope and hoist yourself up if the piece is bomber. If it's questionable, don't clip the rope – clip in direct. The extra rope out will increase your fall unnecessarily. Remember that the follower needs to get up this section too, so keep them in mind before you reach down and backclean anything.

Following a pitch is possible in this style without resorting to jugging up the rope, but is more difficult because the follower needs to clean the gear he/she is using to stand on. If the follower is able backclean then it's not so hard. If backcleaning is difficult, you could make a string of slings to clip to the higher piece, lower down and backclean, then use the hand-line of slings to get back up.

Pre-clipping gear with a **stick-clip** or rodeo clip isn't necessarily aiding, but doing so and then using the rope as a pulley to hoist yourself up is. For whatever reasons, this is considered cheating in aid climbing circles if you actually care about what other people say or think. Rodeo clipping requires a fixed draw and is usually used to avoid ground falls on high first bolts or the 2nd bolt on a severely overhanging route. Take a bight of rope and swing it around like a lasso to clip the draw. Yes, it works.

If you are simply hangdogging up a climb, do the belayer a favor and clip in direct to the gear with a quickdraw on your belay loop. Thick nylon sport draws make much better grabbing surfaces than thin Dyneema draws.

Using the Gear You Have
For climbs with just a pitch of aid, or a few points of aid, but French-freeing would be too strenuous, you can rig up a decent system with the gear you have. Two or three shoulder slings girth hitched together makes a pretty good ladder if you have enough to spare. Your cordalette makes a pretty good aider as well. Just tie knots in it every few feet to make several footsteps. Put a piece of gear in, clip your makeshift aider into it, test the gear by stamping on your aider if the gear is questionable, and then climb up the ladder. You can clip a daisy chain to the clipping spot on your aider to keep it attached, and also a use quickdraw clipped to your belay loop to clip into various points of your daisy (or aider) to stay balanced as you climb up the aider. If the piece is good then clip the rope into it, but if it's questionable, wait until you are at least waist level before clipping it to avoid falling farther than you need to. Repeat until you get past the aid section.

Using Aiders
Bona fide aid ladders are the way to go on climbs with long stretches of aid. The more difficult and steep the aid, the more aiders you'll want. Most straightforward easy aid climbs can be done with just two aiders. Clip an aider to a high piece, transfer your weight to it, reach down and get the other aider and clip it to your harness. Climb until you are in the top step, and repeat.

Introducing a **3rd floating aider** that you clip to the biner of the aider you're about to stand in lets you balance better and is easier to climb higher up on the aiders. This is the most commonly used system on most aid pitches.

Floating aider on left is clipped into biner of main aider. It can be now moved to the aider on the right.

Two sets of aiders, with each set clipped into the same biner allows for the greatest stability and is helpful on full-on aid climbs with overhanging terrain, but is total overkill for almost all climbs. One of the most common errors is forgetting to reach down and clean the aiders on the piece you are no longer standing in. Once you are off the old aider and on the new, the old aider is useless and does nothing for additional safety, so grab it before it's out of reach.

Get comfortable top-stepping. Most fixed gear is just out of reach in lower steps, and you'll save hours by making fewer placements. The grab loop can be used as an extreme top step, or it can be the top step in some lighter alpine aiders. Having something to tension off of while top-stepping steep or overhanging terrain can be really helpful. Simple solutions would be to pull on your daisy or quickdraw clipped to the top loop for active tension. For more security, length, and adjustability, you can use an **adjustable daisy chain or an adjustable fifi hook**. You could also girth hitch a runner or two to your harness, run it through the top of your aider, and use the other end to pull tension. Munter hitches on a biner with a length of cord with one end on your belay loop and the other clipped to the gear are also highly adjustable. Micro rope clamps (like a Ropeman) and a cord also work.

Tensioning a top-step with a cord attached to the belay loop and munter hitched to a biner on the aider.

The fastest way to use your aiders is to not connect them to daisy chains. Seriously consider this unless your gear is questionable. **Daisy chains**, especially two, makes for a lot of clutter, and they will inevitably get twisted in the aiders and rope requiring you to pull everything through and untwisting many times per pitch. If possible, use different colored daisies and aiders. Daisy chains are solely used to for jugging and to keep your aiders and piece you are weighting from falling into space if your gear blows. Many veteran wall climbs still do not use daisy chains on questionable aid. They just make sure that they grab the aider when the gear blows. This sounds dicey, but you are almost always grabbing the aider or gear with your hand and will most likely reflexively grab harder if you fell.

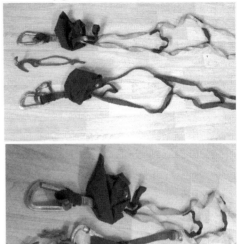

Two pocket aiders (no daisy) and a fifi hook (girthed in belay loop) does the trick on most aid pitches. An adjustable daisy with a ffii can also be useful.

Daisy chains are also helpful to **fifi hook** for balance. They are not designed to save you from falling further. If your gear blows, you'll fall regardless. And since you are literally standing in ladders, there's no reason you should fall if your gear holds! Remember that falling directly onto any sling, especially a daisy creates huge forces on your gear. Besides speed, this is another reason why you need to clean your previous set of aiders if using daisies when transferring your weight onto the higher aider/piece of gear. If your new piece popped, you will fall onto the piece you just cleaned your aider/daisy off of. If you left your aider/daisy still clipped to it, you will fall directly onto your daisy and generate much higher force onto that piece that you would if you just fell onto the rope. Your normally good gear could now rip. If you leave a piece of gear instead of backcleaning it with your aider, you must clip the rope into it.

If a pitch is fairly steep, you will want something to keep you in balance so you aren't pumping yourself out holding onto your grab loop. The most commonly used item is a fifi hook girth hitched to your harness. You can also just use a quickdraw for short sections of aid. If you aren't using daisies then just hook right into your aider. You can use an adjustable fifi made by Kong, but I personally despise them. Climbing Technologies recently came out with a three-hole adjustable fifi that may or may not be better. Adjustable daisies are great on steep terrain, and you don't need a fifi if using them because they do dual purpose. Never ever use them to attach yourself to an anchor, they are body weight only (as are regular daisies, but even more so with adjustable ones). You can rig your own with some cord and a Ropeman, Camp Lift, or other micro ascender.

Using two adjustable daisies is great on really steep terrain, but they create the same tangle and hassle as regular daisies, maybe even more so. One trick is to just use one adjustable daisy and put a biner and fifi hook tied as short as possible to it. Use it just like a normal fifi hook for easy not so steep sections, and extended it for deep crack placements or for balance as you work up the ladder or top step. Use the normal biner clipped right next to the fifi at the end for dicey placements when you might lose your aider and gear if it blows. Have a 2nd PAS daisy clipped to your harness for added safety jugging, for clipping into the anchor, or when you need to use it on your other aider.

Girth hitch fifi hooks to your tie-in loops, and your daisies to your tie-in loops or belay loops. Harnesses with two belay loops are very helpful when aid climbing. Don't keep your daisies girthed to your belay loops forever. Periodically check your belay loop, and reposition the location of your daisies to ensure your belay loop is sound.

A **non-locking keynosed biner** is the best way to clip your aider to a piece of gear, not an oval biner. If you really want to climb fast you can also put fifi hooks on your aiders to simply hook gear. If you forgot to backclean your lower aider, simply kick it out. You actually don't even need to attach your daisies to your aider biner with lockers. For jugging, you'll probably want the top daisy to be a locker (and the top daisy to be a PAS for added safety and clipping the anchor), so one may already be on your harness regardless.

When placing gear (from your top-step and as high as possible of course), clip or hook the piece in the highest structurally sound point as possible to get maximum height. If you add your floating aider in, be sure and clip it on top or to the biner of the aider you are standing in. Otherwise it may be pinched and become extremely difficult to remove when switching it to the next aider. You may not always want to place a piece as high as possible if a lower, better placement is available. Many leaders have wasted hours trying to get in an A3 placement when a much more solid placement just a few inches above the gear they are standing on would give them additional reach and a better new placement option higher up.

Using a stick clip is considered poor form, but for some reason using **stiffened quickdraws** isn't considered poor style for clipping hard to reach fixed gear. Tape up a quickdraw, including the biners so they don't flop over. A Mad Rock **Trigger Wire** biner is a great top biner to use on this mini cheater stick. If clipping a suspect piece, don't use the lead rope! Use the tag line or a bunch of connected slings to climb up on instead of using the rope so you don't fall that much further if it pops.

"Crack Jumaring" is another way to quickly aid a pitch. Tie a small loop of ½ - 9/16" webbing or 5 mm cord to the end of your aiders and put the most common sizes you'll need on a single biner. If your clip in loop is big enough you can skip the webbing loop and just use that. Instead of going through your rack to find the right size, your gear is right there on your aider. To make this effective, you must backclean a significant amount, so this is best done one easier aid pitches. Stick in the cam, hike to the top of your aider, place the next piece/aider, and backclean. Some common pieces are a fifi hook, cam hook, and a few cams of various sizes (or the size of the crack ahead if you can tell).

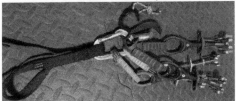

The fastest way to aid is to be in "crappy free mode". Free climb until you give up and grab a piece. Clip in direct, do a little more French-freeing or use your aiders sans daisy, and try resume freeing. This system works great on long routes with short or straightforward aid sections like the Nose or Half Dome. It takes more energy, but is much faster. Get your brain out of "aid-mode". Once you enter aid-mode, it is very difficult to get out. Gear is gear and falls are falls no matter how your setup is rigged.

If you are worried about your aiders hanging up while free climbing you can always leave them, free a section, lower down to grab them and pulley yourself up the to-prope. This is still much faster than resorting to aiding for aiding's sake. If you wear free climbing shoes while aiding, you will be much more likely to free. A great way to move from free to aid is to use a shoulder sling instead of your aiders on the last aid piece. While hanging on that last piece, you can do what you will with your aider (bunch them up, put them in their pocket, etc.), maybe put your rock shoes on, and then have the belayer take your weight. Unclip yourself from the gear, stand in the sling, and make the free moves.

Remember that your fifi, a quickdraw, or adjustable daisy should be used to rest and balance on – not the belayer! Many novice climbers freak out and call take on each piece. So give your belayer a break and use your systems correctly.

When testing suspect placements you first want to be sure that the resulting blown gear doesn't result in you falling, especially if the gear below you is bad. Keep your aiders on the lower piece and clip your daisy into the high piece to bounce test instead of the aider stomp method. A full strength daisy will work much better for this method than using a weaker adjustable one. There is little point testing solid gear that you wouldn't test while free climbing.

Great Setups for Quick Aiding (if the terrain isn't steep for long stretches)

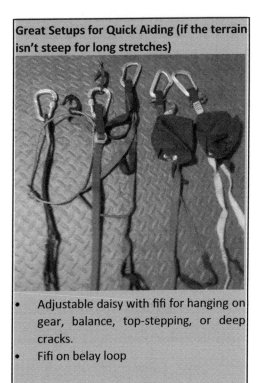

- Adjustable daisy with fifi for hanging on gear, balance, top-stepping, or deep cracks.
- Fifi on belay loop

- 2 Ladder (Russian) Style Pocket Aiders with keynosed biner, along with selection of key gear on each ladder.
- PAS with light keynosed locker girthed to harness but only clipped to ladder on sketchy gear, or another adjustable daisy if steep terrain.
- 1 floating pocket aider with a light keynosed biner not attached to a daisy if terrain is steep.
- *PAS with locker only clipped to aider when needed, fifi on belay loop, adjustable daisy with Fifi, floating aider (optional), 2 pocket ladder-style aiders*

Emergency Aid Kit (Sans Bolts)

If you're free climbing on a first ascent and get to a blank section, it's helpful to have some trinkets to pass a section you can't with standard nuts and cams or bolts. You'll need a hammer.
- Slider Nuts: Camp Ball Nuts #1, #2
- Beaks: Moses Tomahawk #1, #2
- Hooks: Black Diamond Talon(s)
- Copperheads x2
- Pins: 2 long Bugaboos, Baby Angle #1, #2

INEXPERIENCED PARTNER

Here are some other techniques that work with a partner that may or may not be up to the job of following well. Don't climb anything close to your limit if you don't trust their belay. A GriGri is great here, just tell them never to touch that black lever. Short-roping (tying in short to have them simulclimb) works well on easy terrain you'd normally solo. Do shorter pitches so you are always in visual or at least vocal range. Expect traverses to be a problem, even pitches that wander you wouldn't consider traversy. Put them on rappel and put yourself on rappel below them so all they have to do is unclip from the anchor and rap. Give them a fireman's belay for reassurance, and they'll probably rap faster.

If they simply can't get up and you are belaying them off of the anchor on with a guide-mode belay device, lower the brake strand down to them with a locker and have them clip it to their belay loop. The leader pulls up while the follower pulls down on loop lowered. This makes a 3:1 assisted hoist. If the climber is too tired to even pull, you can lower that loop and locker down with a prusik and foot sling to be placed on the brake side of the rope (not the rope the climber is tied to).

Brake strand lowered to climber (shown as the fig-8 knot). Device is in guide mode.

If you don't trust your partner to clean an anchor safely or quickly when toproping and the anchor setup allows for it, you can feed the rope through the chains but use biners on the anchor to keep the rope from rubbing through the chains. The partner or client would climb to the anchor and simply remove the biners to be on the anchor chains without unclipping or wearing down the chains by directly toproping off of them.

Following

Your job as a follower is to get the gear out and up to the next belay as fast as possible. Unless you've got plenty of time, don't try and style the pitch. Climb fast and less cautiously as the leader. You're on toprope; now's your chance to see what you can get away with grabbing and standing on, assuming the belay is good and the rope isn't way off to the side. Be fairly aggressive about organizing gear as you clean the pitch. If you have a gear sling, organize it for your lead on the go. If clipping to your harness, clip cam biners to cam biners in stacks, and clip slings to slings in stacks assuming there's too much gear to clean to have everything clipped individually to your gear loops. Take nuts off the slings and draws and clip them all to the same biner. A cam biner works well compared to a sling biner because you'll most likely see the nuts while re-racking on your sling. If you can, redouble up shoulder slings. If not, put them around your shoulder. If you can't let go to rack the gear, just take it out of the rock and let it hang from the rope until you come to a rest stance. If you have trouble cleaning the gear, yell up and ask how it was put in. If it went in, it can come out. If you are in a hurry and the gear just won't come out, don't take longer than 10 minutes unless that piece is absolutely essential or you have all day. To avoid dropping the gear, leave it clipped to the rope while removing it. If the rope is too tight on the piece, clip a shoulder sling to the rope and gear to give you move room to work. If you have to hang to clean a piece, do the leader a favor and put in a piece to hang on while cleaning.

If the climb is popular and clean, think twice before reaching for a hammer or rock to start whacking away to get the gear out. Split the cost of left or dropped gear with your partner – it could have happened to either of you. When you get to the belay, always say, "nice lead!" It's polite, and inspires confidence for the climb ahead. After you give the leader his or her props, you can then critique the stupid or unsafe things that they did.

Ascending the Rope (Jugging)
There are several reasons why you would ascend a fixed rope, and you should be very familiar with some common methods. The first reason is getting out of a bad situation (self-rescue) - otherwise you could be stuck forever. The next reason is to get up a section of a climb that is too difficult to free climb. This could be in an aid-climbing situation, or following a pitch or section of a pitch that's too hard for you. Again, if you can't reach the belay on a multipitch climb, you're kinda screwed so knowing how to jug and rig one quickly using minimal gear is a very important skill. Finally, jugging is faster than following a pitch in difficult terrain. Anything that you can't cruise on that requires speed should be jugged. Some of the following systems use minimal gear for getting past short sections or improvised self-rescue, while some use dedicated gear when you know you will be jugging.

If you can tie a **prusik-type knot** (prusik, Klemheist, Bachman, or autoblock) you're most of the way there to rigging a basic ascension system. If you have **gloves**, wear them. The leader must make sure the rope isn't running over any sharp edges if he or she expects you to jug. Redirect the rope with slings, or pad edges with something.

Prusik

Klemheist

Bachman

Autoblock

Method One: Texas Kick (Crevasse Self-Rescue or Insufficient Gear)
The following system is commonly used in self-rescue in a crevasse fall, or for getting up a rope when you weren't planning on jugging.

To jug a line using just prusiks you will need a **prusik loop for your waist**, and a **prusik loop for your foot** with something to stand in clipped to it. The waist prusik loop must be long enough to wrap around the rope plus almost full arm extension. This gets put on the rope above the leg prusik and clipped into your harness with a locker. For the foot prusik you can rig a two foot setup, aka Texas Kick, by trying a loop in the middle of a long length of cord to attach the prusik knot to the rope, and two overhand knots on the tails of the cord to girth hitch over your feet. If pre-rigging a Texas Kick, you will want the length of cord to be long enough to reach down to your feet after all the knots are tied, biners clipped, and feet girth hitched. Err on the slightly short side if in doubt. You don't need a loop for each foot, only one loop for standing on a single leg usually works fine. The one-leg system works well when you have something to press off of, like a rock wall or crevasse wall. The two-leg system works better for free hanging terrain. You may want to tie into backup knots along the way up. **Micro ascenders** are great if you have them for a backup.

You can rig this whole system up with just shoulder slings, your cordalette, or dedicated prusik slings. The leg prusik goes below the waist prusik on the rope. This is one of the main differences between this system and the "Frog" system below. If this setup is pre-rigged for glacier travel, either stuff the leg prusik in your pocket, or bunch them up with slip knots and clip it to your harness gear loop. Long prusiks make hauling less efficient, and you can shorten them with a simple overhand knot when using them to haul.

To ascend the rope, sit on the waist prusik, slide up the foot prusik, stand up, slide the waist prusik and repeat. Anyone that's ever used this system knows it sucks (but requires no extra gear besides some extra slings). Remember to fully rest on your waist prusik when sliding the foot prusik up the rope. Practice before you actually need to use this system! Also, see if you can climb out on belay from above if it isn't too steep in a crevasse before attempting to bother prusiking up. If you are wearing a pack, you should clip a **sling to the pack** (pre-rigged on a glacier) and clip it to the loop of rope between your foot prusik and your tie-in. This will also help put some tension on the rope to make jugging easier. If you are in dire straits and seriously low on gear, don't forget about using a foot wrap or a garda hitch instead (including a prusik and foot sling for the upper ascender).

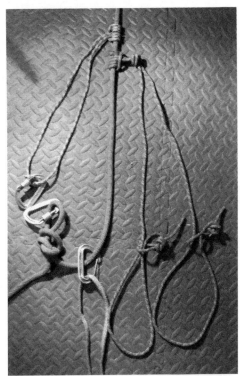

Climber clipped to rope on butterfly knot and locker as their initial tie-in for glacier travel. This could also just be your normal fig-8 tie-in. Above the tie in: chest prusik (top) clips to belay loop, foot prusik on rope below chest (feet go in girth hitched loops), pack clipped off on sling (bottom).

Method Two: Frog

The Frog system is best used to jug overhanging terrain compared to the two ascender system described below. It is a great system to use if "fixing and firing" when you don't want to bring a lot of ascenders and extra gear, although I recommend the extra weight of using real ascenders for the upper jug if possible.

<u>This is a great system for the follower to get up a short section of terrain too difficult for them to free</u> and the leader wasn't kind enough to leave slings to pull through. Fi-

nally, this is a great way to get back up if you fell on an overhang or while rope-soloing. Because this technique uses a closed system on the lower ascender (your device can't come off the rope like a handled Jumar-style), it is a safer system if you can't or don't want to tie backup knots. That said, I should probably say that you should tie backup knots. If the second is using this technique to get past a difficult section, you can belay up the slack created if they clip in directly to (good) gear.

This system is like the Texas kick system, but uses a **non-handled mechanical ascender or ratcheting pulley** attached directly to your waist and the foot prusik is placed above. This system is much faster and easier, but will only work if you have a device that slides easily up the rope. Most autolocking belay devices, like the **GriGri** work quite well. Assisted locking devices like the Smart and Jul, and belay devices that can be rigged in guide mode like the Reverso or GiGi will also work, but not well. A garda hitch can also be used here. The best devices are the ones that slide incredibly smoothly, like the **Microtraxion/Rollnlock, Microcender, and Camp Lift**. Ropemen will work, but not great. Tiblocs don't work at all, and you'll have to experiment with other devices. You can also use a normal ATC or other tube-style belay device with a prusik above it and clipped to the locker. The ATC acts as a prusik minder. Personally, I'd rather use the Texas system than that option, but it's there. Most likely you'll just have a GriGri if free climbing. For the upper prusik you can use slings, a cordalette, an ascender (best), or micro ascenders like a Ropeman or Tiblock with a grab loop. For the leg stirrup that attaches to the upper ascender you can use a couple of slings, a cordalette, or an aid ladder (best). Like the Texas system you can have a stirrup for one or both feet depending on the length of the jug or steepness of the line.

To set this system up on the ground or ledge, attach the upper prusik (or whatever) to the rope and clip your daisy or a tether to it at almost full arm extension. Clip your aider or slings to this as well. If using a cordalette you need to tie two knots below where you tied the prusik to create a small clip in loop for your daisy. The remaining tail can be used for your stirrup. If your cordalette was untied and is long enough, you can make a couple loops for each foot.

If you are using this system to get past a short hard section and don't have a daisy or enough slings for a tether, you don't absolutely need one. Finally, attach your GriGri (or whatever) to the rope below the foot system and to your harness with your belay locker. If you are setting this system up while hanging on the rope you will need to pull yourself up to the prusik and clip in to it so there is enough slack to attach your GriGri between the prusik and tie-in knot.

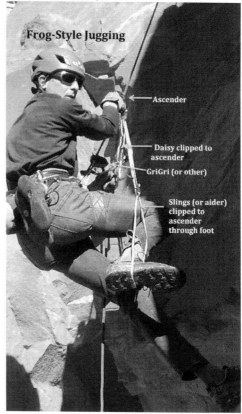

Frog-Style Jugging
Ascender
Daisy clipped to ascender
GriGri (or other)
Slings (or aider) clipped to ascender through foot

To ascend you need to pull in the slack through your GriGri and rest on it. Slide the upper prusik up as high as you can, stand up, and pull the slack in again with your GriGri. Common mistakes are to press down with your feet while trying to slide the prusik up. Relax on your GriGri. If you find that this system pumps you out and you're not using a Microtraxion/Rollnlock which slide incredibly easily, you can clip a **pulley** to your upper ascender to redirect the brake hand of the GriGri so you pull down, not up.

On really low angled terrain you could just pull on the rope with your hand instead of using an upper ascender/foot loop, and "Batman" up the rope, pulling in slack with a belay device. This is commonly used to get back up a short section of rope on rappel with a fireman's backup.

If you are using the GriGri method mentioned for setting up the rope for glacier travel and for setting up crevasse hauls, use the frog system to jug out of a crevasse. Your upper prusik will need some foot slings, so have a couple shoulder slings or a cordalette somewhere on your harness at all times. You can't drop your pack with this system because you'll be fighting it when pulling up on the GriGri. A **chest harness**, even a shoulder sling around your neck and shoulder, clipped to the rope may be helpful to reduce fatigue with a big pack. You could clip the pack off to the GriGri locker (like rappelling with a haul bag described later), but it may be too tricky.

Putting a prusik above your belay device can be an option. Clip the tail loop of the prusik to your belay loop.

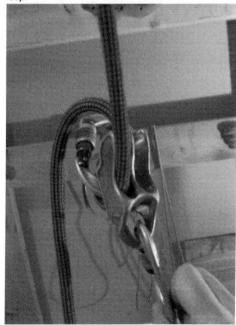

A plaquette like the Reverso can be set up on your belay loop in a pinch. Clip the anchor biner to your belay loop.

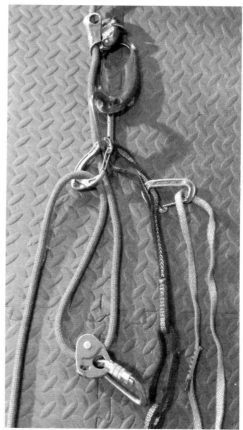

Rope redirected through a pulley (Revolver Biner) off the upper ascender to aid in pulling the rope up. A Microtraxion is being used as the ratcheting pulley on the belay loop, and a shoulder sling is clipped to the PAS low enough to be used as the foot sling.

Method Three: Two Ascenders and Aiders

The above two photos shows an excellent method for a follower to jug past cruxes while on belay. To set this up, attach a prusik on the rope as high as possible (using a prusik, sling, or cordalette). Clip off to the prusik as short as possible with your tether so there is some slack in the rope between your tie-in point and the prusik. Attach your GriGri (or any other variation of a self-ratcheting pulley discussed) to the slack in the rope and your belay loop. If you have an extra sling(s), clip them to the prusik to stand up on. Now you can jug frog-style past the crux. Clip in direct to a piece of gear, undo the system, and have the leader pull in the slack.

To really cruise on slabby to steep terrain where you've got something to help push off of, use the standard fare **two aider, two Jumar, two daisy** system. Once you get good at this, it is much less tiring on steep terrain as well. This system only works well if you have two Jumar-style handled ascenders and were planning on jugging a line. However simple this system is, you can get incredibly pumped and take forever if you haven't practiced. Before you hop on a wall where you'll be jugging many pitches, for the sake of your partner and parties waiting below, please get this system dialed!

Clip a daisy to your upper ascender at almost full arms extension. If your daisy is adjusted too long you won't be able to rest on it. Clip it too short and you won't be able to jug as fast. If you get it the right length and you are still having issues, your feet are placed incorrectly in your aiders. If using a standard daisy chain, don't forget to use TWO biners to shorten it. Clip your daisy directly to the bottom hole in the Jumar with a locker and the aider into the daisy locker with a standard biner. Lockers are still optional considering the weak link is still probably the teeth on the ascender, but you'll probably regret that decision – at least on the upper ascender. The bottom ascender is attached the same way, but the daisy can be at full extension as you won't be resting on it.

Put your foot in the 4th step from the top on the upper aider and the 3rd step from the top on the lower to keep your feet even and at a fairly normal length. You may need to go up or down steps depending on your situation. Slide the upper ascender until it's tight on the daisy and sit on it if it's steep. If the wall isn't very steep you won't need to sit on your daisy often. Now slide the lower ascender up, step down on it, and then move the upper one up again. If the upper ascender isn't moving, you're weighting it. If the lower one isn't moving, you're standing on it (or your leg is pressing down out of instinct). The lower ascender won't slide on its own until the weight of the rope is heavy enough, making the first part of the pitch a pain in the ass. On lower angled terrain once the rope is tight, you should be able to cruise like you're walking uphill. Using a **chest harness** in conjunction with your daisy and upper ascender will drastically improve your ability to rest on the upper ascender compared to coming directly off your waist loop on very steep terrain.

Tie occasional backup knots in the rope below you just in case the ascenders fail. If someone else will be jugging a line behind you, chances are you will not be able to tie backup knots. You can alternatively attach a **3rd backup ascender** below both main ascenders and skip the knots if you can find something that slides very easily. A Tibloc with just the right biner can work, but usually is too much friction to slide nicely. Microcenders and Microtraxion/Rollnlocks work great. By using the backup ascender, you can immediately switch to the Frog System if it gets steep.

The nice thing about the Microcender as your backup is that you can take it off the rope while still clipped in to it if you need to move it around gear while cleaning. You can also place a small backup above your Jumar like a prusik or Tibloc and clip it to your harness on a long sling. Your ascender will push it up with you. The drawback of having it above you is falling onto it for whatever reason may be damaging to the rope. A longer sling can help eliminate this.

You can also clip a **biner into the hole above the teeth** on your upper ascender to ensure it doesn't come off the rope, but don't use a nice biner – it will get trashed. Clip the upper hole during any traversing sections.

Cleaning Gear, Low Angled and Sketchy Jugging

Gear can be really hard to clean if the rope isn't running straight up and down. Clipping in direct to the piece, then freeing the lead line first can help.

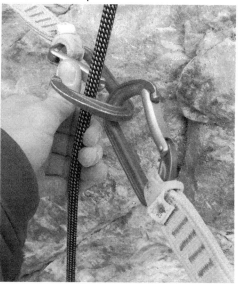

If this isn't a good option, move your upper ascender above the piece to be cleaned (where backups come in very handy), weight the upper ascender, and disengage the cam on the lower ascender. This puts you in the fall line, not the gear. Hold onto the piece this whole time in case you wind up traveling well off to the side.

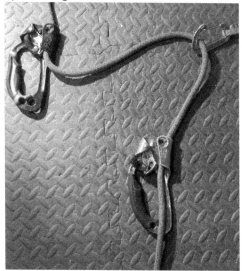

Upper ascender moved above gear, lower ascender's cam disengaged to lower out onto the upper ascender. If the lower ascender won't disengage, pull down on

Two ascender setup with a backup microtraxion. Both ascenders have a daisy and locker with the ladders clipped to the daisy locker. Upper daisy shortened to arm's reach. Microtraxion clipped to belay loop as a backup (optional).

Prusik above jumar (and clipped to belay loop).

Front and tail clipped.

the rope (don't open the cam up fully, however). The lower ascender may now be moved above piece to clean if necessary.

If you begin to jug fairly horizontally, there can be a lot of torque on the cam of the ascender. **Tail clip** your ascender, and possibly also clip a biner through the hole above the cam for safety to keep the ascender from prying off the rope.

If the terrain becomes really easy low angled low 5th or 4th class type terrain, jugging becomes really difficult compared to just climbing. If the line wanders and it's also chossy, things can get dangerous. Tell the leader that they should put you on belay and pull up the slack. Rake off your ascenders and start climbing. If it's still pretty steep, jug a little, stop and let the leader belay up the slack. If it's medium angle, just use the upper ascender to tram up the rope, taking off the aiders and the other Jumar, and have the leader occasionally pull in the slack. You can also take in coils and tie backup knots occasionally instead of the leader belaying and pulling in slack.

If for whatever reason you have a dangerous jugging situation, maybe you'll be jugging an 8 mm line, or maybe you weren't planning on jugging and don't have the best gear for whatever reason, you can always use another rope, like the haul line, to serve as a **backup belay** from above. If less than half a pitch, use the other side of the rope to toss down and use to belay. Of course someone needs to have gotten to the top to do this for you.

Unknown fixed lines, fixed lines left out for a while, fixed lines running over sharp lips, fixed lines subject to rock fall, or super skinny fixed lines all offer a lifetime of nightmare material. If you have another rope and can put in pro on belay from below while jugging, do it. Often times this isn't the case. There's really no safe way to do this, but to either suck it up and hope for the best, or go home. The first one up should be prepared to knot-off sections of unsafe rope for the lucky 2nd who owes the first person up big time.

FOLLOWING A TRAVERSE

Mentioned earlier, the leader must protect the traverse for the follower's ability level, not the leader's. A second rope could also be used as a hand line. Occasionally the traverse will require that the leader does not place any gear, or at least backcleans all of the gear until they are high up enough that the direction of pull on the follower is up and not to the side (or even worse below them). Always think about how the rope will be running for the follower when traversing, or climbing down and back up again.

Clip the hole on the top of the Jumar for even short traverses. Use an old wiregate, it will get trashed. The quickest, but not the safest method has you only on the lower, then only the upper ascender for a moment. Bring both ascenders close to piece, weight the lower ascender and very quickly move upper ascender past the piece and re-clip it to the rope. Tail clipping the upper ascender to the rope keeps it from getting torqued, but is slower if there's a lot of gear that needs cleaning. Now lower out onto the upper ascender by pulling down on rope below the lower ascender and opening up the cam slightly. When you are in line with the next piece, quickly bring lower ascender past the piece so you can then remove the gear. You may be able to clean the gear without removing the lower ascender.

Upper ascender moved while lower weighted

Upper ascender is now weighted. Pull down on the rope below the lower ascender and release the cam just enough to be able to lower onto the upper ascender. Quickly move the lower ascender below the upper and clean the gear.

You can switch to a GriGri as your lower ascender and frog-style just before the traverse. This makes it easier and safer to lower out. Try both out before committing to either on a real climb.

A foolproof, but slower way to clean a traverse or roof is to clip your aider and daisy to the piece past the one you want to clean, stand on it, and backclean. This is basically re-aiding the pitch without placing the gear, but instead just backcleaning. The leader should have placed enough gear for you to do this within reach. **Hooks** instead of biners make this go faster. You need to tie a solid backup knot, as you'll be fully committed to one piece of gear. If you are using the frog system with a GriGri for this, tie a backup knot below the GriGri. You could also tie in short and have the leader belay you, which is probably the safest and fastest system unless the leader is dealing with the haul or can't hear you.

PENDULUMS

Leading a pendulum is easy – clip a piece, lower down, and swing. For all setups described below, it is much safer to lower through a **leaver biner or quicklink** than it is to run the rope directly through webbing. Carry some spare biners even on trade routes just in case.

If you're the leader and you do a pendulum, you must backclean your gear on your way back up until you are at least above the pendulum point if the follower plans on just swinging across (if it's safe), and to minimize rope drag. If you aren't comfortable with a lot of backcleaning then belay down low after the pendulum. If the leader places gear low enough to reduce drag, but the follower can't safely swing across, the follower will need to use some rope tricks described next. If the climbing is dicey right after the pendulum, the leader could leave gear until the climbing eases (or gear gets better) and be lowered to backclean before climbing back up on toprope.

Following a Short (<30') Pendulum

If you are following a pendulum, about thirty feet or less, use this system. You need slack (3x the amount of distance traveled), so if the pendulum occurs early on don't let the leader pull in too much rope for fixing, and if free climbing you will need to call for slack. First clip in directly to the anchor point. The leader will have to leave gear if a fixed point isn't established. Leaving a leaver biner on the master point of the pendulum anchor makes things go faster for the follower.

If jugging, stay about five feet below the anchor on your jugs or things get ugly. If you are sketched about clattering across the rock on your jugs, tie a backup knot just below your bottom jug. After you are secure to the fixed point, unclip the lead rope from the pendulum point.

Pass a bight of rope from your tie-in through the anchor and clip it to a biner on your belay loop. The slack end of the bite coming out of the biner off your harness is your brake hand. Hoist yourself up with the brake hand until you are weighting the anchor with the rope, not your tether. Unclip the tether and lower yourself out with the brake hand. You should come tight on your Jumars at the end of the pendulum/lower-out. Since you are now safe on your Jumars, unclip and pull the loop through the anchor. No untying is necessary. If you are sketched about lowering out with just the loop of rope as your brake, you can replace the biner on your belay loop with a belay device.

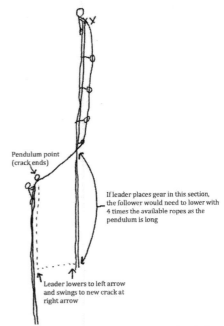

Short pendulum logistics. 3x amount of slack rope needed to follow.

Pendulum to the right: bight passed through anchor point (leaver biner) to lower with. Stay attached to ascenders that were moved past anchor point.

On a short pendulum you could theoretically get your webbing back (see the section on retrievable anchors below). But this combination of skills is PhD level trickery, and you'll probably screw it up and die.

Following a Longer Pendulum

The simplest method of following a long (or any) pendulum is just to rappel off with **another rope**. This is also the heaviest method as you'll need another rope. You may wind up climbing with four ropes if long pendulums and haul bag lower outs are necessary. If you aren't using another rope to simply rappel off of, there are two methods you can use. If the leader plans on leading up after the long pendulum, he/she must back-clean a very long distance. The follower will need 2x the amount of rope as the pendulum is long.

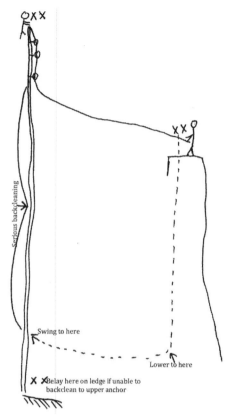

Long pendulum logistics. If using the same rope, the follower must have 2x rope available as the pendulum is long.

- **Method One**

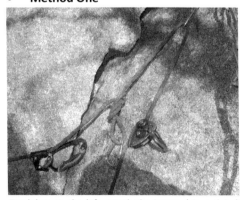

Pendulum to the left: attach the jumar, (via a daisy), knot, and GriGri into your harness. Lower with GriGri.

Clip into the anchor used for the leader's pendulum. Put your ascenders on the new side of pendulum and tie a backup fig-8 on bight below them, clipping that knot into your belay loop. If you are cleaning the leader's biner and sling and going directly through the pendulum point you have to untie and pass all the slack through the fixed point. Tying back in isn't 100% necessary if you are attached to a backup knot, as you will need to untie later. Put your GriGri (better) or belay device on the non-pendulum side (side you jugged up on) of the rope and haul up until weighted. Unclip from the anchor and lower out until you are back on your ascenders. Dismantle the belay device, untie the end of rope if still tied in, pull it through the anchor, and tie back in.

- **Method Two**

This method is fast and assumes you are belaying with a GriGri. Otherwise use method one. After the leader is off belay, keep the GriGri on the rope. Attach your upper ascender with daisy above the GriGri. Untie and pass all the extra rope through the anchor – away from pendulum. You don't have to tie back in, but tying back is safer. Put yourself on rappel on a standard belay device on the side of the anchor you originally jugged on, and lower down until you come tight on the GriGri and ascender. Finish jugging the pitch frog style.

Pendulum to the left: attach jumar (via daisy), GriGri, and belay device into harness. Lower on belay device.

Descending

SINGLE PITCH RAPPELLING/LOWERING

To avoid the dreaded dropped rope on top of single pitch anchors, pull up a bunch of slack up and clove the rope to a draw on the anchor before you untie. Feed the end through and tie back in if lowering. Double check before you undo your tether to the anchor. Clipping your tether to just one bolt isn't the safest idea – you never know. Do yourself a big favor and use another sling to clip into the other bolt for a backup.

If you are rappelling instead of lowering, you could still drop the rope if you let go before enough rope has been lowered down on the short side after unclipping the backup knot. Either be very careful, or pull a ton of rope through the anchor before undoing the backup knot. You could also tie an overhand into the end of the rope, and then undo the backup knot. This way even if the rope slip through, the overhand would jam in the anchor (assuming the anchor point is smaller than the overhand knot).

ANCHORING THE ROPE

Before tossing down your ropes and trusting your life to the anchors, give them a thorough inspection. Rap tat, even on popular routes, should never be trusted. It will eventually fail, and what was good for the first thousand climbers may not be so good for you. No matter how new the tat looks, follow it around the entire length of whatever it's going through including the knot. Give it several solid hard tugs (clipped into something else of course). If it looks questionable replace it with new tat or cannibalize your cordalette or some slings. Don't use Dyneema if you intended to cut and knot it! Pack the old tat out with you please.

If you think it's good, still back it up. To back up the anchor, place a piece of gear and clip it slightly loose to the non-knot strand of rope (in case the 2nd forgets to pull it out so the rope won't get stuck) so the backup isn't loaded when the first person raps, but would hold a fall if the tat breaks. To trust the anchor enough to pull the backup, have the heaviest person go first and give them the rack, pack, and knife. If the anchor held and you still trust it, pull the backup.

Leaver biners, quick links, and rap rings will keep **rap webbing** from being damaged from the rope sliding over it when rappelling. If your leaver biner is an old piece of junk you found or are retiring, use two. Just rapping off webbing is ok for bailing on non-established anchors or remote first ascents. If you find an anchor without some sort of metal rappel point, assume that it isn't safe and back it up. Rap rings are very light, but less user friendly than small lightweight quick links or cheap lightweight biners. Quick links are a great commodity for rappelling with a pull cord. The small opening on small diameter quick links prevents the pull cord knot from passing through the anchor which leads to a stuck rope, and the jamming of the knot also creates a backup if the pull cord breaks on rappel. What size and strength rated quick link you feel safe to rap off of is up to you. You can always back it up for the first person. Never assume that even a small diameter rap link (quick link, biner, etc.) will be small enough to keep a knot from pulling through! People die from this happening.

If using a small diameter quick link with a sketchy tag line, still put both ropes through the rappel device. That way the knot won't be pulled into the quick link and possibly pop through, and if the pull cord broke for whatever reason, the knot could still save you by jamming in the anchor. There is no reason to not rap on both the lead rope and pull cord at the same time. If you aren't using a very small quick link to jam the knot, you could rap off of tat tied with a hole just small enough to allow a rope to fit through, or use some athletic tape to shrink the size of the hole – expect the pull to be miserable. Sometimes anchors can pinch the rope when pulling it and this can jam up the knot. To minimize this you want the knot (pull side) on the bottom side of the anchor. Remember, this is a "just in case the skinny cord breaks" scenario. Don't trust that knot to stay jammed by rapping on both lines.

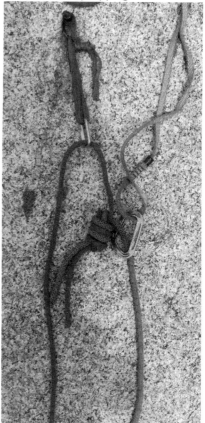

1/4" quicklink to jam knot in case pull cord breaks (pretend the rope on the right is the pull cord). Remove backup sling (connected to a tree out of sight).

If your pull cord is super skinny and sketchy and you also don't trust the knot to jam in the anchor if the pull cord breaks, you'll want to back it up with a knot. Set the rappel up with the knot on the pull cord side (and on bottom side of the anchor). Pull out a little more lead rope through the pull side of the anchor and tie an overhand on a bight or clove hitch. Clip the knot to a locker and to the lead rope on the non-pull side of the anchor. If the pull cord breaks, the lead rope will hitch to the anchor. The big downside of this setup is first the starting friction of pulling a skinnier cord and the backup sliding over the lip sucks. The backup is also going to be more prone to getting caught. If it gets caught and the lead rope is out of reach from the anchor you're pulling from, you've got problems.

Pull cord backup with jamming knot on lead rope

The best way to avoid rappel snafus is for the first person down to do a significant test pull. If doing a full length test pull be sure to knot the end of the lead rope in case the test pull winds up being a real pull, stranding the 2nd rappeller! Don't forget to remove the knot when pulling for real!

If you trust both ropes and have the choice to pull either the lead rope or the pull cord, pulling the lead rope is an easier pull and gives you a lead rope to use in case the rope gets stuck. But, there is a higher probability of the pull cord getting stuck while tumbling down when pulling with the lead line. The **Esprit Alpine Escape** rope is nice because it is stiff and slippery and has a much less likelihood of getting stuck on the way down. If the route is wandering or bushy, you probably want to pull the thin cord. If you are pulling the thin cord, the knot will travel up into the anchor when rappelling, so be advised as this can jam and create a stuck rope.

Anything used to protect a climb or make an anchor can be used to rap off of. Rap anchors get a lot less force than what a lead anchor is designed for. However, rappelling could involve a lot of bouncing, which generates larger loads than just bodyweight. Since you are 100% relying on your anchor for rappelling, you want to test it. Place pro on rappel clipped to the non-pull side of the rope (in case the follower forgets to remove them or needs to leave them) for a catastrophic backup on very sketchy rappels. Thankfully the stretch of the rope, friction of the rope on the rock, and friction of the rope over the edge of the cliff all significantly reduce the loads on the anchor. A rope going over a 90° angle can reduce loads by $2/3^{rds}$, and a 45° angle could reduce loads by as much as half. The friction of the rock the rope is laying on also takes a lot of weight off. This is how folks can hold the weight of a single climber on body-anchor raps and belays.

If you are rappelling on two solid lines of similar diameter, all you need to tie is an overhand knot, aka the **Euro Death Knot** (EDK) with plenty of tail (at least 8"). Dress the knot so there are no twists or overlaps and pull all 4 strands tightly. The EDK is safe with enough tail. It can loosen if the knot flips, which is why you want plenty of tail. However, too much tail can wrap around the lines and cause enough friction to get the ropes stuck.

Never mess with the knot after it has been tied. If you need to get the knot on the other side of the anchor, then it's ok to untie and retie it. The EDK has the advantage of being less likely to jam or hang up on the way down, and stuck ropes can be deadly in the right circumstances. Tying two EKS's tight against each other is a good backup, especially if your ropes are wet. If your ropes are of very different diameter, either tie a rewoven fig-8 (Flemish Bend - so the tails are on opposite sides), or two EDK's tight on each other because the smaller diameter rope can slip out in an EDK.

If both ropes are strong and you aren't worried about the thinner rope breaking, don't use the knot jamming backup system by tying off one of the ropes described above as this increases the likelihood of stuck ropes.

ROPE MANAGEMENT
Good rope management is the key to tangle and stuck-free rappels. If you are using one rope, a clearly visible middle mark makes a world of difference. Guessing the middle on shorter rappels can get you hurt or killed, and guessing the middle on long raps is simply idiotic. If you don't have the middle marked take the time to find both ends and feed them together through the anchor.

Tossing the rope down is the first opportunity you have to create a mess. Simply shoving a pile of rope off a ledge is great if you are tired and don't give a damn, but better to take the time and coil the rope in butterfly coils. If you don't have a clean toss or your hands are too small make two separate coils. Hold onto the end coil and throw the coil closest to the anchor first. Now toss the end coil. This little trick greatly improves your chances of a clean toss.

If you have a pile of double ropes, tossing them together may be better than coiling them individually. If the ropes get caught up fairly far horizontally from the fall line in separate directions you may set yourself up for some dangerous swings. If there are tree branches horizontally out from you, it can be a real disaster if they get stuck above or directly across from you. Tossing a skinny pull cord separately from the lead line is a better idea as the lead line is less likely to stray from the fall line, and the two ropes will tangle wildly if tossed together.

Toss the middle coil first, then the end coil for a clean toss.

Toss rocks and other objects that could fall on you (or cut the rope) off before you toss the ropes. If you have no clue how far the next anchor is, or know that it is a rope stretcher, then knot the ends of the ropes separately, but never together. The only real drawback to knotting the ends are that the knot could jam in a constriction below or way to the side of the next anchor during the rope toss and make it impossible to pull the rope up. This is a manageable situation, but can be dangerous. Worst-case scenario is you need to cut the rope. This happened to me, only the rope jammed in a chimney so deep I couldn't reach it and the rope needed to be cut. The problem was that I didn't have enough rope to reach the next anchor! I cut the rope, and had to rappel off the newly stuck rope as a new anchor (crack was to big to leave a cam). So yes, ropes stuck from below can be bad.

The easily avoidable, but truly awful other scenario is when you forget to untie the backup knot when pulling the rope. How to avoid it? Always hold onto the rope being pulled up – you'll feel the knot at the last moment. Holding onto the rope being pulled up is a really good idea if the pull doesn't go as planned so you can use it to pull the rope back to try and fix the problem. If you let go and it floats out in space, unreachable, you're screwed. You're also screwed if the wind picks up and twirls the end around something. So hold onto the end.

Saddlebagging the ropes and clipped into the ends on rappel

Most institutions argue that backup knots save lives much more than dangerous situations they can create. I believe it is situation dependent. Tying a fig-8 on a bight at the ends instead of a stopper knot could allow you to clip into the ends of the rope - very useful if straining to reach the next anchor safely. Tying in to the ends of the rope while rappelling is by far the safest methods, and can help with getting your ropes snarled by tossing them. Stack the ropes on your harness with some slings, like saddlebags, to keep everything organized. If you aren't into this, then you probably should tie stopper knots on the ends of your ropes unless the situation (windy, bushy, flakey) dictates otherwise.

Another big rope management concern is letting the ropes twist. This is an extremely common cause of stuck ropes. The first place to check is right at the anchor. It's easy to thread the ropes in weird way that causes a twist right at the anchor. The first person down may not notice, as the twist may not appear until the ropes are tight and down the wall a bit. As the second, it is your duty to check for this. If combination isn't an issue, identify which is the left or right strand to the climber down at the lower anchor to aid him/her threading the rope. You can put a leg through the ropes below you to help untwist, and also clip a biner between the ropes above your belay device (with a sling to keep it there). Sometimes long knot tails from joining ropes can get stuck in the anchor so make sure they are ok.

Rope twisted in anchor

The two biners got pressed together creating a situation that could really pinch the rope.

The next rope management duty of the last rappeller is to try and rappel in the direct fall line of the rappel. The first person down may have had to wander around a bit to scope the rappel or fix ropes. The last rappeller must check for objects that will cause the knot to get jammed or the rope falling down to get caught on and direct the rope out of their way as much as possible (the first person down does this also). Better to leave slings and gear to direct the line out of the way of trouble.

If constrictions are present at the lip, the last rappeller needs to slide the knot down along with him/her to clear these. This can only be done if the rappel wasn't a rope-stretcher. Communication between the person at the anchor and last rappeller is critical in these situations.

Sometimes tossing ropes down in coils is a bad idea. There could be a ton of loose rock to knock of, it could be super windy and your ropes will go everywhere, or there could just be a lot of stuff that could hang up the rope like bushes. Pull cords are notorious for being difficult to toss in coils. One solution is to stuff the rope into a **stuff sack** (end tied to the draw cord) and throw the stuff sack full of rope. This works well, and makes a fun toss. You can tie a **heavy roundish object** to the end of the rope to toss or lower it down. Clove hitching the end of a pull cord to a round rock works pretty well, and the rock falls out after it served its purpose. Don't use a cam - it will get stuck. And obviously be aware of anyone below. If these options sound equally un-enticing, you can always sling coils of rope to your harness or put coils in the back and have the feed while you rappel for a zero tangle system.

Make sure no one is below you and if you throw it, you may need to chop a foot or two off the ends if the rock damages the rope.

Lowering the first person down is another, and very safe way to get the ropes down tangle free. Once to the anchor, the first person that you lowered could then lower you down if you tie into the end or tie in short (to avoid passing a knot). To avoid losing the ends or having them float into space if windy, you can tie into the ends of the rope while going down as well. Finally, when pulling the rope either feed the pull side through the anchor as you pull, or tie the pull side off to the anchor to make sure the rope doesn't come down and get away from you, stranding you with no rope at all.

RAPPELLING SAFETY

First make sure your biner is locked and both loops of rope are through the belay device and biner. If rappelling on skinny lines or you need more friction try adding a **2nd carabineer.** If rapping on two strands of super skinny rope, you could put both ropes through just one hole on the rap device. You can also extend your belay device on a daisy chain or sling hitched to your harness and put a Munter hitch on a locker below the belay device with the rope. Extending your device allows for more control and works with a backup autoblock knot better. If using a daisy to extend the rap device be sure to shorten in with another biner as discussed earlier.

Figure-8 devices are useful for rappelling thick and icy ropes, like fixed lines on a big mountain. They don't provide enough friction for most situations. If your new partner has one on their harness, be concerned. The safest thing is to add a redundant backup in case you let go with your brake hand, or need to let go to deal with rope issues. If you're going second, a fireman's belay from the first person down is the polite and fastest thing to do. This simply means the first person down pulls on the ends of the ropes if the rappeller slips.

Belay device extended and backed up with an autoblock knot clipped to leg loop. The gate on the autoblock locker can get unscrewed by the rope. This method is the best and safest way to rappel. There is never a bad time to use this unless you have a fireman's belay from below. This setup uses a PAS, but is clipped with the end locker as should be done with a flab webbing daisy.

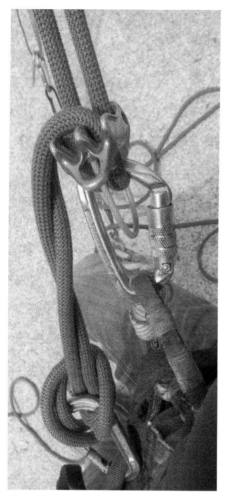

Munter added for friction. I should have extended the device (next photo) and made sure the strands weren't twisted.

knot. The **autoblock knot** is choice, and it goes on the brake strands and gets clipped to your leg loop. To get more length and also control, extend the belay device out on a sling or daisy as mentioned. If the autoblock is too long, it will get jammed in the belay device and won't grip. The **Sterling Hollow Block** cord is the perfect autoblock cord. Leg wraps work in a pinch, but you have to be in control to use them, making them useless for accidents.

Leg wraps

Petzl Shunt

The first person must supply his/her own backup. There are a few double rope auto-locking belay devices that will stop your rappel if you let go, like the **Smart, Jul, and Alpine Up**. The one's I've used are really jerky and are a total pain on low angled terrain. A **GriGri** works, but you can only use one rope and it can also be very tiring. To make this work, tie off the lead line and rap down on this assuming the next person down remembers to undo the tie-off. A **Petzl Shunt** also works as a backup, but is way too bulky and heavy to bring just for this.

The lightest, smoothest, and one of the safest methods is to use a prusik-type backup

Rappelling or getting lowered while cleaning gear can be difficult or dangerous, especially if the route wanders. A fireman's backup with a person ready to pull hard to reduce a swing is helpful. The best way to clean an overhanging route is while being lowered is to clip into the other rope with a quickdraw and tram down the line.

Retrieving draws on an overhanging rappe by tramming the line and the ground person pulling the climber in with the ropes.

If the rope is pulling hard against the gear making it impossible to unclip, clip in direct from your harness quickdraw to the biner the rope is going through (photo shown earlier in jugging). This takes the tension off the rope and you can unclip the rope. Re-clip into the other rope with the draw and quickly unclip the gear, preparing to swing out a bit. If rap cleaning and you wind up way off to the side, you can tag up another rope (or use the end of your rap rope if long enough) and have someone pull sideways to keep you from swinging.

If you don't have a belay device, don't worry. A **Munter hitch** with or without an extra wrap works great, even on two ropes. You can also fashion a carabineer brake bar by clipping two regular biners to your belay loop, pop both ropes through the center of both, and clip the loop with two other biners. Make all the gates opposite and opposed. Be careful about dropping the two biners not directly clipped to the rope. Andy Kirkpatrick suggests putting a nut through these to keep them safe. A Munter will most likely be your choice between this and a brake-bar.

Biner brake with nut clipped to upper biners to keep them falling off when unclipping.

Always find the middle of your rope. If using two ropes of different lengths, be sure to remember this when sliding down. Consider a backup knot in the short end. If rapping first, always have the rack, slings, and a knife just in case.

PULLING THE ROPE / RAPPEL SEQUENCE

Tether into the anchor, check the anchor, and back it up for the first rappeller. Feed the connected ropes through the anchor. Tie off one or both ropes (if you haven't connected them you) if there is a chance that the ropes can get away from you leaving you stranded. Make sure you will be pulling the rope you want to, and backup the pull side if necessary. Have the knot on the bottom side of the anchor and make sure your knot is good. The heaviest person goes first and deals with rope issues and finds next anchor. It is common courtesy for the person waiting to rappeller next to pull up the rope and hold it for the first rappeller to get it more easily into his or her belay device. I know some climbers who use this as a test for a good partner! It's a good idea to have an autoblock knot and the ends of the ropes knotted. You could also lower, rappel with the ropes coiled on you, or be clipped into the ends of both ropes.

The first person down clips into the anchor and checks it before taking him/herself off belay. Do a test pull (communicate this) to ensure a smooth pull and that everything was setup properly. Yell, "Off rappel!" really loud and then feed the pull end through the anchor. Give the next rappeller a fireman's backup. Do not let the free end of the rope get away from you! Remove the backup knots unless the rap was a real rope-stretcher.

The last rappeller puts themselves on rappel and pulls the backup and confirms which rope will be pulled. They reposition the knot past lips if necessary. They rap down making sure the ropes don't twist, they are going in a straight line down to the next anchor, and looking out for rope and knot snagging obstacles. The climber at the anchor helps the last rappeller tether into the anchor, and controls the free ends of the rope and pulls the stopper knots on the rope ends if they already haven't.

Pull the rope until the knot comes down to you. One person should be pulling while the other person coils and tosses the first rope through the new anchor. If you are not alternating pull ropes, tie both ropes off to the anchor near the knot with a few feet of slack so the knot can be retied for the correct rope to be pulled again. Keep pulling until the 2nd rope comes tumbling down. Don't stop pulling the falling rope, you may have a chance to keep it from getting stuck. Do not jerk the rope just before it's ready to tumble down, the resulting elasticity may create waves and make the rope stick on something. If everything went well, the other rope made it down safely. If it zipped all the way down past you, you may not need to pull it up and coil/toss it again. If being extra careful, pull it up and toss it correctly.

Things are obviously a lot simpler with single rope rappels. Just be sure to find the middle and keep the rope from twisting.

LOWERING

For any lowering scenario, putting an **autoblock or prusik** below your brake hand (as in rappelling) can greatly improve safety. To lower off your harness you can re-direct the climber side of the device through the anchor to help control.

Lowering directly off the anchor is easy to control if you clip a biner right next to where the belay device is anchored (or slightly above) and clip the brake side through that. This creates a redirect with a very small angle, increasing friction.

Redirecting brake strand through another biner and using a prusik (clipped to belayer) backup. The belay device shown attached to the anchor is NOT in guide-mode. See below for lowering in guide-mode.

If you are lowering someone from the top of a cliff so they can toprope out (like ice climbing in Ouray), communication is vital between the climber and the belayer. The climber could get lowered too far and be unable to climb back out. Figure this out beforehand! The climber being lowered should have the gear and know how to ascend out if they cannot re-climb the pitch.

If lowering someone off a guide-mode belay device, most devices allow you to stick the nose of carabineer or nut-tool into a smaller hole to act as a lowering lever. This method offer a less control than other methods and a prusik backup should be used on the brake.

Releasing guide-mode with the nose of a carabiner and a prusik backup.

Sling coming down on the right is attached to harness. Prusik not clipped to harness for clarity.

A quick and dirty method is to just pump the carabineer going through the rope up and down. This offers a lot of control but is slow – a good method if the climber just needs a few feet of slack.

Pumping the biner to give some slack

Stuck devices require a re-direct or a block and tackle. Using one or more runners through the spine of the device (or the little hole if it has one), put the runners up through the anchor and down to your belay loop. Squat down and lower while holding the brake hand and use a prusik backup on the brake strand.

To lower one climber when simultaneously belaying two, tie off the climber who is fine, and use whatever lowering method seems appropriate. Hold the brake hand with either method and use a prusik backup. Redirecting the brake strand through another carabineer can also help with control. If the climber needs a bunch of slack for whatever reason and doesn't need to be lowered, the easiest method is to have them take their weight off, release the device by hand (just pull up on the rope carabineer or tilt the device up), and pull out some slack. If they need slack and can't unweight the rope, put a prusik on the weighted strand to the anchor with a load-releasable knot, release the device by hand or with a biner lever, pull out the slack, and release the prusik.

Block and tackle. Prusik'd on rope, overhand tied above prusik and clipped to biner. Remaining cord wrapped between two biners for mechanical advantage.

If you are lowering off a single bolt or questionable anchor you can still back yourself up in case the anchor fails. To do this, attach a prusik to yourself and the rope going through your gear. Slide the prusik down with you as you are lowered and are cleaning your gear. If the top anchor fails, your prusik will save you and the fall would be similar to a lead fall onto the next piece you haven't cleaned yet.

To lower more than one length of rope, see the Rescue chapter.

Do not forget to tie off the end of the rope if lowering! Two cases in particular are when lowering a climber down below you and you aren't tied into the end of that rope, or when lowering a leader above you from the top of a climb that you aren't 100% positive is less than half your rope!

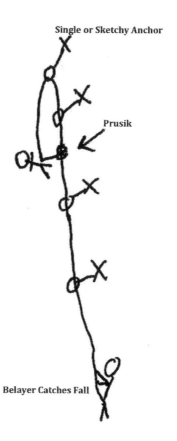

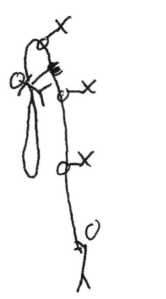

Backup prusik between gear will catch a fall if the anchor fails. Belayer is lowering climber and will catch the fall.

SPEEDY RAPPELLING
Simul-rappelling really can speed up a descent if the anchor is bomber and you don't screwup. It's a really good idea to use autoblock knots or at least knot the ends of the rope. You both need to weight the rope at the same time, and unweight the rope at the same time or the person still weighting the rope will go for a ride.

Another option is to do a tandem or assisted rappel where both people rappel using one device. This is useful for rescues or rappelling with an inexperienced person. The rappel device is extended on a daisy or sling as described above, but both climbers clip into it, or one clips into the other's locker. You can also tie a cordalette or sling so it has two arms of different lengths. Put the belay device in the main loop and have each climber clip into one of the two arms.

In this setup, each climber would clip into an arm of the cordalette. A backup autoblock should be employed here.

If there are other parties on your route you can speed up a rappels by hooking up with them. Send two climbers down with all of the collective ropes to simul-rap and setup all the rappels. The last two simul-rapper's must pull and carry all of the ropes to the last rappel, so buy those guys a beer.

OTHER WAYS OFF
If there's a walk-off or easy down-climb you can probably get off faster and safer unless raps are clean straight up and down affairs. Climbs with sketchy descent steps can be belayed or rappelled with a cordalette if you don't want to undo 200' of rope for 10' of climbing/rappelling. Backcleaning gear with a daisy chain similar to the solo method described later but in reverse could work too.

Some summits allow for a heli pickup. Kind of expensive and ridiculous, but a good way to impress a date. Skiing off is always a blast if you managed to bring the skis. Basejumping off the summit is the all-time coolest way to get down. Why not solo with a chute, aka "Free Basing" while you're at it. Please do not let loved ones find this book if you do that, however.

Glissading, scree surfing, and plunge stepping are really quick ways down snow or loose rock. Being good at this is a necessary skill for speed and safety as slowly going down increases your chances of falling and twisting an ankle. The key to quickly plunge stepping or not falling on sandy terrain is to fall forward, letting momentum carry you, instead of trying to brake with every step. In snow, sand, or small talus, landing on your heel is the best way to plunge down.

PROBLEMATIC RAPPEL SITUATIONS
Bailing on a Big Wall
Many of the following topics will help with bailing on a big wall, especially with haul bags. Don't forget that you can always down-aid sections you aided up. This may take a long time, but may be the only option on severely overhanging or traversing pitches. If retreating with a big ol' bag on a very large wall because a storm is rolling in, it may be one of those special cases where you want to ride out the storm instead. Bailing during a storm with a big bag or very high up a wall could easily kill you for many

reasons. Find an overhang and hide under it. Look out for waterfalls over roof and watercourses (look for black streaks or blank sections). Setting up shop under one of these in a big storm will most likely kill you.

Passing the Knot on Rappel

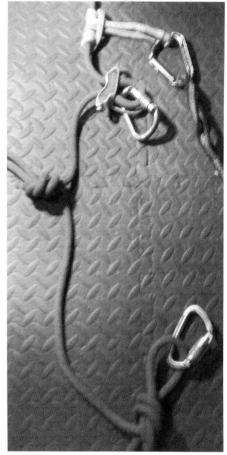

First photo: weight on prusik, backed up below knot. Second photo: Belay device moved below knot with autoblock backup. Next step would be to remove upper prusik.

Passing a knot on rappel usually occurs when you weren't expecting to, so it doesn't hurt to practice. To do this, rap to just above the knot but don't let it get sucked into your device. Put a rope grabbing knot or ascender on the rope above the belay device and get your weight onto it. Tie a backup knot with the rope below the joining while you remove your belay device and reattach it below the knot. The trick is now to remove the prusik and get onto the belay device. The easiest method is to put another prusik or ascender below the belay device and use a sling or aider to stand in (foot wraps work in a pinch) so you can unweight the upper prusik, remove it, and lower your body down onto the rappel device.

A slightly more difficult method, but offering smoother transitions is to tie an autoblock or prusik above your belay device and attach it to your belay loop with a Munter-mule. Use this as your backup on rappel if you have the foresight, or tie it hanging off your normal autoblock. When near the knot, back yourself with a knot below the rope-joining knot. Take your rappel device off and place it under the joining knot and put a new autoblock on below the belay device. Either slide the upper prusik on the load releasable hitch down until you are weighting the belay device, or undo the load releasable Munter mule knot and lower yourself with the Munter onto the belay device. Don't let the upper prusik get too far out of reach to remove it!

Belay device moved below knot with autoblock prusik backup below it. Munter mule undone to lower and transfer weight onto belay device.

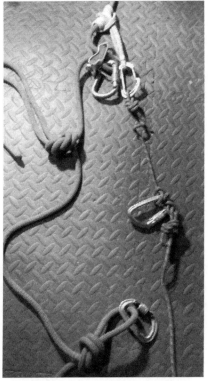

Weight on upper prusik with a munter mule attached to prusik and harness. Backup clipped to harness below knot.

One final way to really quickly pass a knot, besides down-jumaring, requires you to join the knots so two the tails are long enough to tie an overhand on a bight in each. When you get to the knot, clip into the loops of tail and hang on them. Move the belay device to the lower rope. If you can't get off the loops, clip a sling or ladder into one of the loops, stand on it, and lower down onto the belay device. Remove the extra knots.

613

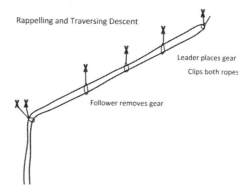

Clipped into tail knots directly with a locker. Stand on sling clipped to knots to remove and replace belay device.

Rappelling Traverses and Overhangs

If a route traverses so your ropes are nowhere near the lower anchor, you can place gear above you, clipping the gear into both strands to keep you in line until your reach the anchor. Put the 2nd on a fireman's belay and they rap and pull gear. You may need to down-aid while on rappel (use a backup knot or autoblock) to get past roofs and still be close to the wall to reach the next anchor.

Rappelling and Lowering Haul Bags (or Victims)

Rapping with a heavy bag on your back is really dangerous, and having the bag hang off your harness gives you little control. The best method is to clip the haul bag into your belay biner or to your belay device extended on a tether so the weight is on your belay device and rope, not you. Use a backup, like an autoblock! You may want a ladder handy to help you getting on and off the anchor.

Belay device extended on PAS, bag clipped to extended device. Backup autoblock on rope as well.

You can also ride the haul bag down while rappelling with it. To do this, attach a locker and rappel device directly to the haul bag's full strength loops. Attach yourself to the rappel device by clipping another locker to your belay loop and to the belay device locking biner. Yeehaw!

You may want to lower the bags instead. Fix both ropes or strands of one rope to the anchor, and lower the bag while the other climber rappels on the other rope or strand and guides the bag down and into the anchor like a tram. If there are overhangs or traverses, the first person raps on a single fixed line and attaches it tight to the new anchor. The haul bags are lowered on another rope or strand and clipped into the tight line to guide the bags down. If another rope is available then it can be used by the climber at the new lower anchor to help guide the bag and pull it free if it gets caught. To transfer a heavy haul bag on and off the anchor you need to attach it to the anchor with a Munter mule and backed up with a tether. See photo at bottom of page.

A counterweight rappel can also be used. If dealing with a victim instead of a haul bag, they will need a chest harness clipped into a prusik tied at chest level on their rope to keep upright if they are unconscious. Put one end of the rope through the anchor and tie it to the bag/victim. Put yourself on rappel on the other side of the anchor, and then put a prusik going from you to just above the victim's prusik so they don't get away from you. Use an autoblock knot on your brake hand.

If you have two ropes, tie them together and do the counterweight rappel on the first rope just until till just about at the knot connecting both ropes. You will have to pass the knot, which will really suck. See also lowering and tandem rappels.

Counterweight Rappel

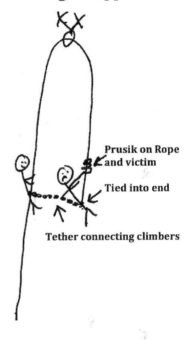

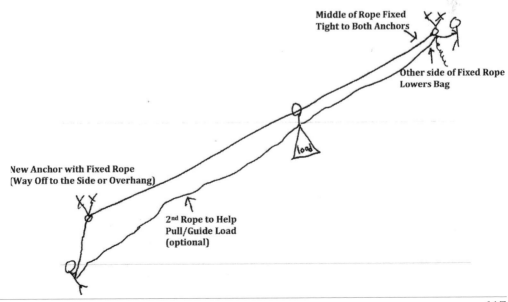

Not enough Rope
If for some reason your rope just doesn't reach the next anchor, or you REALLY want to get away with bringing just one rope and think you can pull it off, try this trick.

First lower your partner down to next anchor, or fix enough rope on one side to have them rap down to the next anchor and pull up any extra slack. At the upper anchor, tie a bight or clove hitch on the short side and clip it with a locker to the long side so it will jam in the anchor when you rap just the long side. Rappel down the long side. When you reach the end of the short rope, start attaching things to it to increase its length to reach the next anchor. Get creative, you probably have enough stuff to get thirty feet easy: clothes, shoelaces, pack straps, linking the rack end-to-end, etc. If worse came to worse and it doesn't reach, you can always jug back up and leave gear for another rap. You can't use this trick with double ropes.

A jamming knot is employed at the anchor, similar to backing up a pull-cord. Rap on longer side (right). I strung together some cams (I clipped the holes on the cam lobes to extended their length), and the hip belt on my pack to reach the ground and pull the line.

Another option if using two ropes that don't reach, would be to extend the rappel anchor itself, but you'll leave more cord behind.

Anchor extended 20' with a cordalette.

If you are very close to the ground, but don't want to zip off the end of the rope, you could put in gear and down-aid/climb, attach a cordalette and/or slings to the end of the rope to use it as a hand line, or attach a cordalette to the end and rap it as well. This needs to be done on the non-pull side of the rope, or even safer, by joining both ends of the rope together in case the knot flips through the anchor. After your partner is down you'll need to get creative to retrieve your rope, mostly likely standing on a sling off the anchor to reach. If it winds up being too far, you should have done another rappel or extended the anchor.

Anchor Far to the Side
If the next rappel anchor winds up being quite far to the side, the first person down can place protection as they go, clipping the pro to both ropes above them to reduce the angle as they go, and help the following rappeller. If this isn't an option, the first person down should put a rappel backup on the ropes and pull up the ends to knot them if not already done. The first person down must combine pendulum, tension traverse, and some desperate grabbing if the angle is huge. To help out the following rappeller,

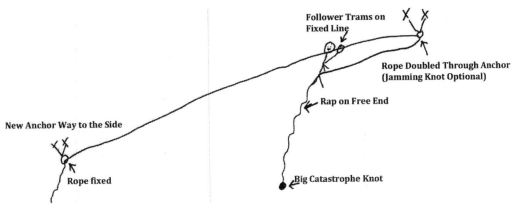

the first person down can fix one of the two strands to the anchor. There must be excellent communication to the following rappeller because they will then rappel down on the non-fixed strand only. If they screw this up they'll die. As they rappel on the single non-fixed strand, they are clipped to the fixed strand and use it as a tram to guide them to the anchor.

STUCK ROPES
Aside from a serious medical emergency, exposed unplanned bivy in the rain or cold, or a major catastrophe like dropping the rope or rack halfway off the wall, stuck ropes are hands down the worst thing that can happen to you climbing. The best thing you can do is to follow the advice already given and not get your ropes stuck in the first place. Take the factory tape off the end of rope ropes while you are at it. Those suckers can hang up on microcyrstals and support the weight of two people pulling with all their might.

Rope Immediately Stuck
If your rope gets stuck immediately or within a foot or two, check to see if you're pulling the wrong end. Keeping track of which end to pull can be difficult after a bunch or raps or when you're exhausted. Sometimes the knot will get

jammed. To fix this pull the other end to free it so you can start over. Flip the rope you're pulling to see if you can avoid this the second time around, or if the ropes somehow twisted around each other.

Whipping the rope in a rhythmic waving motion can do the trick with stuck ropes. If whipping the rope doesn't work, try pulling down quickly and letting go to see if the dynamic recoil of the rope pops it free. Your angle of pull may be pressing the rope into a crack or lip. Try moving out as far as possible, and then to different sides. If it isn't freeing with moderate force, pull the rope back up. Pulling too hard too soon will make it worse and other efforts useless. I've pulled so hard

with a partner that we actually snapped both ropes over a sharp edge. If none of that works, then it's time to pull hard. You may need to both put yourself back on belay and jump up and down in unison. Make sure you're clipped in to the anchor with enough tether to keep you from hurting yourself if the rope does free. If the rope comes free from a very hard pull, the odds of something else coming down with it are high so look out!

If nothing is working you either need to chop the rope and use what rope you've got left, or climb back up and fix the problem. Be the better partner and volunteer for the job.

Both Ends Are Down

If the other end of the rope is out of reach you will have to lead on the rope that's down and available until you can reach both ends to safely jug both. The easiest method is to have your partner give you a fireman's belay and "batman" up the rope with your belay device. The **Alpine Smart, Alpine Up, and Edelrid Jul** auto-lock on two ropes, making them the perfect tool. If it's too hard to do this, you can put prusiks over both ropes at once. You can ascend via any method up one side of the rope if you have your partner tie off the non-pull side. If you don't know what side that is, or are worried the knot may pass through the anchor, tie off both sides, or tie backup knots on the other rope to clip into just in case. If rope is going over webbing you shouldn't jug on one rope, it will create a sawing action and cut the webbing.

If the rope is pulling through metal and feeding smoothly, but you need to get back to the anchor for whatever reason, you can use the slingshot method. Tie a bight on the side of the rope without the knot and clip into it on your belay loop with a locker and put both prusiks on the other rope. If the rap was long, just tie into the end. Jug as normal and you'll slingshot up the rope. If you tie the original bight or end, and clip in and your partner belays the other rope in, you may not need to jug. Expect to pass the knot with your prusik if using two ropes joined with a knot, or your partner will need to pass the knot if belaying you. If you forget this, the belayer could tie you off and use a Munter as the 2nd belay device.

Slingshot method: clip into the knot you tied on non-knotted side of rope and jug with prusiks (or whatever you have) on the other strand. Do not use this if the rope is going through webbing.

Only One End Down

Hopefully you were able to pull enough rope down to lead/aid up on it. If there isn't enough rope to lead up, you have to rope-solo on the rope that is hanging still down. As with any rope-soloing situation, you need a good anchor, so tie the rope off to the anchor. If you've got a partner, have them put you on belay as well. This adds them into the system to provide a more dynamic belay, and they can control the slack at the same time. Climb back up using the clove hitch method (described later under rope soloing) on the stuck line, placing gear often. You may be able to free the stuck rope before you climb all the way up to it, so keep trying as you climb.

If the terrain is unclimbable, you will have to jug a single line that is stuck on an unknown obstacle. This probably the most dangerous thing you will ever do in your life. The possibility still exists of placing gear even if you can't climb up, so bring the rack and have your partner belay you. Jugging up with prusiks and/or a GriGri will harm the rope the least if you fall. If there is any other way down, even if it means doing 50 rappels on 30 feet of rope and losing your rack, or down aiding, choose that option.

RETRIEVABLE ANCHORS
Rigging retrievable anchors is complicated and dangerous. A $2 quick link, an old carabineer, or ten cents worth of tat really make retrievable anchors seem like a stupid idea. However, there could be situations where you need the gear back for more rappelling ahead, "normal" gear won't fit or stay put, or if you really don't want to leave trash. Canyoneers call this ghosting.

Sling Retrieval
This is the only way to get your sling back with a higher margin of safety, assuming you rappel on the correct strand. This is also the most useful retrievable anchor described. You can get your sling back from a fixed anchor point but you need to be less than 1/3rd of the way up from the belay with one rope, or less than halfway up with two ropes.

First clip in and hang. Put half of a sling through the anchor point and untie from the rope. This can be tricky if you are hanging of a quickdraw and a bolt because you'll have to struggle to get the sling under the draw you're weighting. Pass 1/3rd or ½ (if using two ropes) of the rope through both loops of the sling draped through the anchor. The two strands coming down are what you rappel from. Connect the other free end of rope to the stitching side of the sling – this is your retrieval line. Accidentally rapping on the pull side is a major no-no. Once down, pull the rope through and then pull on the strand you tied to the sling. Make sure your sling doesn't get accidentally girth hitched or catch on something, or it won't come down and you won't want to be jugging of that!

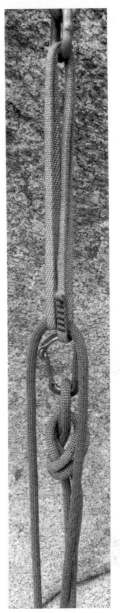

Rap on ropes not clipped to draw.

The Daisy Chain of Death
This is a method used primarily in the Alps for descending long routes with much down-climbing and many short rappels, or by eco-conscious canyoneerers. This is not a safe technique by any stretch of the imagination and should only be used on short rappels. You could use this on longer rappels, but you would be very brave.

tight that you can't undo it from below. Back the system up twice. The first backup is for the first person down in case the knot comes undone during the rappel. The other backup is connected to the sling for a test pull to ensure it will work, but you won't lose the rope in the process.

The Death Macramé

Rap on fixed end

Without a sling shown: Middle of rope draped around anchor (tree). One strand is passed through middle.

Other strand is daisy chained (slipknotted) through the loop created in first picture. Rap on the first strand passed through middle (the one that doesn't undo everything).

A daisy chain is pre-setup for this, but a closely knotted sling also works. You could even use the climbing rope itself to accomplish this. Wrap your daisy (or knotted sling) around or through the anchor. If using one rope, tie a bight in the middle and clip a locker to it and the end of the daisy. If using two ropes, tie them together, tie a bight above the knot joining the ropes, and clip the bight to the end of the daisy with a locker. This is the end you rap from. Push a loop just above the loop your locker is in through the analog loop on the other side of the daisy. Take a bight of rope from the pull side and feed a few inches of rope through the daisy loop you pushed through the other daisy hole. Take the next loop up on your daisy, and do the same thing, pushing a bight of rope through. Depending on the thickness/stiffness of your rope, you may want to repeat this with several more loops. The loops need to be small and about the same size, and should not be pulled so

This is very similar to the daisy chain of death idea presented above. Use this to get your sling back if you need to use more than 1/3rd of your rope (otherwise use the sling retrieval). You can put your rope directly around a large object sans sling if that object were to provide way too much friction to pull the rope completely around when pulling. With a sling, put ½ the rope through one side of the sling, which is looped over an anchor point. Take a bight of rope from the apex of the rope going over the sling and push it through the other loop of webbing. Next make a series of slipknots from the length of rope going through both loops of webbing, starting with the original bight pulled through both loops of webbing. As in the daisy chain of death, make your loops small, even, and not overly tight. The more loops the more secure but more difficult it may be to retrieve. Back it up for the first person and backup the sling so you don't lose the rope during a test pull. Rappel on the rope not slip-knotted. To go directly off an anchor, like a tree, take the middle of the rope and pull a bight around the object. One of the two strands is used to tie the slipknots by passing it through the bight around the anchor, and the other strand is rappelled on.

The Fiddle Stick of Death
This rope retrieval system has a few advantages and some major disadvantages. The gist of this system is to be able to tie a knot that comes apart when you pull on the pull cord so both ends of both ropes come down free. No tedious pulling of the pull cord on this one. The advantage here would be a scenario where the anchor point is far enough back or at a weird enough angle that friction would make pulling the rope through impossible or difficult without extending the anchor a ludicrous amount. Also knot-jamming grooves are far less of a problem. The final advantage is that you don't need to use any webbing on the anchor if slinging an object – unless the object is so big that friction creates and issue. The major downside to this system is that if you weight the pull cord you die. To avoid this, the pull cord is de-tangled and placed as carefully out of the way as possible by the first person down.

The lead line is tied to your anchor point with an upward stone knot at one end. Normally a locking carabineer traps the strands in the knot and keeps it from coming undone, and this should be the case for all but the last person down. Enter the fiddle stick. The last person down swaps out the carabineer with the fiddle stick: a stick that a pull cord is attached to. When the pull cord is tugged on, the stick pops out of the knot, the knot comes undone, and both ropes tumble down. The fiddle stick is commercially available from Imlay, but I seriously doubt anyone in their right mind would ever want to pre-plan on using this in a climbing scenario. So you have to make do. A piton, branch, a pack stay, axe, or pole could work – just hope it doesn't snap in half when weighted! Better yet, figure out a safer plan of getting your ropes back and save this trick for the canyoneering nerds.

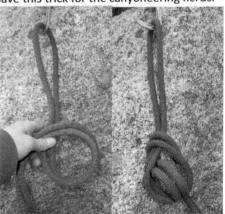

A stone knot is essentially a slipknot. Form a twist as in the fist photo, then pop the tails through the twist as in th second photo. Put fiddle stick through loop poking out to trap slipknot from undoing itself.

In this case a nut tool was used to trap the knot (terrible choice!). The pull cord is clipped to the fiddle stick.

Heads Up! The Retrievable Ice Axe, Picket, Ice Screw, Wood Block, and Sandbag of Death

For any of these, keep the first rappeller on a backup and have them tie both ends to the next anchor so at least the last rappeller will be attached to something (albeit a 400' fall) when they pull the backup.

All of these retrievable anchor scenarios are really REALLY dangerous because what you are trying to get back isn't something you want falling down on you. There is also a high probability that these setups won't work.

Before considering this rappel, can you leave gear, a deadman of some sort, or spare an ax or picket? If you can't, are you sure you can't downclimb on belay, place gear, and belay the other climber as they pull gear? If considering this because you are being cheap, you are an idiot. Put the book down and go find a job.

To setup your axe or picket for retrieval, prusik a length of nylon cord to the center of the rope (or pull side if two ropes are used), run it through the hole in the head of the ax or top hole of the picket, then run it down the shaft to the base, attaching the end to the spike or bottom hole. Sink the ax or picket and loop the rope behind. When you pull on the prusik side of the rope, the cord should pull up from the bottom of the ax or picket and pop it out. Weight both strands equally, lest you pop it out on rappel! You can add another ax or picket in a horizontal trench in front of the sunken ax or picket to make a better anchor (same setup as a T-slotted set of pickets). To get the horizontal ax or picket out, make an exit hole on the side of the prusik and clip it to the vertically sunken ax or picket. Try not to weight the rope too much by down-climb/rappelling if possible. Before you rap off your most valuable piece of equipment, check you and your partner for head injuries based off your poor judgement process.

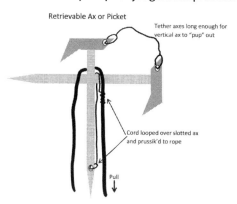

This gets my vote as the worst idea in the book.

I can see wanting to get an ice screw back on a long alpine route, especially if your rack is skeletal. This method isn't especially dangerous (except you are weighting a single screw), but chances are low that it will work. Worth a try in a pinch. Ask yourself first, why aren't you using a V-thread? To do this, first screw and unscrew the ice screw a bunch to loosen it, then take it out and clean the hole in the screw. Use the longest screw you have, 22 cm being ideal. Attach the end of a length of nylon cord to the hanger and place the screw, winding the nylon cord around it. Place the screw as deep as you deem safe to rap on, but leave at least an inch sticking out. The hanger needs to be pointing up when you are done. You can attach the end of the cord to the rope with a prusik (needed to be done before wrapping the screw), clip it to another prusik, or trap the end with the knot used to adjoin two ropes (these are options for any of the setups in this section: ax, picket, screw, lumber). Put the rope over the screw, and rap down weighting both ends evenly. A quick firm pull spins the screw out if you're lucky.

Pull the side with the prusik to unwind the screw out.

On sketchy remote climbs with no anchors, rock is too poor for any anchor, and/or your commitment to not placing bolts or leaving gear is extreme, wedged lumber can work as a rap anchor. Wedged rocks can also work, but good luck getting them back. Getting your lumber back depends on the shape and placement, but usually rotating it out of place with a pull cord attached to a levering point works. One method developed by desert climbers is to lay a piece of lumber over a chimney and have another perpendicular piece of lumbar attached to it on the base (like a capitol T). The top of the T adds some support, and the stem of the T is used to rappel from. A pull cord is placed on an arm of the T that is off the side of the cliff a bit, and the whole thing rotates and comes crashing down when you pull the cord.

Retrievable Wood Blocks

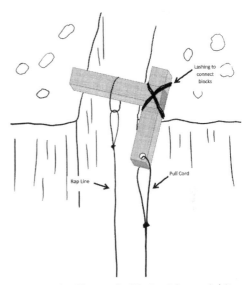

To rappel off a pack filled with sand (dirt, rocks, whatever) and get your pack back, here's what you do. Anchor the rappel rope to the front of the pack (facing the edge of the cliff). Attach the pull cord to the back of the pack. When you rap and pull the pull cord, the pack tips and spills the contents until it is light enough to pull down.

Be sure and reinforce anything that could fail on a pack by tying slings onto several strong points (in this case the grab loop and both shoulder straps).

If using two packs, put them side-by-side and clip the rappel rope to one pack and clip the other pack through the lead rope with the pull cord attached to that biner. The lead rope will weight both packs, but the pull cord will only pull one.

Lead line on left, pull cord on right.

First pack down is retrieved with pull cord as it slides down the lead rope. Lead rope pulled next.

The dangers of these setups should (hopefully) be extremely obvious. First you need the attachment to the pack to be strong enough to support weight – you may need to use slings, cord, or tat to beef up the attachment. The next big risk is that the pack may not hold your weight. Try and increase the angle of the rope going over the edge as much as possible to increase friction. A slick surfaced pack may not provide enough friction. I'm assuming this scenario would only come into play when there is nothing available to anchor off of, so the only way to back this system up would be to have the other climber attach him/herself to the system to provide a bodyweight backup. Besides the system failing, the big concern should be having a pack full of debris fall down on you. Tie the ropes off to the new anchor before pulling so when the pack(s) come bombing down and you run away quickly, you don't lose your ropes. The other major concern should be if the pack doesn't come down and you having to jug back up! I love my pack, but unless this was a very short rappel, I think I'd overload the pack and just leave it.

The Fifi of Death

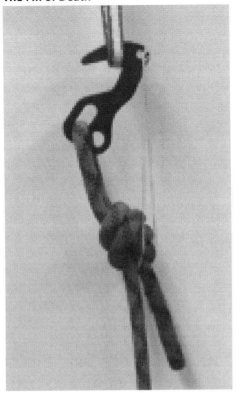

Photo courtesy Jim Nelson

This trick allows you to rap the entire length of a single line and get your rope back. You need a **fifi hook and a hefty rubber band**.

This trick is a last resort for when there is no intermediate anchor and no amount of re-climbing/aiding back up will do. Obviously you need to have a rubber band and fifi hook - not something common in your kit unless aid climbing with a pony-tail. Paying attention on the way down should make it so you never have to use this. Practice this while rapping on another rope fixed to the anchor.

Fix the end of your rope to the bottom hole in your fifi. The location of the knot you used to fix will become important. Put the fifi through the anchor and toss your rope (back it up so you don't drop it accidentally). Now girth hitch a rubber band to the top hole in the fifi and loop the rubber band around the bottom of the knot you used to fix the rope to. The band should be very tight if the knot is far enough down the rope when weighted. The theory is that when the rope is unweighted, the rebound of the rubber band will pull the hook of the fifi out of the anchor. Not only could the fifi come off, especially if you accidentally unweight the rope during your rappel, it may not come off at all – making ascending back up truly dangerous. Good luck!

HAULING

What fun! Not only is hauling one of the least fun activities involved in climbing, it's one of the most complicated. Why not just take a day laborer job and get paid for this much work? I will attempt to demystify hauling for those that really don't want to deal with the hassle, but still want to do a wall at some point, and to geek out a bit for the aid aficionados. Be sure to have bomber anchors if hauling! Not only does hauling put a lot of stress on the anchor, but the weight of the bag and you standing on it (commonly done) can be really heavy. A bag that cuts loose from the anchor can kill your partner, another team, or totally strip your anchor killing you.

RATCHETS AND PROGRESS CAPTURE PULLEYS

Any device or knot that holds a rope hands free can be substituted for another. Once you re-direct the rope, it becomes a ratchet. Adding a pulley to the redirect point greatly improves efficiency. When the two are combined into a single device (or a prusik minding pulley is used), they become a progress capture or ratcheting pulley. Never jug a haul line that's held by a pulley or clamp (especially a toothed one).

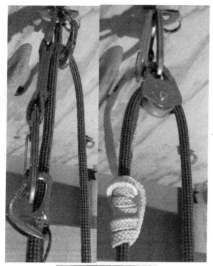

Ratcheting pulleys: Tibloc and Revoler, Sterling Hollow Block and prusik-minding pulley, GriGri

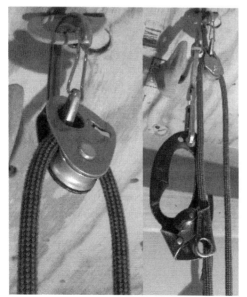

Ratcheting pulley: Microtraxion, pulley and Petzl ascender

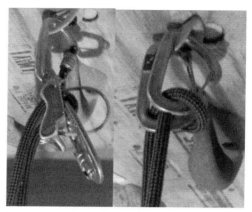

Ratchet, no pulley: Petzl Reverso (or any plaquette), garda hitch

Knots

The prusik, Bachman, Klemheist, and autoblock knots all work to hold the rope depending on what you have available (cord vs. webbing). They can be made from whatever you have on you and are great for emergency rigging. Because they don't have teeth, they are easier on your rope. Sometimes a short prusik is helpful while other times a long prusik (usually made from a cordalette) is helpful, especially when used to tie a load releasable hitch on the other end. You can always use the loop off the tail of a smaller prusik to extend it with more slings or cord. A garda hitch and locking Munter both work as ratchets, allowing you to pull down on the redirected rope and keep it there. Friction on the rope is what makes these knots work, so their efficiency is very low. They are great for when you've got nothing else. The block and tackle knot is a load releasable knot that can be used to quickly haul a short distance. It's load releasable with enough wraps, or finished with a mule. The more wraps, the more mechanical advantage, the less wraps, the less friction.

Pulleys

There are several stand alone pulleys out there made in various strengths and efficiencies. Combo devices like the **Microtraxion** or **Rollnlock** make the main haul point or even a redirect to create a 3:1 haul simple. Get a pulley that is strong enough to handle your loads, but light enough to not be overkill. A simple light crevasse rescue pulley is good enough for most medium to low weight hauls. **DMM Revolver biners** save a lot of weight and are useful when leading to reduce forces and rope drag, but are not nearly as efficient as a dedicated pulley. **Prusik minding pulleys** are nice, but don't always work. They are an inexpensive solution to either using a combo ratchet/pulley or using a micro ascender in combination with a simple pulley.

GriGri or Similar Device
The big drawback is the added friction - the rope will not slide easily. You cannot combine a pulley with these devices.

Reverso or Guide-Mode Belay Device
Even more friction than a GriGri but light and usually on the rack. If you have an old style Reverso with no hole to insert the nose of a biner to lower in a loaded guide-mode, get a new one. You will hopefully never have to use one of these for hauling or ascending. There is no way to attach a pulley to add efficiency safely.

Handled (Jumar Style) and No-Handle (Basic) Ascenders.
Some basic styles do not use teeth and slide more easily. **Handled ascenders** are kind of big and bulky, but the handle is very nice. The main reason for these are comfort when jugging a line. Petzl and Black Diamond are the most commonly used handled ascenders. **Basic ascender**s are more compact, but there is little use for them in most climbing situations. These are usually only used for dedicated hauling or as a chest or backup ascender. **Toothless ascenders** slide much more easily, but are less secure. Some popular basic ascenders are made by Petzl, Camp, Ushba, and Kong. These can all be combined with a pulley.

Micro Ascenders
The main micro ascenders are the **Tibloc, Ropeman, Microcender, and Microtraxion/Rollnlock**. The Microtraxion is made be Petzl and the Rollnlock is made by Climbing Technologies. Both are excellent and deserve a spot on the harness. The Tibloc is the lightest, weighing not much more than a prusik cord and far easier to attach. It slides easily, but not as easily as ascenders, Microcenders, or Microtraxion/Rollnlocks. Its main function is for unintended hauling, ascending, and rescue. Because there is no spring, it must be weighted to clamp the rope. It does not work well for the main hauling ratchet, but can be used in place of other rope clamps in the system.

Ropemen (there are several) are a bit heavier than a Tibloc, but are very small and the teeth are spring loaded. It does not slide easily on its own as the clamp adds a lot of extra friction. This is a good thing because it won't skate down the rope when unweighted like a Tibloc would. Microcenders slide very well and are toothless. They can also be put on and off the rope while still clipped to you or weighted. They work well as a backup ascender, 2nd ascender, or 2nd rope clamp in a haul. The Petzl Shunt is similar in concept, but just doesn't work as smoothly. Its only safe and useful function is as a rappel backup for double rope rappelling.

The Microtraxion/Rollnlock are the smoothest and one of the lightest options. They also contain a very efficient pulley, and can be used for anything from the main haul point to a 2nd ascender to a backup ascender and do not require an additional pulley. The Microtraxion is as strong as its cousin the Minitraxion, but lighter and more efficient. The **Minitraxion** is useful for ropes 11-13 mm. Tiblocs, Microcenders, and Ropemen can be combined with a pulley.

Wall Haulers
The **Protraxion, Wall Hauler, and Kong Block Roll** are a large progress capture pulleys, and are only useful for the main haul point on very heavy loads. The Mini and Microtraxion/

Rollnlock are excellent wall-haulers for lighter loads.

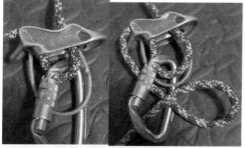

Tying off a weighted system with a mule knot: brake, pass brake strand through biner, twist and make a slip knot, tie off slipknot. A mule knot is a load releasable hitch.

With a mariner's knot: wrap around biner, wrap around itself and backup. This is a load releasable friction knot.

Tying a garda hitch, an autolocking friction knot.

HAUL SYSTEMS

To minimize bringing extra gear, work a haul situation out on paper noting how many lockers, biners, ratchets, pulleys, slings, cordage, etc, you need for hauling a bag or a crevasse rescue haul and rope travel. Next work out what you need for the climb itself, including anchor material. Cross anything off one of the lists that will never be used at the same time. Also, pulling up on the load side of a haul system with your hand or another ascender drastically aids in mechanical advantage when hauling as it tacks on an additional 2:1.

1:1 Hauling

Hauling doesn't have to be a complicated system of pulleys and ascenders if you keep the bags light. The easiest way to haul is to just hoist up the bag hand over hand, or redirected through the anchor. Simple hand over hand hauling works fine for small loads like a pack full of overnight gear. A DMM Revolver biner works great for the redirect biner.

To prevent back-slippage, you need to construct a ratchet. A garda hitch or locking munter makes a simple no-equipment necessary ratchet to haul. A Tibloc with a keeper sling clipped to the redirect biner will also prevent slippage. A prusik and a prusik minding pulley will do the job, as would a pulley and standard ascender. Any pulley to reduce friction on the redirect and something to prevent back-slippage will do. The best tools for up to moderately heavy loads (any standard wall) are the Microtraxion and Rollnlock. They reduce friction and slide wonderfully, are full strength, incredibly simple to use, and weight next to nothing. All you need is a biner (doesn't always have to be a locker) to clip it to the anchor. To get some mechanical advantage, use some type of ascender or knot on the pull side of the rope attached to your harness and use your body to pull. An aider clipped to the pull side and using your legs to push helps if using your body isn't working well.

To really help, pull up on the load side while pulling down on the haul side (creates a 2:1 for you nerds). You can haul heavy loads very quickly using this method, and for most, is a much more desirable method than constructing 3:1 or greater hauling systems. Some people like to clip a backup sling from the ratcheting pulley to the rope in case it broke. You must do this with heavy loads. To quickly help someone hanging on the rope get up a short section, all you need to do is create a progress capture pulley on the anchor, attach yourself to the pull-down side of the rope with a rope clamp or prusik, and squat down while simultaneously pulling up on the victim's rope. Back yourself up to the anchor with enough slack to provide a long enough squat down. Unless your partner is a waif, you probably can't haul them very far with this method.

A 1:1 haul is simply a redirect and can be confusing since it kinda looks like a 2:1. For a 2:1 to work, force needs to be pulled up on the load in one direction and also in the other direction. Think of it like this. You are hanging on a toprope. If you pull up on the rope above your knot to go higher you are pulling all of your weight. Likewise, if the belayer pulls down on the rope coming out of their belay device, they are still pulling all of your weight. But if you pull down on the rope going down to the belayer you are now pulling just half of your weight.

2:1 Hauling
Dropping a line fixed to the anchor down to the haul bag and pulling up on it (put a pulley on the bag) creates a 2:1 system of mechanical advantage, aka the C-drop. This would make a 100 lb. bag feel like a 50 lb. bag, but you have to pull twice as much rope up. The main problem with this is that it is fairly impractical if pitches are longer than half a rope length. This is a pretty good system to use in a crevasse fall if you can get a rope to the victim by either rapping down to them, or if they are conscious but unable to ascend. Use the slack in your drop to drop the loop, or another rope if you've got one.

You can create a 2:1 system at the anchor without a drop-loop. This is a very complex system. If you can figure it out, it's a great compromise for heavy loads but quicker haul times. Big wall vets swear by the complex 2:1 setup for several reasons: minimal "resetting" in cramped belays and more efficient than a 3:1 (less hauling). Once you have rigged the system you can toss it in a stuff sack and it's ready to deploy. The system needs to be perfectly setup to provide maximum efficiency and there are a lot of tweaks you need to make to get it just right. High efficiency pulleys really help. Practice this at home to get it perfect - you'll need to.

The system consists of two parts. The first part of the system consists of a hauling ratchet you use to pull the bag up made with a dedicated piece of cord, called the Zed cord (15 foot 5 mill Technora or Tech Cord), two high efficiency pulleys, and an ascender. The second part of the system is a holding ratchet to support the weight of the bag and move the haul rope through. Both systems attach to a power point, but the holding ratchet (Microtraxion/Rollnlock) must be extended. A 4" quickdraw or nut with double lockers on both works well for this.

The ascender used in the hauling ratchet must be directly below the holding ratchet. The teeth should be extremely close (almost touching) so the pulley connected to the hauling ascender is side by side with the pulley on the holding ratchet. One way to get everything in a straight line is to use a large locker on your holding ratchet and clip it to the upper pulley of the hauling ratchet that actually spans the length of the pulley. To haul, tie into the Zed cord with a clove to your harness and squat down. At the bottom of your squat, the ascender with the pulley on it on the hauling ratchet will lift up with the bag. Pull the haul line slack through the holding ratchet. Putting a grab loop on the hauling ratchet ascender will aid in resetting it and standing back up. If you set it up correctly, the motions should become apparent. Practice on a heavy bag to really get the kinks out of the system. Clear your afternoon schedule to figure this one out. See photo next page.

3:1 Hauling
The most common scenario for hauling heavy loads is the 3:1 pulley system, or Z-pulley. Before you bother, see how hard just redirecting the rope though a Microtraxion or Rollnlock would be using a 1:1 system, especially after the haul bag lightens from using water or when the friction is low on free hanging hauls. Set up the haul as usual by putting the rope through the Microtraxion/Rollnlock (or whatever). Clip another pulley to the anchor (or DMM Revolver). Clip an ascender (or any rope grabbing setup) upside-down on the haul bag side of the rope with a pulley or Revolver. You may need to weight the lower ascender to maintain correct orientation on the pulley. Take the pull side of the rope and put it through the pulley on the lower ascender and then up through the anchor pulley. All you have to do is pull, and reset the lower ascender as it creeps up to the anchor pulley. The upper pulley is not technically part of the 3:1 system, but is used to redirect the rope for easier pulling. To summarize, construct a 1:1 ratcheting pulley on the anchor, put another ascender and pulley on the loaded rope below, and redirect the rope you are pulling with through the lower ratchet. Simple.

Another 3:1 setup is the Spanish Burton System and is a bit more complicated, but only requires a ratcheting pulley on the anchor (like the Microtraxion/Rollnlock) and one other pulley. Put the rope through the anchor ratchet from the haul bag, and clip another ratchet directly below the anchor ratchet on the pull side. Now clip a pulley directly to the new ratchet (or have the ratchet be another Microtraxion/Rollnlock) hanging off the pull side of the rope. Clip the end of the haul line to another 3rd ratchet that is placed on the load side of the rope coming off the anchor ratchet and feed the rope coming from the lowest ratchet through the 2nd pulley/ratchet system and pull from there. You can tie a foot loop from the rope you are pulling to help. The lower ratchet/pulley may need some weight clipped to it to orient the pulley correctly if not using a combo device.

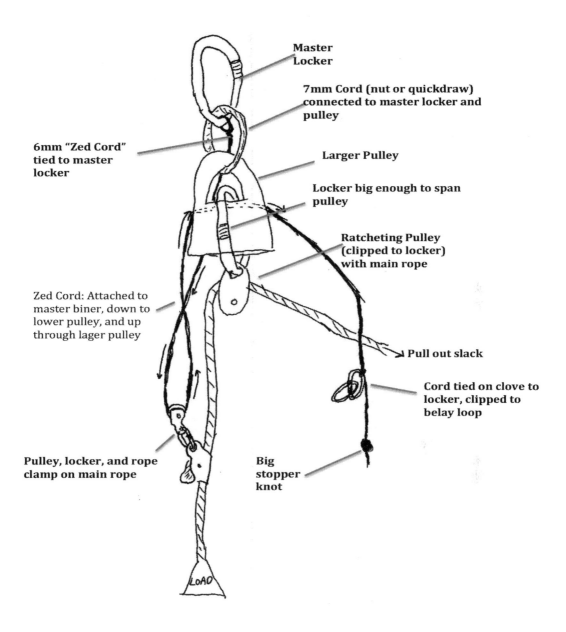

3:1 Haul

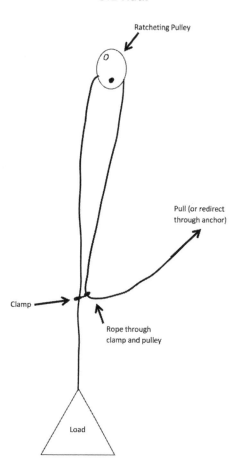

The "clamp" could be something like a prusik or Tibloc and the ratcheting pulley could be a microtraxion, GriGri, or Reverso

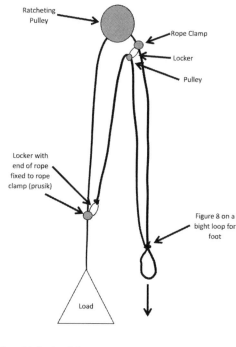

Spanish Burton 3:1

5:1 Hauling

To create a 5:1 haul from a standard 3:1 setup, first take the rope out of upper redirect pulley (if you used one) and the pulley out of the lower ascender, swapping it out with a biner. Now put a long sling through that new biner. Clip one end of the new sling to the anchor and put a pulley on the other end of the sling. Put the rope coming out of the initial ratcheting pulley and through the new pulley attached to the sling. Pull up or redirect it though the anchor.

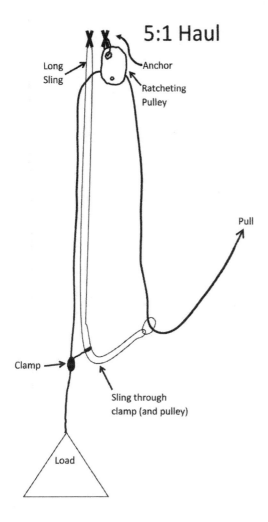

5:1 Haul

6:1 Hauling and Crevasse Rescue

The simple 3:1 and drop loop 2:1 described above are most likely the same systems you would use for hauling a victim out of a crevasse. The 6:1 combines at 2:1 and 3:1, and is probably total overkill for hauling a bag. It would be much quicker to do two hauls on an easier system. Tiblocks, Ropemen, prusiks on prusik minding pulleys, or just simple prusiks will be adequate. A Microtraxion/Rollnlock is totally suitable for this as well, as would a GriGri. This will be explained in a crevasse rescue scenario with two people. With more people you can share pulling power and various tasks, and use anther rope if needed.

When you self-arrest the fall, get an anchor built and transfer the weight from your foot prusik to the anchor. If using stopper knots you can plunge your ax, ski, or picket right into one of the loops. You may need to pass knots if you are using stopper knots, but it can be done fairly easily. Next, beef up the anchor and tie off the rope with a load releasable Munter mule to backup the foot prusik. Don't leave a lot of slack with the backup. If using a GriGri method of travel, tie off to the anchor with the upper prusik and clip the GriGri to the anchor to escape the rope.

Now will you need to prusik to the lip of the crevasse to scope the scene using your chest prusik. Probe around to find the edge of the crevasse, you don't want to fall in too. In any of the scenarios below, pad the lip with an ax backed up to the rope or another ax.

A new device, the **Mammut RescYou**, is a self-contained 6:1 hauling system. It is basically a low friction block and tackle ratcheting pulley. Simply attach it to the anchor and two rope clamps to the rope and haul. The victim can also use it to ascend the rope out of the crevasse. It easily and safely passes stopper knots. I have not used it yet, but it looks like you could easily drop one or more redirects inside the device to make a 4:1 or 2:1 haul system out of it safely. This could possibly make it usable for hauling bags on walls as well. Pretty cool! I really don't see any reason not to use one of these rigs considering how complicated these systems can be in real life with real stress.

Courtesy Mammut

The following are three options to haul a victim out from this point in the scenario. The Microtraxion method and C to a Z are used when the victim is conscious and you have enough lead rope or another rope available. The Z to a C is used when you don't have a lot of rope left or the victim is unconscious. When you initially attach the rope to the anchor you will want to use a load releasable knot if constructing a Z to a C. I recommend doing this even if you plan on using the drop loop to a Z system, just in case you wind up with not enough rope. The whole reason behind the backup load releasable knot is because you are attempting to haul a preloaded system. If simply hauling a haul bag, you can skip the backup knot stuff because you set the system up before your partner releases the load.

- **Microtraxion (simple 2:1+)**
  Drop the fixed end down to the victim with a Microtraxion (or GriGri) on it. They clip into it and you pull them out while they pull up on the fixed end. Simple.

- **C to a Z, aka Drop-Loop to a Z, or Canadian Drop Loop (2:1 + 3:1=6:1)**
  See if your buddy is ok. If they are you can drop a line and haul their pack out. If they are unable to prusik or climb out on a belay from a dropped rope, but are at least able to grab things, send the slack rope down after getting their pack out with a pulley and locker if they don't already have one. If anything on the system gets a pulley, it is the victim. The rope coming back up from the victim/pulley is your 2:1 haul.

  Bring this rope back up to the anchor and put it through a ratcheting pulley. This is where the GriGri is nice, but a Reverso can work well too if you don't have a GriGri or Microtraxion. Now you have a 2:1 drop-loop with a redirect off the anchor. Next, attach a rope-clamp (prusik, ascender, etc) and a pulley (if you have one) onto the stand coming out of the ratcheting pulley and going down to the climber. Redirect the pulling strand through this and, viola, you've got a 6:1 haul. If needed you can redirect the haul through the anchor if needed.

- **Z to a C (3:1 + 2:1 = 6:1)**
  If you can't drop a loop to the victim or are low on rope, you can add the 2:1 on top of a 3:1. To do this, get your Texas foot prusik clipped to the anchor to unweight you from the rope and back the lead rope up to the anchor with a load-releasable knot. After you checked on the victim and padded the crevasse lip, construct a ratcheting pulley on the anchor. If you were using a GriGri, you're psyched. A Reverso or Microtraxion would work great too. If you were just using prusiks, then the foot prusik (currently backed-up with the rope) will be it, hopefully combined with a pulley. Whatever you have, put the slack rope (just past the load releasable backup knot) through the ratcheting pulley and create a 3:1 by redirecting it onto the loaded rope with a rope-clamp and a pulley. You can use your chest prusik (already on the rope) and a pulley for this. You now have a 3:1 setup.

Next you must add a 2:1 on top of your 3:1. Take the end of the 3:1 you would normally pull with and fix it to the anchor. It does not have to be load-releasable, but it never hurts. Now take the free end of the rope that is coming off the newly fixed rope and redirect the rope with a rope-clamp and pulley onto the rope located between the fixed rope (the one you just tied) and the 3:1 re-direct pulley. You may now undo the original backup knot on the rope to load the system and begin hauling. You will need to reset the 3:1 and 2:1 rope clamps as they travel toward the anchor. The ratchet attached to the anchor keeps everything from sliding backwards.

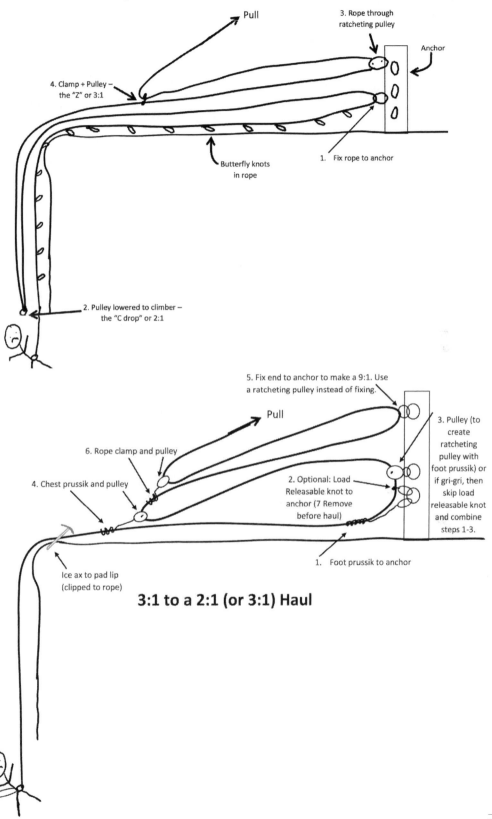

9:1 Hauling

You can add another 3:1 on top of your existing 3:1 on the previous setup. Instead of fixing the rope when adding the 2:1, make another ratcheting pulley on the anchor with the pull strand, tack on another prusik/pulley onto the loaded side of this new redirect, and bam 9:1! See the previous photo. You'll lose time and efficiency with this system unless you've got a ton of pulleys and mechanical ascenders – otherwise plan on resetting a lot of prusiks. This setup may be the only way a single person can haul a heavy climber with a big pack out of a crevasse alone.

SPECIAL HAULING SITUATIONS
Hauling Past Knots

For long hauls, like after jugging several fixed lines in a row on overhanging terrain, you will need to pass the knots. To do this you need to put an ascender or prusik below the knot and transfer the weight onto this. Then extend the haul point with a longer sling so it can be reassembled below the knot. To get slack to transfer weight with lighter loads you can clip a biner about a foot higher and use brute strength.

Rope is going through Microtraxion. Ascender takes weight off the Microtrax on the new side of rope. The Microtraxion must now be lowered below ascender. A shorter sling on the ascender would probably have been better.

Lowering Out the Bag

Most pitches require that the follower lower the bag out in line with the direction of pull from above to keep it crashing across the cliff. Even a little off to the side and the bag will crash across the wall. Do not let the leader pull all of the slack out of the haul line if using the remaining slack for the lower out! Tie the haul bag in short to the remaining slack, and lower it when the leader yells, "Rope is fixed!" Then yell, "Ready to haul!" and lower the bag out when you feel tension from above. You will need a **lower out line** if the pitches are rope stretchers or the lower out is huge because you won't have enough lead line left. You may want to rig a small pulley and belay system to lift the bag off the anchor and control the lower out. A Munter hitch works well for doing both.

Avoiding the Big Bag

You can pack small heavy stuff in the jugger's pack (like water and things you'll want en route that day) to lighten the haul bag. Jugging with really heavy packs is usually more miserable than hauling, but it can be a lot quicker if distributing the load makes both jugging and hauling manageable. If your bag is really heavy (+200 lbs.), it can be easier to use two haul bags and do two separate hauls. If using one huge bag, then the 2nd can jug and clean the pitch after lowering the monster bag out (he/she will need to do a mini haul just get the bag off the anchor) and help the leader haul. Sometimes it is nice to haul two moderate sized bags in tandem than one huge bag. Use a length of 9 mm cord to attach multiple haul bags together, staggering them.

Docking Cords and Far End Hauling

Docking cords of 8 mm line can be very useful on your big haul bags. Use about **15' doubled-up cord** clipped into the bag with a fig-8 on a bight and a locker. When attaching the bags to the anchor, there will be two loops. Make a Munter hitch out of both loops and finish with a mule or mariner knot this is backed up with a biner.

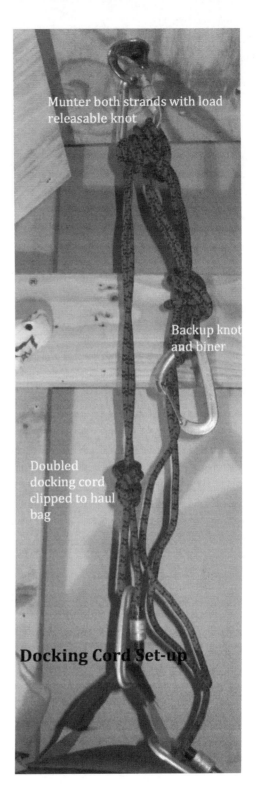

Docking Cord Set-up

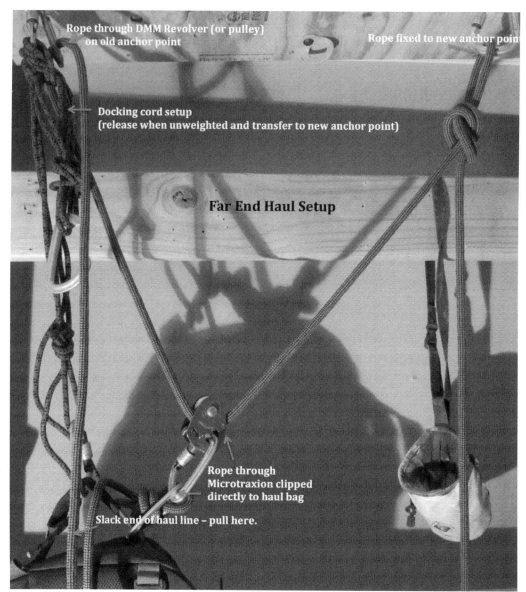

Far End Haul Setup
- Rope through DMM Revolver (or pulley) on old anchor point
- Rope fixed to new anchor point
- Docking cord setup (release when unweighted and transfer to new anchor point)
- Rope through Microtraxion clipped directly to haul bag
- Slack end of haul line – pull here.

Also, putting a Microtraxion/Rollnlock on the haul line near its tie-in point and clipped to the swivel or main haul point, oriented so it slides away from the bag, can be very useful if you need to lift the bags or move them to another anchor point. Fix the haul rope coming out of the Microtraxion/Rollnlock to the new anchor point. Take the rope coming out of the other side of the Microtraxion/Rollnlock (going to the haul bag) and put it through a pulley on the original anchor. You now have 2:1 system to hoist the bag up to the new anchor. Now undo the docking cord and tie it to the new anchor. Release the cam on the Microtraxion/Rollnlock to lower it onto the new anchor. Put the pull side through your GriGri to aid in hoisting the bag and also taking weight off to release the Microtraxion. This technique is known as a "far end haul," and if useful for whenever you need to move the bag around near the anchor. See photo top of page.

Solo Hauling

If soloing on a big wall, not only do you have to rap down and clean your gear, you also have free the haul bag and then haul it up. Pendulums and traversing pitches need to be carefully planned out or you could get yourself into a very dangerous situation. Don't clean all your gear on rappel to keep you in line. Do it on the way up, or rappel the haul line. If you rap the haul line and lower the bag out, be sure to have the haul system setup at the upper anchor first, and backed-up!

Before rappelling, haul the bag a few feet so when you get to it, it's easier to unclip it, and lower it out (you won't be able to rap the haul line if you do this). One way to save time, but can be a little sketchy, is to haul while you rappel. You need a haul and a rap line for this. Pull up the slack on the haul line and feed it through a ratcheting pulley. The haul bag below needs to be attached to the anchor (a separate anchor is ideal) with a fifi so you can detach it from the anchor from above. Once the ratcheting pulley is weighed, tie pull end to you. Rap down on the other line while body hauling the bag up.

The term "continuous loop" is commonly applied to the following system. If you are rope-soloing alone on a wall and don't want to trail the haul line, you can join the free end of the lead line to the haul line to tag up gear. It helps to stack each line (the lead and haul line) in separate rope bags and place the joining knot between the two bags so the knot doesn't catch up on loose loops of rope in the bag. You can use this to your advantage to tag up additional gear, placed in a tag bag – a bag full of extra gear/whatever. If you want to climb light, you could attach the tag bag direct to the lead rope, or attach near the joining knot (on the haul line side). Once you tag up your gear, you can leave the tag bag there and re-stack the rope. This is why you need **two rope bags**, as the rest of the haul rope still needs a home at the lower anchor.

You'll need to attach the tag bag to your anchors with a fifi hook so you can pull it up. Tie the rope to the pull cord on the top of the fifi, and back it up to the rope below this. You can attach both the fifi pull loop and the backup with prusiks, as it is nice to adjust the length on the tag bag occasionally. You can go crazy and attach a **2nd lead rope** to your tag rack with a **secondary tag bag** attached to the end of this. You still only have two strands of rope hanging off you: the lead end going through your pro and attached to the anchor, and the loose end of the free rope which is connected to your haul line and tag rack. Once you pull up the slack and finally get to your tag rack with the 2nd lead rope clipped to it, you can pull that 2nd rope up and grab your secondary tag rack as well! This is useful for super gear intense leads when you want a **3rd rope** for big-wall shenanigans and to have a backup lead rope. Hauling up a tag line hand over hand can be really tiring – splitting it into two tag racks as just described works, as does setting up a mini-haul on mini-anchor mid pitch.

One issue with this is on traversing pitches where the weight of the loose end of rope may cause the stacked rope to tumble out and release your tag bag onto you after it falls for however much rope you have left! Petzl makes a **directional fifi** that locks up if this happens. Use a **quick link** in the groove for this particular fifi for it to work well. Another option is to tie a "slippery knot" in the lead line near the joining knot, which will come apart as you climb, but will hold if the fifi comes off the anchor. A slippery knot is just multiple slipknots daisy chained together that unravel when pulled in one direction but stay when pulled in the other. Both options (can be combined) still don't prevent the rope from tumbling out of the rope bucket, but at least prevent the tag bag from plummeting out, unless you tie a bunch of slippery knots along the way on the loose end of the rope. Your main haul bag, if attached to the anchor with a fifi, probably won't fall off if the haul line winds up falling out of the rope bucket on traverses mainly because your haul bag should be backed up to the anchor (unless you planned on simul-rap-hauling which you probably wouldn't do on a traversy pitch anyway) and weighs a lot more than the haul line. Be sure none of your ropes (lead, tag, haul, etc.) are twisted or loops of rope get caught under flakes, gear, or other bags, or your haul bag and/or tag bag will get stuck.

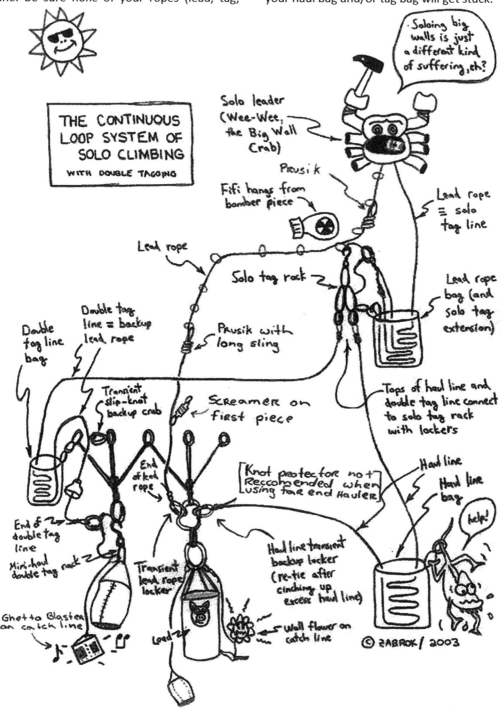

Drawing courtesy Peter Zabrok

Rope-Soloing

True rope-soloing systems use a device strictly designed for this use. Things can get confusing very quickly. Start easy and use lots of backups knots. Always think, "What would happen if...?" It can be very easy to mistakenly tie in the wrong way or unclip yourself completely. If soloing with a haul bag, do not underestimate its weight. If you screw up and the haul bag loads you or the anchor, you could die. Transferring the load of a haul bag in changeovers and while rappelling is a nightmare. Get your systems dialed and quadruple check everything at every transition point. If a climb goes over a roof, has traverses, or pendulums, then plan ahead. Practice on the ground, and practice your systems on a small cliff with a toprope backup and/or close to the ground. Never trust one item of gear to save you except the rope (which could sever over an edge). Back everything up! Use a good rope that you know works with your solo device. Carry a phone or a radio. Finally, there are no guarantees that I wrote this (or anything) in this book correctly. Use your brain. If you screw-up, it's on you.

Soloing can be very dangerous because of increased loads on anchors and greater length of falls. It's also easier to mess up, especially since you've got no one to check your systems. Don't mess up. Quadruple check you system at every transition point (leading, rappelling, jugging, on/off the anchor) when soloing. Because cross loading can actually be an issue when soloing, some climbers attach their solo device with a quick link. If doing this, only use extremely high strength quick links sold by a climbing manufacturer, not Home Depot.

Toprope Soloing

Toprope soloing is the most common form of rope-soloing and can be pretty safe if done correctly. The most dangerous part can be getting to the top anchor to set it up. Occasionally rope-soloing while aiding up a straightforward crack or stick clipping up a bolted climb is necessary to reach the anchors. Asking a party to setup your rope when they are done also works. Also, if you carefully tape the end of your rope to theirs, you could get your rope through the anchor. To fix it for soloing, use the slingshot method describe for ascending.

To setup a TR solo system, you need to fix a rope to an anchor and weight the bottom of the rope with a pack. Weighting the rope allows the ascenders to slide up the rope without your constant attention. Make sure your rope isn't running over a sharp edge. This can happen very easily, so be extremely vigilant about using rope protector and/or padding lips. Redirect the rope with slings to reduce pendulums if you fall. If the gear is solid and the pitch wanders, you could clove hitch certain pieces leaving a bit of slack to move around on and also reduce the rope rubbing from above.

You will need at least one ascender to move with any sort of fluidity. Clove hitches and prusiks take too long for any sort of reasonable fun or challenging free climbing. Petzl does not recommend using a Shunt (but still very popular) or a Tibloc because they can easily get disengaged by pressing into the rock. **Jumar-style ascenders, Microtraxion/Rollnlocks, Microcenders, and basic non-handled ascenders (Petzl Basic and Croll, Camp Lift, Ushba Basic)** and similar items by other companies work well. GriGri's take too much effort to pull in the slack as they won't slide up on their own. Tying in to one end of the rope and belaying yourself on the other side of the rope with a GriGri is also not recommended.

Clip the ascender to your belay loop with a locker or bomber quick link and to the rope. Climb up, being very careful not to cross-load your locker or ascender. Using just one device isn't very safe, and I certainly don't recommend it. You have options. You can use the other side of the fixed rope if it's less than ½ a pitch, or another rope to attach a second ascender to. Now you have two ropes and two ascenders. If you only have one ascender, you could tie overhand knots every few feet down the other rope and clip into them as a backup to your main ascender. This requires a lot of effort.

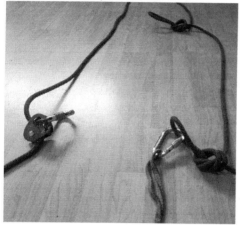

Using a Microtraxion on one fixed end and backup knots on the other.

You could also use two ascenders on one rope. The danger here is having only one rope that could get shredded, but this is highly unlikely unless you have the rope running over sharp edges.

Two microtraxions on one rope, clipped to the belay loop.

Some folks just clip two ascenders directly to their harness. This should work unless one device gets sucked into the other causing both to fail. Another option is to wear a **chest harness** and use something like a **Croll** well above the lower ascender. This is a great system, and the center of gravity keeps you upright in a disastrous fall, and a fall won't shock load the rope as much since the Croll (which is specifically designed for a chest ascender) is higher up. You can use a quickdraw with lockers or quick links on both ends by attaching it to your harness and connection between the upper ascender and chest harness to keep things in line and more safe.

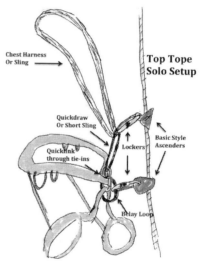

My favorite system besides using a second ascender with a chest harness uses a Microtraxion/Rollnlock on my harness and a Jumar-style ascender on a PAS. I can quickly zip the upper Jumar up the line and hang on it instead of falling onto the one on my harness. The Silent Partner can be used as a toprope belay and to rap off in the exact same setup used for lead soloing (below).

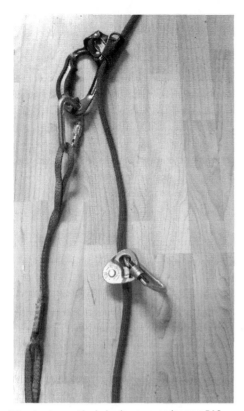

Microtraxion on the belay loop, ascender on a PAS.

Silent Partner

Solo-Aid (courtesy Rock Exotica)

GriGri: *flap removed (not recommended by Petzl).*

GriGri: *swaged cable added (not recommended by Petzl).*

If you need to unload the ascender to rappel down (keep a GriGri or belay device on you) you can simply do a foot wrap on the rope to stand up on it. Or you can use the system described in the jugging section (the system used to get on the GriGri and prusik when following a tough section).

Self-Belay Systems
Types of Devices
There are three legit devices you can use to self-belay: **Clove Hitches, the Silent Partner, and Aid Soloist**. GriGri's, Eddy's, Cinches and other auto-locking belay devices can be rigged to self-belay but the manufactures recommend against it. I highly recommended that you do not use the Soloist (not made anymore). I also cannot recommend that you use any device not meant for rope-soloing. If I mention their use for systems they are not designed for, it is because they are commonly used regardless. Using anything in a non-manufacture recommended situation is your decision.

Any device that won't hold an upside-down fall needs to be used with a chest harness (everything but a clove hitch or Silent Partner). The Silent Partner is by far the safest device, but it is heavy and expensive. It locks via acceleration through a clutch, so slow slabby falls can increase your fall distance. I've never heard of the device not locking, but if you try and grab the rope it could. Try practice falls on a toprope backup with a bunch of slack (watch your landing so you don't sprain your ankle) to gain confidence in various falling scenarios. Check the rope size specs on whatever device you are using before using a skinny rope in a device meant for thicker ropes.

The GriGri is the most commonly used self-belay device (clove hitches coming in 2nd) for short-fixing on walls, but again, it still isn't recommended by the manufacturer for this purpose. Many climbers drill a hole in the device and swage a cable or thread cord through it to keep it oriented correctly and to attach to the chest harness. Climbers also sometimes go a step further by cutting off (and smoothing down) the triangular metal flap on the brake side of the device to help the rope feed smoother. One prolific rope-soloist uses the Edelrid Eddy over a modified GriGri because he states that rope feeds smoother, locks better, and if the release handle is accidentally pulled back (a major risk on these type of devices) the Eddy incorporates an emergency stop. Some climbers completely remove the brake lever off their GriGri. I have never used an Eddy, but I have heard concerns about it compared to the GriGri, and issues with it not braking.

No matter what device you use, tie backup knots close enough to at least prevent a ledge or ground fall! You can't sit down on a Silent Partner and have it lock and hold you weight – it needs acceleration. At first this is unnerving, but in order for other devices to do this, you would still need to be below a piece or within arm's reach. If this is the case, you could simply clip into the gear directly and weight it. Besides just the diameter of the rope being compatible with your solo device, you also want a moderately used rope that isn't so fuzzy it catches

on the device constantly, but isn't so slick from dry treatment that it slips through the device without it engaging either. As long as the rope is rated to your device, it should be fine and catch. Many prolific soloers use a 9.1mm rope to aid in it feeding. Test your rope before committing to it, and tie back-ups!

Basic setup

Two backup knots are employed here

Use one or two super burly locking carabineers clipped into your tie-in points, or better yet, a steel locking biner. If only using one locker (not recommended), make sure it doesn't become cross-loaded. Biners or belay loops that prevent cross-loading should be used. Tie one end of the rope to an anchor (specifics below). The brake side of the device should have the rope attached to the anchor going up into it, and the free rope comes out of the climber side. The Silent Partner uses a large clove hitch, but you can still screw up the direction you clip it in. Do some test pulls to make sure it feeds and engages (do this with all devices). This is pretty much the reverse of a normal lead setup where you would be belayed from the end of the rope farthest from the anchor.

You should tie into the end of the rope if your climb is higher than half a rope length as the last resort backup so you don't slip off the end of the rope if the device does not lock. If the ground is less than ½ rope then you wouldn't reach the tie-in knot by the time you decked, but the weight of the rope could theoretically slide out of the device. As you climb, the slack rope is pulled through the device from tension off the anchor. To test which rope is the end you clip gear into, give a pull if visual clues aren't present. It can be confusing. Put gear in and clip it to the rope going down to the anchor.

When you reach the top of a pitch you need to rap back down and jug or toprope solo to get your gear back. Leave what you don't need at the top anchor (extra rack) and bottom anchor (pack) respectively. If you climbed less than half a rope length, you can rappel down the free end. If you climbed more than half a pitch, you can still rap back down the line with a little bit of slack still left in the system. Rappelling down the lead line could make the re-ascent dangerous on traversing or wandering pitches. Also, if you haven't tied into the end of your rope, it could slide out of your device, leaving you stranded on long pitches. When rapping, tie knots in the end of your ropes. With all the rope work involved, it can be easier to rap off the ends. You can use your self-belay device to act as your toprope solo device, but you'll probably just want to jug if there are many more pitches to go, or were aiding.

Using cloves hitches as your solo device is simple, yet tedious. It is essentially just using backup knots sans device. This is an ok system to use on aid climbs where you are pretty sure you're not going to fall and the knots are purely there as backups. Backup knots are extremely recommended on any system. Have at least two keynosed beefy lockers clipped to your harness so you have two backups at all times. Tie clove hitches down the slack side of the rope at distances close enough to prevent at least a catastrophic fall. When the knot reaches your solo device (or tight on the biner if just using cloves) unclip the knot, and the next backup knot in line locker is now your primary backup. Haul up some slack and tie another backup. Either gauge how far a fall would be to hit a ledge or dangerous object, or estimate how far the next section of difficult climbing will be to estimate backup length. Every so often, give a tug on the line down to the anchor to see if excess slack has started to build up. If it has, readjust your solo belay device. Anticipate longer falls on low angled terrain with a Silent Partner by using more backup knots.

Solo Anchors
Rope-soloing increases the forces on you, your gear, and anchors. Your falls will also be longer. This means placing ultra-bomber anchors. Keep this in mind if using established anchors. Some areas, like the Fisher Towers, have really scary fixed belays that you can't beef up too easily. You may want to clove off some bomber gear on the way up if your anchors are sketchy. Your lead anchor needs to have a large upwards pull since falls pull up on the anchor, not down. It needs to have some downwards pull to keep your gear from falling out due to gravity, and God forbid that you fall directly onto the anchor. The anchor also needs to resist and outwards pull to keep gear from popping or zippering out. Good bolts do all of this. If tying off gear on the way up to either backup the main anchor or to take some rope weight off and reduce slack in the system be sure the gear is placed to withstand a large upwards pull.

Making an anchor with an upward resisting pull can be a challenge, especially on the ground. Giant boulders and bent-over tree stumps can hopefully be found if no cracks are present near the ground. Since almost no climbs have bolts on the ground for an anchor, you may occasionally need to put the anchor on the first bolt of a climb. This is a chore to setup, and is dangerous because you really don't want a single bolt as your only anchor. Clove the rope into the next bolt or two as well. The top of a bolted first pitch gets things back on track with a normal anchor, hopefully. For natural or gear anchors, get them as non-extendable as possible, and equalize mini-anchors into one main point over trying to equalize everything. Use load limiters on any gear less than bomber, or use a load limiter at the master point. In fact, use load limiters on any suspect gear on the lead as well. Remember, there isn't much dynamic belay going on when soloing and any load limiter will increase the length of your fall.

Tie the end of the rope into a beefy locker (or two) in the master point of the anchor. Clip the **load limiter** into the master point with a biner and clove it to the rope with a non-locker as well leaving enough slack in the rope between the clove and the end of the rope to allow the screamer to fully extend. If the first piece is a bolt, consider placing your load limiter on this instead of the anchor. To add another level of force reduction, you could tie your pack loaded with some rocks or heavy haul bag to the master point of the anchor to simulate the weight of your belayer being lifted up. This will reduce the load to the anchor even more, but add the length the pack travels into your fall distance.

Your next anchor off the ground and all subsequent anchors will need a larger downward pull while rappelling down and jugging up than the ground anchor did. You will need two sets of anchor material and gear as well. Because rope drag isn't an issue, you can get away with longer pitches. When you reach an anchor you can clove hitch it until you run out of rope and build a gear anchor to get the most use out of your rope and speed things up. You also won't be worrying about the comfort of the belay since you won't be staying there for very long. Build an anchor for a downward pull, rap down, jug up, and either use the established anchor you passed, or the gear one you built.

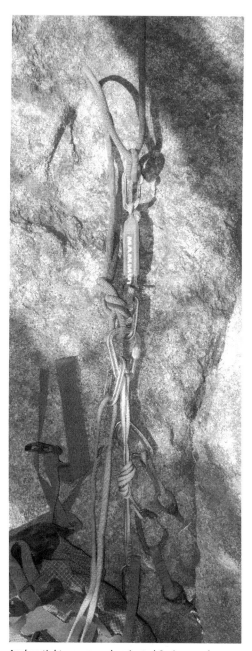

Anchor tight on upwards oriented 3-piece anchor on a cordalette. Rope is tied to anchor, and shortened with a screamer. Backpack clipped to anchor to act as ballast.

The Silent Partner can be used to lower after leading a pitch and then to climb back up in the same configuration. It can also be used to lower out on pendulums. To do this pull up the slack on the brake (anchor) side of the rope to disengage the lock (if it is locked) and slowly let the rope feed through. You won't have the control of a belay device, but it will lock if you let go (you'll fall some first).

Be sure to have a way to jug the line if a fall leaves you dangling in air. Keep this in mind if leaving your jugs at the lower anchor.

Rope Management
Stack the free rope neatly at the bottom anchor. Rope tangles mean you can't climb higher, and you'll need to make an anchor and rap down to fix things. Climbing with the extra rope feeding out of your pack can solve this problem, but you will be climbing with extra weight. Due to the angle, the rope may not feed well through the device. One or two rope buckets can really help things along. Get a large stuff sack and stiffen the brim by feeding or sewing 6-7 mm accessory cord or baling wire. Add a 3' length of ½" webbing to a single point on the opening of the bag to use as an attachment to the anchor. The **Metolius Big Wall Stuff Sack** works great as a rope bucket. When you want to coil the rope in the bag, just clip it to the anchor and hand-over-hand the rope into it. If using slings to hold the rope, be extra vigilant when stacking it. A double length sling with the rope neatly stacked doesn't add any weight. The stacked rope should be higher than the fixed end and off to the side a bit to keep the coils from binding up.

Unless you're a true master, you'll find that you'll be climbing well below you limit, and the scare factor triples even when aiding...so you might not notice the extra weight. The more rope you have out, the harder it becomes to feed rope through the device. It may start jamming up once you've gotten around a half a pitch, or actually back-slipping through the device as the weight of the line fixed to the anchor pulls out slack. One option would be to clove hitch the rope to a piece of gear. This takes the weight off the rope below the clove-hitched piece, but it essentially makes that piece your new anchor as it will absorb all the weight of a fall (in an upwards pull). This may or may not reduce the force on your anchor if the gear pulls.

Another option is to clove hitch the rope to a plastic carabineer or use an easily breakable 2 mm prusik to take some weight off the solo device. There is a pretty scary chance that clove hitching a biner that is designed to break could sever the rope with any sharp fragments exposed, or a 2-3 mm cord could slice the line as well. Use a **thick rubber band** if you are concerned. Keep a couple around your wrist. A cheap **hair-tie** may also do the trick.

Unweighting the rope with a rubber band.

Big wall stuff sacks, courtesy Metolius Climbing

Another trick some climbers use is to put a micro ascender (Ropeman, Microtrax, Rollnlock) on their gear loop and pull 15' or so of rope through it on the loose end - shown above. This helps by giving you the right amount of slack to make clipping gear easier. Too little slack, however, and it could get sucked into the braking mechanism. This will also seriously interfere with backup knots, a compromise between speed and safety. Using a **Metolius Safe Tech harness** with full strength gear loops may add an element of safety.

One nice thing about rope-soloing is that runners are not very as useful since you aren't pulling the rope through the gear like a normal belayed scenario. Use runners and draws to avoid zippering gear by orienting the line of fall with the placement, and to help you rap back down or jug back up in a straighter line if necessary. If you are hauling, be sure to not get lines crossed up - this could be disastrous.

Speed Climbing Systems

Safe Methods
Blocking Leads

Blocking leads means that the leader gets a predetermined number of pitches or even better, a predetermined amount of lead time before swapping blocks with the follower. The advantage of blocking pitches is to keep the momentum going, avoid having to sit through two belays, and to give the follower a break. If a leader is in the zone, why not maintain that momentum? After the block, the leader can turn off his/her brain and relax as the diligent follower. Blocking requires quick changeovers at the belay. The rope needs to be flipped or restacked, or the ends of the rope need to be switched. One method of quickly switching ends is to tie in with locking biners instead of knots. Use two lockers. I still prefer just switching ends, but check your knots! If trying to move fast or keep warm, lead in blocks.

Teams of Three and Four

Climbing with three people on long routes can actually be quicker or wind up expending less energy. With three people you now only have to lead $1/3^{rd}$ of the route instead of half of it. You also have to carry $1/3^{rd}$ as much group gear instead of ½ of it, or at least take fewer turns carrying the weight. If both followers get belayed simultaneously, then one person can totally relax at the upper belay and do nothing. Team of three should only take one to three more minutes per pitch if done properly. If belaying both followers, you can use two ropes and either stagger the climbers (in a crack system) or have them climb side by side (on ice curtains). This works well with half ropes. It can be done with twins, but can be a little freaky on difficult or chossy/sharp terrain. You can also haul and short-fix at the same time easily with a team of three, something that you can't do easily with a team of two. If using two ropes of quite different diameter and belaying off the anchor (really the only way to do it), the thinner rope may not catch as easily in the belay device. Put the better climber on the thinner rope.

You can climb with just one rope and have the first follower tie in several feet ahead of the other follower. Use a butterfly knot, or even better an overhand knot on a bight with a slipknot in its center. A butterfly is good because if the last follower falls, the angle of the knot makes it so most of the weight is only felt by the belayer. The overhand with slipknot also works this way, but allows for the middle person some wiggle room to not get pinned with the tension of the belay and a slow or hangdogging final follower.

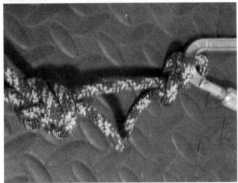

Slipknot inside an overhand on a bight for tying in short.

One way to keep the rope moving is to just belay one climber up at a time. The first follower gets to the belay and either leads the next pitch or the leader resumes leading the next pitch. Either way, the new belayer has to do double duty of belaying the leader and belaying the follower. It's stressful, but efficient. The most efficient system would be for at least one of the followers, if not both, to jug. This prevents double duty belaying.

If you are hauling, the first follower can bring up a fresh lead rope and save a lot of time by belaying and hauling at the same time. Having the first person jug the haul line (carrying the fresh rope) can allow the leader to climb without waiting for the pitch to be cleaned. The leader gets a gear resupply after the 3rd climber jugs and cleans.

The best thing about a team of three is the camaraderie. You now have two people to taunt you and joke around while you lead, and most folks are at their best with a little extra friendly peer pressure. Spirits are high at the belay and aren't nearly as boring with someone to laugh and joke around with.

Teams of four act as two independent teams but join forces on a single objective. This can help ensure success on a big hard route. One team could do the leading for the day while the other follows and brings up gear.

Fix and Fire
Fixing pitches saves time if you can't complete a wall in a day, especially on walls too hot to climb during the months with more daylight. Fix and firing has you climb to a high point and then fixing the ropes down to the ground where you can comfortably sleep and jug the ropes the next day. Fixing above a bivy ledge saves time for the next day, but if you have a portaledge, you may as well just climb until you can't anymore and just stop there. You can really speed down a wall on fixed ropes since you don't have to pull them. Direct the rope out of harmful cracks, choss, and edges with gear. Pad edges and/or the rope with tape, clothes (tied off), or **rope protectors**. Leave the gear you won't need to get down or back up at the top or the last good ledge to avoid jugging with extra weight, mindful if it may rain. It is tempting to just make a rat's nest of gear at the top, but it makes hanging out and sorting in the morning after a tiring jugging session miserable.

Have the last rappeller pull up most of the slack and fixing that to the anchor. Leaving a bunch of slack rope could get caught up. Don't tie off your ropes between pitches too tight or you won't be able to rap down. Wind can also cut into a tightly fixed rope. Too loose and wind could blow the rope out of line of the jug the next day and create real problems. If a fixed line is really long and a bit sketchy, you can tie it off to intermediate gear on your way down. Don't have both people jug the same rope unless the intermediate gear is totally bomber and the first climber is past it and re-fixes it.

Fixing over a big overhang, or fixing straight down to offer a straight shot back up, may require tying a bunch of ropes end to end for one long fixed line. Expect a solid case of butterflies in your stomach when jugging this line the next day. You will need to pass knots on rappel on your way down, and jugging back up the next day. To pass the knot with ascenders on rappel, use backup knots and down-jumar to transfer weight onto to belay device on the lower rope. To pass knots on the way up, just do as you would cleaning gear on the route.

If there are significant traverses on your fixed lines, you need to leave plenty of slack while fixing traverses so there is enough rope left to do the rappel. If there isn't, be sure and tail clip your ascenders so they don't get torqued off the rope. Jugging past large overhangs on fixed ropes offers a similar solution by lowering yourself out from the wall with a belay device. Again, you need slack to do this, so don't fix too tightly. On popular routes where fixing would be unusual, try and keep the fixed lines out of the way of the climbing route. If a route is a really popular aid climb, it isn't uncommon for someone to sneak in early and jug your lines. Jugging fixed lines is one of the spookier aspects of climbing. No matter how many backups you have on your jugging system, you still are relying on one rope to remain intact. The first person jugging up the fixed lines most likely will not be able to clip into backup knots because ropes are fixed on each side, and you may pull the end of the rope out of reach for the following jugger. **Static ropes** make much safer fixed lines, so consider bringing a thick static line instead of a second lead rope. As mentioned earlier, placing pro on the way back up and tying it off, or belaying the next jugger can add some safety.

OTHER (MORE DANGEROUS) METHODS
The best way to climb quickly, just like the pros, is to climb fluidly and with intention. You don't have to race. The other best tactic is to not waste a moment during transitions. Using those tips over the ones below is safer and makes the following tips almost unnecessary. Once you stop wasting time when leading, following, or transitioning you should then employ a fancy tactic.

Simulclimbing
Simulclimbing is the fastest method of climbing short of free soloing. To keep it safe, there are some important details. The leader should always place gear in anticipation of the follower as well as for his/her own protection. This means placing gear on easy terrain if the follower is still on difficult terrain. The more rope out, the less the leader will feel the weight of the second but the more potential there is for rope drag. To avoid drag, the leader could tie in with an adapted Kiwi coil to pay out rope as needed. A really quick method has the follower keeping the leader on belay with a GriGri to pay rope in or out as needed. The follower can move through easy sections by pulling in slack while the leader moves slowly, or if the follower is on hard terrain and the leader is at a stance and piece the follower can self-belay by pulling in slack through the difficulties. To reduce drag, the rope could be folded in half turning it into a 30 m (if using a 60 m) double rope. On routes like the Nose where there are a lot of pendulums, the leader can counterweight pendulum off of the follower (leader hangs and pulls up on the follower) while simuling.

Tiblocking

If the leader is really concerned about the follower, he/she can put a Tibloc (Microtraxion/Rollnlocks work very well) on a piece. Clip a locker to the piece, and put the Tibloc with the rope through it on the biner. The rope must be running through the biner so that it enters the biner from below and exits above, otherwise a lead fall would directly load the Tibloc. Because some extra friction is created by the Tibloc, the rope may lift up on the gear. Not only can this pull the gear out, but it can also create a lever that can pull the leader off the wall. The unfortunate reality is that the longer the sling the worse the effect, but the shorter the sling (none is best) the worse the rope drag (compounded by the friction of the Tibloc and amount of rope out).

Correct. Rope is through the biner.

Long sling lifts up, creating a lever. If follower fell, the rope would pull down on the leader.

Incorrect

Simul-Soloing and Short Roping

Simul-soloing is just free soloing with a friend. Some routes are fun this way. You can protect short sketchy sections when soloing by using a short section of rope or even a cordalette to give a short belay. Falling on a cordalette would be pretty messed up, but is at least some insurance for cruxy or exposed short steps. Short-roping (carrying coils with a small amount of rope between climbers) is an excellent way to move fast over moderately technical or exposed easy terrain. The leader is just a moving anchor (and obviously mustn't fall) and can use terrain to provide protection.

Short-Fixing

Short-fixing means climbing to an anchor and then rope-soloing off the anchor while the follower jugs the line to keep the rope moving up the wall. When the leader gets to the anchor, he/she pulls the slack up and fixes the rope for the follower to jug. With the spare rope, the leader sets up a rope-solo rig (often a GriGri) using the anchor the follower is going to be jugging on. When the follower reaches the anchor, the leader rests on some gear and tags up the fresh rack while the follower puts the leader on belay. The leader now has a fresh rack and plenty of rope to keep doing this for as many pitches as he/she wants. This transition must be done on bomber gear because once the solo device is dismantled, there will be slack the belayer needs to quickly take in. The anchor must follow the same rules as any rope-solo setup (upwards pull, etc.).

The leader and follower never meet until they switch roles. The leader must have enough slack to pull up the fresh rack, or a trail line (clipped through the anchor so it doesn't get away). With short-fixing the follower must always jug the line, and if there's a haul bag, the follower also needs to do the hauling. The haul bag can't get hung up, and if it does, the whole point of short-fixing falls apart due to the huge amount of time wasted having the follower free up the bags. If the follower is going to haul, the leader needs to set up the haul and get the bag off the anchor for the follower. A team of three solves this dilemma.

Short-fixing can be a good solution (if the 2nd is jugging) if you can't reach the anchors due to inadequate gear. Just build an anchor, start rope-soloing until you're on your last good piece, and wait for a rack reload to arrive.

Short-Tagging
On hard, gear intense pitches, another alternative is to bring more gear and have the belayer hold onto the spares. There are two ways for the leader to get the spare gear. The first and simplest option is for the leader to tag it up on a haul line. The next option requires foresight and only requires one rope. The leader begins the pitch tied into the middle of the rope, preferably with two locking biners. The leader is belayed on one of the two ropes. It is crucial the leader knows which rope to clip! Once the leader is near the end of the halved rope, they construct a good anchor and tags the rack up on the trailing line. Once the leader gets the gear, he/she ties into the end of the trailing line, unties from the middle, and the belayer pulls in the slack and put the leader back on belay. There is no rope soloing involved.

By tying into the middle of a single rope, you can also alternately clip gear on wandering pitches just as you would a half rope. It is harder to keep which side is which when doing this, however. Blake Herrington has a simple way to tie into the middle of the rope without using a biner. Put of bight of rope through your belay loop and pass the bight over your body to girth hitch into the middle of the rope.

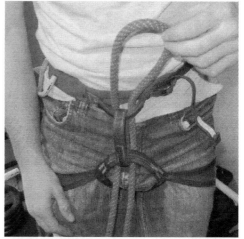

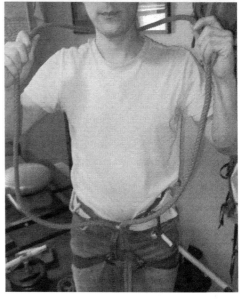

Girth-hitching into the middle of the rope

Movable Anchor
If you are free soloing easy ground and come to a short step that's a bit too hard or exposed for your comfort levels, you can use one to three (three best) daisy chains (or sections of cut and knotted rope if you want some dynamic force absorption) like lobster claws to clip a piece, pull the move, and either unclip and pull the gear, or set another piece before backcleaning. This is how Yosemite free soloists get through difficult sections or through A0 moves (not really free soloing but who cares). Remember that falling onto a tether of any kind (sling, daisy, PAS, etc.) creates huge forces and you gear can rip or sling break very easily.

Yosemite Loop
The next system is known as a Yosemite Loop. Colin Haley used this system to rope-solo the Cerro Torre with the 6 mm Esprit Alpine Escape Rope by leaving his gear and retrieving it on the way down. Besides simply not using this system, I strongly urge that you use a real rope and not do this for entire pitches or routes.

From an anchor or fixed piece, loop the rope through and pull as much slack as you need to get past the crux or as far as you think you can safely climb without falling. Tie in with one end and tie in short on the other strand to make a loop of rope long enough to get where you need. At the end of the loop's reach, establish another anchor and pull the rope through the lower anchor to get out of the system or to start again. You can put gear in along the way to reduce the fall as you climb higher, but the amount of rope out is still constant. In other words, a fall just at the lower anchor would have you fall the length of loop you pulled through and falls higher up a pitch right at a piece of pro would still be the length of the remaining slack in the loop. Falls above a piece of pro would be twice the length between you and the gear plus the remaining slack. You could keep extending the length of the loop as you climb higher to reduce the fall distance or to be able to climb farther.

To get your rope back, simply untie and pull it through the lower anchor. This system is not safe, but it is much faster and hassle free than a standard rope-solo setup. It works fastest for soloing short sections, or climbs that you rappel the way you came up. You must bring enough gear to leave without running out. Otherwise, to get your gear back you would have to rappel back down and climb/jug back up.

Adding a moveable anchor (3 daisies or equivalent) to a Yosemite loop is a way to speed more safely through aid sections, like traverses.

The Infinite Loop
The following is a method of short-fixing for free climbing that allows almost continuous movement of both climbers, a pitch that never has to end, and you never run out of gear. I can almost hear the record screeching off the needle. Be warned, this is by no means a safe system as it is essentially simul-rope-soloing. This is one of the most advanced systems in the book, do it (along with everything else of course) at your own risk. The benefits of this system is almost no down time at a belay, a slightly more dynamic system than a standard rope-solo or short-fix setup, and shorter "pitches" means you can bring less gear or have more gear

available to the leader which may or may or not also help with the psychological drain while leading rope stretching pitches. Unlike short-fixing, the leader does not have to anchor in while the follower pulls through all the remaining slack. The cons of this system are that rope-soloing is dangerous and you can screw it up and die. You also need to use it on pitches with good gear – a bomber piece every 20 feet, and two really bomber pieces every 80 feet or so. Here's how you do it:

Fix both ends of the rope together with an in-line figure eight knot (Flemish Bend) and stack the rope so the middle is on the bottom. A good middle mark is very handy at the start. Marking ¼ rope with a different mark can also help. There needs to be a "mini anchor" at least at by these exact distances for this to be super useful. The leader attaches to the rope with a solo device (usually a GriGri) just past the knot and the follower puts the leader on belay with a GriGri on the other side of the knot. The leader leads up, placing gear as normal. If the leader falls, the follower catches the leader like normal, but the leader will also be caught on his/her rope-solo device as well. Don't screw up how you attach yourself! Tug firmly to see if the solo device catches. If the device does not engage, the leader will fall half a rope length! Use backup knots (impossible if the loop of rope is fully extended).

For the sake of clarity, let's just assume the leader doesn't run out of gear after he/she leads up the available amount of rope. After half (or less) the rope is led out, the leader now puts in a mini-anchor. This mini-anchor is fixed to the lead side of line with a butterfly knot near the rope joining knot, on which the follower will now proceed to jug or preferably toprope-solo off of. The mini-anchor should have two solid and equalized pieces and should not take much longer to build than protecting the climb as usual.

The upward pull resistance on the anchor is mostly taken care of by the dead weight of the follower. With the line now fixed, the leader continues up as usual, but is now self-belaying, paying out rope from the non-lead side through their solo device. The leader continues to place mini-anchors as the two climb on an endless loop of rope.

Both the leader and follower will wind up passing the knot joining the two ropes. This is a good spot for the leader to build a mini-anchor who can then tether in quickly and pass the knot. The follower can pass the knot easily by tying a backup knot in the rope below their self-belay device while they maneuver it above the connecting knot. The follower cannot use a toothed ascender to jug because they are essentially always belaying the leader.

The leader will only be able to tag up fresh gear from the follower on the non-lead side of the rope when they are ¼ rope apart or less. This can be accomplished by making mini-anchors every ¼ rope (50-60 feet), or to just have the follower catch-up: whatever naturally plays out or happens first. Mini-anchors should still be placed every 80 or so feet. The follower should have the rope fully weighted off the mini anchors at all times – pretty easy to do considering they are jugging or toprope-soloing. The leader should be extra careful not to fall when the follower is passing the knot, however. The backup knot would save the day, but the mini-anchor could receive a big upward pull (and the follower would probably lose a finger or drop their GriGri).

The follower never cleans a mini-anchor until the leader has put in a new one. The leader can make more than one, but the newest anchor would then need to be fairly tight to the old one and probably add a piece for upwards pull considering there will still be a bit more slack in the system. There always needs to be at least three bomber pieces of gear between the leader and follower. The closer the follower gets to the leader, the easier it is to tag up gear, but the gear between them needs to be bomber, and with less rope out, fall factors are higher. If the leader is more than ¼ ways out and needs gear, the rope could just be pulled all the way through both the leader and followers devices.

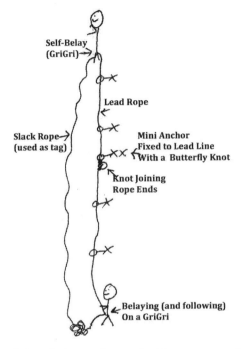

If the climb requires a double rope rappel, connecting two ropes together would probably be big-time overkill and you would need to bring twice as much gear. Since tagging gear up on the remaining rope or pulling through the devices accomplishes the task, you do not need a trail line. Keep the spare rope in the followers pack if you need it to descend, or have both climbers remove their devices (while both attached to solid gear).

YoGo Method

Like simulclimbing (with or without placing Tiblocs), short-fixing, and the infinite loop system, this is a speed system to get both climbers moving up the wall at once. There is no rope-soloing involved and there isn't a chance of pulling the leader off or loading the leader's gear placements. This method is best done if the follower jugs instead of toprope-solos. The basic system is that the leader is being belayed while the follower jugs on a separate fixed rope simultaneously. The belayer will be standing around belaying some of the time, but much less so than with short-fixing.

To do this the leader trails two lead ropes, belayed on one rope while trailing the other. The belayer is tied into both ropes and belays with a GriGri. At an anchor the leader takes up the slack on the lead rope and fixes it. The leader then switches to the trail line as the new lead rope. The follower now belays the leader on the new lead line while simultaneously jugging and cleaning the pitch on the fixed line. To retrieve gear, the leader simply pulls up the slack on the trail rope he/she is currently trailing after the follower gets to the anchor it was fixed to. When the leader reaches the next anchor, he/she repeats the process.

The leader can't have climbed more than ½ a rope after first anchor from the ground to tag gear up. Mark your middles, use different colored ropes, and be extremely clear about switching ropes and belays. A trail line extension or 3rd rope could be used to get the rope back after the gear has been tagged up if planning on leading more than ½ pitches before a new anchor is established. When the leader switches ropes, he/she must obviously clip the anchor or bomber gear. Because there is no way to avoid an upward pull on the follower if the leader falls, expect longer falls for the leader. The follower could also be pulled up into a roof or into uncleaned gear. The Gri-

Gri needs to be monitored for cross loading, too much slack, short-roping the leader, as well as maintaining a grip on the brake hand at all times. Use at your own risk, this system has not had a lot of climbers testing it. There may be unforeseen disasters. Hauling is not going to happen with this system. Thanks to Chris Gonzalez and Robert Yoho for making up this creative, yet simple system, and to Hans Florine for alerting me to its existence.

Rescue and Self-Rescue

To Bivy or Descend

Deciding to bivy versus heading down in a storm or whiteout can be a life or death decision. Will waiting out a storm whose duration is anyone's guess just waste food, water, supplies, energy, and warmth? Can your injured partner wait? Are you willing to put other people's lives at risk as search and rescue or other climbers will inevitably start to look for you? If you are truly pinned down by life-threatening winds and avalanches, digging a snow cave or finding some kind of shelter may be worth the risk of waiting. Descending extremely technical unknown terrain or climbing up terrain at night that is very hard to route find is another good reason to wait, especially if the terrain you descended/rappelled is not re-climbable. If you are lost, take the extra time and energy to climb back up to get back on route so you can descend to safety.

But waiting out a storm just because there's a storm can be equally unsafe, and if there is no storm, one can come in and really pin you down. At least getting down out of the winds and heavy snow into trees, making it to a road or trail (even if it's nowhere near your camp or car), keeps you moving, warm, and closer to safety. Bring pictures and topos of multiple aspects of the mountain in case you need to descend one of those routes. There have been many needless bivies that have killed or seriously detained and exhausted climbers when a little extra effort and technical knowledge could have saved them by just going down. It's impossible to have any hard and fast rules. It all depends on the situation. Just know that bivying for the sake of bivying makes no sense, and getting stuck in a storm, whiteout, or being off route isn't automatic cause for bivying or calling for a rescue.

Calling For Rescue

It's truly incredible listening to stories of climbers and adventures caught in a dire situation and getting themselves out on their own. With the advent of cell phones and personal locator beacons more and more people are calling for help when they could have dealt with the situation on their own. Don't get in over your head, or worse: blindly agree with your partner's decisions to avoid confrontation. Listen to the little voice inside your head telling you that you are right – whether to question a bad decision or to voice your desire to bail. Swallow your pride and check your ego. It will save you. Read as many stories on epics and back issues of "Accidents in North American Mountaineering" published by the American Alpine Club as you can to learn from the mistakes of others.

If you or your partner are in need of immediate medical attention, that is you will die or lose a limb by the time you extricate yourself to safety, then calling in a rescue is acceptable by anyone's standards. Being uncomfortable or missing work the next day is an unacceptable reason to jeopardize safety or future access for others. You will deserve the Internet flaming that will inevitably ensue.

If the decision is made to get help, you first have to figure out a way to contact someone to get rescue. **Phones and PLB's** have been discussed already. A good trick with poor service and a low battery is to send out a group text message to other climbers who can serve as interpreters to authorities who may not know very much about the route you are on. Not all areas have competent search and rescue teams. You'll be in great hands in the Tetons, but may be at the mercy of local Good Old Boys in less popular areas. You climbing friends may be able to hook up with the SAR team to help. Text as much information as you can, including a statement that you will check in every hour to half hour. Then turn your phone off to save battery life. If you can't get a signal and can move, find a high point. If you're pinned down, so be it. But if you can get to a location that will help limit the technical and time consuming rigging that may occur, or get to a more visible location then do so. If your partner is injured and you can't get a message out, you may have to leave them there and high tail it out to initiate a rescue. If you did get a message out, stay put. Not only could you wind up getting hurt going out solo, your partner could really use the company or help if he/she deteriorates.

If you are stuck at night, flash SOS with your headlamp – someone may see if from a long way off. **SOS in Morse Code is three short (S), three long (O), and three short (S) flashes. Three sharp blasts in succession from a whistle also means help.** The sign for help from afar is **both arms up for yes, one arm up for no**. Waving frantically, even waving a jacket, can be misinterpreted as someone just being psyched to see a plane and are waving hello, unless you are sure they are specifically looking for you. Making a fire to get located is one thing, but making one to initiate a rescue may be futile – you're just someone camping. Building **three fires in a triangle** is a signal for help. For a ski plane to land you need to pack down a landing strip: 5 x 60 meter ropes (1000') by a quarter rope length (or about 50 feet). Helicopters need about a 30 meter diameter landing pad unless they are really gung-ho.

HAVE A PLAN

It is a very good idea to let someone know where you are going, what you are climbing, and when you plan to be back by. Write down the information for your significant other, including phone numbers of other climbers that have at least heard of your route who can assist or assure and number or who to contact in case you are late like the local SAR or park service. It's hard to decide what a good "freak out" time should be if you don't call by a certain time. A good rule of thumb is by midnight for a short day and noon the next day for a big day. If spending multiple nights in a remote area give yourself a full extra day to get to the car and then get cell service.

Always have a rescue plan, even if just cragging. In the back of your mind think what would you do if an accident occurred? Does your partner know what to do? If you can't answer yes, you are seriously underprepared and are putting the both of you at risk. Just because a crag is near your car doesn't mean you'll get to a hospital in time. It could be hours away, or it could take hours to get your partner to the ground.

Always have a plan for getting down a route besides the guidebook's descent instructions. If you have a rope and gear you can get down - it just might be expensive. But before committing to terrain that involves difficult traverses above huge roofs or blank terrain, have a solid discussion about continuing on. Have a turn-around time and stick to it, or suffer the consequences if you think it's worth it. Plan on ropes getting stuck when planning gear and timing, especially when doing double rope rappels. Unexpected whiteouts and increasing avalanche conditions can make your plan of descent worthless. Plan for this.

PRACTICING SKILLS YOU ALREADY KNOW

Self-rescue conjures up complicated systems you'll never remember. This doesn't have to be the case. You should have some equipment and knowledge to get out of almost any situation. Knowing basic systems and having proper equipment are tools you can use to create your own scenario as long as some basic, obvious rules apply: always be anchored in to something and use backups when trusting anything your life depends on that isn't absolutely bomber.

Even basic skills need practice. Some skills require a degree of skill that needs refining like self-arresting, some require being able to not only understand the principles but to quickly and smoothly initiate them, like performing a beacon search and extraction. Finally, some skills need practice to be able to improvise without having the information handy. For instance, you may know how to tie certain knots, make pulleys, etc., but if you can't remember to actually use those skills when the time is right, they are worthless. Having the tools fresh in the top of your mind will allow you to at least improvise effectively. Don't rely on this book, but it wouldn't hurt to put a copy on your phone.

IMPORTANT SKILLS TO PRACTICE

Knots There are many other knots but you can get away without them.
- Munter Hitch
- Friction Knots: Prusik, Autoblock, Klemheist, Bachman, Leg Wrap, Foot Wrap
- Fig-8 Follow Through, Fleishman's, Water Knot, EDK, Fig-8 and Overhand on a Bight, Clove Hitch (one handed), Girth Hitch, Basket Hitch, Slipknot, Double Fisherman's
- Load Releasing Knots: Mule/Slipped Half-Hitch, Mariner Hitch, Block and Tackle

Systems
- Transferring Victim's Weight Off You
- Belaying off the Harness, Anchor, and Redirect
- Jugging with Knots and Slings, Belay Device, and Mini Ascenders: Two Prusik System, Frog System, Two Ascender System
- Lowering with Redirect, Backup Prusik, and off a Reverso-like device in Guide-mode
- Backing up a Rappel: Extending Device, Autoblock, Pull Cord Backup
- Counterweight and Tandem/Assisted Rappel
- Passing a Knot while Lowering and on Rappel (and Hauling if Applicable)
- Hauling 1:1, 2:1 (C-drop version), 3:1
- Basic Aiding with Slings or Cordalette
- Basic Rope-soloing with Clove Hitch and GriGri

First Aid
- CPR
- Rescue Breathing
- Stopping Bleeding
- Choking
- First Aid and Emergency Bivy Kit: Check you kit to make sure you've got the very basics

Snow and Ice
- Self-Arrest with Ax, Skis and Poles, Hand/Arms
- Avalanche Rescue: Beacon Search, Multiple Victims, Shoveling and Probing
- Avalanche Evaluation
- Crevasse Rescue: Jugging, Snow Anchors, and Hauling including 2:1, 3:1, 6:1, and 9:1 Systems

Rescue Gear. You should have these items whether you're the belayer or leader to help extricate you and your partner. Provide this gear to your partner if they forgot. Other emergency items and first aid items are not listed.
- Knife
- Belay Device
- Lockers (1-2)
- Spare Biners (1-2)
- Autoblock Rappel Backup Cord (i.e. a Prusik Loop)
- Extras Slings and a Nylon Cordalette (very useful to have, but not always necessary)

With this information you should be able to figure out how to deal with most scenarios from passing a knot, to becoming hands free on the belay, and rescuing a leader or follower via hauling, lowering, or ascending the rope. I've tricked you by already going over 90% of self-rescue situations. If I put them all in one section, you probably wouldn't have read it. Big wall climbers have a leg up since a victim is essentially a haul bag that may or not be able to help. Do a wall that involves some jugging and hauling to make it more fun.

THE MOST IMPORTANT THING TO KNOW:
TRANSFERRING THE VICTIM'S WEIGHT OFF OF YOU

You can't do much just standing there holding the rope except to lower the victim to the ground or safe ledge, which is great if it's possible. The "belay escape" commonly taught as step 1 is a misnomer, you don't want to escape the belay unless you abandon your partner. You just want to get their weight off you. There are many solutions, like the one described below. You should be able to figure out how to do this (and everything else) on your own. If you can't, you don't have a good understanding of what's on the list above.

Most climbers belaying the follower are belaying right of the anchor on a Reverso or GriGri. Yay, you're done! In every other situation other than a simple lower to the ground or safe ledge below, you need to transfer the weight off you. Teach this easy setup to your uninformed partner:

- Tie a mule knot on your belay device biner with the brake strand of the rope so you can let go of the brake hand, or tie a backup knot below an auto-locking belay device. Now your hands are free.
- Put a friction hitch (or any rope clamp) on the loaded rope and attach it to the anchor with a load releasable hitch (Munter Mule or Mariner Mule) and ease the weight onto the friction hitch. You may need to beef up your anchor. Now your body is free, almost done.
- Back up the friction hitch/releasable knot cord with the rope to the anchor. A Munter mule works well for this backup, as it may be useful for a lower later on.
- Don't take the belay device or prusik off the rope just yet - you may need it!

Brake strand mule'd off

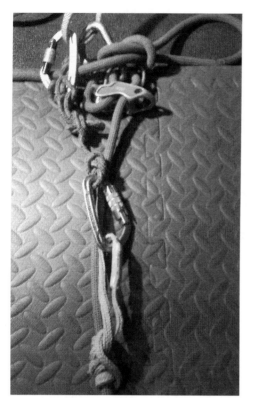

Weight transferred to prusik on loaded strand and tied to anchor with a munter mule knot.

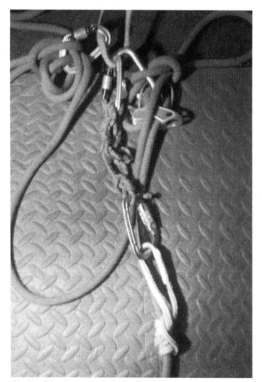

Slack of brake strand tied off to anchor with a munter mule. At this point you could remove the belay device, release the munter mule on the prusik, and remove the prusik leaving the loaded rope attached to the anchor on a mule'd off munter hitch.

You also don't always have to transfer the load to the anchor. Think before you act. You may just be wasting time by following rescue formulas. Always tie backup, aka catastrophe knots, usually just an overhand on a bight tied to you or the anchor in the event a prusik doesn't hold, accessory cord breaks, or you screwed something up. Belaying off the anchor with a guide-mode belay device or GriGri opens up many rescue options and is easier to transition from. Make sure when loading anything with the victim on the rope, you can unload via releasable knot or belay devices/knots. Sometimes it may be easier to go up than down, but It is almost always easier to lower and create a new anchor.

Counterweight is your best friend: use it to get down and even go up. If your partner is conscious, have them help. They're like a haul bag with arms, legs, and a brain (if conscious).

Lowering Past a Knot

If you need to lower more than a rope length you'll need to pass the knot. When you get near the knot when lowering on the first rope, follow the steps in how to transfer the victim's weight onto the rope. The weight should be on the load releasable prusik with a backup. Put the new rope on the other side of the knot through the anchor on a Munter Mule (or another belay device) with a brake hand backup (can use the old one) to continue lowering. If you tied the loaded rope off with a Munter mule as your load releasable knot, you can ease onto the new rope without shock-loading the new Munter (or belay device).

If originally lowering off a Munter, you could feed the joining knot through the Munter while the weight is off of it. You could also pop the knot through the Munter by simply lowering until the knot jams in the Munter, tie off the brake hand to your harness, and work the knot through. The main problem with this simple solution of popping the knot is if it doesn't work (it usually does). Lowering is a great way to get scared partner past two short rappels with just one rope or by passing a knot.

RESCUING THE LEADER

If the leader wants to be lowered but is more than ½ of the rope is out (won't reach the ground), he or she could be lowered to the last piece within reach of the end of the lower, tether to it, pull the rope through the upper anchor, and then get lowered of that piece. This only works if the gear is good. The gear will be left there.

If the leader is using two ropes or a trail line, the leader could rap on the trail line while belayed down on the lead rope while cleaning gear if the chances of anchor failure are high.

If the leader needs rescue, you can counterweight climb up to them. The dead weight of the leader acts as a belay, and as the belayer climbs, the leader is lowered. If the leader is fixed in place, you can jug off of them. If the leader is conscious, have them back up the last piece or something within reach. If jugging off them, have them clip into an anchor they made there.

If you question the leader's gear you're counterweight climbing or jugging off of, you may need to back your climb up by also rope-soloing off the lower anchor (like in the stuck rope with only one end down scenario). Rescuing an incapacitated leader is a lot like getting a stuck rope or haulbag down.

CARRYING A VICTIM
On the Wall
Getting a victim down the wall while on rappel is best done with one of the lowering methods described above. There may be an occasion when you need to have them on your back if for whatever reason their weight can't be fully on the rappel system or you need to move them over low angled terrain.

One way you could carry a victim is to punch a couple leg holes in their (not your) pack. Other options are using extra webbing or extra rope to construct a piggyback setup by running the rope/webbing around the victim and rescuer in a big figure-8. Whatever you do, employ backups galore, secure the victim so if they came "undone" they won't swing or shock load the system, and pad any pressure points. An improvised chest harness connected to the rope with a prusik or ascender will help immensely if supporting the climber on rappel.

On the Ground
The following can also be used to carry a victim once off the cliff as well as the methods shown above. The simplest method is the fireman's carry, but you can't go very far this way.

Courtesy United States Navy

If you've got a full rope to spare you could construct a split-rope carry, aka Tragsitz.

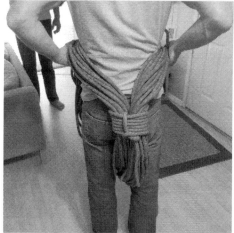

With your rope in a mountaineer's coil, split it in half and have the victim step inside. The victim pulls the coils up wit the knot behind their back and the rescuer puts the coils over their shoulders.

If you have two people you can try a rope litter once on solid ground. Beyond that, rigging stretchers out of branches, ropes, skis, or poles. If rigging stretchers, consider putting the victim in a sleeping bag or tarp. This will not only keep them warm and reduce pressure points, it will add to the stability of the stretcher. If worse comes to worse you could use clothing to put the stretcher arms through. Simply dragging someone injured enough to not even have a supported hobble out will take so long you may as well just go for help. Dragging will probably injure them more (or give them hypothermia on snow). I can personally attest that dragging one's self for miles usually results in skin grafts. Insulate and pad a victim during transport!

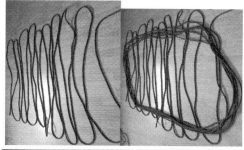

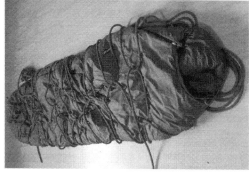

To make a rope litter lay out the rope like the first picture, then lay the round around the coils. Pad as much as possible, then with the free end starting at the legs, snake the rope through the loops back and forth.

Chapter Twelve: Other Aspects

First Ascents, Ethics, and Stewardship

First Ascents

Climbing a route for the first time ever is probably the most exciting and rewarding thing you can do in climbing. Creativity and motivation are the two main ingredients in putting up a new route. Just because a wall or an area hasn't been developed doesn't mean it isn't any good – even in popular areas. The best way to find a suitable line is to get to know the area a bit so you get a lay of the land. Take pictures of features you wonder if they have been climbed before. Look in guidebooks and journals and scour the Internet for more information. Talk to local climbers and guidebook authors. You may be surprised how easy it is to chat with a local legend. If you can't find any information, there's a good chance no one's been there.

After finding a possible objective, you need to get a good idea what the climbing will be like. Knowing the rock type of the feature and what nearby climbs are like will give you a pretty good idea of what the first ascent will entail and what equipment you need to bring. Onsight ground-up first ascents are usually the goal, but some climbs may require extensive cleaning, drilling, and attempts. Spotting scopes, topo maps, and satellite imagery will help you pick a line. Chartering a plane or helicopter ride to fly over is extremely helpful on remote routes, and is one of the more fun things you can do.

Grants

There are many grants available for future first ascents. You don't have to be a high-end climber putting up a modern test piece to get a grant. A good place to start is by checking with the American Alpine Club and your local climbing organization. The local club may not have a published grant, but may find your idea intriguing enough to help with some funding.

Impact of Your New Route

Take into consideration what impact your climb will have on the environment and local climbing community. Radically varying from the local normal standard of practice won't make you any friends. Check with governmental laws regarding permits and fixed anchor policies. If you want others to climb your route safely, take the time to establish long lasting anchors and fixed gear. Making half-assed anchors, like bolts equalized with webbing or rope (come on, make it last, you took the time to put the damn bolts in), or using cheap crappy chain is just plain annoying. If you're going to do it, then do it right. At least come back soon and finish the job. Otherwise just do your first ascent with minimal fixed gear and let others know that you think it would be nice to have it properly equipped and give the blessing. The same thing goes with setting up rappels. If you're going to bolt a rappel, you might as well take the time to make it a clean rap. Setting raps up for 30 meters instead of double ropes is just a good neighborly thing to do.

If reporting the climb, follow local grading customs (or be willing to change the grade), and accurately report any dangers or issues future parties may have like huge run-outs, or no fixed anchors for the descent. You don't have to equip a route for the masses, but at least alert them of the route's difficulty, seriousness, and other important information – unless it's painfully obvious. Try and clean up as much loose rock as possible, at least the death blocks. A hammer with a cleaning pick is a very useful tool, and pitons are still ok to use. Bringing two ropes (or more) is also pretty standard fare.

663

If you bolt a route, it is your duty to clean it until it is safe. Cleaning rock like untouched limestone can take a day per pitch. Come equipped with tons of hard brushes, crowbars, brushes, and old ropes.

If you put up an alpine classic, you should alert the land management officials that they should expect an increase in traffic to that peak, and a proper trail may need to be made. Do you really want a pristine mountain face to have a bolted ride up it?

Being a Jerk About Your First Ascent
If you do a first ascent, remember that you do not own the route (unless it's on your property). Our lands are public and for everyone, and if you didn't climb it, someone at some point would have. Climbing law still dictates that the first ascensionist has the right to deny others to add additional bolts or fixed gear. However, this should really be up to the local climbing community at some point. If the community agrees that adding a fixed anchor or an additional bolt or two is a good idea, calm your ego and agree to it. The same goes with agreeing to remove unnecessary fixed gear.

The first ascensionist does not have the right to deny others from replacing dangerous fixed gear. This doesn't mean that all routes should be safe or for the masses, and luckily the climbing community at large is much more in favor of keeping things adventurous than individuals are. The situation usually comes into play when someone puts up a dangerous route in a popular area or an over-bolted route in a wilderness area.

You don't have to report your route to anyone. But it is not your right to keep others from knowing about it. If you develop a "secret crag" that you and your friends can climb, the minute you tell someone about it, then the information is public domain. Keeping an area pristine is noble, and it makes sense to still have areas with a sense of adventure. The juggernaut of civilization may descend down upon the area, like it has with Yosemite, Indian Creek, etc. But keeping secrets only lasts so long. It's either a matter of time before your crag or route gets overcrowded or it may never happen. So chill out and don't send nasty emails and death threats if someone winds up posting beta about your crag on the Internet. Remember, you don't own it.

I've been amazed at how good an area can be and never seen a soul. Places like Montana had a top-secret hush-hush nature to their climbing all throughout the 80's until present, but anything but roadside crags and high profile cliffs are still desolate. If those types of areas get sieged like paranoid locals worry about, then everything everywhere would be overrun with people and we've probably got more serious environmental/societal issue to worry about than crowed crags.

If you don't report your first ascent and someone else comes along and reports it later, think about your values and reasons for climbing before all of a sudden coming out of the woodwork and claiming it all of a sudden.

BOLTING IMPACT AND ETHICS
Bolting and fixed gear provides just about the biggest source of differing opinions and Internet arguing as anything in climbing. If you decide to bolt, expect criticism. You may deserve it. Squeezing in routes, overbolting, under-bolting, putting the bolts in terrible sports, poor bolt placement, bolting next to cracks, bolting anchors, or placing any bolts at all can and will get you in trouble or at least get you severely criticized. If you can't respect the local bolting flavor and do a good job bolting, do not do it. If you are too cheap to place good gear and the best choice of gear, do not bolt it or fix it. If the locals don't come out for a mid-

night chopping party, then someone may get hurt and it will be your fault.

A local community may be totally cool with grid-bolting the crap out of a local chunk of rock to provide a nearby "gym" and hangout. Just get a general idea on the local flavor. If there is no local community in the official sense, ask around gear shops, talk to guidebook authors, guide services, etc. Call the Access Fund and the American Alpine Club's local chapter. If there's nothing, start your own! You'll probably get thrown some money to buy some bolts and trail maintenance gear.

One new concept in putting up bolted routes is to bolt the route for the leader of that grade. Many easier climbs have extremely spaced bolts, with run-outs and ground fall situations because 5.12 climbers were putting them up and deemed the route too easy to protect well. It should make sense that if you're going to bolt a 5.8, you should bolt it for the 5.8 leader, as harder routes are bolted for leaders of that grade. Of course there are the test-pieces of a grade that are highly committing and much of their character and reputation comes from the heady lead. But honestly, what's the point of making a heady 5.8 test piece?

Of course each crag has its own flavor and a tightly bolted route may not fit in with the ethic of the crag. The point being made is to check your ego before bolting a route and think of who will be the one climbing it. When bolting a route, it should be bolted for others, not you, because of the permanency of the bolts. Making a runout scary easier pitch on a longer difficult climb is one thing, but at local crags that get a fair amount of beginners and regular folks it's kind of a jerk move. Why are you even bothering to bolt it if it's so beneath you? Of course not everything should be made easy for the lowest common denominator, but like I said, check your ego beforehand.

Will future climbers need a bolt ladder, or should you equip it for a free climb attempt? The bolts probably won't be in the same place if bolting for freeing (the East Buttress of Middle Cathedral is a good example). With advances in free climbing and aiding, bolt ladders are seriously frowned upon. Please end your route prematurely or recruit a better climber than you instead of making bolt ladders.

Chopping Routes/Gear
Chopping routes you don't agree with, in this author's opinion, is an egotistical waste of time. I don't agree with unnecessary bolts or routes, but there are so many ways you can better mankind or help other life forms on the planet than chopping routes. If a metal stud in a rock gets you that upset, maybe you need to re-prioritize your life. It's only climbing. Go volunteering at a soup kitchen or clean up some garbage first. If it really must go, get your local climbing community's input. Make it a clean a crag day. But sneaking off in the night with a crowbar just reeks of misplaced enthusiasm and ego.

Replacing Fixed Gear
One conundrum is replacing bolts that are considered "historical". That fifty year old bolt wasn't a fifty year old bolt for the first ascensionist so why should you be required to continue using it? But leaving it is a testament to those who came before, and having a little bit of history during your climb is kinda cool. Many bolt upgraders leave a few old pieces for historical significance and maybe to leave a bit of spice. There is no simple answer. It's pretty contrived to let routes become dangerous that weren't originally, but expect wrath, bodily harm, and or damage to personal property if you start pulling historic bolts and gear. Many old bolts remain because no one wants to

be the one to deal with the wrath. Contact the ASCA and ask their input. It is this author's opinion that anchors should be replaced if the bolts or fixed gear becomes questionable.

Pitons and other fixed gear are fair game when leading a first ascent, but pitons do not last. Yes, some last an incredibly long time, but it is very difficult to guess which ones are suspect and which ones are bomber. Emotionally, clipping a fixed pin vs. clipping bolt may feel more "alpine," "trad," or adventuresome. Both pitons and bolts are similarly sized chucks of metal hammered into the rock you simply clip and go when repeating established routes. Both scar the rock – bolts initially damage the rock and pitons scar more over time. Drilled pitons really scar the rock compared to even a beefy bolt. Pitons also fill in a crack that could be protected by modern clean gear. So the argument that pitons are more "trad" gets a bit turned around when they actually limit trad placements. Of course no one wants to lug a drill or take the time to hand drill on a big climb to replace a piton with a bolt. I advocate that if the piton scar accepts good gear, pull it. If the gear placement is sketchy (or requires a weird esoteric piece) and that placement is pretty crucial, I'd favor a bolt.

If you do wind up pulling out a fixed piece by accident or on purpose, let others know. Other climbers may be counting on that fixed gear, or it may serve as a warning to similar fixed gear in the area placed around the same time. Post it on the Internet (like Mountainproject.com) and if you can, leave a note at the base or trailhead. Better yet, climb the route again and replace it with a better piece if the fixed gear is considered part of the route's protection after discussing it with the first ascensionist and local climbing scene. They may consider the fixed gear a needless relic and no longer necessary, or a replacement with a bolt may be decided upon. The bottom line is that it's your responsibility to let the climbing community know for the safety of others. Get the climbing community's approval if you feel an added bolt to an established route must go, or if you feel a first ascensionist went a little bolt crazy. Purposely removing fixed gear may seem like the pure ethical thing to do, but taking a step back it sounds really arrogant and stupid. Don't act alone, you own the rock as much as the bolter. Get the local community's approval.

Leave No Trace

Although the spirit of climbing is all about freedom and personal fulfillment, we still have an obligation to abide by some rules. The Golden Rule is don't ruin it for other climbers and future generations. This means minimizing environmental impact of the ecosystem you are traveling in, and minimizing impact on the rock itself. Minimizing impact on the ecosystem basically means abide by Leave No Trace principles that apply to climbers and non-climbers alike.

- Plan Ahead and Prepare
- Travel and Camp on Durable Surfaces
- Dispose of Waste Properly
- Leave What You Find
- Minimize Campfire Impacts
- Respect Wildlife
- Be Considerate of Other Visitors

The member-driven Leave No Trace Center for Outdoor Ethics teaches people how to enjoy the outdoors responsibly. This copyrighted information has been reprinted with permission from the Leave No Trace Center for Outdoor Ethics: www.LNT.org

- Minimize your carbon footprint *(I added this one and don't care if you reprint it).*

When talking about impact to the rock, the impact is mainly only impacts other climbers. This means:

- No chipping or gluing holds
- Thoughtful fixed gear placements
- No chopping fixed gear without consensus of the climbing community
- Minimizing visual impact of chalk including tick marks

- Minimizing visual impact of bolts
- Minimizing visual impact when cleaning a route

Visual impact of chalk and cleaning routes can be disturbing. Cleaning a route of lichen and vegetation can make your route as visible as a neon arrow. I'm surprised chalked cliffs haven't been shut down due to their visual impact. If you put up a crag near a trail or easily visible to non-climbers, expect it to get covered in chalk. Will this create an eyesore and threaten future access? Tick marks are really only an eyesore to climbers unless they get out of control: please clean them off if you must place them. Fixed draws may be fine at some crags that only climbers would visit, but crags near hiking trails or visible from roads or parking areas may be a visual eyesore. Leaving fixed draws is always a gamble that someone may steal your gear so don't piss and moan on the Internet if they get stolen. Unless a climb is your personal project you've just bolted, it is presumptuous to assume that other climbers are cool with you leaving them up. Drytooling can leave scratches on the rock. Drytooling on summer rock routes is almost always unacceptable. Besides scratching up the rock, picks and crampons can shear off holds much easier than you think. Leave a climbing area cleaner than how you found it. That means picking up after yourself (and others).

Etiquette
The Ethics Committee

There is a huge difference between climbing for yourself and climbing for others. You can do whatever the hell you want as long as you aren't ruining things for others. Climbing for other means doing a climb for, or using the accomplishment you've already done for attention, money, or competition. The moment you step into one of those three reasons, including reporting a climb (fits under attention), you are subject to the "Ethics Committee". I'm joking about there being such an establishment, but it does exist in the form of morality and good sportsmanship. It may truly exist as an entity for actual climbing competitions. You are accountable for representing your achievement accurately and honestly in the style in which you climbed a route if recounting your exploits to friends and co-workers, guidebook authors, journal entries, magazines, etc. If you were guided, your story of your Everest summit must include this detail. If you hung or aided, you need to report this. If you used performance enhancing equipment or drugs that are not considered "the norm", you need to clarify your ascent with those aids. Saying "I climbed so-and-so route" to someone when you aided a section is fine, but saying you freed it is lying. Bottled oxygen and Diamox are both considered performance enhancers because too many climbers have shown that they aren't necessary. Does any of this mean you can't aid, hang, suck down O2, etc? No! Especially if you're climbing for yourself. The minute you benefit from your achievement monetarily or egotistically or claim to have set the bar higher, you need to be honest about the style in which you did it.

There is nothing wrong about being egotistical and climbing. It has inspired and driven many climbers, and it is a major driving force in everything in our lives. Without it the only challenge would be from within, and most us want to quit when things are hard without external motivation. That said, making other people feel bad for not climbing at your level, using same gear you used, or doing the route as fast as you did, etc., is just as bad. We don't all have the same genetic gifts, upbringing, and privilege. A fumbly 5.6 climber you're about to mock may have battled cancer, gotten a PhD from a destitute upbringing, and raised thousands of dollars for children in Somalia.

Being a better climber does not make you a better person in any way, even if you worked hard to climb at the level you do now. There will always be someone better than you, and you will always be forgotten at some point. A 5.10 for you may feel like 5.12 to someone else. This doesn't mean the route wasn't 5.12 for that person – ratings are subjective. So to belittle a climb's grade because it felt easy for you doesn't mean it's easy for others.

The typical response is to downgrade everything that feels easy and call anything that's hard "sandbagged". I do think many climbs, especially modern bolted routes, feel quite soft compared to other older established climbs. However, downgrading everything to the lowest common denominator but keeping the scale linear would probably make the test piece 5.15's at about a 5.12+ considering how hard some 5.9+'s are. Allowing excuses for yourself, but not for others is bullshit. Tall people, skinny people, and those with a large ape index (arms longer than height) clearly have an advantage. But they love to tell someone who is short that, "Lynn Hill is only five foot one and can...," or fat that, "Those beer bellied Brits can pull down E7..." The reply to this should be, "Ok, then you should be sending 5.15!"

Good Beta
Call or write guidebook authors to give updates or correction to routes. Posting to regional forums and submitting to regional publications is better than nothing, but also submitting to the American Alpine Journal or posting the climb on Mountain Project will keep the information alive and accessible. For those of you wanting to preserve the adventure then don't post about it, don't look at the guidebook, and don't read (or post) online beta. If complaining about this, you should have a long list of first ascents to your name.

If you didn't lead the pitch, do the route, or actually followed your own advice then your beta needs to clarify this. Take online beta with a huge grain of salt. Generally easier routes have bad beta because hundreds of inexperienced climbers are posting info on them, and hard routes get sandbagged beta. The most common errors are passionate suggestions not to bring certain gear, especially wide gear. As long as you aren't using the gear to aid, bringing that extra #4 Camalot doesn't invalidate your ascent in any way. Saying you don't need a piece does not always mean that you can't place it. In fact, that #4 you "don't need" may wind up being the most bomber piece of gear in a pod on that tips crack route. Another common inaccuracy is that one guy who stated that you can rap the route with a 70 meter rope. It's quite amusing to read subsequent posts that state that you actually cannot! Wait for a second opinion to confirm this, or run the risk of coming up short. Not all 70 meter ropes are created equal.

If you are an amazing and fast climber then say so in your time estimate and gear beta. Don't sandbag danger ratings or opinions about routes. What may be "not that bad" for you, could hurt someone that isn't at your skill level. If you suffer from Alpenheimers like I do, you are forgiven. Be able to empathize with people other than yourself. There is no need to punish climbers worse than you, they have every right to climb as you do and you may have forgotten that you were once there too. If you feel a climb was scary or sandbagged, please voice your opinion. Someone may disagree with you, but if someone gets angry with your opinion, then you can rest easy knowing that they have issues of inadequacy – especially if their response turns into a series of ad hominem attacks. There's nothing wrong with admitting you took a #4, broke up a pitch into two, or thought it was sandbagged and run out. Chances are that jerk on the Internet thought so too.

Finally, if someone asks for beta, then don't withhold route info. You visit other places, so others can visit your crag too. Not posting your crag on Mountainproject.com makes sense, not everything needs to be advertised. But if someone asks about an area online send them an email and ask them not to post your info online to keep the area low-key. If someone else posts information about your secret route or area on Mountainproject or elsewhere, you really have no claim to be upset. They found the area just like you found the area (even if it wasn't by the same means) and chose to share. You don't own the land.

Noise Pollution and Dogs
If you're alone it can be a lot of fun to blast tunes and create a ruckus at the crag or campsite. But the minute you share the area with another party either keep it down or approach the other party and tell them that either you'll be partying and they may want to camp elsewhere. If there aren't other options for them to camp, first ask them to join you. Don't ask if it's okay, nice people say yes even if they don't mean it. If they decline to join you, then that means they also don't appreciate the noise. Believe it or not, not everyone enjoys a drum circle, Dave Mathew's Band, or your acoustic guitar.

Your lovable dog may not be as behaved as you believe it to be. Dogs get anxious and scared when you are climbing. Besides their incessant whining or barking, scared dogs attack (or pretend to attack) people they don't know coming up on them while you climb. I once found a dog with an upside-down water dish tied to the base of a twenty pitch climb. My partner and I barely made it out without being bitten when we refilled its water dish. Your unleashed dog, however behaved in your sights, may wander around and get into other climbers food bins or backpacks – or pee on them. Finally, your dog does not belong in the backcountry. It does not know how to behave around true wild animals because it is not a one, and you are setting yourself and your dog up for injury. I watched a nice sheepdog get gutted and flung down a slope by a mountain goat after explaining this to a hiker. Three pitches up while witnessing this, my partner yelled, "told you so!"

Waiting in Line and Passing
The best way to avoid waiting to get on a route or passing a party is to avoid it in the first place. When you get to the base of a climb, get ready and go. <u>Don't screw around at the base and all of a sudden get going when another party arrives</u>. It's just rude, and creates a bottleneck. If you are slow then please don't hop on a long popular route that's going to be a test piece for you. If you do, and we all do this, then please let people pass. Tell them to pass you, and get an insanely early start. Don't hop on a trade route with a party of 3 if you don't have your systems totally dialed, or gang bang a popular long route or crag with your large party or group. Even if you are climbing in pairs, hopping on a trade route with a group isn't fair to others. If you are top-roping a popular route and a party comes up to lead it, give them the route and ask the follower to tail your rope to re-establish your TR. If you are in line to climb a route and decide to pass the time cragging nearby, you lost your place in line. If two climbs share an anchor but are not dangerous to climb at the same time, then you cannot lay claim to the other line for your leading or toproping pleasure.

Some routes should be expected to be crowded and slow. Deal with it or climb somewhere else. Passing people on hugely popular easy trade routes is just as bad as clogging up a route you shouldn't be on unless there are only one or two well-spaced parties on it. Don't expect a climber on a difficult or scary pitch to be ok with you passing them. Plead your case, and offer to help them by giving them a TR or to jug your line. They should be expected to say no. In this scenario, passing anyway is a jerk move.

So when is it okay to pass? Parties above you earned their place on the route because they got there first and you don't own the route. But if you catch up to them quickly and the route is really long and there aren't other similar routes nearby that your rack is adequate for, or they are clearly over their head, you should be allowed to pass.

To pass someone you must have either proved yourself by catching up to them, or the party above proved their passable status by taking forever. If both of your parties are at the base, tell them you are fast and that everyone will be happier with the decision to let you go first to avoid cramped belays and having someone chomping at the bit below you all day. If they say no, wait for them to finish leading the 2nd pitch and then pass. If this happens higher up, it may be better to ask for forgiveness than permission. Tell the slow party in the nicest way possible, but not apologetically, that you are passing them. This is where diplomacy is crucial. Be super nice in a chatty friendly, "nothing to see here, what a lovely day, isn't this fun, I like your backpack, etc.," sorta tone. If they seem agitated, then just tell them how it will go down. Tell them that you can clip their gear with your own draws to speed up the transition. Tell them that you have no problem if they start leading or following while you are on top of them. If they do, you should not have a problem with them cleaning the gear you clipped off to. I really can't offer any advice if they clearly deserve to be passed and won't let you. Just be friendly and go for it. Unless they are crazy, they shouldn't physically restrain you from passing. Don't worry, you won't be seeing them again!

Helping/Rescuing Another Party
The best way to not have to rescue or help another party is to avoid it. If you see a group or party that gives you really sketchy vibes, there's nothing wrong with going somewhere else so you aren't morally obligated to help since you weren't there to see it go down! But if you see an accident or know someone needs help, then you need to help. Yes, your day or climb is most likely ruined, but unless you're a sociopath, you should help. If they say they are fine, give yourself a good solid gut check before you leave them. If you are unable to help them, suck it up and go down or drive into town and make a call.

GIVING BACK

Great White Icicle Superbowl Sunday BBQ. Yes, that is a couch hauled two pitches up.

A lot has already been talked about with replacing bolts, anchors, and reporting routes. Giving back to the climbing community is so important since most climbs and crags have zero price of admission. If you don't want to be the one to do the work yourself, please join and donate money to:

- The Access Fund
- The American Safe Climbing Association
- The American Alpine Club
- A Regional club or organization such as the Mazamas, Mountaineers, Salt Lake Climbers Alliance, Friends of Indian Creek, or Washington Climbers Coalition - just to name just a few

Many of these clubs and organizations have organized cleanups and events to improve a local crag you can participate in. They also may have important petitions or lobbying you can sign your name to or write a letter to a politician. Better yet, start your own volunteer effort. Host a barbecue, slideshow, fundraiser, or good old-fashioned kegger. Here in Utah we have "No Star Tuesdays" where obscure routes are rediscovered, and have barbecues on top of desert towers or even ice climbs. This is a fun novel way to raise awareness and get people to participate.

You may notice that a single person is responsible for the vast amount of new routes and anchor installation. That person deserves a beer and some money. Chances are they frequent the local gear shop. Leave them some bolt money, or donate a rope. They will really appreciate it.

The best thing any of us can do is to leave an area better than we found it. Next time you visit an area keep this in mind.

Traveling and Back Home

TRAVEL AND LODGING

If you're going to be car camping, you might as well do it right. Car camping "alpine style" is only fun for about a night. See the gear checklist for some ideas to make life more comfortable. If you're not the type that likes to cook, but doesn't want to spend a ton of money eating out, planning menus and shopping is most likely a nightmare and makes packing for trips stressful. The best way to deal with this is to have a **cook kit pre-packed in a storage tub** that all you need to do with it is freshen propane, paper towels, and consumable spices. Then after you've picked up your climbing partner, stop at a grocery store after driving for a few hours. This way you'll probably enjoy the break from driving, and will have a partner in crime to plan a menu by just walking down the aisles and getting what looks good. Eating the same meals at camp is a lot less of a headache. If you can't cook, be the cleaner upper.

Vehicle Setup

Having a livable vehicle is a compromise between livability, gas mileage, drivability on bad roads, and stealthy camping. There are options to maximize space and comfort for cars of all sizes.

Smaller cars can still tow smaller trailers to sleep in or store gear. Aerodynamic rooftop storage boxes provide extra storage space on top of your car. You can even install a collapsible tent made of waterproof canvas on the roof of a car. None of these options are cheap unless you are a serious do-it-yourselfer or find a sweet deal on a used item. They also affect your gas mileage quite a bit. They are much cheaper than buying a second vehicle, and allow you to soup-up your fancy around town hybrid. A small trailer is probably the best livable option that still allows for some stealth camping. The major drawback is cost and poor (if any) performance on 4x4 roads and snow.

Photo courtesy Autohome

Trucks with canopies are the most common compromise as they allow you to do it all, especially if you add a camper top. The biggest drawbacks are cost and slightly more cramped living than a trailer, but the ability to drive on bad roads and snow. Like a trailer, you can still stealthily camp, but not as stealthily as in a van. The cheapest option is to sleep in the back of the truck with a standard or slightly raised canopy. Bolt it on good and tight, I've lost a few. Canopies, especially large ones are still expensive, but used ones are fairly easy to find. You can fix up the canopy with a light, add some curtains for privacy, and rig up some storage space. There are a lot of ways to rig storage space, mainly by elevating the sleeping area with some framing and sliding gear underneath. You can make storage boxes by framing the sides (over the wheel wells) and putting a sliding piece of plywood that fits over a lip to create a level surface on top of the boxes but still allows access. Slide the plywood below the lip and on the floor of the truck bed for seats or to make room for bulky loads. Carpeting the plywood with durable stain resistant carpet is a must. Some folks pad the sleeping area with eggshell foam so no air mattresses are needed. This can make sliding gear in and out more difficult, however.

Storage boxes and elevated sleeping in a pickup truck. Slide a board on top to sleep (a lip on the side to support the board negates the use of the cross beams shown). Photo courtesy Ryan Megenity.

Giant bouldering pads and Paco Pads make decent mattresses as well. The problem with sleeping in the back of the truck is there is little stealth, and if you have a lot of stuff, it will be pretty obvious you're sleeping in the back when crates are stuffed in the front seat or outside the truck. Livability is low without a camper top.

Action Packers *make the best durable storage containers.*

Vans are the ultimate in stealth camping and livability short of having no vehicle at all for stealth, or a bus or RV for livability. Some vans can even get up some serious 4x4 terrain, but at a much higher sticker price and fuel consumption. Pop-top VW vans are the standard. They aren't always the most livable, break down all the time, go super slow and burn fuel like crazy. You are also a target for police, rednecks, and it's pretty obvious you're camping in one.

Besides paying a ton for a dream van like a Sprinter or something similar, consider a conversion or delivery-style van. You can do a lot with the inside of a conversion van, they aren't too expensive especially if bought used from a company that owns a fleet, and camping inside is pretty low-key.

If you can, a hybrid model is choice for fuel savings. But diesel engines are also very efficient and hard-core dirtbags can make their own biodiesel. No matter what you decide, spend hours, even days, researching your options and scouring the Internet for deals. Make friends with a good mechanic to make any engine modifications, and make friends with a carpenter to help you with making the inside totally tricked out and awesome. A true dirtbag owns a tiny ultra fuel efficient car from the late 80's with all of his or her gear somehow crammed in, cooks meals on a white gas backpacking stove, and sets up a tent every night.

There are a lot of nifty **12-volt accessories** you can put in your car to make like more comfortable, especially if living out of your car. Have some spare fuses handy for when they inevitably blow a fuse.

Car Trouble

This may sound dumb, but just because you are at your car doesn't mean you're out of the woods. Not all trailheads are frequented by other climbers and hikers, so if you can't use your car you may as well be up on the mountain. Leaving the keys locked inside is quickly solved with a rock, but what if you lost them? Did you leave the lights on and need a jump? What will you do if no one's around? Having emergency equipment in your car can be as important as a first aid kit. Learning how to pick locks and hotwire a car are excellent skills to learn – just not in this book. Always park facing downhill just in case you need to get a dead battery going. If you have a clutch, pop it when in 2nd gear.

Here is a small list of emergency car equipment:
- Battery Charger – Even better than jumper cables
- Boards - To clear ditches or get out of the snow.
- Chains
- Chainsaw - To clear a fallen tree over the road (or firewood where appropriate).
- Compressed Air – Deflating your tires will get you through sand traps.
- Crowbar - To move rocks.
- Extra Gas - Optional if you remember to fill up. Using white gas for your stove will work, but it could ruin you engine as well, especially if your car requires a high octane fuel.
- Extra Oil, Brake Fluid, Windshield Washer Fluid, Antifreeze.
- Extra Set of Keys - In the car to retrieve with a rock, or magnet box if you trust it. You could use a cordalette to slide between the top of your door and handle side with a slip knot in the middle to catch a tab-style lock, or use a thin pack stay or tent pole to push an automatic lock.

- First Aid Kit – This is where you can keep those heavier items you don't want to pack.
- Fix-a-Flat - For that second punctured tire.
- Jumper Cables – You still need another car or battery. I've head of climbers stringing together nuts when neither vehicle had cables!
- Shovel - For getting out of the snow.
- Spare Tire, Jack, Tire Iron and knowing how to use them.
- Spare Water and Toilet Paper
- Tool Kit – A multi-piece tool kit and a roll of duct tape will always come in handy.
- Wikihow.com/Hotwire-a-Car. Print this out and keep it in your car or phone.
- Winch and Tow Rope - If you don't want to ruin your climbing gear by setting up a haul.
- Extra Fuses

You don't want to know how long it took to make this work: Using cord to unlock a door by sliding it in the door frame and hitching the lock with a slipknot. A rock is quicker.

Respect the need for a working vehicle in the winter. Be extra anal retentive about keeping your battery fresh, tank filled, keys where they should be, etc. An emergency battery with jumper cables is cheap and can be a lifesaver. Make sure your antifreeze and windshield washer fluid is rated for cold winter use. If your window fogs up try turning on the A/C with the heat together, and crack the windows. A set of chains can save you hours of shoveling and winching. Although wasteful on gas, bringing a second car (or 4wd truck is more like it) into a place you really don't want to get stranded, especially in winter, can add a lot of peace of mind. It's always a good idea to get your car checked out by a good mechanic and tell them what you plan on doing. Don't trust drive through oil change services to put everything back where it should go. Finally, although it may take longer to get there, walking a few extra miles can save you hours when you get your car stuck.

Free Camping
For every pay campground there is at least an equal number of free camping spots in the Western USA. A godsend website is freecampsites.net – other options are topo maps from your phone or GPS and detailed **Delorme Road Atlases** for each state. Look for BLM or National Forest land near the climbing area and find dirt roads you can drive to find "the spot". If there's not even a pullout or dead-end side road to be seen, you can always try and get away with one free night and then play dumb when you get busted in the morning. The main issue with finding free camping spots is many times you have to pack it up in the morning, or drive quite a bit further to the climb in the morning. Some trailheads allow for camping, but most do not. Vans are perfect because it's impossible to tell if you are camping or still out climbing. Rangers can't enter you van, so if you play it cool when they shake and pound on your van and you could get away with it. It isn't illegal to cook or pack-up at your car, so parking at a trailhead and then bivying in the woods out of

sight is another option. Unless there are special restrictions, camping should be free in USFS and BLM areas. Don't bother with state parks, they are almost always very expensive.

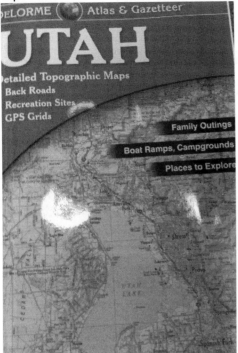

Before the advent of smartphones. These babies are bivy gold!

Some of the best climbing stories involve a sketchy side of the road bivy. Doing any of this in a heavily patrolled state or national parks will probably result in a ticket and getting booted from the park. Sometimes bivying in town is a safer option than attempting it inside a park. Church parking lots, malls, casino parking garages, and Wal-Mart's are sometimes ideal places to bivy inside your car, as are innocuous residential streets. They are also great places to leave a car if meeting someone. Rest stops are probably the sketchiest places to sleep in your car. Getting in late, not paying, and leaving early rarely works. It's amazing how seriously campground hosts take their jobs, and considering most of them are retired seniors, they probably still get up earlier than you. Having a **bicycle** can really improve the prospects of camping for free. A bike is really easy to hide off the road, and you can leave your car parked in an overnight lot. Parking your car in a group site or walk-in lot and then sleeping in the bushes well away from your car is another option. Any illegal camping is on you, I am just providing information. Sometimes paying for camping, especially if it's right inside the park and has nice facilities, is worth it. Still $20 or more a night to camp seems un-American.

Huts, Hostels, and Couches

If you pack enough people in, a motel room can be cheaper than camping. Some motels have small cabins, or larger rooms with kitchenettes. However expensive, a motel room, especially on an ice climbing trip or extended road trip, can be a trip (or relationship) saver. If planning a rest day, remember that you don't get the room for the day after you sleep there. Plan on two nights if you need a full rest day. Most motels will negotiate on price, so it's worth it to haggle, especially if you pit motels against each other. Motels may check to see if you are a AAA member, but none will check to see if you truly are a member of the American Dental Assistant Association (or whatever) and will offer a discount on any ridiculous trade organization membership you throw out. Priceline.com and Hotwire.com are great websites to use to book a cheap room if you are flexible.

Hostels and huts can be great ways to still be inside with a bed, but save some money. Some hostels are just like fancy hotels or bed and breakfasts (and may cost as much), while some are not much better than spending the night in jail (always a free shelter). Bring **earplugs**. There will be someone who snores, guaranteed. Being a member of a climbing or skiing club can get you deals on huts and hostels in some areas. Finally couch surfing websites are a gamble you may be willing to take. Many people have had great experiences with couchsurfing.org, especially when traveling abroad.

Cheap Travel

The cheapest way to save money on gas is to stay in one area as long as possible. Hitchhiking can get you to the climb, or killed (or worse). The main problem is dealing with all your climbing and camping gear. The vast majority of dirtbaggers have their own vehicle. You can get away without a car in popular climbing areas like Yosemite by posting ride share requests on the message board. You can try your luck on ride share websites or climbing forums. Unfortunately public transportation usually won't get you close to a climbing area, unless the area is extremely popular. To finish the journey you'll have to hitchhike, or better yet, bring a bike with a trailer and ride the final miles. Ride sharing through websites like Craigslist, Ridejoy, and others can help you save money on gas by offering rides to folks going your way. It may be hard to get rides this way as most climbing areas are off the beaten path and getting back could be tricky.

Flying to places cheaply usually depends on the days you are willing to travel. Being flexible allows you sign up for cheap flight deals, or price bidding on sites like Priceline. Some fellow dirtbags have gone so far to sign up for courier jobs to get one-way flights. If you can handle a credit card by paying it off completely every month, cards that offer air miles are great. The big drawback is that you can't use them on most deals, and airfare is usually full-price. Cashback cards or using your points on other purchases like hotel rooms may be more economical, but for some reason "free miles" can be better reason to spring for plane tickets in the first place.

Flying Logistics

Packing for air taxi to the glacier

Packing for a climbing trip and then getting it onto an airplane has become a serious hassle and really expensive. **Scales** at home will help unexpected and expensive surprises. One way that sometimes works is to give the bag to the curbside check-in with a generous tip. They may not weight it. You can bet that that baggage check inside the terminal will, however. What you wear and carry-on are your secret weapons. Put everything heavy in your carry-on and wear things like mountaineering boots onto the plane. You may not get away with packing an ice ax, crampons, or stove, however. Some airlines have special deals for "sporting equipment" like skis and golf bags. If so, pack a ski bag full of climbing kit. It can be well worth it to join a milage club not only to get free miles, but to reap the rewards of extra free baggage. It is almost always better to have too many bags than an overweight bag when it comes to fees.

Buy your food when you get there, including gas for the stove. Many large grocery stores now carry canister fuel. If you are meeting someone, they should be supplying the majority of group gear to keep your baggage weight down. Finally, you could ship yourself some of your equipment, but chances are that the fees for extra bags or weight will still be cheaper.

United's excellent multiple bag policy. Photo courtesy Willie Benegas.

Consider airplanes a petri dish in the sky. You're touching all sorts of common objects and sharing a small airspace with potential sick people or un-sick people carrying a bug you aren't immune to. Carry **sanitizing wipes or gel**, wash your hands like mad, and even though they may not work, load up on **Emergan-C, Airborne, Echinacea**, or whatever you think works.

Jet Lag and Travel Fatigue

Expect to be really tired and worn out after a long travel day(s), or if arriving at a new time zone. If you dash from the car, plane, or even a grueling day at work straight to the crag or trailhead, you can be wiped and not recover for the remainder of the trip. Plan in a rest day, take a shower, and refuel and rehydrate, as traveling is always a dehydrating activity. If you cross multiple time zones it may take a few days of rest to recover. Sometimes it may be necessary to be awake for much longer than you want upon arrival to avoid the desire to get to bed much too early or much too late. Sometimes skipping a meal to eat dinner at the new local time zone can help your body clock readjust. For low scale time-zone changes try and eat on the local time schedule and get a hearty breakfast, lunch, and dinner beforehand along with lots of water. If you cross several time zones then try to get a full days rest per time zone crossed, if possible. In any case, get plenty of rest once there and try and stick to the local schedule. An **empty carry-on water bottle** (especially a collapsible one) is worth its weight in gold to stay hydrated. Bring **snacks and some powdered sports drinks** in case it is difficult to get meals immediately. Increase your protein intake a bit to offset the travel stress. Try taking **melatonin** at the bedtime of your target time zone.

ROAD TRIPS AND EXTENDED STAYS

The key to a successful road trip is flexibility due to unforeseen issues and weather. One of the newer road trip problems is the availability of communication. Change your voicemail greeting and generate an automatic email stating that you are unavailable and will not be checking messages until you are back. Check in with loved ones every so often to keep them happy, but avoiding contact with the outside world keeps the outside world from randomly requiring you or your partner from needing to go home immediately. Most road trips start to go downhill after the two week mark. The cure is either just planning on two weeks, or to budget some motel-bound rest days and if an alpine trip, and pack in some sport climbing to keep you sane. If your trip is longer than a week, be vigilant about taking rest days.

Even with a lot of climbing, you can get out of shape and off your diet very easily on a road trip. Everything becomes an excuse to be lazy on trips. Try and eat healthy, avoid fast food or gas station snacks, and get exercise besides just climbing. Have a few exercises you planned out to stay balanced, and to shake off joints and muscles weary from being cramped inside a car, tent, or harness for days on end. Have a good selection of music and podcasts on your iPod or phone and download some movies to watch when you're sick of campfire and talking about climbing. If something looks fun on a road trip, do it. Spur of the moment decisions, whether climbing related or not, are the spice of life and always lead to unexpected fun or at least a funny story. Plodding on with the plan can start making you wonder why you like climbing or road trips to begin with, and thoughts turn to home. If your partner agrees to do something stupid, repay the favor when he or she recommends an activity or climb you don't feel like doing.

Finding Partners
Being a dirtbag is usually a solitary mission and finding partners may be more challenging than the climbing. Message boards and partner requests on local or mainstream climbing sites should get you some bites. Make a **big sign** and put it on your car or campsite clearly stating you need a partner. You will most likely need to be gregarious and approach people for the majority of the days. Some suggestions to making yourself approachable or pitiable have already been discussed (like rope-soloing). Plain old asking works pretty well too. If you want to climb remote stuff, start in crowded areas and make plans with new partners there.

The Opposite Sex
Here's my small amount of bad wisdom. That elusive climbing girlfriend won't happen unless you make one from scratch. Your odds of finding a girl who you find attractive, climbs, is single, and wants to be with you are slim to none. If it does happen, she's probably crazy and it will end in disaster. Better to find someone that likes you for you, and get them to start climbing. Before you send me a pipe bomb in the mail for being sexist, wait! This can be the case for finding a climbing guy to date, but the odds are astronomical that he is single and wants to have sex with you. He'll be bat shit crazy and loaded with emotional problems too, but you can always dump him and find another replacement easily. Mold the girls, cycle through the dudes. To actually get the date? It's just like making friends in grade school – everyone likes the pretty popular rich kids and no one likes the brooding eccentric loner. Be super confident and assertive without being a total asshole (with brief moments of kindness and humor) and then slowly let them see the self-conscious crazy loner dork that you really are.

Climbing with your significant other can be a great relationship building experience or a relationship ender. I am going to assume you are the dominant climber for this discussion. Treat climbs and climbing trips as a fun way to spend time together - not to push you or your significant other's limits. No matter how frustrating it is for you, try and keep from shouting advice and playing "coach" unless they specifically ask for help. This is annoying to the person climbing and for everyone else around! If a climb is too hard or frustrating, apologize and don't force them to finish.

After you figured out the types of climbs that make him or her happy, do those. Save trying to tick off your list or push the grade with your buddies. It's also a good idea to lay of the hardcore alpine climbs with a significant other - even if they are just as good or better than you. You have to act callous and sometimes yell at your partner on big hard climbs, and that usually doesn't work so well when that person is your lover. Of course this doesn't apply to all couples, and if you're fine and both want to climb hard stuff all day, then obviously ignore this advice. Just don't be selfish.

Sex can get a little gross after a few days on the road so plan for this. See the section on outdoor hygiene, or better yet, get a motel. Everyone likes a romp in a motel room, and you get a bonus break from the road and the tent for a night. Packing a small package of wet wipes, condoms, and/or a little Platypus of wine and a closed cell foam pad can make your time on the wall or at the summit an experience to remember!

Food
The biggest image that comes to mind when mentioning dirtbagging besides living in a car or van stuffed full of climbing equipment is of course dumpster-diving and finishing other people's meals in cafeterias. Dumpster diving is mostly done by posers and Trustafarians looking for an excuse to feel okay about driving dad's Jeep Cherokee than it is by your true dirtbag. Eating food someone else didn't finish is definitely a lot more sanitary than dumpster diving, but it's still gross and gives climbers a bad name. Food costs aren't that high when camping and climbing. The important thing to do is make menus that share similar and cheap ingredients. You can spend just a couple bucks a day on food if you plan well and take the time to cook. There are usually discount grocery stores, food outlets, or at least a Trader Joe's or Costco somewhere near a climbing area.

The biggest food expense is eating on the road. Planning road meals and taking the time to stop and cook takes a huge amount of discipline. Pack your car with this in mind so the thought of digging out the stove and cooking gear doesn't drive you straight to a fast food restaurant. Eating your own food on the road is also a lot healthier. Invest in some quality **airtight containers, a vacuum sealer** (just the handheld pump and corresponding Ziplocs are enough), **and a solid cooler.**

Jobs and Money
Most dirtbags save up money to take a year or season off. How much money you need depends on how big of a dirtbag you plan on being. Make a budget and don't forget to include bills you need to take care of that aren't part of your extended vacation like mortgages and student loans.

If you plan on making money on the road you'll need a job that you can do anywhere or have a trade that you can sell to climbers at popular crags (don't expect much cash flow here). Finding jobs on the road is nothing like it used to be, so getting a dishwasher job may not be so easy these days. Check out temporary job services and websites. Getting a seasonal job is probably your best bet unless your jobs can be done from a computer or offers travel options (like nursing). Seasonal jobs also allow you to crash or rent a room for non-car living and spend a season in a particular area. Many seasonal jobs force you to work like crazy during the season, like guiding or ski jobs. To combat this you could get a temporary job during the winter or shoulder seasons in a non-climbing location. Many of these jobs pay very well and can bankroll a several month road trip. Use your climbing experience to your advantage and apply for high angle rigging, construction, Alaskan fishing, or other dangerous jobs.

Jobs that offer graveyard or swing shifts can be great for climbers that want to get in pitches during their workweek. Blocked schedules like 7/7 or 8/6 shifts can be appealing if you plan on taking lots of trips. They can be a mixed blessing as you may not be able to climb at all during your block on, and only get a few to a couple of days on your time off without the possibility of taking a longer vacation.

No matter what your work situation, realize that the grass is always greener, and if you don't enjoy your job, any work schedule sucks. High paying jobs usually mean long hours, stress, and responsibility that will all cut into your climbing. But, you will be able to pay for gear and plane tickets. If you plan on making a lot of money you should maximize it by living in a cool town regardless of its location to good climbing as you'll be working anyway. The rewards are being able to fly as often as you have free time, living in a nice city or town, and the possibility of retiring early. If you don't think you'll be making any money, might as well live right next to your favorite climbing area. You can live cheaply anywhere and you'll spend a lot less money on traveling. The worst-case scenario is not making any money, working your butt off, and not living near good climbs. Might as well be a dirtbag climbing bum instead, or go back to school and live on financial aid.

Down Time

If you need to be constantly entertained then dirtbagging isn't for you. It can be so lonely and boring you'll start studying for that Bar Exam, GRE, or MCAT you swore you'd never take within two weeks of leaving home. You still need to do something on your rest, bad weather, or partnerless days.

To stay active, develop an exercise routine to keep healthy. Active rest days can be a really fun way to stay active but enjoy the outdoors in other ways. Hike, bike, run, ski, canyoneer, scramble, surf, boat, fish, kayak, spelunk, do some cleanup and trail work, scope out approaches and descents, find a hot spring, whatever! If you need some indoor time go to an exercise class like a much needed yoga class, or buy a day pass at the local exercise or climbing gym. Some towns have cheap rec centers that you can exercise, swim, and shower at.

Sometimes you don't need to be outdoors, and an indoor hangout may be needed to maintain sanity. Popular dirtbag places to waste an entire day are libraries (aka homeless shelters), bookstores, coffee shops, shopping malls, and giant retailers like Costco. Finding free or cheap showers and a laundry is a key rest day activity. Movie theaters that you can jump from show to show can keep you entertained and cool.

Start a new hobby or craft. Learn a language. Take some online classes at the local community college or adult learning center. When you are at wits end and your endless freedom starts feeling like a cage, nothing helps like getting a motel room for a night or two and just totally vegging out. **Smartphones, laptops, iPods, and books** can keep you busy. Smartphones are gold for dirtbaggers and travelers alike. Besides their obvious benefits, many have been discussed already; you can also find deals on gas, food, or just about anything.

INTERNATIONAL TRAVEL AND EXPEDITIONS

If you are going on a big expedition in the U.S. to places like Alaska, or traveling to another country, logistics and planning will be just as difficult as the climb itself. Don't just show up; plan everything. The American Alpine Club is great place to start gathering information as well as wikitravel.org. Post online to see if you can find someone that's been where you're going before to get their advice. Consider local expedition companies, guides and trekking agencies, a travel liaison, and consulting the U.S. Embassy for the area. Non-climbing travel books can be very useful.

Your **visa, ID, passport, and permits** are extremely valuable to you. Protect them, and find out who is legally allowed to take them from you before casually handing them over. Find out local bribing customs. A pack of smokes and stack of porno magazines can get you past checkpoints where 16 year old boys are shoving guns in your face. The same offer could get you killed. Make sure your passport isn't close to expiring or you may not get in or out. At least 6 months from expiring is a safe bet. If carrying prescription drugs, keep your doctor's prescription available at customs or checkpoints.

Expect a radical change in diet and meal preparation. Expect fees for everything. But most importantly, learn the local customs/culture and behave in a similar fashion. Don't be a stupid American.

Be sure and have a **MasterCard or Visa** credit card that isn't refused in certain areas or countries like Discover and American Express. **Traveler's checks** are good insurance, but small businesses or street vendors probably won't take them or they may charge you a crazy exchange rate. Depending on what country or region you visit, you could double the value of your U.S. currency by exchanging with local merchants (off the grid), or get totally cheated. Don't forget to get your passport early, **immunizations and documentation**, drugs from the doctor, **voltage adaptors, international SIM card** for the phone, and **locks for your luggage**. If taking antibiotics, consider some **prebiotics** as they can really irritate your gut. Also, you may be able to get a SIM card locally much cheaper than in the States.

Paying for all of this is next to impossible for your local climbing bum. Grants are a good place to start, but consider getting sponsors. The obvious choices are the gear companies, but consider sponsorship from unlikely places and companies. Tacking on a "cause" can help. Even if you do believe your own bullshit that you're actually climbing for a cause (how bout not going climbing and working for the cause), you can at least use this as an excuse to beg for money and to host fundraisers (how about not spending money on a bunch of beer, food, and giveaway schwag and putting that money toward said cause). Another way to get people to give you their money is through a crowd-funding site on the Internet, like Kickstarter.

The book "Climbing: Expedition Planning" by Soles and Powers is an extremely useful book for going on big expensive remote expeditions. Check the following websites when traveling to another country:

- http://wwwnc.cdc.gov/travel
- http://www.travel.state.gov/travel/cis_pa_tw/tw/tw_1764.html

INSURANCE

It's sad that many climbers can't afford health insurance and a travesty that basic health care and emergency care cost anything to begin with (Affordable Care Act aside). Find catastrophic health insurance at the very least. Insurance with a high deductible may sound worthless until you get hurt and rack up tens of thousands of dollars. Many doctors and rehab therapists are climbers. Get online and prey on their goodwill if you do wind up needing care, you might at least get a discount. If you are broke and wind up in the emergency room, tell them you cannot afford to pay. Unless some agreement is made, you will be stuck with the bill and be hounded by creditors. Withholding your social security number, driver's license number, or any identifying information is up to you.

Life insurance is something to think about. It should be almost a requirement if you've got a family. But even most dirtbags have parents, and death-related costs can add up. Getting a life insurance policy when you are young and staying on it can really help your decrepit future self out at ton by getting on a policy early. Do not lie about your activities. Insurance companies make money by not paying, so don't give them a reason not to. Instead, take your time to find a company that doesn't care that you climb. Unfortunately, mountain guides may wind up being denied completely.

Rescue insurance is included in a membership with the American Alpine Club and should make sense that it's worth the cost of membership alone. You may get away with not needing it or health insurance when you are young and can bounce back, but if you can afford to travel abroad then you can afford a membership. Not all areas offer free rescues, and the bill may ruin you.

If your credit card or car insurance doesn't offer decent roadside assistance for cheap, get a AAA membership. Since cars love to break down in the middle of nowhere, make sure your towing coverage allows for more than just a few miles. Most offer tows to at least the nearest service station.

The other kind of insurance you should think about is travelers insurance. You can get super cheap trip protection in case something comes up to cancel your trip and avoid paying out the nose to change flights or get a refund. Not all "for any reason" policies mean canceling a trip because the weather forecast changed from bad to worse. Read the fine print and find a doctor friend to write you a note. Using certain credit cards to buy tickets can get you really good cancellation policies. Some cheap travel policies also include some medical and gear loss insurance. Renters and homeowners insurance may also cover lost or stolen gear even if the gear was lost/stolen outside your home. Your credit card or auto insurance company may also cover lost/stolen items as well.

BACK TO CIVILIZATION
Back to the Car
Sometime I think we just go climbing in order to appreciate our cars more judging by the rush to get back to dump the pack, take off the shoes, and crack a beer. Nothing is more disappointing then getting back to the car and not having **fresh clothes, snacks, and cold beer.** Plan ahead! Bring a **cooler** if it's hot out and fill it with beer (or soda), sandwiches, chips, etc. Drinking your old climbing water and snacking on unused GU packets is just plain uncivilized. Not only does packing some post-climb food aid in recovery, many small towns near climbing areas restaurants are closed by the time you get there, or are outrageously expensive. Even if you didn't pack a fresh pair of pants and shirt, a pair of **flip-flops or slippers** takes most of the edge off a long drive.

Driving home after a long climb can be dangerous. More climbers have fallen asleep at the wheel and flipped their car than I've thought possible. Stash some **instant coffee** and a way to heat water to make a cup of coffee. Keep a **gallon jug of water** for emergencies, and to make **Gatorade from instant powder** instead of spending ten times the amount at the gas station. Grab a huge stash of **napkins, coffee additives, and sauce packets** at the gas station instead. A **backup roll of toilet paper, trowel, wet-wipes, and hand sanitizer** are super handy. You never know how well stocked the trailhead outhouse will be.

Bringing **extra gear and guidebooks** for nearby climbs or climbing areas on the way there or back could get you more pitches in if there's time on the way there or back, or if the weather or situations call for a plan B. Your ice climbing trip could easily become a sport climbing trip if the weather says doesn't cooperate.

Back at Home
When you get back home, hopefully you have a vacation from your vacation day lined up to sleep in and deal with all the crap that becomes instantly important. Getting back into a good training routine can be difficult, but starting back up as soon as possible prevents you from putting it off completely. Putting away and cleaning gear as soon as possible helps you remember all the repairs and maintenance you noticed on your trip, and will set you up for the next trip with less frantic last minute repairs or purchases. Keeping a **pen and pad of paper,** or using your smartphone or laptop to jot down to-do lists can keep you organized on trips. Long trips and extended periods of inactivity like traveling always make you think of things to do, music you like, books to read, etc, and keeping it all in your head is usually unreasonable.

Write in your climbing journal, put notes in your guidebooks, and update or add routes to Mountainprojrect.com for you and other's future reference. Update your tick list based on what you saw or your partner kept spraying about. Reflect on your climb and make note of what did and didn't work, or what you'd like to change or improve on. Make a plan and act on it. Share your photos and Facebook the crap out of your trip. Write trip reports on local sites, Supertopo.com, SummitPost.com, or Mountainproject.com. Beef up your 8a.nu scorecard!

Check your important gear every so often for cracks, holes, tears, cleaning, replacing, modifying, replenishing, recharging, updating, or tweaking. Go through your protection, slings, biners, and ropes at least once a year to check for cracks and overuse. Go through your training plan and tweak it for the next project and go back to page one.

THE END!

Thank you for purchasing this book. I hope you found something useful in these pages, and I appreciate your feedback.

Sincerely,

APPENDIX

EXERCISE LIST

I have included a handy list of exercises for you to help tailor a program or WOD. I suggest that you create your own. Download the list @ sites.google.com/site/climbingbeyondthebasics

Cardio Protocols
Aerobic Endurance
Aerobic Threshold
Anaerobic Threshold

Strength Protocols
Endurance
Strength
Strength-Endurance
Power

Climbing Specific Protocols
Strength
Strength-Endurance
Power
Power-Endurance
Endurance

Warm-Up
Climbing
Abdominal Breathing
Cardio

Full Body
Overhead Air Squats
Squat Jumps
Burpees
Inchworms
Foundation Exercises
Weighted Postural Training

Neck
Neck Retractions
Isometric Neck Retractions
Isometric Hold
AROM Reps
Face Clenches

Hand, Wrist, Elbow, Finger
Chinese Balls, Putty,
Squeeze Balls
Wrist Circles
Flipper
The Groper
Finger Spreads
Pronate/Supinate
Alphabet
Screaming Barfies

Shoulder
Arm Circles/Scissor
Shoulder Sweeps
High Reaches
Around the World/Clap
Empty Can Raise
Field Goals
Toy Soldier
Pec and Lat Foam Roller
Weight Balance
Kipping Pull-Ups
Circumduction
Wall Walks
Wand ROM

Scapula
Serratus Punch
Reverse Dips
Wide Grip Lat Pulls
Shoulder/Scapula Rolls
Angels

Lumbar
Cat / Camel
Active Knee to Chest
Pelvic Tilts / Circles / Fig-8
Pelvic Tilts w/Ab Breathing
Superman
Swimmer

Core Stability
Dead Bug
Quadruped
Bridge
Reverse Bridge
Floor Roll
Helicopter

Hips
Leg Kicks
Rapid Toe Touches
Lunges
Lunge Jumps
Over Under
Dynamic Hip Stretch
Glut Squeeze and Pumps
Standing Hip Dips
Leg Circles
Clamshell
Side Leg Raise Lower
Double Leg Raise Lower
Lower Leg Raise

Knee
Knee Extension
Eccentric Quad Machine
Straight Leg Raise
Reverse Lunge
Quarter and 1/2 Squats
D1 Soccer Kick
D2 Snowplow
Jumps/Hops

Foot & Ankle
Alphabet
Toe and Heel Walk/Rock
Short Foot

Balance
Balance Exercises
Sit to Stand
1/2 Foam Roller Walk
Squats
Ball Toss & Catch
Provocation
Visual Tracking
Slack Line
Balance Lean

Yoga & Pilates

Intense Core
Abs Isometric
Side Plank
Abdominal Plank
Supine Plank Twist
Plank Twist
Front Levers & L-Sit
100's

Abs General
Crunches
Full Extension Crunches
Wood Chop
Hanging Sit-Up
Pike
Kettlebell Swing
Medicine Ball Toss Sit-Up
Obliques
Bicycles
Chop and Lift

Lateral Benders
Windmill

Lumbar
Hip and Back Extension
Lumbar Isometric Hold
Leg Extension and Hip
  Flexion
Romanian Deadlift/Good
  Mornings
Hip Extension

Agonists & Stabilizers
Shoulder Pushing
Push-Press
Handstand Pushup
External Rotation

Shoulder Stabilizers
Abduction
Field Goals
Y's

Horizontal Adduction
Shoulder Extension/Gorilla Pull
Combining Field Goals through Extension
Internal Rotation
Functional Shoulder
Sword and Seatbelt
Cross Body Lift and Press
Chest Pulling
Rows
Reverse Fly
Arms Pushing (Triceps)
Dips
Triceps Curl
One Arm Pull Down
Hammer Throw
Wrist & Hand Antagonist/ Stabilizers
Reverse Wrist Curls
Weight on a String
Finger Extension, Opposition, & Abduction
Pronation
Tyler and Reverse Tyler Twist
Radial and Ulnar Deviation
Lower Body Antagonist/ Stabilizers
Tibialis Anterior
Foot Eversion and Inversion
Leg Internal and External Rotation
Toe Flexion and Extension
Toe Adduction and Abduction

Stretching
Whole Body
Relief Posture
Yoga
Neck
Upper Traps
Posterior Cervicals & Levator Scap
Neck, Sub-Occipitals, & Lev Scap
Sub-Occipitals
Rotation
Extension
Scalenes
SCM
Passive Neck Traction
Chest
Pectorals
Nerve Flossing
Ulnar
Median
Radial
Musculocutaneous, Axillary, & Median
Shoulder & Arm
Whole Arm

Shoulder Traction / Bar Hang
Rhomboid Stretch
Latissimus Dorsi
General Rotator Cuff
Subscapularis
Supraspinatus
External Rotators
Posterior Capsule
Triceps
Hand & Forearm
Forearm/Wrist
Fingers
Wrist Traction
Hip & Thigh
Gluteals
Low Squats
Piriformis
Hamstring
Psoas
Egoscue Stretch
Quads
Groin
TFL and ITB
Hip Traction
Leg
Calf
Tibialis Anterior
Plantar Fascia
Lumbar
Pelvic Blocks
Extension, Lat Flex, Flexion
Cobra
Rotation
McKenzie and Williams
Lumbar Traction & Inversion

Non-Climbing Supplemental Exercises
Upper Body
Pushups
Bench Press
Medicine Ball Toss
Pushup and Row Combo
Biceps Curl
Lat Pulls
Lower Body
Outdoor Activities
Indoor Machines
Step-Ups
Box Jumps
Side Step-ups, Step-Downs
Lunges
Front Squat
Back Squat
Goblet Squat
Reverse Squat
Wall Squat
One-Leg Squat
Pistols
Leg Press Machine
Leg Extension Machine
Mountain Climbers

Hamstring Curl
Calf Raises
Pulling a Tire
Upper & Lower Combo
Turkish Get-Up
Thruster
Wall Ball
Burpee
Sumo Deadlift High-Pull
Olympic Lifts
Cardio
Circuit
Speed Climbing
Running
Hiking/Skinning Uphill
Biking
Spin Cycle
Treadmill
Elliptical
StairMaster
Versaclimber
Rower
Cross Country Skiing
Jump Rope
Swimming

Climbing Specific
Strength
Grip
Fingerboard Standard
 -Advanced
 -Ice Tool & Pinch
Grip Trainers
Farmer's Carry
Wrist & Forearm
Wrist and Finger Curls
Pull-Ups
Biceps, Lats, Shoulders
Staggered / Archer Pull-ups
Kipping Pull-ups
Frenchies
Negative Pull-ups
Muscle ups
Lockoffs
Core
Body Tension
Figure 4 & 9

Strength-Endurance
System Holds
Timed Climbing
Laps
Moving Hangs
Pyramids
4x4, 6x8, etc.
Very Difficult Climbing
Weighted Climbing
Grip Trainers
Farmers Carry
Lock Offs
Pull-ups
Staggered/Archers
Frenchies
Negative Pull-ups

Muscle Ups
Figure 4/9's
Power
Power Dyno
Wrist & Finger Curls
Grip Trainers
Pull-ups
Muscle ups
Power-Endurance
Campusing
 -Deadpoint
 -Single Dyno/Ladder
 -Double Dyno
 -Drop Downs
 -No Feet Boulder
 -Stacking Fingerboards
 -Bachar Ladder
 -Rope Climb
 -Pegboards
Repetitive Hold/HIT Strip
Power Boulder/Toprope
Weighted Climbing
Endurance
Climbing
Lock offs
Kipping Pull-ups
Grip Trainers
Farmers Cary
Frenchies
Jugging with Weight
Jumar Hang
Jumar Hang and Squat
Ice Tool Squat and Reach
Skills
Falling Progression
Fast/Dynamic
Dynamic
Fast
Deadpoints/Dynos
Skip Holds
Follow Through
Slow/Static
Slow
Find Rests
Shake Out
Balance
Weight over feet & Body Tension
Straight Arms
Traverse One-Arm
Body Extended
Body Scrunched
Rock-over High-step
Same Hip/Hand Straight Arm
Body Tension
Hips Under Hand & Over Feet
Twist Lock/Tripod/X/Frog
Hips In / Out
Forearms 90° to Hold
Sloper Balance

Movement		Specific Conditions	
Twist-Lock	Fingernail Crimp	Ad-On	Climbing Fast
Flagging	Sloper	Weight Off	Crampon Type
Drop Knee	Pinch	Open Feet/Hands	Boot Selection
Stem	Pockets	Down-Climb	Ice Conditions
Back-Step	Layback	Top-Roping	Screw Placement
Frog-Step	Non-Traditional Holds	Re-Climbing Redpoint/	Ice Features for Pro
X-Position	Compression	Onsights	Angle Transition
High-Step & Rock Over	**Crack**	Vary the Terrain	Resting
Heel Hook	Tips	Climbs you Hate/Flail	Rock Type and Holds
Toe Hook	Tight Fingers	**Specific Conditions**	No Crampons/Tools
Kneebar	Finger	Night Climbing	Pick and Tool
Bicycling	Off Finger/Rattily	Cold Weather Climbing	Leashless/Leashed/
Lock-off & Straight Arm	Ringlocks	Cold Tolerance	Umbilical
Cross-Through	Tight Hand	Rain	Stashing Tool
Step-Through	Hands	Snow	Practice Clipping on Rock
Rose Move	Off Hand	Windy	Rock Gear
Matching and Swapping	Fist	Dehydrated	**Big Wall**
Hands/Feet	Off Fist	Hungry	Aider Systems
Roofs	Fist Stacks	Exhausted	Jugging
Mantling & Down-Palming	Chicken Wing/Arm Bar	Hot	Hauling
Deadpoints, Single, Double	Smear	Altitude	Pendulums/Traverses
Dyno	Toe Jam	**Sport**	Aiding Quickly
Figure 4 and 9	Foot Jam	New Shoes	Short-fixing & Rope Soloing
Steep to Slab	Foot Cam	Clipping	Placing Special Gear
Feet	Off-Foot Cam	Jamming	**Alpine & Mountaineering**
Maximum Foot Pressure	Heel-Toe	Fig 4 and 9	Self-Arrest
Outside & Inside Edge	T-Stacks	**Trad**	Minimal Ice
Use Feet Like Hands	Calf/Knee/Thigh Jam	Limiting Gear	Axe and Foot Positions
Push with Feet	Flaring Cracks	New Brands of Pro	Steep Snow Traverse
Velcro Feet	Leavittation	Different Shoes	Glissade/Plunge/Scree
Climbing with Fists	Inversion	Find Difficult Placements	**Ability**
Slab Climbing	Sidewinder	Chockcraft	Comfort Zone/Ticking
Approach Shoes	Worm and Shoulder Scrunch	Pitoncraft	Routes
Faceholds in Jams	Chimney	Natural Pro	Redpointing
Hands	Body Stem	Hand Drilling	Wire Climb Solid
Soft Grip/Relaxed	**Route-Finding**	Linking Pitches	Head-Pointing
Velcro Hands	Visualization	Back Cleaning	Very Difficult Climbing
Undercling	Trust Gut	Racking Gear Differently	Solo TR, Rope Solo,
Thumbercling	New Area	Sport and Bouldering	Bouldering
Gaston	**Feedback**	**Snow/Ice/Mixed**	Onsighting / Revisiting Old
Side-Pull	Video Feedback	Sinker Swings/Kicks	Climbs
Reverse Side-Pull	Partner Feedback	Thin Ice	Strength-Endurance Climb
Open-Hand Crimp	Coach Feedback	Holding the Tools	Technique Endurance Climb
Crimp	Movies/Online Video	Rock Moves	Good Day Cragging
	Combination	X vs T	

Gear List

I have tried to include just about everything in this list, but it still is not all-inclusive. I've tried to avoid duplicating items across categories. I highly recommend making your own list organized how you want. Download the list @ sites.google.com/site/climbingbeyondthebasics

Approach	Autolocking Belay Device	Minitraxion
Bear Spray	Block Roll	ProTraxion
Bike & Repair Kit	Croll	Prusik Minding Pulley
Canoe, Kayak, Inflatable with PFD &	Hand/Foot Speed Ascender	RescYou
Paddles	Jumar	Rollnlock
Trekking Poles	Lift/Basic	Rope Protector
Water Shoes	Microcender	Ropeman
Ascenders & Pulleys	Microtraxion	Slings, Knots, Hollow Block

Small Pulley
Texas Kick
Tibloc
Wall Hauler
Bags
Approach Pack
Climbing, Approach Pack
Crampon, Ax Covers
Crampon and Screw Bag
Day, Leader Pack
Duffel
Haul Bag, Swivel, & Knot Protector
Pack Cover
Ski Bag
Sled
Stuff Sacks, Ditty Bags, Mesh
Bolting
5-Piece, Wedge, Triplex/Legacy
Blow Tube, Bulb, Compressed Air
Caulking Gun, Gun, Mixing Tip
Chain
Chalk Bag and Belt
Cold Shuts
Drill Batteries, Gas
Drill Case, Holder, Sling
Eye, Wave, Staple, Titanium Glue-In
Glasses
Glue Stick
Glue-in Drill Adaptor
Hammer, Holster, Sling
Hand Drill
Hanger
Lock Tight
Quicklinks
Rag
Rap Rings
Rappel Bolts
Rappel Ring Bolts
Removable Bolt
SDS Bits
Torque Wrench
Tuning Fork
Wilderness Bolts: Button Head, Z-Mac, ¼-Inch, Copperhead, Self-Drilling & Perfo Drill
Willy-Stick
Wire Brush
Wrench & Sling
Climbing Gear
Aiders
Astroturf Square
Autolocking Belay Device (GriGri)
Bail Biner, Tat, Quicklink
Belay Biner(s): Light, Standard, Cross-load
Belay Plate/Plaquette
Belay Seat/Bosun's
Brushes, Cleaning Tools
Chalk Bag
Chalk, Liquid Chalk
Chest Harness: Full, Slings
Crash Pad, Shield

Double Rope Belay Device
Fifi Hook, Adjustable Fifi
Figure-8
Gear Sling: Looped, Double, Padded, Webbing
Harness: Aid, Light, Diaper, Padded
Helmet: Light, Standard
Knife, Multitool
Locking Biners
Pull Cord/Haul Line
Racking Biners
Rope: Normal/Fat/Skinny/Twin/Half, 30/50/60/70/80m
Rope Bag
Rope Buckets, Stuff Sacks, Rope Hook
Spare Biners
Stick Clip
Stiff Draw
Topos/Guidebook
Tubular Belay Device: ATC/Reverso
Clothing
Head
Balaclava: Warm, Silkweight
Ball Cap
Bandana
Belay Glasses
Buffs
Bug Hat
Eyes
Face Mask
Fog Wipes
Glacier Glasses
Glasses or Contacts
Goggles
Hair Ties
Headband
Ice Climbing Visor
Light Warm Hat
Medium Warm Hat
Neck Gaiter
Nose Protector
Safety Glasses
Sunglasses
Thick Warm Hat
Visor
Torso Base-Layer
Base-Layer Wool, Nylon
Cotton T-shirt
Long Sleeve Sun Shirt
Offwidth Shirt
Sports Bra
Stuff Sack for Harness
Tank Top
Torso Mid-Layer
Fleece
Hybrid Fleece
Light Insulated Jacket: Down, Synthetic
Torso Outer
Belay Jacket: Down, Synthetic
Cagoule

Hardshell
Poncho
Soft,Hardshell Hybrid
Softshell
Umbrella
Waterproof Insulated Jacket
Wind-shirt
Legs
Bibs: Hardshell, Softshell
Canvas Pant, Jeans
Down Pants
Hardshell Pants
Insulated Overpants
Long Underwear: Heavy, Light
One-Piece Down Suit
One-Piece Long Underwear
Quickdry Pants
Shorts, Zip-Off Pants
Softshell Pants: Light, Heavy
Tights
Underwear, Panties
Windpants / Track Pants
Knees
Protective Kneepads
Rubber Kneepads
Hands
Athletic Tape
Belay Glove: Fingers, None
Belay Gloves
Crack Gloves
Drytool Gloves
Elbow Sleeve (for O/Ws)
Glove Stuff Sack
Handwarmers
Insulated Mittens
Leather Insulated Gloves
Light Ice Gloves
Liner Gloves
Medium Ice Gloves
Overmits
Pre-Tape
Spring Gloves
Windstopper Gloves
Feet
Aid Climbing Shoe
Ankle protector (½ sock)
AT Boots
Barefoot Shoe
Belay Slippers
Fingered Socks
Fruitboots
Gaiters: Small, Large
Half Socks for Thin Cracks
Hiking Boots
Insole: Orthotic, Warmth
Light Approach Shoes
Light Mountaineering Boots
Midweight Mountain or Ice Boots
Orthotics
Overboots
Plastic Boots

Rock Shoes: All Day, High Top, Aggressive Sport, Moderate Trad/Sport, Thin Crack
Rubber Band
Running Shoes, Sandals, Flip-Flops, Boat Shoes
Socks: Liner, Cotton, Hiking, Ice
Sorrel-type boots
Supergaiters
Supportive Approach Shoes
Synthetic Booties
Toe Protector (½ sock)
VBL Socks/Plastic Bags
Warm Double Boots

Cooking Systems
½ - 1.5 Liter Aluminum or Titanium Pot, Lid
2-3 Liter Aluminum Pot, Lid
Alcohol Stove and Fuel
Biolight Stove
Canister Fuel
Canister Insulation
Canister Stand
Cup, Mug, Measuring Cup, Folding Bowl, Water Bottle, Cut-Off Plastic Bottom
Cutting Knife
ESBIT Stove and Fuel
Hanging Stove Kit
Heat Exchanger: Standard, Copper Wire
Heineken Beer Pot
Inverted canister/modular stove
Jetboil, Reactor
Knife
Lighter, Matches
Liquid Gas Containers
Liquid Gas Stove Alpine
Liquid Gas Stove Camping
Liquid Gas: White, Kerosene, Unleaded, Diesel
Pot Grips
Spoon
Spork
Windscreen: Commercial, Foil

First Aid-Rescue
Accessory Cord
ACE Wraps
Altitude Drugs
Antibiotic Ointment
Antihistamine
Band-Aids
Book on First Aid
Broad Spectrum Antibiotics
Calamine Lotion
Cavit
Cell Phone, Sat Phone, PLB
Clove Oil
Cold and Cough Medication
Compass
Cortisone Cream
CPR Mask
Dental Emergency Kit

Drinking Tube
Duct/Gorilla Tape
Electrolyte Tablets
EMT Shears
Epi Pen
Extra Batteries
Extra sunblock. Sunglasses, Chapstick
High Calorie Bar
Fifi + Rubber Band
Flint and Steel
Firestarter Tinder
Flares, Smoke Signal
Gamow Bag
Handgun
Handwarmers
Hemorrhoid Cream, Suppository
Hydration Kit
Imodium AD
Iodine
Knife
Latex Glove
Laxative/Suppository
Leaver Biner, Rap Ring, Quicklink
Leukotape
Membrane Bandage
Needle and Thread (Floss)
NSAIDs & Prescription Pain Killer
Pepto-Bismol, Rolaids, or Zantac
Prescription Meds & Med Tags
Prusik, Hollow Block
Pulse Oximiter
Quick Clot or Celox
Rain Shell: Garbage Bag, Storm Shell
Razor Blade
Reflective Bivy
Safety Pins
SAM Splint
Second Skin
Signal Mirror
Spare Lighter
Spare Tiny Headlamp
Sterile bandaging
Sterile Gauze
Steri-Strips
Sun Clothing
Syproflex
Syringe: Injection, Irrigation
TAT
Tecnu
Thermometer
Tibloc, Microtrax, Rollnlock, Prusik
Tincture of Benzoin
Tweezers, Tick Remover
Vaginal Infection Medication
Whistle

Food & Water
Alcohol
Bagels
Bars: Candy, Granola, Energy, Protein
Breakfast Bar
Car Snacks, Beer

Cereal, Dried Milk (NIDO)
Cheese
Chocolate
Cookies, Crackers, Chips
Crash Kit
Dried, Fresh Fruit
Electrolyte Pills, Drink
Energy Drink/Gum/Strips
Ensure
Freeze Dried Meal
Gels, Chews
Halva
Hard Boiled Egg
Hard Meats, Jerky, Salami, Etc.
Hot Drink
Instant, Low Cook Time Dinners
MRE
Nuts
Oatmeal
Olive Oil
Pastries, Confections
Peanut Butter, Nutella
Salt, Pepper, Spices
Sandwich
Sauce Packets
Soda, Energy Drink, Beer
Sports Drink
Supplements
Taffy, Hard Candy
Tortillas
Trail Mix
Tuna
Vacuum Sealed Dinner

Food & Water Equipment
1-2 Liter Water Bottle
2 Liter Soda Bottle
Alarm
Alcohol Container
Alpine Straw
Bear Container
Chlorine Drops, Tablets
Cooler
Fancy Cooking Gear
Fishing Equipment
Flow Meter
Fry Pan, Spatula
Garbage Bag
Insulated Bladder, Tube
Iodine
Recovery Food
Spice Containers
Steri Pen, Miox
Stuff Sacks, Grocery Bag
Thermos
Vacuum Sealer
Water Bladder, Dromedary
Water Bottle Parka
Water Filter, Bandana
ZipLocks

Ice Protection
Conduit
Flukes
Hooks

Ice Clips, Tape, Pipes, Sling
Ice Screw Bag
Ice Screws: (10,13,17,22cm)
Icepider
Leaver Screw
Petzl Screw Sharpener
Pickets
Rock Gear
Snarg
Stuff Sacks for Deadman
V-Threader, First Shot, Tat
Warthog

Navigation, Communication & Electronics
Alarm Clock
Altimeter Watch
AM/FM Radio
Binoculars
Camera
Camera Case, Leash
Cell Phone/Old Flip-Phone
Compass
Earphone Splitter
External USB Charger
Extra Batteries
GoPro
GPS
Headlamp
Headphones
IPod
Map, Topo
Memory Card
Paper, Journal
Pen/Pencil
PLB
Satellite Phone
Signal Mirror
Smartphone
Solar Charger
Speakers
Spotting Scope
Tablet, Laptop
Tent Lantern
VHF/UHF Radio
Walkie-Talkie
Wands & Grease Pencil
Weather Radio
Whistle
Wind Gauge
Wrist Watch

Personal Items/Hygiene/Minor 1st Aid
Allergy Medication
Aloe Lotion
Anti-Diuretic
Anti-Friction Stick
Antiperspirant
Athletic Tape
Birth Control
Blister Pads
Bug Clothing
Bug Dope
Chap Stick
Citronella Candles/Coils
Clorox Wipes
Compost Poop Bag
Contact Lens Kit
Ear Plugs
Eyedrops
Extra Laces
File or Emory Board
Floss
Foot Powder and Antiperspirant
Freshette + Mesh Bag
Hand Salve & Lotion
Hand Sanitizer
Lysol Spray
Nail Clippers
NSAIDS
Nu Skin or Super Glue
Prescriptions
Permethrin
Piss Bottle
Poop Tube, Bag & Kit
Q-Tips
Shaving Kit
Sleeping Pills
Soap: Dish, Hair, Laundry
Solar Shower, Dromedary
Sunscreen
Tampons
Toilet Paper, Napkins
Toothbrush, Paste
Trowel
WAG Bag
Wet-Wipes

Repair
Accessory Cord
Air Mattress/Soft Water Bottle Patches
Baiing Wire
Bike Repair Kit
Duct/Gorilla Tape
Eyeglass Repair Kit
Fabric Repair Patches
Floss
Hose Clamps
Knife
Needle and Thread
Pole Splint: Tent, Trekking Pole
Safety Pins
Ski Straps
Ski, Binding, Skin Repair
Seam Grip & Accelerant
Stove Repair
Speedy Stitcher
Tent Repair Kit
Zipper Repair Kit
Zip Ties

Rock Protection
Beaks
Big Bros or Big Cams
Bolt Wrench
Cam Hooks
Cams: Three Cam, Micro, Offset, Four Cam, Link Cams, Fat Cams, Supercams
Funkness Device
Hammer, Holster, Sling
Heads, Center Punch, Chisel
Hexes
Hooks: Talon, Cliffhanger, Grappling, Logan/Bathook, Ibex, Modified, Blue Tack
Nut Tool
Nuts: Standard, Offset, Micro, Brass
Pitons: RURP, Pecker, Tomahawk, Knifeblade, Angle, Lost Arrow, Z-piton, Universal, Spectre/Bulldog, Titanium, Sawed, Notched
Rivet Hanger: 3/8-5/16", or Wire
Slide Nuts
Tie off and Hero Loops
Tricams
Wood Blocks

Sleeping Systems
Bothy Bag
Broom
Bug Tent
Compression Sack
Cook Tent
Double (Spooning) Bag
Double Wall Camping Tent
Double Wall Expedition Tent
Ensolite Hardman Pad
Ground Cloth
Ground Stakes
Half-Bag, Belay Jacket
Handwarmer
Light Inflatable Pad
No Bottom Insulation Bag
Normal Sleeping Bag: Down, Synth
Pack Padding
Pillow
Portaledge with Fly, Pole
Quilt
Ridge, Z-Rest
Single Wall Sil-Nylon Tent
Single Wall Tent
Snow Stakes, Deadmen
Space Blanket
Sponge
Synthetic Overbag
Tarp Tent
Tent Lantern
Tent, Tarp Fly
Thick Inflatable Pad
Triangle Sleeping Bag Extender
Ultralight Down Bag
Ultralight Inflatable Pad
Ultralight Stakes
Ultralight Synthetic Bag
VBL
VBL Clothing
Very Warm Bag:Down, Synth, Waterproof
Vestibule

Water Bottle	Ice Ax: Ultralight, Durable	Car Camping Double Burner, Grill
Water Resistant Bag Cover	Ice Pick	Car Repair: Keys, Battery Charger, Cables, Gas
Waterproof Bivy Sack	Ice Tools: Alpine, Light, Ergo Mixed, Ergo Ice	Cards, Chess, Checkers, Backgammon
Slings, Draws, & Anchor	Inclinometer	Change of Clothes
1-2 Biners, Sling	Knotted Pit-Test Cord	Cook Table
Cordalette: Nylon, Sewn Dyneema, Rabbit Runner, Snake, ARC	Leashes, Umbilicals	Couch
Docking Cord	Mixed Pick	DWR Spray
Double Runners, Rabbit Runner	Pack Leash	Extra Guidebooks
Dyneema Shoulder Slings	Regular small wooden hammer	Firewood, Newspaper, Starter
Long Draw	Shovel	Frisbee, Hackey Sack, Hula-Hoop
Nylon Shoulder Slings	Skis, Bindings, Crampons, Skins, Leashes/Brakes	Gear Cleaning Detergent
Prusik, Autoblock Knot	Small File	Glover Drier
Revolver Biner	Snow Saw	Guidebooks
Screamers, Load Limiters	Snowshoes	Hammock
Short Draw	Spare Pick, Tool	Large First Aid Kit
Tat	Trekking, Ski Pole, Ax Attachment	Leather Conditioner
Tether: Slings, PAS, Daisy, Adjustable, Dynaclip	**Solo Gear**	Myrazime
Tied Runners	Aid Soloist	Nail Polish
Top Rope Slings, Webbing, Lockers	Breakable Sling, Band, Biner	Plan B Gear
Snow & Ice	Modified GriGri	Propane Heater
3rd Tool	Silent Partner	Road Food
Adz, Hammer	Soloist	Road Maps, Atlases, Smartphone, GPS
Aermet Pick	**Travel/Basecamp/Home**	
Airbag	12-V Accessories	Road Repair/Stuck: Chain Saw, Crowbar, Boards, Chains, Winch, Shovel, Fuses, Compressed Air
Alaska Pick	After Climb Snacks/Beers	
Avalanche Probe	Barge Cement	
Avalung	Big Ax, Crampon File	Rope Marker
Beacon	Blank Checks, Travelers Checks	Scale: Small, Pack
Bush Saw	Board Game	Stealth Paint
Crampon & Tool: Strap-On, Semi-automatic, Automatic, Horizontal, Vertical, Monopoint, Spurs	Book	Storage Bins
	Boot Drier	Stove Fuel
	Cam Lube & Cleaner	Tool Kit
Curved Pick	Camp Chairs	Towel
Holster	Camp Kitchen	Training Equipment
		Water Jugs

REFERENCES

Most of the information in the book has been painstakingly learned through my own trial and error, critical thinking, experimentation, countless climbing partners, and from my undergrad and postgraduate education. I have listed books, DVDs, and websites that I have read and found to be useful and will provide you with further information. Some specific references are found throughout the book. Please check out **https://sites.google.com/site/climbingbeyondthebasics** for more links.

APPS

- Avalanche Conditions
- Access Fund
- Boulder Trainer
- Flashlight
- Gas buddy
- Instant Heart Rate, Stress Check, (pulse oximeter coming soon)

- Map & Topo: Backcountry Navigator, Google Maps, Google Earth, MyTracks, Peak Finder, Peaks
- Mountain Project
- Rakkup Topo
- Ski Report

- Slope Finder: Inclinometer/Compass, Theodolite, Mammut Avalanche, Geocam, Level/Protractor
- Time: HIIT Timer, ReMind Alarm

- Weather: Weatherbug Elite, NOAA, Climbing Weather, Barometer, Thermometer, Wind Sensor

BOOKS AND DVDS

The following books are either the gold standard in their subject matter, contain unique information somewhere within, or are at least the most useful put-in-to-practice references available. There are certainly more books and resources available than the following, but I felt these were the best supplement sources of information. *Starred* books totally stand-out as amazing, or contain info not found elsewhere.

Alpine, Snow and Ice
- *"Allen and Mike's Really Cool Backcountry Ski Book" – Clelland & Obannon. How could you not like this book?
- "Backcountry Skiing" - Volken. Excellent info on ski mountaineering.
- *"Glacial Mountaineering: An Illustrated Guide to Glacial Mountaineering and Crevasse Rescue" –Tyson and Clelland. Easy to read and understand, but still chock full of information.
- *"Ice and Mixed Climbing: Modern Technique" – Gadd. Written by the master and offers wisdoms from years of experience. If you ice climb then read this book.
- "Mixed Climbing" – Issac. A good supplement to Gadd's book.
- *"Staying Alive in Avalanche Terrain" – Tremper. An outstanding book that puts avalanche science into a usable format for the backcountry user.

Backpacking
- "Allen and Mike's Really Cool Backpackin' Book"– O'Bannon and Clelland. Great tips by great authors.
- "Trail Life" – Jardine. Written by the guy who invented cams and reinvented backpacking. See his website rayjardine.com for more info.

Big Wall, Expedition, and Aid
- "Big Wall Climbing: Elite Technique" - Odgen. Best book to date on aid climbing.
- "Driven" and "Hooks" – Kirpatrick. The best, if only, books on pitons and hooks.
- "Expedition Planning" – Soles. One of the few books available on planning international expeditions.

Bouldering
- *"Better Bouldering" – Sherman. Great info on landing and spotting, holds and movements. One of the best instructional books ever written.

Cardio
- "Breathe Strong Perform Better" – McConnell. A ton of information on breathing physiology and training. Great for high altitude climbers and speed alpinists.
- "Chi Running" – Dreyer. One of the three running methods.
- "Dr. Nicholas Romanov's Pose Method of Running" – Guess who it's by? One of the three running methods.
- *"Evolution Running" DVD – Mierke. One of the three running methods.
- "Heart Rate Training" – Good info on training your cardiovascular system for alpinism or mountaineering.
- "Lactate Threshold Training" – Janssen. Another good cardio read with a few minor flaws.

Climbing Performance
- "Building Your Own Climbing Wall" – Lange. The price tag of the book will pay for itself by doing it right.
- "Climb Strong: Power Endurance" – Bechtel. Lots and lots of supplemental climbing drills to improve power endurance.
- *"Masterclass Vol 1" – Neil Gresham (DVD). The best reference I have ever seen regarding climbing movement, balance, and training for both sporto's and tradsters. Get it.
- *"The Rock Climber's Training Manual" - Anderson & Anderson. Hands down the best book on the subject on training for rock. Published just days before this book went to press, I still had time to skim it and loved it!
- "Self-Coached Climber" – Hague and Hunter. Great supplemental info on balance, movement, and center of gravity.
- *"Training for the New Alpinism" - House & Johnston. The best book out there for those more concerned with training for mountaineering, big alpine climbs, and climbing at altitude.

General Climbing
- *"1000+ Climbing Tips" and "High – Advanced Multipitch Climbing"– Kirkpatrick. No I didn't just fluff out Andy's pointers from his e-books, but it was refreshing to find someone as paranoid as I am! I may have become his biggest fan after reading some of his more esoteric and obviously learned the hard way tips. Andy has many useful tips not presented in this book so spend the extra $5 or whatever and download these e-books.
- *"The Complete Guide to Rope Techniques" – Shepard. How did so much useful information get crammed into such a little book? Every climber should own a copy.
- *"Mountaineering – Essential Skills for Climbers and Hikers" – Richardson. Yet another excellent book that goes the extra mile from "Freedom of the Hills". Also contains some good ski mountaineering and expedition planning information.
- *"Rock Climbing: Mastering Basic Skills" – Leubben. An amazingly well written book on how to rock climb.
- *"The Mountaineering Handbook" – Connally. If you do general mountaineering or general alpine climbing get this book. Wonderful info on forces, navigation, camp, and loaded with very useful information. Like this book, you may not agree with everything in it (like backing up a rap ring), but it is worth taking the author's opinions under consideration.

General Exercise Performance
- "5/3/1" – Wendler. A unique and effective training program from building general strength. Not for climbing, but a good off-season approach.
- "Advances in Functional Training" – Boyle and other books by this author. Good general info on the subjects presented.
- "Conditioning for Outdoor Fitness" – Musnick et all. Jam-packed with functional training exercises. Mostly useful if you are looking for that "one exercise" not described elsewhere.
- "Exercise Physiology" – McCardle. The best book on the subject.
- "Facilitated Stretching" – McAtee. A great resource for more information on active stretching.
- "Fit" – Kilgore. Another great fitness primer.
- "Maximum Strength" – Cressey. A great off-season training book.
- "Olympic Weightlifting" – Everett. A great primer on the subject if you're into this kind of thing.

- "Periodization" – Bompa and other book by this author. Good general info on the subjects presented.
- "Starting Strength", "Practical Programming for Strength Training" – Rippetoe and other books by this author. Good general info on the subjects presented.
- "Supertraining" - Verkhoshansky and other books by this author. Good general info on the subjects presented, although a bit thick.
- *"The Athlete's Guide to Recovery" – Roundtree. One of the best training books you can own and very well written and researched.

Nutrition
- *"Advanced Sports Nutrition" – Benardot. Hands down the best book out there on all things sports nutrition. Start here.
- *"Nutrient Timing for Peak Performance" – Skolnik. Not only is this book an excellent primer on nutrition and physiology, but also an in depth look at what, when, and how much to eat.
- *"Performance Nutrition" – Austin & Seebohar. Another excellent book on sports nutrition with some advanced concepts for those looking to perform their best, including altitude, heat, and cold.
- *"Power Hungry: The Ultimate Energy Bar Cookbook" – Saulsbury. Original and knock-off recipes for popular bars and chews!
- *"Racing Weight" and "Racing Weight Quick Start Guide" – Fitzgerald. Excellent books on attaining a performance level of weight loss.

Rehabilitation
- "Anatomy Trains" – Myers. An amazing book on fascia, movement, and how it's all connected. Good for manual therapists, but an interesting read for all.
- *"Assessment and Treatment of Muscle Imbalances: The Jana Approach" – Page et all. One of the best books available regarding muscle imbalances and how to correct them.
- *"Athletic Body in Balance" and "Movement" – Cook. In the first book, Cook presents 5 basic movement patterns as a self-test and then shows you how to correct imbalances in those movement patterns. The second book is a more advanced look at the topic presented in the first book on how to assess and correct functional movement syndromes. Excellent.
- *"Becoming a Supple Leopard" – Starrett. Like most things CrossFit: hip, hyped, a rebranding of previously known and popular concepts, but a must have resource for self-massage, and properly performing some Olympic lifts and basic exercises including some surgical insight.
- *"Corrective Exercise Solutions to Common Hip and Shoulder Dysfunction" – Oscar. A very useful book on postural and movement imbalances and how to correct them with functional training.
- "Fascia: The Tensional Network of the Human Body" – Schleip, et all. The bible on fascia. For therapists.
- "Fixing Your Feet" – Vonhoff. The bible on self-treatment for foot conditions.
- *"Framework", "Framework for the Lower Back", "Framework for the Shoulder" & "Framework for the Knee" – DiNubile. All great books on common conditions, surgery, and rehab. A good place to start. One of the few decent books for the layperson.
- *"Foundation" – Goodman & Park. Ten wonderful exercises for back pain and other good information on weight loss and general exercise. The DVD may be more useful if you just want the exercises.
- *"Healthy Shoulder Handbook" – Knopf. Full of very good shoulder exercises.

- "Heal Your Knees" – Klapper & Huey. Although dated, this is another excellent book. Lots of great pool exercises.
- "Human Locomotion" – Michaud. A PhD level book on foot through low back disorders. All you could ever want to know regarding gait, orthotics, and diagnosis and treatment of lower extremity (hip to foot) disorders.
- *"Movement System Impairment Syndromes of the Extremities, Cervical and Thoracic Spine" – Sahrmann. Incredibly detailed look at how changes in movement or posture can contribute to injury and dysfunction. The book dissects extremely subtle changes in movement rather than gross discrepancies and may be too advanced for the layperson (or most therapists!).
- "Overcoming Back and Neck Pain" – Morrone. Very good book on the subject, especially the recommendations on use of pillows and supports for sleeping if you can get past the Jesus crap.
- "Pain Free" – Egoscue. A treatise in postural syndromes. Dry as a bone but interesting for dorks.
- "Rehabilitation of the Hand and Upper Extremity" – Skirven et all. Only a couple thousand pages on all things injury-related from the finger up to the shoulder. Most of the focus is on surgery and post-op recovery. An amazing reference, but save your money for the therapist and surgeon.
- *"Rehabilitation of the Spine" – Liebenson and all other books/DVDs by this author. Ground-breaking book on spinal related disorders and functional exercises.
- "Stability, Sport, and Performance Movement" – Elphinston. A useful reference on stability training.
- "The Carpal Tunnel Handbook" – Fried. A great book on this syndrome. Dated, but useful.
- *"The Foot Book" – Rose & Martorana. One of the best books out there on just about every foot condition imaginable from a medical standpoint.
- *"Therapeutic Exercise for Musculoskeletal Injuries" – Houglum. An excellent reference in easy to understand language which covers a broad range of principles and techniques. At about 1,000 pages it covers more than you would expect from the title.
- "Treat Your Back without Surgery" – Hochschuler. Ironically enough, a good resource for surgical options.
- *"Ultimate Back Fitness and Performance" and "Low Back Disorders"– McGill. The first book is an amazing reference to train the low back or to rehab an injured back and also includes excellent functional exercises for general conditioning. If you have back problems, want a strong core, or want to avoid future problems than get this book. His other book is more clinical and thorough but more conceptual and academic.

Weather
- "Northwest Mountain Weather" – Renner. Much of the same information contained in the Woodmencey book, but more tailored to the Pacific Northwest.
- "Reading Weather" – Woodmencey. Packed with tons of great information in a tiny little book.

Wilderness Medicine and Rescue
- "Accidents in North American Mountaineering" – American Alpine Club. Reading this book can help you learn from other's mistakes or misfortune. A must!
- *"Altitude Illness: Prevention and Treatment" – Bezruchka. A ton of information packed into a little book.

- "Medicine for Mountaineering" – Wilkerson et all. A bit drier that the other books, this has a great chapter on altitude related illnesses and fills in the gaps of other texts.
- "Medicine for the Outdoors" – Auerback. One of the best layman's guide for first aid in the wilds. The author's "Expert Consult" edition is much more detailed, but vastly more expensive.
- "SAS Survival Handbook" – A really good resource on survival.
- *"Self Rescue" – Fasulo. The best book on the subject.
- *"Wilderness Medicine" – Forgey. My favorite wilderness medicine book. Down to earth and sprinkled with lots of DIY field remedies.
- *"Wilderness Survival" – Davenport. Another great survival book.

GEAR
Gear Companies and Distributers

- 40 Below
- ABS
- Acopa
- Adidas
- Adventure Medical
- Alive Nutrition
- Alpkit
- Arctyrx
- Asana
- Atomik Holds
- Backcountry Access
- Backpackers Pantry
- Bald Eagle
- Beal
- Belay Specs
- Bellaggles
- Beyond Clothing
- Bibbler
- Big Agnes
- Biolite
- Black Diamond
- Black Rock Gear
- Blue Ice
- Blue Water
- Body Glide
- Bradley Alpinist
- Brooks Range
- Brunton
- BSN Nutrition
- Camelbak
- CAMP USA / Cassin
- Canyoneering USA
- Cascade Designs
- Cilogear
- Clif Bar
- ClimbTech
- Cold Avenger
- Cold Cold World
- Coleman
- Delorme
- Deuter
- DMM
- Dynafit
- Easton
- e-climb
- Edilrid
- EFS Nutrition
- Eidelweiss
- Enlightened Equipment
- Esbit
- Esprit
- Evernew
- Evolv
- Exped
- Feathered Friends
- First Ascent
- Fish Gear
- Five Ten
- Fixe
- Flashed
- Flylow
- Franklin Holds
- Garmin
- Gear Aid
- Geigerrig
- Goal Zero
- GoLight
- GoPro
- Gossamer Gear
- Granite Gear
- Gregory
- Grivel
- GSI
- GU
- Hammer Nutrition
- Hilleberg
- Home Depot
- Honey Stinger
- Hydroflask
- Hyperlight Mountain Gear
- Ibex
- Icebreaker
- IceHoldz
- Imlay
- Ininji
- Integral Designs
- Iron Mind
- Jacks R Better
- Jet Boil
- Julbo
- Katabatic
- Kenyon
- Kind Bars
- Kinko
- Klymit
- Koflatch
- Kong
- Krukonogi - Russian ice and big wall gear. Custom Petzl picks.
- Kuhl
- La Sportiva
- Leki
- Liberty Mountain
- Lifelink
- Light My Fire
- Lorpen
- Lowe Alpine
- Mad Rock
- Mammut
- Marmot
- McNett
- MEC
- Metlious Climbing
- Millet
- Misty Mountain
- Mont Bell
- Montaine
- Moon Climbing
- Moses
- Mountain Equipment
- Mountain House
- Mountain Kakis
- Mountain Laurel Designs
- Mountain Tools
- Mountain Hardwear
- MSR
- Mueller
- Nalgene
- Nemo
- Nicros
- NOLS
- Norona
- Nunatak
- Nuun
- NW Alpine
- Occun
- Olukai Ohana
- Omega Pacific
- OMM
- Optimus
- Orbworks.cz
- Organic
- Ortovox
- Osmo Nutrition
- Osprey
- Outdoor Research
- Pacific Health Labs
- Paco Pads
- Patagonia
- Pat's Backcountry Beverages
- Petzl
- PhD Designs
- Pieps
- Platypus
- Powerbar
- PowerBreathe
- Prana
- Primus
- Probar
- Rab

- Raw Revolution
- REI
- Revolution Holds
- Rock Exotica
- Rogue Fitness
- Runout customs
- Saltic
- Salt Stick
- Salwea
- Sanuk
- Saywer
- Scarpa
- Schmoolz
- Scratch Labs
- Sea To Summit
- Send - sticky rubber knepads
- SicGrips
- Sierra Designs
- Singing Rock
- Six Moon Designs
- Slingfin
- Smartwool
- SMC
- Snowpeak
- So iLL
- Softshell company
- Soto
- Starbucks Via
- Stealth Paint
- Sterling
- Stevensons Warmlight
- Stonelick
- Superfeet
- Suunto
- Tarp Tent
- Tenya
- Terra Nova
- The North Face
- Thermarest
- Totem
- Trail Designs
- Trango
- ~~Ushba~~ (RIP)
- Valandre
- Valley Giants
- Vargo Titanium
- Vibram
- Voodo
- Westecomb
- Western Mountaineering
- Wild Country
- Wild Things
- Yamma Mountain Gear
- Yates
- Zpacks

Gear Services
Expert welders, sewing experts, and machinists could also be utilized for making custom equipment.

- Dave Page – Resoles for those in the PNW
- Grizguides – Ice screw sharpening
- Mountain Tools – Cam and gear re-slinging service (can send to the company that made the gear too)
- Ouray Mountain Sports – Ice screw sharpening on a Grivel machine
- Rainy Pass Designs – Custom gear mods and repair
- Ramutas – My favorite resoler!
- Rock and Resole – Resoles for the Colorado folks
- Rubber Room – Resoles for the Sierra climbers
- Runoutcustoms – Cam re-slinging, custom jobs
- The Cam Doctor – Fix your broken cam trigger wires.
- Wired Bliss – Cam repair
- Yates – Cam Re-slinging

WEBSITES

There are tons of great blogs and websites that share trip reports, sell gear, or post news feeds. These focus on sharing tips and information relating to the info in this book, and I feel are the most useful. I used the person's name when possible as blogs change names and locations on the net. Don't expect these all too still be active. Some great climbers aren't great writers, and some great writers just don't write about anything useful. Some aren't even great climbers, but at least post intelligent information. This is a select list. If you know exactly what you are looking for try searching Google, YouTube, and Vimeo first.

Beta and Travel
- Alpine Club of Canada - Huts and Hostels
- American Alpine Club - Searchable AAJ, Teton Ranch
- Cascadeclimbers.com - The best climbing forum on the planet
- Canyoneering USA – Great info on SW canyons and tech tips
- Center for Disease Control (CDC) - Info on vaccinations and disease in other countries
- Couchsurfing.org - Find places to crash
- Craigslist - Great place to find couches to surf and rides to share
- Freecampsites.net - Maps to free campsites with reviews
- Hotwire.com - Great cheap hotel site
- Northwest Mountaineering Journal - Where folks still put up long routes in the USA!
- MountainProject - Online Route and Conditions Info. Offline app coming soon!

- Pataclimb - Rolondo's amazing website for beta on Patagonia, South America, and the Teton Traverse
- Priceline.com - Great cheap airfare
- Ridejoy - Find a travel companion to split gas
- RockClimbing.Com - Yet another place to find route info
- Stanford.edu/~clint - Topos for obscure or out of print areas assembled by Clint Cummins
- State Department - Info on current warnings for international travel
- SummitPost - Another place to look for route/area info. Kinda wanky but still useful
- Supertopo - Good route info for Cali, and other areas published by Supertopo. Excellent Spray as well
- Teton blog – Current conditions in the Tetons
- Wikiboulder.com - Bouldering wiki
- Wikitravel.org - Excellent recourse on international travel destinations
- Yosemitebigwall.com – An amazing companion to their guidebook showing excellent topos of the Yosemite big wall routes.

Blogs with Great Info on Many Subjects

- Blake Herrington
- Climbing house
- Climbingnarc
- Crankenstein
- Dave Burdick
- DPM Climbing
- Kelly Cordes
- Kris Hampton
- Marvinclimbingeng.blogspot
- Matt McCormick
- Micah Elconin (educatedvegetable.blogspot)
- Paul Fearn
- Phil Requist
- Pullharder
- Raphael Slawinski
- Robotclimbing
- Ryan Palo
- Sean McColl
- Sonnie Trotter
- Splitterchoss
- Steph Davis
- Steve House
- Stevie Haston
- The Cleanest Line (Patagonia)
- The Climbing Lab
- Upskill Climbing
- Veticulture (Outdoor Research)
- Will Gadd

Bolting and Access

- Access Fund - Also lists local climbing organizations
- ASCA

First Aid and Rehab

- Highaltitudemedicine.org - Info on high altitude medicine and travel
- Red Cross - CPR and First Aid
- Steadman Clinic - One of the very best ortho clinics in the world with "scholarships" for climbers
- Wilderness First Responder (WFR) - NOLS, wildmed.com, SOLO, several others

Forums

- 8a.nu
- Alpinist
- Backpackinglight
- Bigwalls.com
- Cascadeclimbers
- Climbing.com
- Climbinglife
- CrossFit
- Gripped

- Mountainproject
- Planet Fear
- Planetmountain
- Rockandice
- Rockclimbing.com
- Summitpost
- Supertopo
- Ukclimbing

Gear Info / Tips
- http://youtu.be/SOE28brAcEc - Fancy shoelace tying
- Howardjohnson.name/Backpacking/Stove/Stoves.htm
- Outdoorgearlab – Comparison reviews and good how to choose articles
- REI – does a good job a providing accurate weights, and efficiency of bag, pads, and stoves if they sell the product. Good how to choose articles.Guiding

Guiding
- AMGA - guide courses and some articles/tips, good place to find a guide.

Ice Climbing Conditions
MountainProject or your local climbing forum are a good all-around beta sites for ice conditions.
- Alaskaclimbing.com
- Lillooet - westcoastice.wordpress.com
- Cascades - wastateice.net or cascadeclimbers.com
- Montana and Wyoming - montanaice.com
- Cody - coldfear.com
- Canadian Rockies - gravsports-ice.com (Will Gadd's Site)
- Colorado Ice - iceclimbingcolorado.com
    - skywardmountaineering.com/ouray-ice-climbing-conditions
    - climbinglife.com
    - totalclimbing.com

Navigation
- Gmap4 - mappingsupport.com
- hillmap.com
- Google Maps
- Bing Maps

Nutrition
- Healthnotes - great resource for nutritional related health conditions, supplements, and medication
- Linus Pauling Institute - best info on vitamins, minerals, and micronutrients. Keep in mind that although Pauling was a Nobel winning chemist, he kind of went nuts (similar to what happened to Dr. Heimlich) on the whole vitamin C and later vitamin recommendations. The LPI has different recommendation than the late Dr. Pauling.
- USDA – nutrient data on thousands of foods and supplements
- Gatorade Sports Science Institute – great professional nutrition and sports performance related articles. Ironic since Gatorade makes terrible products marketed to non-athletes.

Training, Injury, and Tech Tips
- Alli Rainey - training and injury
- Andrew Pacey (climbstrong.com)
- Andrew Shannahan, DC (climbingtrainingproject.com)

- Andy Kirkpatrick - Tech tips galore
- Atomik - how to build a wall
- Beastmaster.co.uk - Training
- Black Diamond QC Lab
- Bodyrock.tv - Home exercise videos
- Chongo Chuck - big wall genius or insane?
- Chris McNamara - great aid videos on YouTube
- Climb-strong.tumblr - Training
- Clyde Soles - cam conversion chart
- CrossFit – Online exercise, WODS, and forums
- Dane Burns (Coldthistle) - Gear reviews
- Dave Macleod - Training and injury
- DMM - gear safety videos
- Eva Lopez training blog
- FISH - Bolting and big wall tips
- Gym Jones – Good online content with a subscription
- Julian Saunders - Injuries
- Mark Hudon - Big Wall
- Mark Twight - Training
- Metolius Climbing - build a wall, how to tape, other info
- Mike Anderson - training blog
- Mike Barter - no specific site, technical videos all over web
- MobilityWOD - Training and rehab
- Moon Climbing/Ben Moon - Training
- Mountain Athlete – Online exercises and WODS
- Ned Feehally - Training
- Neil Gresham - Training
- Nicros/Eric Horst - Training
- Nuclimbing.com - (section on training)
- The North Face Mountain Athletics - Training
- Pamela Pack - Offwidth info
- Pass the Piton Pete - no website, but tons of aid advice on various websites
- Petzl - great pdf instructions on equipment
- Randy Leavitt - (vimeo.com offwidth video)
- Rosstraining - Make your own gym equipment
- SIET (expeditiontraining.org) - great tech tips
- Steve Bechtel - Training
- Steve Maisch - Training
- Summit Strength Training
- Supertopo - Cam conversion chart
- The Alpine Training Center
- Wide Fetish - offwidth info
- Wild Country - Tech and training on vimeo.com
- Zuzkalight - Home exercise videos

Weather and Avalanche
- AIARE - avtraining.org
- Avalanche.ca
- Avalanche.org
- Climbing Weather
- How to shovel out a victim & perform a beacon search (many site)
- Weather.gov (NOAA)
- Weatherspark
- Windguru.cz

About the Author

Michael has been climbing alpine rock and ice routes for twenty years, including many first ascents in Alaska, British Columbia, Nevada, Oregon, Utah, and Washington. He has appeared in Alpinist, Climbing, Rock & Ice, and U.K.'s Climber magazines for his first ascents and climbing accomplishments. He was the recipient of the 2006 Fred Beckey Award for several bold first ascents, including what was called "the most significant climb [in the Pacific Northwest] in the past 50 years," on the East Face of Mox Peak, just days after completing a Grade 6 first ascent on the other side of the range.

When Michael isn't climbing, skiing, mountain biking, or running, he has worked at several rehabilitation clinics, at the University of Utah sequencing and analyzing DNA of infectious & esoteric diseases, as an advisor for insurance companies and the Affordable Care Act, and as a mountain guide for Wasatch Mountain Adventures (formerly Exum Utah).

Dr. Layton received his Doctor of Chiropractic from Western States Chiropractic College in Portland, OR and received his Bachelor's in Exercise Science from Western Washington University in Bellingham, WA. Michael has also been invited to attend Stony Brook University's class of 2016 Masters of Science Physician Assistant Program in Long Island, NY. Michael is happily married to his amazing, intelligent, & beautiful favorite climbing partner, Britne.

WWW.DMMWALES.COM

A TOUGH NUT TO CRACK
The Alloy Offsets - This versatile nut will fit right in

Alloy Offsets

5 SIZES AVAILABLE

Alloy Offsets are the most versatile nuts on the market - their distinct and dramatically offset sides let them fit perfectly into pin scars where many other nuts might only be marginal whilst the deep cutouts on each side let you place them in irregular and highly textured cracks with confidence. If you climb in Yosemite, Zion, the Adirondacks, Index and Lovers Leap then they are an essential part of your rack. DMM Offsets - versatile and bomber.

FEATURES

- Offset alloy nuts on wire
- Wire recessed into top of nut and full wire radius for extra strength
- Lightening holes
- Colour coded for easy recognition

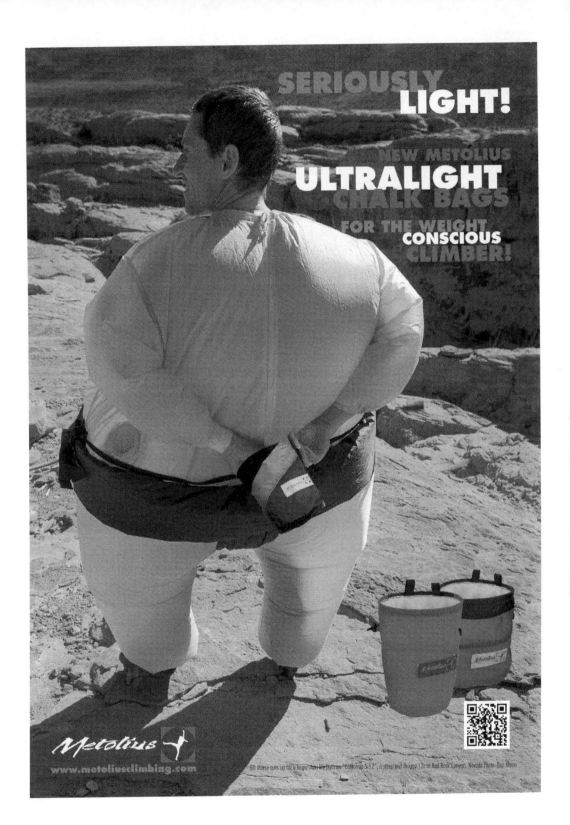

Access the inaccessible

Photo © John Evans

PETZL

CYPHER
For every problem, there is a solution.

SAM PERKINS on TRINITY RIGHT 5.12A
Little Cottonwood Canyon, Utah

Liberty Mountain
Distributed in the United States by Liberty Mountain
www.cypherclimbing.com
For a dealer near you call 1-888.90.CLIMB
Photo ©Nathan Smith - www.pullphotography.com

NOTES

Made in the USA
Charleston, SC
20 July 2014